# THE ARABIAN SEAS

## The Indian Ocean World of the Seventeenth Century

R. J. Barendse



VISION BOOKS
(Incorporating Orient Paperbacks)
New Delhi • Mumbai • Hyderabad

ISBN 81-7094-518-6



This book is an extensively revised and expanded version of the author's *The Arabian Seas, 1640-1700,* Leiden: CNWS, 1998. The publisher gratefully acknowledges the permission of CNWS to publish this new edition.

This edition published in 2002
in arrangement with
M.E. Sharpe, Inc., USA
by
Vision Books Pvt. Ltd.
(Incorporating Orient Paperbacks and CARING Imprints)
24 Feroze Gandhi Road, Lajpat Nagar-III
New Delhi-110024, India.
***Phone:*** (+91-11) 6836470/80
***Fax:*** (+91-11) 6836490
***e-mail:*** visionbk@vsnl.com

Printed at
V. K. Printers
C-114, Okhla Industrial Area, Phase I
New Delhi-110 020, India.

Aan mijn ouders

*E verreis o Mar Roxo, tão famoso*
*Tornar-se lhe amarelho de enfiado*
*Verreis de Ormuz o reinho poderoso*
*Duas vèzes tomado e subjugado*
*Ali vereis o Mouro furioso*
*De suas mesmas setas trespassado*
*Quem vem ora contro os vossos*
*Que se resiste, contre si peleja.*

And you see the famous Red Sea
Turning green with envy
You see the powerful King of Hormuz
Twice fallen, twice subjugated
You see them trespass
On the very holy lands of the furious Moor
Who now still turns against you is sure
That if he resists, you will defeat him.

Camões, *Os Lusiadas*
Canto II, poem 49

# Contents

# Abbreviations

| | |
|---|---|
| A | Manuscritos Azuis |
| AHU | Arquivo Histórico Ultramarino, Lisbon |
| Ajuda | Biblioteca Pública da Ajuda, Lisbon |
| *Annales ESC* | *Annales économies, sociétés, civilisations* |
| ANTT | Instituto dos Arquivos Nacionais (formerly Arquivo Nacional) Torre do Tombo, Lisbon |
| ARA | Algemeen Rijksarchief, The Hague |
| ARU | Algemeen Rijksarchief in de Provincie Utrecht, Utrecht |
| BAC | Biblioteca da Academia das Ciênçias, Lisbon |
| Becarri, *Rerum* | C. Beccari (ed.), *Rerum Aethiopicarum scriptores inediti a saeculo XVI ad XVII*, 14 vols., Rome, 1903–13 |
| *BMGN* | *Bijdragen en Mededelingen betreffende de Geschiedenis der Nederlanden* |
| BNL | Biblioteca Nacional, Lisbon |
| *Boletim* | *Boletim da filmótheca ultramarina Portuguêsa* |
| BPL | Manuscripts of Bibliotheca Publica Latina, University Library, Leiden |
| *BTLV* | *Bijdragen van het koninklijk instituut voor Taal- Land- en Volkenkunde* (formerly *van Nederlandsch Indië*) |
| *Cal. St. Pap. Col.* | N. Sainsbury et al. (eds.), *Calendar of State Papers. Colonial Series: America and West Indies*, 42 vols., London, 1860–1969. |

| | |
|---|---|
| *COACM* | A. and G. Grandidier (eds.), *Collection des ouvrages anciens concernant Madagascar*, 9 vols., Paris, 1903–7 |
| Cód. | Códice |
| Coll. | Collectie/Verzameling |
| Con. d. Gr. | Convento de Graça Manuscripts, Torre do Tombo, Lisbon |
| *Court minutes* | S. Sainsbury (ed.), *Calendar of Court Minutes of the East India Company*, 16 vols., Oxford, 1913–37 |
| CR | Criminele rol van het kasteel Batavia |
| Cx. | Caixa |
| *Dagregister* | J.E. Heeres and A. van der Chijs (eds.), *Dagregister gehouden in 't kasteel Batavia rakende 't principaelste gepasseerd daer ter plaetse*, 31 vols., Batavia, The Hague, 1887–1931 |
| DRI | Documentos remettidos da Índia |
| *EHR* | *The Economic History Review* |
| EIC | East India Company |
| *English Factories* | W. Foster and C.H. Fawcett (eds.), *English Factories in India*, 17 vols., Oxford, 1906–55 |
| Estado | Estado da Índia |
| Évora | Bibliotheca Publica, Évora, Portugal |
| FG | Fundo Geral, Bibliotheca Nacional, Lisbon |
| GAA | Gemeente Archief, Amsterdam |
| GAR | Gemeente Archief, Rotterdam |
| *Gaz.B.Pr.* | J.M. Campbell (ed.), *The Gazetteer of the Bombay Presidency*, 26 vols., Bombay, 1877–1926 |
| Geleynssen | Collectie Geleynssen de Jong, Algemeen Rijksarchief, The Hague |
| *Generale Missiven* | W.P.H. Coolhaas and J. van Goor (eds.), *Generale missiven van Gouverneurs-Generaal en Raden aan de Heren XVII der Verenigde Oost-Indische Compagnie*, 8 vols., The Hague, *RGP*, 1960– |
| H. | Handschrift |

| | |
|---|---|
| HAG | Historical Archives of Goa, Panjim, Goa |
| HB | Verbalen van het Haagsch Besoigne |
| HRB | Verzameling Hoge Regering Batavia, Algemeen Rijksarchief |
| *IESHR* | *The Indian Economic and Social History Review* |
| *IJAHS* | *International Journal of African Historical Studies* |
| *JAH* | *The Journal of African History* |
| *JAS* | *The Journal of Asian Studies* |
| J.d.T. | Junta do Tabacco |
| *JEH* | *The Journal of Economic History* |
| *JESHO* | *Journal of the Economic and Social History of the Orient* |
| KITLV | Manuscripts in the collection of the Koninklijk Instituut voor Taal- Land- en Volkenkunde, Leiden |
| Knuttel | Pamphlet in Koninklijke Bibliotheek, The Hague, catalogued in P.C. Knuttel (ed.), *Catalogus van de pamfletten-verzameling berustende in de koninklijke bibliotheek*, 9 vols., The Hague, 1889–1916 |
| LH | Archief van de Directie voor de Levantse Handel, Algemeen Rijksarchief |
| LM | Livros dos Monções |
| *MAS* | *Modern Asian Studies* |
| Mç. | Maço |
| NAI | National Archives of India, New Delhi |
| *NYCD* | B.R. O'Callaghan and B. Fernow (eds.), *Documents Relative to the Colonial History of the State of New York*, 15 vols., Albany, 1856–87 |
| OB | Overgekomen brieven uit Azië en van de Kaap |
| PA | Particulier Archief, Gemeente Archief, Amsterdam |
| *Plakaatboek* | J.A. van der Chijs (ed.), *Nederlands-Indisch Plakaatboek 1602–1811*, 17 vols., Batavia, The Hague, 1885–1900 |
| PRONI | Public Record Office Northern Ireland, Belfast, The Londonderry Estate |

| | |
|---|---|
| Resende | Pedro Baretto de Resende, *Livro do Estado da Índia Oriental* (BNL Mss. Illuminado, 139). |
| RGGR | Resolutie van de Gouverneur-Generaal en Raden |
| *RGP* | *Rijksgeschiedkundige Publikatiën* |
| RXVII | Resoluties van de Heren XVII |
| St.Gen. | Archief van de Staten-Generaal, Algemeen Rijksarchief |
| SV | São Viçente Collection, Torre de Tombo, Lisbon |
| Theal | G. McTheal (ed.), *Records of South-Eastern Africa*, 9 vols., London, 1898–1903 |
| UB | Uitgaand briefboek Batavia |
| UBL | Universiteitsbibliotheek, Leiden |
| VOC | Verenigde Oost-Indische Compagnie, Archives of the Verenigde Oost-Indische Compagnie, Algemeen Rijksarchief |
| *VSWG* | *Vierteljahrschrift für Sozial- und Wirtschaftsgeschichte* |
| *WHS* | *Works Issued by the Hackluyt Society* |
| WIC | West Indische Compagnie |
| *WLV* | *Werken uitgegeven door de Linschoten-Vereniging* |
| XVII | Brieven van de Heren XVII aan Gouverneur-Generaal en Raden en kantoren in Azië en aan de Kaap |

# Preface

## Preface to Dutch Edition (CNWS, Leiden, 1998)

*Certains auteurs, parlant de leurs ouvrages, disent: "mon livre, mon commentaire, mon histoire," etc. Ils sentent leur bourgeoise, qui ont pignon sur rue et toujours un "chez moi" à la bouche. Ils feraient mieux de dire "notre livre, notre commentaire, notre histoire," etc. vue que d'ordinaire il y a plus en cela de bien d'autrui que de leur.*

—Blaise Pascal, *Pensées* no. 43

Pascal's words certainly apply to this work too, although it is a supremely individual work on which—I am ashamed to confess—I have toiled, intermittently, for thirteen years. The present work constitutes a much revised version of my Dutch Ph.D. dissertation from 1992: "Koningen, Compagnieën en kapers: de Arabische zeeën 1640–1700." My voyages, like those of Sindbad the sailor, have been long, adventurous, and often arduous. But ever and ever again magnificent vistas upon a long-forgotten and long-disappeared past have lured me to pursue.

I am grateful to the Leids Universiteits Fonds for giving me a small grant to cover the costs of the trip from The Hague to Amsterdam, and to the Cultuur Accoord Nederland–India for financing a most rewarding stay in India in 1987–1988. I thank the International Institute of Asian Studies in Leiden both for a financial contribution toward the publication of this book and for funding a (too) long stay in Portugal in 1994. There are, obviously, still many more archives and libraries that would beckon further research (Copenhagen and Cairo, as much as London or Lima; Moscow and Madrid, as well as Rome and Rio, Sa'na, or Spanish Town) but such an endeavor would be beyond the means of a single researcher.

It is a pleasure to thank the many archivists and librarians who always provided ready support throughout my interminable quest for dusty, and often incredibly weighty, old volumes. In the Netherlands I should extend my gratitude, first and foremost, to the staff and directors of the Algemeen Rijksarchief, where I worked for more than six years and who have given me moral as much as muscular support. Thanks should be extended as well to the librarians and archivists of the Universiteitsbibliotheek in Amsterdam and in Leiden, as well as to those of the Koninklijk Instituut voor Taal- Land- en Volkenkunde, of the Instituut Kern in Leiden, and of the Economisch Historische Bibliotheek in Amsterdam. In India I should thank the staff and directors of the National Archives of India and the Indian Council for Historical Research for a most pleasant reception in New Delhi, as well as the staff of the Gomantak Archive in Panjim and the Xavier Center for Historical Research in Bicholim, and in particular Dr. V.B. Shirodkar for allaying my financial and other panics.

In Portugal, finally, I should extend my particular thanks to the staff of the Arquivo Histórico ultramarino—where the dishes are as interesting as the documents—and to the lovely ladies of the Arquivo Nacional Tôrre do Tombo and the Bibliotheca Pública da Ajuda—not least for trying to provide some heat during an unexpectedly cold winter. Since this work has been very much a part of my life during the last thirteen years, it is almost impossible to thank all those who have in some way or another provided support—the longer the book the longer the list of people who have suffered the sorrows of its completion.

Among the scholars, pride of place should surely be given to Professor J.C. Heesterman for his support during the years required for completion of my Ph.D. dissertation, but even more because of his unfailing assistance with the completion of this book during my indescribable ordeal in the *brandwonden centrum*—and his private ordeal.

I should also like to thank Professor J.C. Bruin (who intervened during several critical moments for me personally as much as for my research); Professor D.H.A. Kolff for originally proposing this book for publication, among other things; Professor A. Gunder Frank for his constant attention to both the burns on my hands and my work; and finally to Professor W. Stokhof, whose abiding enthusiasm never ceases to amaze me.

During the work on this volume I have had the pleasure to work and talk with or write to many historians involved in one way or another in the history of trade and of Asia and who, indubitably, will recognize their own ideas here—albeit in mangled form and context. I should mention in simple alphabetical order: B. Bhattacharya, G. Bouchon, S.B. Dale, A. Das Gupta, V.B. Gupta, the late A.P. Meilink-Roelofs, L. Nachtegaal, M.N. Pearson, Om Prakash, E. Pijning, N. Steensgaard, W. van Schendel, and G.D. Winius.

It is a yet more demanding—and often more painful—task to acknowledge those who have manned the ship during my navigation of the Arabian seas. I ought to thank Ella Goubitz and Professor Joke Wigboldus, who—with neither pay nor much reward—have revised the convoluted Dutch of the original Ph.D. dissertation. Among the sailors I should surely also mention are Pim Been, Maarten Bode, Mario Rutten, and the mariners who left the ship before reaching the port: Olga Nieuwenhuijs and the true buccaneer-girl Cynthia Brown—though she will neither read nor understand this.

## Preface to the U.S. Edition

*Arabian Seas* has gone through several incarnations, this being the third one. This new version was written partly at the Australian National University (Canberra) in 1998, partly at the IIAS branch office in Amsterdam in 1999. I am, as always, grateful to the IIAS for this (and other) support.

For the accomplishment of this American edition I ought to thank the CNWS-publicaties for permitting the reissue of this book; A. Gunder Frank (again) for his relentless plugging of this book with various publishers; Doug Merwin and staff of M.E. Sharpe for putting up with the surely often inordinate demands of this "flying Dutchman"; and last but not least Mark Selden, my indefatigable guide through the labyrinth of American (and, dare I remind him, British) publishing. Yet the heaviest debt can only be expressed in the dedication of both the Dutch and the U.S. editions.

There have been a number of changes between the two editions—inevitably so, as research and intense academic debate continue on many of the questions discussed here. In particular the appearance of A. Gunder Frank's book *Reorient: Global Economy in the Asian Age* and the controversy surrounding it have prompted me to sharpen my argument, which is still fairly tentative in the Dutch edition, on whether or not there was a linked world economy before the eighteenth century.[1] On the whole I now tend to think there was.

Furthermore, the recent work of what J. Goldstone calls the "California school of historians/sociologists" has rightly alerted us to the danger of "historical triumphalism": of discerning putative weaknesses in the Asian (or African) economic structure merely because Europe "won." Up to the late eighteenth century there was not really any great divergence in productivity and wealth between Orient and Occident, the California school has been arguing, and that is a position I fully share.[2]

I should add, though, that much of the work of California historians, while speaking broadly about "Asia," is really mainly referring to—and in some cases seems to be somewhat biased toward—China. It is much weaker on South and Southeast Asia, very weak on the Middle East, and totally ignores East Africa.[3]

Yet East Africa is an integral part of the trading world of the Arabian seas that cannot be dismissed easily. The major difference between the U.S. and the Dutch editions is hence that East Africa is now being dealt with at some length, while in the Dutch edition I paid only scant attention to this "western half" of the Arabian seas. This is partly because, in particular, M.N. Pearson's recent study *Port Cities and Invaders* has convinced me that East Africa was neither so isolated nor as different from the rest of the Arabian seas as I originally supposed.[4]

But this book is also an attempt to write World history, or rather world history with a small *w*. It is an attempt "to provide a historical perspective," in J.H. Bentley's phrasing, "that transcends national frontiers" and, not the least important, spans the boundaries between the academic discourses of Indianists, Iranists, and Africanists—the difference between Asianist and Africanist discourses being particularly glaring—and provide a perspective on a "regional, continental and global scale."[5] The essential task of world history is, then, to seek connections across space and across academic disciplines at the same time, rather than comparisons within disciplines across time.

This approach is sure to conflict with established national schools of historiography and with the established methodology of "area studies," both on European expansions and on the societies in the Arabian seas. I can only hope it may prove useful. Again, with such a large topic there are bound to be errors, either in judgment or in fact.

Above all, however, I hope that the topic of this book will captivate the mind and the imagination of the reader as much as it did mine. May the monsoon rustle through these pages.

## Notes

1. A. Gunder Frank, *Reorient: The Global Economy in the Asian Age* (Berkeley, 1998).
2. See, for example, the recent works of R. Bin Wong, *China Transformed: Historical Changes and the Limits of the European Experience* (Ithaca, 1997); and K. Pomeranz, *The Great Divergence: Europe, China and the Making of the Modern World* (Princeton, 2000).
3. For, as Pomeranz (*The Great Divergence*, p. 40) admits: "a combination of enormous variety and weak data"—and, I'm also afraid, rather uneven research—"make it particularly hard to generalize about South Asia, or even to make the sort of statements about subregions that are possible for China, Japan and Europe." And if that is true for South Asia it is doubly true for Iran and Iraq, not to mention for East Africa, Madagascar, or the Arab Peninsula.
4. M.N. Pearson, *Port Cities and Invaders: The Swahili Coast, India and Portugal in the Early Modern Age* (Baltimore and London, 1998).
5. J.H. Bentley, introduction to the first issue of *Journal of World History*, 1 (1) (1990), p. iii.

# THE ARABIAN SEAS

1

# Introduction

To the merchants and mariners of the seventeenth century, the wide waters of the Indian Ocean appeared of vast, even colossal scale. An eternity was spent crossing it and there were myriad perils to be overcome during journeys that adversity could extend from months to years—truly, like those braved by the gallant Sindbad. The Indian or Arab dhows, frail vessels, would linger in their ports of call for months to wait for next year's favorable monsoon. It might easily take them two or three years to traverse the entire ocean round trip.

And for their later historian those boundless sweeps of ocean are a formidable obstacle as well. If we include the South China Sea, the waves of the "large" Indian Ocean sweep shores inhabited by most of humankind and encompass most of its recorded history. So, I propose to divide this vast sweep of ocean into three parts: the seas of and around the Indonesian Archipelago, the Bay of Bengal area, and the western Indian Ocean. I call the western Indian Ocean the Arabian seas, encompassing the Arabian Sea and the interior of the Persian Gulf and the Red Sea, as these two seas have both long been tied to the expanse of the Arabian Sea, and extending to the waters off the East African coast.

If still large, this is an area with old and deep commercial linkages, one bound by common characteristics and by common networks, which merits consideration as a whole. I would defend that historically those "lands before the wind" stand apart from the Bay of Bengal, from the Indonesian Archipelago, and from the South China Sea. And in many respects this is the historic core area of the Indian Ocean.

One might term the Arabian seas a "world economy" within which all trajectories could be covered in one monsoon. This made it feasible to send bulk products not only along the coast but also from one side of the sea to the other without incurring prohibitive transport costs.

The Arabian seas during the seventeenth century and in the centuries prior may be perceived not so much as a closely interlocking or unipolar system, like the modern world economy, but as a much looser series of networks. J. Voll defines it as "a social system that had boundaries, structures, member groups,

**Map 1. The Indian Subcontinent and Burma**

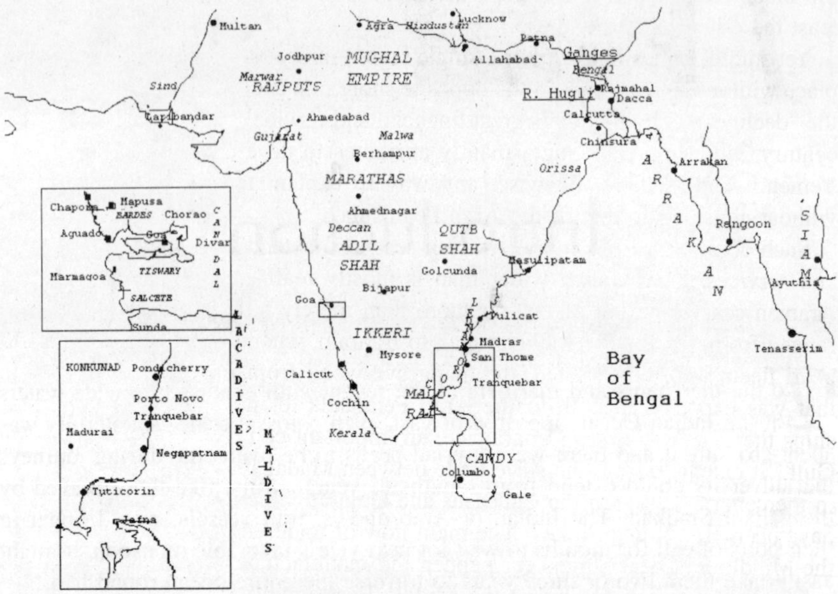


rules of legitimation and coherence" with ties over a wide area, but whose commercial nodes penetrated the rural economy only to a very slight extent. It also lacked a central location where prices throughout the system were fixed, like Wall Street or the City of London nowadays, and a single hegemonic center, like Britain in the nineteenth century and the United States in much of the twentieth.[1]

Yet commercial ties ranged far and wide—far wider, in fact, than is commonly recognized in most studies of Asian trade, linking areas seemingly as remote from the world market as the interior of Rajasthan or Malawi to a flourishing trade centered on the Arabian seas and extending beyond it. For the Arabian seas were linked by far-flung trading networks that extended into Europe, Central Asia, East Asia, Southeast Asia, Central Africa, and the Americas.

First and foremost, then, this study is an extended brief for "globalism," for in exploring and focusing on linkages within and beyond the Arabian seas, it tries to overcome the limits of the area studies approach. In far too many studies what was happening in, say, the Safavid empire is seen as fundamentally incompatible with and unrelated to what was happening in the Mughal empire. The task ahead is not so much to compare the developments in those two empires as to causally link them.[2]

This seems to be a particularly pressing issue for the Swahili Coast. Because of the deep institutional and theoretic academic cleft between Asian and African studies, this area continues to be studied—by both Africanists and historians of the Indian Ocean—as if it were evolving in isolation from Asia and not in the least the other way around too.[3]

Yet studies on a single city or a single region rarely can explain what is taking place without taking those on the opposite shore into account. Take, for example, the "decline of Surat," India's great financial and service center, in the eighteenth century, which A. Das Gupta mainly attributes to developments in Persia and Yemen.[4] And is there, likewise, any way to explain the history of Zanzibar without considering that of the Arab Peninsula?

Such commercial ties in the Arabian seas also extended to an array of goods and services that is much wider than is mostly realized. For the trade of the Arabian seas consisted of far, far more than merely silk, textiles, or spices. It ranged from the trade in Malabar teak to Bahrain, where the vessels used in the pearl fleets were constructed, the mangrove wood from the Lamu Archipelago that was exported in bulk to the Arab Peninsula to make masts and rees for ships there, and so on to Canara rice, an important commodity for cities in the Gulf.[5] It extended from the slave trade between Madagascar and the Gulf to that in mercenaries between the Caucasus and Gujarat, which surprisingly appear to have been closely interlinked. The main flow of trade, though, was bullion from the Middle East, exchanged for pepper and manufactured goods from India.

The link between India and the Middle East comprised the largest volume, although it certainly was not the most profitable branch of trade in the Arabian seas. A secondary but still substantial trade linked India and East Africa, and East Africa and the Middle East.

Yet the entire region was crisscrossed by such overlapping networks, and these were in turn linked to global markets extending overseas to Europe, China, Southeast Asia, and the Americas as well as overland to Central Asia and Central and West Africa.

Muslim merchants often dominated trade in the Arabian seas, and Islamic kings mainly ruled the shorelines. But the Arabian seas were not an "Islamic sea" and this was not an era of "Islamic dominance over trade."[6] Sailors and traders of many creeds were present. If Arab and Persian traders controlled a sizeable share of Surat's trade, for example, Gujarati and Sindi *bania*s (members of the merchant caste) were ubiquitous in the Gulf. Again, while there were a few hundred Indians from Goa resident at Mozambique, there were thousands of Africans resident at Goa, which was as African as Mozambique was Indian. Ethnic, national, or religious labels are of limited use in a pre-national and—in a way—"ecumenical" age.[7]

Rather than discerning one dominant group, we should perceive the Arabian seas as an "archipelago of towns" (or rather towns and their wide surroundings) populated by traders, mariners, and fishermen living within various *natio*s, autonomous communities that linked the various coastal areas. The population of those cities often strongly differed from the hinterland and they linked the coast to the interior; such cities were called *échelles*, or "scales," in the Levant. These were often like windows offering a glance on an alien environment.

Now, while we will navigate wider seas than regional studies and address more issues than essays that deal with a group of traders or a company, this study still focuses on an area and time span that can be explored on the basis of original sources. It is the reliance on primary sources that distinguishes the present work from numerous broad syntheses relying on the secondary literature, of which there have been several recently.[8] For although indigenous material is rather scanty for the seventeenth century, the prodigious quantities of European archival and documentary sources left allow an examination of trade and society in the Indian Ocean in far greater depth than has so far been attempted. That is even true for regions where indigenous sources do exist, such as Yemen.[9]

The secondary literature tends to perpetuate certain disciplinary biases too. There is, for example, a huge anthropological, linguistic, and archeological literature on Kenya and Tanzania. However, this literature focuses either on the period before 1500, for which there is a good archeological record, or on the period after 1800, for which the anthropological and linguistic data are much fuller. A further problem of these studies is their area studies bias—since students of the Swahili Coast are Africanists they tend heavily to stress links of the coast to the African hinterland. To a relative outsider like the present author it would sometimes seem as if the "essentially African character of the Swahili" is something like a mantra among the specialists.[10]

This is obviously a major problem for Madagascar. If, by way of example of such an area studies bias, with M.C. Hornton we assume that "Asiatic colonisation of the East African coast remains an unlikely and unproven hypothesis," we have a big problem with Madagascar.[11] For not only the Malagasy language but also many tools, tomb styles, and religious practices on Madagascar can be traced to Indonesian origins.[12] Madagascar (and the Comoros) was really more closely tied to the Indian Ocean and to the Arabian seas than to the "African history" to which it is assigned by conventional academic boundaries.

There is also in the literature a tendency to locate East Africa in a peripheral position, destined to underdevelopment, because it had few contacts with Europe.[13] This tendency is in many ways also found in the literature on Iran, which emphasizes the (few) commercial contacts with Europe and slights the overwhelmingly important links to India. If in the seventeenth century Iran or East Africa stood in a relationship to any "world-system," it was to that of the Arabian seas rather than to that of Europe.[14]

The Arabian seas had at least since the Hellenistic period been one of the crossroads of global social, military, and cultural exchanges as well as of commercial ones. And commodity and bullion movements in the region had long had conjunctural fluctuations in common.[15]

In the seventeenth century the Arabian seas continued to link major regions of the world economy. As A. Gunder Frank has recently persuasively argued against J. Abu-Lughod, the ancient world-system did not simply disintegrate in the fifteenth century despite heavy strains in the system. Rather it persisted right through to the industrial revolution. Indeed, though disagreeing on many details, this study is a prolonged demonstration of Gunder Frank's main point: the continued vitality of the ancient world economy—a vitality that extended even to the classic case of decline, the silk route.[16]

Production and accumulation, however, were not hierarchically arranged on the scale of the system as a whole. The ancient "ethnosphere"—to borrow a term from L.N. Gumilev[17]—was a multiethnic, multipolar network of cultural and commercial exchange without any dominant center rather than a unipolar world-system. In the seventeenth century prices of goods and labor were still not linked throughout the global system, "world" prices were still not fixed at one location, and there was not as yet a hierarchical organization of production processes within the system as a whole.

Throughout much of the period from the twelfth to the seventeenth century, world trade in many ways still pivoted on China (the heartland or core put forward by Gunder Frank for the sixteenth to eighteenth centuries) and had another major center in the Arabian seas, including Sudan, Ethiopia, and the Swahili Coast (Abu Lughod's candidate for heartland in the twelfth and thirteenth centuries).[18] Indeed, the core of the modern unipolar world-system, based on the Atlantic, and whose origins may be traced to the sixteenth century, arose side by side with, and was to some extent dependent upon, earlier dynamic trading nodes, including the Arabian seas, the Bay of Bengal and the South China Sea.[19]

Besides describing this trade we will—inevitably, as they cannot be ignored—also have to examine and compare the roles of the various European states active in the Arabian seas, studying their institutions, the organization of official and private trade, and the relation between the state and its servants.

This concerns principally the Portuguese Estado da Índia, the Dutch Verenigde Oost-Indische Compagnie (VOC), and the English East India Company (EIC). The Danish role in the Arabian seas was small, and the French were mainly confined to Madagascar. The French Compagnie des Indes was—until the eighteenth century—of only marginal importance to European trade within the Arabian seas. I will only briefly consider the Italian, Spanish, and Russian trade too. For the impact of the latter was mainly limited to the Caucasus and to Central Asia, that of the Italians to the Levant and the overland routes stretching from there, and that of the Spanish to the Pacific and Southeast Asia.

In the seventeenth and eighteenth centuries the Arabian seas region extended its linkages with the expanding modern world-system or the world economic order as we now know it. The territories surrounding the Arabian seas specialized in the production and trade of textiles, silk, and saltpeter as well as providing some agricultural commodities, particularly coffee, cotton, and sugar, and labor. Capital flows within the Arabian seas became ever more closely linked with worldwide bullion flows and credit systems.

Already in the late seventeenth century, products from the Arabian seas not only were marketed globally but also faced increasing pressure from competitors worldwide, whether located in Southeast Asia (for pepper, indigo, and sugar, and later coffee) or in the Caribbean and South America (for indigo, coffee, and cotton).

While this involved only a few products, and trade was still overwhelmingly conducted within the Arabian seas rather than with areas outside, it marked the initial stages of the region's peripheralization or—in plain English—the "development of underdevelopment."

In the beginning of the seventeenth century the contribution of the Arabian seas to world trade mainly centered on bullion, gold, pearls, diamonds, pepper, and to some extent silk. By the end of the seventeenth century, worldwide trade had emerged in various bulk products from the Arabian seas demanding a massive outlay of land and labor, including sugar, indigo, coffee, saltpeter, tobacco, cotton, and even rice and grains, as well as bulk-manufactured goods like calicoes. One can also speak of a growing world market for labor: not only slaves but also indentured labor and mercenaries.

Trade in the greater Indian Ocean was, until the late sixteenth century, organized through a system of interlocking circuits of trade, centralized in entrepôts from Kilwa to Canton. In the seventeenth century this was increasingly replaced by direct links between ports throughout Asia. Although indigenous shipowners certainly profited, the biggest beneficiaries were the VOC and the English private merchants engaged in "country trade" within the Indian Ocean. The country trade emerged as a dangerous competitor for the indigenous merchants, dealing in the same goods and sailing the same routes in the Arabian seas as Indian vessels.

In the course of the seventeenth century the growing system of direct commercial links and of production of bulk products in the Arabian seas and greater Indian Ocean began to fall under European control. VOC fleets controlled many of the major seaways of the Indian Ocean, which, ironically, mainly benefited the British, as the British state backed British country traders, interlopers on the VOC monopoly. By contrast, Asian merchants were not actively supported by their states, which generally remained aloof from conducting trade themselves and did relatively little to protect the position of their own merchants. The massive amounts of capital accumulated in London also favored the development of the British country trade linking the Indian Ocean and Europe.

Yet by 1700 the eventual British primacy was by no means a foregone conclusion. The present literature on India and the Indian Ocean, however, is largely based on British documentation, which has produced an image of the seventeenth century as prelude to a triumphant British dominion, ignoring the more voluminous Dutch documentation as well as that of the Portuguese "losers." But if there is no denying British dynamism, the seventeenth century nevertheless may best be characterized as the era of Dutch/Iberian rivalry in the Arabian seas. The VOC—and not the EIC—was the major European trader in the Arabian seas, while the Portuguese presence after 1640 has been unduly neglected.

Moreover, company studies have focused on official trade and contacts with Europe, which are more easily quantifiable than are private trade, intra-Asian or country trade, and smuggling.[20] These latter activities were of basic importance to Europeans (and Americans) in the Arabian seas, though. This has resulted in an underestimation not only of the true extent of Portuguese activities in the seventeenth-century world economy (for much of the Portuguese trade was conducted not by the state but by settlers, *casados*, in Asia as much as in Potosí or Angola) but of the activities of the Dutch as well.[21]

As the overwhelming bulk of the available documentation puts severe limits on the period that can be studied on the basis of primary material, this study focuses on the Arabian seas in the years 1640–1700. Power in the Indian Ocean shifted to the decisive disadvantage of Portugal in 1640 as that nation attained its independence from Spain and simultaneously became embroiled in a lengthy conflict with Spain. "Because of the war with Spain we are unable to make a major effort to aid India," the Portuguese sovereign council for the overseas possessions (Conselho Ultramarino) warned the settlements there in 1644.[22] The VOC seized this opportunity.[23] Portuguese fortresses throughout the Indian Ocean were rapidly conquered by the Dutch, resulting in a decisive shift toward Dutch dominion in the region and beyond.

The end point is surely arbitrary. I can frankly adduce no better apology than Clio's well-known love for round figures. One might, however, consider the period 1690 to 1710 a turning point.

Around 1710 English country trade surpassed the Dutch intra-Asian trade. Its growth was related to the burgeoning trade between Europe and Asia, a boom that began around 1690 and lasted until 1724. Around 1700 several new companies were chartered, partly conditioned by this boom: the Scottish Company, the association of English merchants trading in the East Indies (the English Company, competitor of the EIC), and the Portuguese *junta do comércio*. Old companies were provided with new charters, like the Danish one. Trade under flags of convenience flourished, favored by the economic boom.

The year 1690, therefore, was the beginning of an age of wild speculation that ended with the collapse of the "bubble companies" in the 1720s. But interloper traders had come to stay. The period from 1640 to 1700 may be seen, then, as the age of Dutch predominance in the waters of the Indian Ocean, and in a broader sense the era of the great monopoly companies. These had yet to face cutthroat competition from myriad interloper and "bubble" companies.

Even more important is the fact that after 1690 European demand for a number of new products from Asia rapidly increased, first in the coffee boom and then in the "tea madness." Those terms well convey the feverish nature of this traffic. The center of gravity for commerce shifted from India to Arabia and China. Trade with Asia in the second half of the seventeenth century was mainly characterized by the growth of the commerce in piece-cloth (the "calico craze") and spices.[24]

The seventeenth century was an age of Omani ascendancy in the Arabian seas too: this Omani presence is a thread connecting all shores of the Arabian seas, if one that is far less noted in the literature than the Dutch presence. And finally—but most importantly—this was an age in which the coast was dominated by empires centered in the hinterland: the Ottoman and the Safavid empires, the Zaidit imamate and the Mughal empire, and—to a very minor degree—the Monomotappa confederacy. The disintegration of these states in the early eighteenth century would pose vast new problems to the merchants in the Arabian seas. Those states protected the routes to the hinterland on which the *échelles* in the Arabian seas depended.

For, as we shall see in the following chapter, what is now sometimes called maritime (that is, what was once called "colonial") history of the Indian Ocean—a tale of ports, merchants, mariners, and Companies—cannot be written without constant reference to the camels, porters, and caravans of the hinterland, the classic domain of Islamicists, African anthropologists, and Indologists.[25]

## Notes

1. See J.O. Voll, "Islam as a Special World System," *Journal of World History* 5 (1) (1994), pp. 213–27; N. Steensgaard, "The Indian Ocean Network and the Emerging World-Economy ca. 1500–1700," in S. Chandra (ed.), *The Indian Ocean: Explorations in History, Commerce and Politics* (London, 1987), pp. 223–35.

2. As was already—though somewhat tentatively—tried by M. Athar Ali, "The Passing of Empire: The Mughal Case" *MAS* 9 (3) (1975), pp. 385–96.

3. Thus, as is already evinced in the title, K.N. Chaudhuri in *Asia Before Europe: Economy and Civilisation of the Indian Ocean from the Rise of Islam to 1750* (Cambridge, 1990), writes as if China is located in the Indian Ocean and as if East Africa is not.

4. A. Das Gupta, *Indian Merchants and the Decline of Surat* (Wiesbaden, 1976).

5. VOC/OB 1246, 6 February 1664, fo. 778.

6. See, for example, P. Risso, *Merchants and Faith: Muslim Commerce and Culture in the Indian Ocean* (Boulder, CO, 1995), p. 6.

7. Thus, the critical error in C.A. Hromnik, *Indo-Africa: Towards a New Understanding of the History of Sub-Saharan Africa* (Cape Town, 1981); A.M. Pescatello, "The African Presence in Portuguese India," in P. Manning (ed.), *Slave Trades, 1500–1800: Globalisation of Forced Labour* (V. Aldershot, 1996), pp. 279–91.

8. Such as A. Toussaint, *History of the Indian Ocean* (London, 1966); A. Wink, *Al Hind* (Leiden, 1991–), three volumes so far; and see the summary of the whole project in "*Al-Hind:* India and Indonesia in the Islamic World-Economy," *Itinerario* 12 (1) (1988), pp. 33–70; Chaudhuri, *Trade and Civilisation in the Indian Ocean: An Economic*

*History from the Rise of Islam to 1750;* K. MacPherson, *The Indian Ocean: A History of the People and the Sea* (New Delhi, 1994); and R. Hall, *Empires of the Monsoon: A History of the Indian Ocean and Its Invaders* (London, 1996).

9. As has recently been shown in C.G. Brouwer's exemplary *Al Mukha: Profile of a Yemeni Seaport as Sketched by Servants of the Dutch East India Company 1614–1640* (Amsterdam, 1997).

10. R. Wilding (ed.), *Swahili Bibliography of the East African Coast* (Nairobi, 1990).

11. M.C. Hornton, "Asiatic Colonisation of the East African Coastlines: The Mande Evidence," *Journal of the Royal Asiatic Society* (1986), p. 20.

12. There is a vast literature on this problem of Malagasy origins, for it has fascinated linguists for a long time. Even one of the very first Dutch visitors, Frederick Houtman, who in 1613 compiled a short dictionary of Malagasy, could already not fail to notice the resemblance with Malay and speculate on the origins of the language. D. Lombard (ed.), *Le "Spraak ende Woorde-boeck" de Frederick de Houtman. Première méthode de malais parlé (fin du XVI siècle)* (Paris, 1970), p. 5.

13. For example, in A.M. Sheriff, "Trade and Underdevelopment. Economic History of the East African Coast from the 9th to the 15th Century," *Hadith* 5 (1975), pp. 1–23.

14. J. Foran, "The Making of an External Area: Iran's Place in the World-System," *Review* 12 (1) (1989), pp. 79–119.

15. And the Arabian seas had, long before the Portuguese, been the object of "imperialist" grand politics to control its trade. See, e.g., for the politics of Byzantium in the Arabian seas: N. Pigulewskaja, *Byzanz auf der Wege nach Indien. Aus der Geschichte des byzantinischen Handels mit dem Orient im 4 bis 6 Jahrhundert* (Berlin, 1969).

16. J. Abu-Lughod, *Before European Hegemony: The World System* A.D. *1250–1350* (New York, 1989). See also R. Palat and I. Wallerstein, "Of What World-System Was Pre-1500  'India' a Part?" in S. Chaudhuri and M. Morineau (eds.), *Merchants, Companies and Trade* (Paris, 1996).

17. L.N. Gumilev, *Etnosfera: Istorija lijudej i istorija prirody* (Moscow, 1993).

18. For, although Abu-Lughod ignores Africa, Egypt looked south and east as much as north and west. If Egypt survived the economic contraction of the fourteenth century better than did China and Europe—as Lughod (note 16, above, p. 356) plausibly argues—that may well be related to her links with the trans-Sahara routes, with Ethiopia and the route to India through the Red Sea. Commerce along all of these routes appears to have flourished in the fourteenth century, contrary to that to the Middle East and Europe.

19. Cf. I. Wallerstein, *The Modern World-System* (New York, 1974–), 3 vols. so far.

20. Thus K.N. Chaudhuri, *The Trading World of Asia and the English East India Company 1660–1760* (Cambridge, 1978), deals with English participation in Asian trade in some 4 pages while allotting more than 400 to trade with Western Europe.

21. L. Hanke, "The Portuguese in South America, with special reference to the Villa Imperial de Potosí," *Revista de História de América* 51 (1958), pp. 1–48.

22. AHU, [Papeis vultos da] Índia, Cx. (old numbering) 17, 5, 5 October 1644.

23. See the discussion on what policy one was to follow upon the restoration of the Portuguese monarchy in the High Council of the Indies in 1641: as long as one did not have a definite confirmation from the Estates General and there merely existed a truce between Holland and Portugal, one should grab as much territory as possible (VOC/RGGR, 664, 11 September 1641).

24. On the "calico craze" see in particular C. Mukherjee, *From Graven Images: Patterns of Modern Materialism* (New York, 1983).

25. This alludes to the "epistemological wall" between the discourse on the hinterland and that on the coast, which is particularly strong in Indian studies, where "coast" and "hinterland" studies are virtually two distinct disciplines. (See F. Perlin, "Pre-Colonial South Asia and Western Penetration from the Sixteenth to the Nineteenth Century: A Problem of Epistemological Status," *Review*, 4 (2) (1980), pp. 276–306.)

2

# Ports and the Hinterland

We will now move to the period around 1670 to navigate the Mozambique Canal, the Persian Gulf, the Red Sea, and the west coast of India. This was a time of depression across the Arabian seas. Yet—and this will be the main theme of this chapter—the ports on the Arabian seas weathered this harsh economic climate very differently.

The unity of the Arabian seas is given by the monsoon. These are the lands before the wind, as the great Arab navigator Ibn Majid put it—poetically and aptly.[1] With a small *bombara* or *zambucca* or *bagla* (a female mule, the Arab name for the dhow, the workhorse for the navigation in the Arabian seas) one could sail from Basra to Bandar Abbas in three weeks, Basra to Cochin in three and a half months, Surat to Bandar Abbas in six weeks, Malindi to Goa in two months, northwest Madagascar to Muscat in two months, and so forth. Yet when sailing from Basra to Java there was a chance that one would "miss the monsoon" and would have to seek shelter at Cochin or Calicut. In the late seventeenth century it was still usual for Indian vessels from Surat, coming from the Philippines, to spend the winter on the Malabar Coast. Likewise, the uncertainty and short span of the monsoon winds necessitated that ships wanting to cross from Africa to India along the East African coast winter either in Mozambique or in Kilwa. This was the main reason, too, why Arab vessels did not venture much further than Sofala, which lay beyond the monsoon winds.[2]

Of course vessels of the Companies as well as large Indian ships might sail over the open ocean from Basra, or Mozambique, to Java in one season. But most Indian, African, and Arab shipping preferred safety to speed and tended to navigate, if possible, in sight of the coast. This is clear when considering the itineraries of Indian ships leased by the Companies or with an Arab and Indian pilot: the *Snoek,* for example, in 1645, which, since the currents of the Gulf were imperfectly known, was piloted by an Arab navigator and sailed in the "native fashion."[3]

A ship would, leaving Bandar Abbas, first touch at Kung to take pilots aboard, then port at Sheikh Sho'yeb to fetch fowl and goats and follow the Persian coast to Kharg. There the pilot from Kung would disembark and the ship would take on pilots for Basra and fresh water. Next it would moor off the estuary of the Kharun, so pilots for the Shatt al-Arab could go on board, and wait there for a few days more—while bartering provisions—until arriving at Basra. In all these small anchorages the vessel might linger up to two or three days, selling some merchandise to pay for supplies. The whole trip might easily take a month—while it was possible to cross the Gulf in two weeks if one were in a hurry.

But most were in no hurry, as the costs of the leisurely pace of navigation—tramping, one is tempted to say—were redressed by small transactions in the ports along the way and by a safer passage. The Persian Gulf, the Red Sea, the Mozambique Canal, and the Gulf of Cambay are dangerous and shallow waters filled with shifting sandbanks, coral reefs, and cliffs.

So ships generally sailed slowly from anchorage to anchorage. And, indeed, the Arabian seas can be seen as a linked array of narrow seas or "marine zones." Each was like a small archipelago plied by fishing boats, sloops, and small sailing vessels, and mostly populated by closely related communities of peddlers and fishermen.[4] This coastwise shipping fetched merchandise and provisions between ports in the narrow seas and rarely ventured beyond them. Such coastwise navigation comprised the bulk of shipping in the Arabian seas; trade along the littoral was the backbone of commerce.

The governor of Muscat estimated, for example, that 5,000 rowboats (*terradas*) could be found along the coast of Oman. This was probably an exaggeration. More realistic would seem another figure of about 250 small vessels that could be mustered by the imam of Oman. Again, the total number of available boats at Bahrain and surroundings was given as more than 500.[5] To take a case from the west coast, the number of crafts touching at Mangalore in 1682 was estimated at 125. The smallest were only 32 tons, the largest 60. But in total these sloops fetched 3,500,000 to 4,500,000 pounds of rice to Gujarat and Goa.[6]

This coastwise trade was pretty much the pursuit of small peddlers. To own a sloop one did not need to be wealthy. As to the Gulf: "if the Company would not trade here, this place [Bandar Abbas] would soon decay to but a fishermen's village. For the ports on either side of this Gulf are not places of big trade, except for the *bania*s, who with some goods—though in small quantities—go there like peddlers and hucksters. And since they can live soberly and survive on very little they are able to sell their goods for a meagre benefit."[7]

On the west coast, Pilaji, Vitoji, and Balaji—"carpenters, resident at Tana"—had equipped a boat to bring rice from there to Goa. They had borrowed money to pay for this venture but—eight of their sailors having fled to Candal—were unable to reimburse this and thrown in jail. On some sloops the captain might own part of the cargo and the sailors the rest. In others the mariners would be allowed to take some goods along, while the rest of the cargo was owned by a partnership of small hawkers. Govind Das and Musem Das, Gujaratis, requested of the governor of Bassein that they be relieved of the debt on a loan they had signed for making a trip with a sloop to Cambay to trade rice from Bassein. It had been damaged in a storm and they were unable to pay the interest. They supplicated "on behalf of the merchants, the dealers [*trattantes*], the owners of the ship [*os donos da nau*], the sergeants [*mocadais*] and the sailors," who all had a share in this voyage.[8]

It was a large step for a trader from coastwise trade to oceanic navigation, which was far more hazardous and demanded long-term outlays. The *bania*s, "traders, presently in Daman," requested of the captain there that they be acquitted of a bottomry contract, which they had signed with the captain for taking ivory from Mozambique. They normally traded in salt between Daman and Broach, overland and on small sloops, and the long-distance trade was far too risky. "It is a long voyage and they have creditors in this land. They are unable to pay when the term for remuneration is this long."[9]

In general merchants do not appear to have known a great deal about the empty, hostile coastlines that intersected the narrow seas plied by coastwise trade. Companies or the Estado had never charted large parts of the Arabian seas—and there was no need to do so, as vessels followed long-established routes.

Knowledge of coastlines, sandbanks, or cliffs was jealously guarded by a hereditary guild of pilots who were reluctant to lose income by giving information. When the Dutch wanted to establish the position of reefs and sandbanks from Mocha to Hodeida nobody had the slightest knowledge of it except two old "Arab navigators." This applies to the Persian Gulf, the estuary of the Indus, the Mozambique Canal, and the Gulf of Cambay as well. It is not amazing that few Indian maps of the seaways between India and the Red Sea or the Gulf have so far been found. There was an ancient store of orally transmitted—and secret—navigational knowledge, as Indian or Arab navigators sailed along the same routes for hundreds—if not thousands—of years and seem to have rarely ventured beyond these.[10]

The collaboration of indigenous pilots was therefore a crucial local contribution to the rise of European empire. The Portuguese supported the families of pilots established at Kharg to guide them through the dangerous, often inhospitable, waters of the Gulf, for example. In Mozambique, again, piloting ships was one of the main sources of income of the Swahili community and one of the main reasons why the Portuguese, however reluctantly, had to allow their presence there.[11]

Politically the Arabian seas in the late seventeenth century present us with a rather ambiguous picture. On the one hand, on land, most of the small buffers—city-states that had existed in the late sixteenth century—had been subdued or become a tributary of great empires in the hinterland: Zeila of Ethiopia, Basra of the Mamluk, pashas of Baghdad, Hormuz, and Bahrain of the Safavid empire. But at sea no single state, like the Portuguese in the sixteenth century, controlled the ocean. Dutch control was confined to the Indonesian Archipelago and Ceylon. The sovereignty over the waters of the Arabian seas had devolved to a number of small chieftains, vague feudatories of land empires. Angão Island (Sheikh Sho'yeb) was in 1673 nominally still a fief of the long extinct Turanshah dynasty of Hormuz, for example. Nobody had claimed sovereignty over this place although it was one of the key locations of the Gulf.[12]

In the late seventeenth century this vacuum was partly filled by a new power that asserted paramountcy over former Portuguese, Ottoman, and Safavid tax gatherers in the narrow seas: the Ja'ariba imamate of Oman.[13]

This Ja'ariba ascent was particularly marked on the Swahili Coast. Because of the ancient close ties between the Arab-Wangwana elites on the Swahili Coast and those of the Arab Peninsula, when the Portuguese lost Muscat in 1650 this was bound to have instant repercussions in East Africa. Pemba, Pate, and the queen of Zanzibar revolted against the Portuguese and sided with Oman in 1652. While the captain of Mombasa extinguished the uprising at Pemba—with Muzungulo aid—there were insufficient means to attack Pate and Zanzibar. And the inhabitants on the mainland were much less supportive of the Portuguese there. Those two cities turned to staunch anti-Portuguese bulwarks on the coast.[14]

There ensued a long and bitter war between the Estado da Índia and Oman, fostered on the proceeds of the East African trade, which the Portuguese were losing by 1690. And this was because of the Portuguese inefficiency as much as because the Muscatis were paradoxically more "progressive" than the Portuguese. The Muscati field artillery (mostly fabricated in Muscat) assembled during the siege of Mombasa far outclassed the Portuguese artillery, although the fall of Mombasa to the Muscatis was far more due to cholera than to guns. And they not only outgunned the Portuguese but outpriced them as well; the only way to outclass Muscati traders on the Swahili Coast, it was asserted, would be to give away textiles.[15] And, finally, Portuguese commanders, who had mostly bought their command, tried to make this investment pay by indiscriminate ransacking and plundering of the Swahili Coast and of the Gulf. Such was by 1690 the main pursuit of the Portuguese, which surely did not endear them to the inhabitants of either.[16]

Mombasa was under siege from 1696 to 1699. When this stronghold fell, the former Portuguese allies on the Swahili Coast were forced to side with the Ja'ariba imam. Thus in the case of Zanzibar, which was directly subjected to Muscati rule, its ruling family was evicted by the Muscati governor. Or they were forced to flee, like the king of Ampassa—in the Lamu Archipelago and then one of the major ports of the Swahili Coast—who went into exile in Goa.[17]

In other areas too, Muscat emerged as a successor power to the Estado. The Muscati fleets devastated Kung in 1693, bombarded Mocha in 1696, attacked Bahrain in 1694 and 1698, assaulted Zeila in 1702, and conquered Mukalla in 1689. By 1700 the Muscati Arabs were, ubiquitously and aggressively, present in the Arabian seas. At Surat, the Omani trade flotillas had their own wharves and fortified compounds while being allowed reduced customs. They were well armed and manned; the oared vessels of the Mughal fleet could not brave them. The Omanis threatened in 1696 to bombard Surat if they were not allotted rights to fortify their factory. Along the west coast of India, Oman had erected a system of fortified warehouses, like at Janjira on the Konkan Coast and at Cananore. Ministers named by the governor of Muscat mostly administered those magazines.[18]

## Brides of the Sea

Some ports in the Arabian seas, such as Basra, Cambay, Surat, Siyu, Calicut, Cochin, or Pemba, although they were centers of trade too, were mainly agricultural market towns obtaining goods from their farming hinterland. The first four possessed a fairly large manufacturing industry as well, fabricating not just goods related to the port but commodities for the internal market too. These were exceptions: the life of most ports depended entirely on the maritime trade, making them true "brides of the sea."[19]

As to their institutions, we may draw a distinction between fairs and communities, or in the Swahili terminology—where fairs were normally makeshift wooden huts surrounded by a palisade—"wooden" and "stone" ports. "City-states" one may call the latter, even if they often recognized an overlord like the Estado, the Zaidit imamate of Yemen, or chiefs in the immediate hinterland.

Thus, for example, at Mombasa, where a given percentage of the customs revenues was reserved for the neighboring "kings of the Muzungulos"—or the Mijikenda (the "six cities"), as they were later known—goods fetched by the Muzungulo chiefs from the hinterland were bought by the Portuguese *feitor* at favorable prices and exempted from duties, and the chiefs were closely linked to the ruling families of Mombasa, so that each leading family there had its counterpart on the mainland. Although the Muzungulo-Mombasa relationship is exceptionally well documented, other ports on the Swahili Coast like Querimba, Seguju, Pemba, and Kilwa had a similar relationship with neighboring chiefs.[20]

Those towns boasted an ancient history and communal institutions and a sultan chosen from the old established families, whose genealogies would trace their descent to the Prophet. They paid scribes to write chronicles of the town. They might have a council of aldermen running their affairs. Commercial profits were invested in mosques or Koranic schools.

Many ports of the Hadramawt, like Khisn, Mukalla, and Aden, may be termed city-states, as may some ancient ports on the Swahili Coast, like Mogadishu, Brava, Malindi, Kilwa, or Pate. The tiny Comoro islands of Mayotte and Anjuan may be considered communities as well, and so too the ancient Islamic settlements in Kerala like Panani and Cananore. The latter places were all, to some extent, transplantations of Hadramawti city-states to the tropics.[21] Basra, an ancient metropolis with intricate urban institutions and a convoluted urban politics, was an independent city-state during the first half of the seventeenth century, vaguely tributary to the pashas of Baghdad too.[22]

The fairs had but a recent history and there existed no real civil feeling. Such ports were generally ruled by a governor presiding over higher jurisdiction, a lord of the castle controlling the garrison and military jurisdiction, and a portmaster or *shahbandar*. Communal representation was limited to handling the occasional petition. The various *natio*s of merchants inhabiting those fairs were autonomous and would settle disputes within their own circle. Apart from a few laborers and soldiers of the garrison, most of the population of Hormuz, Kung, Bandar Abbas, or Mocha resembled a band of gypsies encamped in tents, as around Kung, or dwelling on the flat rooftops (to escape the sweltering heat of summer) at Hormuz and Bandar Abbas.[23] There was no manufacturing industry. At Mocha and Bandar Abbas it was not even possible to repair ships; one had to take these either to Muscat or all the way to Surat.[24]

Those fairs completely depended on the routes connecting them to the interior. If these routes shifted, the towns vanished as if blown away by a volcanic eruption. Some are now only fields of ruins: Hormuz, for example, or Laribandar. Others have virtually withered without trace: Kung, for example, or take the case of Miani in Sind, which was a very significant port in the early seventeenth century—its share in the Mocha trade being more significant than those of the English and Dutch combined, in fact—but had turned into a mere fishing village by 1670.[25]

Such ports were mainly, to use a term from the Levant trade, *échelles:* places where seaways were tied to routes to the interior. This involved not just disembarking goods and loading them on bullocks or camels, but a whole array of financial transactions too: insuring the goods, writing bills to pay for procuring goods or their delivery, and handing advances to the caravans for paying customs along the way. Banking would grow along with maritime trade and some towns seem to have remained financial centers if shipping declined.[26]

The *échelles* often differed from their surroundings and hinterland with respect to language, population, or customs.[27] For the port cities were, as we shall see, major killers of their population by famine as much as by epidemics. Thus they had constantly to be fed by new immigrants from across the seven seas lest they die out rapidly. The population of the Strait of Hormuz, for example, is Arab. Yet Hormuz was a multinational—Persian-speaking—mart inhabited by crowds of Persians, Turks, Armenians, Jews, Indians, and Coptic and Syrian Christians, as well as the occasional Ethiopian and Italian merchant. Such a multitude of drifting traders, blown along with the monsoon, gathered there "that some believe this city is the center of the world." They were "people of the sea" attracted to it by maritime trade—but there were few Arabs.[28]

The meteoric growth and equally abrupt decline of such ports only marginally concerned the communities in the vicinity: the 200 Arab families, the original inhabitants of Hormuz—fishermen mostly—dwelled on the island before the rise of the town and settled amid the ruins after its fall.[29]

This may also be said of many of the stone towns and certainly of the wooden towns on the East African littoral, either fairs connecting the Swahili towns to the hinterland or makeshift villages on the mainland where the urban elite and "middle classes" had their gardens and plantations. Such extensive rural "suburbs" surrounded most towns: normal East African kraals—unlike the stone towns with their Arab appearance. But—as we now only see the ruins of the stone cities, whereas the wooden cities have disappeared—it is easy to exaggerate the extent to which the Swahili cities were cut off from the immediate surroundings. But they drew both supplies and manpower from their *umland,* as it is now called in the literature on port cities. If only for their food and cattle, the stone towns depended on the wooden cities. Manufacturing—leatherwork, woodwork, net making, and so forth—was also concentrated in the wooden towns. And, indeed, some towns on the Swahili Coast, like Siyu, were mainly centers for the manufacturing industry and conducted little trade.[30] It might be argued that Swahili itself, with its mixture of Arab, Persian, Portuguese, and Bantu words, reflected this symbiosis between stone and wood cities. By extension, the Swahili (the "people of the coast") were originally probably shore folk rather than an ethnic group, tribe, or civilization: drifting people of the coast on the African littoral, of many different origins.[31]

For tribal, ethnic, or national boundaries were of limited relevance to the people of the coast in the Arabian seas and were spanned by matrimony as much as by the invention of genealogies. To take a concrete example: there is a petition from 1685 signed by all members of the elite of Pate in which they pledged to subject themselves to the Portuguese king. Almost all names are unmistakably Bantu rather than Arab. But, in spite of that, Pate was—as mentioned already—pretty much the fulcrum of Omani power on the coast in this period. Was Pate any less "Arabic" and Islamic if its elite was by and large African?[32]

But although the raison d'être for these *échelles* was the long-distance trade and they often stood apart from their surroundings, they did have an immediate impact on and were closely tied to their *umland,* economically as much as ecologically. The repair of ships required wood, for example, just as did the construction of houses and the making of charcoal. A great port would thus deplete the forests nearby. This was the case at Bassein, where the Portuguese had cut down the teak forests on the hills near the town. By 1640 all the woodland nearby had been exhausted and trees had to be obtained from Manora and beyond. Lumber had become too expensive for profitable trade, though at the beginning of the century Bassein had exported this in quantity to Goa.[33]

The rise and fall of the *échelles* in the Arabian seas, which we will survey here, depended on shifts in the caravan routes linking the coast with the interior. Except for those cities that commanded an agricultural hinterland, the ports wandered too—along with the people inhabiting them.

## East Africa

The East African coast is commonly divided into four—the Banadir Coast, the Mrima Coast, Mozambique, and Madagascar. The last is—and was—really a continent in itself. Like its fauna, the cultures of Madagascar too constitute a "museum" of groups, usages, and beliefs from throughout the Indian Ocean, often long forgotten elsewhere. Material artifacts and beliefs derive as much from Borneo as from Sofala and Zimbabwe, and minorities range from the Barra hunters in the southwestern interior, who must derive from Africa, to the clearly Indonesian Hova; from Jews, speaking an ancient Egyptian version of Hebrew, to Gujarati *bohras*, or farmers. The Comoros are, likewise, both for navigation and in cultural terms, a critical stepping-stone between Madagascar and the mainland, and another museum.[34]

South from Cape Garadafui to Lamu is the Banadir Coast, a desert area. Amid the empty plains are some sand dunes and mostly empty riverbeds. Astride these dry riverbeds are a few ancient trade centers, of which Mogadishu and Brava are best known.

The coral islands of the Lamu Archipelago, on which several rival trade cities are located—of which Pate had succeeded Lamu as the most important in the seventeenth century—are the northernmost border of the Mrima Coast.

> For the traveller approaching East Africa from the sea a charming and alluring prospect awaits the eye, as though a damask cloth were spread out and thereon was displayed a delightful repast. Pearl-white beaches, breeze-cooled palm groves; the quiet surge of the warm coral sea and hush of the trade winds all combine to create an enchanting and tranquil sphere. In this beneficent and paradisical setting where the senses savour the unmistakable and indefinable tang of the East, thoughts arise as to what further delights lie behind such an inviting threshold.[35]

Thus writes a very poetic R.W. Beachey—albeit, for Europeans, all this beauty was in the seventeenth century more than offset by the malaria endemic here. However enchanting the coast might have seemed, few survived more than a year's stay here. And it might well be argued too that malaria, cholera, and smallpox, more than any other factor, forestalled access to the hinterland until the nineteenth century.[36]

For, though the dry savannah of the Nyaka plain beyond the coast is not a very hospitable area, it is not a true desert either and certainly no inaccessible barrier: there are several corridors leading across the Nyaka with sufficient water. Along the coast are, often closed off by sandbanks, many inlets, some of which are easily accessible from the sea, and tiny coral islands. On these islands, or on tongues of land, mostly isolated by swamps, are located many old cities, such as Mombasa, Malindi, Pemba, and Zanzibar, tracing back their history to the Arab settlement on the coast from the ninth to the thirteenth century. These cities on the Mrima Coast are the ancient heartland of the Swahili language and culture, which in the seventeenth century spanned the coast from Mogadishu north to Mozambique and south to the Comoros.[37]

In the seventeenth century most of these cities were small independent sultanates, consisting of the core city, suburbs, and gardens on the mainland or on nearby islands. These "plantations" might stretch for extensive distances along the coast, as at Pate, where the urban elite had claims on plots throughout the Lamu Archipelago, but mostly only a few miles inland. The city-states were dominated by a number of lineages (Arabic: *taif*) mostly tracing their origins either back to Arab or Persian colonists or to the legendary founders of the city, hidden in the distant past. Under this ruling aristocracy was a middle class of merchants, shipowners, and owners of gardens; a lower class of sailors, workers, and small farmers; and finally a substantial underclass of slaves.[38]

This regime was quite fluid, however, as there was a constant circulation of elites: one could be adopted into ruling lineages, or subordinate groups could weld an alliance by marriage or concubinage. Furthermore, the ruling families were divided into several factions, which assumed power in the city-states in turn.[39] Factions were linked to those in other city-states, and since lineages might stretch along the entire coast and ruling families were closely related, there existed an intricate balance of love and hate between the Swahili cities.

South of Kilwa the coast is sheltered by the coral islands of the Querimba Archipelago and yonder by lagoons and sandbanks. Kilwa was the southernmost frontier of the "house of Islam" in East Africa. Beyond were located the dry and unsettled plains of the Macua territory, where a few remote Swahili outposts, with only a few hundred inhabitants, such as Angoche in northernmost Mozambique and Mozambique itself, led a precarious existence.[40]

The Mrima Coast produced sufficient food and some towns such as Pemba were even able to export substantial quantities of fruits, yams, and rice to Soccotra, Mogadishu, and occasionally Yemen. But the cities in northern Mozambique were deficient in it and had to rely entirely on the precarious incomes of trade to subsist. In the northern part of Mozambique various great rivers run into the sea: the Rovuma, the Zambesi (or Cuama, as the Portuguese called it), and the Limpopo. The estuaries of these great rivers are quite green and densely populated. South of the Zambesi the coastal forests slowly give way to arid savannah—few people lived there, "subsisting on little else but fishing." But, although the area might hold great riches like pearls and cowry shells, neither was exported in any quantity because of insufficient labor. Green inlets of the sea, of which a few were densely populated, interrupt this dreary region.[41]

In 1685 Pieter Clarton and the *Jan en Marie* (Dutch rendering), obviously a

British interloper, was hired by the VOC at Cape Town to survey the southernmost tip of Mozambique (Maputo): Dela Goa Bay. This was then still a rather obscure spot but destined for greatness under the name Lourenço Marques.[42]

The *Jan en Marie* was anchored from July till January in the bay near a large island, which was called St. Mary (not to be confused with its namesake at Madagascar).

> We went ashore to trade with the natives every day, in well-armed sloops for we do not trust them a great deal—sometimes too they came on board with their canoes; to vend their goods; we faked we were not interested and bartered but small quantities.

Clarton mainly bartered rough *bafta* (textiles), pearl beads, and coral against ivory, gum, and ambergris. One piece of ivory weighing 100 pounds would cost only 20 beads—much cheaper than at Mozambique.

The land was fertile and densely populated. The Tsonga inhabitants, spread in kraals along the coast, hunted elephants, fished, and cultivated coarse grain. Various small kings ruled here; the most important was nicknamed João Joaquim by the Portuguese. Clarton gifted him with a bottle of spirits.[43]

The Portuguese conducted barter up to 100 miles into the interior. As a base, they had constructed a reed settlement of 100 houses and a church, which the traders would vacate between the monsoons. In December the Portuguese tuned up indeed: a small vessel of only 160 tons, filled to the gunwales with peddlers from Mozambique. "The skipper and 6 to 8 others were native Portuguese, the others mostly kaffirs from Mozambique, as well as 25 to 30 *lascarins* from Goa."[44]

What a paradisiacal spot, Clarton exclaimed, and what a waste to leave it to those stupid Portuguese! He thought it would be an excellent location to build a fortress, and he urged Cape Town to do so. Cape Town was at first reluctant to embark upon this risky venture but in 1721 finally decided to construct a stronghold on Dela Goa Bay, mainly to buy slaves and ivory, but also to possibly gain access to the gold trade from the Rozvi dominion.[45]

The main trading center of this southern Mozambican region was the Portuguese fortification of Sofala. Sofala had known its balmy days in the fifteenth and sixteenth centuries, when it was a booming center for the transit trade to the periodic markets in the hinterland and had boasted a flourishing community of Arab/Swahili traders. Yet as the Portuguese moved further and further inland, it lost much of that function. Sofala still had some importance as a center for the gold trade to Torwa—a vast domain to the south of Monomotappa, of which the Portuguese had only a vague notion and where they were not admitted—and for coastwise trade in ivory, cattle, rice, wax, and grain from the surrounding Kiteve kingdom to Mozambique. But the settlement was in rapid decline. To the decrepit fortress—in 1652 they briefly considered tearing it down altogether since it was totally beyond repair—manned by a dozen Indian and African soldiers in rags, which was gradually being eaten away by the sea, still clung the huts of a few dozen Afro-Portuguese *casados*. Sofala town had in 1636 about 150 inhabitants, with 1,300 people in the villages surrounding it.[46]

The Portuguese capital in East Africa, on the island of Mozambique, was described by the VOC in 1678 thus:[47]

> Mozambique is one and a half miles in width and about a long musket shot in breadth. It is surrounded by sandbanks and coral reefs with about 5 to 7 fathoms of water. On the north side is a fortress with four strongpoints, about as large in circumference as that on the Cape of Good Hope. It is built of coral stone and its foundations are built on cliffs on which severe waves break. One can approach these to a stone's throw distance. The garrison consists, in our estimate, of sixty men, including mestizos. It is a very unhealthy place, for the Portuguese, who live there, look as if they are all severely ill [*als ofte half vergeven waren*]. The scarcity of food contributes much to this but the brackish water most. The village has only one or two straight streets and it is a musket shot from the fortress. Between them is a level square, so that nothing can obstruct the view from the fortress. There are a few palm trees there but most of these as well as most of the village were destroyed by the Arabs five years ago.

In 1688 Mozambique had 15 Portuguese inhabitants, 17 Indian merchants, 400 Africans on the island, and 1,500 on the mainland opposite. And, indeed, as the VOC rightly concluded, the trade of Mozambique, which had reached its apogee around 1600, was in decline, as commerce was shifting from there and from Angoche northward to Querimba and Kilwa and southward to Quelimane. Quelimane was obviously closer to the gold trade than Mozambique; it had—unlike that sterile island—sources of fresh water nearby, and was, finally, the main port for the slave trade on the coast.[48]

The shift to the north might partly, but not entirely, be explained by shifting routes in the interior. The Maravi kingdom—which had arisen at the beginning of the seventeenth century—blocked direct access to Mozambique. Meanwhile a new route from Kilwa and Querimba to Lake Nyasa and the rich elephant hunting grounds of the Shire valley was opened by Yao traders, coming to the coast around 1610 in search of white *bafta*—as Yao oral tradition has it. The trade of Mozambique to those towns in the north was concentrated in the indigenous town. This Swahili suburb was, significantly, located well out of reach of the guns of the fortress—for the relationship between Portuguese and "Moors" was tense, to say the very least. But the Muscati raid on Mozambique in 1674 inflicted severe damage on the shipping of the Swahili traders established at Mozambique. Another cause for the decline of Mozambique, then, was that Muscat offered merchants an alternative to the old Portuguese trading circuit. Muslim traders in particular moved to ports not as dependent on the Portuguese as Mozambique. Ever fewer cities on the northern coast of Mozambique were welcoming Portuguese merchants for fear of possible Muscati retaliation.[49]

This ruined the trade of the Portuguese from Quelimane and from the sultanate of Angoche with Madagascar as well, where Afro-Portuguese *casados* briefly had a factory in St. Luce Bay, on the southern coast, in the early seventeenth century. They also traded with Anjuan on the Comoros, which had a vague tributary relationship with the Portuguese, and where there was a small resident community of Afro-Portuguese *casados*.[50] But although Portuguese merchants still occasionally sent dhows to Madagascar—whether to trade or to plunder—in the late seventeenth century most of this trade was conducted via Kilwa and Querimba.[51]

As recent excavations in the frame of UNESCO's Boina Bay project have shown, Madagascar is—despite the obvious Indonesian ancestry of many inhabitants—not nearly as isolated from the history of the Swahili Coast as might appear.[52] The "island of the moon," as the Arabs called it, had been a pivot of trade in East Africa since the ninth century. And its commerce was very much tied to that along the Swahili Coast.

The northwest coast of Madagascar, in particular, was the hub of a complex maritime zone in the Mozambique Canal, linking the fishermen and merchants of Kilwa, Pemba, Mozambique, and Angoche via the Comoros to the thriving Arab/Swahili settlements there. These were connected via the rivers to the Malagasy hinterland, which was a major supplier of rice to the East African littoral. This dominance of the northwest coast of Madagascar is also due to the better connections to the hinterland, the link to the Swahili Coast, and natural causes as well. Most of the unending coastline of western Madagascar was "all wasteland with here and there a scrappy bush growing" and it is open to the notorious hurricanes of the Mozambique Canal. There were only a few deep bays with fresh water on Madagascar, so trade tended to concentrate in a few locations.[53]

However, the metropolitan administration was not very concerned about all that. To Portugal, Mozambique was mainly important as a way station for inward-bound Indiamen—but a miserable one. "There is so little food available there," the viceroy complained in 1703, "that the soldiers have to eat in taverns which costs them their allowance for paying the rent, so that many are forced to subsist on alms." And apart from this Mozambique island was infested by cholera, so that often more people died in that hellhole than on the trip from Portugal.[54]

Few of the commodities sold at Mozambique were sent to Portugal. Mozambique's trade was overwhelmingly directed toward India, and the governor and *casados* there conducted most of it, whereas the Portuguese crown was little involved. That was to its anger, though, and we shall see later how the crown tried in vain to control this commerce more rigorously in the second half of the century.

Until 1752 the Captaincy of Mozambique was an administrative dependency of Goa. The relationship between Goa and Mozambique was a fairly uneasy one, for—as Lisbon well realized—the area was really too large and remote to be administered from India. Schemes to separate Mozambique from Goa had been under consideration in Lisbon as early as 1634 but were constantly shelved, as it basically would have been too expensive either to administer Mozambique directly or to institute a separate administration.[55]

And, besides, Mozambique and Mombasa had too many unruly Portuguese subjects to be easily administered at all. Mombasa was normally, Mozambique often, used as a penal colony, as (because of the epidemics) "it is difficult to send people there in any other way." That a large part of the population of either consisted of criminals did not contribute greatly, of course, to a good understanding between Portuguese and Africans.[56]

### *Exporting Feudalism*

From the island of Mozambique convicts, missionaries, and merchants began to fan out into the interior from the late sixteenth century, fleeing from their dreary existence as convicts or tempted to go there by the vast mineral riches the interior was—rightly—held to contain. On the Zambesi and in the Kiteve kingdom they were very much following the Arab/Swahili example, as there were already small groups of Muslims in the hinterland. And these also remained—since for Kiteve and Torwa there are references to powerful "Moorish" merchants and medicine men established there right into the seventeenth century.[57]

These settlers can appropriately be styled "explorers of the bush" (*sertaneiros*) or transfrontiersmen—crossing from a European to an African lifestyle—for Mozambique, coastal Madagascar, and the seas surrounding it were in the seventeenth century the true frontier of the Arabian seas. These vast bush lands were thinly populated by small agricultural communities, which mainly conducted shifting cultivation, and were intersected by vast stretches of waste over which groups of herders roamed. These typically combined pastoralism with trade in ivory, gold, and occasional service as mercenaries: the Maasai and Galla along the Mrima Coast; the Sakalava on Madagascar; the Yao, Lundi, and Maravi in Mozambique. The lower reaches of the Zambesi are poor lands, plagued by irregular rainfall. The Zimbabwe plateau, on the other hand, has a moderate climate and is quite fertile, but frequent epidemics, the tsetse fly, and sleeping sickness (trypanosomiasis) as well as high infant mortality appear to have deterred the growth of dense settlements.[58]

Since the yields of agriculture in the hinterland of Mozambique were low and villages were constantly on the move, these areas lacked the consolidated state systems, based on agricultural taxes levied by a bureaucracy, that were found elsewhere in the Arabian seas. Kingdoms rapidly rose and fell apart again on the savannah.[59]

This is even true for the largest and oldest state in East Africa, the Shona kingdom of Mweni Mutapa, or Monomotappa, centered on its shifting ritual focus, the *zimbabwe*s (the word means "stone dwellings") on the Zimbabwe Plateau. This was rather a loose ceremonial confederacy of various Karanga kings, or more appropriately chiefs, than a consolidated "bureaucratic empire." Monomotappa was in many ways a classic example of the African segmentary state, where the king and his officials (or rather members of his family and their entourage) tried to monopolize some spheres of activity, like the gold and ivory trade, but left local autonomy in all other spheres virtually unscathed.[60]

And though there were agricultural kingdoms in the far hinterland, Malawi and Buganda in present Uganda, these had only ephemeral contacts with the coast. Basically, the lack of rivers and huge transport costs made contacts between the coast and the deep interior quite difficult, though certainly not impossible. From Sofala to Dambara textiles increased sixfold in price, for example.[61]

Cattle were too highly prized as both bridewealth and a source of scarce protein to be used as draft animals, so that everything had to be carried by porters. But porters, and guides even more so, were scarce since these were highly specialized professions, requiring great physical strength (an elephant tusk weighs more than 50 pounds) or experience in discerning landmarks in the monotonous savannah.[62] The Portuguese were, for example, well aware that there were vast deposits of copper in Zambia. And copper—used for making tips of spears—had long been a major good for long-distance trade in the interior. But it proved impossible to export this overseas via Mozambique due to the prohibitive transport costs involved.[63]

Commercial contacts between coast and hinterland remained confined to a few lightweight goods such as Indian cotton piece-cloth and occasionally arrack, rum, and—on the Mrima Coast—porcelain, of which some has been found as far inland as the Buganda kingdom. Persian porcelain, often cheap imitations of Chinese models and mostly brought there via Muscat in the seventeenth century, appears to have largely been substituted for Chinese porcelain, which played such an important role in an earlier period.[64] With the exception of the trade in salt, iron, gold, and ivory—the last drawing on an extensive network involving most of interior East Africa to the great lakes—long-distance trade mainly consisted of "commodities" that could walk: slaves and cattle.[65]

The *sertaneiros* were followed much later by commissioners of the crown and by its armed forces. In the early seventeenth century Lisbon was not very interested in Mozambique. And neither was Goa, until the short-lived euphoria over the Monomotappa ruler's subjecting himself as vassal to the Portuguese crown in 1632 and later converting to Christianity. Yet his vaunted "conquest of Monomotappa," on which the then-viceroy Linhares prided himself so much, was, Linhares's successor Pedro da Silva muttered, merely a grandiose term for getting rid of a few ill-disciplined mercenaries by exiling them to the Zambesi. "These lands have been conquered by the Portuguese who stay there, without them recognizing that they are vassals of mine," the king grumbled.[66]

The crown grudgingly conceded in the beginning of the seventeenth century that it was facing a fait accompli by trying to frame those settlements of freebooters up the Zambesi Valley into a system of fiefs (*prazos*). The recipient was to enjoy the usufruct over the land for one to three generations, after which it was to revert to the crown. In return for such a grant those feudatories were to pay a quit-rent of gold dust to the crown yearly and raise a couple of armed men to defend it.

In theory *prazos* were only bestowed by the king on "subjects who, in this kingdom, have been of great service to me." And—a much more onerous condition—they were to be granted only to those who were willing to move with their family to the Zambesi too. In practice, though, *prazos* were also auctioned or donated to "creatures" of the viceroy or of the governor of Mozambique. This spawned a serious problem of absenteeism, as few were willing to move to this unhealthy, lonely, and dangerous place. Estates were thus often either an empty claim, administered by mayors (mostly clerics), or absorbed by others.[67]

Isaacman calls these feudatories *prazeiros*. The *prazeiros* controlled the communities in the immediate surroundings of their properties with gangs of armed retainers and slaves; the peasants there were often forced to work three days a week on the estate. They also extorted occasional tributes in livestock and grain from the wider surrounding area, which, in the bush, could easily amount to hundreds of miles. Such conquistadors mostly also reserved a monopoly on the gold dust gathered from their lands and on the first tusk of a dead elephant. Both were traditionally prerogatives of African chiefs, a position the *prazeiros* mostly assumed by simple right of arms or, rarely, by being allotted such a position by the Monomotappa kings.[68]

In 1636 there were 76 *prazeiros*.[69] *Prazos* located on crown properties—mainly those surrounding the Portuguese settlements at Sena, Tete, and areas neighboring Mozambique—often consisted of large agricultural estates with several dozen villages that were directly controlled by Portuguese landowners and whose the inhabitants were little more than serfs.

Out-*prazos*, on the other hand, stretching over vast areas in the interior, and located on what was—at least nominally—Monomotappa land, mostly consisted of rights to levy market dues (the *curva*—originally an impost on traders traveling to Monomotappa) or shares in the gathering of ivory. The Monomotappa formally leased such rights in return for military support or merchandise. Most *prazos*, located "on lands of the *fumos*," or the African chiefs—who might or might not be tributary to the Monomotappa—were in principle granted by them to the Portuguese for a fixed term too. In return the Portuguese were to deliver to the *fumos* piece-cloth or a contingent of armed men.[70] There was a thin line between politics and war in the Monomotappa confederacy, though, as chieftains were ranked according to the amount of Indian piece-cloth they could deliver.

Finally, the Portuguese crown might bestow *prazos* to *fumos* as well: to wit, Inamcara, which was seen as the *prazo* of the *fumo* Mamboro. This also applies to distant Sofala and its surroundings where the "chiefs" or *muzungo* families, to whom *prazos* were given in the early seventeenth century, were really chiefs of the Kiteve kingdom with no ties with Portugal whatsoever except maybe a token Portuguese name and equally nominal Christianity.[71]

So, as those examples illustrate, the *prazos* arrangement was partly a translation of African customary law into European legal norms or—the other way round—a way for Shona chiefs to gather symbolic recognition by collecting European legal titles and documents. A major difference with European fiefs was the uncertainty prevailing about the fixed territorial location of *prazos* and their lack of clearly defined boundaries. For example, the *prazo* of Sebastião da Silva comprised "the savannah [*sertão*]—approximately—located between the Guari and the Gionique River." And a *prazo* in Mozambique was primarily tied to a people rather than to the territory on which they lived. The *prazo* of Antônio de Comora loosely encompassed "lands of the Zungos," for instance.

Again, *prazos* were generally inherited along the female line—in accordance with the African tradition. The deliveries of ivory and grain as gifts to *prazeiros* on the out-*prazos* tallied with African systems of rule too. Thus, Antônio de Alveilar's *prazo* consisted of a yearly right to receive gifts of a fixed quantity of sorghum from a number of stray villages.

Yet while the *prazos* had some African elements, the *prazeiros* did not enjoy the hereditary ritual prerogatives of the Shona chiefs—such as their special capacities as rainmakers—or their direct access to spirits. As their holders had no hereditary access to spirits to boast of and thus no inheritable legitimacy, *prazos* proved to be more unstable than African chiefdoms. They were subdivided, or rights to delivery of ivory or presents expired with the demise of the primogenitor's family. During the division of a *prazo*, outlying villages might forswear the former overlord, often leading to bloodshed as subordinate collectors or heads of village tried to assert their independence.

There is an economic element involved in this transient aspect of the *prazos* too. Many owners of *prazos* were primarily cattle-drivers and gold-and ivory-traders, who could be absent from their property on wanderings that might take years. The whole arrangement being largely premised on obtaining gold by trade rather than on developing agriculture, the cultivation of wheat, sorghum, or cassava was mainly undertaken to barter these at the various periodic markets in Zimbabwe. Of the many *feiras* in our period, those held at Masapa, Luanze, Ongoe, and above all the royal mart at Dambara, stood out. If the barter of gold there obviously attracted most European attention and was also the branch of trade most directly controlled by supervisors of the Monomotappa, the bulk of goods traded were local agricultural products: cotton, cattle, wax, honey, locally made textiles, iron, salt, and other bulk products.[72]

A settled feudal arrangement was thus uneasily wedded to a more nomadic lifestyle. This was another cause for the instability of the *prazos*. Furthermore, this system was erected on a low-yield, extensive agriculture, which, too, did not allow for a settled urban life. Even the Portuguese "metropolises" of Sena and Tete had only a few thousand inhabitants. This was not altogether a solid foundation for the system of central control that Lisbon sought to establish over Mozambique via the *prazo* system.

In spite of the normal reference to Mozambique as the "Cuama conquests," the Estado da Índia really ruled over the Zambesi by consent of both its own feudatories and the *fumos* then. Yet it needed the *prazeiros* as their trade caravans provided access to the periodic markets, even if they brought "rather cloth than arms." The *prazeiros* were—beyond Sena and Tete—merchants and mercenaries rather than yeomen, and this angered the Portuguese crown, which saw Mozambique as a possible plantation colony: a new Brazil.[73]

The occasional inspector from Goa or Lisbon might feel himself very alien in the "Cuama conquests," though. For one thing—to touch on a difficult issue—there were neither white nor Indian women on the Zambesi. The Portuguese there had been marrying African women for a century. Most of the "Portuguese" there were really black Afro-Portuguese and had often but the faintest of relationships with metropolitan Portugal.[74] And so were the priests: Sofala claimed that the Dominican mission there was entirely run by Africans and a few Indian priests.[75]

For another, the lifestyle on the Zambesi resembled African rural life rather than Portuguese: most of the *prazeiros* in Tete were living in kraals with pointed, thatched roofs rather than European-style villas. Huts for the African clientele surrounded these and a high mud wall enclosed the "mansion." In the deep interior the Afro-Portuguese settlers were living in walled compounds together with several wives and dozens of children, truly like African chiefs.[76]

### *Trade and War in Mozambique*

The trade to southern Mozambique differed from the trade along the Swahili Coast and in Sofala. Unlike along the Swahili Coast and in Sofala, where the Arab merchants had long been trading inland, there were no pre-existing trade networks or Arab merchant colonies there on which the Portuguese could construct their own. Sofala appears to have been the southernmost limit of Arab navigation in the Arabian seas.[77]

The commerce from Mozambique to the areas south of Sofala was conducted with small vessels, rented by the governor, or by the monopoly (the *estanco*) running the trade. These were granted concessions to sail to Sena Bay and Dela Goa Bay. Shares in such voyages were then auctioned to the Indian and Swahili sailors and soldiers at Mozambique, to Christian Indians from Goa (the *canarins*), or to the Portuguese settlers (*moradores*) on the island. The captain of the ship held about one-tenth of these; the *canarin* or Swahili crew of the vessel carried out the rest of the trade to Sofala and Dela Goa Bay. They would each carry along a few pieces of textile and barter these for one or two slaves, some pieces of ivory, pearls, or cowry shells, the latter two "mostly fetched by the Indian sailors" on their own account.[78]

Let us now examine these Portuguese settlements south of Mozambique in more detail. The VOC ship *Voorhouten* surveyed Quelimane, the center for trade on the estuary of the mighty Zambesi—which was, however, very dangerous because of sandbanks in 1676. The Portuguese then had a large settlement there, which was surrounded by a palisade of clay. Within was a village of forty houses. The country was fertile and around the settlement stretched fields that seemed as green as Holland in May. In this pleasant spot were cultivated grain, yams, and coconuts.[79]

Eight miles beyond this settlement was the stronghold of Maromeu and south of it Inambane Bay. "The people there are polite and interested in bartering but they are tributary to the Portuguese, who yearly sent a ship to collect what the inhabitants have gathered." From Maromeu one could sail in tiny crafts to Sena, a town with about 150 Portuguese inhabitants, according to the VOC; along the Zambesi lived another 500 Portuguese, ruling over more than 70,000 Africans, of whom most could handle firearms.

This is a huge number and quite an unfamiliar one to the historian of European expansion, who is used to counting the strength of European armies overseas in the hundreds rather than in the thousands.[80] Yet it was not an unrealistic estimate at all. Felipe de Mascarenhas estimated in 1634 that the Portuguese *prazeiros* on the lower Zambesi alone could muster 9,000–10,000 musketeers—which would also give us a quite acceptable figure of a population of about 50,000–70,000 for the Zambesi.[81]

If the core of the Monomotappa army was made up of a small professional bodyguard, the bulk of it was made up of a mass levee, contributed by the subordinate *fumos:* young men who were promised a bride upon having participated in battle. These "militias" were only vaguely connected to the Monomotappa and constituted a vast reservoir of manpower, eager for women and plunder, which the Portuguese *sertaneiros* could use once they got accustomed to the political arrangements on the Zambesi after about 1610. Mozambique was conquered and held by those mercenary armies; Portuguese troops were of little avail, as they were rapidly depleted by illnesses. But such were private militias, raised and entertained by the *prazeiros* with little to no connection to the army of the crown. The number of Portuguese soldiers on the Zambesi was never more than a few dozen.[82]

From Sena Portuguese and Indian merchants would move upstream on the Zambesi—the left bank of which was controlled by the Portuguese, the right by the Maravi, with whom the Portuguese had an "armed peace"—in canoes to Tete, loaded with *bafta*, iron, and copper. Tette was the last place that could be reached by sloops moving up the Zambesi; the rest of the great river was dangerous to navigate due to the Cabora Baça rapids. The metropolis of the interior was a small place of about 3,000 inhabitants surrounded by a high palisade, mostly consisting of mud houses.[83]

Beyond Tete stretched the arid, flat bush, spangled with huge boulders. In Tete were mounted expeditions of Portuguese merchants with hired porters and retinue, hundreds of men—and women as temporary wives—strong, carrying rusty muskets, for the bush was then as now full of robbers, and huge horns to announce their coming to the villages they passed through. Carrying an array of merchandise, ranging from cloth and cattle to honey, they would hike to the *feiras* of Dambara or Ungoe. At the *feira* of Dambara, about twenty days' march from Sena and the major mart for the trade of the Monomotappa kingdom, assembled peasants, pastoralists, and peddlers from the wide surroundings near a small Portuguese kraal, which was only inhabited during the trade season. The *prazeiros* financed a small garrison of African soldiers there to watch over their merchandise.[84]

Such expeditions for trading to the interior, taking flocks of cattle along for barter and milk, could reach right up to the shores of Lake Malawi and to southern Zimbabwe (Baroe and Tongwa, maybe even as far as the modern Witwatersrand) and might easily last up to two years.[85] One could ramble through the bush for months without meeting another living soul. The *sertaneiros*—really African long-distance traders, not so different from the Yao or the Maravi—were trying to tap the vast inland network of transcontinental barter and migration, of the extent of which they had only a faint notion, but which has meanwhile been painstakingly reconstructed by Africanists from oral tradition.[86]

The Conselho Ultramarino pondered, for example, that in southern Zimbabwe salt was imported, which might be fetched from Angola—and indeed salt was exported in bulk from the Lunde kingdom on the upper reaches of the Congo River to Zimbabwe. At the latter place, on the other hand, rivers seemed to be flowing from Mozambique. Could Portuguese expeditions not be mustered to take gold right up to the Atlantic, if that appeared possible, for salt? One overlooked the distance involved, however. Though both Luanda and Sena outfitted parties to search for a route to the Atlantic, both got lost in the bush and were not able to reach their goal.[87]

Beyond *feiras* the "barter" conducted by those armed Portuguese trade expeditions was virtually indistinguishable from plunder. This was particularly so where one could not haggle slaves from the chiefs, as in Dambara or in the district of Chicova. Instead, raiders burned down villages and enslaved the able-bodied inhabitants. Wild raiding for slaves appears to have increased after the 1670s. For with the expansion of the gold trade and the consecutive growth of agriculture on *prazos* around Sena after 1660 the demand for slaves also boomed. Moreover—although the crown nominally prohibited this, as it infringed on a prerogative of African chiefs—*prazeiros* also began to use slaves to shift gold from the rivers and to scout for silver themselves.

And in the poor lands on the lower Zambesi a pastoral economy developed. Livestock was easier to control than farmers, did not revolt, and could walk to the markets. Portuguese *sertaneiros*, in *prazos* remote from any kraal with troops of the crown, evicted or enslaved African villagers to make room for cattle. The authorities at home vehemently denounced such practices. In Lisbon they even considered sending soldiers to protect the subjects of the Monomotappa—who was nominally a protégé of the crown after all—against the inroads his majesty's vassals made on his territory.[88]

During the years 1684–86 there were poor harvests; this was due to a simultaneous influx of both cattle and settlers in Zimbabwe after 1678, fleeing pestilence on the lower Zambesi, which triggered an outbreak of a devastating cattle plague, apparently a trypanosomiasis epidemic, in 1685. This not only ruined the gold trade, but wreaked havoc on the Monomotappa empire too. The conversion of the Monomotappa to Christianity had disquieted both many confederate chiefs and members of his family. Gungo, one of the Monomotappa's brothers, had sided with the rebels and was conducting a guerrilla war from the bush, with Monomotappa and Portuguese auxiliary troops trying in vain to track him down. And the guerrillas could increasingly count on wide support: if subjects of the Monomotappa were dying in the thousands, was that not a sign that the ancestral spirits no longer favored this dynasty?[89]

And, besides, there were very good reasons to revolt. The Portuguese were grabbing lands from the subjects of the Monomotappa without authorization by either king. And the "general of Mozambique" was treating him, the Monomotappa warned the king of Portugal, "as if he is some kaffir, a captive of his, while your majesty is treating him like a king." Manica revolted in 1680, an uprising that was smothered by a combined Portuguese and Monomotappa army "with much bloodshed of the vassals of your majesty." Mining declined as inhabitants fled epidemics, drought, and oppression.[90]

To add to the troubles besetting the Portuguese, the *prazeiros* were involved in incessant internal quarrels. The mighty *prazeiros* were by 1680 adjudicating their many differences by means of pitched battles between their militias in front of Sena's palisades. By 1686, through violence as much as bribes, smaller Portuguese landowners had been robbed of their rights. The benefits from agriculture on the Zambesi, as much as the market dues of the *feiras* and the rights to organize expeditions to Dambara, had been usurped by a mere ten major *prazeiros* and by the captain of Sena, who was normally part of that claque. The Cuama conquests by 1680 were rapidly drifting into anarchy by the force of the same audacious but reckless greed for gold, girls, and plunder by which they had been acquired in the first place. "Today the great rivers are almost unpopulated and in revolt and if the government does not intervene from outside very soon we surely are going to lose them."[91]

However, though Goa and Mozambique might condemn this, there was precious little they could do (or perhaps wanted to do) about it. For neither was able, or willing, to allot sufficient troops to the settlements on the Cuama. If the custom stations (*alfândegas*) of Mozambique fetched but meager benefits to them, it appeared superfluous to spend these sums on protecting *feiras* in the far hinterland.

And yet not only the Portuguese there were worried, as the Monomotappa emperor had been solemnly supplicating the Portuguese crown for more armed support as early as 1665 to restore order. The *zimbabwe* (shifting) of the emperor was still protected by a mere twenty Portuguese musketeers, he warned. It might easily be overrun. The Dominican friars at the Monomotappa court concocted this request for more aid, Lisbon surmised. The Christianity one was supposed to defend in Zimbabwe had little in common with what was called thus in Portugal. Should one then risk Portuguese lives for it? And while the Portuguese forces were already thin on the ground, the commanders were spreading them even thinner by mounting expeditions during a wild-goose chase in the eighties for silver veins that were supposed to have been discovered in Torwa or Malawi.[92]

This led to the disastrous invasion of Dambara by Xangamira Dombo, usurper of the old Torwa crown and founder of the new Rozvi kingdom in 1693 on the old territory of Torwa. Upon the defeat of the Monomotappa's main army in 1687 and the desertion of many of his subordinate *fumos* to Xangamira, Sena's mercenary army merrily marched out to give them "a good bruising"—as the British would have said two centuries later. They had merely a few thousand to face hosts from Torwa, the campfires of which, in the night before battle, stretched from one end of the horizon to the other, but no cause for worries, the Portuguese thought. Once the muskets fired, the "Rozvi barbarians" would flee. To their horror, however, they discovered that Xangamira's warriors were not scared away by bullets. Xangamira had administered a magic ointment to his men that would protect them. The auxiliary forces fled from the battle in terror. Upon the defeat of the remaining few dozen Portuguese, the African forces of the entire presidency of Sena fled, refusing to face the wizard king, who even was said to command deadly swarms of bees.[93]

The Rozvi thus overran the *feiras* in the interior as much as the *zimbabwe* itself, forcing the Monomotappa into exile. "Women are raped and churches profaned by the barbarians." And the trade of Mozambique collapsed, as it very much depended on its links to the *feiras*. In 1693 the customs revenues of the captaincy dropped from 15,000 xeraphins yearly to a mere 5,000 and remained at that low level for the next years. The inhabitants of Sena began to barricade themselves, expecting an attack, but fortunately for them, Xangamira died in 1696. "The rivers are full of tears," the inhabitants of Sena wrote in 1700, proving they had at least not lost their very Portuguese sense of the melodramatic, for the situation was not so bad as it seemed. The Rozvi still needed the Portuguese intermediaries to gain access to the world market. However reluctantly, therefore, a few Portuguese traders were already permitted back into Rozvi territory by 1700. But the Portuguese lost their link to the *feiras* on the Zimbabwe plateau forever, since the Rozvis continued to block the access thereto. The Portuguese defeat also caused a temporary decline of Mozambique's gold trade in the early eighteenth century, as the Rozvi were not willing to have the Portuguese scout for gold in their lands. Tete's trade had recovered by 1720, however, and its population and that of Sena were on the increase again.[94]

For—seen in the long run—the fall of Monomotappa might be seen as a normal dynastic cycle on the savannah in which a central kingdom disintegrated after a series of bad harvests, as had happened in Zimbabwe before. Since the prestige of the Monomotappa king was primarily built on his access to the spirits, confederate chiefs forswore him when he appeared to have lost it. The Portuguese penetration was certainly not crucial here. And the other way round, it might be argued the Portuguese had been acting as a normal African kingdom in trying to build up a state around an agrarian core territory (Tete and Sena) by exploiting revenues of trade and trying to systematically overcharge the neighboring state of Monomotappa, occasionally plundering it. It was, however, unavoidable that this unfortunate neighbor would withdraw from such an unequal exchange sooner or later, causing a collapse of the state outside of its core territory.[95]

## Yemen

Let us not ponder these broader implications any longer but rather continue our trip northward until reaching one of the main island entrepôts of the Arabian seas: Suqutra. This island stepping-stone between India, Africa, and Yemen was still often used by the Portuguese to store wood, cattle, and water after the long, dreary trip along the arid Banadir Coast. But in 1636, when the VOC described it in detail, only a few rusty guns on the fortress above its capital would remind visitors that Suqutra had until 1563 been a Portuguese possession, partly to protect the mainly Coptic population there. The Christian communities on Suqutra appear to have suffered heavily from the influx of traders, shepherds, and peasants from Yemen after 1570, when the island was subdued by the sultan of Khisn on the Hadramawti Coast, and most were apparently converted to Islam by 1640.[96]

The population of Suqutra loathed the Portuguese, yet happily conducted a busy trade with Goa throughout the seventeenth century all the same: one to three ships yearly, loaded with reed and aloe. Probably because of Portuguese attempts to block traffic to the Ottoman Red Sea, much Indian trade shifted to Suqutra and Khisn in the late sixteenth century. This allowed the sultan of Khisn to buy 25 to 40 small vessels in Surat and Dabhul. The sultanate traded with Mogadishu, Mombasa, Pate, the Persian Gulf, Dabhul, and Miani. The trade in slaves and aloe was monopolized by the sultan.

During its heyday from about 1600 to 1630 this tiny thalassocracy ruled the narrow seas between Cape Gardafui, the Somali coast, and many of the Hadramawti ports. Suqutra dealt mainly with Mogadishu, which delivered slaves, wheat, and mire (a perfume, much appreciated in both India and the Middle

East) in exchange for salted meat, butter, milk, and textiles. Its other major port was Khisn. Major indeed: like the other inlets on the Hadramawti Coast, Khisn was a very small settlement of no more than 400 houses. Indian ships, mainly from Dabhul and Diu, traded textiles and cotton for hides, lacquer, East African ivory, and aloe there. The sultanate fell apart in 1630 when as-Shir and Dhofar subjected themselves to the Ottoman governors of Yemen in order to be protected from Khisn.[97]

Tanar was located in a broad bay surrounded by "evil, cruel mountains." Suqutra was "inhabited everywhere, but mostly along the shore, which is very beautiful; a few also inhabit and have their houses along the side of the mountains, some live in the valleys and in the countryside there is only the said city as the inhabitants dwell in widely dispersed villages." Unlike in the sixteenth century, when there appears to have been still some forest left on Suqutra, in the seventeenth it was a dry and barren island covered with thorny bushes. Rice and wheat had to be imported from Mogadishu and India. The population mainly subsisted from offshore fishing and especially on "the milk and flesh of goats of which there is no lack." While Suqutra was mainly an entrepôt between the Banadir Coast, the Hadramawt, and India, it did have one valuable export: the famous aloe (a crimson tincture). "It comes from small bushes, standing on the mountains, this aloe is the sweat or fluid which these produce. It is gathered in bladders by the inhabitants and then sent to the king in Quisn."[98]

Nearing the coast of Yemen now, the Hadramawt offers the sight of rugged mountains piercing a serene blue sky. This coast had to be approached near Cape Ra's al-Fartakh since the eastern coast of Oman was notorious for hurricanes. From Cape Ra's al-Fartakh a strong current pulls a ship to the twin narrows of Bab al-Mandeb. Inlets and small ports wedged between those steep mountains and cliffs enlivened this forbidding view. However, J.S. Wurffbain—who surveyed the Hadramawti Coast in 1643—was not enthusiastic about the possibilities those harbors offered to shelter oceangoing ships, for the anchorages were fenced off by cliffs, sandbanks, and severe waves.[99]

This rough coast is isolated from the agricultural hinterland, the Valley of Hadramawt, by impenetrable deserts. The staunch race bred by this harsh land was forced to send their junior sons far away. The Hadramawti Coast was the place of origin of Islamic colonies—consisting of warriors, priests, and merchants—scattered throughout the Indian Ocean from the Laccadive Islands to the Swahili Coast (which the proud Yemenites more or less saw as hereditary lands) and on to Madagascar. Some families might equally well have sons on the Comoros as in Pontianak in Borneo.[100]

The most famous of the Hadramawti ports was Aden, and indeed, Aden was the most ancient city of the Arabian seas, with at least a 2,000-year history behind it.[101] The sight of Aden is awesome. It is located at the foot of a steep mountain wall; the extinct volcano overlooks the long and deep bay. Massive walls surrounded Aden, dating back to prehistoric times. Above these walls towered many-storied dwellings. The cyclopean walls of Aden were the awe of visitors, but the palaces, mosques, and merchant houses were disintegrating. While in the sixteenth century Aden was still the hub of trade to the Red Sea, it fell into deep decline in the early seventeenth. This was due to the rise of Mocha and other boomtowns, which suddenly sprang up amid the dunes of the Tihama. These places thrived on coffee, which was picked in the fertile foothills of the mountains of high Yemen. But Aden was more an oceanic entrepôt than a center for trade to the interior. Mountain and desert isolated the town from Yemen and hampered communications with the Hadramawt. Aden was independent from the Zaidit imamate too, which stimulated the ports along the Tihama Coast with tax exemptions for merchants who would settle there.[102]

Of its ancient wealth only the pepper trade remained of vital importance. Aden also dealt in cotton and indigo, sold from there to Egypt, and in Egyptian opium, fetched to Kerala. Yet, through its reversals of fortune, the rugged community strove to survive: Aden still conducted a busy coastwise trade with Mocha. Mocha supplied Aden with coffee and textiles; Aden provided incense and of course the famous Arab sap. This was tapped from the bushes planted on the wasteland stretching between city and mountains.[103]

Across—on the African shore—was a barren coast where hills with sparse bushes gave way to the endless plains of boulders and salt of the Danakil desert. Amid those gloomy hills lay the small town of Zeila: a flourishing small port with 2,000 houses.[104] It conducted a busy coastwise trade with Somalia and the Swahili Coast with saffron and Indian textiles exchanged for butter, salted meat, slaves, and ivory, primarily sold to the Haramawt.[105]

Zeila mainly lived from the revenues of those narrow seas, for the town was practically closed off from the hinterland. Passing to the Ethiopian interior, there was nothing but water and trackless desert for three weeks' march. This wilderness was controlled by the Islamic Galla warrior nomads, who exacted high fees for both protection and providing guides. Crossing the Danakil was not unlike crossing the Indian Ocean itself. It could only safely be traversed by well-provisioned, well-armed caravans, thousands of merchants strong, and those convoys arrived at best once every year. Until 1699, when the town was conquered by a Zaidit fleet, Zeila was a city-state independent from both Ethiopia and the Ottoman empire.[106]

Past Bab al-Mandeb the African shore became more mountainous and forested. Vessels sailed along the Eritrean shore, where many Indian ships would anchor to load water and woodwork.

In Ethiopia, an empire "where uprisings are as normal as the waves are to the sea," there had been an anti-Catholic insurrection in 1634. This had prompted the *negus negast* (the Ethiopian emperor) to evict the Catholic missionaries. The land was closed to Christian outsiders and—in spite of an unsuccessful attempt of the court to communicate with the VOC through the Armenian merchant/adventurer Hodja Murat—remained so for the remainder of the century.

The *negus* did entertain regular contacts with Yemen, Egypt, and Persia, though. The status of Abyssinia as "hermit kingdom" was perhaps caused by the daunting problem of communicating with the interior rather than by any conciously followed policy.[107]

Whatever the main reason, in the late seventeenth century Abyssinia had become a dimly known realm: the enchanted kingdom to Europeans. Was it true that the horns out of which one drank ale there were of the unicorn? Gentlemen XVII—the board of directors of the VOC—inquired.[108] European sails rarely entered the Red Sea. The Ottoman authorities officially forbade this, and one would need a permit from the sherif of Mecca to do so.[109]

Europeans had only heard at that time about the quadrangular Ottoman fortress on the island of Massawa and the crowded bazaar there. Ethiopian traders bartered grain, salt, ivory, and slaves there for various forms of quasi-currency—fake coral beads and mirrors—and treasures like luxury cloth and, first and foremost, firearms. The arms were obviously mainly intended for internal consumption; the other articles were partly circulated within Ethiopia and sold to herdsmen from the interior. Massawa was an Ottoman campsite but its *ataliq* had to send a quarter of the customs revenues to Ethiopia. The administration of the port was in effect shared between khalif and *negus nagast*. The walls of the fortress had by 1640 crumbled. Within the compound survived a few dozen Ottoman soldiers, devoid of arms and scratching out a living with some barter.[110]

From Massawa four to five caravans, presided over by a chief merchant named by the *negus* and an armed escort several hundred men strong, ventured to the hinterland every year. The two weeks' passage to Ethiopia's main fair, the periodic markets at Domvia, where the camel caravans met the caravans of porters fetching goods over the Ethiopian mountains, led through desolate mountains and wastes, but there was plenty of water obtainable. The main demand in Domvia was for manufactured products from Yemen—steel, iron, and copper wire—but there was also some demand for Gujarati textiles. So there was a small *bania natio* there: thirty adventurous Indian merchants, commissioners of the Indian merchants in Massawa, who were in turn working on behalf of the great merchant houses of Diu or Cambay. In Massawa there were about two hundred *bania* residents.[111]

The total trade of Massawa and Zeila would not amount to more than 1 million guilders—insufficient to warrant venturing on such a risky trade for the VOC. This trade was, and remained, a virtual preserve of the *bania*s and apparently particularly those from Kathiawar. Whereas the Portuguese had been humiliatingly banished in 1642, the *negus* wrote a letter to Sam Das Parek—the *nagarseth* of Diu—that the exclusion of foreigners from Ethiopia did not pertain to Indian merchants in Portuguese territory. They, please, should continue to trade with Abyssinia.[112]

Likewise, Europeans had only heard of the Ottoman fortress of Suakin. This capital of the Ottoman province of Ethiopia had played a very important role in the sixteenth century. Thence the galleys of the Porte ravaged the Eritrean coast and a stream of arms and mercenaries was flowing to the frontier of the Islamic conquest in Harrar (Somalia). With the failure of the Islamic conquest of Abyssinia and the loss of the Tihama to the Zaidit imams of San'a in 1632–34 the Ottoman empire lost its former vital interest in the settlements there. Suakin exercised a weak hold upon some fishermen's cottages on the coast of the Sudan and was to outfit a few oared vessels to protect the shipping to Mecca.[113]

Yet Europeans certainly beheld the *jilbas* "named after Jidda"—large flat-bottomed crafts tied together with ropes, without any use of nails—which were crossing the Red Sea from At-Tur and Suez to Jidda, Hodeida, or Mocha. It was a narrow and dangerous passing because of coral reefs and strong currents.[114]

At Suez arrived caravans from the Nile and goods were loaded on the *jilbas:* grain, rice, textile, cotton, and arms. These were brought to provision the caravans of the hajj and to serve as yearly Egyptian subsidy to the scholars and the sherif of Mecca, who was—after the Sheikh al-Islam of Istanbul—the highest-ranking religious authority of the Ottoman empire. From Damascus and Cairo tens of thousands of pilgrims crossed the Hidjaz: true cities on the move, guarded by a small army. Those caravans were loaded with merchandise and gifts to the shrines. Assembling the faithful from the entire house of Islam, the hajj was the largest bazaar of Islam too.[115]

To Jidda, port of Mecca, would sail twelve to fourteen Indian ships from Surat, Cambay, occasionally from Cananore and Calicut, and *jilbas* with traders from Sa'na and Tarim.

> Where usually they await the two caravans arriving from Gran Cairo; one arrives three months and the other a month before the celebration of Abraham's sacrifice. Upon the arrival of the latter the grand and entire commerce both with selling and buying the goods received has to be finished within 20 days and then, after the pilgrimage, everybody departs.[116]

Having to arrange the stay of all those people in Mecca, the sherif was highly interested in any revenues one might attract. The revenues of the sherif would have to derive from the taxation of shipping from Jidda to At-Tur and Suez. One sought to lure merchants from Mocha to Jidda by instituting lower customs, or guaranteeing the Hindus free exercise of religion. This succeeded to some extent, for the coffee trade was still an important attraction of Mocha. Yet Indian ships after 1670 regularly passed Mocha by and sailed to Jidda directly. Surat's merchant prince, Abdul Ghafur, in 1700 also attempted to send his ship, the *Suleimani*, to Suez without touching at Jidda. The authorities at Mocha seized it. The sherif protested at Sa'na and insisted that Cairo was in the future to forestall such trespasses as well.[117]

Like mirages, the shabby boomtowns of Hodeida and Gameṛan emerged from the sands of the Tihama, both essentially new foundations catering to the coffee trade. Most vessels anchored at the densely populated and fertile island of Gameran to take on provisions. There was a fortress but the dangerous coral reefs of the Jabil as-Sukar were a more effective deterrent to entering the Red Sea than was the stronghold. One could easily enter the Bay of Gameran and take on water from wells, which were out of range of the guns.[118]

Mocha was situated on an endless, flat, desolate plain stretching as far as the eye could see. Fenced enclosures of Ethiopian slaves were speckled around the town; oases could be descried in the far distance. In the town "it is unbearably full of flies, so one cannot sit down without having somebody to chase them away. Also, full of white ants. Many cats and dogs live from the streets and roam peacefully on the dung-heaps searching for food."[119] Insufferable heat alternated with sandstorms "and when there's a little rain and dewfall, the next morning two hours of sunshine fill the streets with white salt."[120]

The sailors must have loathed Mocha. The crews of ships anchored at its roadstead were usually decimated by malaria. This was somewhat compensated for by the goodwill of the inhabitants. Anyone who arrived with a sloop at Mocha's sea-gate would be cheered by a crowd: children mainly, who were begging for candies. The exhilaration would soon yield to boredom, though; there was not much entertainment at Mocha, a place devoid of female companionship.[121]

C.G. Brouwer estimates the total number of inhabitants around 1640 at no more than 20,000 and that is likely over- rather than underestimated. Mocha was basically a fair where traders from Gujarat, Canara, and Kerala encountered those from Egypt, Syria, and Yemen. The few dwellers were either agents of merchants established elsewhere or connected to the garrison of the town. In January, when the merchants from up-country arrived, proprietors of houses departed to the countryside and would lend them to the itinerant merchants, who had to pay a year's rent. Most houses were empty for the rest of the year.[122]

When one was emerging from the bleak desert, Mocha resembled an oriental rhapsody: white walls, palaces, and minarets. But this fair vision evaporated when coming closer. Merchant H. Cloeck considered it a melancholy, wretched hamlet. Mocha measured only one mile in circumference. Most buildings were decrepit. The town largely consisted of wooden shanties. There were 200 (in 1700 450) stone constructions—mostly ruins. Of five mosques only one was in regular use; the others were wrecked. The caravanserai was in shambles too. Most avoided staying there anyway, since it was full of robbers and other low-lifes. The garrison consisted of ragged riffraff hardly distinguishable from the mob of mendicants. Plenty of goods were for sale during the trade season but how dusty and dirty was this bazaar! One did find "an unbelievable number of cauwa [coffee] inns, which are generally of straw and reed," however. The Arab, Cloeck noted contemptuously, idled his days away and would rather miss a decent meal than opium or coffee.[123]

The Bab al-Mandeb, or "the Babs" for short—in North America trips to Asia were called "voyages to the Babs"—was a mousetrap. The Babs were squeezed between high mountains and located in an area of dangerous currents and winds. If a vessel safely passed the dangerous coral reefs near Mocha, its pilot would have to choose between Scilla and Charybdis: the "small gate" between Perim and the Arab coast, and the "large gate" between Perim and the African one. The currents were unsteady. One had to keep far away from Perim, as this island was surrounded by razor-sharp coral reefs and whetted cliffs lined its shore.[124]

The western monsoon meets the northwestern monsoon at the exit of the Bab al-Mandeb in April; there were then either storms or lulls. It often occurred that vessels bound to India had to await a favorable wind for days in sight of the Babs. Because the supplies of water were rapidly dwindling and Indian ships used to carry fabulous treasures and crowds of hajjis, who were mostly slow and badly armed, the passengers panicked if the ship got stuck in the doldrums. And well they might—for the desolate bays on the African coast were a hideout for pirates. It was the ideal spot for an ambush. Most losses of Indian ships to European pirates occurred on the journey home near the Bab al-Mandeb.[125]

## The Gulf

The total surface of the Persian Gulf is almost 460,000 square miles; it is 678 miles at its broadest point, 140 in the Strait of Hormuz, and 365 miles long. Although the Indian Ocean influences the winds, the weather is mainly dependent, in winter, on the front of high pressure above the Persian highlands and, in summer, on low pressure above the Makran Coast. The interaction between the two causes a strong and unreliable gale, called the *shamal*. The *shamal* is mainly a danger to shipping in April. During the shipping season from December to March dhows could ideally cross the Gulf in two weeks, but in April there prevailed a strong, variable bluster that often swelled to the strength of a hurricane. The shipping season at Bandar Abbas was closed after the tenth of April.[126]

The westernmost port of the Persian Gulf is Basra, at the mouth of the Tigris—then 22 miles from the estuary of the Shatt al-Arab. The Ottoman province of Basra extended from there to a lake where the Euphrates joins the Tigris. On an isle in this lake was situated Gordolan fortress. From this island to Basra stretched a strip of fertile land, two to three miles broad. The date groves renowned throughout the Islamic world were found there.[127]

Beyond Basra the river divides into a maze of islands, swamps, and gullies. Only two were navigable for large vessels. The Shatt al-Arab was one of the most dangerous waterways in Asia. Wrecks littered the river and its current changed constantly.

Though it had known better times during its long history, Basra was still the largest city in the Gulf. Europeans detested the place: for them it was a rat hole.

**Map 2. The Middle East**

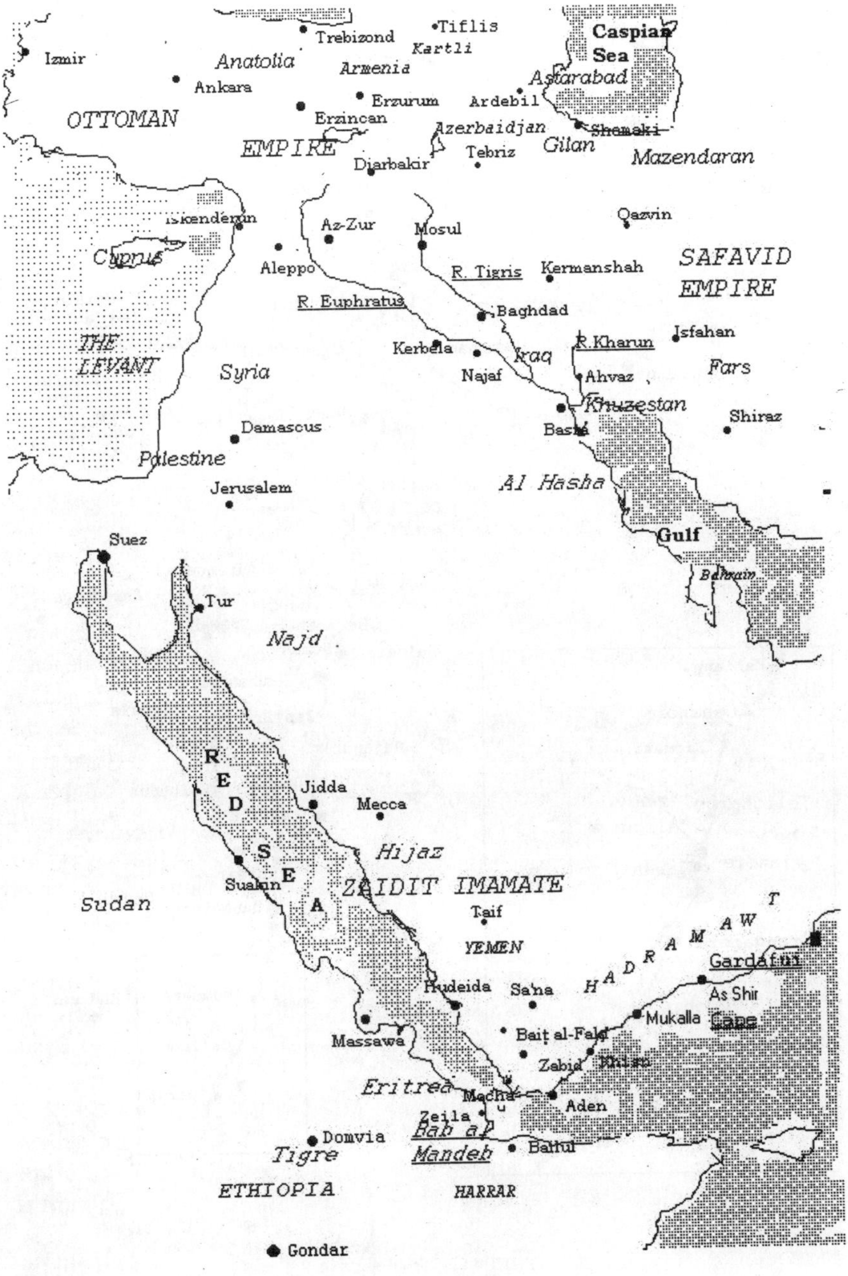

## Map 3. The Indian West Coast

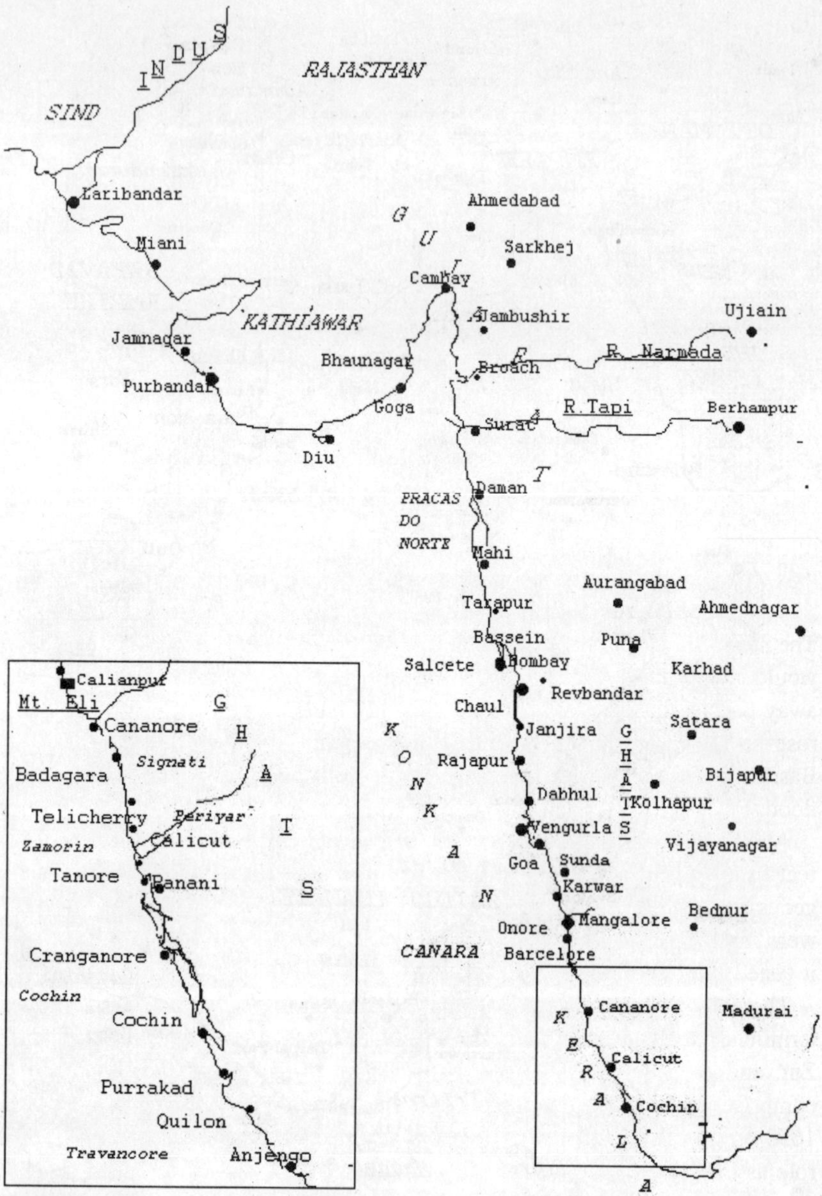

**Map 4. The Persian Gulf**

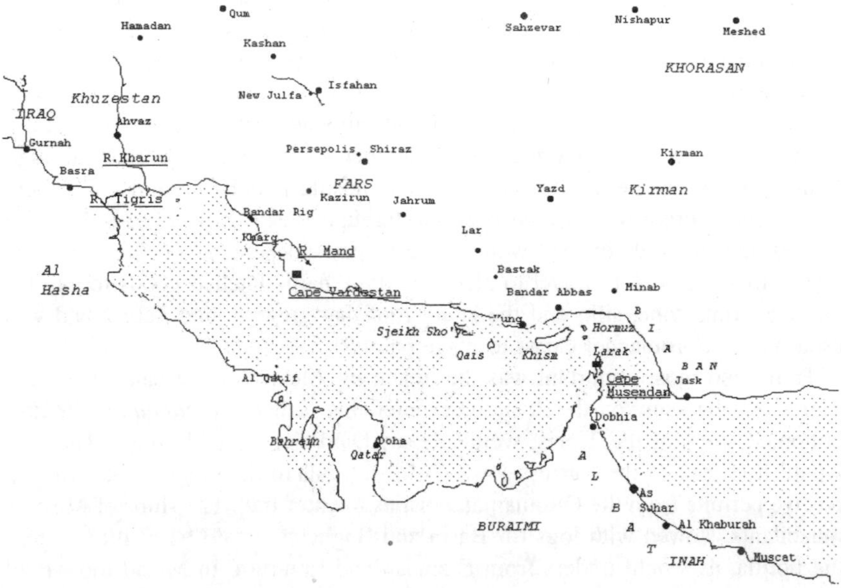


The stench in town was unbearable. Waste was dumped into the Tigris, which would sweep the dirt along during the rainy season. But often the river washed away part of the town too, as it was mainly build of earth. In 1687 the waters rose so high that the city seemed to float amid an interminable swamp. Yet Basra's welfare depended upon the fertile soil the river deposited during the floods.[128]

About forty thousand people were crowded within a narrow wall of 1,700 feet in circumference. For a small house one would have to expend the outrageous rent of 1,700 reals a year, three times more than at Bandar Abbas. There were insufficient wells and in summer water had to be fetched from the Tigris; it tasted salty and foul.

The trade of Basra depended upon the three great routes of which it was the terminus. First, slow caravans departed twice a year from Basra to Kerbela, az-Zur, and Aleppo. Until 1650, and then again in the eighteenth century, these comprised hundreds of camels for freight and stallions for breeding. But from 1650 onward the trade along this route declined. One reason was that Aleppo's role as the hub of the Levant trade was taken over by Smirna, reached through Anatolia. Another was that the desert became increasingly unsafe as Ottoman garrisons were withdrawn from al-Hasha. No great tribal confederation, like the Muntafiq in the eighteenth century, then provided safeguards for caravans to traverse the desert, and robbers roved the sands.[129]

Second, there was the link to Shiraz, overland by way of Kirmanshah or Ahvaz or overseas from Rig. Rig also traded grain to Basra, which was deficient in supplies. Silk was fetched from Persia. Part of this was sent to Baghdad for the manufactures there, and part was used for the textile industry of al-Hasha, which mainly specialized in carpets. By far the most important traffic with Persia was the pilgrimage, however. If a Shiite pilgrim had visited the shrines in Iraq, he might wish to travel to Mecca. He might then either journey overland through Jerusalem—where he had to put up with a hostile population and harassment by Ottoman authorities—or go overseas through Basra. In the fifties 5,000 to 10,000 pilgrims did so: they would have to pay—depending on their prosperity—8 to 15 tomans to travel to Jidda.[130] Many hajjis fetched goods to pay for the trip: fruit, wine, silk, and the *ruina* root that grew around Tebriz and was used on the Coromandel Coast to make paint.[131]

Third, and most important was the link from Aleppo to Diarbakir along the Tigris. As the snow on the Anatolian mountains melted, the *tanaqin*s, the flat-bottomed ships of the Tigris, would depart Diarbakir's muddy quay. This trip would first lead to the fortress town of Mosul, where they moored in order to receive permits from the Ottoman authorities to enter Iraq. The ships of Mosul's inhabitants, stowed with logs for Basra and Baghdad, would be waiting to join the flotilla, as would traders from Erzincan and Erzurum. In Mosul too would be anchored galleys with provisions and munitions for Baghdad and Basra—the frontier of the Ottoman empire. Those galleys were packed with *janitsar*s, resembling peddlers rather than soldiers. The trip to Basra led through barren deserts, where the single sound was the distant wail of hyenas. No other human beings were seen for days; sometimes on the far horizon appeared campfires—of robber tribes? At night guards were put out so bandits would not swim to the *tanaqin*s. Arriving at Gordolan, one had to carry one's goods ashore and wait for permits to proceed to Basra.[132]

Once the river fleet had arrived at Basra, everything had to go quickly. The longboats from Rig arrived in March and had to depart before the onset of the *shamal;* the other ships had to leave in May. For two months Basra was a buzzing beehive, but during the other months it would slumber.

To the south of Basra came the inlets and scattered hamlets of as-Shamil and thereafter the Najd—an unknown land—and, to the east, the barren wastes and the ruined fortresses and hamlets of Khuzestan/Arabistan. The prolonged Persian-Ottoman wars, the conflict of 1632–38 in particular, seem to have devastated the fragile irrigation works around Ahvaz. They were not regularly maintained and, partly intentionally, were wrecked by the armies. While Ahvaz (Lhasa), a drab little town of clay edifices drifting amid swamps, was still a minor transit center in the beginning of the century, at its end Ahvaz's trade had dwindled.[133]

Avoiding the coast with its many sandbanks, vessels would next sail toward Kharg—a rocky island with a high cliff on the north side, a beach on the south.

Sheltering under the promontory to avoid the gales, they waited for provisions fetched from Bandar Rig to Kharg and sold to the sloops supplying the pearl fleet at Bahrain. These sheltered at Kharg against storms and the dreaded *nakhila* sea rovers, who preyed on the pearl vessels too. The hamlets of fishermen along the Persian coast supplemented their paltry subsistence with piracy since times immemorial.[134]

West was the tiny port of Rig. Sloops peddled between Rig and the ships at anchor, which had to avoid the sandbanks in front of the island. Along the Mand River near Rig were irrigated lands, and fine grain was cultivated there and shipped to Basra and Bahrain. It was too expensive to be exported beyond the maritime zone of the lower Gulf, however. The grain was largely paid with exports of cash from Basra and Bahrain.[135]

East of Rig ships now approached Cape Vardestan, announcing the desolate plains with mountains of the Persian coast looming in the distance. Keeping within sight of the shore, ships would have to remain four to seven miles out and take constant soundings of the dangerous rocky seabed. In front are scattered uninhabited islands and cliffs.

Yet vessels sailed along the Persian shore and avoided the Arab coast, not only since it was imperfectly charted and the narrow inlets closed by sandbanks were ideal hideouts for pirates, but also since the access to Bahrain was restricted by the Safavid empire. European traders needed safe-conduct documents from the sultan of Bandar Abbas or Kung to go there. This flat Arab shore was one of the most isolated areas in the world. Lone fishing hamlets were disseminated in the waste—like counterpoints in the perennial symphony of sand and violet sea. The inhabitants lived on fish; even the meager goats were fed on fish flour.[136] Bahrain was "a flat island, a humid and fertile place with many palm trees. Wherever one digs, one finds water immediately but it is very unhealthy, which causes great epidemics, particularly from September to February, when all noblemen go to Qatifa so as not to get ill too."[137]

From Leghorn, Marseilles, and Venice, mostly Jewish merchants conducted overland trade along the Syrian caravan route to Bahrain and neighboring Qatif.[138] This involved substantial capital: at the end of the seventeenth century about 2–3 million guilders in cash yearly. Greek merchants also traded with Bahrain over the Caucasus and from there to Muscovy and Poland.[139] The trade from Bahrain to India was predominantly in the hands of *bania* merchants, who made a 30–40 percent profit on it. About 3–4 million guilders were invested in this at the end of the seventeenth century. Although people dived for pearls in south India too, Bahrain pearls could command a ready market there. Those pearls did not turn pale from the oils and perfume that Indian belles rubbed in "when these people are having a feast."[140]

The trees and minarets of Sheikh Sho'yeb Island announced Kung. Sloops were sent ashore to buy fowl and goats. Kung was situated on a sultry plain next to the Bani Kung, a brook that generally was nothing but a dry bed. Whitewashed houses blinked in the ever-fierce sun; one could see a few date groves, gray shadows of mountains in the distance, and sails in front of the roaring swell. Yes—from afar Kung was an impressive sight.[141]

But Kung, an odd location for a major port, was vexed by all kinds of problems. The ships had to remain far from the shore with its many constantly shifting shallows and sandbanks. Ships were not in reach of shore-based artillery and could not be protected against Muscati or Portuguese corsairs. The port was not sheltered against gales; when the *shamal* blew, the ships then had to seek refuge at Khism. The desolate plain surrounding Kung grove was as sterile as it was arid and the water was brackish. Potable water had to be fetched from Khism. The scant vegetation provided little shade and, though Kung was not as infernally hot as the "oven," Bandar Abbas, the sandstorms in the summer were equally depressing. And on top of it, connections were terrible: the track to Bastak and Shiraz was but a stony trail, hard to tread even for donkeys.[142]

Yet, despite those inconveniences, Kung had grown from but a hamlet with 200 Arab fishermen in 1626 to the major port of the Gulf around 1680. The Portuguese "Gulf fleets," cruising off Khism, were instructed to "gently persuade sails coming from Surat to go to Congo," but this would not appear to be the only explanation for the rise of Kung.[143]

Due to the busy coastwise trade within the Gulf, there was only a 3–4 percent price differential between Bandar Abbas and Kung. The customs in Kung were 4–6 percent, but in Bandar Abbas the merchant was crushed by them: 7 percent on cotton yarn and up to 13 percent on tobacco. Merchants were also burdened there with a host of added impositions, such as the weighing-house taxes (4 percent) or the 45 mahmudis to be paid on transporting goods ashore.[144] Furthermore, the customs revenues of Bandar Abbas were farmed and each tax farmer might not only replenish his income by bribes but might impose even more taxes as well, to pay for his ever-increasing retinue. Such a suite could amount to so many persons that the merchants of Bandar Abbas had to send petitions to the Safavid court to have at least some dismissed.[145]

Generalissimo (*sipahsalar*) Allah Verdi Khan and Admiral Ruy Freyre de Andrade had agreed in 1626 that the *vazir* of Shiraz, Allah Verdi Khan, was to grant half the customs revenues of Kung to the Estado da Índia. A similar arrangement existed between the English and Persians relative to Bandar Abbas. Unlike the Portuguese, the English used arguments rather than arms to collect their share, though, so they seldom or never obtained it. It was, therefore, not in the court's interest to levy high duties in Kung, for the Portuguese might be the main beneficiaries. And the arrangement was signed by the *sipahsalar*, not by the shah, anyway. Kung seems to have become a responsibility of the grand vizier later, who occasionally sent a commissioner to gather taxes. When Kung was brought under direct rule of the court around 1684, the city came under the supervision of the sultan of Bandar Abbas, who rarely gathered the incomes of Kung and elected to stay at Bandar Abbas. The merchants themselves largely ruled the town. The *nakhuda geral* of Kung, with whom the Portuguese generally negotiated their share of the customs, appears to have been a representative of the merchant community. Traders hence preferred Kung's few comforts and fewer taxes to the security and high levies of Bandar Abbas. Additionally, Kung was located closer to Shiraz, the hub of the horse trade.[146]

Divided from the mainland by a narrow strait, the dense forests of the long and narrow island of Khism adorned the Gulf. Khism would have been a logical location for a major port but because of sandbanks in front of the coast the small ports on the island, like Bashidu—"a miserly little village completely consisting of ruins"—were not accessible to seagoing vessels. There were about 40 villages on Khism, an isle of forest and plains, a checkerboard of walled gardens. Fruits, vegetables, and some grain were cultivated and mainly sent to Bandar Abbas.[147]

Sailing to the east now, one could discern the shape of a barren rock of sulfur and salt: Hormuz. If ships requested to take on ballast at the island (one had to obtain a special permit for this), they could see in the distance the vaults of palaces, churches, and minarets. Edifices that were demolished served as building materials for Bandar Abbas and were exported as ballast throughout the Arabian seas. Seasonal laborers would quarry the jagged rocks of salt, which soared above this abandoned city, too—terrible work, especially after a rain, when the salt formed crystals. Salt was one of the main sources for Hormuz's former prosperity, as it was a favorite ballast for ships. The sulfurous earth was much used for making porcelain: it would give a deep red tinge, which could not be achieved with any other earth, and was even exported to distant Japan. Given these primary materials and a strategic position comparable to Gibraltar's, it was but logical that in the sixteenth century, "if the world was a ring, Hormuz would have been its diamond."[148]

Gamru—the caravanserai on the mainland of Hormuz—was named "felicitous port of Abbas" (*Bandar mobarak ye-abbasi*) in 1624, though the Europeans persisted in giving the site its old name. As evinced by its new name, the choice of Gamru had been a political one. Not many reasons could be thought of to single out Gamru as a good location for a port. The ships had to anchor three to four miles out of the roadstead, which was shielded by sandbanks. Just like Kung, Bandar Abbas was open to the northwesterly winds. So most ships, when unloaded, proceeded to the desolate island of Larak, where some repairs could be carried out. The keels, while taking on ballast, were there protected by the guns of a fortress too—unlike at Bandar Abbas. However, Gamru did have a good and safe link with the hinterland: to cater for the traffic to the new port of the empire the Safavids had also constructed several new caravanserais. This royal highway linked Bandar Abbas to the prosperous little town of Lar and thence to Shiraz, Kirman, or the metropolis Isfahan.[149]

To Europeans this "felicitous port" resembled a haphazard heap of bricks rather than a grand emporium. It consisted of single story houses, generally of earth; a skyline of towering ventilation chimneys (*badgir*) built to catch the few breaths of cool air in the summer; cramped and dusty streets; a dilapidated palace of the sultan and a ramshackle fortress. Most worthy of note were the factories of the English and Dutch Companies: compact blocks of brick centered on cramped courtyards. The town was situated on a bleak, windswept plain.[150]

Bandar Abbas was such a desolate sight because the town was constructed as a camp rather than a residence. Most dwellings were not erected for eternity but were only shelters, empty most of the year and rented to merchants arriving there from Isfahan and Lar in October. During the summer the town was practically empty except for a few Arab hawkers and sailors stranded ashore, unfortunate peasants pressed into the local militia (*mulazim*). And only mad dogs and Dutchmen stayed in the sun. For the Dutch rank and file was forbidden to leave the town except by special permit of their director, who normally went to cooler places in summer, like to Shiraz, to pursue the pleasures of wine and the hunt.[151]

Next, ships would sail along the plains of the Biaban, where only a few hamlets of fishermen enlivened a boring view of barren rocks over which roamed skinny goats and sheep. A hill announced the land tongue of Jask, until the fall of Hormuz the only seaport of the Safavid empire. Sailors sent ashore in 1645 to survey this site "saw one camel, decaying houses, stone graves, some woodwork on which they saw cruciforms, and three to four crosses to which were nailed skins of goats. That is everything they saw."[152]

The glory of Hormuz vanished practically overnight, but this was fairly typical of towns in the Gulf, and it is not that difficult to explain: "Eight months a year it is terribly hot and the air is very pestilent, causing major epidemics and fevers, so not only many of us but many inhabitants too die every year. One hour they are healthy, the next ill and unconscious and the third they are dead." Thus wrote Ysbrand Goske: if not replenished by constant migrations, the population of cities in the Gulf would be decimated in no time.[153]

Passing to the Arabian side of the Strait of Oman, the ships now neared Cape Musendan: cliffs, bays, and knurled mountains. High above the bare rock walls towered this grey promontory, which was surrounded by cliffs sharp as razor blades. "There is no anchoring ground there or you will have lost your hook."[154] But to the east of this awesome cape were prosperous hamlets and sheltered coves. Rugged Portuguese watchtowers and fortifications were raised on the slopes of the hills. In 1645—when the VOC made a detailed survey of the area—a Portuguese captain and ten wretched soldiers still raised a frayed flag above Dobhia, a barren outpost of the Portuguese empire. It was to be their last year: Dobhia was conquered by Ja'ariba troops in 1647. The English in 1648 considered building a fortress there: caravans from the interior of Oman might be routed to the Musendan area, they thought. It was not an unrealistic scheme. There was a fairly extensive caravan trade between Dobhia and al-Hasha. Piece-cloth and horses from al-Hasha were exchanged for rice from India and fruit and cattle from al-Batinah and the Omani hinterland there. Dobhia was an entrepôt for slaves too, who were brought from India and the Swahili Coast and nourished after their long journey before being sold on the slave markets in Basra, Kung, and Rig.[155]

In 1670—on establishing a factory of the VOC at Muscat—the flute *Weesp* was sent to survey the al-Batinah coast. Those shores offered a grim picture. In the 1620s al-Batinah was a land of densely planted date groves, busy shipping, and abundant fishing. Suhar, the main town, was then a fairly large settlement. It was an Arab town of whitewashed clay houses next to a Portuguese fortification on a wide plain, planted with groves; irrigation canals were drilled in the mountains to water it.[156]

But in 1670 Suhar and the other ports along this coast were only ruins. In front of the crumbling fortifications erected by the Portuguese lay abandoned villages and groves, swallowed by the advancing dunes. The area was suffering from overgrazing. The Portuguese had brought in herds of cattle and herdsmen from Buraimi to feed the fleets: these flocks were chasing the peasants away, either to the interior or to the booming city of Muscat.[157]

To quote A. Hamilton:

> The city of Muskat is very strong, both by nature and by art; but the buildings very mean as most fabricks are under the œconomy of a people who abominate luxury and pride as the Muskat Arabs do. The cathedral built by the Portugueze, still retains some marks of its ancient grandeur and is now converted into a palace for the king when he resides here, which is generally a month or two yearly. The walls of the town that faces the harbour has a battery of large cannon, about 60 in number and there are 8 or 10 small forts built on the adjacent rocks or mountains which guard the avenues to the town both by sea and land; and there are none permitted to come in or go out of the harbour between sun-set and rising.[158]

Muscat controlled the entrance to the Gulf, for vessels sailed along the Arab shore, not along the Makran Coast. That was a shelter of sea scum, plagued by hurricanes in summer. Yet Muscat's location, while making it invulnerable to attacks from the land and the sea, was its curse too. The caravans that linked Muscat to the interior had to climb forbidding mountain passes to reach the town. Foodstuffs were prohibitively expensive to transport from the hinterland: the only regular fare in the town was fish. Two products were received from the hinterland, though: horses and sugar.[159]

To nourish Muscat was therefore bound to be a major concern of any power controlling the stronghold, and this would require ships from the entire ocean. The Portuguese brought rice for Muscat from Barcelore and grain from Mombasa, Rig, Sind, and Gujarat. The Ja'ariba *vali*s (viceroys) of Muscat stretched those arteries of supply even further—to Suqutra and Malindi, to Pate, Mogadishu, and the Hadramawt. They were quite successful, but at the cost of draconian penalties: prices of provisions in Muscat were tied to rigid schedules and infringement of these met with severe corporal punishment.[160]

And that was not the only offense met with such punishment: the naval wars that were conducted from Muscat attracted mercenaries from throughout the seven seas, but its puritan legislation contrasted to that rowdy crowd.[161] Drink, a good smoke, dancing, gambling, unbecoming conduct with women—for anything one might be mutilated or whipped. This was still a minor discomfort, however, compared to the climate—reputedly even worse than at Bandar Abbas. As the city was surrounded by cliffs, "noxious vapours" could not be blown away.[162]

Nonetheless, the town flourished in the late seventeenth century under a succession of very capable imams. It was a precarious prosperity, however; Oman itself was only a small market and the bulk of the merchandise imported in Muscat was smuggled to the opposite shore. The customs at Muscat amounted to a mere 2.5 to 4 percent and many ships engaged in coastwise trade within the Gulf and from Sind paid no customs at all—quite a difference from Bandar Abbas![163]

## Gujarat

After the long trip along the dreary coast of the Makran the first landmark of the Indian coast, if ships were heading for Gujarat, was greeted with joy. This was the densely forested hill of Girnar, which the Europeans called the "highland of St. John." Diu, the first port one would touch, is located on a barren island dotted by palm groves. Duarte Mathias had the following verdict on it in 1681:[164]

> There is no wood and there is no water, except what is assembled in autumn in cisterns; there are no white women and one can not count an old man in this town of which the climate, as everybody agrees, is more unhealthy than that of Goa.

The strength of Diu was its strategic location at the entrance of the Gulf of Cambay; it was an excellent port but a bad entrepôt, for there were few good roads crossing Kathiawar. The island is two miles long by three wide. The harbor was sheltered against the winds and two to three fathoms deep. More than 100 ships could anchor there. Piers and quays ensured that ships could be quickly loaded. Two fortresses guarded the entrance to the inner port, and these were provided with 15 guns. This inner port could be locked with a chain, so Diu was reputed to be impregnable from the sea. To profit from this marvelous anchorage Indian ships had to pay high customs, however: 10 percent on merchandise, 2 percent on cash.[165]

The center of Diu was not the Portuguese citadel with its massive fortified church and hospital, but the "black town" with its temple and mosque—adjacent to the Portuguese *castelo* and surrounded by an earth wall. The *banias* had financed the building of the Jesuit seminary and three churches in Diu, in exchange for being allowed to retain their temple.[166]

But the Indian population there had—according to Antônio Bocarro, writing in 1634—declined from 10,000 "fireplaces" in 1600 to but 1,000 in 1630. Bocarro—a very critical observer—blamed this on extortion by the governors. Taking a "fireplace" to mean about four persons, this would be a dramatic decrease indeed. The Hindu community of Diu agreed with Bocarro, though; Diu's population had fallen from 46,000 fireplaces in 1620 to 1,000 in 1644, they estimated. Next to those Indian crowds lived 59 Portuguese families, according to Bocarro; in 1642 there were 50 Portuguese and 100 Indian Christians. "Because of the continuous maladies there, however, they mostly flee to the mainland." The Christian community on the island had practically disappeared by 1680.[167]

If the ships now turned toward the Gulf of Cambay, they would gaze at a densely populated, fertile land with many villages that were cultivating grain and fishing in the rich waters of the gulf. The distant hills of Kathiawar, the hinterland, were ruled by independent Rajput dynasties and politically stood largely apart from the Mughal province (*subah*) of Gujarat. Yet those black hills have long played a part of their own in the trade of the Arabian seas, if a less conspicuous one than the *subah* of Gujarat. There was a gamut of minor ports there: Jamnagar, Purbandar, Namanah, and Goga. From Surat the ports of Kathiawar obtained iron, lead, spices, fibers, and coconuts, "which are fetched inward thence."[168] They exported agricultural products: *paddy*, fish, and grain from the coast; clarified butter and wood from the interior; and manpower—Diu's garrison mostly consisted of soldiers "from the mountains."[169]

Goga was the main port of Kathiawar: "a mean little town, inhabited by rude moor sailors." Goga went through a span of prosperity in the early seventeenth century as one of the ports favored by Mughal shipping; the Portuguese then also had a customs station there. The town's importance declined after 1650. Goga was mainly a center for recruiting mariners. Sailors from Goga largely manned Diu's ships. And it was an excellent port since the ships could, due to the strong tide in the Gulf of Cambay, be easily unloaded. It was a minor center of shipbuilding as well.[170]

The inlet of the stream leading to Cambay was announced by a number of small bays, brimming with fishing boats and sloops loaded with merchandise. Even past its balmy days in the sixteenth century, in the seventeenth Cambay was still the second port of Gujarat and the main entrepôt for goods from Ahmedabad and for the products brought from Mozambique and the Swahili Coast. Some Europeans thought Cambay was more favorably located for the textile trade than was Surat and one might better move the factory there. But the place suffered from two major disadvantages.

First, there was the notorious tidal bore: a wall of water rising up seven fathoms. It could wreck ships in an instant. This made the roadstead on the entrance to the river of Cambay perilous even for sloops.[171] There were sandbanks in the river, and their position constantly changed. This stream got ever more shallow. This was one reason why Cambay was overtaken by Surat around 1620. Second, Cambay also did not dispose of the financial facilities of Surat. It was possible to repair ships there while there was plenty of manpower available. But one could not easily insure ships or cargo, or take up bottomry there.[172]

Sailing southward, ships passed along the fertile district of Jambushir, where indigo was cultivated, mostly used by the textile industry of Gujarat. Next, they reached the estuary of the Narmada, leading to the important city of Broach—a major center of the textile industry. Many small crafts taking textiles to Surat were moored at isles in the estuary, rented by textile traders to dry piece-cloth.[173] And then one approached the most famous and largest city of the Arabian seas: Surat.

This metropolis, "a city as large as a kingdom" (and probably the second largest of the Mughal empire around 1700, after Ahmedabad), had about 100,000 inhabitants around 1660, maybe up to 200,000 around 1700.[174] Despite its recurrent famines, epidemics, and violence it grew, on and on, "with vast numbers of people, moving thither from every area." "The *banias*"—in this case Hindus in general—"house in unbelievable confusion in the tiniest of nooks and crannies where they not only live among appalling filth, but also put everything grubby in front of their door and on the public streets, women and men, with great indecency."[175]

According to independent attorney (*fiscaal*) J. Deodati, Surat was a pigsty; to the all-pervasive stench of excrement was added the suffocating smoke of chalk ovens and charcoal fires, to the human filth the industrial. In addition to the congestion in the inner city—where squatters occupied any piece of open land—there was an interminable belt of slums along the river. As most of Surat consisted of wooden shanties, there were constant fires—particularly in the slums in the inner city, where iron furnaces were located. The government tried to fight this hazard of fires by forbidding blacksmiths to establish their trade within the urban parameter but to little avail.[176]

The metropolis would probably have died out if not for being fed by constant migration from the entire continent. Contagious disease, cholera apparently, was endemic in Surat.[177] Moreover, a large part of the population was malnourished because of the perpetual lack of foodstuffs that plagued the town. The Mughal government was concerned but utterly unable to deal with the problem of supplying the *bandar-i mobarak* or combating its urban predicament.

It did try to effect some improvements, though. In 1685 a scheme was considered to pave the main thoroughfares and provide for lighting at night. This failed because of the resistance of the *nagarseth*. He feared, rightly, that such improvements would have to be paid for through additional taxes that most inhabitants could ill afford. Still, the Mughal government did look after some amenities—it had founded a bathhouse (*hamam*) that everybody could visit free of charge. And it had established a good Koran, school, which only charged a nominal fee.[178]

The Mughal governor of Surat also took draconian measures to forestall the speculation in grain. Such speculation troubled the government, as there were frequent riots in the town that were mainly directed against grain traders but occasionally against the tax gatherers of the state as well.[179] The grain merchants were regularly summoned to the governor's audience chamber to be upbraided for selling cereals to the Marathas instead of to the poor of Surat, and for withholding stocks when the government tried to fix food prices. The governor in 1694 had all stocks seized and the dealers who withheld grain from the starving population lashed in public. But he was unable to do much about this problem: the empire did not control the routes to southern Gujarat and Malwa from which most grain was imported.[180]

The inner city of Surat measured 12 miles in circumference. The castle and the great square (the *maidan*) were the center of town. There, tents owned by various nations and merchant princes were piled with goods on their way to the customs house. To the left was the customs house, to the right the palace of the governor. Near the *maidan* too were the palatial dwellings of famous merchant princes, of Abdul Ghafur for instance. From this *maidan* extended a maze of narrow, winding streets. The center of each neighborhood of Surat was a caravanserai, often named after governors who had founded them or after the various *natios*. (There is incidentally still a neighborhood at Surat called Vallanda Bandar—the Dutch harbor—located on the site of the former VOC wharf.)

The gloomy, black fortress—the landmark of the metropolis—was reputed to be unassailable. But it was badly manned, badly armed, and in decay. "No Europeans are permitted to enter it but this is apparently in order that these defects should not become public knowledge." The earthen inner wall of Surat, hastily and shabbily constructed in 1676, was repeatedly washed away by the monsoon rains. In any case, the suburbs were situated higher than the inner city, so that the town could not have resisted an artillery bombardment.[181]

We are of course well informed on the Companies' buildings. Shacks from the early seventeenth century still housed the Companies' personnel in 1756. To quote Jan Schreuder on the VOC's factory: "In short: it is not possible to imagine a building as irregularly constructed, as inconvenient, as inefficient and as depressing as the one we are forced to live in." However, Europeans were not permitted to build another factory outside of the walls. The Mughal authorities, with due justification, feared they might construct a fortress.[182]

A. Das Gupta has called the rise of Surat a "gift of the Mughal Empire." The Mughal empire linked Gujarat to the trade routes of northwestern India, he argues. This is certainly so, although Rander was already a major port in 1560: the Mughal empire was building on foundations laid by the Gujarati sultanate. Surat's prosperity was a token of the Mughal empire in two other respects as well.[183]

First, the Portuguese had conceded that the two or three ships built by the Mughal empire would be provided with navicerts. These were huge vessels taking as much cargo along as 15 or 20 small craft, and charging lower freight than the Portuguese. While this concession was to apply to shipping to Yemen and Persia alone, by 1620 the *nawab* of Surat was dispatching ships under the Mughal flag to Atjeh as well. It would be but a matter of time before the trade of Diu would be ruined by this Mughal competition.[184]

Second, it seems Surat took over the position of leading entrepôt of the Arabian seas from two other ports: Laribandar, on the mouth of the Indus, and Dabhul, in the Konkan. Around 1600, Laribandar was the largest center of trade of the Arabian seas with—according to Resende—up to 150,000 inhabitants. It was mainly a port for trade with Persia, both overland and overseas. The *terradas*, navigating the Indus from Laribandar, connected the port to the indigo- and sugar-producing lands of the Doab and the Punjab and to the centers of textile production there. But—taken by ships over the Ganges to Agra and from there by caravans to Lahore—textiles were received from as far away as Bengal. It would seem Laribandar's trade reached its apogee at the turn of the sixteenth century since it was the port of Lahore, the seat of a dazzling court that attracted manufactured goods from the whole of India.[185] When the court moved to Agra and Shahjahanabad the link over the Indus appears to have been replaced by communications overland through Rajasthan. In the first half of the seventeenth century this was a rapid and cheap means of transit since one could use bullock carts, which were cheaper than camels.[186]

This caravan trade through Rajasthan declined in the latter half of the seventeenth century. After the Rajput rebellion against Aurengzeb in 1676 the customs in Rajasthan skyrocketed, while roads fell into decay and it became necessary to fetch the goods by camel instead of by bullock cart.[187] Goods from Hindustan were now brought to Gujarat through Malwa via Burhanpur. One had to pay about 5 percent local customs along this road and it took much longer than through Rajasthan (four weeks against six weeks).[188] But the road through Malwa was free from robbers and accessible to bullock carts. This was a boost to the trade of Surat. While Surat was the terminus of the latter road, Cambay was the terminus for the one through Rajasthan: the Narmada was a major obstacle if traveling to or from Surat.[189]

Surat's wealth thus sprouted more from the humble bullock cart than from the splendid sails crowding the roadstead. And, indeed, Surat was a rotten harbor. The Tapi—and Suali, its estuary—was a nightmare for sailors. The river was silting up, with nobody apparently caring at all. People were even throwing ballast into the river. Rander—where the Tapi in 1600 led into the sea—was in 1700 one mile distant from the present anchoring place. One then distinguished a new and an old Suali. Old Suali, the mouth of the river in 1660, was inaccessible even for flat-bottoms in 1700. The shore was covered with rubble of dilapidated warehouses; wood of wrecked ships drifted on the muddy waters.

New Suali had developed when dunes were washed away into the sea. At low tide it was dangerous because of the shoals. It was not covered against storms, while batteries on shore could not protect the estuary. Because of sandbanks, tides, and wrecks the river was very difficult to navigate even for the flat-bottomed *houris*, which were used to ferry goods from the ships at Suali to Surat.[190]

## The Konkan

Further to the south was the key of the Portuguese northern quarters, Daman: a mighty citadel with walls reputedly 30 feet thick and surrounded by moats and trenches.[191] It was a fine port protected by the water bastion, a stronghold with 30 cannons. Ships could be hauled ashore under the protection of this fortress.

The town was famous for the wood from the forests on the hills near Daman, renowned for its strength and durability. This was exported to Surat to make furniture and doorjambs. The captain of Bassein and of Daman enjoyed the *cola* monopoly: the right to send parties of lumberjacks to cut the best trees. It was the main income of the captains. Rice, sugar, and coconuts were cultivated near Daman and even some wine was made. "In short"—G. Pelgrom noted in 1650—"it is a very pleasant place."[192]

South of Daman began hillocks. These girdle a coastal plain, some miles broad. Rice and sugar fields, dense groves of palms, white churches rising above reed huts, and sprawling villages hidden under the high trees—such was the sight of this plain, the Portuguese northern quarters or Praças do Norte, from the sea.

This area was granted to his "brother," the Portuguese king, by the sultan of Gujarat in 1578, on provision that the rights of subordinate rajahs to levy their fixed "protection" fee (*chauth*) on the revenue of the area would be respected. This *chauth* generally amounted to about 15 percent.[193] The area was considered legal "wasteland" by the Portuguese crown. In accordance with the normal Portuguese practice when dividing wasteland, the lands were partitioned in fiefs (*foros*) granted in emphyteusis to retired soldiers, who had to pay a sum to the crown annually. The holder of such a fief had to take care of the defense of their lands: entertain armed men and Arab horses. They were not allowed to lease or sell the land, which legally remained the property of the crown. They were not permitted to divide it among their sons either, and if a girl inherited a property, she was to marry a Portuguese soldier named by the crown.[194]

As to the status of the Indian inhabitants of the Praças do Norte:

> They are commonly called *abunhados das aldeais* [those tied to the villages], which is roughly comparable to *glebae adscripti*. They have a perpetual obligation to work there—an immutable one so that, if a serf flees to another proprietor, he has to be

> given back to his former owner immediately, as he is a part of his property. Thus the best and most profitable village is not the hamlet with most land, but the village with the largest number of *abunhados*, for if they are lacking it is abandoned and lost.[195]

As Portuguese private trade became an ever more risky affair, investors withdrew to the haven of investment in land, mainly in the Praças do Norte. In 1610 people were complaining that the area had become depopulated since the Portuguese took over, as the *foreiros* invested in trade and luxury goods rather than in farming and rice.[196] There was no cause to complain later on. Some formerly small hamlets in the Praças do Norte had by 1630 grown into substantial agricultural towns, like Tarapur, which boasted some 30 Portuguese and 750 Christian "fireplaces," or Tana with 25 and 500.[197]

Bassein, playground of those landlords, was situated on a tongue of land, surrounded on three sides by marshland, flooded during high tide. At the end was the fortress in which were situated a large warehouse, the Jesuit convent, the parochial church of Bassein, and the house of charity—the *misericórdia*. According to Boccaro 400 Portuguese *casados* and "many" *fidalgos* (noblemen) lived there with 300 rich indigenous Christians—each of whom boasted a retinue of three or four black slaves from Mozambique and many Indian serfs. The former were employed in household work and in the sugar-cane plantation. Father Manuel Godinho S.I. counted 300 *casados* in 1664. At the high ground opposite the tongue of land was the Kasbah or Indian town of Bassein, which may have counted about 30,000 inhabitants.[198]

Ships now followed the forested, hilly coast of Salcete. Near the southern extension of a hillock one could discern the silhouette of a large temple. There unfolds the sight of the Bay of Bombay, which is one and half miles broad and five miles long. In the distance one can make out the mountains of the mainland, the two mountains of Kanjeri Island and the rocks of Elephanta Island. The bay becomes ever more narrow to the west, where the mountains of the mainland hug those of Salcete. Separated from the mainland by a narrow creek, surrounded during the monsoon by an extensive swamp but in summer by muddy flats and salt pans, were the six islands of Bombay. Bombay was a stronghold forged by nature. Ships could throw out their anchors at any season in the deep, sheltered bay, where they had access to provisions from the fertile island of Salcete.

Under the Portuguese the lands of Bombay consisted of the fishing and market town of Kasbah Bombay, the agricultural area of Mahim—a land of wet-rice cultivation with 56 villages—and Mazagao (Malabar Hill), "the garden of Bombay" with dense palm groves. Hardly a booming metropolis, but no stagnant backwater either, as one might gather from the literature. There were some substantial estates and Kasbah Bombay was a flourishing little town. The total value of all property in the area was estimated at 620,100 xeraphins. The transfer of Bombay to the English by the Portuguese crown in 1661 thus certainly grieved the Portuguese vassals in India. The English promised to pay the revenue of the estates in Bombay to the Portuguese. But after the siege of Bombay by the Mughal army in 1688 they ceased doing so, as they claimed the land had been conquered anew by the English.[199]

In 1665 the English started to build a fortress on the southernmost island. The islands were gradually connected through the construction of dams and salt pans. Around 1700 a small town of about 20,000 inhabitants was located on the southern isle, surrounded by bulwarks. On the other islands were found fishermen's cottages and the humble abodes of workers in the salt pans. Although it was a reasonably healthy place, Englishmen considered it morose and boring; only the arrival of the Indians would interrupt the dreary routine.[200]

In the distance, south of Bombay, one saw the steep basalt cone of the Karnala Mountain and on top the fortress—or Moro—of Chaul. The town at the foot of this stronghold consisted of two cities: the town of Revbandar—Portuguese "downtown" Chaul near the sea—and some miles up a small stream, "uptown" Chaul with its temples and minarets under the domination of Ahmadnagar, later Bijapur and the Marathas. The Moro was the southern key to the Praças do Norte. A memory of many sieges was tied to this stronghold. The ominous shape of the fortress on the mountain was to the merchants of uptown Chaul the symbol of the Portuguese grip on the trade of the Arabian seas. A true frontier, the Portuguese had always to keep a watchful eye on the surroundings: skirmishes were common there. The hostile territory of Ahmadnagar started but one musket shot away from the Moro.[201] Yet this station at the frontier was until 1630 like "another Venice, because of the great traffic conducted here." Prosperity was partly due to the Portuguese protection, but Chaul had been the privileged port of the Ahmadnagar sultanate too. And Grand Vizier Malik Ambar had been very active as a trader. The 200 Portuguese living below the citadel were around 1630 one of the wealthiest communities of the Estado da Índia. Trade was conducted with Mombasa in ivory and Sind in textiles, "the major traffic of this town," Persia and Yemen in rice and textiles and in steel—for Chaul was the smithy of the Estado da Índia.[202]

But Chaul was hit hard by the destruction of the Ahmadnagar sultanate at the hands of Bijapur and the Mughal empire in 1630. Merchants then either fled to Surat or to Dabhul, which was under Bijapuri protection. Later, Chaul was hit by the Portuguese war with Muscat as well. The badly armed ships built there were ideal prey for Muscati corsairs. By 1700 dense jungle had engulfed uptown Chaul. Revbandar was a decaying fortress below containing the crumbling dwellings of 54 *casados*. The long-distance trade of Chaul had largely disappeared.[203]

South of Chaul the hills reach close to the sea and enclose a narrow coastal plain: the Konkani Coast. Along the seaboard moved hundreds of small crafts loaded with fish, coconuts, rice, and fruit. Konkan was a densely populated area.

The Saraswat Brahmin communities and the fishermen have traditionally been heavily involved in trade and seafaring, for this was a poor land: the soil was threatened by salinization, the harvest by the erratic rains. Saraswat communities were seeking fortunes beyond their native land, on land and sea: one met them wherever one went in the Arabian seas.[204]

The main port of the Konkani Coast was Dabhul. But when Surat boomed, Dabhul decayed. It was around 1600 the main outlet for trade to Hormuz and "the merchants of Daphol may well be said to control the trade" with Suqutra and Yemen.[205] The decline of the port was evident when the Dutch ambassador to the Adilshah, J. van Twist, visited it in 1638. Though the Bay of Dabhul could still harbor hundreds of vessels, there were none at anchor—just wrecks strewn around the roadstead. Houses were in ruin, bulwarks and temples on the hill above Dabhuḷ had been swept away by the rains, guns were corroding on the seashore. By 1700, Dabhul was a port of mere local significance.[206]

This decline was partly caused by the silting of the entrance to the anchorage. It was dangerous to enter in 1638, due to sandbanks. But this is not the only explanation. Dabhul's trade was also tied to a number of ports and city-states in the Middle East and East Africa that were in decline: Hormuz, Zeila, Khisn, Mogadishu, and Mombasa.

Dabhul was the main outlet of Bijapuri trade on the Konkan coast, not only since Adilshahi grandees largely conducted its shipping but also because it depended upon the roads to the hinterland protected by the Adilshah. Dabhul's bulk goods: textiles—like sailcloth and cheap piece-cloth—were woven in Belgaum and Kolhapur. The cotton, saltpeter, and grain exported were mainly from the Maratha Deccan. But the road linking Dabhul to Bijapur over Karhad was already dangerous in 1638 and virtually impassable after the rise of Maratha power in the hinterland. The saltpeter trade, perhaps the main trade of Dabhul, collapsed. This was partly due to the danger of the road. It was also because saltpeter became a royal monopoly under the Maratha ruler Shivaji and its export was curtailed.[207]

Luxury textiles were transported to Dabhul from the Bijapuri Carnatac overland. This was a precarious trade, which depended upon Adilshahi control of the overland routes. Most products sold at Dabhul were brought to the Coromandel Coast and to Gujarat, however; its immediate hinterland, the Maratha Deccan, was only a small market. Dabhul's decline may have had two further causes, then. On the one hand there was the destructive fighting between the Mughal and Maratha armies in its region in the 1680s; on the other was a shift of the trade of the Deccani hinterland from Dabhul to the Coromandel Coast around 1670. However, as was the case with other ports, while shipping declined, Dabhul was, under Maratha rule, still the abode of a powerful community of Arab and Persian shipowners and bankers, who financed the shipping and commerce from other harbors, like Rajapur.[208]

There existed several more—and better—ports in the Konkan besides Dabhul, but none assumed its former paramount position. The deep Bay of Rajapur, for example, was for a while the privileged port of the Maratha dominion. On a hill was located the small compound of a factory that was in turn occupied by the English and the French Companies.

Ships now had to steer carefully as they approached the treacherous sandbanks of the Ilhas Queimadas. In the distance one might distinguish sloops on the lookout for ships from Portugal that approached the shore here. A number of small streams flowed into the sea from behind low hills. At the foot of one of these mounds lay yet another of those small ports: the VOC stronghold of Vengurla. The prosperity of Vengurla very much depended on the protection of the VOC and the demand of the "offensive fleets," sent by the VOC to blockade Goa.

Vengurla had probably been founded around 1570 by Saraswat brahmins expelled from Bardes. During its heyday around 1670 it was still but a hamlet containing about 8,000 inhabitants, located on the edge of a small stream amid swamps and salt pans. It was a bad port: ships had to anchor at the entrance of the brook and wait for sloops to take the goods upstream. Around 1673 the fortified VOC factory and the palace of the VOC's broker Timoji Nayak dominated the place. Vengurla consisted of huts for the workers in the salt pans; of a "*lascarin* quarter," which was partly inhabited by refugees from Portuguese territory (black slaves from Mozambique mainly, some serving as mercenaries for the Company); and of the "hookers' neighborhood" (*het hoerenkwartier*)—no comment needed.[209]

A trip of half an hour led along the white beaches of Bardes to Aguado Heights. The fortress on top controlled the entrance to the Mandovi River. In front of it, one could discern the Portuguese galleons, provided with supplies at the small settlement of Panjim. The roadstead of Panjim was a dangerous one. It was too shallow for galleons, which had to be unloaded almost a mile from Aguado—far out of reach of its guns. It was also open to the southwesterly winds and not sheltered from hurricanes. Storms, time and again, wrecked the sails anchored at Aguado.[210]

The voyage to Goa would take one and a half hours, the flat embankment of Tiswary Island on one shore, the hills of Bardes on the other. Then would appear the white church of Ribandar—beyond Ribandar the tiny islands of Chorão and Divar and finally the forest of masts at the quay (*ribeira*) of Goa. The *ribeira* was the main dockyard of the Portuguese crown in Asia, employing about 300 workers and a small administrative staff. Goa was situated on the island of Tiswary, three to five miles in size, from which five shallow fords led to Candal and Punda.

Candal was alien, yet closely linked to the city of Xavier. There was very little love lost between the Portuguese and the Bijapuri provincial governor of

Candal, the rajahs of Candal, and the Savant family. Nonetheless, those rulers of the mainland were closely dependent on—and financially involved in—the trade of the Estado and of Goa.[211]

Goa was surrounded by a bunch of busy market towns on the mainland, which furnished it with grain and cotton. Without regular imports of provisions from the mainland, Goa would soon have starved. Though outwardly Goa might appear a colonial enclave, wedded to the Indian Ocean trade, the city in fact heavily depended on the trade with its surroundings and the other way around—the *umland* depended on regular supplies of rice and salt from Goa.[212]

Van Twist thus described Banda, the second largest town of Punda:

> A very large agricultural town. It is built on the river Kerj, which flows into the sea there. It has broad avenues and various beautiful heathen temples. The inhabitants conduct a very busy trade with those of Goa with all kinds of European manufactured goods, in exchange of which they deliver 2 to 3000 candil pepper yearly and various provisions. Through this trade the city is flourishing.[213]

Even though Goa was first and foremost a port, the total income from the tax farms of customs stations located on the passages across the fords between Goa and the mainland (the *passos secos)* surpassed by 1660 those of the *alfândega* of the port. As was the case with many other ports in the Arabian seas, the trade with the *umland* hence generated both more employment and more aggregate income than that overseas: the "stone town" is unthinkable without the "wooden town."[214]

Pearson arrives at a figure of 30,000 inhabitants of Goa in 1600; this number may be too low. According to the administrative council in 1656, Tiswary had 35,000 Christian "fireplaces" in 1630, and 750 to 850 Portuguese families. The mostly reliable Resende counted 20,000 Christian "fireplaces" in 1634, 5,800 Portuguese with "many" slaves, and 20,700 Hindus. The first dependable census from about 1710 arrives at a total of 37,402 inhabitants on Tiswary, of which about 30,000 lived in Goa. Yet a wall spanning three times its present compass still surrounded this small town. Goa's population may—counting slaves and Hindus, which were not included in population figures—can be estimated at around 35,000 at the end of the seventeenth century, down from 70,000 at the beginning of the century. Bardes had in 1710 48,508 Christian inhabitants, Salcete 70,449 Christians and 10,000 non-Christians. It seems that the population of both rural districts had rapidly increased in the sixteenth and seventeenth centuries. One source claims that it had more than doubled, partly as a result of migration from the mainland. Those overpopulated areas were thus unable to provide the city with sufficient food.[215]

When going ashore one would certainly be "welcomed" by suspicious customs officials—but if lucky, perhaps by a Portuguese nobleman too, dressed in raven black, under a canopy borne by black slaves. Despite the calamities that plagued it, these *fidalgos* were still proud of their town.[216] Leading the visitors around, they would boast that the city of Xavier was still the second town of the Portuguese empire, if not in size then in noble deeds. They would lead the visitor along the Rua Direita, the main street of Goa, with its shops selling everything from arrack to jewels. The visitor would be shown the *misericórdia*, the palace of the archbishop of Goa, the extensive complex of secretariat buildings, and the palace of the viceroy too. But most of these edifices were in a critical state of decay. Viceroy Linhares used to cherish his crumbling palace—"my dungeon"—and his successor, Pedro da Silva, agreed.[217]

Churches and monasteries eclipsed those rather pedestrian buildings. Places of worship like the church of Nossa Senhora do Rosário, on top of a hill—where the great Viceroy Afonso de Albuquerque had been laid to rest—or like the elegant Nossa Senhora do Monte, overlooking the city from a hilltop, stood out. There was also the vast Santa Catarina cathedral, under construction since the sixteenth century—the largest freestanding European edifice in Asia. Behind its baroque facade this cathedral was a ruin too; it was hastily patched up in 1682, most of its furniture having been sold and the building unusable for services because of falling stones. On Tiswary Island there were 26 parochial churches, on Salcete 45, and on Bardes 34.[218]

Most sumptuous, however, were the monasteries. There was the extended complex of church, monastery, and seminary of the Jesuit St. Paul's, where pupils from all over Asia were educated. There were the São Roque convent, the Augustinian and the Franciscan monasteries—which boasted of being the richest in the world—and the huge nunnery of Santa Mônica. Yet the most precious church of "Goa *dourada*" was the Bom Jesú monastery and church. The baroque Bom Jesú church with its three naves rivaled the cathedral and included the relics of Francis Xavier, the unofficial patron saint of Goa.

But on this blithe arrival followed the plague: malaria and cholera in particular, which spread from the stagnant irrigation lake near the gates of Goa. It was not exceptional that one-third of newly arrived crews would die within one year. This mortality assumed catastrophic proportions at the end of the seventeenth century.[219]

Goa was undergoing a creeping decay in the second half of the seventeenth century. Urban services, like sewage and pavement, were paid by a house tax levied by the municipality. As the number of inhabitants dwindled and more and more inhabitants claimed exemptions from this *renda do verde* because they were too poor, the urban services began to decline too. In the second half of the seventeenth century the city was smothering in filth. Inhabitants were supposed to spend some money to paint and restore their houses, but in 1690 most were in decay. A major income for the few inhabitants left was the sale of wood from dilapidated dwellings. "This city nowadays resembles rather a cemetery for the dead than an abode of the living."[220]

In 1689 the Portuguese crown decided to move the capital elsewhere—Goa was not just a graveyard, it was indefensible as well. The administration was to move to the fortress of Marmagoa, on a bare, windswept hill. It was more defensible and supposed to be healthier than Goa. However much the crown pleaded for this, no special funds were allotted to the construction of a new capital. The inhabitants of Tiswary were unwilling to pay; the wealthy were disinclined to abandon their commodious houses in the countryside and the poor were unable to move.[221]

## Canara and Kerala

But let us raise anchor again, heading for Cochin. At Cape Rama, the border of the Portuguese possessions, the mountains lining the sea start again. These mountains too are the frontier between Hindu and Islamic kingdoms, the historic border of the Vijayanagar empire. After the destruction of Vijayanagar's host at the battlefield of Talkotta by the united armies of the Deccani sultanates in 1565, generals of Vijayanagar had established their own kingdoms—the most important of which were the Vodiayar dynasty of Mysore in southern Karnataka and the Nayakas of Ikkeri/Bednur in northern Karnataka.[222]

In the distance one could discern the fortress Citakul; at the foot of it was the small town of Karwar, where an English factory was located. Karwar was located in the mountainous, densely forested small state of Sunda, a split-away chieftaincy of Vijayanagar too. Sunda was, in the seventeenth century, a tributary of the Adilshah, later on of the Marathas. The Adilshahi king had to confirm the nomination of the rajah. Aside from the white deer of its nearby forest, Sunda was mainly known for pepper, exported by the English and French Companies to Europe.[223]

Onore, the main city of the northern coast of Canara, is situated astride the narrow Sharavati River. On a steep hillside, which commanded the stream, was a Portuguese fortress overlooking the busy trade with sloops on the Sharavati.

The Portuguese lost this fortress and that at Barcelore to the kings (the *nayakas*) of Ikkeri in 1653—a sorrowful loss, one Portuguese memorandum noted in 1656, for Goa obtained both pepper and most of its rice from Barcelore and Onore. But it was only to be expected that those strongholds would be lost sooner or later. There were now no easy victories anymore—like in the sixteenth century. The "natives" had become quite adept at handling siege techniques and firearms. And there was no way the Portuguese could recapture a fortress defended by seven hundred Indian musketeers.[224]

Near Onore the hills give way to the plains of the southern part of the Canara Coast. Various broad rivers flow into the sea here. This was a fertile and densely populated land of plenty, the rice bowl of the Arabian seas, where one might harvest three or four times every year. On the riverbanks were various ports specializing in the rice trade.

Best known was Barcelore, where a quadrangular fortress of the Portuguese was situated. Next to it was a drowsy little town. The VOC had a small stone warehouse there to store rice. In its heyday at the beginning of the sixteenth century Barcelore had been the center for transit trade with Vijayanagar's metropolis—one of the largest cities in the world—near the present-day village of Hampi. When it was abandoned, Barcelore declined too. It was still an important center for the rice trade, but the foreign merchants there—Persians, Turks, Italians, Portuguese, Jews, and Armenians—seem to have moved to Dabhul, Calicut, and Cochin after 1590.[225]

The southern coast of Canara resembles a long beach, interrupted by hills. In the south was Mangalore, which toward 1680 had taken Barcelore's place as the major port of Canara. On the broad and up to 17-fathom-deep Netravali River even seagoing vessels could load rice. Mangalore was situated along the river and dominated by a large fortress on an island in the estuary of the Netravali. It was mainly a port trading with Goa and with Muscat. In 1672 the Portuguese had been allotted the right to construct a factory and collect half of the customs gathered there. This share was partly paid in rice. At the end of the seventeenth century, apart from the Portuguese, English sails became more conspicuous there.[226]

The monotonous sandy beaches merged with dense palm groves. In the distance the Ghats were discernible. The small town of Calianpur was the historic border of Kerala, a region announced by the bulge of Eli Mountain, soaring from the plain and covered by dense woods. In the bays surrounding Eli, many barges were moored. For here grew the famous pepper renowned as the best of the world. The Romans had already heard of this mountain, which attracted traders from throughout the world: Syrians, Copts, and Arabs, long before the advent of Islam.[227]

Arab merchants had settled on these shores since the sixth century and mixed with those of the indigenous population who had converted to Islam. Their descendants differ from North Indian Muslims, both as to their language (they speak and write Malayalam) and as to their customs. They are called *mappila*s, indigenous (*deshi*) Muslims of Kerala, as opposed to the *paradeshi*—North Indian, Persian, and Arab Muslims who controlled the trade of Kerala in the century before the coming of the Portuguese.[228]

Northern Kerala, Malabar proper, was one of the most dangerous areas in the Arabian seas. Many a tiny island and deep bay sheltered the notorious Malabar pirates. According to Rijkloff Volckertszoon van Goens those redoubtable warriors traced their descent to the Turkish hero of the seven seas, Sidhi Ali Re'is. There were huge numbers of them—more than 100,000, van Goens estimated—and they were brave men, expert at firearms. The most notorious pirates lived in the realm of the rajah of Badagara, nominally a feudatory (*kaimal*) of Cananore.[229]

Cananore, situated just outside of the European fortress, was a small, walled town with about 20,000 inhabitants. The sumptuous dwellings of rich Muslim merchants, both *deshi* and *paradeshi*, and the apexes of mosques dominated it. This "bazaar" of Cananore was the busy center both of seaborne trade and of a small maritime kingdom.[230]

Legend tells that one of the daughters of the *colathiri*, the ruler of Cananore, had borne a child to the chief of the Arab nation at Cananore, the Marakkar family, around 1470. This Arab was adopted into the *colathiri*'s family and given the title Azhi rajah. As with many other events in the history of Malabar, the lore is too lovely to disbelieve, but the pattern bears a suspicious resemblance to the immunities granted to *janmis*. Hereditary lines of wardens (*janmakar*s) also guarded *janmi* land. The Marakkar family might thus have been the *janmakar*s of the bazaar of Cananore, a position that may have been granted to the head of the Arab *natio* in the fourteenth century.[231] Since the Europeans were mainly interested in the trade of this bazaar, the Azhi Raja would appear a prince to them—a ruler equal to, if not surpassing, the rather shadowy figure of the *colathiri*, who was protected by the Portuguese and the Dutch against the might of the Azhi Raja. And, indeed, the Azhi Raja did have his own realm in the Laccadive Islands, which may have been conquered by his flotillas in the fifteenth century.[232]

The Portuguese fortress of Cananore was in 1663 a ruin. "It will not be able to resist the enemy for more than a few days," went one prediction—and indeed the VOC conquered it in the same year. The fortress was rebuilt in 1667 by the VOC as a strong citadel. There were 40 soldiers stationed here. Within its walls was a village with 1,000 inhabitants. There was an inn, a storehouse, a parade ground, and 4,000 coconut trees planted there.[233]

Passing Badagara, next one encounters Kerala—the land of clouds. Afar is a rim of blue mountains with a necklace of haze; near, along the shore, runs a ribbon of palms with the cabins of humble fishermen like brown specks in the verdure. The fertile coastal rim of Kerala was very densely populated indeed. Pieter van Dam, attorney of the VOC, estimated the number of *nayyar* men who could be mustered along the coast already at a mind-boggling 1,540,000, apart from "an incredible number" of other people who were also able to bear arms. Every available piece of land had to be used. Floods were a severe threat, since dwellings were built everywhere, including on the most dangerous locations on islands or astride the streams.[234]

But this densely populated—perhaps overpopulated—coastline was bordened by virgin jungle, a forest that was both a threat and a blessing. It was a sanctuary for wild boar, which threatened the harvests of the village on its edge. Tigers were another menace. It was a hideout for wild men too: slave raiders who had raised strongholds in the bush. They occasionally looted the villages and sold children and women to ships plying the never distant sea. Yet the forest also provided plenty: wax, honey, and wood.[235]

But in the surroundings of Cochin, and in the mountains surrounding the Palghat Gap, the logging of timber, for shipbuilding and charcoal, seems already to have devastated this pristine woodland. There were complaints in 1693 that no cheap lumber for charcoal could be transported over the Periyar. Forests accessible by water had all been cut down. Panani, with its access to the jungle by the river, was suffering from similar problems.[236]

The cities straddling the coast appeared almost as rural dwellings along the wide tracks lined with palms. Calicut—seat of the powerful *zamorin*—was a quiet, rural town that differed so markedly from the image conjured by its famous name that legend spread that the historic metropolis had disappeared in the sea. At low tide, it was said, one could discern the shapes of stately edifices at the bottom of the sea. In spite of its dreamy appearance and its open roadstead, Calicut was still the major port of Kerala. This was in part because the trade of Cochin was obstructed by the VOC and also because Calicut had good connections with the hinterland through the Palghat Gap.[237]

South of Calicut the sailors could discern earthen walls and wooden palisades and the broad Baypore River, where many dhows were moored. Above the greenery rose the white steeple and edifices of the seminary of the Jesuit monastery of Tanore. Further on there was a broad bay, then the walled town of Panani, the religious center of Kerala's Muslims. This place—and the fortress of Kotte, to the south of Panani—was the ancestral home of the redoubtable Muslim Kunjali corsairs, who were vague vassals of the *zamorin*. The Kunjalis had always defied the Portuguese and later challenged the Dutch, though to be sure there was nothing like the same animosity between the Kunjalis and the VOC as there was between the Kunjalis and the Estado. The heavily armed oared vessels of the Kunjalis clawed in and out of Panani without accepting the navicerts of unbelievers.[238]

Rains from the Ghats flooded over the shallow parts of the coastal lint. There was first a stretch of high land and then a wreath of lagoons, stretching from Cranganore to Coylan. The trip along those backwaters was, according to Rijkloff van Goens Jr.,

> so pleasing that it is really worth seeing how nicely the embankment on all sides has been divided into small and some large village plots by trees and houses, and how everywhere around these villages there are beautiful large and small islands, planted with grain, as far as the eye can gaze. Everything looks so pretty and green that every view pleases the heart and every time, through the beautiful colors and perspective, the sight is equally enjoyable. And not least pleasing are the many small dikes, gullies and other creeks, the cattle grazing here and there, fences of long reed around the houses and nets very finely braided. Many different kind of crafts from one piece of wood float to and fro, some only one fathom long, in which men are standing upright, carrying some goods.[239]

One then passed Trichur, where a deep blue bay opens to the sea. This mouth of the Periyar was the border of the kingdom of Cochin. In the far distance one could discern the stronghold of Cranganore—in 1663 a dilapidated Portuguese bulwark and an unfinished cathedral. This fortress served to guard the waterways to Cochin. Under the Portuguese the captain was allowed to tax the sloops going to Cochin, on condition that he protect the waterway. The stronghold was reconstructed by the VOC in 1674. The Dutch probably used the stones of the cathedral for it. Yet, with the Dutch occupation, the backwaters became very dangerous, for the VOC tried neither to tax nor to protect them.

The land of Cochin resembled a string of palm forests, above which sometimes churches were raised—about 7,000 Indian Christian families lived there. Beyond the forests were two fingers of land with, in the distance, a green speck of islands drifting on brownish waters. One was covered with forest; on the other stood the town of Cochin, which "due to its favourable location, beautiful river, prosperity and abundance of all kinds of provisions is the most favorably located roadstead on the coast of Malabar—uniting in itself all advantages, usually divided amongst many ports."[240]

The bay was 5 miles long and 20 broad. Sandbanks sealed the entrance. And "by the mud, during the stormy season, the waters and the rollers are abruptly broken. So, it would seem as if the tides are withheld by a dike." The waters of the bay were tranquil "like an interior sea." This bay was 6 to 6½ fathoms deep and more than 100 seagoing vessels could anchor there safely.

Cochin consisted of three towns: Ernakulam was at the opposite side of the bay, where several temples were sited. Matancheri, or "downtown" Cochin, was where the palace of the rajah stood, surrounded by a number of busy bazaars; though it had a quiet, rural appearance, Matancheri was a fairly big town and a major port. Finally there was "uptown" Cochin, or the European settlement.

Since ancient times the Bay of Cochin had been a crossroads of peoples and creeds. Cochin harbored two unique religious communities. The Jews of Cochin had come to the Malabar Coast in the fourth century and had received privileges in the eighth. In the seventeenth century they consisted of about 6,000 families. Most lived in Matancheri, where the synagogue was located too. Under the Portuguese the position of the Jews was rather singular: on the one hand, they were sometimes persecuted by the Inquisition. But, on the other, many ministers (or *rajadores*) of the king of Cochin were Jews—like Samuel Ezechiel, chief minister of the king in the early seventeenth century. Those *rajadores* controlled the deliveries of goods to the Portuguese.[241]

The other community was the Thomas Christians, about 12,000 families, living throughout Kerala in 163 villages around 65 churches. The Thomas Christians trace their ancestry back to the apostle Thomas, and probably came to Kerala around the fifth century. Some of the Thomas Christians observed Catholic ritual with some modifications; some were Monophysites, following the patriarch of Antioch, who named the bishop of the Thomas Christians. The Portuguese had tried to reconcile the Thomas Christians with the Catholic faith. This led to a schism in the church between Catholic and "orthodox" Thomas Christians. The Jews and the "orthodox" Thomas Christians thus initially welcomed the Protestant VOC. Some children of Thomas Christians were educated, at the cost of the Company, at a primary school in Cochin to serve as interpreters for the Company. The VOC often used Jews as interpreters too.[242]

However, the position of both communities may have initially worsened, for the VOC generally used Saraswat Brahmins as middlemen in its trade and its relations with the rajahs—rarely Jews or Thomas Christians. It is probable that Thomas Christians still worked as intermediate dealers in pepper, as they did a century before and after. But there is little proof of this, for it largely concerns the hinterland, Vadakumkur and Tekumkur, realms not as well documented in European sources as the coast.[243] The rise of Jewish merchant princes at Cochin and of Thomas Christians at Travancore is an eighteenth-century development that has yet to be adequately explained.

Obviously, the indigenous Catholics did not welcome the Dutch. Although they had to take an oath in 1663 that they would remain loyal subjects of the Company, these Catholic *topazes* were not trusted at all. Some attempts were made to convert them to Calvinism but without much success, while many a servant of the Company was led back to the fold of the mother church by his Catholic *topaz* wife. Since the Jesuits were suspected of encouraging sedition among the *topazes*, they were forbidden to enter Cochin. There was an attempt to have mass celebrated by Indian priests, but they appeared to be as hostile to the Company as the Portuguese were. Therefore, the VOC arranged with the Vatican in 1665 that the Carmelite friars would administer the services. They followed the Holy See, not the Portuguese patronage of the church. The Vatican named the bishop of Cochin too. Obviously, this caused constant arguments between the Jesuits at Tanore—supported by the Portuguese crown—the Portuguese bishop of Cochin in exile, and the Carmelites in both Cochin and in Goa.[244]

When the VOC conquered Cochin castle—or the city of the holy cross, as the Portuguese called it—in 1663, it took what was essentially a walled town, for the place was 4,000 feet by 1,500 feet. It was a walled town. But while the Portuguese Senate of Cochin had begged for subsidies to have the fortress repaired, this was "in order that the glorious memory of the Portuguese shall not be lost rather than to serve any practical use or defensive purpose." For, in reality, most *casados* lived outside the grim walls of this castle in pleasant country seats spread along the entire bay.[245]

This area contained about 12,500 inhabitants, a number that had strongly declined during the turmoil of the last two decades and the siege by the VOC. Portuguese Cochin may have had about 25,000 inhabitants in its heyday at the beginning of the seventeenth century. Churches then dominated the city of the holy cross: seven parochial churches, the Jesuit monastery with its tall bell tower, and the cathedral. The huge customs house of Cochin—its other curiosity—had been ruined by the fighting, as, indeed, most of the town had been.[240]

Field Commander van Goens concluded the city of the holy cross was indefensible. It was therefore decided in 1664 to demolish the town and build a new one. Atop a Portuguese town slowly arose a Dutch village. This Dutch Cochin was a heptagonal citadel, each bulwark named after a Dutch province. It measured 6,000 feet in circumference and was surrounded by a moat. On the main square, where the troops would parade, were the secretariat and the former cathedral. There were 200 houses, resembling those in Dutch provincial towns but painted austerely white in the Iberian fashion, where about 3,000 persons lived.[247]

Cochin was the only settlement of the VOC in the Arabian seas that could choose between various applicants for office and not just because it was a healthy place. One could go for a stroll, hunting, and fishing in the countryside. There existed other, less innocent, pastimes too: the stout mestizo women attracted many a Dutch male. In 1671 they were struggling with the problem that homeless white orphans roamed Cochin. A branch of the orphanage (*weeskamer*) was founded in 1673 to care for them.[248]

## Conclusion

There was thus a huge variety of landscapes along the great maritime arc of the Arabian seas. And there was a vast array of different ways of economic organization—or modes of production—ranging from simple (but not necessarily primitive, for optimally adapted to the ecological conditions and often deeply involved in sophisticated long-distance trade) hunter-gatherer societies and nomads, such as the Yao of the Great Lakes, to the merchant tycoons and sweated laborers of Surat. There was in the seventeenth century as big a gap between "developed" and "underdeveloped" areas as nowadays, but the gap ran primarily *through* civilizations and countries rather than between them. London was not "more developed" than Isfahan, but there was as huge a difference between the sophisticated urban culture of Isfahan and the Biaban as existed between London and the Scottish highlands. Neither did those different modes of production necessarily have to penetrate each other, nor did there have to be a "dominant articulation"—they might happily exist next to each other for centuries.

In Mombasa, to take a concrete example, the representatives of Indian "portfolio capitalists" rubbed shoulders with the famous Maasai nomad warriors. The Maasai had long been in contact with the Swahili Coast whether as mercenaries or as cattle traders (for the beads around the necks or wrists of the Maasai women were probably often Indian-made), yet there is not that much difference between the lifestyle of the Maasai in 1580 and that in 1880.[249] Except for some ornaments to serve as brideprice, the coast had little to sell the Maasai. In East Africa nomadism was a largely self-sufficient activity, unlike in India or Iran, where it was a specialized activity, closely linked to the demand for bullocks and camels for transport, horses for the army, or—in Persia—wool for trade to

Turkey and Europe. (Both the Dutch and the English East India Companies purchased modest amounts of wool in Kirman.)

Indeed, Swahili customs before the nineteenth century recognized this cleavage between different modes of production and irreconcilable—but not hostile—cultures quietly living next to each other without having much of a mutual impact, separating *uungwa*, the civilized city dwellers, from *wa ushenzi*, the uncivilized strangers from the hinterland.[250] And in many ways—as we shall see in chapter 7—the critical difference on the Mrima Coast was not between Arabs, Africans, and Portuguese *casados*, all *uungwa*, but between them and the *wa ushenzi*. And that was not only the case on the Swahili Coast, as we have already observed.

Yet all these areas were attracted by the magnetism of the Arabian seas, and all experienced their pulse. It was above all the seas that tied all these lands together, and it was above all the seas, too, that provided overriding elements of unity. There was the garland of harbors along the coasts—*échelles*, where maritime trade met the land routes—yet the land routes also existed to serve those port cities. It was said in the nineteenth century: "If they play the flute in Zanzibar, they dance on the Lakes," and this could be repeated for Malwa and Surat, or for the massif of Yemen and Mocha.

The *échelles* attracted coastwise navigation too. For the Arabian seas were not only a complex of port cities; they were also a complex of overlapping maritime zones, and the overwhelming bulk of navigation and trade was conducted within these maritime zones. It often makes more sense to write precolonial economic history in terms of what was happening in "zones," more or less ignoring borders, rather than by colonial boundaries. There was, for example, a busy navigation between Sind and the opposite shore of Arabia, but was this "international trade" between South Asia and the Middle East, or was it simply trade within a single linked zone?

There was the current of new products cultivated—moving generally westward to eastward, like tobacco, coffee, and maize from Persia to India in our period, and from the ports and their *umland* to the hinterland too. For maize and tobacco were planted by the Portuguese on the Mrima Coast in their gardens on the mainland in the mid-sixteenth century, and the cultivation of those crops then rapidly spreading to the hinterland.[251]

There were the "trade coins," like the ubiquitous larin in the sixteenth century, the Mexican real in the seventeenth—used as unit of account from Batavia to Madagascar—and the Maria Theresa taler in the eighteenth.

And there were the communities of traders and sailors, some of which were girded with the sword: the Arab and western Christian merchants. Two main currents of maritime expansion were of decisive importance for the history of the Arabian seas in the seventeenth century. The Islamic expansion was one current: it involved Arabs, Turks, and Persians and took place in India, along the Swahili Coast, and in Madagascar—most conspicuously involving the merchants and mercenaries from Oman, but there was an important Yemenite element as well, which is often overlooked in African studies.

For armed European expansion flowed along a parallel course with that of Islam. It is tempting to see the propagation of Islam in the Arabian seas as a "peaceful" and "indigenous" process—as opposed to European "intolerance" and "violence"—yet on the frontier of Islam in Madagascar, the Comoros, or Sofala the faith was spread by fire and sword too. It might be argued that the buccaneers on Madagascar were merely following in the footsteps of earlier groups of Persian, Yemenite, Galla, and Swahili *ghazis*: warriors for the faith and merchants as well as witch doctors and magicians, which is how they are best remembered on the Malagasy coast, for example.[252]

The other current was, obviously, the expansion of the western Christian *natios*, to whom in many respects the Armenians, and to a lesser extent the Persian Jews, were very closely related. For—as we shall see—the Western Europeans in Iran had an intimate relation, commercially and carnally, with the Armenians. In both Western and Eastern Europe there were large resident Armenian communities who were in Europe more or less perceived as European—and in Russia as Orthodox—merchants and allotted privileges by states as well as by East India Companies. Let us, therefore, now take a closer look at the Europeans.

## Notes

1. T.A. Chumkovsky (ed. and trans.), *Três roteiros desconhecidos de Ahmad Ibn Majid. O pilóto Árabe de Vasco da Gama* (Lisbon, 1960), pp. 17, 20.
2. J. Poujade, *La route des Indes et ses navires* (Paris, 1947); B.A. Datoo, "Influence of the Monsoons on the Movement of Dhows along the East African Coast," *East African Geographical Review*, 12 (1974), pp. 23–33. On timing, winds, navigation, and distances used in the VOC's navigation, see in particular the series of standard regiments for navigation (*zeilageorders*) in VOC, 359; VOC, 360; and VOC, 1432.
3. Geleynssen 280 c, "Log kept by Michiel Willemsz."
4. On this concept see J. Warren, *The Sulu Zone, 1768–1898: The Dynamics of External Trade, Slavery and Ethnicity in the Transformation of a Southeast Asian Maritime State* (Singapore, 1981).
5. Ajuda 46-X-17, fo. 484; ANTT, DRI, 43, 1641, fo. 20.
6. VOC/OB 1379, 1 May 1682, fo. 2352.
7. VOC/OB 1476, 20 September 1690, fo. 484 vo.
8. BAC, A 499, 26 November 1678; BAC, A 500, 20 December 1678.
9. BAC, A 499, 16 November 1678.
10. Thus accounting for the—in my view striking—anomaly that Arab seafarers appear to have been unaware of the existence of the Mascarenhas and western Australia, both apparently being discovered by Europeans, although the Arabs had been sailing the same ocean for a millennium before them.
11. L. Varadarajan, "Traditions of Indigenous Navigation in Gujarat," *South Asia* (New Series) 3 (1) (1981), pp. 28–35; B. Arunchalam, "The Heaven-Finding Art in Indian

Navigational Tradition and Cartography," in S. Chandra, *The Indian Ocean,* pp. 191–221; AHU, Índia, Cx. 19, 5, Exhibit no. 47, "Orders for Commodore Dom Gonçalço de Silveira"; Theal, iv, p. 439.

12. AHU, Índia, Cx. 29 bis, 171, 29 May 1674.

13. C. Bathurst, "Imamate and Maritime Trade: Two Principal Themes in the History of Oman," in D.K. Hopwood (ed.), *The Arab Peninsula: Society and Politics* (London, 1972), pp. 93–126; on Oman see too J.B. Kelly, *Britain and the Persian Gulf 1795–1880* (Oxford, 1968); P. Risso, *Oman and Muscat: An Early Modern History* (London, 1986); J.C. Wilkinson, *The Imamate Tradition of Oman* (Cambridge, 1987); W. Philips, *Oman: A History* (Beirut, 1971), pp. 24–61; M.A. Darwish, *Saltanat 'Uman fi'l qarnayn al-thamin ashar wa al-tashi ashar* (Jidda, 1992).

14. J. de Vere Allen, *Swahili Origins* (London, 1993), p. 209; HAG, LM, 30, 3 August 1652, fo. 383–86, and, 27 September 1652, fo. 381–382 vo.

15. HAG, LM, 72, 20 December 1699, fo. 405, and 19 March 1699, fo. 177.

16. For example, VOC/OB 1266, 8 November 1668; and VOC 9115, Mocha diary, 20 February 1705.

17. C.R. Boxer and L. de Azevedo, *Fort Jesus and the Portuguese in Mombasa* (Nairobi, 1962); Ajuda 51-VII-24, 18 December 1700, fo. 143; AHU, Índia, Cx. 41, 96, 3 March 1700.

18. For the Muscati policy in South Arabia see A.A. Hamid Hiyed, "Relations Between the Yemen and South Arabia during the Zeydi Imamate of Abd al-Qasim" (Ph.D. diss., Edinburgh University, 1973), pp. 118–21. In order to protect the ports in the Gulf from Muscati attack, the Safavid empire had in 1720 stationed a permanent rapid-deployment force in the Gulf—see R. Schimkoreit, *Regesten publizierter safawidischer Herscherurkunde* (Berlin, 1982), p. 426; HAG, LM, 67, 5 December 1702, fo. 11; Rao Bahadur Ganesh and D.B. Parasnis, *Selections from the Satara Rajahs and Peshwa's Diaries* First Series, *Shahu Chatrapati,* 2 vols. (Puna, 1432 v.), i, doc. 361, p. 209.

19. F. Broeze and K. Mc Pherson (eds.), *Brides of the Sea: Port Cities of Asia from the 16th–20th Century* (Honolulu, 1989).

20. T. Spear, *The Kaya Complex: A History of the Mijikenda People of the Kenya Coast to 1900* (Nairobi, 1978).

21. J. Kirkman, *Men and Monuments on the Swahili Coast* (London, 1964), is probably still the best introduction on the Swahili Coast. See also R. Hall, *Empires of the Monsoon* (London, 1996), which is unreliable on India but quite good on the Swahili Coast; J. Martin, *Comores: quatre îsles entre pirates et planteurs,* 2 vols. (Paris, 1983). For the chronicles of Aden see O. Löffgren (ed.), *Arabische Texte zur Kenntnis der Stadt Aden im Mittelalter,* 2 vols. (Uppsala, 1936, 1950).

22. See S. Longrigg, *Three Centuries of Modern Iraq* (London, 1956).

23. BNL, FG, Cód 28, fo. 19.

24. VOC/OB 1224, 9 December 1657, fo. 276.

25. BNL, FG, Cód. 28, fo. 19; Resende, fo. 142; VOC/OB 1168, Mocha diary, 1 March 1647; 28 March 1647; Brouwer, *Al-Mukha, stelling* IV.

26. A. Charles-Roux, *Les Échelles du Syrie et du Palestine au XVIIIe siècle* (Paris, 1928). This may be compared with Polanyi's concept of a port of trade; the difference is that *échelles* are mostly not gateways to two different economic systems, merely to two different economic circuits, although this *does* apply to the *échelles* on the northwest coast of Madagascar. K. Polanyi, "Ports of Trade in Early Civilization," *Journal of Economic History* 23 (1) (1963), pp. 30–45.

27. See M.N. Pearson, "Littoral Society: The Case for the Coast," *The Great Circle* 9 (1987), pp. 1–12.

28. J. Wycki (ed.), *Documenta Indica Societate Iesu,* 26 vols. so far (Rome, 1956– ), ii, p. 77.

29. A. Fiorani Piacenti, *L'emporio ed' il regno di Hormuz (VII fino XV secolo d. chr.): Vicende storiche, problemi ed aspetti di un civiltá costeira del Golfo Persico* (Milan, 1975).

30. H. Brown, "Siyu: Town of the Craftsmen," *Azania* 23 (1988), pp. 101–33.

31. R. Wilding, *The Shorefolk: Aspects of the Early Development of Swahili Culture* (Mombasa, 1987). There is a very large literature arguing how to put the "Swahili tribe or people" in an anachronistic ethnic or linguistic framework. See, for example, T. Spears and D. Nurse, *The Swahili: Reconstructing the History and Language of an African Society* A.D. *500–1500* (Philadelphia, 1984); F. Guennec-Coppens and P. Caplan (eds.), *Les Swahilis entre Afrique et Arabie* (Paris, 1991); or J. Middleton, *The World of the Swahili: An African Mercantile Civilization* (New Haven, 1992). This may be related to the unwitting "tribalism" that pervades African studies as much as "casteism" tends to pervade Indian studies. In either case it is because the researcher has to start from colonial classifications of populations, which in India used the caste as building block, in Africa the tribe.

32. HAG, LM, 52, "Propostas que fêz o Rey Bara Sanu e os fidalgos de Patta ao Illustríssimo Senhor Rodrigo da Costa," fo. 260–64.

33. ANTT, DRI, 60, 13 December 1650, fo. 261.

34. See, for example, M. Brown, *A History of Madagascar* (London, 1995). As P. Ottino, "À propos de deux mythes malgaches du début du XVII ème siècle," *Taloha* 6 [Antananarivo, 1974], p. 84, rightly puts it: "isolated and 'rustic' regions if compared to the brilliant civilizations of Ceylon, Java, and of Bali, like Madagascar, the Comoros and maybe the Maldives, assume considerable importance precisely to the extent that their social and political organization, their religious ideas and myths testify to contacts, amalgams and syncretisms of which the very memory has been lost in history and by the people themselves."

35. *A History of East Africa 1592–1902* (London, 1996), p. 1.

36. Theal, iii, pp. 164–68; see J. Koponen, *People and Production in Late Precolonial Tanzania: History and Structure* (Jyväskylä, 1988), pp. 150–70.

37. H. Yajima, "Some Problems on the Formation of the Swahili World and the Indian Ocean Maritime World," *Senri Ethnological Studies* 43 (1996), pp. 319–55.

38. HAG, LM, 52, "Propostas," paragraph 15.

39. The cause of these fractional politics is, amazingly, rather obscure. Traditionally it is presumed that the Ibadi Islam and the Yemeni version of Shi'ism are very different from the Shafi'a Islam dominant on the Swahili Coast. Factions therefore fell apart between Ibadi and Shafi'a, and between old residents and newcomers, but Risso (*Oman,* pp. 22–23) thinks these differences have been much exaggerated. One might wonder whether they are related to overlapping claims on plots of land.

40. Angoche had about 30 Portuguese and 1,500 Swahili households with a few thousand slaves in 1636 (Resende, fo. 16).

41. Ajuda 51-VII-39, "Papel de Notiçia sobre Sofalla," fo. 49. For Mozambique in general the reader is referred to E. Axelson, *Portuguese in Southeast Africa 1488–1699* (Cape Town, 1963); F. de Oliveira Marques, *História militar e política dos Portugueses em Mozambique,* 2 vols. (Lisbon, 1953, 1956); and the quite brilliant study of M.D.D.

Newitt, *A History of Mozambique* (London, 1995), attempting to present an "indigenous" perspective on the history of Mozambique. And see too S. Welch, *Portuguese and Dutch in Southern Africa* (Cape Town, Johannesburg, 1951). This study has been severely criticized by Boxer—in my view excessively so. Much material in this book cannot be found anywhere else, and Welch, to my experience, is quite reliable on African details, though perhaps less so on the Indian Ocean.

42. VOC/OB 4022, "Extract from a diary kept by Pieter Clarton." For the Dela Goa and Cape Correntes trade see S.H. Carlson, *Trade and Dependency: Studies in the Expansion of Europe* (Uppsala, 1984), pp. 128–50 (a fine study of the trade of the Trieste Company on the Dela Goa Bay marred by a lot of modish and totally irrelevant theory); A. Smith, "Dela Goa Bay and the Trade of Southeast Africa," in J. Gray and D. Birmingham, *Pre-Colonial African Trade: Essays on Trade in Central and Eastern Africa Before 1900* (London, 1970), pp. 267–77; and A. Lobato, *Quatro estudos e uma evocação para a história de Lourenço Marques* (Lisbon, 1961).

43. A methodological observation is in order here: In the literature on Dela Goa Bay two major kingdoms are discerned, but is it legitimate to speak of kingdoms if the dominion of the "king" of Dela Goa Bay was but 12 to 15 miles with about 2,000 subjects (Theal, ii, p. 458)? This may result from a wider terminological slant in the literature. Since most of the literature on African kingship derives from West Africa, where there were large kingdoms with a consolidated system of taxation, bureaucracy, and a standing army, there is naturally a tendency to adapt this terminology in East Africa too. Yet there is little evidence that the small chieftainships in Dela Goa Bay had anything in common with, say, the Ashanti or Yoruba kingdoms. If they can be termed states at all, rather than a system of dominant lineages, they were at best early states. However, the term *early state*—which seems perfectly legitimate for the Sakalava or Hova kingdoms—is dangerous too, for it suggests an evolutionary line toward mature states, which did not evolve in Dela Goa Bay at all.

44. On the Portuguese trade there see Ajuda 51-VII-27, "Informaçáo," Rafael de San Martino.

45. J. de Coetzee, *Die Kompagnie se besettinge van De La Goa Baai* (Pretoria, 1947); Marks and Gray, "Southern Africa," p. 410.

46. Theal, iii, p. 450; Resende, fo. 26; HAG, LM 29, Februari 1652, fo. 20, and Ajuda 51-VII-39, "Notiçia," fo. 37. For the trade of Sofala see also A. Nogueira da Costa, *Penetração e impacto do capital mercantil Português em Moçambique nos séculos XVI e XVII, o caso de Muenemutapa* (Maputo, 1982), pp. 125–38.

47. VOC/OB 4012, "Brief explanation of Mozambique island," fo. 1018.

48. AHU, Índia, Cx. 29, 5, "As deposições annexes são as sequentes"; A. Rita-Ferreira, *Presença luso-asiática e mutações culturáis no sul de Moçambique até 1900* (Lisbon, 1982), pp. 113–17; Theal, iv, p. 439, iii, 437, 451.

49. Theal, iv, p. 267, 288; iii, 437; AHU, Cód. 1224, 8 December 1672, fo. 17, and 3 October 1675, fo. 9 vo.

50. R.K. Kent, *Early Kingdoms in Madagascar* (New York, 1970), p. 132; Theal, iv, p. 247; S. Leite (ed.), *Os dois descobrimentos da ilha de São Lourenço* (Lisbon, 1970), p. 289. Their "Portuguese" credentials can be disputed, though: the Dutch referred to them as "black Portuguese" (*COACM*, i, pp. 265–67), which probably means either Indians or, more likely, Afro-Portuguese. VOC/OB 4021, "Brief description of Anjouani," fo. 656 vo.

51. E.A. Alpers, *Ivory and Slaves in East Central Africa* (London, 1975), pp. 53–

58; AHU, Índia, Cx. 10, 81, 27 February 1633; AHU, Cód. 1221, 14 December 1675, fo. 374; Theal, iv, p. 247.

52. H.T. Wright et al., "The Evolution of Settlement Systems in the Bay of Boeny," *Azania* 31 (1996), pp. 37–75.

53. P. Verin, *The History of Civilization in North Madagascar* (Rotterdam, 1986); C. Allibert, *Mayotte: Plaque tournante et microcosme de l'Océan Indien oriental* (Paris, 1984).

54. HAG, LM, 75, 20 January 1703, fo. 265; C.R. Boxer, "Moçambique Island and the *Carreira da Índia,*" in *Océan Indien et Méditerannée,* pp. 95–133.

55. AHU, [Papéis vulsos de] Moçambique (henceforth Moç), Cx. 1, 77, 16 November 1634; AHU, Índia, Cx. 30 bis, 171, "Sobre o socorro da Índia."

56. Theal, iv, p. 315; AHU, Moç, 1, 66, "Informação do desembargador Pedro Álvarez Pereira"; ANTT, DRI, 60, 25 November 1650, fo. 280.

57. Évora, CV/2–7, "Discurso sobre a conquista da Monomatappa," fo. 42. See, e.g., R.E. Gregson, "Trade and Politics in South-East Africa: The Moors, the Portuguese, and the Kingdom of Mwene Mutapa," *African Social Research* 16 (1973), pp. 413–46.

58. See J. Ford, *The Role of the Trypanosomiases in African History* (Oxford, 1971); and J. Giblin, "Trypanosomiases Control in African History: An Evaded Issue," *JAH* 31 (1990), pp. 59–80.

59. See A. Salim (ed.), *State Formation in Eastern Africa* (Nairobi, 1984).

60. S.I.G. Mudenge, *A Political History of Munhumutapa c. 1400–1902* (Harare, 1988), pp. 77–165. This is the most extensive treatment of Monomotappa history and institutions to date, but the book perhaps suffers from the romantic idea that there was such a thing as a single, unified "Monomotappa national state." See the comments by D. Beach, *The Shona and Their Neighbours* (Oxford, 1994), pp. 102–8.

61. A. Lobato, *Estudos Moçambiquanos: A expansão portuguêsa* (Lisbon, 1959–1963), iii, pp. 362–65.

62. Theal, iii, p. 451; J. de Barros and D. do Couto, *Da Ásia dos feitos que os Portuguezes fizeram na conquista e descobrimento das terras e mares do Oriente,* 25 vols. (Lisbon, 1780; facsimile reprint Lisbon, 1974) (henceforward, *Da Ásia),* Decada IX, Cap. XXII.

63. J.F. Mbwiliza, "The Hoe and the Stick: A Political Economy of the Heru Kingdom c. 1750–1900," in *La Civilisation ancienne des peuples des Grands Lacs: Colloque de Bujumbura* (Paris, 1981), p. 110; AHU, Índia, Cx. 12, 76, February 1635.

64. See C. Sassoon, *Chinese Porcelain in Fort Jesus* (Mombasa, 1975); Verrin, *History of Civilization,* pp. 227; P. Garlake, "The Value of Imported Ceramics in the Dating and Interpretation of the Rhodesian Iron Age," *JAH* 9 (1) (1968), pp. 29–30; and information by D.A. Lowe (Canberra) on Buganda; compare the fascinating article by R. Finlay, "The Pilgrim Art: The Culture of Porcelain in World History," *Journal of World History* 9 (1) (1998), pp. 141–87. Interestingly enough—to illustrate this quality of porcelain as pilgrim art—shards of Dutch Delftsblauw porcelain have been found in bulk in East Africa. At the moment it is quite obscure how it came there since the VOC did not trade in porcelain to East Africa. One may surmise it was brought there by the Trieste Company—maybe from Oostende too—in the late eighteenth and nineteenth centuries from Hamburg; maybe by the French from Mauritius.

65. That traders did not venture inland was due to this rather than to ignorance. For the Portuguese were actually well aware of the existence of Lake Nyasa, which they inferred might be the source of the Nile (Theal, iv, p. 186) and the map of East Africa

in Resende. See further: M. Ylvisaker, "Ivory Trade in the Lamu Area 1600–1870," *Paideuma* 28 (1982), pp. 221–31; M. Posnadski, "Connections Between the Lacustrine People and the Coast," in N. Chittick and R.I. Rotbert (eds.), *East Africa and the Orient* (New York, 1975), p. 216.

66. ANTT, DRI, 57, 15 December 1646, fo. 51.

67. Theal, iv, p. 328; M.D.D. Newitt, *Portuguese Settlements on the Zambezi* (London, 1973), pp. 55–67; A. Isaacman, *Mozambique: The Africanization of an European Institution: The Zambezi Prazos* (Madison, 1972), pp. 16–25. The best exposition on the metropolitan judicial background to the *prazo* is, however, A. Lobato, *Colonização senhoral no Zambési e outros ensaios* (Lisbon, 1962), pp. 235–52; AHU, Cód. 432, "Regimento das alfândegas," 22 March 1637, fo. 67–69.

68. ANTT, DRI, 55, Memorandum Antônio de Barros, 1637, fo. 129; Theal, iii, p. 250.

69. The main source for the following paragraphs is ANTT, DRI, 55, "Titolo das terras dos Rio de Cuama." Thus—contrary to Pearson's argument (*Port Cities and Intruders,* p. 149)—*prazos* were already the dominant institution in Mozambique in the seventeenth century; the only difference is that sources on the eighteenth century are more copious than on the seventeenth, so that it is often assumed in the literature that they arose in the eighteenth century.

70. There is considerable disagreement on the significance of the *curva*—mainly relating to whether this was levied on all or mainly on Islamic merchants—though see Mudenge, *Political History of Munhumutapa,* p. 133.

71. Theal, iii, 441; Newitt, *History of Mozambique,* p. 137.

72. BNL, FG, Cód. 10.836, fo. 13, 15.

73. AHU, Moç, Cx. 1, 32, "Relation by Dom Jerónimo de Almeida."

74. Ajuda 51-VII-27, "Relação de Rafael de San Martino." Compare to the difficult issue involved here for apartheid historiographer Hromnik, *Indo-Africa,* p. 81, who argues that if the Portuguese in Sena were obliged to marry their concubines by the crown these *must* have been of Indian descent, rather than African.

75. AHU, Moç, Cx. 3, 120, 22 June 1697. The crown had proposed the establishment of a seminary in Sena for the education of the children of Africans to the church office, but this never materialized because of the crown's continuous financial problems in Sena (AHU, Índia, Cx. 39, 123, 20 November 1694).

76. BNL, FG, Cód. 8548, "Notices on Mozambique and Senna" (ca. 1720), fo. 189 vo; HAG, LM, 44, "Resumo dos homens brancos."

77. This is a highly contentious issue, I should add, as there is a considerable amount of controversy on whether—and if so, how deeply—Islamic merchants penetrated into the hinterland on the Zambesi. See, e.g., E.A. Alpers, "Towards a History of the Expansion of Islam in East Africa: The Matrilineal People of the Southern Interior," in T.O. Ranger and I.N. Kimambo, *The Historical Study of African Religion* (London, 1972), pp. 172–201, who argues the "Moorish merchants" the Portuguese refer to were Swahili-speaking; and Beach, *The Shona,* p. 105, who argues they were Shona-speaking.

78. Theal, iv, p. 494; HAG, Regimentos de Moçambique, 2780, 1681, fo. 1: "Condições que ha de fazer o feitor real para a tratta do Cabo dos Correntes"; BAC, A 513, 15 December 1696, fo. 34.

79. VOC/OB 4013, "Diary of the ship *Voorhouten* during its trip to Madagascar," 18 October; 23 September 1676; AHU Cx. 29, 22 January 1673; see, too, the picture of the Portuguese settlement in Sena Bay in ARA, Coll. Aanwinsten 1987, xix, fo. 7.

80. See the essays collected in D.M. Peers (ed.), *Warfare and Empire* (Ashgate, Variorum, 1997).

81. AHU, Índia, Cx. 12, 76, February 1635.

82. See, for example, AHU, Ìndia, Cx. 12, 75, 8 July 1636; C. Serra, *Para a História da arte militar Moçambicana* (Maputo, 1983); W.W. Gray, "Portuguese Musketeers on the Zambezi," *JAH* 12 (4) (1972), pp. 563–65.

83. Ajuda 51-VII-27, "Informations by Rafael de San Martino"; Évora, CV/2–7, "Discurso sobre a conquista," fo. 419.

84. For archeological research on the *feiras* in the *veld* of Zimbabwe see H. Ellert, *Rivers of Gold* (*Zambesiana* no. 21) (Gweru, 1993), pp. 90–123; Newitt, *History of Mozambique,* pp. 193–217; Ajuda 51-VII-39, fo. 37 vo.

85. For the trade with Malawi—"the land of clouds," as the Portuguese aptly called it—see AHU, Moç. Cx. 3, 106, 24 July 1685.

86. For example, S. Marks and R. Gray, "Southern Africa and Madagascar," in R. Gray (ed.), *The Cambridge History of Africa,* iv, *From 1600 to 1790* (Cambridge, 1975), pp. 408–10.

87. AHU, Moç., Cx. 1, 104, 12 February 1656.

88. HAG, LM, 75, 2 November 1702, fo. 297; HAG, LM, 58, 19 December 1694, fo. 275; AHU, Cód., 212, 11 March 1677, fo. 78 vo; AHU, Moç., Cx. 3, 99, 3 July 1682.

89. HAG, LM, 52, 23 June 1687, fo. 403.

90. AHU, Índia, Cx. 34, 129, 23 June 1687; AHU, Cód. 212, 9 January 1681, fo. 123.

91. AHU, Índia, Cx. 32, 64, 24 January 1683; Ajuda 51-VII-35, fo. 48 vo.

92. AHU, Moç, Cx. 3, 95, 22 March 1681; AHU, Moç, Cx. 2, 119, 20 April 1665, and 16 February 1666.

93. Ajuda 51-VII-37, fo. 50–52. There is an extensive literature on the Rozvis, the reconstruction of the history of which by D. Abrams from oral testimony was long seen as vindicating the use of oral history in African studies in general. But Abrams has come under sharp criticism. See Mudenge, *A Political History,* pp. 285–295; Beach, *The Shona,* pp. 119–22; H. von Sicard, "Reiche und Königstum der Rozwi vom Ende des 17 bis zum Anfang des 19e Jahrhunderts," in *Festschrift für A.E. Jensen,* 2 vols. (Munich, 1964), ii, p. 653.

94. Axelson, *Portuguese,* p. 137; Lobato, *Colonização,* p. 85; Isaacman, *Mozambique,* pp. 18–24; HAG, LM, 72, "Enformação Joseph Fonseca de Coutinho," fo. 196–98; AHU, Moç., Cx. 3, 120, 22 June 1697; I.S. Mudenge, "The Role of Foreign Trade in the Rozvi Empire: A Reappraisal," *JAH* 15 (3) (1974), pp. 379–91.

95. These remarks refer of course to the "African mode of production" as a separate "mode of production" with the state premised on the exploitation of trade, as was argued by Catherine Coquery-Vidrovitch—see, e.g., her "Political Economy of the African Peasantry and Modes of Production," in P.C. Gutkind and I. Wallerstein (eds.), *The Political Economy of Contemporary Africa* (Beverly Hills, 1976), pp. 90–111.

96. J.F. da Costa, "Soccotra e o domínio Português no Oriente," *Anais. Academia portuguêsa da história.* Segunda série. 24 (1) (1977), pp. 323–77; Frey Gaspar de St. Trinidade (F. Lopes, ed.), *Conquista espiritual do Oriente,* 3 vols. (Lisbon, 1967–69), iii, pp. 20–23; Barros, *Da Ásia,* Decada II, Livro I, Cap. 31; C.R. Boxer, "The Principal Ports of Call in the *Carreira da Índia,*" in *From Lisbon to Goa* (London, 1984), p. 38.

97. ARA, Coll. Sweers/Manis 9, "Brief representation by A. Bechers," fo. 120–24;

Beccari, *Rerum,* xi, p. 514, xii, pp. 62–64; Trinidade, *Conquista espiritual,* ii, pp. 23–26. For shipping of the sultan of Khisn to Diu compare the list of *cartazes* handled by the viceroy in M.N. Pearson, *Coastal Western India: Studies from the Portuguese Records* (New Delhi, 1981), pp. 145–47.

98. De Costa, "Soccotra," p. 254; VOC/OB 1133, "Report by W. Carstensz on the cruise for the carracks from Lisbon," fo. 221 vo.

99. VOC/OB 1134, "Report by J. Sigismundi Wurffbain," fo. 161.

100. On these ports see Niebuhr, *Reise,* pp. 286–88; L. de Albuquerque, "Diário de viagem de Dom Álvaro de Castro ao Hadramaute em 1548," *Revista da Universidade de Coimbra* 23 (1973), pp. 157–221; G.B. Martin, "Arab Migration to East Africa in Medieval Times," *International Journal of African Historical Studies* 9 (1) (1978), pp. 368–90; A.W. Forbes, "Southern Arabia and the Islamisation of the Central Indian Archipelago," *Archipel* 21 (4) (1981), pp. 55–91.

101. R.B. Sergeant, "The Ports of Aden and Shihr," in *Les Grandes escales dans le monde (Recueils de la société Jean Bodin)* (Brussels, 1974), pp. 207–44.

102. A. Barades, "Tractato de sitio de Adem," in Beccari, *Rerum,* iv, pp. 331–35; W.P.H. Coolhaas (ed.), *Pieter van den Broecke in Azië,* 2 vols. (The Hague, *WLV,* 1963), i, pp. 106–8; G. La Roque, *Voyage dans l'Arabie heureuse* (Amsterdam, 1711), pp. 52–54.

103. See BNL, FG, Cód. 7640, "Breve relação de Ethiopia."

104. E. Celabi, *Seyhatnâmesi,* 6 vols. (Istanbul, 1985), vi, p. 675.

105. M. Abir, "Southern Ethiopia," in R. Gray and D. Birmingham (eds.), *Pre-Colonial African Trade: Essays on Trade in Central and Eastern Africa* (London, 1970), pp. 128–30; VOC/OB 1625, "Report by N. Welters," fo. 158–61.

106. VOC/OB 1603, 23 August 1698, fo. 1698; VOC/OB 1323, "Questionaire regarding the present state of Ethiopia," paragraph 12; VOC/OB 1625, "Report by N. Welters," fo. 158.

107. ANTT, DRI, 49, "*Propostas* by the patriarch of Ethiopia," fo. 236. On the Portuguese role in Ethiopia in the sixteenth century see. M. Abir, *Ethiopia and the Red Sea: The Fall of the Solomonic Dynasty and European-Muslim Rivalry in the Region* (London, 1980). The "European" credentials of the Afro-Portuguese *casados* resident in Ethiopia can, by 1600, be questioned too, however. E. van Donzel, *Foreign Relations of Ethiopia 1642–1700: Documents Relative to the Journals of Khodja Murat* (Istanbul, 1979); E. van Donzel (ed.), *A Yemenite Embassy to Ethiopia 1647–1649: Al Haymi's Sirat al-Habasha* (Stuttgart, 1986).

108. VOC/OB 1248, "Report by Jan de Vogel," fo. 2163 vo.

109. VOC/OB 1132, "Report by Pieter van den Broeke," fo. 1311; Beccari, *Rerum,* xiii, pp. 301–3.

110. R.B. Pankhurst, "Some Notes on the Historical and Economic Geography of the Mesawa Area," *Journal of Ethiopian Studies* 13 (1) (1975), p. 101; J. de Castro, "Roteiro do Mar Roxo," in A. Cortesão and L. de Albuquerque (eds.), *Obras de Dom João de Castro,* 2 vols. (Coimbra, 1971), i, pp. 231–33; A. Barades, "Tractatus tres," in Beccari, *Rerum,* iv, p. 210; M.W. Arregay, "A Reappraisal of the Impact of Firearms on the History of Warfare in Ethiopia," *Journal of Ethiopian Studies* 13 (1) (1975), p. 118; ANTT, DRI, 44, fo. 24.

111. VOC/OB 1625, "Report by Nicolaas Welters," fo. 159–61; for the trade from Massawa to Domvia see also the report by T. Zas in VOC/OB 1625, 12 August 1698.

112. ANTT, DRI, 49, fo. 236 vo.; R. Pankhurst, "The Banya, or Indian Presence at

Massawa, the Dahlak Islands and in the Horn of Africa," in C. Mehaud (ed.), *Mouvements des populations dans l'Océan Indien* (Paris, 1979), pp. 107–27.

113. ANTT, ut supra.

114. On the vessels in use in the Red Sea in the sixteenth and seventeenth centuries, see C. Orhonlu, "XVI-asrin ilk yarasinda Kizildeniz sahhilerinde Osmanlilar," *Türk tarih Dergisi* 12 (1962), p. 4.

115. See W. Foster (ed.), *The Red Sea and Adjacent Countries at the Close of the Seventeenth Century* (London, *WHS,* 1947), pp. 66–72; H.O. Üzünçarşili, *Mekke i-müherimije emirleri* (Ankara, 1970); S.J. Shaw, *The Financial and Administrative Organization of Ottoman Egypt* (Princeton, 1962), pp. 238–51; S.J. Shaw (ed. and trans.), *Ottoman Egypt in the Eighteenth Century: The Nizâmname i-Misr of Cezzâr Ahmad Pasha* (Cambridge, MA, 1962), pp. 40–44; M.N. Pearson, *Pilgrimage to Mecca: The Indian Experience* (Princeton, 1996), pp. 123–39.

116. VOC/OB 1330, "Report by J. Wyns," fo. 962 vo.

117. Pearson, *Pilgrimage to Mecca,* p. 161; VOC/OB 1409, fo. 1670 vo.

118. J. Baldry, "The Early History of the Yemeni Port of al-Huddaydah," *Arabian Studies* 7 (1), 1985, pp. 37–53: Foster, *Red Sea,* p. 73; Niebuhr, *Reise,* pp. 228–31; G. La Roque, *Voyage,* p. 90; VOC/OB 1130, "Report by Pieter van den Broecke," fo. 1312 vo.

119. ARA, Coll. van Hoorn van Riebeeck 12, "Description of Mocha, its present site, inhabitants and trade."

120. PRONI D 654/31/15, 8 June 1724.

121. K. Glamann, *Dutch-Asiatic Trade 1620–1740* (The Hague, 1956/1981), p. 189; Brouwer, *Al-Mukha,* p. 208 ff.; ARA, Coll. van Hoorn van Riebeek 12, "Description of Mocha."

122. Brouwer, ut supra, p. 373; VOC/OB 1134, "Report Wurffbain," fo. 168.

123. VOC/OB 1383, "Relation by H. Cloeck," fo. 649–53.

124. VOC/OB 1330, "Description of Bab al-Mandeb," fo. 763–67; see Castro, "Roteiro," pp. 218–25.

125. VOC/OB 1383, "Report by H. Cloeck," fo. 678.

126. For the Persian Gulf see in particular the classic work of L. Lorimer, *Persian Gulf Gazetteer,* 3 parts in 6 vols. (Calcutta, 1903; London, 1969); D.E. Long, *The Persian Gulf: An Introduction* (Boulder, 1977). For the meteorology of the Gulf see *The Cambridge History of Iran,* i, W.B. Fischer (ed.), *The Land of Iran* (Cambridge, 1968), pp. 212–49. A good (Persian) historical atlas is *Atlas ye-naqsahija ye-jugrafiya va asnad bara-ye tarikhi dar Khalig i-Fars* (Teheran, 1971).

127. The following is mainly based on VOC/OB 1179, "Description of Mocha" (actually a description of Basra), 1652, fo. 963–66.

128. VOC/OB 1425, 26 September 1687, fo. 466.

129. C.P. Grant, *The Syrian Desert: Caravans, Travel and Exploration* (London, 1936), p. 99; D. Carruthers, *The Desert Route to India* (London, *WHS,* 1929); W.P.H. Mandeville, "The Ottoman Province of al-Hasha in the Sixteenth and Seventeenth Century," *Journal of the American Oriental Society* 90 (3) (1970), pp. 1179–83.

130. A. Karim Rafiq, *The Ottoman Province of Damascus in the Eighteenth Century* (Beirut, 1966), p. 62; VOC/OB 1204, Basra diary, 28 October 1651; VOC/OB 1206, "Description of Mocha," fo. 965 vo; *English Factories* 1646–1650, p. 86, 219; VOC/OB 1307, 16 March 1676, fo. 638.

131. See R.W. Ferrier, "An English Account of Persian Trade in 1618," *JESHO* 19 (1976), p. 202.

132. On this trip see Grant, *Syrian Desert,* pp. 70–125; VOC 9033, Basra diary, 1725,

23 August, 7 March, 24 April, and for the wood trade of Birecek see A. Baião (ed.), *Itinerários da Índia athé o Portugal por terra* (Coimbra, 1923), pp. 273–83; and D. Ohlson, *The Ottoman Siege of Mosul and Ottoman-Persian Relations* (Bloomington, 1974), p. 23.

133. Évora, CXV/1–5, fo. 60; Frey Gaspar de San Bernadino, *Itinerário da Índia athé a ilha de Chypre por terra* (A. Reis Machado, ed.) (Lisbon, 1953), pp. 183–85.

134. Geleynssen 102, 4 November 1645; on Kharg see too A. Hamilton, *A New Account of the East Indies,* 2 vols. (W. Foster, ed.) (London, 1930), i, p. 59; *English Factories* 1637–1641, p. 245.

135. VOC/OB 1315, 20 January 1677, fo. 638; VOC/OB 1355, 15 May 1681, fo. 405.

136. C. Niebuhr, *Reise nach Arabien* (Graz, 1969), p. 311; V.V. Minorsky, *The Tadhikarat al-Muluk. A Manual of Safavid Administration* (London, 1943), p. 172.

137. BNL, FG, Cód. 28, fo. 17.

138. P. Tuson, "Lieutenant Wyburd's Journal of an Excursion into Arabia," *Arabian Studies* 5 (1979), p. 33; V. Guinet, *La Turquie de l'Asie*, 4 vols. (Paris, 1892–96), iii, pp. 332–34; S.B. Miles, *The Countries and Tribes of the Persian Gulf* (London, 1919/1969), p. 416; W. Floor, "Pearl-Fishing in the Persian Gulf in 1757," *Persica* 10 (1982), pp. 215–19; Lorimer, *Persian Gulf Gazetteer*, i, c, pp. 2227–34; BNL, FG, Cód. 32, fo. 11; VOC/OB 1476, 15 November 1694, fo. 603; VOC/OB 1416, 9 April 1685, fo. 1676 vo; VOC/OB 1425, 8 August 1687, fo. 448 vo; VOC/OB 1425, Memorandum by Jacob Willemsen, fo. 696; VOC/UB 880, "Memoir for those who are sent to buy pearls in Bahrijn and Catijf." On the pearl trade of Qatif and the fortress there see NAI, Foreign Miscellaneous 189, "Captain Salgier's mission to Arabia," fo. 68.

139. VOC/OB 1245, fo. 369 vo.

140. VOC/OB 1251, 6 April 1667, fo. 1332.

141. Geleynssen 280 c, Diary of Willemszoon, 3–12 July 1646; sources on Kung are enumerated in J. Aubin (ed.), *L'ambassade de Gregório Pereira fidalgo à la cour du châh soltân Hosseyn* (Lisbon, 1971), pp. 11–13.

142. VOC/OB 1125, Diary by Leonard Winnincx, 20 November; VOC/OB 1266, 8 November 1668, fo. 155 vo.

143. Resende, fo. 233; AHU, Índia, Cx. 30, 41, February 1674.

144. ARA, Coll. Aanwinsten 1903 xix, "Dastur al amal bara-ye bandar-i mobarak i-Bandar Abbas." In practice the situation was even worse than on paper: The Armenian trader Hovhannes had to pay for his indigo not the official rate of 12 percent but 17 instead. So these burdensome impositions tended to weigh upon Armenian merchants even more heavily than upon the European ones: L. Khachikian, "Le registre d'un négociant Arménien en Perse, en Inde et au Tibet," *Annales ESC* 22 (1967), p. 255.

145. VOC/OB 1241, 15 February 1663, fo. 725 vo.

146. *Diário do terceiro conde de Linhares*, 2 vols. in one (Lisbon, 1937–43), ii, p. 179; AHU, Cód. 210, 11 February 1643, fo. 238; HAG, Regimentos e instruções, 1423, 11 February 1658, fo. 8; VOC/OB 1314, 12 September 1675, fo. 136 vo; VOC/OB 1559, "Brief summary of events in Kongo," 4 July 1693, fo. 788; VOC/OB 1250, "Instruction to Adriaen Verdonck," fo. 250–53; VOC/OB 1652, 23 July 1703, fo. 1004.

147. M.A. Sadid as-Saltanya Khanbabi, *Bandar Abbas va Khalig i-Fars* (A. Iqtidari, ed.) (Teheran, 1342 [1984 or 1985]), pp. 244–75; L. Lorrimer, *Persian Gulf Gazetteer*, III, ii, pp. 1100–16; a map of Khism fortress with notes can be found in W. Floor, "Het Nederlands-Perzisch Conflict van 1645," *Bijdragen en Mededelingen Stichting Cultuurgeschiedenis Nederlanders overzee Verslagen en Aanwinsten* (1978/1979), p. 4.

148. See Fiorani Piacenti, *L'emporio ed il regno*, p. 123; J. Aubin, "Le royaume de

Hormuz," *Mare Luso-Indicum*, 2 (1972), pp. 190–93; T. Volker, *Porcelain and the Dutch East India Company* (Leiden, 1954), p. 184; VOC/OB 1243, 31 May 1664, fo. 1929 vo.; Geleynssen 133, 22 May 1640. The export of sulfur was a monopoly of the Turanshah under the Portuguese and appears to have been so under the Safavids as well: E. Sanceau (ed.), *Cartas de Dom João de Castro* (Lisbon, 1954), p. 45; VOC/OB 1244, 16 March 1657, fo. 303.

149. See H. Gaube, "Ein Abschnitt der safavidische Bandar e-Abbas-Shiraz strasse: die Strecke von Seyyid Gemal al-Din nach Lar," *Iran* 17 (1979), pp. 39–47.

150. Évora CXV/1–5, fo. 46. An excellent description of Gombroon can be found in O. Dapper, *Asia, ofte nauwkeurige beschrijvinge van 't rijk der grooten Mogol benevens een volkomen beschrijvinge van geheel Persiën*, 2 vols. in one (Amsterdam, 1672), ii, p. 69. This is a strange book—for it is unclear how Dapper obtained his information—yet it is a veritable storehouse of rare data. Although Bandar Abbas is one of the best-documented ports in Asia, it has not attracted a great deal of attention; but see Sadid as-Saltania, *Bandar Abbas*, p. 23 et seq., and L. Lockhart, *Famous Cities of Persia* (Middlesex, 1939), pp. 103–12.

151. VOC/OB 1321, 21 December 1676, fo. 1032; VOC/OB 1307, 29 March 1676, fo. 981.

152. Geleynssen 280, "Journal kept by Claes Janssen on the *Zeemeeuw*," 28 October 1645.

153. ARA, St. Gen. 5740 i, Lias VOC, Report Ysbrand Goske.

154. Geleynssen 280, 1 November 1645.

155. *English Factories,* 1646–1650, pp. 27–28; BNL, FG, Cód. 177, fo. 273; Geleynssen de Jong 102, 10 February 1646; Wilkinson, *The Imamate Tradition*, p. 233.

156. Resende, fo. 177; BNL, FG, Cód. 162, fo. 6 vo.

157. VOC/OB 1259, "A description of a voyage along the coast of Arabia"; BNL, FG, Cód. 1627, fo. 9; A. Bocarro, "Livro de todas as fortalezzas, cidades e povoações do Estado da Índia Oriental," in A. de Bragança Pereira (ed.), *Arquivo português oriental*, (Bastora, Goa, 1932–36), 2 vols., i, pp. 60–64; see also the descriptions and maps of the fortresses along the Arabian shore in A. Cortesão and A.T. de Mota, *Portugaliae monumenta cartographica*, 6 vols. (Lisbon, 1960–62).

158. Hamilton, *A New Account*, i, pp. 44–45.

159. J. Fryer, *A New Account of the East Indies and Persia, Being Nine Years' Travel 1672–1681* (W. Crooke, ed.), 3 vols. (Cambridge, *WHS*, 1909–15), ii, p. 45; ANTT, DRI, 44, "Regimento de Muscat"; Bocarro, "Livro," i, p. 66; HRB 874, "Comprehensive (*radikale*) description of Persia by A. van Rheede Jr.," para 9; VOC/OB 1259, "Description of a voyage," fo. 3376 vo.

160. VOC/OB 1291, "Report on Aman by George Willemson," fo. 584.

161. See, for instance, a case when the fleet under Viceroy Villa Verde had captured three Muscati vessels: "Their pilots were Englishmen and so were their gunners, and there were ten more Englishmen on board who have fled Goa, since I intended to pay them for treason with death" (AHU, Índia, Cx. 38, 54, 15 January 1696).

162. ANTT, DRI, 61, 11 January 1649, fo. 47.

163. VOC/OB 1291, "Report by Willemson," fo. 565; VOC/OB 1297, 1 April 1675, fo. 101 vo., and see the important anonymous memorandum on Muscat and the Swahili Coast (probably by João Correia de Sá) from 1673 in AHU, Índia, Cx. 29 bis, 171. It is possible that these lower tariffs mainly referred to Muslims and that Hindus had to pay higher rates; see Risso, *Merchants and Faith*, p. 121.

164. HAG, LM, 46 bis, "*Pareçer* of J. Duarte Mathias."

165. J.R. Quadros, *Diu. Appontamentos para sua história e chorographia* (Nova Goa, 1899), pp. 43–47; P. van Dam, *Beschrijvinge van de Oost-Indische Compagnie* (F.W. Stapel and C.W.T. van Boetzelaar, eds.), 7 vols. (The Hague, *RGP*, 1927–63), III, iii, p. 105; VOC/OB 1201, 1 March 1651, fo. 889.

166. AHU, Índia, Cx. 14, 110, 1643.

167. Bocarro, "Livro," ii, p. 115; ANTT, DRI, 44, 9 April 1644, fo. 184; AHU, Índia, cx. 14, ut supra; AHU, Índia, Cx. 17, 63, 24 December 1644.

168. ARA, HRB, 836, "Memorandum on merchandise, received and despatched from the Surat customs" (1755).

169. Resende, fo. 164–89; ANTT, Con. d. Gr., Cx. III E, "Relação de que rende."

170. AHU, Índia, Cx. 42, 2, "A petition of the hindus and moors"; VOC/OB 1625, "Report by Johan van den Berg," fo. 187–88; VOC/OB 1279, "Report by A. van Oosterwijk," fo. 193.

171. VOC/OB 1625, 22 November 1698, fo. 28.

172. VOC/OB 1279, "Report by van Oosterwijk," fo. 196 vo.; "Enformação que me deu Joam de Magalhães dos cousas de Cambay," in A. de Almeida Calado (ed.), *Livro em que se tratta muito por extenso dos cousas da Índia e de Japão* (Coimbra, 1957), pp. 57–60; and for the relative costs of naval stores and supplies in Cambay and Surat see VOC/OB 1635, 14 November 1700, fo. 102.

173. VOC/OB 1383, Surat diary, 12 November 1682, fo. 628; for Broach see I. Ray (ed.), "Of Trade and Traders in Seventeenth Century India: An Unpublished Memorandum by G. Roque," *The Indian Historical Review* 9 (1982), pp. 220–23; Dapper, *Asia*, i, p. 291; J. van Twist, *Generale beschrijvinge van Indië* (Amsterdam, 1648), p. 11.

174. For estimates of Surat's population see A. Das Gupta, *Indian Merchants*, p. 29; and for the relative size of this population see H.K. Naqvi, *Population and Urban Centres under the Great Mughal 1556–1706* (Simla, 1972), pp. 112–25. The proportion is relative to the period under consideration, of course; during the early seventeenth century the population of Agra to all appearances surpassed that of Ahmedabad, but Agra's population almost certainly significantly decreased during the second half of the seventeenth century.

175. VOC/OB 1611, "Report Pieter Ketting," 28 April 1698, fo. 292; see also Fryer, *A New Account*, p. 231.

176. A. Das Gupta, *Indian Merchants*, p. 20; B.G. Gokhale, *Surat in the Seventeenth Century: A Study in Urban History in Pre-Modern India* (London, 1979), pp. 9–19; Fryer, *A New Account*, p. 231; J. Ovington, *A Voyage to Surat in the Year 1689* (C.H. Rawlinson, ed.) (London, *WHS*, 1929), p. 191; VOC/OB 1333, 28 January 1679, fo. 640; VOC/OB 1611, "Report Ketting," fo. 292; VOC/OB 1635, 14 November 1700, fo. 77.

177. See, e.g., VOC/OB 1548, Surat diary, 27 February 1693, fo. 421 vo.

178. VOC/OB 1409, Surat diary, 15 July 1684, fo. 1601; BNL, FG, Cód. 864, "A voyage to India," fo. 27. (In spite of its title these are actually the reminiscences of a Portuguese merchant living in Ahmedabad in 1693! Alas, this manuscript is badly damaged by moisture and the title page, which presumably mentioned the author, is lost; we only know his father was governor of Daman.)

179. For a description of a food riot in Surat see VOC/OB 1430, Surat diary, 15 June 1687, fo. 464–67.

180. VOC/OB 1548, Surat diary, 19 April 1694, fo. 456 vo.

181. VOC/OB 1635, 14 November 1700, fo. 79 vo.; Das Gupta, *Indian Merchants*,

p. 23; and to the literature mentioned there add Khafi Khan, "Muntakab al-lubab," in O. Dowson and C.H. Eliot (eds.), *The History of India as Told by Its Own Historians: The Muhammadan Period*, 8 vols. (London, 1867–77; Calcutta, 1954–60), *Aurengzeb*, p. 79. The court mightily worried about the decay of the fortress and the walls and repeatedly ordered that these should be maintained properly but to little avail; see VOC/OB 1475, Surat diary, 27 September 1689, fo. 414 vo.

182. ARA, Coll. Hoppe, Koloniaal Archief (henceforth K.A.), 8448, "Considerations of Jan Schreuder (1740)," ii, para. 96; for the English factory see C.H. Rawlinson, *English Beginnings in Western India 1600–1650* (London, 1926), pp. 96–99, 140–64; VOC/OB 1370, 8 December 1680, fo. 2394–96.

183. A. Das Gupta, "De VOC en Suratte in de 17 e en 18 e eeuw," in M.A.P. Meilink-Roelofsz (ed.), *De V.O.C. in Azië* (Bussum, 1976), pp. 65–67; Couto, *Da Ásia*, Decada IV, book 6, ch. ix.

184. ANTT, Manuscritos da Casa Forte 63, 6 February 1609, fo. 6; Évora CXVI/1–18, "Relação dos rendimentos," fo. 39–40 vo.

185. Évora CXV/1–5, fo. 34; BNL, FG, Cód 580, fo. 11; VOC 4904, "Description of the kingdom of the Grand Mogul," ca. 1620, fo. 9–11; S. Subrahmanyam, "The Portuguese, Thatta and the External Trade of Sind 1515–1635," *Revista da Cultura*, 13/14 (1991), pp. 48–59. And much of the textile industry in Sind was specialized in very expensive silk cloth, often with gold and silver embroideries (such as *nim gul* and *gul dar*), as well as in Kashmiri shawls—obviously mostly produced for the court too; see VOC/OB 1209, "Notice on profit and loss of merchandise," fo. 508, and 5 May 1655, fo. 507.

186. According to VOC/OB 1273, "Memoir for Andries Bonde," fo. 1803, it was almost as expensive to transport goods by bullock cart as by camel, but in the latter case merchandise often was broken or arrived filthy.

187. VOC/OB 1343, 25 January 1680, fo. 565; on this rebellion see R.C. Hallissey, *The Rajput Rebellion Against Aurengzeb: A Study of the Mughal Empire in Seventeenth Century India* (Columbia, MO, 1977).

188. For a description of this road see A. Das Gupta, *Indian Merchants*, pp. 50–57; VOC/OB 1139, 13 May 1642, fo. 306; VOC/OB 1475, 13 December 1688, fo. 214.

189. See, e.g., VOC/OB 1548, Surat diary, 20 June 1693, fo. 504 vo.

190. Das Gupta, *Indian Merchants*, p. 22; VOC/OB 1611, "Report by P. Ketting," fo. 312–15.

191. Henceforth for the rest of this itinerary I have sailed on the course plotted by G. Schurhammer, *Franz Xavier. Sein Leben und seine Zeit* (Freiburg i.B., 1956–72), 4 vols. in two parts, ii and iii, *Asien*.

192. VOC/OB 1201, 11 May 1651; AHU, Índia, Cx. 20, 102, 2 March, 1649; descriptions of Daman are to be found, for example, in "Livro das cidades e fortalezas que a coroa de Portugal têm nas partes da Índia" (F. Mendes da Luz, ed.), *Studia* 5 (1960), pp. 26–28; Bocarro, "Livro," i, p. 132; van Dam, *Beschryvinge*, III, iii, p. 107.

193. Generally—the amount of *chauth* levied was in reality 12 to 27 percent of the revenue and differed from village to village; see AHU, Índia, Cx. 18, 116, 28 November 1643.

194. See A. Lobato, "Sobre os prazos da Índia," in A. Guerreiro and L. de Albuquerque (eds.), *IIo seminário internacional de história Indo-Portuguêsa* (Actas) (Lisbon, 1985), pp. 459–75; and see too A. De Silva Rego, *Portuguese Colonisation in the Sixteenth Century: A Study of Royal Ordinances* (Johannesburg, 1957). Neither is completely

adequate: we are badly in need of a study on the legal aspects of the Portuguese system of donations. This is mainly based on AHU, Índia, Cx. 32 bis, 240, "Pareçer Miquel Nunes de Mesquita."

195. BNL, FG, Cód. 10.703, "Discurso apologético" (1725), anonymous and unpaged, ch. x.

196. Évora, CXVI/1–18, "Relação dos rendimentos."

197. Resende, fo. 230; A. Gerson da Cunha, *Notes on the History and Antiquities of Chaul and Bassein* (Bombay, 1876), p. 167; *Gaz.B.P.*, xiv, p. 344; ARA, Map Room, photostatic copy of British Museum mss. Sloane 53, "Plattaforma da cidade de Taná."

198. Gerson da Cunha, *Notes*, pp. 140–44; A. de Bragança Pereira, "Os Portugueses em Baçaim," *O oriente português* (Nova Séria), 1, (1936), pp. 148–52; M. Godinho, *Itinerário que o fêz no anno de 1663 vindo da Índia para o Portugal por terra* (Lisbon, 1974), p. 25; *Gaz.B.P.*, xiii, ii, p. 552; xiv, pp. 38–43; Resende, fo. 175; ARA, Sloane mss. no. 53, "Pranta desta cidade de Baçaim."

199. BNL, FG, Cód. 10.703, "Discurso apologético," ch. III; AHU, Índia, Cx. 37, 31, 3 December 1693.

200. A. Tindall, *City of Gold: The Story of Bombay* (London, 1982), pp. 66–92; J.M. Campbell (ed.), *Gazetteer of Town and Island of Bombay* (separate volumes considered as vols. XXV–XXVII of *Gaz.B.P.*), i, p. 120; J. Burnell, *Bombay in the Days of Queen Anne* (T. Sheppard, ed.) (London, *WHS*, 1933), p. 20.

201. G. von Mittelwalner, *Chaul. Eine unerforschte Stadt an der Westküste Indiens (Wehr-Sakral-und Profanarchitektur)* (Berlin, 1964); Évora, CXVI/14, fo. 5–12; ANTT, DRI, 55, 8 January 1647, fo. 490; ANTT, DRI, 60, 18 February 1650, fo. 133.

202. Resende, fo. 179; AHU, Índia, Cx. 18, 44, 19 November, 1646; AHU, Cód. 210, 9 January 1640, fo. 76 vo.

203. Mittelwalner, *Chaul*, p. 42–44; HAG, LM, 71, "A list of citizens of the city of Chaul."

204. T.B. Jervis, *Geographical and Statistical Memoir of the Konkan* (Calcutta, 1840); F.F. Conlon, *A Caste in a Changing World: The Chitrapur Saraswat Brahmins* (New Delhi, 1977); N. Wagle, "The History and Social Organization of the Gauda Saraswat Brahmins of the West-Coast of India," *Journal of Indian History* 47 (1970), pp. 498–508.

205. ARA, Coll. Sweers Manis 9, "Considerations by Albert Bechers," 1 July 1624, fo. 120 vo.

206. VOC/OB 1122, "Report Johan van Twist," 30 January 1637, fo. 478–79; A. Das Gupta, "Indian Merchants and the Western Indian Ocean: The Early Seventeenth Century," *MAS* 19 (3) (1985), p. 484; Coolhaas, *Pieter van den Broeke*, i, p. 115.

207. VOC/OB 1278, "Memoir for Rombout Lefer," fo. 1749–51 vo.; Geleynssen 317, 19 May 1642.

208. Geleynssen 319, "Memoir of what could be sold in Visiapour"; Geleynssen 319, 17 September 1642, and 22 October 1642; BAC A 58, 20 May 1677, fo. 223–25.

209. VOC/OB 1170, Vengurla diary, 9 August 1643, fo. 705; VOC/OB 1246, "Statements by P. van Sandvliet," fo. 1679–81; ARA, Map Room, VOC maps, De Graaf, 6; VOC/OB 1240, 13 May 1662, fo. 558; for another description of Vengurla see J.B. Tavernier, *Travels in India*, 2 vols. (V. Ball, ed.) (London, 1887), i, p. 184.

210. ANTT, DRI, 48, 20 January 1641, fo. 35; Ajuda 51-VII-27, "Note on moving the city of Goa to the mountain of Marmagoa."

211. There are sundry texts on the history of Savantvadi, yet no modern history,

although this principality is one of the best documented in India, but see *Gaz.B.Pr.*, xii, pp. 430–34; S.K. Mhamai, *The Sawants of Vadi and the Portuguese* (New Delhi, 1984), pp. 5–10; and the historic documents on Savant claims to sovereignty over Candal, which are collected in NAI, Foreign Miscellaneous, 183, "Several letters etc. relating to the state of Savantvadi." I did not see W. Courtney, *Memoir of the Sawant Wudee State* (Bombay, 1855); and V.P. Pingulkar, *Savantvad samsthañce itihas* (Bombay, 1911).

212. M.N. Pearson, "The Port City of Goa," in *Coastal Western India*, p. 88; VOC/OB 1273, 20 November 1668, fo. 1763; and see VOC/OB 1234, 13 May 1660, fo. 353, and *Dagregister* 1661, p. 211; the VOC repeatedly tried to convince the Adilshahi nobles not to export grain to Goa to starve the town into submission within six months—but to no avail; the nobles were both financially interested in this trade and unable to thwart it.

213. VOC 1122, Report by van Twist, fo. 500.

214. HAG 656, "Arrematações das rendas." The salt exported from Goa to Candal and the Konkan Coast was, according to HAG 1127, "Petições despachadas para o conselho da fazenda," 10 September 1681, fo. 16, mostly used "for salting fish."

215. M.N. Pearson, "Goa During the First Century of Portuguese Rule," *Itinerário* 8 (1) (1984), p. 39; Ajuda 49-I-51, fo. 169; A. Thekkedath, *History of Christianity in India*, vol. 2, *From the Middle of the Sixteenth to the End of the Seventeenth Century* (Bangalore, 1982), p. 483; V. de Albuquerque, *O senado de Goa. Memória histórica-archeológica* (Nova Goa, 1909), pp. 446–48; T.R. de Souza, *Medieval Goa: A Socio-Economic History* (New Delhi, 1976), p. 25; VOC/OB 1204, 1 August 1654, fo. 334; HAG, LM, 36, 25 April 1656, fo. 421.

216. The classic description of Goa is that of Pyrard de Laval, *The Voyages of François Pyrad of Laval to the East Indies, the Moluccas and Brazil (1611)*, 3 vols. (London, *WHS*, 1887–1890), ii, pp. 45–62. For modern descriptions see B. Penrose, *Goa rainha da Oriente/Goa, Queen of the Orient* (Lisbon, 1960); J.N. de Fonseca, *An Historical and Archeological Sketch of the City of Goa* (Bombay, 1878); and a brief evocation in G.V. Scammel, *The World Encompassed: The First European Maritime Empires ca. 800–1650* (London, 1985), p. 243.

217. H. Carita, *Les Palais de Goa. Modèles et typologies de l'architecture Indo-Portugais* (Paris, 1996); ANTT, DRI, 37, 15 December 1637, fo. 407.

218. J. Pereira, *Baroque Goa: The Architecture of Portuguese India* (New Delhi, 1995); AHU, Índia, Cx. 32, 5, 20 September 1682.

219. HAG, LM, 67, 23 December 1703, fo. 136; F. Da Silva Gracias, *Health and Hygiene in Colonial Goa* (New Delhi, 1994).

220. Ajuda, 51-VII-27, fo. 33; AHU, Índia, Cx. 34, 107, 17 October 1689, and 176, 25 August 1688; AHU, Cód. 58, 8 February 1658, fo. 158 vo.

221. J.H. de Cunha Rivara, "A Índia no governo do Vice-rei Conde de Villa Verde 1693–1698," II: "A mundança da cidade de Goa para Marmagoa," *O chronista do Tissuary* 18 (1867), pp. 123–31; the decision and the reasons to move from Goa can be found in HAG, LM, 51 bis, "Propositions regarding the improvement of this state."

222. For the *nayaka*s of Ikkeri see K.D. Swaminathan, *The Nayakas of Ikkeri* (Madras, 1957); and for Mysore see the classic work by J.R. Wilkes, *Historical Sketches of the South of India*, 2 vols. (Mysore, 1932).

223. Hamilton, *A New Account*, i, p. 324; Bocarro, "Livro," ii, pp. 307–11; ANTT, DRI, 47, 16 November 1640, fo. 72.

224. Ajuda 50-V-38, "Relação do soccedido," fo. 169.

225. S. Subrahmanyam, *The Political Economy of Commerce: Southern India 1500–1650* (Cambridge, 1990), pp. 260–65

226. ARA, HRB 542, "Description of Ceylon by Ryckloff van Goens"; VOC/OB 1474, 10 April 1689, fo.318; Ajuda 51-VII-34, fo. 99–101.

227. See in particular the description of Mount Eli in G. Bouchon, *Mamale de Cananore. Un adversaire de l'Inde portugais* (Paris, 1975), p. 7.

228. G. Bouchon, "Les Musulmans du Kerala à l'époque de la découverte portugaise," *Mare Luso-Indicum* 2 (1973), pp. 3–59; E.J. Miller, *Mappila Muslims of Kerala: A Study of Islamic Trends* (Bombay, 1976).

229. HRB 542, "Description of Ceylon"; VOC/OB 1638, 28 December 1699, fo. 26; Antonio de la Cruz in 1620 also noted that the *chulias* mainly used bows but also "lanchas y alcanchias de fuego de que avía mucho cantidad en sus navios y assi escopetas y algunos falcones," most of these apparently being locally made. However, they preferred to grapple rather than disable ships for "los soldados son mariñeros y los mariñeros son soldados" (BNL, FG, Cód. 580, fo. 28).

230. See van Dam, *Beschrijvinge*, III, ii, p. 305; Baldaeus, *Nauwkeurige beschrijvinge*, p. 101; also G. Bouchon, *Mamale de Cananore*, p. 23.

231. ARA, Coll. Aanwinsten 1856, "Malabaers woordenboek" (Malabar dictionary) *sub* Aliraja; see K.N.K. Kurup, *The Aliraja of Cananore* (Trivandrum, 1972); W.W. Logan, *Malabar*, 3 vols. (Madras, 1951), i, pp. 61–67; Bouchon, *Mamale de Cananore*, p. 35.

232. M.A.P. Roelofs, *De vestiging der Nederlanders ter kuste Malabar* (The Hague, 1943), p. 371; Bouchon, *Mamale de Cananore*, pp. 45–75, to which add NAI, Foreign Miscellaneous, 55–57, "Report of the Malabar comity 1793" (this is the settlement survey of Malabar—a veritable cyclopedia of trade and history of Kerala), 2 vols., and one with enclosures, 57, Enclosure no. XIV.

233. AHU, Índia, Cx. 25 bis, 220, 24 January 1664; VOC/OB 1308, 16 January 1675, fo. 732–34; ARA, HRB 542, "Description of Ceylon"; Batavia would have liked to demolish the fortress at Cananore, but Cochin pleaded it should preserved at all costs, being the key road of access to Cochin (ARA, St. Gen., Lias VOC, 5738 ii, Report by P. van Dam, 21 December 1664).

234. BNL, FG, Cód. 36, "Description of Malabar" (ca. 1780), fo. 1; ARA, St. Gen, Lias VOC, 5741 i, Report by Pieter van Dam, 21 December 1683.

235. BNL, FG, Cód. 36, "Description of Malabar," fo. 2.

236. VOC/OB 1474, 13 January 1691, fo. 545–52. On the Portuguese trade in Malabar teak see K.N. Mathew, *Portuguese Trade with India in the Sixteenth Century* (New Delhi, 1975), p. 220; I. Bulhão Patto and A. de Silva Rego (eds.), *Documentos remettidos da Índia ou livros dos monções*, 7 vols. (Lisbon, 1884– ), iii, p. 131. The kinds of wood exported to Portugal were, according to HAG, LM, 30, "Rol das madeiras que podem ir da India," *angelim fino* (fine teak), *angelim preto* (black teak), and *pao preto de Moçambique* (ebony wood)—probably from Madagascar. Albeit, in the second half of the seventeenth century the Portuguese rarely exported wood from India, and it was even proposed one might sell Brazilian *jacará* wood in Goa.

237. A. Das Gupta, *Malabar in Asian Trade* (Cambridge, 1967), p. 3; R.M. Eaton, "Multiple Lenses: Differing Perspectives of Fifteenth Century Calicut," in L. Sears (ed.), *Autonomous Histories, Particular Truths* (Madison, 1983), pp. 71–86; and to the literature mentioned there should be added J. Schouten, *Oost-Indische Voyagie* (Amsterdam, 1676), p. 254; Hamilton, *A New Account*, i, p. 263; W. Lubbock (ed.), *Thomas Barlow's Journal of His Life at Sea*, 2 vols. (London, 1954), i, p. 194.

238. On Panani see Lubbock, *Barlow's Journal*, i, p. 190; there is quite a large literature on the Kunjalis, often not free of a nationalist slant, where they are perceived as

primeval "freedom fighters," thus, for example, O.K. Nambiar, *The Kunjalis: Admirals of Calicut* (Bombay, 1963).

239. VOC/OB 1307, diary kept by Ryckloff van Goens, 2 March 1674.

240. ARA, 2 e Afdeling, Comité voor de Oost-Indische handel en bezittingen, 137, "A brief sketch of Cochin," fo. 136. On the number of *topaz* Christians, which given the exceptionally large size of families and numbers of children among the *topazes* can be guesstimated at about 40,000 persons, see VOC/OB 1406, 11 September 1686, and A. Galetti, *The Dutch in Malabar. Selections from the Records of Madras Government. Dutch Records* (Madras, 1911), p. 15.

241. ANTT, DRI, 40, 29 November 1637, fo. 137; W. Fishel, "Cochin in Jewish History," *Proceedings of the American Academy of Jewish Research* 30 (1962), pp. 37–59.

242. VOC/OB 1307, "Diary by Ryckloff van Goens Jr.," 7 March; H.K. s'Jacob, *De Nederlanders in Kerala 1663–1701. De memories en instructies betreffende het commandement Malabar van de Verenigde Oost-Indische Compagnie* (The Hague, *RGP*, 1976), p. 294. At Cochin too, Dutchmen remained Dutch, however. The VOC at Cochin had yearly to report to Batavia the results in primary school of the Thomas Christian pupils so Batavia was sure the money was not squandered. These lists are among the most touching human-interest documentation I have come across.

243. VOC/OB 1245, 28 January 1664, fo. 478 vo.

244. KITLV H 47 D, "Formula for an oath taken by indigenous Christians at Cochin"; VOC/OB 1304, 14 May 1674, fo. 362; BNL, FG, Cód. 301, "Brief and true relation," fo. 14–18.

245. ANTT, DRI, 60, 21 December 1648, fo. 119; and 15 February 1650, fo. 116.

246. On Portuguese Cochin see Subrahmanyam, *Political Economy*, p. 135; and A.R. Disney, *A decadência do império da pimenta* (Twilight of the pepper empire) (Lisbon, 1981), pp. 23–25; to which add ARA, Sloane 53, "Descrição de Cochim"; Galetti, *The Dutch*, p. 10; Schouten, *Oost-Indische voyagie*, pp. 266–67.

247. VOC/OB 1280, 26 November 1671, fo. 583, ARA Map Room, De Graaf 22 D; ARA, 2 e afdeling, Comité Oost-Indische handel en bezittingen, 138, "Brief sketch," fo. 134; VOC/OB 1344, 16 January 1675, fo. 734; VOC/OB 1377, 14 August 1670, fo. 1170.

248. VOC/OB 1308, "Report and disclosure," fo. 818, 806, 805; VOC/OB 1275, 16 February 1675, fo. 936; Baldaeus, *Beschryvinge,* p. 182.

249. Compare, e.g., Couto, *Da Ásia*, Dec. XI, Cap. XXIII, with A.C. Holis, *The Masai: Their Language and Folklore* (London, 1903).

250. C.M. Eastman, "Service, Slavery, and the Swahili Social Reality," *Afrikanistische Arbeitspapiere* 37 (1994), p. 88.

251. A.K. Gode, "The History of Tobacco in India and Europe," in *Studies in Indian Cultural History* (Hosiapur, 1961), pp. 429–39; E.B. Martin, *The History of Malindi* (Nairobi, 1973), p. 35.

252. And the *ghazis* probably came there in several waves rather than in a single group. Thus, for example, Flacourt's statement that many of the *ombasis* among the Antemoro were sent there quite recently by the "Caliph of Mecca"—meaning the sherif of Mecca—is in my view too easily dismissed by R. Kent (*Early Kingdoms*, p. 101). Instead, Kent argues for an origin in Ethiopia somewhere in the fifteenth century, but might this group not have been reinforced by *ghazis* coming in from Yemen over the Comoros in the late sixteenth century?

# 3

# European *Natios* in the Arabian Seas

One may perhaps argue that, to follow K. Polanyi, the role of the state was crucially important for the creation of a free market in Europe.[1] There the state shaped a legal frame for the free conduct of international trade in which the same set of globally recognized laws applies universally. Precisely the opposite situation existed in the Arabian seas. There the coexistence of various incompatible systems of law, or legal pluralism, was common. Each community ruled itself according to its own customs, its *adat*. While there was legislation regulating trade on the markets within the kingdom, there did not exist a system of international legislation to govern foreign trade or foreign settlement throughout the region.

Individuals, groups, and institutions—like religious sanctuaries—might be allotted an *inam*, which entailed the right to exemptions from trial and customs. Enclaves of separate jurisdiction might thus be created placing an area outside the law of the realm. But an *inam* or a *madad i-ma'ash* grant applied only to the immediate beneficiary, not to those who were only marginally involved with its proprietor. Such rights could only be bestowed by separate allowances and did not apply by extension. In cases of doubt or involving criminal justice—for example, homicide—royal jurisdiction had precedence over privileges allotted by *inam* too.

The rights allotted to foreign merchants were an extension of those commonly bestowed by granting an *inam*. Traders tended to be segmented in regional and religious groups: *natio*s, enclaves of separate jurisdiction apart from that of the kingdom. Those groups arbitrated differences among themselves according to their own law and they represented the interests of the merchants with local authorities.

The Europeans fit within this judicial frame and within this system of *natio*s too. Partly, the European communities consisted of different *natio*s, divided between Catholic (French and Portuguese) and Protestant (English, Dutch, and Danish), for the difference between *natio*s was mostly a religious one. But European *natio*s also closely collaborated, to no small extent because both the states and other merchants in the Arabian seas perceived the European Christians as a single group. At the out-stations, people behaved toward outsiders and interacted among themselves as one community. Thus a certain feeling of common interest underlies all discord amongst Europeans in Asia in the seventeenth and eighteenth centuries. In this chapter we shall first consider the legal frame within which the Europeans operated. Next we shall look more closely at life in the European communities.

If European nations were partaking in an ancient system of Asian *natio*s, they nonetheless stood apart from others. Their representatives acted on behalf of states, while Persian or Indian communities did not. And European states had endowed their representatives in Asia with arms, fortresses, and warships, while Asian states had not (excepting the Ja'ariba imamate to some extent).

This presented the Islamic empires in the Arabian seas with two problems. On the one hand, how to deal with these assertive Europeans? They could not be satisfactorily framed within the existing (Islamic) legislation relative to foreign traders, for the Europeans often arrogated rights to exercise jurisdiction that belonged to the king alone. And, the other way round, how to deal with settlements of merchants from the Islamic realms within the domain of European law?

In the Arabian seas—and even, as we shall see, in Goa and Diu—the advantage of legal pluralism was that inhabitants of Islamic nations could be tried according to the rules of the *shari'a*. But these were not in force in Western Europe. Thus, in a judicial sense the Arabian seas—even Hindu Kerala or animist Madagascar—were *dar al-Islam* while Western Europe was *dar al-harb*. Since European states did not recognize legal pluralism, but substituted for it the nationality principle instead, this meant that the Safavid and Ottoman empires were endowed with jurisdiction over the members of their nationality in Europe. Since these were by and large Christians, this was a task the judicial apparatus of these two empires was neither disposed to fulfill nor prepared for.

## The *Natio*

C.H. Alexandrowicz has pointed to the resemblance between the medieval concept of *natio* and the *millet* (Turkish; *milliya* in Persian/Arab, *nagara* in Tamil/Malayalam, and *torwa* in Kiswahili).[2] It is a legal concept—less embracing yet more precise than the rather vague sociological term "trade diaspora" that is now commonly used.[3] It is essentially tied to a system of many states, involved in commercial exchange and widespread mobility (for instance, of students), where there is no commonly recognized frame of international law to appeal to, so that groups have to adjudicate their internal differences themselves, rather than appealing to the authorities.

If one wanted to become a member of a *natio*, one had to behave in accordance with the rules of behavior of the community. Such mores might or might not be committed to writing. Then—and there might be a considerable span of time involved—one was recognized by representatives or, more generally, by the assembled members as an associate. Only subsequently was one recognized by the local government as such.

The concept of *natio* in use in the seventeenth century may be characterized as a descriptive group, that is, status and identity were derived from within the group, which possessed legally institutionalized autonomy. The *natio* had a formally instituted or informally recognized internal structure of authority. Representatives, and umpires during internal differences, were elected or recognized by the *natio*. These spokesmen were either senior members in terms of residence, age, or social status, or those most likely to be recognized as spokesmen by local authorities.

One's allegiance to a *natio* was primarily determined by one's religion; thus, in Russia, Hindus from Hindustan belonged to a different *natio* than Multanis, Muslims from Hindustan. The Orthodox *natio* might include Russians, as was the case in Bahrain for example. It was defined by language too, and among Europeans in this period nationality increasingly overlapped with its modern significance; one's nationality was defined by the boundaries of the state one belonged to. Yet the *natio* arrangement is at odds with the modern perception of the legal status of foreigners. The *natio* was self-governing and the criteria according to which one became a member of a *natio* were descriptive rather than ascriptive. One had to be accepted as a member. For there existed no means to prove one belonged to a country, like the modern passport, merely the testimony of countrymen.

In the Arabian seas national belonging was not as clearly delimited as was the case in seventeenth-century Europe, since it was not demarcated by interstate conventions. There did not exist a set of institutional arrangements defining the relations among countries as was developed in Renaissance Europe, such as diplomatic missions, commercial treaties, and a host of commercial arrangements like quarantine rules, officially recognized exchange rates and so forth. Instead, the latter type of affairs was settled through agreement among the members of the *natio*. European states generally named representatives to their *natio* abroad. This was rarely the case for indigenous merchants in the Arabian seas. Nor were there institutional arrangements for the payment of representatives of the *natio*.

This lack of bilateral arrangements turned into quite a vexing issue when the Safavid and Ottoman empires were called upon to protect the interests of the Greek, Persian, Armenian, and Georgian traders who were established in Europe. The story of the way in which the Islamic empires dealt with those settlements is a complex one. The few representatives the oriental princes sent to Europe evoked a great deal of interest in Europe, but little or no attention is paid to such missions in Safavid and Ottoman sources. It is thus difficult to ascertain the intentions and the status of such missions.[4]

Basically, the Safavid empire seems normally to have taken care of the concerns of its countrymen's settlements in Europe within the framework of the Armenian *natio*. To assume jurisdiction over Christians in Europe would have conflicted with the autonomy in judicial and religious matters that the Christians had been allowed in Iran.[5] The major representative of the Armenians—both in Iran and abroad—at the court was the "mayor" (*qalantar*) of Julfa. During the reign of Abbas I he had been named by the grand vizier, for Julfa was part of his domain. Later the Julfa alderman elected him, the *qalantar* being subsequently recognized in the traditional Indo-Iranian fashion by receiving honorary robes from the shah.[6] Representatives sent by the Armenian *natio* to Europe to negotiate on commercial matters were answerable to the *qalantar,* not to the court. They were tempted to assume the prerogatives of an ambassador when in the occident, however. Whereas they mostly held no official status in Iran, in Europe they claimed to be emissaries of the king of kings abroad, so that the European courts would have to allot them the concomitant privileges—for ambassadors could, of course, import goods without having to pay customs.

In the Arabian seas the *natio* took care of the day-to-day running of trade without interference from representatives of the state. It would, for instance, look after the exercise of religion, including burial in the cemetery of one's creed, and would safeguard the places for cremation. These were important affairs. The Hindu custom of cremation was a special problem for Indian merchants at Mocha, for example. Cremation apparently offended the local population and the imams repeatedly issued orders to prohibit it.[7]

If there were disputes with local officials, the *natio* would submit a "humble petition" to the central administration. Often it was really not so unassuming: it might threaten that if demands were not conceded to, members of the *natio* would cease business, boycott the port, or abandon it altogether. Only in the very last instance would merchants appeal for the arbitration of the government of their native land. The king might then send an ambassador to mediate. Thus, Persia sent an embassy to Siam in 1685 to negotiate—according to the account bequeathed to us by its secretary Sheikh Ibn Ibrahim—an official right for the Persians to elect a chief for their rapidly increasing community in Ayuthia. He was also to arbitrate internal differences that had arisen within the *natio*.[8]

Some representatives of the *natio* were closely linked to courtiers and therefore enjoyed the status of an official. A case in point is the position of the *nakhuda*s of the ships that the Mughal Empire sent to Mocha in the 1690s. Since the main purpose of those vessels was to convey poor hajjis to the holy places, one may suspect the *nakhuda*s were often a Mughal *amir* or at least a member of the tribe of the Prophet. Standing they certainly had. When arriving at the sea gate, the *nakhuda* "was fetched to town in a palanquin and the entire town was afoot to receive him."[9]

The assembly of the *natio* functioned as court of appeal during commercial lawsuits and for mediation during financial entanglements too. There were in the Arabian seas no centralized or government-sanctioned economic institutions like insurance companies and exchanges, as were found in Europe. Lacking such arrangements to insure against commercial risk, merchants would not—and, better, should not—turn to the government when involved in commercial litigation. For to involve the local government in an internal affair of the *natio* was outrageously expensive: in Persia costs involved in recovering contested property might run to 50 to 60 percent of its value. And the king's mills ground very slowly. In the Safavid kingdom commercial disputes might take decades: verdicts by one governor were often not implemented by the next, so the case had to be staged all over again.[10] In Mughal India the situation was, if anything, worse.

The *natio* also looked after diplomatic attendance at court. For instance, the Armenian *natio* in Agra financed a representative to hand presents to Emperor Aurengzeb on the occasion of his installation to the throne, much to the frustration of the Dutch and English agents, since the Armenian was allowed an earlier audience than his Western European competitors.[11] The presentation at the court of cases involving commercial litigation was generally administered by agents (*vakils*). They were allowed a share of the sums involved in claims.

The *natio* was not a formally arranged institution, however, as was the case among European traders and to an extent the Armenians. Hindu or Muslim traders do not seem to have used written statutes, for instance, to be consulted during litigation and signed when becoming a member of a *natio* like those used by the European traders and the Armenians.

Rather, Indian communities were tied through sects and the veneration of locally sacred objects that were probably linked to analogue objects in India. A case in point is the *bhoti* tree near Kung, which was held in special veneration by Jain merchants. The Dutch broker Sutanji Set got involved in a long dispute when he broke some branches and was obliged to pay a hefty indemnity. Indian merchants could be brought before Brahmin judges. Cases often had to be tried in court in the presence of a Brahmin juridconsult. Brahmin communities overseas, scriptural prohibitions notwithstanding, were not exceptional, as for example in Mocha and Muscat.[12]

Islamic merchants have traditionally been linked through the common veneration either of a saint or of learned men. In due course members of an Islamic *natio* abroad might construct genealogical trees tying them either to the tribe of the Prophet or to a famous place of learning (like Shiraz or Taif).

Whether or not such claims were spurious, they did provide local converts with a niche in Islamic tradition. For nationality and creed were descriptive rather than ascriptive. In describing oneself as of "the Moorish creed" one did not have to be Arab or even strictly adhere to the Islamic faith. It was thus among the Antemoro on Madagascar, where the observance of Islam is largely confined to not eating pork and where the *ghazi*s were seen as powerful "medicine men" (*ombasy*) rather than as propagators of the faith. It meant that one might have developed a pedigree linking oneself to the Arab Peninsula or to Arabian towns and objects. One could choose to be Arabic while having no true ancestral links with the peninsula. In Madagascar, again, the Zafi Ramini (the sons of Rahman) claim to derive from the uncle of Muhammad but their Arab—and even Islamic—credentials appear to be very dubious.[13]

## European *Natio*s in the Arabian Seas

The legal frame in which the European nations, where they did not enjoy sovereign power, traded consisted of "court orders" (*farmans*): writs whereby certain rights had been bestowed on the Dutch, Portuguese, French, Portuguese, and Danish traders, and special relevant regulations instituted (*hasbul hukm* or *raqm* in Persia, *qaulnameh* in Oman and India).[14]

There was a difference between the Mughal empire and Persia, and between the British and the Dutch there. In the Mughal empire the original *farmans*, which granted the English, Dutch, and French freedom of religion and a fixed custom due without additional imposts, were irrevocable. "Later attempts to change or enhance the effect of the original *farman* were either pointless or harmful," P. Ketting noted.[15] In Persia, on the other hand, the *farman*s were brought under renewed scrutiny when a new *shah in-shah* ascended to the throne. The privileges had then to be reconfirmed, for which one normally had to send an emissary. The British position in Persia differed from the Dutch. The British-Persian treaty of 1622, which granted the British free trade and a share of the customs of Hormuz in return for their assistance in expelling the Portuguese from there, was a permanent compact. So too was the Persian-Portuguese treaty of 1626.[16]

Although there were some differences in focus between the *farman*s granted to the Portuguese and to other nations, most stipulated at least the following:

The Europeans could freely move through the territory of the king and trade there. They would have to pay customs, generally reduced ones, at the place where the goods were imported but would not be burdened by new or additional levies or by road dues. They could freely observe religious duties and were free from impositions on religious grounds. They could bury their dead in a Christian cemetery and would not be converted by force. Generally, it was provided that Europeans would enjoy some special advantages over other nations: for instance, stolen goods would be rendered, as would wares salvaged from shipwrecks. Europeans would also enjoy primacy in suits on outstanding debts.

The Portuguese—more attentive to this matter than the VOC or the EIC—generally stipulated that they could freely found mission stations and that missionaries were permitted to spread the Gospel. More importantly, in some cases the Portuguese also obtained the right that converts would be under the jurisdiction of the Portuguese church and sometimes under Portuguese extraterritorial law. The latter prerogative that the Portuguese extorted from the rajah of Cochin was asserted by the VOC, too. So indigenous Christians in Cochin (but not elsewhere in Kerala) were under VOC jurisdiction.[17]

Most important were extraterritorial rights: Europeans could exercise jurisdiction over the members of their *natio*. And Companies and the Estado were at least liable to be heard when a member of their *natio* was involved in a suit involving a "native." The criteria according to which one qualified as belonging to the European *natio* might differ. In general, one was considered to be a member of a *natio* if one's father had the nationality concerned. Others might enjoy some degree of protection too: indigenous personnel in the factories, the broker and—in Persia in the seventeenth century and in Cochin—indigenous merchants operating with a safe conduct of the *natio*. These merchants would pay the reduced customs allotted the Europeans.[18] Generally, other *natio*s did not enjoy this right. However, the protection of indigenous personnel under European law did not extend to immunity from criminal prosecution.[19]

### *Settlers and Colonists*

Those European communities on the shores of the Arabian seas consisted of a few thousand persons mainly earning their living by trade and war. Yet in the thirties and forties ambitious schemes were proposed in France and England to establish agricultural communities in Madagascar as well, a vast and dimly known land that, surely, had more appeal on a map than on the ground. Such designs were partly inspired by the noble motive of sheltering Huguenots and dissenters from religious persecution. But they were intended also to provide a not quite so noble cover for interlopers on the EIC's monopoly, in the case of the British Assade Company, and a cloak for very dishonorable piracy in the case of the first French East India and Madagascar Company of 1640.[20]

The Assade Company, founded in 1646, was to colonize "Assade's Island" (Nossi Bé, named after its ruler) off Madagascar and establish a settlement of Dissenters there. This island, which had long been visited by ships from India could serve as an entrepôt for the navigation to Europe too. According to one Portuguese account, the four ships outfitted by the Assade Company were well received by Sultan Assad—wholly ignorant of the English plans. The English secretly seized an island near Nossi Bé, where they began to plant sugarcane and built a fortress. A Portuguese captain, mindful of his duty to this king and his fatherland, advised Assad to evict the English. Assad attacked the settlement, killed most settlers, and imprisoned the others. A few remaining colonists were hastily evacuated from the island in 1652.[21]

The protracted French attempt to establish the settlement Fort Dauphiné on Antongil Bay (from 1641 to about 1672) was a much more substantial affair, involving more than 5,000 *colons*, largely drawn from Brittany, and huge sums from the French treasury. Yet despite all this effort, it too was an utter failure.[22]

The French were demoralized and decimated by yellow fever and malaria. Those sturdy sons of Brittany's stony soil proved incapable of adapting to the tropical swamps of Madagascar. Foodstuffs did not flourish in those torrid bogs, so the colonists had to barter rice with the interior. Since they were insufficiently furnished with beads, coral, and mirrors from France, supplies of provisions soon faltered.

Prompted by a hungry belly, the French resorted to stealing cattle and rice from the neighboring Antemoro villages. This—as much as the kidnapping of local women by the mainly male settlers—did not endear them to their initially quite friendly neighbors. When the Antemoro began to raid French settlements to obtain the firearms with which the French were terrorizing them, the French were sucked into a maelstrom of looting, slaving, and carnage.

"There are only 77 of us"—director É. de Flacourt wrote to the captain of Mozambique in 1657—"amongst a million barbarians, who are bent on nothing but our loss and destruction." "For four years we have been continually at war with the [white] grandees of this province and with their Negro subjects."[23] The Dutch, English, and Portuguese, of course, were only too eager to provide the Antemoro with guns and ammunition, for they considered Fort Dauphiné, rightly, as a den of piracy.[24]

The hope for a mineral bonanza (for the interior was reputedly rich in iron, gold, and copper) petered out, as did that of selling locally grown indigo and tobacco to the European market. The few products that could have been exported from Fort Dauphiné—cattle, sugar (this crop did flourish), ambergris, and ebony—were burdened by high transport costs. Antongil Bay was not on the normal routes of ships heading for Insulinde or India. Those goods were not fit for ballast nor could they be sold on the European market.[25]

The traders of Nantes soon lost interest in the enterprise. By default the crown had to send succor but this was hampered by continuous disagreements in Versailles on the policy to follow: was Fort Dauphiné to be a colony or merely a trading station? The few surviving colonists were finally evacuated to Bourbon in 1672, though a few may have settled among the indigenous population.

Although these attempts to organize colonies failed, there was in the Arabian seas, as elsewhere in Asia, a difference between large settlements with well-established European communities and the isolated factories and out-stations with their nomadic population of merchants, mercenaries, missionaries, and mariners.

As a major settlement, consider pleasant Cochin around 1700, where one might meet, apart from the VOC personnel (200 Dutch men and a few women), 750 settlers. Those *vrijburgers* included professional men like a surgeon, a clockmaker, two blacksmiths, a gardener, marketers, woodworkers, a bookbinder, a tailor, and a shoemaker; a host of Luso-Indian women in the oldest profession; and even a band of actors and musicians.[26]

Such communities generally consisted, as was the case at Batavia, of "movers" (*trekkers*)—personnel who, after the expiration of their contract with the Company, would be homeward bound again—and "settlers" (*blijvers*) who had founded a family in Asia.[27] *Blijvers* are mainly found among Dutch and Portuguese—the two largest European communities in Asia—but around Tranquebar there was in 1650 also a small community of Danish settlers.[28]

***Women: Caryatids of Empire***

If the pillar of the European household was the father, and the inheritance was generally along the male line, in Asia one could not erect a family on that pillar, for men mostly died younger than women. Living quarters of junior males were cramped and unsanitary both at sea and ashore. They were frequently posted to new assignments with new hazards to their health. They might even die in battle. With their husbands either dead or absent, the continuity of family life was safeguarded by widow or wife. "Gentry" lines, with a hereditary stake in empire, budded in Asia, like Mello e Castro at Goa—the only family from Goa to provide a viceroy in the seventeenth century—generally along the female line.[29] Widows often inherited estates and would run them as capably as any male *fidalgo*. In Mozambique the men were also often away on lengthy voyages to the interior and the African wives or daughters had to administer the affairs of the estates.[30] And, to be sure, such were truly "transfrontier women"—whether in Mozambique or among the buccaneers on Madagascar.

> I will not pretend to compare them to Europeans, and yet I can't help confessing it is with pleasure I think of mine and with concern I remember our parting. For as to their fidelity, behaviour to their husband, good-natured dispositions and agreeable conversation, so far as their little knowledge extends, I think the Europeans must not compare with them.[31]

Thus wrote Robert Drury, but this obviously did not apply only to Africa. The significance of the transfrontier women in the Praças do Norte is attested to by the formidable figure of Dona Inez de Miranda, who—from her fortified mansion at Bombay—continued to defy both the English and the Portuguese crown with continuous suits until 1678. At Bassein and Daman the crown often tried to impose either a guardian or—preferably—a husband upon those formidable females. This was firmly rejected by the Bassein families. Especially resented was the regulation that women were to marry Portuguese men; there were sufficient eligible mates in India. Moreover, many Portuguese were not willing to establish a homestead at all but would rather return home. Quite a number of women remained single and ran their estates on their own.[32]

That women were the pillars of European empire equally applies to Portuguese Cochin and to Goa. Yet Goa was at first sight a rigid, patriarchal society where, as the lusty Pyrard de Laval complained, women were jealously guarded by their menfolk. They were not allowed to go outside if not wearing the veil and were constantly kept under the surveillance of their (Indian) maidservants or even of black eunuchs.[33] Still, Dona Beatrice de Mello e Castro was in the

1660s one of the main shipowners at Goa since her husband was too occupied with being viceroy. That women would effectively partake in Portuguese trade was, in fact, to be expected, as they were often given a share in a "concessionary voyage." The Count of São Vicente, who had been allowed two voyages to China, sent his aunt Isabella Botelho to India to take care of this investment, for example.[34]

As has been pointed out in many studies, European women were at a premium in Asia. Gentlemen XVII, the board of directors of VOC, tried to quench this thirst for female companionship by sending "maiden ships" to Asia. Eligible virgins were to be recruited from orphanages in the Netherlands.[35] Such an "emergency solution" was far too expensive to be used regularly, however. The lower-ranking personnel in particular were forced (if such is the word) to marry Indian or Luso-Indian wives. Admittedly, in Ceylon, where the Company had previously tried to entice servants into wedlock, the "committee of correspondence" of the VOC (the Haagsch Besoigne) was told:

> That there is little furtherance in procreating. That the women are mostly dishonest and have earlier often been prostitutes, so that the soldiers are immediately sorry having married such wives. And that there is no relying on such soldiers during an enemy attack, because they have only one wish and that is to be rid of their wives.[36]

But if the low-ranking man was perhaps forced, high-ranking personnel often chose to do the same. Governor Dianat Khan of Surat invited the most important women resident at the Dutch factory in 1701 to spend a night of "drink and merry-making" with those of his harem. The "black lady" of Chief Merchant van Breen, the "méstizo little girl" (*'t mestieze nonnetje*) of Director Zwaardecroon, and "the four whoring black sluts" (*vier swarte hoeren van meiden*) Assistant Merchant A. Schlosser had recently brought with him from Agra gladly went. But Deodati—our informer here—would under no circumstance allow his three daughters to attend. "My love for my daughters is so great that I cannot allow them to hear the sinful talk commonly used by those luxurious and lascivious Moorish women."[37]

Indian spouses were not only a major factor in the acculturation of the Dutch personnel; they might also provide them with an important link with Asian traders. This applies in particular to Surat and Persia in the early seventeenth century. The pristine Companies' trade was then conducted by vigorous teenagers, constrained neither by conventions nor by regulations of the Company. The Companies' fortunes depended upon the initiatives of their servants—the amorous ones as well. Their sweethearts would provide them with an important tie to Asian traders. At Surat and Isfahan this included Armenian merchants engaged in the overland trade—elsewhere, as at Laribandar, *banias*.[38] Jan Smidt, the Dutch envoy to Shah Abbas I, tells us, for example, that the factory of the honorable Company at Isfahan was, during the term of office of director Hubertus Visnich, not a neat trading station but rather a messy Armenian household. Visnich had the factory rebuilt at a cost for the Company of 20,000 guilders "to dwell there with his mistress and her ilk."[39]

Likewise the Portuguese (and certainly the Spanish) crown had vehemently objected to Portuguese soldiers betrothing heathen women. The crown tried to recruit eligible virgins, *orfães do rey* (orphans of the king), to be sent to Asia. But we had better leave the question of their virginity aside: girls sent to India in 1636 were mostly "of questionable reputation." If a soldier was willing to marry such a maiden, he would be rewarded at least with an honorable discharge from military duties, or even—as on the Zambesi, where the lack of white women even more than of men was particularly acute—with a *prazo*. "It seems your majesty is mainly sending soldiers to India to provide grooms for poor families here," Chancellor A. Cotta muttered. Yet these official attempts to constrict the marriage market easily turned into a heavy burden. The number of *orfães do rey* should not be underestimated: there were 400 of them at Goa in 1684. For, with ever more people in Goa getting ever poorer, ever more girls were sent to the orphanage. In 1684 people were seriously concerned that the *recolhação* (state orphanage) would have to be closed because of this. Viceroy Count of Alvor proposed getting rid of the surplus by marooning female orphans on the Zambesi, which might lure males to go there too.[40] Even so, the newly arrived soldiers preferred the free market for both their sexual and material needs.

There exists a whole lore, sweet as cherry pie, about the Indian nautch girls (*bailardeiras*) that those virile warriors preferred in their crib. Yet even then, people not only told tales about lascivious Indian women but also earned a lot of money on them. Goa was, in spite of the ubiquitous sermonizers, a society of loose morals where arrack was distilled and love was for sale. As at Macao, while Goa's trade declined, new outlets were found after 1663 in gambling, drinking, and fornication, so that—according to Canter Vischer, a vicar—"merrymaking and prostitution has mounted to a summit of unholiness" there. Many a *fidalgo* would put his women slaves or serfs to work in taverns. In Bassein *foreiros* (Portuguese landlords) would adopt slave girls in their households. They would learn to dance and sing and, when they reached adulthood, be sold to temples on the mainland. It would seem most *bailardeiras* were serfs, in both Goa and Macao.[41] Those booming inns and brothels could welcome visitors from a wide area. There was Fort São Estevão (at Chapóra-Bardes), for example, of which the viceroy had heard that "wine is sold in a tavern there and after food and drink, not only inhabitants but Hindus from the other shore as well, often take a nap."[42]

There were bitter complaints about the *bailardeiras*, who, it was thought, should be expelled "both to advance the health of our inhabitants and their Christian faith," as the viceroy exclaimed in 1703. Bestowing more money on his mistress than his wife ruined many a *fidalgo*. The *bailardeiras* from the mainland were to be banished from Goa—the sooner, the better—by threat of penal labor and flogging, it was decreed. This did not have any results. But fortunately, the Inquisition noted in 1722, most prostitutes came from the mainland, though it was worth reproach that a few good Christian girls could also be encountered in houses of ill repute.[43]

Yet there was an economic as much as a sexual attraction involved, since a liaison to Indian maidens might allow Portuguese *soldados* to gain access to the (overland) trading networks of their Saraswat or *bania* family. Or—both in India and on the Swaḥili Coast—marriage might serve to convert commercial ties into blood ties, to cement strategic alliances, or to "bend" genealogies to serve the most convenient interests of commerce or politics.[44]

Thus the *senado da câmera* of Goa proposed that poor Portuguese soldiers should marry the daughters of rich Brahmins. In return for this favor such Brahmin families should be permitted the right to assume offices. This was partly to provide poor soldiers with an income, partly to provide for offspring willing to take up arms, unlike Saraswat Brahmins, "for their sect does not allow it." Love and marriage takes two families, though. While *soldados* were perhaps well willing to espouse Indian girls, Brahmins were extremely reluctant to betroth their daughters to Portuguese: what prospects did they have to offer? They rather sought grooms from wealthy families from the mainland.[45]

## Soldiers of Fortune

Life was short in the Indies—many a fortune was soon gained and sooner lost. Wealth was generally not acquired through inherited nobility, but gentry position through wealth. This even applied to smug Bassein, "a town where everybody takes such pride in his title that it is generally known as *Dom* Bassein," to quote Manuel Godinho. A scrutiny of the register of dues paid for fiefs (*tombo*) of Bassein reveals that many scions of the "ancient nobility," whose worn tombstones still pave the Bassein churches, were originally not of noble descent at all. They were merely referred to as *soldado*, or commoner. But in Bassein individuals considered themselves noblemen if they possessed an estate, and would behave and title themselves likewise.[46]

That was the case not only in Bassein. Thus friction occurred in Portuguese India between the *índicos*, with their recently acquired or invented noble titles, and the *reinois*, the "second sons of illustrious nobles" with whom the ships from Portugal yearly encumbered India. And the *índicos* had cause to be disgruntled. There were many seasoned soldiers, born in India, with an excellent record of service, the Conselho Ultramarino agreed with the Governors of India in 1691. They were much more capable than the silly youngsters habitually sent from Portugal. But those people, the Conselho Ultramarino decided, simply did not have the necessary "standing" (*aquelles respeitos necessarios*) to qualify for commanding a fortress.[47]

Europeans were linked with each other not primarily through institutions of government but rather through ecclesiastical and charitable ones. In this respect the European *natio* fits with the other *natio*s in the Arabian seas. For these too grouped around priests and places of worship rather than around state institutions. This applies in particular to the Luso-Indian communities, indistinguishable from Indians were it not for their Catholic shepherd and sometimes for their representation by an elected *senado da câmera*.[48]

Equally important was the link to charitable institutions: the orphanage at Batavia with branches at Cochin and Colombo in the Dutch case, the lay brotherhood of the "holy house of charity" in Goa, Bassein, Cochin, Mozambique, Diu, and Chaul in the Portuguese case. Although the *misericórdia* was as closely related to Portuguese expansion as were the knightly orders, the *misericórdia* was not an institution tied to empire as such. In the late seventeenth century subsidiaries of the Goa *santa casa da misericórdia* were established at such dens of freebooters as San Tomé and (perhaps) Tanore.[49]

To be on the board of a *santa casa da misericórdia* was a manifestation of "being somebody" in the Portuguese empire, as was being a regent of the *weeskamer*. By participating on the board of the charitable institutions a member of the local elite could distinguish himself. And, indeed, one needed to be very wealthy to be nominated as *provedor* of the *misericórdia*. One was expected to make a substantial donation, which in Goa was to consist of 3,000 xeraphins at least. The *misericórdias* were completely autonomous. This was not the case with the *weeskamer*, where the governor-general, "considering the opinion of respectable citizens," named the board.[50]

Such a devotion to charity was not only prompted by Christian brotherly love. In the Portuguese empire the estates of the deceased and homeward-bound were deposited in the treasury of the *misericórdia*. These were converted in bills, which could be cashed throughout the Portuguese empire. Putting money into the *misericórdia* was an excellent way to hide unlawfully acquired property. This induced Pedro da Silva to plea for at least rigorous control of the elections to the *misericórdia*. A tiny circle of "wealthy families and their clients" now ruled it, and as a hive of fuzzy deals rather than as a haven of Christian brotherhood, Pedro da Silva suspected.[51]

Dutch free merchants and free burghers throughout Asia also used the *weeskamer* as a clearinghouse to remit property within Asia or to Europe. They were a member of the Dutch nation through the *weeskamer*.

As to the importance of ecclesiastical institutions, there was—of course—a difference between the Dutch and English on the one hand, and the Portuguese and Danish—and to a lesser extent French—settlements on the other. The church played a dominant role in social life in those establishments; this was not so in Madras or Batavia. These places were perhaps more secularized, or at any rate outwardly more devoted to earthly gain. However—as L. Blussé and H. Niemeijer have argued—in the Dutch settlements too the church was an important instrument to glue together the rather heterogeneous communities established under the guns of the Company's fortresses, in particular since the Protestant church propagated a norm of conduct that at least provided a common standard of immorality.[52] This would, no doubt, apply to Madras as well.[53]

Cochin and Bombay differ from these Protestant settlements: these were by and large Catholic towns with a slight Protestant minority. This drove a wedge between the Catholic and the Protestant populations. However, at the out-stations one could not be too demanding as regards the church attendance of the flock. For example, the tiny French Jesuit mission post at Surat was looking out for the Portuguese as well, although it sometimes appeared as if the only agreement between the Portuguese and the French mission in the Orient was to disagree.[54]

We can make a rough distinction among various social groups within the European *natios*, which was rather an elusive social divide than a tight judicial one, however. First, there were the higher personnel ashore, represented on the board of a factory by the captains and helmsmen of Company ships, or ships with a commission from the crown (for the French and Portuguese). In the French and Portuguese cases these individuals were generally to be present during meetings of the board of a settlement. This might cause quite a stir, since French and Portuguese admirals of the fleet presided over the chief merchants and members of their *natio*. This was bitterly resented by the Portuguese *natio* at Surat, for example, when faced with the haughty admiral Duarte Barbosa de Machedo, who—after a quarrel with the viceroy—had left Goa in anger. By his high-handed conduct de Machedo immediately antagonized everybody in Surat and was finally assassinated by his own countrymen.[55]

Second was the lower personnel servicing crown or Company, to whom we shall return in a moment.

Third, we have individuals named in the citizen register in settlements with the franchise, like Madras, Bombay, Goa, Bassein, Colombo, and Chaul, or listed in a muster roll of local citizenry, such as was drafted by the VOC at Cochin.

Fourth were free burghers who were permanently established in Asia but not registered as burghers. Legally, the difference between citizens and noncitizens was an important one, particularly in the Portuguese settlements, where the citizens enjoyed protection by the city. But in practice this was a most vague distinction. Chaul was supposed to have 39 citizens. Ten of them were dead or had somehow "disappeared," while 10 other Portuguese did have a say in sessions of the senate but were not citizens. In reality, one apparently became more of a citizen the whiter one's skin was.[56]

Fifth, there were "natives" professing Catholicism and generally speaking creole Portuguese: mestizos or *topazes*, generally the underclass of the European communities.[57] This was, as we have seen, a significant group in Goa and in Cochin, where the *topazes* were organized in rival groups under four captains—local strongmen who took care of the recruitment of mercenaries among the community. The *topazes* at Cochin were largely earning a living through soldiering.[58]

The *topazes* of low-caste descent and even the Christian Saraswats were subjected to a great deal of racial discrimination in the Portuguese settlements. There were plenty of able Indians in the Estado, but if one were to allow "natives" a captaincy, the bishop of Cochin considered, Portuguese would no longer apply. Again, in 1650 Dom Phelipe de Mascarenhas had written Lisbon that it would be logical if services in parochial churches in Bardes and Salcete would be administered by native clergy, "as they know the language." This was also a lot cheaper than delivering the services by the Franciscan and Augustinian orders. The crown would not permit it: the natives "are untalented and display no drive to overcome any difficulty they might face."[59]

Such racism was not confined to those born in Portugal. Most of the *fidalgos* making up the Daman senate had probably but the faintest tie of blood with Portugal. Still, one of them successfully insisted that "a branch of blacks, which we call natives and are the offspring of moors and Hindus," should not be allowed to acquire land. And, though they might be married to Indian women, there was racism by poor whites too. In 1700 the viceroy drafted a special writ to protect Indian soldiers sailing on board of Portuguese vessels from insults and beatings by their Portuguese mates.[60]

All the same, some *topazes* might acquire a considerable fortune, like Louis Tayspil, who was acting as representative of the VOC to the rajah of Cochin. But according to Commander C. Zwaardecroon, Tayspil belonged back in the gutter where he came from.

> One has to remark in this respect that he is a mestizo and of lowly descent, for his mother has been here a certain lady of easy virtue, called Cassa Moqua. And it certainly merits consideration that such a guy [*soodanig eenen borst*], whose father never married his mother, has obtained so much influence over the affairs of the Company.[61]

Finally, there is an important, but hard to identify, group of roaming freebooters (*lançados*), who had established themselves under the sway of indigenous kings. The Companies and the Catholic church made vague claims to jurisdiction over them. We shall return to that group later.

## Collaboration and Strife

The administration of all Companies and of the Estado tried to limit access to Asia to its countrymen and exclude foreigners. Dutchmen were not permitted to sail to Asia on foreign ships, for example, and in principle the Company was able to imprison any Dutchman found on such a vessel.[62] Yet at the out-stations their servants participated in a closely linked European face-to-face community, complete with the tensions inevitable within small and closed communities.

One might, for example, cite the constant petty quarrels in Surat between the French on the one side, the English and Dutch on the other. Strife erupted on such seemingly trifling issues as French attempts to raise the flag after a victory of the French arms or set off fireworks in honor of the birthday of the Sun King. With trials and petitions the others tried to forestall this, right up to the highest authority: the Mughal emperor himself. Quarrels cost several lives too. It was near farce in 1688: solemnly hoisting the colors, celebrating mass upon yet another victory of the invincible hosts of France, and other such distractions were about the only pursuits of the Sun King's loyal subjects at Surat. They had received no goods to trade in whatsoever. But this was in the age of the baroque, after all—rank was a matter of the utmost importance.[63]

Moreover, the Indian bystanders were expecting insistence on such matters. For the Europeans were always closely observed by a host of servants and an undifferentiated "crowd of natives." Whenever anyone left the factory in Surat or a house in Goa he was immediately engulfed by spectators. The Europeans acted as if on a stage (or were performing "colonial mimicry," in the currently fashionable terminology) and were well aware of it. The Portuguese crown objected, for example, against the violent quarrel that erupted among the chapter of the cathedral of Goa in 1659 "since it causes a general scandal, even amongst the natives."[64]

Yet, in spite of this incessant bickering, the Companies were closely interlinked. When sending messages to Europe all Companies and the Portuguese used the services of the Carmelite missionaries at Basra and Baghdad. These were French priests.[65] The VOC and Estado da Índia often entrusted dispatches to English or Danish ships from Macassar to Goa, to Batavia from Surat, or from either to the homeland. Gentlemen XVII often suspected captains of English and Danish Indiamen of peeping into the correspondence of other Companies, but generally everybody seems to have respected the rule that one was not to open a competitor's mail.[66]

Again, the Europeans often used the same indigenous personnel. Vira Sen, the broker of the VOC at Mocha in 1699, acted on behalf of the English, Dutch, and Danes. The VOC was not altogether glad of this and ordered him to toil for the Dutch alone. Vira Sen argued, convincingly, that the VOC traded too rarely at Mocha to have this pay and the VOC had finally to agree: he had a great deal of influence on the government of the town—so much so that he succeeded in obtaining a writ by which he was named sole broker of all Europeans.[67]

At Surat where, Danes excepted, in 1700 all Europeans were represented, it was usual that when an important member of the European *natio* was buried, a funeral procession (*lijkstate*) was arranged. English, Dutch, Jesuits, and French chief representatives would ride to the Company's burial ground in their oxcarts "accompanied by a moorish horse-guard." One attended the funeral and afterward rushed to a copious dinner. "And truly it is a disgrace that when mourning, one has so little attention for the deceased," Deodati sourly remarked.[68]

During merry occasions as well the Europeans would be constantly in touch. The English parson baptized children born in the Dutch compound. The English chief merchant often acted as godfather. Dutch usually attended the English sermon. The Dutch lecturer from the Gospel (*krankbezoeker*) at Surat, when submitting a petition for advancement to vicar, adduced he had been schooled in theology by the English parson and in philosophy by a Portuguese Jesuit.[69]

Friendships might flourish. At Bandar Abbas English and Dutch personnel would visit each other's factory weekly "and it's a miracle if they part sober: He, that holds out longest, makes it a matter of triumph and values himself for it as a boon companion would on the same score in England," J. Lockyer discovered.[70] The voyage of a combined Dutch-English fleet sent to combat the Portuguese in the Gulf in 1626 appears to have been quite a merry trip as well. English and Dutchmen "were utterly drunk and the chiefs were indulging in fun, like throwing pillows at each other with the fillings and cotton flying all around—a scandalous sight to witness."[71]

The Dutch and English Companies would sometimes collaborate when faced with a common commercial challenge. For example, the two Companies drew one line in buying coffee at Mocha in 1646 when the price, due to a poor harvest, threatened to mount. Personnel often preferred obtaining a "great cargo" above sound commercial reason, however, and tried to outwit their competitors without much regard for the price. VOC director C. Overschie in Persia—to mention a notorious case—tried to oust both the English competitors (and the possible competitor of a mission that had just arrived from the German principality Schleswig-Holstein) from the trade in Persian silk by attempting to buy the entire crop in 1636. He was recklessly borrowing money to attain this, which was to cause the VOC lots and lots of trouble later on.[72]

If we are well informed about troubles brewing between Europeans in the tavern, we are not nearly as familiar with commercial dealings.[73] But such mutual trade, illegal for VOC servants, was of some importance. J. Vernati, chief accountant at Batavia in 1640, used English ships to transport privately traded goods to the Netherlands. He was handed beer and wine by the English chief merchant at Banten, which he sold at a considerable profit in Batavia. We know too that in the first half of the seventeenth century the English offered more favorable rates for bills of exchange drafted on their homeland than did the VOC. The Dutch often invested in this. We will deal with other cases, and with the much closer cooperation between English and Portuguese, later on.[74]

The Europeans were also forced to act together when faced with a common threat. When Surat was, for instance, threatened by Maratha invasion, the EIC and VOC servants, and the French later, would deliberate over how to face this. During Shivaji's sack of Surat in 1664 the Dutch also lent a number of soldiers to the sorely pressed English factory. But the French always remained hypersensitive. If they were consulted by the Dutch, they had to be consulted first and not the English; the English would not accept this in turn and so forth. This rather often wrecked such plots.[75]

Very often such unity was short-lived when one of the Companies, or the Portuguese, took up arms against a perceived common threat. The president of the Board of Directors, Sir J. Childe, for instance, justified the English war with the Mughal empire in 1689 by pointing out that Mughal depredations harmed all Europeans alike. The Dutch would at least not interfere with, and at best support, the good English cause, he hoped.[76]

Indeed, VOC director G. Vosburg at Surat pleaded to the Mughal officials to treat the English gently—in any case not to throw them in a dank dungeon. However, Vosburg was immediately prepared to swallow those pleas when threatened with penalties. Perhaps this Mughal behavior was not as abhorrent to them as they claimed it was. Surat may not have forgotten how the English had, five years previously, forestalled a Dutch attempt to blockade Bandar Abbas by immediately selling the right to wave an English flag to the highest bidder. The situation was, by the way, worse in Bengal, where the English attempts to block the entrance to the Hugly River in 1692 led to gunfights with Dutch ships.[77]

After having paid attention to the core of the European *natio,* let us now return to a marginal group: the European freebooters active in Asia.[78]

## European Freebooters in Asia

In general, Europeans no doubt went to Asia for lust of adventure, and—first and foremost—"*pour faîre ma fortune*," as J. Chardin put it very candidly.[79] And no doubt too it was possible to make a fortune by ascending in the Company's hierarchy through merit alone. This, as we have remarked in the case of Bassein, was not impossible in the Portuguese case either. Undoubtedly the administration of the Estado was studded with idlers, chosen because of their birth—as critics never tired of pointing out. But a glance at the petitions to obtain an office still leaves one with the impression that in most cases the title *fidalgo* was not an automatic qualification for a position. One's past record of service was seriously considered and, at least in the Conselho Ultramarino, debated.[80]

To climb this stairway to the clouds one had to overcome both the Asian and African climate and—not the lesser problem— the fact that at the factories there was no lack of backbiting, petty hatreds, and jealousies, of which we shall witness plenty of cases in chapters 7 and 8. Even then success was far from assured. This was especially so for the Dutch East India Company, which, unlike the English and the French, did not respect seniority when naming personnel.[81]

It is understandable that many tried to escape this suffocating environment. And this was not very difficult, since a deserter could easily hide and look for a job among European settlers or in an indigenous court.

Part of the European settlers in Asia consisted of people who had come to Asia on their own, either on a Portuguese ship or along the overland route through the Levant. Even though the Portuguese crown had in principle to countenance any passenger bound for the Indies, and the empire was to be reserved for Portuguese alone, those regulations were not very strictly adhered to. For one thing, in the early seventeenth century—and even as late as 1672—Portuguese captains rarely bothered to draw up a muster roll, and *carreira da India* ships often had many stowaways on board.[82] But anyway, one could hardly be very fastidious about one's personnel, given the lack of available men.

For another thing, the Portuguese crown and Portuguese private traders had invested heavily in the diamond trade with Golconda, which was mainly conducted by free traders and new-Christian merchants. This greatly disconcerted the crown, which ordered in 1626 that all foreigners and heretics be banished from the Estado's territory. Some efforts were made to implement this measure, but the prohibition was not executed by force, as this would have led to a collapse of the diamond trade. The crown did, however, admonish Goa to closely monitor the foreign residents and register them in a muster roll.[83]

The second road may sound rather adventurous to modern readers. But the Syrian desert was still a highway of commerce in the seventeenth century and it was quite possible even for humble folk to traverse these wastes. The Portuguese did try to dam the flow of traders shuttling between Aleppo and Hormuz by demanding that traders bear a safe conduct from the captain of Hormuz. The price differential between the various entrepôts across the desert made it feasible to earn the costs of the trip through small transactions. There were several relay stations, which were connected to the European settlements at Aleppo, at Baghdad, and at Mosul. Only small means were necessary to pay for the trip. The journey through Anatolia was more hazardous, yet it was also by no means impossible to make this crossing.[84]

For example, on board the ship *Delfshaven* anchored at the Basra roadstead in 1646, G. Bouwman (boatswain) was put on trial. He was accused of having conspired together with the sailmaker of the *Pauw* and with S. Leven, assistant merchant, who had come to Basra in secret. They intended to escape to Baghdad and from there to Aleppo, aided by a French merchant who may have been connected to the French consul at Aleppo.[85]

It is not of much use to attempt to divide freely established Europeans into neat professional categories. Many freebooters, like the famous N. Manucci, regularly changed their business. However, most were nominally blacksmiths, painters, watchmakers, surgeons, and jewelers.

As to the first three groups, there was some demand in the Persian and Mughal court for knickknack-like puppets, "curiously barking toy-dogs from Nuremberg," "wax statues of women," and so forth. It was habitual for the Mughal and Safavid emperors to occasionally exhibit such wonderful things from far lands to the deeply impressed nobles. Perhaps for the same purpose a clock was also on display at the gate of the *ali kapu*. These, obviously, had to be repaired. There was also some demand for paintings, for which European artists were enlisted, like P. Angel, who was lent to the court by the VOC in 1651. European hirelings may have painted some of the Italianesque frescoes still adorning the Chihil Sutun palace in Isfahan.[86]

European surgeons were often used by Safavid and Mughal nobles, and one Dutch surgeon was even frequently consulted by the Zaiditic imam. The small settlement at Ahmedabad the VOC had a surgeon attached, not because the four servants there were continuously ill, but because Mughal nobles often consulted him.[87]

As mentioned already, trade in diamonds is a different case: gems are light and their purchase and sale require a lot of expert knowledge. The trade was controlled by a small circle of specialized dealers—mainly Sephardic Jews—who maintained a wide international network of contacts, extending from India to the Sephardic communities in the Ottoman empire and in Azerbaijan. They would often travel overland. For example, A. Pereira, a Jewish diamond trader for whom the Estates General requested a passport from the Venetian senate in 1666, wanted to sail to Smirna and depart from there with his family to India. There were Sephardic communities at Tebriz and at Isfahan, which were linked to the Jewish communities in the Levant and on the Indian coast, trading in diamonds and pearls. Those diamonds were mostly sent overland to Venice or Marseilles.[88]

Such Jewish adventurers would often travel from Goa to Golconda itself to procure diamonds there. This caused irritation in Goa; the state was drained of silver to benefit the trade of Jews and heathens in precious stones, it was objected. In 1615 the crown prohibited its inhabitants from dealing with such traders on the mainland; whatever the real impact of this decree, Jewish overland trade to Golconda appears to have declined after 1630.[89]

While these Jewish traders were closely linked to the Companies and the Estado, this bond was not as intimate as that between Latin Christian free traders engaged in the diamond trade and the Companies. It was a small but well-documented group of merchants, as some of them—J.B. Tavernier and J. van Couteren, for example—happened to be talented travel writers. Tavernier often operated on behalf of the VOC.[90] To mention two bad writers but better merchants (Tavernier went bankrupt in 1658), in 1628 the French diamond merchants F. Marineaux and J. de l'Étoille transported goods to Mocha, mainly on behalf of the VOC's director at Surat, van Hassel, in such quantity that the ships were unable to transport any other merchandise.[91]

As was the case in Europe, traders in diamonds often also dealt in precious metals. Many diamond traders doubled as bankers to the companies. For instance, the French (probably Jewish) merchant I. Baudet was, in 1641, with a backlog of 700 tomans, the major creditor to the VOC at Isfahan after Hodsia Ahmad. The Company was in debt for 250 tomans as well to one J. Adelar (Dutch spelling), an English free merchant.[92]

Most European mercenaries, active at the indigenous courts, were derived from this group of free merchants, deserters, and converts to Islam. Yet the Companies and the Estado occasionally lent personnel to the courts as well, like Angel or Corporal K. van Eeden, who was in 1673 seconded by the VOC to the Safavid court to assist in the training of Persian gunners. This might involve tangled problems relating to jurisdiction, however, particularly if such guest workers incurred debts. Thus it was problematic to rescue van Eeden from his ungrateful employer, for example. In view of those difficulties the VOC was generally extremely reluctant to lend personnel.[93] The French and English appear to have had much less vacillation.[94]

If the role of Western European mercenaries was not pronounced in the Persian administration, since one could easily buy either Russians or Poles as slaves or hire them, their role in the Deccan sultanates was very important. The mission in Bijapur existed mainly to cater to the spiritual needs of runaway slaves from Goa, who appear to have been employed in the Bijapuri army and lower administrative echelons.[95]

The Marathas in the eighteenth century mustered whole battalions of mestizos, and such a reliance on foreign manpower was somewhat of a tradition. For the Deccan sultanates had always heavily depended upon foreign recruitment. In the case of Adilshah, for example, slaves from Ethiopia or the Swahili Coast or recruits from Iraq were used. The sultanates depended upon those new recruits; they did not yet dispose of entrenched landed interests. So they constituted a group largely dependent upon the sultan, which could be helpful given the incessant fighting between opposing factions at the court.[96]

In 1638 the commander of Bijapur fortress was a certain Niamat Khan, born in Rome. A. de Witt from Brussels was enlisted by the emir Sidr Jaqut Khan as a painter and doubled as a Portuguese spy. It was customary to bestow a "fief" (*vatan*) on mercenaries. For instance, P. Andrieszoon, surgeon to Grand Vizier Mustafa Khan, received neither wage nor allowance, "but he was always told to rely on the incomes of some villages, which he did not receive either."[97]

Wherever one went in the Arabian seas one was likely to encounter a European mercenary as surgeon, painter, or military advisor. Although this concerns but a small group of people, these hirelings deserve some attention.

The sale of expertise, military in particular, in the use of firearms and, more basically, in the drill of soldiers has played an important role in the European penetration of India since in the long run Indian courts began to rely upon such know-how. This was not a new development in the eighteenth century, when European mercenaries assumed a critical role in Indian politics. European mercenaries were in fact already established in India before its "discovery": the *zamorin* had enlisted Genoese mercenaries to fight the Portuguese in 1502, for example.[98]

But the main source for military expertise, tapped by Indian courts, was the Ottoman dominion. However, by the late seventeenth century the know-how of Turkish mercenaries, particularly regarding siege artillery and mine laying, began to fall behind contemporary European knowledge. Manucci, who had a close-up view of Mughal artillery, judged that Indian fortresses would not be able to withstand a European siege train and poured scorn on Indian military discipline. The imperial host would easily give way to a few thousand European soldiers, he thought. It is possible the court was aware of this and began to recruit among Europeans, as it had always previously enlisted Turks and Persians. The Mughal court then regularly sent a commissioner to seek out European hirelings at Surat. These "consist of deserters and converts from many nations, and we are unable to inhibit these practices in this country," according to the VOC.[99]

Furthermore, these mercenaries provided the Europeans with information on the interior. The vision of most Europeans was confined to what was happening on the coast. One often relied upon hearsay or travel accounts for the hinterland. The intelligence derived from mercenaries was thus crucial for policy making. These informants would include Manucci too, who was acting as spy for the Portuguese viceroy at the Mughal court in the 1680s.[100]

Unlike Manucci, J.B. Potvlied, surgeon to Prince Azzam Tarra at the court at Aurangabad in the late seventeenth century, has not bequeathed us his memoirs. Officially, the VOC dealt through its "court informer" (*vakil*), Gokhale Das. Gokhale Das was mainly the intermediary of Dutch brokers to the court at Surat. The VOC distrusted the brokers, however, and increasingly relied on Potvlied, who was to receive a percentage of the money concerned in those disputes for which intercession at court was needed (as was the normal arrangement for a *vakil*). He was also entrusted with presents and bribes to hand to Mughal nobles. As it turned out, in 1705 Potvlied appeared to have pocketed most of the sums received without ever bringing them to the court's attention. It was thus in his own interest that the Company should quarrel with the court or, at least, that disagreements not be settled. This, then, was the fellow whom the Company was using as its intercessor at the Mughal court, a realm in which was conducted the major trade of Asia![101]

Those European mercenaries at Indian or Persian courts had already existed in the Middle Ages and such activities were given a boost by the Portuguese discoveries. For the discoveries did not destroy the ancient overland routes between Europe and Asia, along which there always flowed a trickle of migration to Asia. Various Venetian firms active in Aleppo extended their overland trade to the west coast. Whereas the Venetian role declined in the second half of the seventeenth century, firms from Marseilles—established at Aleppo—entertained a network of correspondents in Anatolia, Azerbaijan, and Iraq.[102]

There was also a small but steady trickle of slaves flowing from the Crimea to Istanbul. Some were sold to Persia and probably to Yemen too; they were mostly Polish and Russian, but there were Germans and, once in a while, English and Dutch as well. Thus Corporal J. Struijs, who was captured by the Tartars when in Russian service and subsequently sold to the Caucasus, wrote a fascinating account of his experiences in Circassian captivity.[103] Struijs's case was by no means unique: there was a small European community, mainly Germans and Poles, resident at Shamakhi on the Caspian shore in the early eighteenth century, mostly runaways. Some slaves might end up much further afield: Shuja'at Khan, the *subehdar* of Gujarat, had in 1691 a bodyguard of 30 Polish and Russian slaves.[104]

To this trickle along the overland route was added a torrent from Portuguese territory. We saw already that the Portuguese settlers normally had familial links to the interior, links that might prompt them to seek their luck beyond the Estado. J. De Silva, for example, was still listed as sergeant in Chaul in 1677 but had long since made a fortune in trade and moved to Surat.[105]

Again, in any given year about 20 to 30 *soldados* normally fled from Goa to Maratha territory. There was little possibility to forestall this, the Portuguese king sighed in 1657: "some flee because they are badly paid, others to escape punishment for crimes they have committed."[106] By 1650 there were more Portuguese soldiers in foreign service than in Portuguese forces. Perhaps they might be tempted to re-enter Portuguese service by a general pardon? The Conselho Ultramarino first wanted to consider only minor misdeeds like theft and lese majesty "both divine and profane"; it next extended the amnesty to sodomy and finally to homicide, but with no result.[107]

The violence of the VOC impoverished many *casado* communities, especially in Portugal's "southern conquests" like Malabar and the Coromandel Coast, where the *casados* out of dire need "with their family and households go to live in the land of Hindu kings, forgetting they were ever called Portuguese [*esquecendo-se do nome Português*]."[108]

The Dutch, as a matter of policy, banished "white" Portuguese from their conquered territories; this "treacherous breed" of people was seen as a potential threat to the Company. But the refugees from Cochin in 1664 were not in a position to be a menace to anyone, since they rather resembled "a ragged bunch of beggars." Some of these *casados* fled to Goa, where the council of state was soon pondering decent ways to get rid of them. Some were thrown ashore by the VOC at Surat to beg for alms at the Capuchin monastery: "they swarmed all over them like bees." And some fled to Calicut, where apparently they were given a warmer welcome. There was, at least, a sizeable Portuguese *casado* community in Calicut at the end of the seventeenth century, which conducted a busy trade with Yemen—mostly deriving from refugees from Cochin.[109]

Those Portuguese settlers were later replenished by free merchants and a drifting "European sea proletariat," as F.C. Lane would have called them: impoverished English and Dutch free burghers, their younger children, deserters, and converts to Islam.[110] In several places in the Arabian seas, for example, Bombay, Calicut, and Mozambique (where, as we shall see later, there were also buccaneers from both the American colonies and the West Indies), there were sizeable communities, and even at Surat there were in 1696 about 40 European freebooters. Again, in some cities in the interior there was a European citizenry: in 1615 there were already—to the amazement of the Spanish ambassador Don García de Silva y Figueroa—several hundred European residents at Isfahan.[111]

Let us meet two representatives of this European "sea proletariat." I will take not a case from the Arabian seas but one from Hugly. For we happen to possess a list of all European free burghers resident in Hugly in 1686 and enjoying English or Dutch protection.[112]

D.J. Jongeling went to Asia in 1662 aboard the pirate ship of H. Hugo. He deserted from this vessel in 1664. Jongeling then departed to Pulicat, where he established a household under VOC protection, married, and was blessed with two children. In 1669 he came with his family to Bengal and settled on the bazaar next to the VOC's factory at Chinsura. With his small vessel he sailed with an English passport between Bengal, the Coromandel Coast, and Arracan.

D. Joachimi came to Asia aboard a vessel of the Danish Company. He was working in the Danish settlement at Banten until this town was conquered by the VOC in 1683. The high and mighty Company then decided to send Joachimi, his wife, and three children to Batavia. Rather than going back to Denmark, Joachimi chose to remain in Asia and settle at Chinsura. There, Joachimi ran an inn, which was much frequented by Dutch sailors. Most people established at Chinsura shuttled between sailing on "Moorish" vessels, small retail trade, and work in taverns.

These were true "sea proletarians"—without a fatherland, like many of the sailors and soldiers on the factories and ships, not only since they were recruited from all over Europe but also since many were recruited in the Arabian seas.

## Rank and File

In French and Portuguese society the sailors were often considered "scum of the earth." Perhaps with some justification: in the 1630s Spanish nobles would habitually complain about the Portuguese sailors sent to India. They were insubordinate and underskilled but overpaid. Practically the only way one could attract Portuguese sailors, it appeared, was to offer them merchandise to take along in their "liberty chests" to sell at Lisbon. In 1638 it was proposed that the fleets might be better manned with sailors from Biscay or Flanders than from Portugal.[113]

And the few sailors who were available in Portugal were not likely to enlist. Most means and manpower of the monarchy were devoted to the war in Brazil; India received only the "offal." Yet "India was won by brave men, not by merchandise," the viceroy Count of Aveiras warned the crown.[114] Throughout the century sailors were badly paid, treated, and fed aboard Portuguese vessels in India, and often aboard French ones too, which caused many deserters of those two nations to repent of their act of enlisting with them.

In spite of the traditional martial spirit of the Portuguese empire, the professional capacities of the troops sent to the Orient were not rated very highly either. On the Tague, drums were beaten to announce that mercenaries were sought; "in such a small kingdom one may be sure that they will come to Lisbon" but ever fewer enlisted. Sometimes it was necessary first to entice soldiers aboard ship by announcing they were heading for Brazil and then lock them up until the ship had left port. The crown had to resort to sending convicted criminals to the East Indies—a counterproductive strategy, many there muttered, for convicts who had to choose between going to jail or to India were not very likely to risk their lives for king and fatherland.[115]

Every penitentiary in the Mediterranean thus had to be scoured by Portuguese recruiters.[116] Hirelings were enlisted not only in Portugal, but also in Italy, Spain, Germany, Flanders, and even distant Ireland. Apart from this, Dutch, English, and French deserters were also gladly accepted—especially the Frenchmen, "who are very well versed in the art of throwing grenades and are good sailors."[117]

By contrast, Dutch soldiers were held in much lower esteem than were sailors and there was often considerable friction between the two. As is well known, soldiers and sailors from all four corners of the earth manned the VOC.[118]

The situation among the English was almost identical, though the EIC may have recruited fewer personnel abroad than the VOC. To the ancient friction between soldiers and sailors in England should be added the considerable tension between the underpaid soldiers of the Company and those of the crown, who enjoyed both higher standing and higher pay. Such grudges of the English soldiers were evinced by the mutiny of Captain Keigwin at Bombay in 1683, which was prompted by long-standing grievances concerning the abysmal housing, continual arrears on payment, and general mistreatment of the soldiers. Their clothing, their rifles, and even their rations were withheld. The soldiers had to buy these goods from their officers, on which the latter were making "an excessive profit." But then again, the English soldiers were not all of the best quality, to put it mildly: they were an insubordinate lot and were keener on trafficking than on glory. It is questionable whether they were English soldiers at all, for the garrison at Bombay largely consisted of *topazes* and "Moorish" mercenaries lured from the mainland by the extravagant pay of the English: 12 pardaos, which was twice the rate in Goa. The English obtained them from the same recruiters as did the Portuguese.[119]

The Portuguese regiments too had to be replenished by gangs recruited by *fidalgos*—which generally consisted of black slaves from Mozambique—and by Asian mercenaries. These mercenaries were enlisted throughout Asia. In the direct surroundings of Goa Indian recruiters in Portuguese service often hired foot soldiers and rowers for the coastal fleets.[120] Although these *lascarins* occasionally fought together with Portuguese troops, they generally had their own leaders and were not subjected to regular drill. The Portuguese recruiters were angling in the same pond as the Marathas, and sailors generally served on both Maratha and Portuguese warships. The Portuguese *foreiros* in the northern quarters were supposed to raise private armies too. This operation had been bestowed on one Indian chief contractor: Essoji Raja Pattecar. Essoji Raja in turn had a network of subcontractors who recruited in the wide surroundings. The Portuguese army at Daman was in 1686 "aided" by a motley gang of *sidhis*, for example. They were more a danger to the Portuguese themselves than to their Maratha foes, however, as they enthusiastically looted any Portuguese village they passed through, but ran away when hearing gunshots.[121]

The Portuguese recruited much further away. Assyrian Christians were often enlisted as sailors by the Gulf fleets. "They are brave soldiers," it was said, so viceroy Count of Linhares tried to induce the entire community, consisting of about 12,000 persons, to relocate to Portuguese Ceylon, but without much success. Since they were not used to the climate, the few who did move soon perished.[122]

But those elite foreign mercenaries were, as in Mozambique, purely auxiliary to the massed peasant levee of the Portuguese. In Goa—and Cochin—there was an urban militia, financed by the guilds, that paraded every Sunday, and if they were lacking weapons, they surely did not lack spirit during their colorful cavalcade. On paper, the Portuguese could raise up to 13,000 men in Goa. Peasant militias had even before the Portuguese conquest existed in the countryside of Bardes and Salcete, where every village had to muster a number of musketeers. The peasants were to train every month, ideally under the supervision of a Portuguese captain. But, according to the Dutch in Vengurla, "they are not as reliable as the Portuguese, since the natives want to be freed of the Portuguese yoke and wish we became masters of Goa."[123]

Those mercenaries and peasant-soldiers owed an often fanatical loyalty to their leader but little or none to the king, let alone any country.[124] In Muscat the Portuguese were assisted by *lascarins* recruited in Baluchistan; there were 160 stationed there normally, "and when more are needed more can easily be drafted from the Makran Coast." "These moors haven proven valorous, gallant men: braver, in fact, than the vassals of your majesty," the viceroy believed.[125]

But since these troops were dedicated to their leader and not to any fatherland they had little objection to deserting when they thought they were treated improperly. Like the Europeans, they were part of the drifting sea proletariat. Whether the Europeans looked upon desertion as treason can be doubted, though it might be punished with keelhauling or, among the Portuguese, even with capital punishment.[126] In case of dissatisfaction, one simply moved to another employer, be it a European or an Asian one.[127] Regulations that outlawed this were of little avail in the Arabian seas and, surely, to most of the European rank and file would have appeared purely arbitrary. An English captain might conduct trade in Asia as a free skipper if he could show a license of the Company. If he did not have such a document, or wished to sail between Europe and Asia, he was an interloper who was infringing on the Company's monopoly and liable to punishment—but the possession of some official scrap of paper mattered little to him.

**Desertion**

Therefore, as was the case in Europe, armies and navies of the Portuguese and the Companies suffered constant attrition by both sickness and desertion. Resende estimated that at least one-third of the soldiers on the muster roll of the Estado were normally missing.[128]

It is logical that most servants of a Company would desert in places with a European community. (Desertion in places like Basra or Mocha was rare.) One could easily hide under the flag of another Company, and recruiters were mainly active there. After having deserted, a sailor or soldier might join the ranks of Europeans who fulfilled all kinds of jobs aboard Company, interloper, private traders', or pirates' keels. Although the Companies very often lent sailors to ships of Indian nobles, and service of European freebooters on Indian keels was relatively common in the early seventeenth century, this appears to have declined when, with the rise of the "country" fleet, more opportunities arose for employment aboard English ships. This obviously depends on how one defines "European," for Luso-Indians were commonly sailors on Indian ships.[129]

Dutch and English were both officially Protestant and would frequent the same services and places of entertainment—so desertion led to almost constant altercations between those two. After 1692 the exasperated exchange of notes between the Dutch in Surat and the English in Bombay or the Dutch in Chinsura and Calcutta on the mutual abduction of personnel became a yearly ritual. In Surat the VOC lost 30 to 40 men yearly to the English. Ten to 20 Englishmen were engaged in turn. This loss was further compensated as 10 to 20 Englishmen deserted yearly at Ceylon and Anjengo. Nonetheless, the VOC probably lost more men to the English than the other way round. It was English policy to man country ships with deserters since they were not paid by the Company. The VOC hesitated to do so—for the opposite reason. If Englishmen were to be engaged, this was mainly intended as retaliation for the British recruiting the Dutch.[130]

Why did men desert? Obviously this was often because of simple fear of the whistle of bullets. When in 1678, for example, the Portuguese fleet anchored in Bassein, half the sailors and some of the soldiers on board fled to Bombay when rumors spread that they were going to be sent to the dreary Persian Gulf.[131] During the wars with the Dutch, many Portuguese undoubtedly fought heroically; many others did not, however. The crown had the greatest of difficulty in preventing soldiers from escaping to Portugal before the expiration of their contract and inhabitants from fleeing back home as well. The Portuguese had to post guards on homebound ships to search for stowaways. They also enlisted in droves on Dutch vessels to escape to Europe, and the Dutch were annually gaining more Portuguese by desertion than they received on the *carreira da Índia.*[132]

In some cases, soldiers and sailors deserted to escape punishment for some misdeed. The Dutch skipper M. Stuyvesant, guilty of the "terrible sin of sodomy," fled to Goa in 1642, where he intended to put up a business. He was extradited by the Portuguese to the Company and after a summary trial thrown in the sea with a stone tied to his feet. This was long overdue, Batavia wrote. One ought to have dumped him immediately: "this horror has to be out of mankind's eyesight: the sooner, the better."[133]

In Catholic towns, like Cochin, the VOC accused the Jesuits of abducting Catholic sailors either for the French or, more rarely, for the Portuguese. But generally, as was the case with conversion to Islam, the "renegades" would follow the voice of their heart. The Mughal empire surely aggressively promoted love's temptation, though; the *qazi* of Surat was accused of constantly having two barbers around to instantly circumcise any Christian who had shown but the slightest interest in the creed.[134]

In the more common case of desertion of VOC servants to the English, one motive for desertion was certainly the possibility of earning more aboard an English vessel. It appears, however, that sailors on country ships were often rewarded by permission to take their own merchandise along. Salaries may have been lower than on ships of either the Dutch or the English Company. The Compagnie des Indes and the Estado paid less than the VOC or the EIC.[135]

A more important motive for desertion than money seems to have been that men thought their earnings were less than was their due, were involved in one of the ubiquitous quarrels on the factories, or were passed over during promotions. And sailors were often forced aboard by press gangs. In Surat, the EIC, the Compagnie des Indes, and the VOC engaged in such practices. All three vehemently denied this while claiming that their competitors did so, of course. The press gangs were paid per recruit and conspired with innkeepers, gamblers, and "other friends of the drunken sailor" skulking along the Company's wharves.[136] Mariners, pledging the VOC to reengage them after having deserted to the English, told a tale that smacks of boys' adventure books. One might be forced to enlist aboard a country trade ship to pay outstanding debts at the inn. Or one awoke, after a long night of merrymaking, on board a brig. The victim would try to jump overboard only to be caught and locked in the hold of the ship until it was at sea.[137]

But it was often not necessary to use force; sailors often changed their employers and countries as easily as they would their shirts. Let us consider an example: C. Teerman, born in Cleve (Germany) in 1660, departed to the East Indies aboard a Portuguese vessel in 1691. From Goa he went to Macao, where he married a wealthy widow. From there he sailed the South China Sea. In 1696 Teerman enrolled at Canton as boatswain on the Armenian-English ship *Rebecca* for a trip from Canton to Surat. He visited the inn run by the widow of free skipper T. Coolidge there, and quarreled with free captain J. de Bremer, engaging in a knife fight. Coolidge's tavern being adjacent to the VOC's factory and under the Company's protection, the VOC intervened and imprisoned both. Teerman had, before his capture, just signed an agreement with J. Annesley, the director of the EIC, to sail on his ship as first boatswain from Madras to Bengal.[138]

Teerman and Bremer are two fortuitously well-documented cases of the drifting sea proletariat. As there became more opportunities in free trade it became more attractive to desert, even if gathering a fortune was not likely.

And there were ample reasons for the rank and file to be disgruntled, for what was the life of the average soldier or mariner like on the outposts in the Arabian seas? Consider a petition that 18 humble *soldados* submitted to the king of Portugal in 1643—Portuguese soldiers were probably worse off than Dutch or Englishmen, but similar sentiments could have been voiced by the others too. The king should not think that only Goa or Lisbon rejoiced in the restoration of the national monarchy. No, his humble subjects on the desolate outpost of Mozambique had exulted too. Why did "ministers named by a tyrant" rule them, then? Majesty—please note that your ancestors have allotted us a meager salary of 10 cruzados, barely enough to survive. "Yet, if some viceroy happens to pass through these lands, 4 cruzados are taken from us, which adds to our woes in this land." They were living 16 men to a barrack—sleeping on planks: a life "worse than the smallest crofter in the most barren of mountains." Most of them were youngsters, from 15 to 20 years, who even had to share a blanket. "Furthermore, your majesty should know that we have not even an infirmary here and if someone is ill, as we experience daily, he will die without remedy—all of us are threatened by a death to which there is only a divine but no human cure."[139]

One might perceive European life in the Indies as life along the frontier, as does C.R. Boxer. In this "*fronteira cercada de tantos inimigos*"—as the Portuguese habitually described it—life was brutal, nasty, and often short. And not only because of the constant threat of ailments but of a violent death too. One always bore arms: "when in Portugal you count so many assaults, in India you count so many casualties." In Daman, when "the Portuguese or their sons go to the countryside they, and their family, are always escorted by musketeers."[140] This escort was intended to protect the Portuguese against their enemies as much as the Portuguese masters from their Indian bondsmen and black slaves. "The quest for liberty is a natural inclination of man, so it may always pass that the kaffirs revolt."[141]

However, European violence was framed within an extremely violent and heavily armed society. In 1693 a band of *sidhi*s did not hesitate at all to threaten burning down an entire neighborhood of Surat in order to secure the release of one of them, whom the governor had imprisoned for manslaughter.[142] Such practices were little different from the vaunted Portuguese "cruelties."

And if the Dutch, Portuguese, and English occasionally shelled and blockaded towns, so did the Ja'ariba fleets: take the bombarding and looting of Kung in 1694 by those fleets, for example, which caused more apprehension in Persia than similar practices by the Portuguese. In 1697 at Barcelore the fleet of Muscat, "when the queen of Canara did not allow them to establish a factory, heavily damaged their temples and sacked the town."[143] But while there was plenty of violence in the Arabian seas, brutality was curtailed by certain norms. It was to be aimed at obtaining ascertainable targets that were negotiable, and the defenseless were to be spared.

The brutal behavior toward fellow human beings found in slavery on St. Helena or Mauritius has no counterpart in India, Persia, or the Swahili Coast. Actually the Dutch, English and Portuguese occasionally used slave labor at Bandar Abbas, Diu, and Surat: "our [free] workmen are more prone to steal than to work" at Surat. But the slaves were better treated under Islamic law than under Christian law, and when abused they might flee. Diu town was surrounded by settlements of refugee Portuguese slaves, as was Goa.[144] The casual and random cruelty of the buccaneers too, normal in the Caribbean, was alien to maritime practices in the Arabian seas, though piracy was quite common there too.

Violence was curtailed by the set of norms and arrangements, the informal "law of nations" shared by the society in the Arabian seas to which the Europeans had to conform if they wanted to trade successfully. And there was—as yet—no social divide between "Europeans" and "natives," merely one between the humble and the mighty, serfs and masters, hillbillies and city dwellers. Europeans were wont to put up with alien kings and laws as best they could. Though they would normally spurn powerful traders, noblemen, or kings as "niggers," they had to deal with them as equals in wealth and status.

Let us now examine more closely the norms that regulated behavior among the Europeans themselves, and between Europeans and indigenous states.

## Notes

1. This view was first expounded by Polanyi in his classic *The Great Transformation* (New York, 1944), and later on elaborated in various other essays. For a systematic exposition of Polanyi's thought see J.R. Stanfield, *The Economic Thought of Karl Polanyi* (London, 1986). And for an enthusiastic presentation (perhaps overly so) of his views see R.C. Dalton, "Karl Polanyi's Analysis of Long-Distance Trade and His Wider Paradigm," in C.C. Lamberg and K. Sabloff (eds.), *Ancient Civilization and Trade* (Albuquerque, 1975), pp. 63–112. While Polanyi has had a lot of influence on the study of economic history of classical antiquity and—due to his posthumous *Dahomey and the Slave Trade*—some influence on African studies, in Indian and Middle Eastern studies his influence has been practically nil.

2. C.H. Alexandrowicz, *An Introduction to the Law of Nations in the East Indies* (Oxford, 1967).

3. P.D. Curtin, *Cross-Cultural Trade in World History* (Cambridge, 1984); for *natio*-like institutions in force in the trade of medieval South India, see C.S. Hall, *State and Statecraft in the Age of the Imperial Colas* (New Delhi, 1981), p. 53 et seq.; and in general see also A. Wink, *Al Hind* (Leiden, 1989), i, p. 62. The literature on the *natio*

in the Levant is very extensive; see, for example, A.H. De Groot, "The Organization of Western European Trade to the Levant," in L. Blussé and F. Gaastra (eds.), *Companies and Trade* (Leiden, 1981), pp. 231–41, or B. Homsy, *Les Capitulations et la protection des chrétiens au proche Orient* (Harissa, 1956).

4. There is a score of books on this topic, though mostly of fairly mediocre quality. See, however, B. von Palombini, *Bündniswerben abendländischer Mächte um Persien 1453–1600* (Wiesbaden, 1968); N. Steensgaard, *Carracks, Caravans and Companies: The Structural Crisis in the European-Asian Trade in the Early Seventeenth Century* (Copenhagen, 1973), part 3. But see especially the brilliant work of P.P. Busev, *Istorija posolst'va i diplomaticheskich otnoshenii Russkogo i Iranskogo gosudarei v 1586–1612 gc.* (Moscow, 1976).

5. V.B. Moreen, "The Status of Religious Minorities in Safavid Iran 1617–1661," *Journal of Near Eastern Studies* 40 (1981), pp. 128–52.

6. According to Geleynssen 283, Isfahan diary, 11 October 1645, fo. 220 vo; VOC/OB 1379, 6 March 1682, fo. 2656 vo.

7. G. La Roque, *Voyage dans l'Arabie heureuse* (Amsterdam, 1711), p. 135; ARA Coll. van Hoorn van Riebeeck 12, "Description of Mocha."

8. J.O. Kane (ed. and trans.), *The Ship of Sulaiman* (London, 1972); see also J. Aubin, "Les Persans au Siam dans le règne de Narain," *Mare Luso-Indicum* 4 (1980), pp. 95–126.

9. VOC/OB 1660, "Report of the Mocha chiefs," fo. 781 vo. See also C.G. Brouwer, *Al Mukha*, p. 271.

10. See, for example, VOC/OB 1455, 25 November 1687, fo. 1396; ARA, HRB 877, "Comprehensive description of Persia," by van Rheede.

11. VOC/OB 1233, 3 June 1660, fo. 134.

12. A. Das Gupta, "Gujarati Merchants and the Red Sea Trade," in B.B. Kling and M.N. Pearson (eds.), *The Age of Partnership: Europeans in Asia Before Dominion* (Honolulu, 1979), p. 201; VOC/OB 1379, "Memoir by Cassembrood," fo. 2702 vo.; F. Valentijn, *Oud en nieuw Oost-Indië* (Dordrecht, 1724–26), v (1), p. 202; ANTT, DRI, 36, 28 March 1636, fo. 421; the assistant of the customs at Muscat in 1636 was, for example, "hum bramene por nome Bomba" (ANTT, DRI, 44, "Regimento de Muscat").

13. G. Ferrand, *Les Musulmans à Madagascar*, 3 vols. (Paris, 1902), ii, pp. 120–75.

14. Alexandrowicz, *The Law of Nations*. See for examples of *farmans*, *hasbul hukms*, *olas*, and the like concerning the European settlements: A.H. Aitchinson (ed.), *A Collection of Treaties, Engagements and Sunnuds Relating to India and Neighbouring Countries*, 8 vols. (Calcutta, 1862–66); J.F. Biker (ed.), *Collecção de trattados e concertos de paz que o Estado da India fêz com os reis e senhores delle*, 14 vols. (Lisbon, 1883–87); J.E. Heeres (ed.), *Corpus diplomaticus Neerlando-Indicum*, 6 vols. (The Hague, 1907–53); A. Martineau (ed.), *Lettres et conventions des gouverneurs de Pondichéry* (Pondicherry, 1914).

15. ARA, HRB 838, "Memoir by Jan Schreuder," fo. 77–86.

16. L. Lockhart, "European Contacts with Persia," in, L. Lockhart and R. Jackson (eds.), *The Cambridge History of Iran: The Timurid and Safavid Period* (Cambridge, 1986), pp. 373–412.

17. See A. Moens, "Oorspronkelijk gedenkschrift," *Selections from the Records of Madras Government: Dutch Records* 2 (Madras, 1908), pp. 79–81.

18. *Travancore Archeological Series,* 8 vols. (Trivandrum, 1908–15), iv, p. 11; VOC/OB 1571, 26 February 1695, fo. 127–35.

19. See, for example, VOC/UB 913, 9 November 1686, fo. 744, for a case in which

the Dutch factory provided safe haven for two Dutch freebooters who were accused of manslaughter and was nearly stormed by an angry Indian crowd.

20. L.P. Boiteux, *Richelieu: Grand maître de la navigation et du commerce de la Françe* (Paris, 1955), pp. 57–75.

21. W. Foster, "An English Settlement on Madagascar," *The English Historical Review* 27 (1927), pp. 239–50; *English Factories 1650–1654*, pp. 42, 103; R. Brenner, *Merchants and Revolution: Commercial Change, Political Conflict and London's Overseas Traders 1550–1653* (Cambridge, 1993), pp. 171–72; AHU, Índia, Cx. 28, 94, Anonymous memorandum 1669.

22. F. de Malotet, *Étienne de Flacourt ou les origins de la colonisation française à Madagascar* (Paris, 1858); and H. de Froidevaux, "Madagascar du XVIe siècle à 1811," vol. 6 of G. Hanoteaux and A. Martineau (eds.), *Histoire de l'expansion française dans le monde* (Paris, 1933), pp. 21–52.

23. AHU, Moç., Cx. 2, 106, "Copy of a letter of the commander of the French resident at the island of San Lourenço."

24. VOC/XVII 318, 18 September 1662, fo. 540; Gentlemen XVII (VOC/XVII 317, 16 April 1657, fo. 500) advised the personnel on the Cape and on Mauritius they should engage the French on land and at sea and demolish the fortress at Augustin Bay.

25. See, apart from the above, also G. de Rennefort, *Rélation du premier voyage de la Compagnie des Indes Orientales en l'isle de Madagascar* (Paris, 1668; Ann Arbor, 1987); and Étienne de Flacourt's relation in *COACM*, ix. This is, however, mainly based on VOC/OB 1237, Report by Jan de Swart, fo. 303–12 vo.; Ajuda 51-V-37, fo. 234; and "The history of the war with the white man," probably the oldest Malagasy text, which has been edited by G. Mondain as *L'histoire de l'Imoro d'après un manuscrit arabo-malgache* (Paris and Algiers, 1910).

26. See, for example, VOC/OB 1529, Cochin muster roll, or VOC/OB 1474, "Summary account of all servants of the Company"; VOC/OB 1308, "Report and disclosure," fo. 818. Cochin's population may be compared with that of contemporary Colombo, for which see G.J. Knaap, "Europeans, Mestizos and Slaves: The Population of Colombo at the End of the Seventeenth Century," *Itinerário* 5 (2) (1984), pp. 84–101.

27. For the following part see especially a gem of an essay by L. Dermigny, "Les Européens aux 'Indes' du XVI au XVIIIème siècle," in C. Mehaud (ed.), *Mouvements des populations* (Paris, 1979), pp. 209–16.

28. *Dagregister 1661*, p. 367; *Danmarks historien*, vol. 9, O. Feldbaeck, *Kolonierne i Asien og Afrika* (Copenhagen, 1988), p. 100.

29. E. Sanceau, *Mulheres portugueses no ultramar* (Porto, 1979); C.R. Boxer, *Mary and Misogny: Women in Iberian Expansion Overseas* (Duckworth, 1975); L. Blussé, "The Caryatids of 17th Century Batavia," in *Strange Company: Chinese Settlers, Mestizo Women and the Dutch in VOC Batavia* (Dordrecht, 1986), p. 158; for the Dutch "womenfolk" at Cochin cf. J.H. Canter Vischer, *Malabarse Brieven* (Leeuwarden, 1743), pp. 40–49.

30. ANTT, DRI, 55, "Titolo das terras dos Rios de Cuama."

31. P.S. Olivier (ed.), *Madagascar, or Robert Drury's Journal During Six Years' Captivity on That Island* (London, 1890), p. -171.

32. A.C. Germano de Silva Correia, *História da colonização portuguêsa na Índia*, 6 vols. (Lisbon, 1948–58), iv, pp. 277–81; AHU, Índia, Cx. 28 bis, 180, 28 February 1669, and 27 January 1670; AHU, Índia, Cx. 26, 170, 5 March 1665; AHU, Índia, Cx. 32, 165, "A petition of Daman"; see also HAG 3067, "Tombo geral de Baçaim" under Timóteo Britto et al.

33. Sanceau, *Mulheres portugueses*, p. 170.

34. ANTT, Con. d. G., Cx. III E, 10 March 1687, fo. 83; AHU, Índia, Cx. 27, 116, 8 March 1666.

35. C.R. Boxer, *The Dutch Seaborne Empire* (London, 1988), pp. 224; VOC/RXVII, 221, 25 March 1649, 25 August 1670.

36. VOC/HB 4457, 12 April 1677, fo. 171 vo.

37. VOC/OB 1649, 21 March 1701, fo. 460.

38. D.H.A. Kolff, "La nation chrétienne à Surat au début du XVIIe siècle," in R. Goutalier (ed.), *La Femme dans les sociétés coloniales* (Aix en Provence, 1984), p. 12.

39. ARU, Coll. Huydecooper 621, "An exposition of some things which happened to me in Persia."

40. T.J. Coates, *Degredados e orfãs: colonização dirigida pela coroa no império português* (Lisbon, 1998), pp. 239–59; ANTT, DRI, 37, 26 March 1636, fo. 367; AHU, Índia, Cx. 33, 50, 29 October 1675; AHU, Cód. 212, 30 August 1680, fo. 99–100 vo.

41. J.H. Canter Vischer, *Malabarse Brieven* (Leeuwarden, 1743), p. 80; see C.R. Boxer, "Fidalgos portugueses e bailardeiras índianas" *Revista da Historia* (São Paulo), 50 (1961), pp. 83–105; BAC, A 396, 5 December 1677; AHU, Índia, Cx. 40, 28, 12 December 1696.

42. HAG, Cartas e ordens para o conselho da fazenda, 2597, 1 March 1697, fo. 22 vo.

43. HAG, LM, 73, 22 December 1700; HAG, Cartas e ordens para o conselho da fazenda, 2597, 17 October 1680; J. Wycki (ed.), *O livro do pai dos christãos* (Lisbon, 1969), p. 230; T.R. de Souza, "The Voiceless in Goan History," in J. Correia-Alfonso (ed.), *Indo-Portuguese History: Sources and Problems* (Bombay, 1981), p. 126.

44. J. Middleton, *The World of the Swahili* (New Haven, 1982), p. 22.

45. M.N. Pearson, "Banyas and Brahmins: Their Role in the Portuguese Indian Economy," in *Coastal Western India* (New Delhi, 1981), p. 96; V. de Albuquerque, *O senado*, p. 291; HAG, LM, 31, 21 January 1653, fo. 79; ANTT, DRI, 61, 30 December 1648, fo. 163; AHU, Índia, Cx. 30, 146, March 1676.

46. Godinho, *Itinerário*, p. 63; C.R. Boxer, *Race Relations in the Portuguese Empire* (Oxford, 1963), p. 67; A.I. Amançio Graçias, *Floreal da nobrezza da cidade de Goa* (Bastora, 1905). Most of the Bassein nobility is listed in Germano Correia, *História da colonização*, and in *Armas e inscrições do forte de Baçaim* (Lisbon, 1975). HAG 3067, "Tombo geral de Baçaim." This *tombo* material is excellently suited for prosopographic research, which, however, is lacking. The grand effort of the Viceconde de Goa, *Grandes e humildes na epopeia portuguêsa no Oriente*, 2 vols. (Lisbon, 1942, 1943), has come no further than the letter A.

47. AHU, Cód. 212, 15 November 1691, fo. 205.

48. J.R. Magalhães, "Uma estrutura do império português. O município," in *1o Ciclo de conferências Portugal e o Oriente* (Lisbon, 1994), pp. 67–91. It should be noted that, oddly, the municipal gatherings were not very important on the Zambesi, being largely replaced by patronage ties between the governors and their claque. This probably reflects the more rural character of the Portuguese settlements there.

49. J. Wycki, "Die Laienbruderschaft der Misericórdia in portugiesisch Asien," in *Das Laienapostolat in den Missiones. Festschrift für Dr. J. Bechman* (Schöneck, 1961), pp. 79–97; C.R. Boxer, *Portuguese Society in the Tropics: The Municipal Councils of Goa, Macao, Bahia and Luanda* (Madison, 1965); A.J. Russel-Wood, *Fidalgos and Philanthropists: The Santa Casa da Misericórdia of Bahia* (Berkeley, London, 1968), pp. 24–45; J.F. Feirrera Martins, *História da misericórdia de Goa*, 3 vols. (Nova Goa, 1910–

14); for the institution of the *weeskamer* see J.K.J. de Jonge (ed.), *De opkomst van het Nederlands gezag in Oost-Indië Verzameling van stukken uit het oud-koloniaal archief*, 11 vols. (The Hague, 1862–83), iii, pp. 245–85.

50. AHU, Índia, Cx. 29, 138, 30 September 1673.

51. ANTT, DRI, 40, 29 November 1637, fo. 108.

52. Blussé, "The Caryatids," p. 166; H. Niemeijer, *Calvinisme en Koloniale stadscultuur: Batavia 1619–1725* (Academisch Proefschrift, University of Leiden, 1996). This is not to say that the Protestant church had a monopoly since there was a Catholic church-in-hiding at Batavia—see *Plakaatboek*, ii, p. 370.

53. English social life in India has been quite well researched; see, for example, P. Spear, *The Nabobs: A Study of the Social Life of the English in Eighteenth Century India* (London, 1963).

54. ANTT, DRI, 57, 9 April 1657.

55. AHU, Índia, Cx. 36, 15, 12 February 1692.

56. BAC, A 58, fo. 179 vo.

57. See the classic work of D. Lopes, *A expansão da lingua portuguêsa no Oriente durante os séculos XVI, XVII e XVIII* (Barcelos, 1936); the fight between Dutch and Portuguese in the Dutch factories in Insulinde, which ensued in a victory of Malay, has been documented by K. Groeneboer, *Weg tot het westen: het Nederlands voor Indië 1600–1950. Een taalpolitieke geschiedenis* (Leiden, 1993), pp. 34–65.

58. AHU, Índia, Cx. 31, 58, "Information on Cochin"; VOC/OB 1406, 11 April 1684, fo. 810 vo.

59. ANTT, DRI, 35, "Pareçer do Bispo de Cochim", fo. 58; ANTT, DRI, 61, 27 February 1651, fo. 295.

60. AHU, Índia, Cx. 12, 135, 6 October 1637.

61. VOC/OB 1593, 10 December 1697, fo. 11.

62. ARA, St. Gen., Lias VOC, 5737 ii, "Writ by the Estates General in which it is prohibited to everybody to sail to the East Indies on foreign ships." The English had comparable regulations; see *Court Minutes* 1677–79, p. 95.

63. See for example, *English Factories* 1670–77, i, p. 216; VOC/OB 1355, 30 January 1681, fo. 353; VOC/OB 1360, 7 June 1681, fo. 1854 vo.; VOC/OB 1454, 28 August 1693; VOC/OB 1480, 10 October 1691, fo. 166.

64. AHU, Cód. 53, 6 April 1662, fo. 295.

65. R.J. Barendse, "A Long Road to Livorno: The Overland Messenger-Service of the Dutch East India Company in the Seventeenth Century," *Itinerario* 7 (2) (1988), p. 37.

66. See, for example, VOC/RGGR 677, 18 December 1666; AHU, Índia, Cx. 20 bis, 126, 8 October 1649. Even when the Dutch remitted mail from Aleppo to the Netherlands they occasionally used English ships—Geleynssen 220, 15 October 1642; VOC/HB 4455, 13 April 1661.

67. VOC/OB 1603, 23 August 1698, fo. 1688–90.

68. VOC/OB 1636, "Diary Deodati," 8 August, fo. 353; compare H. Yule (ed.), *The Diary of William Hedges*, 3 vols. (London, *WHS*, 1877–89), ii, p. cccviii.

69. GAA, P.A. 379, "Archief Nederlands-hervormde gemeente," 5, Enclosure to letter of 13 September 1666.

70. *An Account of the Trade of India* (London, 1711), p. 230.

71. ARU, Coll. Huydecooper 614, Report by Wouter Tenhaeff (1630).

72. Geleynssen 284, 19 August 1646; and for Overschie's reckless buying see VOC/XVII 316, 12 September 1639, fo. 256.

73. At Bandar Abbas emissary W. Bastinck was admonished by Batavia to obtain a *raqam* from the court to inhibit the brewing of arrack by Jewish innkeepers because there were continual fights between Dutch, Persian, and English drunken soldiers (VOC/OB 1165, "Instruction for W. Bastinck going to Ispahan," 20 February 1647, fo. 1992 vo.).

74. VOC/HB 4455, 26 February 1657; VOC/RGGR 664, 18 June 1641; VOC/RGGR 681, 9 September 1666, fo. 196; VOC/HB 4456, 3 April 1666; Boxer, *Dutch Seaborne Empire*, p. 277; *Plakaatboek*, ii, p. 180.

75. VOC/OB 1548, Surat diary, 13 March 1693, fo. 436–41; 8 September, fo. 528 vo.; VOC/OB 1246, "An extract from the Surat diary," fo. 750; see S.N. Sen (ed.), *Foreign Biographies of Shivaji* (Calcutta, 1927), p. 74.

76. W.W. Hunter, *History of British India*, 2 vols. (London, 1899, 1900), ii, p. 272.

77. *Generale missiven*, v, p. 153; VOC/OB 1464, 24 January 1689, fo. 461, 474; VOC/OB 1448, 10 January 1689, fo. 405–8 vo.

78. See G.V. Scammel, "European Exiles, Renegades and Outlaws and the Maritime Economy of Asia c. 1500–1750," *MAS* 26 (4) (1992), pp. 642–63.

79. J. Chardin, *Voyages du chevalier Chardin en Perse et en autre lieu de l'Orient enrichis d'un grand nombre des figures* (L. Langlès, ed.), 11 vols. (Paris 1811–14), i, p. 3.

80. And the Portuguese did have a general muster roll and pay office (*matrícula geral*) so that the metropolis was well aware who was getting which position—in the seventeenth century nominations were formally not through patronage of the office holders as, apparently, in the early sixteenth. See Évora CXV/1–41, fo. 21–75.

81. F. Lequin, "Het personeel van de Verenigde Oost-Indische Compagnie in de achttiende eeuw, méér in het bijzonder in de vestiging Bengalen," 2 vols. (Academisch Proefschrift, University of Leiden, 1982), i, p. 55, 65.

82. HAG, LM, 40, "Regimento geral para a carreira," fo. 32; Évora CXV/1–41, 2 January 1626, fo. 60; ANTT, DRI, 39, 17 March 1637, fo. 66.

83. E. Stols and C. Verberkmoere, *Aziatische omzwervingen. Het levensverhaal van Jacob de Coutre. Een Brugse diamanthandelaar 1591–1627* (Berchem, 1988); J.C. Boyajian, *Portuguese Trade in Asia Under the Habsburgs 1580–1640* (Baltimore, 1993), pp. 136–40; Bulhão Patto, *Documentos remettidos*, ii, p. 490; ANTT, DRI, 32, 3 January 1635, fo. 61; ARA, St. Gen., Lias Portugal, 7016 i, 11 December 1691; and see on foreigners taken aboard Portuguese vessels, ARA, St. Gen., Lias Portugal, 7015 i, 29 February 1684; VOC/OB 1406, 20 May 1684, fo. 989–91 vo.

84. For a description of the overland routes to Persia see G. Emerson, "Ex occidente lux: Some European Sources on the Economic and Social Structure of Safavid Persia" (Ph.D. dissertation, University of Cambridge, 1968), pp. 69–167; A.R. Disney, "The Estado da Índia and the Caravan Trade" (paper presented to 31st International Conference of Human Sciences in Asia and North Africa, Tokyo, 1983); BAC, A 96, 1621, fo. 87.

85. Geleynssen 280 c, "Register of cases tried."

86. See C. Cipolla, *Clocks and Culture* (London 1965); VOC/OB 1370, 10 June 1681, fo. 2452 vo.; S. Schuster-Walser, *Das safavidische Persien im Spiegel europäischer Reiseberichten (1502–1722)* (Baden Baden, 1970), pp. 51–53; VOC/OB 1209, 5 April 1653. Paintings were also donated by other Companies, like the Compagnie des Indes: see VOC/OB 4026, "Mémoires de ce que on a besoin au Bengalle," fo. 1175: "des portraits du Roy pour présenter dans les occasions aux gouverneurs. Aussi des portraits des principaux personnes de la cour et particulièrement des dames, mais il faut remarquer que il ne faut point de ceux où les personnes sont representées avec des habites Romaines; aussi quelques tableaux représentantes des combats de terre et de mer."

87. ARA, Coll. van Hoorn/van Riebeek 12 no. 279, 1701; VOC/OB 1241, 22 November 1663, fo. 592 vo.; and in same, "Batavia register regarding the good housekeeping [*mesnagie*]," fo. 561–66 vo. or, for example, VOC/OB 1224, 5 January 1656, fo. 140 vo.

88. G. Yogev, *Diamonds and Coral: Anglo-Dutch Jews and Eighteenth Century Trade* (Leicester, New York, 1978), p. 55; ARA, St. Gen., Lias Barbarije, 6910, Estates-General to serenissima, 28 October 1666.

89. Évora, CXV/1–39, 16 March 1616, fo. 96; and 22 February 1611, fo. 75.

90. Stols and Verbermoère, *Aziatische omzwervingen*; on Tavernier see C. Joret, *Jean Baptiste Tavernier* (Paris, 1883).

91. ARU, Coll. Huydecooper 621, "Relation Ten Haeff."

92. Geleynssen 247, "Register of bills, loans etc. outstanding in Spahan and Gombroon"; and in same, 17 September 1646, fo. 431; VOC/OB 1236, 6 September 1660, fo. 775; VOC/OB 1245, 24 June 1665, fo. 568 vo.

93. VOC/OB 1295, 5 January 1673, fo. 493; VOC/OB 1297, 12 July 1675, fo. 1017; see also VOC/UB 887, 10 October 1663, fo. 464.

94. Thus, for example, ARA, St. Gen., lias VOC, 5741 i, Letter by Pieter van Dam, 8 June 1685.

95. ANTT, DRI, 61, 20 December 1651, fo. 372.

96. S.N. Sen, *The Administrative System of the Marathas* (Calcutta, 1976), pp. 268–71. For the European mercenaries in Golcunda see A. Martineau (ed.), *Mémoires de François Martin,* 3 vols. (Paris, 1931–34), ii, p. 253 (there is an English translation by L. Varadarayan under the title *India in the Seventeenth Century*; references here are to the French edition); T. Bowrey, *A Geographical Account of the Countries Around the Bay of Bengal* (R.C. Temple, ed.) (London, *WHS*, 1905), p. 111; J.S. Cummins (ed. and trans.), *The Travels and Controversies of Frey Domingo Navarette,* 2 vols. (Cambridge, *WHS,* 1962), ii, pp. 314–6; most published references to *habsi* slaves have been gathered in R. Pankhurst, *An Introduction to the Economic History of Ethiopia* (London, 1964), appendix 2.

97. VOC/OB 1122, "Report Johan van Twist," fo. 483 vo.; VOC/OB 1334, 20 October 1639, fo. 189.

98. S. Bidwel, *Swords for Hire: European Mercenaries in Eighteenth Century India* (London, 1974); D. de Gois, *Crónica do Sereníssimo Senhor Rey D. Manuel* (J.M. Teixeira de Carvalho and D. Lopes, eds.), 4 vols. (Coimbra, 1926).

99. VOC/OB 1660, 7 May 1701, fo. 938 vo.; N. Manucci, *Storia do Mogor or Mughal India 1653–1708* (W. Irvine, ed.), 4 vols. (London, 1907–8), ii, p. 443; see W. Irvine, *The Army of the Indian Moghuls* (London, 1902).

100. Ajuda, 51-VII-23, 20 September 1684, fo. 449.

101. VOC/OB 1559, 21 November 1697, fo. 991–94; ARA, HRB, 834, Report by Zwaardecroon, fo. 136–40; ARU, Coll. Huydecooper 621, "Specification of such pennies as the company could and should reclaim"; VOC/OB 1660, 2 October 1701, fo. 883 vo.

102. R. du Mans, *Estat de la Perse en 1660* (C. Schefer, ed.) (Paris, 1890), pp. 361–63; R. Cessi, "Mercanti Veneziani nella 'India' nel secolo XVI," in *Studii in onore di Armando Sapori*, 2 vols. (Milan, 1957), ii, pp. 1098–105; E. Ashtor, *The Levant Trade in the Late Middle Ages* (Princeton, 1983).

103. J.J. Struijs, *Drie aanmerkelijke en seer rampspoedige reysen door Italiën, Griekenland, Lijfland, Moscoviën, Tartarijen, Mediën, Persiën, Oost-Indiën, Japan en verscheydene anderen gewesten* (Amsterdam, 1676); Struijs's ransom cost the VOC dearly, for which see VOC/OB 1284, 7 March 1671, fo. 2336.

104. *Letters édifiantes et très curieux des pères de la mission*, 12 vols. (Paris, 1780), iv, p. 65; BNL, FG, Cód. 864, "Voyage to India," fo. 50.

105. BAC, A 58, fo. 171.

106. HAG, LM, 35, 3 May 1657, fo. 207.

107. AHU, Índia, Cx. 25, 43, 4 November 1661; Évora CXV/1–39, 9 April 1661, fo. 168.

108. AHU, Índia, Cx 25, 45, 18 December 1660.

109. HAG, Petições despachadas para o conselho da fazenda, 1127, 1 February 1683, fo. 36; VOC/OB 1256, 29 March 1666, fo. 82–83 vo.; VOC/OB 1240, 3 May 1662, fo. 1005; VOC/OB 1236, 28 October 1660, fo. 185; P.P.S. Pissurlencar et al. (eds.), *Assentos do conselho do Estado da Índia*, 6 vols. (Bastora and Goa, 1953–74), iv, p. 35; AHU, Índia, Cx. 25, 147, 1 February 1663; AHU, Índia, Cx. 38, 71, 1696.

110. *Venice: A Maritime Republic* (Baltimore, 1973), p. 166.

111. Don García de Silva y Figueroa, *Commentarios de Don García de Silva y Figueroa de la embajada que de parte del rey de España Don Felipe III hizo al Rey Xa Abbas de Persia*, 2 vols. (Madrid, 1903, 1905), ii, p. 254; compare Ajuda, 46-IX-19, "Relazione degli carmeliti scalze," fo. 219: "ci sono [in Isfahan in 1601] ancor d'Europa mercanti diversi: Portughesi, Francesi, Inglesi, Olandesi, Veneziani"; VOC/OB 1592, 27 September 1695, fo. 327 vo.; for other places compare, for example, the case of the community of Portuguese renegades in Lahore: "Missões jesuitas na Índia," in *Documentação ultramarina portuguêsa*, iii, (Lisbon, 1963), pp. 279–91.

112. VOC/OB 1403, "Notice regarding free burghers at Hugly."

113. AHU, Índia, Cx. 11, 6, 4 February 1635; and Cx. 13, 10, 8 January 1638.

114. AHU, Índia, Cx. 13 bis, 128, 24 January 1639.

115. C.R. Boxer, *The Portuguese Seaborne Empire 1425–1825* (New York, 1969/1989), pp. 313–15; AHU, Índia, Cx. 11, 58, 23 March 1633; ARA, St. Gen., Lias Portugal, 7015 i, 27 February 1685; ARA, St. Gen., Lias Portugal, 7014 ii, 4 March 1681; AHU, Índia, Cx. 25, 45, 18 December 1660.

116. The Dutch ambassador in Lisbon dryly noted that if the Portuguese had obeyed a request of the Sun King that all French subjects in Portugal were to be extradited, they might as well have closed down all shops and immediately ceased all shipping (ARA, St. Gen. 7015, I, Lias Portugal, 29 February 1684).

117. M.L.E. de Freitas Ferraz dos Santos, *Documentação histórica moçambicana* (Lisbon, 1973), p. 203; HAG, LM, 39, 27 January 1676, fo. 364; see, for example, AHU, Índia, Cx. 37, 23, *Devaça* of Antônio Machedo de Britto, witnesses Jacobo Jerardo van der Novo, "Olandês, pilóto-mor deste Estado, capitão do mar e guerra," and Hieronimo Francisco, "Veneçiano"; and in same, 98, 6 November 1694.

118. Boxer, *Dutch Seaborne Empire*, p. 81; on the rank and file on the VOC vessels, see in particular the classic articles of J. de Hullu, in *Op de schepen der Oost-Indische Compagnie. Vijf artikelen van J. de Hullu* (J.R. Bruijn and J. Lucassen, eds.) (Groningen, 1980); and more recently R. van Gelder, *Het Oost-Indisch Avontuur. Duitsers in dienst van de VOC* (Nimwegen, 1997).

119. *English Factories* 1678–1684, pp. 142–73; BNL, FG, Cód. 10.703, "Discurso apologético"; VOC/OB 1474, "Appendix to the general letter", fo. 114 vo. Indeed, the rate of pay at Tana was meager, even according to Indian standards: VOC/OB 1649, "Specification of payments of 164 sailors." In the eighteenth century the term *lascarin* specifically referred to sailors, but in the seventeenth century this term was used for indigenous mercenaries in general.

120. For the expenses involved see AHU, Índia, Cx. 24, 77, 15 December 1657.

121. HAG, Correspondênçia de Baçaim, 1249, 2 July 1641, fo. 30; Ajuda 51-VII-25, 25 May 1684, fo. 411; BAC A 496, 12 December 1677, fo. 54, 65.

122. ANTT, DRI, 32, 3 January 1635, fo. 51; BNL, FG, Cód. 7640, "Relação breve dos principais succesos," fo. 60 vo.; AHU, Índia, Cx. 28, 94, 1669.

123. BNL, Pombalina, Cód. 525, fo. 46 vo.

124. See D.H.A. Kolff, "An Armed Peasantry and Its Allies: Rajput Tradition and State-Formation in Hindustan 1450–1850" (Academisch Proefschrift, University of Leiden, 1983).

125. ANTT, DRI, 44, "Regimento de Muscat"; ANTT, DRI, 57, 2 April 1650.

126. BNL, FG, Cód. 8538, "Alvará," 12 March 1603.

127. In principle, Gentlemen XVII did not condone that Dutchmen should work on Indian ships—VOC/XVII 318, 16 April 1660, fo. 276.

128. F. Talett, *War and Society in Early Modern Europe 1495–1715* (London, 1992), pp. 112–25; BNL, FG, Cód. 1783, "Livro das receitas e depezas," fo. 112 vo.

129. Lequin, "Het personeel," i, pp. 134–36.

130. J. Bruce, *Annals of the Honourable East India Company 1600–1700*, 3 vols. (London, 1810; Farnborough, 1970), ii, p. 552; VOC/XVII 322, 6 October 1688, fo. 499 vo. See, apart from various notes on this in the correspondence of Surat (for Surat and Hugly had to report yearly on desertion to Gentlemen XVII from 1692 on); also ARA, HRB, 826, "Protest to Mr. John Annesley," fo. 64; VOC/UB 935, 28 August 1700; VOC/OB 1559, 3 August 1693, fo. 220–21.

131. BAC, A 500, 14 December 1678.

132. VOC/UB 880, 26 September 1645, fo. 496; AHU, Índia, Cx. 22, 15, 20 December 1650; ANTT, DRI, 58, 29 December 1649, fo. 86.

133. Geleynssen 283, 18 March 1645, fo. 96–97.

134. VOC/OB 1277, 14 August 1670, fo. 1709 vo.; VOC/OB 1636, "Diary Deodati," 16 October, fo. 399; compare also, for example, the proceedings against Mathijs Nick from Frankfurt in VOC/CR 9288, 14 February 1655.

135. See, for example, *Dagregister* 1681, p. 272, or the trial of Roelof Pietersz and Claas de Vries, VOC/CR 9286, 8 June 1652 or VOC/CR 9292, 23 June 1682; VOC/OB 1613, "Questionnaire to 7 English deserters," fo. 490–93.

136. VOC/UB 930, 21 August 1697, fo. 991–93; VOC/OB 1593, 21 November 1697, fo. 1008–11 vo.; VOC/OB 1611, 22 February 1697, fo. 134.

137. VOC/OB 1611, "Declaration of deserters," fo. 100; and "Memorandum by the deserters," fo. 106; VOC/OB 1549, Surat resolution, 18 March 1694, fo. 298–300 vo.

138. VOC/OB 1523, Surat diary, 10 September 1694, fo. 593.

139. AHU, Moç., Cx. 2, 35, 5 December 1643. The crown did consider this request and ordered the viceroy to take urgent steps to establish a hospital in Mozambique (Theal, iv, p. 299).

140. C.R. Boxer, "Some Possible Fields of Research in the History of Portuguese India," in J. Correia-Alfonso (ed.), *Indo-Portuguese History* (Bombay, 1981), p. 186; AHU, Índia, Cx. 32, 25, 9 November 1682; and in same, 31, "Alvará que mandou passar o V. Rey"; AHU, Índia, Cx. 12, 135, 6 October 1637; see Évora, CXV/1–41, 15 January 1617, fo. 65.

141. Pissurlencar, *Assentos*, i, p. 359.

142. VOC/OB 1548, Surat diary, 5 January 1693, fo. 386.

143. (Mohammad Mar'ashi-i Safavi (A. Iqbal, ed.), *Majama al-tawarikh dar Tarikh-i inqirad-i Safavija va vaqa-i ba'd* (Teheran, 1328/1345), pp. 31–36. To punish Muscat

grand vizier Muhammad, Taher Vahid first requested Dutch and then Portuguese naval support for arranging an expedition to Muscat to punish the imamate. Although both the Dutch and the Portuguese were interested, the expedition was never staged because the court lost interest after Taher Vahid's death, and it probably was too expensive. VOC/OB 1546, 19 July 1695, fo. 585; BNL, Pombalina, Cód. 439, 15 January 1697, fo. 9.

144. AHU, Índia, Cx. 34, 99, "Statement of Frey Caetano de São Miquel"; Geleynssen 133, 24 March 1641; see too, for example, VOC/OB 1224, 16 March 1657, fo. 316.

4

# Diplomacy and the State

In many respects, the Arabian seas might be seen as a frontier where one was always encircled by foes. Peace treaties and bilateral diplomatic relations between European states were of limited avail there. Instead, European states might have armed collisions, whereas they were allies in Europe. The settlements in Malabar were, according to van Rheede in 1670, won and held by the sword and by the sword alone:

> One is at the frontier here and is never assured against the cunning of white and other nations and does not know when they will implement some devious plot or it may be too late and time runs too short for sending relief.[1]

One had always to be wary of the deceit of either "white" or "black" nations: "beyond the line there are no more friends, and anything afloat is a prize," to quote E. de Flacourt.[2]

This proverbial principle, "no peace beyond the line," was applied as a legal axiom in the latter half of the seventeenth century to soothe possible collisions in Europe over minor quarrels in the colonies. Though this mainly concerned the Caribbean, it applied to the Arabian seas as well.[3] One obvious reason, concerning both Asia and America, was the difficulty in remitting messages to the colonies. One was only at peace there when both parties in a conflict had received definite confirmation from their sovereign authorities of a cease-fire, and that might take more than a year.[4]

There was another reason for the application of this principle, which was specific to the East Indies. Chartered Companies had obtained a monopoly over the trade of certain areas that was legally granted to the Company (and not to its sovereign, Parliament or the Estates General) by force of treaties with indigenous princes. Since the latter were not tied to the European diplomatic system and not connected to any higher sovereign authority, the VOC, and to an extent the EIC, had been granted sovereign power over such areas. Sovereignty could and would be enforced with arms if necessary.[5]

But this would not have applied had there been a common body of natural law in force in international relations pertaining to any kingdom. In that case any state would be a sovereign power and not derive its sovereignty from an external contract. A Company could then not engage in an armed conflict with an indigenous state without the consent of its sovereign authority and could not legally enforce a monopoly. But this would apply only if states in Asia recognized such natural laws and lived up to such perceptions. And according to most European authorities in Asia, the Indian states only respected brute force—so one had always to be prepared to draw the sword. "By nature the kings in India are unreliable and if we suffer but the slightest reverse they will immediately side with our opponents," as the councilors at Goa put it in 1658.[6]

But the authorities in the metropolis were mostly opposed to any use of violence and an involvement in local politics. The costs were unpredictable and it was seen as an incentive to graft. The authorities on the spot, however, tended to perceive a more competitive reality in which sovereignty appeared to derive from the sword. There ensued a contrast between the "hawks"—generally found in Asia—who were pleading for local intervention, and the "doves"—mostly found at home—who were favoring abstention from local involvement and peaceful trade.[7] The Europeans might plead that the Asians were unreliable, but Asian kings might have argued with equal justification that the Europeans were too. Raja Sinha, the king of Candy on Ceylon, could tell some stories about his involvement with the VOC. So too could the *zamorin*. He had been enticed to aid the VOC in its conquest of Cochin by a Dutch commitment that he would have a say in the nomination of the rajah of Cochin and that Trichur and Chalur provinces were to be handed (back) to the *zamorin*. Although this was solemnly avowed, the Dutch never honored their commitments. Instead, they sided with the *perumal* of Cochin afterward—sworn enemy of the *zamorin*.[8]

Yet states in the Arabian seas also impressed Europeans as being unreliable since they viewed trade very differently than the Europeans did. The root difference was quite simple: European states in the Arabian seas directly engaged in trade themselves and used violence to further their commercial interests, while courts in the Arabian seas as a rule did not. (The Ja'ariba imams appear to be the exception.) Most others were mainly interested in the revenues deriving from trade.

Regarding the significance of this pursuit of revenue from trade, N. Steensgaard refers to the theory of F.C. Lane: Lane sees the sale of armed protection as a service rendered by a monopolist to his client for which rent is due.[9] The way in which this "protection rent" is levied differs in various societies. In a capitalist society this is done with capital and income taxes, in military-agrarian or feudal societies with land revenues and the military hold on trade routes. After merchandise was bought, it was burdened with protection rent. Steensgaard says protection rent is "externalized." If the protection rent is already discounted in the price of a product—through excises, for example—the protection rent is "internalized."

In the Arabian seas the state did not sell protection rent alone. It competed with a multitude of small suppliers, ranging from the ubiquitous thieves to local landlords, and—as we shall see later on in the case of *rahdari*—yesterday's thief might be today's tax collector. The former robber became a right honorable *chaukidar* when given a *farman* by the king, allowing him to tax instead of pillage merchants.

For the state was primarily a dealer in legitimacy, rather than in protection. Instead of the centralization of the right to levy taxes, recent studies of India and Yemen have emphasized the wide diffusion of this right within rural society.[10] In view of this diffusion of power, one tried to spread risks by claiming many different shares in the land revenues and as many warrants to legally do so as viable. One would also diversify one's activities and play the game of politics as much as that of trade. This was insurance against bad harvests and political chance. Commercial and political elites shared in an identical circuit of credit, goods, and services, based on the exaction of the land revenue: a political and military game.

Such a competitive reality was far removed from the image of Asian states ruled by an all-powerful tyrant, depicted by many Europeans. But although this view of Islamic empires as centralized despotisms still influences debates on state formation in Asia, it was derived from, and was actually only applicable to, the situation in Europe. Such a view did not accurately depict politics in the Arabian seas and to an extent was not intended to do so either.

## European Views

The Company servants in Asia mainly held two different legal views of the situation there. Some reasoned that Asian and African societies had a completely different character from European ones in terms of both their social and religious manners. European legal norms could not be upheld in the Arabian seas since they applied only to Christians. Others argued that "the law of nature," based on the innate human feeling of right or wrong, was applicable to Asia as well. Our first case in point is a difference of opinion amongst VOC personnel at Surat. Was a deposition in a criminal suit against a Dutchman's testimony given under oath by a Hindu valid? And—in a civil lawsuit—could accounts delivered under such an oath be considered evidence? The directors of Surat, G. Vosburg and J. de Buquoi, reasoned that such was not the case. One had to view such an affidavit as comparable to that of a minor or a slave. For under Christian law only oaths by believers were legally valid. A Hindu's testimony needed to be endorsed by a Christian. Gentlemen XVII were in doubt and submitted the issue to the faculty of law at Leiden University. According to these lawyers the capability to distinguish between right and wrong is inherent in human nature.

Law is derived from this capability and not from faith. An oath by anyone recognizing some deity is valid if delivered on a sacred book or object, since in recognizing a god, one acknowledges an objective standard of right and wrong. Thus, for example, in the Netherlands testimony by Jews was considered valid evidence.[11]

Another case is the view of treaties signed between the VOC and the rajahs in Kerala. According to van Goens, "The Dutch are wont to honor obligations and have to do so because of their religion. But in this part of the world people do not comply with solemnly delivered oaths and easily break commitments." The Company could not place trust in any solemn promise and would have to remain vigilant; Indians would fulfill their obligations only if they were forced to. The Company was well allowed to push demands beyond the limits fixed by the treaties, van Goens argued. If one stuck to the letter of conventions, the result would be that ever more insolent demands would be voiced and no treaty obeyed. "In the name of the Lord—would that I was wrong and that these people had but a dint of conscience or knew a God," van Goens exclaimed.[12]

His successor L. van Dielen, however, reasoned that religion had nothing to do with this matter and that the Indians certainly had a conscience. The rajahs might well have fulfilled their duties if the Company had not imposed impossible conditions on them—in particular that they were to deliver the entire pepper crop of their lands to the Company. This was a demand that conflicted with the intent—if not the letter—of those treaties, and even if it did not, who would voluntarily give up his income?[13] Such an arrangement would have been considered invalid in the European context as well. "If I want somebody to stay in my house, I will have to offer him decent shelter and food. But if I refuse this I should not be amazed if he runs away and steals my belongings," as the anonymous memorandum *Malabars' Interest* put it.[14] The rajahs were to be treated in accordance with universal norms of right and wrong.

The Company's accounts of states are not the objective testimony that scholars like W.H. Moreland considered them to be. The problem is not just that Asian states were perceived through the distorted lens of Roman or common law, but that the policy of the Company was justified by a peculiar interpretation of Asian societies. We will consider the Dutch case here, but comparable arguments were also heard in England or Portugal.

Take the note delivered by P. van Dam, the secretary-general (*advocaat*) of the VOC, to the Estates General relative to an English proposal to concede free trade to the Indies.[15] This is the official view of the VOC on the legal basis of its presence in Asia and is thus well worth consideration. Along with other arguments rejecting the English proposal, with which we shall deal later, van Dam wrote:

> We have had ample occasion to learn that people in the East Indies are in general of an evil and treacherous nature. They do not have the slightest scruple to break

> any commitment and are imbued with a deep hatred for Christians. Therefore, if they have the slightest occasion to do so, they will try to weaken and possibly ruin and exterminate them.

Free trade could not be permitted since the "evil nature" of Asians might necessitate the use of force. But when free trade did prevail, other Europeans might obstruct retaliatory measures.

With the expression "evil nature," van Dam did not intend to imply the Asians were an "evil race" but rather that the law there was not based upon innate respect (*facultas*)—as Hugo de Groot would have voiced it—for "humanity." Humanity here was defined as a moral quality (*aptitudo*) whereby "an individual is competent to have or to do a certain thing justly."[16] For the Asian "nature" was corrupted by the lack of constitutional safeguards to liberty. Asians would only respect the brutal despotism of the ruler. As they did not recognize the innate respect for humanity, they could not be included within a system of international jurisdiction based on this.[17] Natural law, applying to all people (*ius inter gentes*),[18] could not be extended to Asian states. If these were not even minding their own subjects' interests, how could one expect them to consider the common interests of mankind, such as the common right enjoyed by people to trade with one another, for example?

Moreover, if the application of the "law of nations" (*ius gentium*) was to be extended to the territory of Asian states, this implied, in principle, that these would recognize the European system of states. The law of nations is, by definition, multilateral. But Asian states were not part of the European concert of nations.

The exception to this rule was Safavid Persia, which had signed legally valid treaties with England, Spain, Venice, the Holy Roman Empire, Poland, and the Dutch Republic. Treaties like the Persian-Dutch one of 1634 specified privileges of Persian subjects in the Netherlands and of Dutch subjects in Persia. These conventions are interesting in their own right and as a precedent for modern international law.[19] But their practical significance was small. It seems doubtful whether the Safavid state was able to enter into bilateral treaties along European lines with its neighbors in the Arabian seas. This would have implied that the law sanctioned the existence of the government of the other signatory states. For a Shiite state such would seem an odd admission.[20]

Treaties were probably perceived by the Safavid lawyers as temporary expedients, rather than permanent arrangements framed within an interlocking system of international treaties. The VOC—later on—did not particularly like being reminded of the existence of these arrangements either. The Company reasoned it was not bound to honor them. Freedom of movement was linked by the Safavid state to either the payment of 10 percent customs or to the procurement of silk from the treasury. These conditions on freedom were not implied in the treaty of 1634, the VOC in Persia argued.

Dissatisfied with this, Persia—after having consulted Batavia but not Gentlemen XVII—in 1645 used force to obtain freedom from customs by a blockade of Bandar Abbas and a (failed) attack on the fortress at Khism. When the Gentlemen XVII got word of this they were furious: "We understand the matters concerned quite well, even though we are not seated at Batavia," they wrote—underlining the word *Batavia*. The High Government of the Indies in Batavia apparently reasoned, Gentlemen XVII continued, that one could resort to force to sort out any trivial difference of opinion. "Too promptly one argues: we can not accept such conditions, ergo one may attack somebody without looking for any reason or justification. This is a stance we cannot vindicate to ourselves or to the world." The Persian point of view, that one was to pay customs or pack one's bags, was both reasonable in common sense and in law. "For might the king not argue: I am lord and master in my country. Either you will obey the law of the land or, if you do not want to, you may leave."[21]

This case prompted the Gentlemen XVII in 1650 to draw a General Instruction (*Generale instructie*) defining the legal status of the Company in Asia and the line of conduct that was to ensue.[22]

The *Generale instructie* distinguished three different areas of jurisdiction of the Company. First there were those where the Company enjoyed full sovereignty (the Moluccas). Second, there were regions where the Company had received certain prerogatives to exercise sovereignty over indigenous princes (Batavia, Ceylon, and later Kerala). And, lastly, there were lands where the Company did not enjoy any rights to exercise power and was but a humble merchant. In the latter case the Company was to trade peacefully and respect indigenous legal norms. This was as much a pragmatic as a moral position: except in the case of tyranny, when one has exhausted any alternative to resistance, one may not use violence against kings with a divine right to rule on their own territory. For in Calvinist thought God ordains the king.

What were the practical implications of this perspective for day-to-day policy? As Zwaardecroon wrote from Surat in 1702, where one traded in peace "one should behave with leniency, amiability and forbearance, though treated and abused by tyrants like a slave. For one always has to keep in mind the rule of old that one resides here as a merchant and not as a ruler. But one might wish that we were treated like a merchant too, for in that case it would be easier to adapt to the rules of the country!"[23]

One could reason, however, that if the Company was treated in an arbitrary manner it would have a right of resistance against tyranny. There was between the Gentlemen XVII and the High Government of the Indies at Batavia, the Board of Directors and the Presidencies of the EIC, the Conselho Ultramarino and the Conselho do Estado in Goa, a constant friction between two lines of thought.

There were those who argued that one could define on one's own what constituted tyranny in accordance with European legal norms. For if the Dutch, Portuguese, or English *natio*s was permitted preferential treatment, this implied that the area of the factory and the members of the *natio*s were included in extraterritorial law. If such norms were violated, this was an infringement on privileges.

On the other hand, others argued that comparable favors had been allotted to other groups who were not under extra-territorial jurisdiction, like the Saraswats in Cochin or the Jews in Yemen. Consequently, just as Jews in the Netherlands were under Dutch jurisdiction, the factory was not granted exemption from indigenous law. And one had a right to resist tyranny only if this conflicted with indigenous norms and the common feeling of right and wrong, but hardly for any trifling offense against European law. In general, Batavia tended to support the first position, Gentlemen XVII the second.

But the latter position would imply that there existed such a generally recognized system of law in the countries concerned. And according not only to F. Bernier—the best known representative of this stance—but to various directors of the VOC as well, most states in Asia were "despotisms," states where the law is arbitrarily defined by the ruler and not adopted by the general consent of the population, as expressed by diets in Europe. Asian states were thus effectual tyrannies that could not be divinely ordained.[24] Consider the example of the views of K. Hartsink—the director of the VOC on the Coromandel Coast—on the Qutb Shahi kingdom in 1686:

> Here a polity, or a civil government based upon laws, is unknown. The local ruler is sovereign. He acts as he pleases and does whatever may occur to him. The rich and the needy, the mean or the powerful are all equal to him. He pardons or punishes as he pleases and with money he may always mollify the king and his absolute lord. The local ruler is a man living in great pomp. He has as many servants as he likes; he gets free entertainment of 1,200 pagodas a year and free servants and Brahmins—or nosy busybodies [*kijk in den pannen*]—as well. So he cannot do anything, or pocket any present but has to perfectly declare everything or it would cost him his head. This man who here, down under, seems so powerful and pompous is held in little esteem when he comes to Golconda. He may not even sit down beside his lord without permission. There he is plundered and squeezed like a sponge, and the end of a local ruler is generally in poverty and misery. It is highly exceptional for him to retain some respect—and indeed his life.[25]

Because of the general fear of the arbitrary violence exerted by the ruler, the entire body politic was corrupted. Since law did not guarantee life and property, everyone tried to grasp as much money as possible. "With the Moors," Hartsink wrote, "one can obtain everything desired for money, but if one comes to them without gilded arguments they are deaf and plug up both ears for our request." Unlimited power is evil—and leads to moral decay: the king was thus almost inevitably a weakling. Sultan Abdul Hassan Qutbshah, for instance, was "effeminate, vain without ability; he is mainly interested in women and leaves the affairs of state to the Brahmin Madoena; a clever, devious and untrustworthy little fellow [*manneke*]."

This insistence on the unbridled despotism prevailing in Asia often tallied well with the interest of the Companies or of the Estado. If they violated rules of conduct appropriate to European international relations, they could deny this by claiming that these did not apply to Asia anyhow. Hartsink called, for example, for the seizure of Diva Island near Masulipatam and blockade of the port if not allowed lower customs. Mere levy of customs certainly would not have been considered a valid casus belli in Europe.[26] But since Golconda was being "unreasonable," one would have to use the baton to teach the "moors" a lesson.

As many officials of the Companies well recognized, a blanket characterization of very different societies, ranging from Mataram to Bijapur, from Atjeh to the Zaidit imamate, as "oriental despotisms" was too neat to be true.[27] Van Rheede considered it hard to swallow when reflecting on the system of government in Kerala, for instance.[28] Van Goens and others had conveniently labeled the system of government in force at Calicut and other independent states there an "absolute monarchy." If kings did not obey treaties, this could be blamed on the ruthless double-dealing of the sovereign and he would have to be punished.

But, according to van Rheede, Kerala did not fit any neat Aristotelian distinction of the system of government. "One can neither say with good reason that the Malabars are ruled by a monarchy or by a single head of state, nor that it is a republic, or that, thirdly, it is ruled by the common people. Their government really consists of a mixture of those three." When observing the daily running of the government in Kerala, it was clear that there were distinct—if unwritten—limits to power that had arisen because of the innate respect for customs rather than because of "proper constitutional arrangements, laws or through the general consent of the people." For, if such was not the case, how could one explain the existence of myriad small and weak chieftains along the coast that would normally have long been crushed by a more powerful neighbor?

One often took a far too superficial view of what was actually going on at court. The veneration bestowed on the kings would seem at first sight to be "rather fitting a slave than a free people." But if the monarchs appeared to enjoy vast powers, this might was in reality "closely circumscribed and only enforced by the vigor of custom. So it seems more like living up to custom than free and unbridled exercise of power."

Reverence would not be paid to a king because of the sharp edge of his sword but merely because of his impeccable adherence to a vast number of rituals and other rules. Those customs, in effect, inhibited the effective exercise of authority.

Now, one might plead—van Rheede argued—that if rajahs were not observing their promises, they were behaving treacherously. But one had to squarely put part of the blame for this on the VOC too. Treaties between Company and rajahs were, in reality, not valid for they had not been made with the consent of the signatory but under pressure of military retaliation by the Company. "And people behave very differently threatened with fire and sword than when listening to arguments without consequence." One ought not to be angered if rajahs were hesitating to honor commitments. If treaties were not even valid according to European norms, how should the rajahs be expected to comply with them?

## Companies and Courts

### *Merchants and Rulers: Malpractices and Corruption*

Shifting to a consideration of the policy of courts in the Arabian seas toward commercial matters and concerning trade with Europeans in particular, I could do no better than to quote T.B. Macaulay writing on the seventeenth century:[29]

> The most enlightened Englishmen looked on India with admiration. The most enlightened natives of India were scarcely aware England existed. . . . It was probably not known to one of the statesmen in the Durbar of Agra that there was near the setting sun a city of infidels called London, where a woman reigned and that she had given to an association of Frankish merchants the exclusive privilege of freighting ships to India. That this association would one day rule India . . . would have seemed to the wisest of European or Oriental politicians as impossible as that the inhabitants of our globe should found an Empire on Venus.

Indeed, why should the courts bother with such an obscure group of foreign merchants? One has to use a magnifying glass to gather any reference to traders, let alone to European traders, in official chronicles, an absence that is all the more puzzling if one knows that those same chronicles are mostly not altogether short on words.

To study the relation between states and merchants, historians have, therefore, often been prompted to take statements of travelers and Company accounts at face value. And when dealing with indigenous states these documents are full of complaints about "extortion," "bureaucratic interference," and "heavy taxation"—matters that traders are always bound to whine about, of course. Many writers have elaborated upon these complaints to argue that—to quote a very recent exposition of this very old view—"the agents of the Mughal government constituted the greatest source of political danger to the [merchant] community. For the officials of the Empire regarded the exaction of money, jewels and other valuable items from the trading population as a legitimate prerogative of rulership."[30]

It would be easy, too much so, to refute this argument by pointing out that all this oppression apparently did not hinder the accumulation of huge fortunes by the merchants of Surat or of New Julfa.[31] The very fact that the traders of Surat or Julfa are hardly noted in chronicles of the court would seem merely to indicate that they were little involved in the running of the realm. There were, obviously, no bureaucrats administering commerce.

Again, if there were occasional malpractices, in general Safavid and Mughal authorities mostly acted well within the constraints of law when committing what Europeans characterized as "abuses." Close examination of what the Companies considered "arbitrary acts of violence" reveals that such deeds were generally resorted to when merchants or Companies transgressed explicit limits on their freedom. These restrictions were for the most part expressly stipulated in the treaties or were seen as simple attempts to evade taxes.

Thus, to consider one case among many, the heavy additional imposts that the sultan of Bandar Abbas imposed in 1670 were labeled "despicable acts of tyranny" by the VOC. Zainal Khan, on the other hand, claimed these *avania*s—as they would have been called in the Levant—were merely his response to Dutch attempts to illegally fortify the factory and smuggle goods.[32]

Yet the evidence on corruption and administrative malpractice is too extensive to be entirely discounted. Traders and artisans in the Mughal empire or under the Safavids, the Zaidit imams, Bijapur, or the Marathas were indeed plagued by arbitrary impositions and had to bribe officials on a large scale.[33] In that respect, however, I would not vouch for the officials in Spain, France, or, as we shall see, England and Portugal either. As K.W. Swart has hinted in his study *The Sale of Office in the Seventeenth Century*, this practice and the widespread corruption it spawned both in Europe and in the Dar al-Islam may have had the same cause: the easy availability of cash—American silver.[34] In M. Weber's terms, this was the replacement of a "prebendal" by a "bureaucratic" administration.

Basically, both in Europe and in the Arabian seas the cornucopia of American bullion was emptied by the state in payments for a salaried bureaucracy and army. In either case officers, whether *noblesse de robe* in France or men of the pen—*ʿahl i-tajik*—in Iran, saw their position as their private fief rather than as a service to the public. They would resort to peculation to cover the inevitable fluctuations of income. Such oscillations might be caused by inflation, as in Persia in the second half of the seventeenth century, or, as in the Maratha Deccan, by fluctuations of the many local currencies. Or again, as in the Mughal empire, it might be caused by the resistance of local landholders to attempts to impose central authority and central taxation on them.[35]

Both Eastern and Western public functions were increasingly sold: thus, by 1670, in the Safavid empire most subordinate positions were sold. Under the Marathas in the eighteenth century the sale of office reached a unique pitch, but already in the seventeenth century Shivaji and Sjambaji had extensively resorted to selling positions. They were but following in the footsteps of the Deccan sultanates, where offices were also farmed on a large scale.[36]

Moreover, oriental bureaucracies were subject to their own "Parkinson's law." They were always attracting more people aspiring to office than they could entertain by creating service tenures or shares in the land revenue. For, while creating a new bureaucracy and standing army, some niche had also to be sought to accommodate old elites. The consecutive overcrowding of the administration forced new entrants into the administration to grab money by illegal means. We shall deal with the "*mansab* crisis" in the Mughal empire in a different context, but the overcrowding of office was not confined to the Mughal empire. Tensions between old and new elites apparently also occurred in the Zaidit imamate under Imam Muhammad Muta'wakil. The imams were manning the administration with Ethiopian slaves instead of the tribesmen, their former allies, who mightily resented this policy.[37]

The rise of a paid bureaucracy and mercenary armies in Iran under the rule of Abbas I and Abbas II has been reasonably well researched. According to V.V. Minorsky, a major part of the staff of army and administration consisted in the late seventeenth century of *homines novi.* Slaves recruited from Kart'li and Kurdish tribesmen filled the ranks of the army, instead of the Azari Turks who made up the Safavid hosts during the sixteenth century. The administration was increasingly manned by *Farsi ʿahl i-tajik:* Persians, often of humble descent. With much of the land revenue still controlled by older elites, newcomers had to seek an income through graft.[38] A case in point illustrating both the rise of a *noblesse de robe* and of their tendency to dabble in corruption is the biography of Muhammad Saru ("The Blond") Taqi, grand vizier from 1636 to 1643—a striking case, but far from the only case. Saru Taqi, whose father was a baker, had advanced by the grace of patronage of the governor of Mazendaran, who appreciated his administrative abilities—particularly his proficiency in drafting missives. Having no ancestral property to boast of, Saru Taqi was on the take. His ousting from office and subsequent assassination by *sipahsalar* Jani Khan was mainly prompted by his appropriation of royal revenues. During his last four years' stay in office he was thought to have embezzled more than 4,000,000 guilders.[39]

If anything, this tendency of officials to engage in illegal transactions increased in the later seventeenth century as officials saw their incomes in cash dwindle due to inflation. And this occurred despite the efforts of grand vizier Sheikh Ali Khan Zanjah to curb peculation and illegal exaction with draconian measures including scores of beheadings. Officials still had to invent ways to enhance their dwindling incomes, however, be it by trading, by fleecing the treasury, or by straight highway robbery. Moreover, the Safavid empire resorted to farming out, even auctioning, land revenues to gather more money. Public discontent with the constant robbery of both the subjects and the treasury by officials, and with the abuses committed by tax farmers, had reached such a pitch by 1674 that Shah Sulaiman refused to receive any petition from his subjects. The grand vizier was afraid to leave his house for fear of being stoned by angry mobs.[40] Thus, as in Europe, a venal state was a cliff that the "fragile ship of capitalism had to sail around," to use F. Braudel's image. There was a gap, and often an abyss, between the interests of the rulers and the ruled.[41]

But corruption works both ways for merchants. One might groan under heavy impositions, but it was easy to evade these by the liberal use of bribes. A good case, if not from our area of concern, is that the VOC at Bengal for 40 years carefully drew up two lists of imports. One list was to be delivered to the officials of the Hugly *divani*, and one contained the actual imports which, in return for the occasional "present" to officials, were not declared at customs. And—I might add—there could have been a third list of goods illegally imported by the VOC's servants on their private account without authorization of the Company. But already the second list was twice the size of the official one. Of course, such connivance of officials in smuggling might cause the occasional collision between the smugglers and some zealot at the customs house or of the Company trying to forestall those sneak imports—the resulting surcharges would then be "extortions" cherished by the Company.[42]

### Merchants and Rulers: Royal Shipping, Royal Trade

The lack of interest of Persian sources in Europeans raises an important question: Why did states like Bijapur or the Gujarat sultanate permit the establishment of Europeans—particularly of the bellicose Portuguese—on the coast at all? Their armed forces far outnumbered those of the Portuguese and there was only a slight disparity between European and Indian military technology. Were the Portuguese there due to "divine providence," as they would maintain? Or was it rather because those states were not very interested in Europeans and were not willing to risk their expensive and irreplaceable armies to capture some unimportant port towns? Historians do not excel in figuring out godly intentions, but Pearson provides a plausible answer.[43] Most major states in the Arabian seas had their focus of power in the interior, he argues. Their vital source of revenue was agricultural taxation; the average Bijapuri, Safavid, or Mughal grandee was therefore little interested in maritime trade. They took little account of Portuguese depredations on trade and preferred to strike a bargain with them whenever possible. Pearson makes a good case. Of Sheikh Ali Khan Zanjah it was remarked, for example, that "he has garnered most of his experience in wars in the interior and he has little feeling for, and little interest in, maritime or mercantile affairs."[44] Sheikh Ali Khan was the rule rather than the exception.

If most nobles had no interest whatsoever in maritime trade, this might not apply to a minority, however, and that minority often included the king and his closest dignitaries. Since the conditions under which nobles and officials of the state were in business may shed some light on the policy of the state toward merchants, I shall list a number of examples, moving from east to west.

### Kerala

This is obvious: maritime trade was of great importance to minute port-principalities like Badagara or Purakkad, and both operated a fleet. As to the larger states: both the *colathiri* at Cananore and the *zamorin* were officially permitted by the Portuguese—and in their footsteps the VOC—to send two royal vessels to trade at Mocha. In reality this limit of two was soon transgressed, and Calicut operated an entire fleet.

*Ikkeri*

Officials of the Ikkeri *nayak* were engaged in seaborne trade in two directions. First, some of the coastal vessels used in the rice trade with Goa and Cochin were owned by officials. These were mainly the tax gatherers of Mangalore and Barcelore. Portuguese mercenaries dwelling at Barcelore often manned these crafts. Second, Ikkeri sent two or three ships yearly to Kung and Muscat, mainly loaded with rice; one generally brought horses in return.[45]

*Adilshah*

This case is well documented and merits a longer treatment. After the Portuguese-Adilshahi treaty of 1576, the Adilshah dynasty had been allotted the right to send two or three ships to Mocha and Hormuz yearly, which were to be given Portuguese navicerts. Royal goods would not have to pay customs dues. Bijapur would not transport prohibited goods aboard the royal ships—Christian slaves from Abyssinia and arms.[46]

Although the Estado had in the first half of the seventeenth century more pressing concerns than bickering with the Adilshahi empire, there was a great deal of resistance to this arrangement. Little respect was paid to the Portuguese prohibitions on "merchandise," which caused the Lusitanians to demur. Both Bassein and Goa protested that the Adilshah was stretching the terms of the treaty to the limit—and beyond. This led to several clashes where Adilshahi ships were seized and searched by the Portuguese authorities, only to be released from custody after Bijapuri protests. The growth of shipping at Dabhul and Rajapur, mostly with royal vessels, severely harmed the trade of Daman and Bassein, it was muttered there, particularly since lesser grandees, like the *faujdar* of Rajapur, and not just the grand vizier but lesser nobles in attendance at court too were claiming that privileges allotted to the Adilshah applied to them as well.[47] This is logical since many officials connected to the grand vizier, Mustafa Khan, *khan i-khanan* (1636–1645), for instance—the main shipowner on the Konkan Coast in that period, who operated more than seven ships—were immigrants from Persia or emancipated Ethiopian slaves with strong ties to Yemen, the Banadir Coast, and the Gulf.[48] Many officials in the Konkan ports were of such Sidhi stock and settlements of emancipated Ethiopian slaves, soldiering in the Bijapuri armies, may have shared in the revenue of harbors where there were powerful Sidhi communities. It was thus at Bassein and at Danda Rajapur (Gheria), which in the sixteenth and seventeenth centuries were places approaching "Ethiopian"—or rather African—city-states on the west coast that were ruled and mostly populated by the *Sidhi*s. The revenues of those ports were to be spent on arms and oared fighting ships for the Bijapuri campaigns in Sunda and Ahmadnagar. It was obviously important for Adilshah that trade increase. Despite the picturesque hosts that the Adilshahi sultanate could occasionally muster, the empire was continuously walking a financial tightrope. Since the bulk of land was assigned in fiefs, the income of the royal household from land was limited. But the incomes from Rajapur and Dabhul were partly the crown's, partly the grand vizier's revenues; it was important to tap this fountain of prosperity by operating ships and leasing the right to transport freight therein.[49]

In effect, the Portuguese were aiding the Adilshah with this policy. By treaty the Portuguese were to place a representative at Dabhul, who was to hand *cartazes* to ships from Dabhul. The Portuguese might sack ships heading to other ports, provided that half of the goods seized were handed to the Adilshah. Portuguese aid was an indispensable tool for developing the royal revenue, then. Nor was this only the case with the Adilshah: Nizamshah was also to receive half of the customs revenue of Chaul as tribute annually.[50]

### *Bhonsle Svaraj*

This older tradition of direct involvement of states in the Maratha Deccan with the maritime trade of the ports in the Konkan was pursued under the Marathas. L. Leendertsz, chief merchant of the VOC at Vengurla, put it thus:

> The countries, which Shivaji possesses, are poor: there is little trade there and few farmers. And they do not yield but half of the money he needs to pay for the garrisons and the 184 castles he presently possesses. [Therefore his revenue] mainly consists of those derived from the seashore; in particular the customs of a number of ports of which he is the proprietor. Otherwise he would be in severe trouble for the remainder of his income consists of poor land, planted with palms and some rice.[51]

This was certainly an exaggeration: the income from customs was only a tiny portion of the income of the kingdom. But customs revenues were of importance in the local context of the Konkan. For the conquest of the Konkan by the Bhonsles was a slow one: it only involved a few fortresses and market towns occupied by troops of the royal household. Most forts were not under the direct control of the Bhonsles; most revenue from the countryside collected by local landlords. Only in a few ports, Rajapur for instance, were taxes gathered directly by the Bhonsles. Hence the court strove to develop the revenue of those harbors. With such benefits one might engage mercenaries. And thus one might acquire a hold on the division of the land revenues, though only in the very long run.[52]

So, to attract trade, in 1664 the Bhonsles embarked upon an extensive program of shipbuilding. The VOC at Vengurla could not find a carpenter for necessary repairs since all were pressed into service for constructing war and commercial vessels for Shivaji.[53] These were mostly small vessels for coastwise navigation, but in the seventies dozens of small dhows from Rajapur and Vengurla reached Muscat. Most of these were owned by the Bhonsle family and freighted by small merchants.[54]

### *Mughal Empire*

We have already considered royal shipping from Surat, which might be seen as a component of "a mercantilist policy aimed at stimulating the trade of Surat," as H. van Santen suggests. However, the Mughal chronicles—generally not remiss in finding any occasion to praise the ruler—do not give much indication that such a conscious policy was followed. Whose policy was it? should rather be the critical issue here.[55]

Part of the income from the customs of Surat was allotted by Emperor Shah Jahan to his favorite daughter Nur Begam as part of her household income (*sarkar*). She was a shrewd woman with a keen interest in trade. The royal ships, as proven by Persian documents from 1655,[56] were largely keels belonging to Nur Begam and operated on her behalf by the governor of Surat. The merchants of Agra, who paid a part of the freight premium to the princess, mainly used these ships. Nur Begam took an immediate interest in trade and regularly wrote the governor of Surat urging him to send precise accounts of her income from Surat. In 1662, when Aurengzeb confined Nur Begam to the fortress of Agra "to give Shah Jahan relief in his solitude," her ships could not be seized by Aurengzeb (Nur Begam being alive and Shah Jahan merely being "pensioned") and it was therefore thought best to demolish them.[57]

Though this demolition of the huge royal ships made for a dramatic sight, and van Santen uses it to prove the mercantilist policy which the Mughal empire supposedly pursued, it was merely an episode. By 1680 the Mughal empire was again operating "three to four big vessels which depart every year to Mocha with 2 to 3,000 holy men (as they call them). These ships have been built thereto by the king. And, when they return in September, they take some merchandise along."[58]

Prince Azzam on his own behalf also ran various ships that sailed to Atjeh and Banten. While according to the Hugly port registers in Bengal the nobles retreated from operating ships themselves by 1685, in the Arabian seas they both dabbled in Indian shipping and invested in it—as well as in English country trade.[59]

The participation of the Safavid empire and the Zaidit imamate in maritime trade was obviously severely constrained by the lack of wood and difficulties with shipbuilding. The Safavid empire did muster a coastal fleet but it had no oceangoing vessels. It was possible to rent cargo space in Indian ships, however, to take freight to Surat, the Coromandel Coast, and Siam.[60] Yet the major maritime enterprise of a kingdom in the Arabian seas was located on the Omani Coast. Such maritime trade was business, but warfare was big business and its proceeds dwarfed trade. So too was gathering the land revenue, and both in Iran and in India the most profitable transactions were with co-shares in it. Mughal *mansabdar*s had many different portfolios in the revenue, army, and trade, and all might be pursued for both profit and honor. Mahmed Amin Khan, who had the rank of 4,000 *zat mansabdar*—one of the most powerful men at the Mughal court—in 1684 bequeathed in cash and valuables alone a sum estimated at 110 million rupees (by comparison, all assets of the VOC in Asia were then worth about 60 million rupees). And that was still apart from vast flocks (more than 800 camels alone), immense possessions in Bengal and on the Coromandel Coast, and innumerable other estates belonging to his family. Aside from those main pursuits Amin Khan also had some shares in ships on the Coromandel Coast.[61]

Political entrepreneurs on this scale of magnitude would hold the petty, single-minded pursuit of commercial profit in disdain. Mirza Muhammad Sadr Murtuza al-Mulk, councilor of Golconda, was operating several ships and sold rice to the Portuguese at Ceylon. Yet he assured F. de Mascarenhas in 1648 that "your Excellency should believe that I am not a merchant, nor do I want to be. When I am sending merchandise to Ceylon, I am not sending it because I want to conduct trade but merely to serve your Excellency."[62]

As the chronicles testify, in the court too, trade, not to mention Europeans, was rarely discussed. For even in Persia, where European states were after all useful potential allies against the Ottoman empire, the court had only a vague idea of any Christian nation beyond the Russian border.[63] And this certainly applies to the Mughal empire. The majority of the nobles manifested neither knowledge of nor interest in the affairs of European "hat-wearers," let alone understanding of or participation in conflicts among them—such as the fights between the Dutch and Portuguese for example. Yet if the Mughal or Adilshahi court scrupulously allotted equal treatment and privileges to both, either would interpret this as treason.[64]

### Kings and Companies

The affairs of the European "hat-wearers" were of no interest to the court, as such matters should, first, be left to the *natio* to settle, and second, to local officials who were involved in arranging disputes concerning trade. The court's affairs were lofty concerns of politics and war, not petty quarrels among *natio*s.

Such trade as was conducted in a few monopoly goods by the court was not primarily seen as a source of gain. This commerce was rather perceived as an asymmetrical exchange of gifts—amiable taxation—though, admittedly, it was a thin line between bestowing gifts and bartering them for a profit. Monopoly products were often goods with clear military significance, too: horses, sulfur, powder, saltpeter, copper, and lead.

This applies to the monopoly of the Safavid empire in the silk trade with the VOC and the EIC as well—the most striking exception to the rule that the state hardly interfered in trade.[65] Emissary W. Bastinck had bothered Taqi more than enough with his interminable claims that the price of silk sold to the Dutch was to be lowered by two tomans, the grand vizier complained in 1643, for example. "Our friendship does not depend on the price of silk. This is but a merchant's affair; it is of no more value than straw. No, it is based on our grand alliance to strike a blow at our enemies."[66] To the court the prime concern was the grand alliance. This had to be munificently affirmed by giving presents to the court. The VOC should not bother the court with the price of presents or of silk; this should be left to the officials in charge—the *mustauwfa i-khass* in this case.

To the Safavid court the trade of the Company was a revenue matter of local importance, primarily an affair for local tax gatherers rather than for the department responsible for the administration of revenue (*divan*), and still less for the court. But—as the revenues of ports were mostly farmed—the *ali kapu* had, and could have had, but a very limited say in these matters. Affairs concerning the silk consigned to the VOC were handled as a rule by officials from the department of royal estates (*divan i-khass*) like the *mustauwfa i-khass*, the comptroller general of this department; the *nazir*, the treasurer general of the royal warehouses and workshops; and the "stick-keeper" responsible for visitors to the palace, the *icik agashi bashi*. Finally—to make the matter still more complex—during the reigns of Safi and Abbas I, the general accountant of the royal mint (the *sharaf bashi*), Mulaim Beg, was responsible for money received from the Company in return for silk.

These were all minor officials; the highest authority to whom Companies could appeal was the grand vizier, for the incomes from tax farms and the royal domains, from which most silk derived, were his responsibility. If, as was often the case with the VOC and the Portuguese, one desired to speak directly to the "head of state," or addressed letters to the shah, this was considered insolent behavior. It meant that humble traders put themselves on the pedestal of a king.[67] Representatives of European Companies were during audiences assigned the rank of minor Georgian chieftains who had rented some tax farms from the shah and occasionally made a fuss about it.

The same applied to the Mughal empire: here, too, the Europeans were seen as a *natio* among others, and at best as a band of rather unimportant allies—a band of no consequence on the coast. Their main task was to protect the interests of the maritime traders. The court might intervene if such interests were damaged, but rarely did so. The immunities granted to *natio*s had been allotted to allow merchants to carry on their own affairs. It would transgress the limit of competence of royal jurisdiction to intercede in any matter of minor importance. These were to be adjudicated through its proper customs among the *natio* itself.[68]

## Viceroys and Chieftains

Let us now shift the focus from the court to local conditions. As Pearson has noted, there were different measures of involvement of officials in matters maritime and commercial.[69] On the west coast, or in the ports of the Red Sea and the Gulf, the incomes of officials directly depended on revenues gathered from customs. And not only did they rely on this. The customs of Surat, for example, were farmed. Portions of those incomes were assigned to expenses for "foodstuffs, weapons and *sepoy*s" for the Mughal army operating in the Konkan. Local officials were thus bound to be keenly interested in trade. Their very survival depended on it.[70]

Grand seigneurs at court, the VOC at Surat noted in 1658, were a hard nut to crack; one should abstain, if possible, from dealing with them.[71] Local officials, however, were often financially involved in trade and would favor the Company's case. The Company thought they were easier to understand and more pliant, too. Even though they were corrupt, one could fathom their devious plots, whereas it was very hard to glean any precise insight into what was going on at court. The Companies—and the Portuguese—therefore rarely dealt directly with the ruler. They preferred to delegate affairs to Armenian or *bania* representatives whether in Golconda, Bijapur, the Mughal empire, Yemen, the Safavid empire, or Oman.[72]

Locally the Europeans could have a marked impact. There might arise markets and trade networks associated with a Company and often under European protection. Rings of merchants, who were closely tied to the local administration, were dealing with the Europeans too. European private traders began to deal in bulk products, which might infringe on tax revenues. And they recruited and trained soldiers and delivered arms. R. Frykenberg has assessed the impact of such developments on the local politics of India's east coast in the eighteenth century in an exemplary study.[73] What happened, Frykenberg argues, was that Indian magnates asked the EIC for help in the adjudication of various conflicts among themselves. Tussles occurred almost inevitably, for lengthy bargaining between various elite groups, between tax collectors and richer peasants, was always involved in the collection of the land revenue. Frykenberg calls this the "inner logic" of Indian politics. Such bargaining entailed the marshaling of military muscle as well.[74]

Thus an increase in local trade might well give rise to a tangled web of intrigue involving local potentates, mercenaries, and servants of the Company. They would coalesce to steal incomes of their overlords and carve out kingdoms of their own without the cognizance of any central authority. Such deals in the seventeenth century did not yet occur in the Mughal empire, certainly not at Surat, where the Europeans were completely at the empire's mercy. But they did eventuate in the more decentralized, and surely weaker, Bijapuri state, which bordered on the only territorial area under European control—the Portuguese conquests.[75] We will briefly consider Kerala, another area where the Europeans also possessed considerable leverage, later.

Shadowy dealings between Adilshahi nobles, the Savants, and the Portuguese at Goa were the rule in Candal—the three combining or quarreling to extract revenues from the villages in Candal and Bardes. With the rise of the house of Bhonsle on the coast after 1662, a fourth party entered the fray, so the *subehdar* of Candal, the Savants, and the Portuguese jointly opposed this newcomer. "We are the Savants, we are a family equal to the Bhonsles, you will have to entertain us properly," Lukham Savant's representative justified his opposition to Shivaji's ministers. If the Bhonsles did not allot the Savants a treatment commensurate with their standing, they might well restore their rights with help from "hat-wearers" at Goa.[76]

Portuguese involvement was almost inevitable, for Portuguese territory provided a commodious haven for the discontented. Local landholders might appeal, and would appeal, for Portuguese aid while adjudicating feuds involving land revenues, for fights were a normal component of its levy. For example, Narna Sinay and Chandra Vai—landholders from Candal—requested the governor of Salcete to aid them with men and weapons in order to conquer their ancestral properties. They would allot part of its revenue to the Portuguese if they were successful. Shivaji had stolen their lands, they asserted, and its revenue had been sold to tax farmers.[77] Those deals culminated in 1685. Upon having repelled the Maratha forces, who had invaded the island, from Goa, the Portuguese handed funds, arms, and mercenaries to Rama Deva Savant so that he and his allied local landholders (*desai*s) could rise in arms against the Bhonsles in 1687. The Konkan was divided between the two parties beforehand. The Portuguese would receive one-third of the revenue of the Konkan Coast and the *desai*s the rest. This money was to be remitted to Goa by bills of exchange by the *desai*s' brokers there. The *desai*s had long sold grain and bought rice in Goa through middlemen. This deal reared great expectations of the count of Alvor. "The damage which those blacks have inflicted on Sjambaji is incredible." So, "barring some miracle, we will be lord of the Konkan in a few months." There did occur a miracle, as Pate was—more or less by chance—taken by the captain of Mombasa, and Alvor had to hastily dispatch all his forces to the Swahili Coast. This brought his grand scheme to a premature end.[78] Nor was the viceroy alone in participating in local politics: in 1672 the Marathas had seized the territory of Ramnagar. Its former ruler—the "king of *chauth*" (*o rey chauthai*), as the Portuguese called him—had sought refuge in the mountains. "It will be a good idea," the captain of Daman wrote the governor of Bassein, "to favor him with some gunpowder and what more he might require, in order that Shivaji will not completely succeed in becoming lord of his territory."[79]

Besides such local power-mongering there was always an amount of low-key violence surrounding European settlements that normally spilled over into European territory. Tana, for example, was a typical frontier next to hostile lands.

Fearing confrontation with his Maratha neighbors, viceroy Luís de Mendonça Furtado had forbidden the governor of Tana, J. de Mello Perreira Sampayo, to pursue Maratha bands that invaded this territory. This was impossible, the governor of Tana warned.[80]

Every year during the collection of the land revenue, bands of Maratha horsemen would make a sally into the countryside to collect their incomes. They would normally take some cattle, fire some guns, or capture some peasants in the process, for the peasants would never grant the revenue to the Marathas without putting up at least a show of resistance. Those routine raids inevitably extended into Portuguese territory since there was no clear border between Portuguese and Maratha lands. The Portuguese would then have to retaliate with a foray themselves; they too would have to steal some cattle beyond the border and take some hostages, or else their villages would become depopulated or cease paying land revenues to them.

The Portuguese protested against those practices to the Mughal *tanahdar* of Ramnagar, Trimbaji Raja, in 1677, but he pleaded it was not really his responsibility if his soldiers "steal cattle, cows, bullocks or take away rice and other things." For the warriors were assigned to the villages and "every place has its own credit." If they thought the villages were not giving them sufficient income, they would strengthen their bargaining position by a bit of plunder. And it was but justified that they would ransack Portuguese territory too. "We have a right to levy *chauth* on your majesty but you inhibit us to come—this is not fair."[81]

Thus an "unruly frontier" of violence and banditry continued to separate Portuguese from Adilshahi and Maratha territory. By interfering in local politics the European enclaves "created disorder." There was another reason for this. As in Europe, on the west coast troops were mainly recruited from this unruly frontier.[82]

The *senado da câmera* of Daman was worried in 1677 that the territory was open to a Maratha attack. Since 1638 Daman had by and large been at peace with its neighbors. The *foreiros* saw no need to entertain horsemen and troops or to train them regularly. Though the villages were to entertain a contingent of armed men, the matchlocks had been welded to ploughs and the peasants had forgotten the pursuit of arms. Every able-bodied man was used to work in the fields. Here—as probably everywhere on the west coast—most labor tended to be allocated to agriculture unless the agricultural cycle was in disarray due to military operations. This tended to yield surplus manpower in the villages. This could be employed in the army, or disgruntled peasants might turn bandits. And indeed, there was a severe problem of brigandage in Bassein.[83]

This applies even more to cavalry. Horses were expensive: to maintain one horseman in Daman cost 148 pardaos, a professional soldier 40, a rower 12. And one has to add to this the fertile land that had to be put aside as grassland. One would only keep horses if there was empty land available and there was a pressing need to do so. The "unruly frontier" thus tended to be self-perpetuating:

conflict would yield both man-and norsepower and this tended to sustain the friction.[84]

The Adilshah might be a whimsical despot, King Philip IV of Spain gloated in 1636, but "in my land of Bardes and Salcete, there are more than 40,000 trustworthy vassals of mine, all provided with firearms." What did the Adilshah have with which to face this? Only a ragtag host of mounted archers.[85] Two years later Muhammad Razi, the governor of Candal, invited the Dutch to establish a settlement at Vengurla and talked aloud of invading Bardes. Pedro da Silva panicked; one could not possibly resist a Dutch-Adilshahi coalition.[86] So in 1639 *fidalgo* A. Moniz Baretto was sent to Bijapur. He was well received but there was a strain of anger in the polite words of his interlocutor.[87] Just when Moniz had left Bijapur he received a "slanderous pamphlet" voicing Adilshahi discontent with the Portuguese.[88]

This pamphlet alleged, first, that the king had allowed the Portuguese in his territory on condition that they were not to harm traders and that they were to protect the ships of his majesty. Yet the Portuguese had robbed Adilshahi ships on slight pretexts and murdered Bijapuri sailors. The Portuguese had also been allowed to exercise freedom within their jurisdiction, provided they did not engage in hostile behavior. But the Portuguese had repeatedly made inroads on Bijapuri territory and they had built fortresses facing Bijapuri lands—an open declaration of hostile intent. The Adilshah had allowed the Portuguese a right to trade with his subjects, provided they paid customs. Yet the Portuguese were defrauding the royal customs, having put up *alfândegas* of their own. While the objective of the privileges allotted the Portuguese was mutual benefit, the Portuguese swallowed all the benefits.

All of this is just defamation, Moniz retorted. The Adilshahi ships were not sailing with a navicert, so the Portuguese had a right to seize them. Goa was repeatedly invaded by plundering gangs from Candal. The Portuguese had a right to resist such marauders and even to pursue them beyond the border. Bardes and Salcete were the territory of the Portuguese king, not some fief of the Adilshah. And as to the Portuguese defrauding the customs, the Adilshah had a number of vassals who did not pay anything at all. Those chieftains systematically plundered Portuguese merchants, so it was reasonable to occasionally retaliate. The king ought first to tackle his own defiant chiefs before claiming revenue from the Portuguese.

This case constitutes an illustration of the themes treated in this chapter. The Europeans were permitted by kingdoms in the Arabian seas to establish themselves since their trade was of mutual benefit. The king would mostly not interfere directly in this, as it was an affair of subordinate tax gatherers. The European *natios* could carry on as they liked—provided they did not arrogate sovereign rights and were not openly hostile. However, such an official policy of noninterference was in reality negated by the rapacity and ambitions of lower officials. The Europeans might use connections to lower-ranking officials to extend their privileges beyond the accepted boundary of conduct. Thus might they engage in openly hostile acts, like blockading ports, seizing ships, or even making armed inroads on the territory of indigenous states.

Such deeds were justified by pointing to the despotic character of indigenous states: if there were no reasonable laws, and if the only intent of the state was ransacking the merchants, it would then be necessary to behave likewise in self-defense. This was an apology, but not entirely so. The Mughal or Safavid empires were military-agrarian societies where revenues were apportioned by the exercise, or at least the threat, of armed force. This might be innocuous enough if trade was increasing, but in a period of decline and stagnation the state indeed weighed heavily upon commerce.

## Notes

1. VOC/OB 1308, 16 January 1675, fo. 729 vo.
2. *COACM*, ix, p. 319.
3. I have relied heavily for the ensuing paragraph on J. Fisch, *Die europäische Expansion und das Völkerrecht* (Stuttgart, 1984).
4. Which, obviously, one might exploit to one's advantage: the Dutch conquered Cochin half a year after the Dutch republic had signed a peace treaty with Portugal. The Portuguese, therefore, argued the Dutch ought to give Cochin back, while the Dutch pleaded they were not at peace since Batavia had not received the message, although to the Estates General van Dam was well willing to admit this was only a subterfuge for plain grabbing of land. ARA, St. Gen., Lias VOC, 5738 ii, June 1661.
5. J. van der Kan, "De rechtstitels van de Vereenigde Oost-Indische Compagnie," *Mededelingen Koninklijke Akademie van Wetenschappen*, Nieuwe Reeks 5/8 Afdeling letterkunde (Amsterdam, 1942).
6. HAG, LM, 36, 16 August 1659, fo. 383.
7. For this well-known contrast for the eighteenth century, see P.J. Marshall, "British Expansion in India in the Eighteenth Century: A Historical Revision," *History* 60 (1) (1975), pp. 28–43.
8. Ironically the VOC decided in 1663 not to allow the *zamorin* a say in the nomination of the heirs to the throne of Cochin as a mere *ad interim* decision to shore up some support for the Company in Cochin, to which it then stuck right up to 1793 (ARA, HRB 543, "Remarks on the present state of Malabar," fo. 14–28). K.N. Pannikar, *Malabar and the Dutch Being the History of the Fall of Nayyar Power in Kerala* (Bombay, 1931), pp. 24–38, now mostly replaced by H.K. s'Jacob, *The Rajas of Cochin 1663–1720* (New Delhi, 1999), which I received too late to aptly consider in this text. For the complaints of the *zamorin* regarding the treacherous behavior of the Dutch see VOC/OB 1547, "Report of Louis Tayspil," fo. 187, and VOC/OB 1256, 17 January 1667, fo. 11–13. For Ceylon see K.W. Goonewardene, *The Foundation of Dutch Power in Ceylon 1638–1658* (Amsterdam, 1958).
9. F.C. Lane's essays on protection rent have been assembled in *Profits from Power: Readings on Protection and Violence-Contrólling Enterprises* (Albany, 1979); "Violence and the Rise of Capitalism: F.C. Lane's Theory of Protection," *Review* 5 (2) (1981), pp. 247–73.
10. See, for example, F. Perlin, "The Pre-Colonial Indian State in History and Epis-

temology: A Reconstruction of Societal Formations in the Western Deccan from the Fifteenth to the Early Nineteenth Century," in H. Claessen and P. Skalnik (eds.), *The Study of the State* (The Hague, 1981), pp. 275–303; P. Dresch, *Tribes, Government and History in Yemen* (Oxford, 1989). For Iran see the classic work of I. Petruševski, *Ocerki po istorii feodalnie otnošenije v Azerbaidjane i Armenii v XVI–nacale XIX vc.* (Leningrad, 1949).

11. VOC 363, "Advices of legal scholars to the VOC," fo. 19b–23.

12. VOC/OB 1251, 28 December 1665, fo. 555 vo.

13. VOC/OB 1268, 20 January 1668, fo. 1049.

14. KITLV, H. 49, "Malabars interest (ca. 1674)," fo. 15.

15. ARA, St. Gen., Lias VOC, 5739 ii, 19 March 1669.

16. Grotius, *De Iure belli ac pacis libri tres*, book I, chapters 1 and 4.

17. See R. Tuck, *Natural Rights Theories: Their Origin and Development* (Cambridge, 1979).

18. Grotius, *De Iure belli*, book I, chapter 12.

19. C.H. Alexandrowicz, "A Persian-Dutch Treaty in the Seventeenth Century," *The International Yearbook of International Affairs*, 1958, pp. 201–6.

20. The ideological component of the Safavid diplomacy has been badly researched, but see J.L. Baque-Gramont, *Les Ottomans, les Safavides et leur voisins (Contribution à l'étude des rélations internationales dans l'Orient islamique)* (Leiden, Istanbul, 1987), and the discussion between H. Römer and R. Savory in *Iranian Studies* 7 (1974).

21. VOC/XVII 317, 22 September 1648.

22. P. Mijer (ed.), *Verzameling van instructiën, ordonantiën en reglementen voor de regering van Nederlandsch-Indië* (Batavia, 1848), pp. 76–116.

23. ARA, HRB 834, Memoir by H. Zwaardecroon, fo. 141.

24. R. Koebner, "Despot and Despotism: Vicissitudes of a Political Term," *Journal of the Warburg and Courtauld Institute*, 14 (6) (1961), pp. 275–305.

25. ARA, St. Gen., Lias VOC, 5741 i, Report by Willem Karel Hartsink (1654), fo. 8–9; see too van Dam, *Beschrijvinge*, III, ii, p. 151.

26. See A. Knippendorf, *Staatsverfassung und Mächtepolitik. Zur Genese von Staatenkonflikten im Zeitalter des Absolutismus* (Berliner historische Forschungen, 15) (Berlin, 1975).

27. Compare, for example, the Dutch view of Mataram: L. Nagtegaal, "Rijden op een Hollandse Tijger. De Noordkust van Java en de VOC" (Academisch Proefschrift, University of Utrecht, 1988), pp. 23–37.

28. H.K. s'Jacob, *De Nederlanders*, p. 106 et seq.

29. *The History of England from the Accession of James II*, 4 vols. (London, 1843–57/1966), iii, p. 374–75.

30. S.D. Haynes, "Merchant-State Relations in Surat 1600–1924," in S.D. Haynes and G. Prakash, *Contesting Power: Resistance and Everyday Social Relations in South Asia* (Delhi, 1991), p. 246.

31. A point also conceded by J. Calmard, "Les Marchands Iraniens," in D. Lombard and J. Aubin (eds.), *Marchands et hommes d'affaire asiatique dans l'Océan Indien et la mer de Chine 13–20e siècle* (Paris, 1988), pp. 92–102, who, otherwise, rather sticks to the traditional idea that the Safavid empire oppressed the merchants.

32. N. Steensgaard, "Consuls and Nations in the Levant," *Scandinavian Economic History Review*, 14 (1) (1967), pp. 15–17; VOC/OB 1270, 24 April 1670, fo. 886; VOC/OB 1273, 18 June 1670, fo. 1901–6.

33. See, for example, Om Prakash, "The Dutch East India Company in Bengal: Trade Privileges and Problems 1633–1712," *IESHR* 9 (3) (1974), p. 272; H. Mukhia, "Illegal Exactions from Peasants, Artisans and Menials in Eighteenth Century Rajahsthan," *IESHR*, 14 (2) (1977), pp. 176–200; and H.K. Misra, *Bureaucracy Under the Mughals* (New Delhi, 1989), pp. 185–205.

34. K.W. Swart, *The Sale of Office in the Seventeenth Century* (The Hague, 1964).

35. Thus, for example, the interpretation by H.D. Robertson, "Revenue Enclosure in Mr. Chaplin's Report," in *Selections from Papers from the Records of the Government of India*, 4 vols. (London, 1820–26), iv, pp. 399–426; and by R. Clive in K.N. Datta et al. (eds.), *Fort William-India House Correspondence*, 23 vols. (New Delhi, 1949– ), iv, p. 330.

36. A. Wink, *Land and Sovereignty under the Eighteenth Century Maratha Svaraj* (Cambridge, 1989), p. 340. Revenue farming was maybe a reaction to agrarian crises, as Wink argues, though not only under the Marathas but under Bijapur as well; it was also used for the administration of newly conquered regions. It was common in the districts in Canara that were conquered by the Adilshah, for example. Yet I still cannot escape the impression that Wink is looking for deeper motives than really existed, much of the revenue farming being simply a way to externalize "protection costs."

37. Dresch, *Tribes, Government and History*, p. 200.

38. Minorsky, *Tadhikarat al-Muluk*, p, 35; M. Haneda, *Le Châh et les Qizilbâs: le système militaire Safavide* (Berlin, 1987); K. Röhrborn, "Die safavidische Zentralverwaltung," in *Handbuch der Orientalistik II Regierung und Verwaltung des vorderen Orients in islamischer Zeit* (Leiden, 1979), pp. 17–48.

39. This is mainly based on Geleynssen 283, "Extracts from the Isfahan diary," fo. 213–21 vo.; see further N. Falsafi, "Sargozast-i Muhammad Taqi," in *Haft majala i tarikh va adabi* (Teheran, 1342), pp. 163–203; H. Braun, "Ein iranischer Grosswezir des 17e Jahrhunderts: Muhamad Taqi," in W. Eilers (ed.), *Festgabe deutscher Iranisten für das 2500-Jahrfeier Irans* (Stuttgart, 1971), pp. 1–7.

40. V.P. Papazian, *Agrarnie otnošenije v vostocnoi Armenii XVI–XVII v.* (Erevan, 1972), pp. 183–205; VOC/OB 1297, 5 October 1674, fo. 33; VOC/OB 1323, 30 July 1678, fo. 656.

41. Braudel, *Capitalism and Material Life*, ii, p. 554.

42. ARA, Coll. Hudde 14, "Account of merchandise fetched to Bengal."

43. M.N. Pearson, *Merchants and Rulers in Gujarat: The Response to the Portuguese in the Sixteenth Century* (Berkeley, 1976).

44. VOC/OB 1330, 12 August 1677, fo. 970 vo.

45. See, for example, ANTT, DRI, 36, 20 February 1636, fo. 225; ANTT, DRI, 40, "Regiment for Martin Teixeira da Sá," fo. 337; AHU, Índia, Cx. 31, 21, "Conditions of peace between the Rt. Hon. Antônio Pães de Sande and Bassopa Naique, the king of Canarra."

46. K.N. Mathew, "Trade in the Indian Ocean and the Portuguese System of Cartazes," in M.D.D. Newitt (ed.), *The First Portuguese Empire* (Exeter, 1985), p. 75. For the Portuguese-Adilshahi relations see also S.B. Nayeem, *External Relations of the Bijapuri Kingdom* (Hyderabad, 1976), pp. 216–36.

47. See, for example, VOC/OB 1170, 19 April 1648, fo. 658; and Vengurla diary, 2 and 3 April 1648; Geleynssen 317, 30 May 1642; ANTT, DRI, 48, 21 December 1643, fo. 138; AHU, Índia, Cx. 11 bis, 209, "Relação."

48. J. Sarkar, *The House of Shivaji* (Hyderabad, 1987), pp. 82–91. For Mustafa Khan's

role on the Konkan Coast see, e.g., Geleynssen 102, "Copies of passes delivered in Persia 1645," and on the Coromandel Coast see S. Arasaratnam, *Merchants, Companies and Commerce on the Coromandel Coast 1650–1740* (New Delhi, 1986), p. 225.

49. *English Factories* 1646–1650, p. 251; VOC/OB 1122, "Report of van Twist," 16 March 1637, fo. 156; VOC/OB 1132, 20 October 1639, fo. 183. Dabhul and several ports in the Konkan had actually already been in crown domain (*khud-bast i-jama'*) since the fifteenth century, according to Said Ali Husain Tabatai, *Burhan i-ma'athir* (Hyderabad, 1300/1936), p. 137. On the Sidhis in southern Gujarat see in particular Couto, *Da Ásia*, Dec. VII, book 6, Cap. VI–VIII.

50. B.G. Tamaskar, "Malik Ambar and the Portuguese," *Journal of the Bihar Research Society* 33 (1952), pp. 33–35; Évora CXV/1–39, fo. 31.

51. VOC/OB 1278, "Relation by Leendert Leendertsz.," fo. 1761.

52. Wink, *Land and Sovereignty*, p. 305; Ajuda 51-VII-23, fo. 279–81; see S.N. Gordon, "The Slow Conquest: Administrative Integration of Malwa into the Maratha Empire," *MAS* 11 (1) (1977), pp. 1–40.

53. VOC/OB 1245, 16 August 1664, fo. 355.

54. AHU, Índia, Cx. 29 bis, 174, Anonymous memorandum 1673.

55. H.W. van Santen, "De Verenigde Oost-Indische Compagnie in Gujarat en Hindustan," (Academisch Proefschrift, University of Leiden, 1982), p. 77; see also S. Chandra, "Commercial Activities of the Mughal Emperors During the Seventeenth Century," *Bengal Past and Present* 78 (146) (1959), pp. 93–97; Pearson, *Pilgrimage to Mecca*, pp. 119–21.

56. ARA, Coll. Aanwinsten 1936, vii; see also VOC/OB 1168, 12 March 1648, fo. 623.

57. Ali Muhammad Khan, *Mirat i-Ahmadi: A Persian History of Gujarat*, 2 vols. (M.T. Lokhandwale, ed. and trans.) (Baroda, 1965), i, p. 253; VOC/UB 877, fo. 398.

58. VOC/OB 1323, 26 January 1678, fo. 395 vo.

59. Om Prakash, *Dutch East India Company and the Economy of Bengal*, p. 233; VOC/OB 1343, 1 March 1679, fo. 439.

60. See, e.g., AHU, Índia, Cx. 29 bis, 174, Sjeikh Ali Khan to João Correia da Sá; and VOC/OB 1210, 6 March 1656, fo. 783.

61. VOC/OB 1388, 31 March 1683, fo. 2053–55.

62. ANTT, DRI, 57, fo. 461.

63. A characteristic case of the Persian ignorance of things European is the letter from Abbas I to the Estates General in ARA, St. Gen., "Loketkas Perzië," reproduced in L. Feketé, *Einführung in die persische Paläographie* (Budapest, 1977), doc. 89; the Safavid chancellery was completely unaware of the precise function of the Estates General. So the letter was addressed to the "Frank Istandgi," "der Name erscheint im Dokument personifiziert," as Feketé puts it (p. 493).

64. But, in all fairness, both Dutch and Portuguese were unreliable allies too. Van Twist had assured Mustafa Khan in 1637, for example, that "the sun may shine in the darkest night, the moon in bright daylight, ere the Dutch and Portuguese are friends," whereon the Dutch had entered into negotiations with the Portuguese, only four years later, without consulting or notifying their nominal ally at Bijapur (VOC/OB 1122, "Report of van Twist," 16 February 1638).

65. See T.E. Hertzig, "The Iranian Raw Silk Trade and European Manufacture in the XVIIth and XVIIIth Century," *The Journal of European Economic History* 19 (1) (1990), pp. 73–91; the following paragraph is, however, mainly based on R.J. Barendse, "Zijde,

zamboeks en zilver: de Verenigde Oost-Indische Compagnie in Iran" (Doctoraalscriptie, University of Leiden, 1984).

66. Geleynssen 167 B, 14 October 1642.

67. A case in point is the quarrel over diplomatic protocol between envoy J. van den Heuvel and the *vaqa-i navis* in 1685—interesting for Safavid diplomatics too. Since the ascent of Abbas II to the crown, van de Heuvel protested, the court had shifted to styling letters from the VOC from *nameh* (letter) to *arz* (a petition). And the initial invocation of a *farman* from the court had shifted from *farman-i humayun sarf navaz yaft ke* to *farmani humayun šud ma'alum ke*, the formula normally used for subordinate officials. Again, the seal was moved from the front to the back of a *farman*. VOC/OB 1416, 20 October 1684, fo. 1033; VOC/OB 1398, 13 October 1684, fo. 610.

68. Pearson, *Merchants and Rulers,* pp. 118–25.)

69. M.N. Pearson, "The Sixteenth Century," in A. Das Gupta and M.N. Pearson (eds.), *India and the Indian Ocean* (Calcutta, New York, 1987), p. 80.

70. BAC, A 58, 22 May 1677, fo. 219 vo.

71. VOC/OB 1216, "Memoir of Gerardo Pelgrom," fo. 598 vo.

72. And this to the anger of Aurengzeb, who threatened not to take letters merely signed by a representative of the VOC into consideration (VOC/OB 1252, 3 May 1663, fo. 794).

73. R. Frykenberg, "Company Sirkars in the Karnatak. The Inner Logic of Political Systems in India," in R. Fox (ed.), *Realm and Region in Traditional India* (Madison, 1968; New Delhi, 1979), pp. 117–64.

74. Ibid., p. 163.

75. There is a very extensive literature on this topic; see P.P. Pissurlencar, *Maratanche-Portuges riyasat*, translated as *The Portuguese and the Marathas* (Puna, 1974); A. de Bragança Perreira, "Relações do Estado da Índia com os reis vizinhos," in *Arquivo Português Oriental*, I, ii, p. lxii et seq., and in *O Oriente Português*, velha série, 24 (1932), pp. 117–330; A. Lobato, *Índia. Relações Luso-Marathas* (Lisbon, 1967).

76. E.S. Sardesai, *A New History of the Marathas*, 3 vols. (Bombay, 1963–65), i, pp. 114–7; B.R. Parasnis (ed. and trans.), *Shivaji Chatrapati* (Puna, 1932), p. 95.

77. BAC, A 501, 12 August 1679.

78. AHU, Índia, Cx. 33 bis, 124, 24 January 1686; and 181, 10 December 1686; AHU, Índia, Cx. 38, 13, "Capitulations Between the Count of Alvor and Daluy Dev Saunto."

79. BAC, A 58, 18 May 1677, fo. 272 vo.

80. BAC, A 496, 27 February 1678, fo. 55.

81. BAC, A 58, 22 May 1677, fo. 219.

82. F. Perlin, "South Asia and Western Penetration from the Sixteenth to the Nineteenth Century: A Problem of Epistemological Status," *Review* 6 (2) (1980), p. 299; Talett, *War and Society*, p. 91.

83. BAC, A 500, 9 December 1678.

84. BNL, FG, Cód. 1783, "Livro das receitas e despezas"; BAC, A 58, 23 May 1677 fo. 250–54.

85. ANTT, DRI, 36, 28 January 1636, fo. 61.

86. ANTT, DRI, 41, 10 July 1638, fo. 1 vo.

87. ANTT, DRI, 44, 2 March 1639, fo. 254.

88. ANTT, DRI, 44, "Treslado dos capítulos," fo. 414–15.

# 5

# The Merchants' World

Debates on Asian—though not on African—merchants in the seventeenth century are still dominated by the views of J.C. van Leur.[1] There must, however, be as many interpretations of van Leur as there are pages in his (not very voluminous) oeuvre.[2] I shall presume that van Leur intended to say the following:

Indonesian and Indian society were "primeval agricultural societies" (*agrarische oerbeschavingen*). The surplus here was creamed off by labor dues, later by agricultural taxation. With the surpluses of agriculture devoured by agrarian empires and consumed within those empires, trade was only conducted in a small array of luxury products. Furthermore, demand was severely constrained by limited production. Commerce was, therefore, mainly (but van Leur did not claim only) conducted by small peddlers. And because of the small array of goods offered for sale simultaneously by a host of traders, the market was characterized by unpredictable fluctuations.

Steensgaard, following van Leur, has characterized Asian merchants, particularly those operating along the caravan routes in the Middle East, as peddlers, and markets as "peddlers' markets" characterized by unforeseeable fluctuations of prices and of supply. This theory has been criticized by several writers, but I think Steensgaard's argument is partly justified. [3] Peddling trade, whether along the caravan routes, in coastwise navigation, or in the agrarian hinterland, may be considered the ground level of a many-storied building of trade in the Arabian seas, to paraphrase F. Braudel's metaphor. But on top of this ground level there were many higher levels: there was a level of military redistribution of wealth, and a level of monopolist practices, of usury and big commodity transactions; indeed, perhaps rather a floor populated by capitalists than a floor of capitalism.[4]

In a sense the peddler is, in van Leur's view, the sole *Homo economicus* in an economy where surpluses are not primarily sold in the marketplace. But one has to view the merchant as both economic and political as well as hierarchic man. Those elements were intertwined: concerns we might consider marginal to business were of grave economic importance. And the other way around, matters we might consider religious, familial, or ceremonial might involve economic reasoning.[5]

Products were marketed in very different ways. The markets were segmented—in the argot of economics—according to the merchandise involved, the quantities sold, and often according to its destination. When, in Isfahan, one peddled a piece of cloth at the caravanserais of the Russian merchants, one would be offered a very different price than at the serail of the Turks.[6] To turn to an African example: the ties between the Muzungulo chiefs and those of Mombasa might certainly be seen as a political and social arrangement, a traditional African "joking relationship." But it was also a form of long-run market segmentation, protecting Muzungulo merchants marketing one commodity against fluctuations in the price of a different one.[7]

The demand for some products was unpredictable since supplies were inelastic. Supply could not be easily increased or decreased to respond to fluctuation in demand. Such peddlers' markets were almost textbook cases of perfect competition: unlimited numbers of sellers were meeting unlimited numbers of customers there. Yet they deviated from the textbook in that prices did not reach equilibrium but showed wild fluctuation. One cause was that goods could not be stocked. Another—and a more important one—was that information was incomplete, preventing merchants from controlling the market. Access to information thus played a paramount role in the formation of prices in the Arabian seas.[8]

But while the demand for one product might show wild fluctuations, another product might be monopolized by a small ring of sellers who controlled the access to information. This could be done for goods for which the demand could be predicted, supply could be adjusted, or buffer stock could be amassed. In this case the trader could cater to fluctuations by the accumulation of buffer stocks or even by using monopolist practices to restrict the amount of goods brought to the market.

Still, the trader's existence was dominated by insecurity. The main pursuit of an entrepreneur in the hostile environment of the crisis-prone seventeenth century in general was gaining security rather than high profit, as has been stressed by many writers on Europe.[9] The environment of the Arabian seas was even more hostile than that in Europe, and the urge for security an even more paramount consideration. This was not only because of the uncertain monsoon climate and the consequent vagaries of the harvest and the huge distances, but also because the state did not offer many guarantees to trade. It was thus not possible to safely put away part of one's money in a consolidated state debt or in joint stock companies guaranteed by the state.

One hedged one's bets by "portfolio investments," as C.A. Bayly has argued: dealing with a wide array of goods, investing small outlays in many different branches of affairs, and working through a large number of intermediaries.[10] Portfolio investment was primarily in men. Middlemen might function as buffers to smooth the disruptive impact of fluctuations of supply and prices on commerce. Dependent on a network of intermediaries, the merchant would strive to maintain credit with his partners. The creditworthiness of a merchant depended upon his wealth, for sure, but on many other considerations too, which might well run contrary to the pursuit of profit.

As to the role of these middlemen, one may consider the ideas of T.P. van der Kooy on Amsterdam in the seventeenth century.[11] This economic historian argued that in a pre-industrial society trade would tend to be concentrated in a "staple market" or—in the idiom of economic geography—"a primary locus market." Because of the intransparency of supply, the small scale of commerce, the high transaction costs (i.e., the costs involved in buying and selling a good), and the risks involved in trade, markets would be hierarchically organized in space and function. By the concentration of transactions the costs involved could be reduced. The risks of unpredictable price fluctuations could be curtailed by the formation of buffer stocks. To achieve such a centralization of supply and demand, merchants in a "staple market" would specialize in specific activities. Such dealers would function as a buffer to cushion risks. Van der Kooy distinguished three specialized groups of merchants: maritime traders, taking care of imports; "secondhand" merchants, involved in marketing commodities, who functioned as a buffer between supply and demand; and export dealers, looking after the distribution of goods.

No doubt the reality is much more complex than the theory. Merchants cannot be divided this neatly into distinct functional groups. Transport costs interfered with the formation of a hierarchy of markets and so did political hindrances. Yet in the Arabian seas one meets with a somewhat comparable organization of trade too. Through portfolio investment one catered to unpredictable fluctuations of supply and price. For risks were spread over the hierarchy of dealers who arranged sale and distribution.

We shall first consider the constraints on trade through transport costs and access to information. Next we shall consider the character of markets and the operations of merchants in the Arabian seas by considering three case studies. First we will examine two markets that would qualify as typical peddlers' markets: Basra and Mocha. Then we will review the very different case of the markets and merchants of staples in Gujarat.

## Transport: Maritime and Overland

It is virtually a truism—albeit a useful one—that in any economy prior to the steam engine the costs of transport accounted for an important part of the total costs of a good transacted and that the charges for maritime transport were lower than those for transport overland. Land-bound economies were thus constrained to small circles of local consumption.[12]

This was true for Western Europe and it was even more the case for the Arabian seas—as could be observed already in the case of the trade with Ethiopia, the interior of Oman, and between the Mrima Coast and the hinterland—because of the often hostile terrain and vast distances involved. As R. du Mans noted, caravans could roam the wastes of the Persian empire for months orienting themselves on the shapes of the mountains: "it's just like navigation—but on land."[13] At the slow pace of the donkey, Isfahan to Bandar Abbas would take four weeks, Isfahan to Gilan (in summer) three, Isfahan to Mashed six. "The stretches along the roads are wild and uninhabited . . . from halting-place to halting-place one may stride 6 to 8 miles without seeing a human being, only rough mountains." With the complete lack of orientation in the featureless desert, caravans would often march at night to fix their position by the stars. To take 250 camel loads of silk from Isfahan to Bandar Abbas would cost in 1642 527 mahmudi on 52,374 value, but for the leather transported in the same caravan, transport costs already amounted to 470 on 6,300 mahmudi for the leather. If, in the same year, one would have sent 250 camel loads of barley over the same stretch, that would have brought a total of 96 mahmudi compared with roughly 500 for transport costs.[14]

The economy of the giant Safavid empire can thus be perceived as an array of small local circles of supply that were crisscrossed by long-distance trade, pilgrimage, and military movements.[15] There were huge disparities in prices within the Safavid empire. Take the expenses of W. Geleynssen when traveling from Bandar Abbas to Isfahan in 1645. One maund of bread would cost at the consecutive caravanserais of Kuristan 9 mahmudi, at Tang i-dalang 4 mahmudi, at Kormut 12 mahmudi, at Sams i-Sages 24, at Lar 10, and at Jahrum 24 mahmudi, and so forth.[16]

Because of the costs and difficulties involved in transport, the economy consisted of small local circles of supply and consumption. That could surely be said for the African bush—as we saw already—and for the forbidding mountains of high Yemen and Ethiopia too.

It seems to apply to the Indian interior as well, as S. Blake has tried to demonstrate in an attempt to apply G.W. Skinner's model of rural marketing communities to Mughal India.[17] Basically the pattern consists of circles of marketing, bordered by the transport costs, which were centered upon the local market towns; these were in touch with provincial capitals and those in turn with the imperial centers. Yet only a small trickle of luxury products and of forced deliveries of foodstuffs reached the last.[18]

The triad of markets in northern India, a concept developed by Bayly to represent their spatial and functional patterns, is of some help here: it consists of the *hat*, the periodic small rural mart; the *ganj*, the permanent local (grain) market; and the kasbah, the regional market town. Likewise, in Praças do Norte, places were arranged in three categories. The villages; the *pacarias*, small rural marts where peasants would peddle rice and wood to the merchants and where these products were converted into cash; and the kasbah or market town, where products were resold and taxed: Tana, Tarapur, Bombay, and Bassein.[19]

However, the Indian pattern does not completely square with those elementary classifications for two reasons. First, periodic markets and fairs are an aid in the distribution of goods in an economy in which monetary relations have imperfectly penetrated the distribution process. Such was certainly the case in Praças do Norte, where an important part of economic circulation consisted of deliveries of rice by the peasants to landlords and their armed retinue. Markets and fairs are also an aid in an economy where credit has insufficiently penetrated into daily transactions. In other places, especially in the cities, shops took over, running on credit from the big merchants to the shopkeepers and from the shopkeepers to their purchasers. In the countryside of Bardes and Salcete, for example, which was more heavily monetized than Praças do Norte, there were few fairs (except at Mapusa, which was catering to the caravans coming in from the Deccan) but there was an extensive network of small shops. These were generally run on credit. Such shops might sell everything from cloth to candles, spices to salt.[20]

Second, various services tended to be widely spread in the countryside, if only since Rajput, Jat, or Maratha landlords mostly lived in the countryside, not in the towns. Much economic activity tended to concentrate in "manors," such as banking, luxury consumption, or the division of loot. One has to handle Skinner's model of rural marketing with some caution, therefore. The service or intermediate economy—producing war, poetry, prayer, and some luxury manufactures—was only partly based in cities or rural market towns, and in some areas shops fulfilled the function of periodic markets.[21] This would certainly apply to Kerala, where there were many rural fairs but few large market towns and where the *nayyar*s lived widely scattered in the countryside.[22]

There are also many exceptions to the elementary rule that transport costs constrain the area covered by markets and the sale of products. At Basra the VOC had to offer lower prices for Banka tin than at Bandar Abbas, for example. Its demand was curtailed by the import of Cornwall tin, which was transported through the Syrian desert directly from Aleppo.[23] This improbable overland trade in heavy metals over enormous distances was triggered by fluctuations of prices and their regional disparities. For precisely because of the difficulties of transport, prices did not reach one national level. This could make long-distance overland trade remunerative, in some circumstances even with bulk commodities.

The pattern of trade along the caravan routes catered to this. Like coastwise trade, the caravan trade mainly consisted of small local transactions: exchanging a few pieces of cloth for a few coins here, bartering these for some bars of metal there. Just as with coastwise trade, the aim of a caravan trader was not to rapidly take a product from one emporium to another; rather it was to make small profits on as wide an array of goods as possible. For if one brought but one product, a small local market would be glutted and the trader ruined.

Let us consider two concrete cases of peddlers along the caravan routes: Take the Julfa hawker, name unknown, who had received 10 pieces of Indian textiles from VOC second merchant P. de Witt at Isfahan: 180-guilder value. He was to barter this for rhubarb at Mashed, received from Sinkiang by the great caravans coming from Samarkand. On arrival he heard that, as Turkmenian raiders had plundered the caravans, no goods would arrive from Turkestan this year. He decided to buy 20 tufts of silk, received last year from Samarkand, and still for sale at the bazaar. De Witt was far from content and tried to get his profit of 200 guilders back from the merchant with little success.[24]

Another case: Nasr Ali Cagasi, a Turkish peddler, to whom Visnich had handed 15,000 guilders to buy rhubarb at Samarkand on Visnich's account. Visnich would receive two-thirds of the proceeds. When Visnich was murdered in the Syrian desert in 1630, Cagasi kept the money. The next year Cagasi traded between Samarkand and Circassia. In Samarkand he bartered textiles and spices for silk and rhubarb, which he exchanged in Circassia for Christian slaves, whom he sold to the Ottoman dominions. In 1642 Cagasi, who had meanwhile earned a sum of 32,000, went bankrupt. He was locked in chains by the VOC to force him to pay his debts. Nobody wanted to offer bail for him, though, so the Compagnie had finally to release him. In order to pay off his arrears to other merchant houses Cagasi had to sweat as a domestic servant. As an indemnity the VOC had seized one slave, an Armenian boy named Petros, whom he had procured for 60 guilders in Circassia.[25]

Peddlers such as these disposed of small trading capital and stock, and were not able to influence the movement of prices. They were victims of the market. Furthermore, they did not distinguish funds needed for personal use from those needed for trade. To follow A.V. Chayanov, one could compare the peddler's behavior to that of a small peasant.[26] Like the peasant, the peddler was not out to maximize profit but rather to maximize yield. The peddler would sell as much as possible, even when risking his profit. The larger the sales, the more people he could feed. Furthermore, like the peasant, he was interested in minimizing his drudgery rather than maximizing his returns—for a peddler time was not money. Trade was based on self-exploitation: the peddler engaged no labor except his own legs and perhaps those of family members.

So peddling was sluggish commerce: peddlers would remain at the caravanserais for months, to visit holy places, stay with old friends, and wait for a favorable rate in the bazaar.[27]

In a remarkable passage in N. Witsen's *Noord en Oost-Tartarye* we have a description—apparently overheard by VOC chief merchant H. de Jager at Julfa—of a journey made by Armenian merchants about 1680 from Smirna to Isfahan.[28] Next they would depart to Samarkand, then to Kashgar, to finally arrive at Peking. This was the ancient silk route then, which was still busily traveled by merchants. But no one was in a hurry. The journey could easily take three years from one end of the silk route to the other, since traders would often spend months in Isfahan, Samarkand, Kashgar, or Mashed to barter in the bazaars. The silk route was in the seventeenth century not directly competing with seaborne trade to China. For it was not really a highway from Europe to the Middle Kingdom; it consisted of a succession of small local circuits of trade.

Such slow traffic and the network of caravanserais and fairs to which it was connected should be imagined as the backdrop to maritime trade. Most routes in the Arabian seas could be accomplished within two to four months, but behind the inviting threshold of the coast loomed the impenetrable hinterland.

And throughout the Arabian seas transport overland was slow and hazardous. That was true for Africa and the "Empty Quarter" as much as for Iran and India, where the problem with overland transportation was not so much the expense as the risk involved and the slow speed.[29] But here too, overland transport over long distances clearly was an expensive affair. The costs for transporting cloth from Agra to Surat might amount to a hefty 40 percent of the price if one paid customs, and about 25 percent if not. For spices the costs were put at 10 percent.[30]

On the shorter distances the transport costs were less of a problem. From Vengurla to Raybagh on the opposite side of the Ghat the costs for pack oxen amounted to only 1 percent of the cost of the price for spices, 6 percent for cotton. Again, fetching piece-cloth from Ahmedabad and Broach to Surat overland in 1687 would amount to 13–14 percent of costs, and this sum appears to have varied little in the seventeenth century.[31] Rather, the trouble for a merchant on the seashore who was anxiously awaiting the arrival of his goods from the hinterland was the torturous delay involved. For example, when crossing the Narmada one often had to wait for days when no ferry was available. Ships depending on the monsoon could not wait for sluggish caravans.[32] And there was the added hazard of the weather. During the monsoon all communications came to a standstill. In Hindustan tracks would turn to bottomless swamps that could swallow entire carts. Torrential rains could pin down caravans before they reached their destination. Furthermore, the wet season was also the normal season for outbreaks of malaria, so it was not well advised indeed to travel then.[33]

Yet, clearly, the choice between routes, between land and sea transport, in India primarily depended on the protection rent involved. For example: the cost to rent a cart to travel from Surat to Agra (an 86 days' journey) amounted to 40 rupees per cart in 1701; costs for ferries amounted to 16 rupees; the "official" fee to be paid on custom dues was 7 rupees, and 12 rupees were spent during delays at customs stations. But additionally one had to pay 18 soldiers to guard the caravan, for a total of 180 rupees; miscellaneous fees for "armed escort"—a true protection racket provided by local rajas and *zamindars*—amounted to another 324 rupees; and sundry expenditures, such as the unavoidable alms or the "new moon presents" for the drivers of the carts, came to another 35.[34]

In Persia only beasts of burden were used, as its stony tracks were mostly unfit for wheeled traffic. But the Indians there occasionally imported carts from Ahmedabad to Bandar Abbas, perhaps for use during weddings. It is also possible that in the unsettled conditions of the eighteenth century in Persia, tracks deteriorated and wheeled traffic declined.[35] For transport from Bandar Abbas to Isfahan, mules predominated, and transport by mule was generally cheaper than by camel (normally 100 mahmudi versus 140 mahmudi in the nineties). However, conveyance by mule was much slower than by camel. The VOC, whose prime consideration was speed rather than price, mostly used camels to bring its silk from Isfahan to Bandar Abbas.[36]

The weight of the protection rent was paramount when choosing between a mule and a camel as well. It is possible that the rise of Smirna, terminus of donkey tracks to Azerbaijan, was connected to the greater safety of the roads upon the consolidation of the Persian empire after roughly 1620. This made for a preference for this cheaper route above the Syrian desert road that was served through camel caravans.[37]

It seems that donkeys were the normal beasts of burden along the Arab shores of the Persian Gulf too: Muscat was, for example, connected to the interior with donkey caravans. In Yemen camels would mostly be used on the desert routes, like the route from Jidda over Taif to Sa'na, where "one traverses nothing but horrible barren rock and wilderness"; this route was only used in case of dire necessity.[38]

However difficult the Persian roads might be, those tracks were busily traveled, for what never ceased to amaze travelers was the safety of the roads throughout the vast Safavid empire. This was very different from the dangers prevailing along the same roads in the sixteenth century and the many threats for travelers in the Ottoman dominions in the seventeenth. In the sixteenth century, when the Persian paths were crowding with bandits, the Turanshah had to arrange his own caravans—small armies—to link Hormuz to Qazvin.[39] The Portuguese then paid a fixed share of the customs of Hormuz (the *mu'arrir*, lusified to *mucaria*) to the sheikhs in the interior in order that caravans could safely pass their territory. The amount of *mucaria* probably depended on the frequency of traffic and the safety along the road concerned: protection rent in its purest form.[40] But when L. Winnincx traveled from Bandar Abbas to Isfahan in 1645, near Shiraz he could enjoy a nice outing to the spooky hideout of a former robber-chieftain, a highwayman who had faded into the distant past.[41]

This was accomplished by the *rahdari* arrangement for guarding the roads (which, of course, was derived from older Mongol arrangements). The Safavid empire might assign the revenues from a caravanserai and villages allocated to the caravanserai to do forced labor for its repair; or it might sell the right to tax a certain stretch of the road to a tax farmer of the caravanserai. They would have to take care of the road and entertain a few runners in return for a right to tax trade along the track. Since the trend in the administration of revenue in the Safavid empire was toward the substitution of assignments of the revenue by tax farms, the latter system came to prevail under Abbas I. Isfahan was, for example, surrounded by a circle of *rahdari* posts, each of which converged on a caravanserai. The merchants were obliged to bring their goods to one caravanserai, which catered to one particular route. With the revenues of the tax farmers depending on the traffic along their stretch of road, they were keen to attract it. It is obviously but a small step from *mucarias* to *rahdari*. The difference is merely that the latter is levied with the consent of a central authority and is thus generally more predictable.[42]

The traveler did have a high price to pay for this security, however. If the VOC had paid *rahdari* to take silk from Isfahan to Bandar Abbas, it would have paid up to 4 percent additional customs, which may actually have been greater than the "protection racket" paid in the sixteenth century.[43] Many traders were tempted to evade customs whenever they could. This spawned a serious problem of smuggling along the borders of the Safavid empire.

Although for a few products there was a definite choice between overland and overseas trade, between peddlers and Companies the overland trade in India and the Middle East also represents an enduring structure. The volume of traffic overland was little dependent upon fluctuation of trade. For in either case nomadism was linked to overland trade; it is thus extremely hard to ascertain whether movements overland increased or decreased, for nomads are almost by definition impossible to count.

In India, the trade overland was dominated by the seasonal movements of the migratory *banjaras*. Those movements were linked to the migration of cattle in summer from pastures in the Deccan to those in the Konkan. It was also related to a trade in draft cattle between the fringes of the jungle and the village communities. One is dealing with huge numbers here. The long-distance trade overland on the subcontinent was really but an adjunct to such movements of nomads and the cattle trade.[44]

In Bardes, for example, the inhabitants owned 2,000 oxen themselves and another 2,000 oxen were exploited by the tax farmer of the trade of Bardes, who monopolized the trade in arrack and coir rope. The oxen drivers made four trips to and across the Ghats every year. This was partly to procure merchandise, partly to allow the cattle to graze during the dry season. The Conselho da Fazenda at Goa had to grant these oxen drivers exemptions from paying customs. They were mostly poor men and their cattle was indispensable for agriculture.[45]

Moreover, the overland trade in luxury goods was but an adjunct to that in bulk goods. Probably the largest trade between coast and hinterland on the west coast was that in salt: an indispensable commodity in a tropical country. It was a very important source of income for both Daman and Bassein, for example. Every year Daman was visited by caravans of 2,000 to 3,000 head of cattle that would fetch up to 600,000 pounds of salt to the hinterland. Apart from this, small crafts also carried salt, in quantity, to Broach, Cambay, and Diu.[46]

The caravan merchants in India were mostly typical peddlers. Majumdar Sura, a *banjara* trader, had been sent to Daman to buy provisions on behalf of a bunch of Maratha soldiers. His property, "three bullocks and three bags with cloth," was stolen by vassals of the Portuguese king, which would ruin him, he complained.[47] But various forms of insurance and partnership were normal in the caravan trade. It was usual at Surat to insure goods going to Agra, while *banjara* caravan traders normally operated in partnership. The Portuguese generally bought saltpeter from the *banjara* caravans from the Deccan. They negotiated such deals with the *caravanbashi*, acting as spokesman for the caravan merchants as a group.[48]

Turning to the means of transport, as we already observed, most of the traffic across the plains of northern India and of Saurastra was done with bullock carts—even within Surat itself. For, according to Deodati (admittedly no great admirer of the *bandar i-mobarak*), a pedestrian would be covered in mud and filth to his waist. Both the fortunes of Surat and those of myriad humble kasbahs throughout the plains of northern India were linked to the bullock carts. There were infinite varieties of types: *bulubuna*s, *garga*s, *pandani*s, *boico*s, *sultani*s or *assari*s, and more.[49]

But for the steep mountain passes along the Ghats, pack animals were the predominant way of transport. In the case of the salt trade to Daman, for example, pack animals were used to transport salt over the Ghats; bullock carts were used for the trip to Gujarat. Those passages over the Ghats constituted true bottlenecks of trade. In Praças do Norte the donation of a fief (*foro*) of a market town near the Ghats would habitually include the passage over the Ghats as well. This often comprised a duty to safeguard them. This was no light task: the *koli* tribes inhabiting the jungle on the Ghats would often exact dues from the caravans. The passage had to be guarded by wooden hill fortresses, manned by bands of *lascarins*.[50]

As the fortunes of the ports in the Konkan were linked to the traffic across these passages over the mountains, most coastal towns in the Konkan were surrounded by extensive meadows for the cattle. At some particularly steep passages, covered with jungle, even those pack animals could not be used and soldiers and merchants resorted to porters. A hamlet of *koli*s, for instance, was assigned to Agaçerim fortress, located on a hilltop, to bring goods there.[51]

Again, most of the trade of Kerala across the Ghats was done with pack animals. As was noted by Captain Bacx, traveling from Negapatam to Trivandrum, when at the rural market town of Alur near the passageway over the Ghats, "we met in this village with an incredible number of pack animals, either coming loaded from Malabar, departing thereto, or grazing around the village: it is well nigh unbelievable and, as it seems to me, half an hour around the village there were as many as 10,000."[52]

Safety has as high a price as has danger. Roads in India were far more dangerous than in Safavid Persia, but the road dues were often lower. In 1638 Shah Jahan had forwarded a *farman* to the VOC abolishing internal customs in Gujarat. Customs were to be paid only at Broach and at Surat. The VOC decided to present the imperial *farman* to the various tax gatherers. Some "respectfully put the order on their head." Others "cursed the king." Anyhow, one had to pay precisely the same customs as before. Those *chaukidar*s who had previously earned a living from gathering customs now banded together as highwaymen to extort from the merchants precisely as much as they previously gathered in road dues.[53]

A telling example in several respects: the protection rent levied on merchandise in Mughal India was unpredictable at first sight, as the Mughal empire was not the only supplier and because of corruption. But, as mentioned before, this very corruption and competition in the sale of protection also ensured that those heavy dues could be easily evaded and that these would tend to reach equilibrium. Hence, as any economic textbook would predict, the plunder of highway robbers was mostly well known in advance and tended to stay at a stable level. For example, the robbers active around Agra were true entrepreneurs striving to oblige their clients—this is just as one would expect since most were the roving henchmen of the governor of Agra. They could conveniently be paid ransom by drawing a bill of exchange on the broker of the VOC before the caravan set out to Surat.[54]

All the same, during the turbulent last 20 years of Aurengzeb's reign, travel along some routes in Mughal India was very dangerous indeed. There was unrest in the Deccan; Punjab was in turmoil, the Delhi/Agra Doab and Rajasthan in revolt. This seriously upset overland transport, which might spell disaster for some ports, as noted above in the case of Dabhul, and might be a boon to others, as for Surat. This turmoil along the roads, J. de Buqoi at Surat gloomily commented in 1682, "is but a portent of the speedy decline of this state and of all former glory of the Mughal, and one might wonder how long it will take before this gangrenous body politic will have consumed itself and be shattered in pieces."[55]

Let us consider some further instances of rise and decline. We have a list of imports for Ahmedabad in 1643 which indicates that the city was the hub of a very large trade in sugar that was transported overland from the Punjab through Rajasthan, from Ahmedabad to Cambay, and from there to Persia and Yemen. This amounted to more than 3 million pounds yearly.[56] As we have seen, with the Rajput rebellion the roads through Rajasthan became almost impassable, which precipitated a contraction of this trade. By 1700 Cambay was importing sugar from Java, China, and Bengal. Toward 1686 even the small stretch overland from Ahmedabad to Broach and Surat had become so expensive and dangerous that the VOC decided to build three small *houris* to fetch goods over sea from Cambay to Surat.[57] For the traveling man was harassed not only by "bands of angry rebels" but by the bad state of the roads as well, which made a voyage a true ordeal.[58]

The route from Agra to Lahore was also extremely hazardous at the end of the seventeenth century because of the revolt stirring among the Jats in the Doab and the Sikhs in the Punjab. The trade and manufacture of Agra badly suffered. Whole neighborhoods of Agra were by 1690 deserted as merchants and weavers were abandoning the city—maybe fleeing to Lucknow, which was developing into a staple for textiles at the end of the seventeenth century.[59] The Jat horsemen made repeated forays into the suburbs of Agra, where they would burn and plunder. Worse than that, however, was the deterioration of the grand trunk road from Agra to Allahabad.[60]

W. Geleynssen's diary of a trip from Surat to Varanasi in 1636[61]—primary evidence that contradicts many travelers' descriptions of the roads in Mughal India[62]—is still somewhat unreliable. A cheery Geleynssen was clearly enjoying himself and would safely wander off the beaten track to visit sites along the route, like Fatehpur Sikri and the—just finished—Taj Mahal. It was true that midway through Rajasthan "there were rumors that robbers were intermixed among the travelers. So, we all grasped our rifles and sat watching on our bullock carts for half an hour." But despite the occasional adventure it was not a very hazardous journey. And it was quite a picnic at times, like along the grand trunk road from Agra to Allahabad, "which is very pleasantly planted with trees on both sides."

Ever since the war of succession to the Mughal empire (1658–62), however, the North Indian roads were increasingly infested with highway robbers. This often blocked the roads altogether. The banditry did not subside to its normal level thereafter, although "it is a common plague in this country since days of old"—mainly, the VOC asserted, since Aurengzeb had dismissed part of his host and many hangers-on of Shah Jahan's court, who now pestered the traveling man.[63]

We have another extensive letter book from 1690, this time covering the Agra-Lucknow trip. Organizing a caravan to procure indigo had meanwhile become a nearly military undertaking and the risks were proportionate. Caravans resembled armies, with up to 300 armed men. Local *zamindars* sent troops along, and the villages where the traders would buy indigo also provided them with an escort. This was not an honorific one since the caravan was confronted with robbers armed to the teeth near Daryabad. VOC merchant C. Grousius tried to curb the saber rattling and calm his martial retinue of peasants—equipped with rusty matchlocks and bows—scolding the band of Mewati horsemen they faced, but to naught. The caravan got entangled in a shootout with the robbers, in the course of which poor Grousius's hand was battered.[64] There were many other minor nuisances: bridges had collapsed, and at Dholpur one had to wait several days for a ferry over the Jamuna, since all had been occupied "by more than 50,000 heathen devotees, coming from the Ganges."[65]

There was a definite trend toward an increase of seaborne traffic at the end of the seventeenth century and in the beginning of the eighteenth to the detriment of land trade, as is evinced by the growth in seaborne trade between Gujarat and Bengal. The bulk of those commodities had been carried overland in the early seventeenth century. This was mainly caused by the turmoil in the Deccan and northern India.[66]

However, this unrest might also stimulate the overland trade; the *banjara* caravans were as necessary for supplying plundering hosts as they were for peaceful traders. And the choice between carrying goods overland or overseas depended on the commercial circuit of the *natio* involved. The price of information could prevail over the transport costs, as could considerations of creditworthiness. Dealing with close acquaintances made possible the lowering of the insurance premium and the rate of the bills of exchange.

The silk trade between Bengal and Gujarat was a domain of the *khatri* merchants, for example. This community flourished in both Gujarat and Hindustan at the end of the seventeenth century. Because of their close credit ties with the members of their *natio* in Hindustan, the merchants tended to send goods overland. Transport costs, the insurance premium involved, and the interest rate might eat up the profit from the trade in raw silk, which normally amounted to 10 percent or less. But wealthy *khatri* traders could amass buffer stocks of silk to sell at the opportune moment. One needed a web of reliable associates and ancient partnerships to achieve this, though.[67]

This silk was transported along the Ganges to Allahabad and from there overland to Ahmedabad: this traffic amounted to 300,000–400,000 pounds yearly in 1647 and still to 300,000 pounds in 1684. The silk manufacture, indeed the prosperity, of Ahmedabad was said to depend on these regular supplies from Bengal overland.[68]

## Information: The Most Precious Good

News was a crucial component of the price of products as well: its availability had a significant impact on conditions of the market. It was so precious that great efforts were made to keep it hidden whenever possible. Thus, for instance, the Indian merchants at Mocha trading with Abyssinia very effectively scared away competitors by inflating the dangers of this commerce beyond all reasonable proportions. If one were to believe them, one would either be eaten or beheaded when stepping on Ethiopian soil.[69] This urge to exclude outsiders from vital information obviously contributed many a brick to the wall of estrangement that divided European and Indian merchants. To quote C. Zwaardecroon,

> The *bania*s keep their accounts on long scrolls of paper in secret signs and they are so secretive about their content that they will never show them to anybody. So they will have two books: one to show to outsiders and one showing the actual trade.[70]

It is questionable whether many *bania*s kept accounts at all, for many transactions were never committed to writing. This was often not necessary for the *bania* merchants, as many were trained in mental arithmetic from early childhood. Many Europeans marveled at their agility in handling complex calculations. In the Swahili towns, likewise, few transactions were committed to writing, trade being based by and large on verbal agreements. And, sadly for the historian, one reason why there is so little information on the lands beyond the Nyaka is surely that the Yao or Muzungulo middlemen kept hidden from outsiders any such information as they might have had.

If there was a wall of secretiveness around the family and related firms, and another one around the *natio*, this was not an impassable barrier. Armenian merchants were, for example, using printed price lists and trade manuals that were freely sold. A few, covering the Amsterdam and Russian markets, have survived. Such manuals may also exist for Asian markets but have not been published so far.[71]

We have indirect evidence for the wide circulation of price lists among mercantile communities throughout the Arabian seas. There are such lists extant in the VOC archives from distant places like Tebriz, Lahore, Laribandar, and Qazvin, where the Company never had representatives or only briefly. This information was apparently obtained from Armenian or Indian merchants, and it was not very expensive. The VOC at Bandar Abbas and Surat used those price lists mainly in internal communications, not bothering to send them to Amsterdam. At Isfahan the VOC paid a *bania* representative to keep a watchful eye on the market; this representative was one of a large band of commercial informers, or should one say spies? In Surat too, one employed a "bazaar walker," who was to make written reports on the fluctuations of prices of products at a number of shops on the *maidan*, a normal profession there.[72]

But despite such arrangements, communications in the Arabian seas were a sum of delays—and the merchant had always to make decisions constrained by severe limitations upon his knowledge.

This problem was certainly most acute for communications to Europe. As we shall see in the case of the Brazilian tobacco trade in the Arabian seas, the massive problems in communicating with Europe and America virtually precluded the barter of European with Asian goods. Due to the time lag of up to two years between ordering a product to be made in Europe and receiving it, the prices of European goods in Persia or India were completely unpredictable. It was hence not possible to barter merchandise in India or Iran, and goods had to be mainly purchased on credit. Thus the importance of cash in the trade between Europe and the Arabian seas, as it confirmed the creditworthiness of merchants. Besides, silver is much more durable than, say, tobacco, and fetches a relatively high price relative to its weight, so that transport costs bear less heavily on it than they would on tobacco.[73]

The Portuguese very much relied on the transmission of messages overseas. Sending a message overseas would take ten months at least.[74] If, on the other hand, one sent a runner overland—from Goa via Kung to Basra and then through the Syrian desert to Aleppo, or via Kung to Isfahan over Hamadan and from there via Baghdad to Aleppo and then up to Venice or Marseille—three to four months should suffice from Goa to Lisbon and five from Surat to Amsterdam. *Should* suffice, for in reality the stretch still normally took six to seven months, presumably because of a well-justified fear that the Turks might intercept messages, the viceroy rarely sent them. Moreover, Portugal did not maintain a system of consulates in the Levant and the really perilous stretch of the overland route was that between Aleppo and Venice, which was notorious for pirates, rather than the Syrian desert.[75] The services provided by the consuls were much needed. Overland post from Hormuz to Venice seems to have developed only in the Habsburg period. Spain did have a network of representatives in the Levant. They, in turn, corresponded with merchants in Iran: Sephardic émigrés, like the Ximenes family, and Italian traders established in Isfahan, like the Altani, Stropeni, and Bontempeli families. Later, the ambassador of Holstein also offered to double as a private transmitter of messages and a Spanish spy.[76]

With the establishment of the Augustinian mission in Persia the transmission of messages overland by the Estado da Índia passed from private, often unreliable entrepreneurs to an institution that was much more convenient. The friars took care of transmitting messages through their settlements at Muscat, Kung, and Tebriz. Letters were now first sent from Goa to the *feitor* at Kung, from there to the Augustinians in Isfahan, and by them probably to the apostolic legate in Jerusalem.[77] Still, although urgent messages were often sent overland—and even private Portuguese, like the governor of Daman in 1643, repeatedly sent messages overland—the Conselho Ultramarino was reluctant to employ this system. It was expensive, the councilors noted, and key missives might be intercepted by the Dutch. This was a well-grounded fear indeed, for in 1687 the Dutch in Isfahan managed to intercept French letters. Yet if one relied on the overseas conveyance of messages, communications might suddenly break down at the worst possible moment. Such was the case in 1658, a critical year in the struggle with the Dutch, when "due to the lack of ships arriving from India" the Conselho Ultramarino "was completely unaware of any news from India"—and that ignorance lasted for more than a year![78]

Both the VOC and the EIC used the system of overland conveyance of messages from a very early date—at least since 1616. The EIC initially hesitated to send messages from Jask to Isfahan and from there to Aleppo, fearing they might be seized by the Augustinians, who were conceived of (also with good reasons) as Habsburg spies.[79] If those overland communications were subject to many unforeseen delays, dispatches could still be remitted overland in four to six months by the Carmelites. They were more reliable than other conveyors such as the Augustinians and private French and Armenian merchants, since they handed a written receipt of the letters received and undertook to transmit them through the Syrian desert by their own runners.[80]

This enhanced speed of communications had military, social, and commercial significance. The Dutch consul at Aleppo used to notify Bandar Abbas of the prices of spices there monthly. The VOC at Bandar Abbas might thus avert a situation in which spices would be dispatched from the Gulf to the Levant by coordinating the price of spices in Bandar Abbas and that in Aleppo. One paid the consul but a trifling sum; the Dutch consulate at Aleppo was perpetually short of cash, however, and those pennies were much appreciated.[81]

In the sixteenth century not only was Portugal often utterly unaware of what was happening in India, India itself often was too. But in the seventeenth century the Portuguese crown entertained a quite smoothly operating system of runners, such as the one linking Goa to Daman every week, for example. The viceroy had his own *pattamar* and so did the chancellor. The captains of the fortresses mostly hired runners through subcontractors, who also catered to Indian merchants. These *pattamar*s were apparently both a well-paid and well-trained "guild" of specialists. When departing on their trip they had to sign a receipt for letters received. Part of their salary was paid before departure, part on arrival—with fines for lateness.[82] In addition to runners, one also paid spies at Indian courts. For example, Ramoji Naik, a Portuguese agent in the Maratha army, had a number of couriers working for him so that he could, at "great danger to his life, send messages in dark nights."[83]

In Persia the Portuguese settlement at Kung entertained runners as well to link this settlement with Isfahan and Baghdad. Luís da Foz, an Armenian courier, requested of the Conselho Ultramarino in 1694 that he be paid a salary henceforth, instead of the usual piece-rate per letter conveyed, because of his high expenses along the roads. His father had already served the king of Spain, he alleged.[84]

One of the major initial investments of the Companies as well was to hire both runners and informants. At Isfahan, for instance, three regularly employed and sundry hired runners maintained connections between the VOC's factory there and Bandar Abbas. One of the couriers, "Simeon," was paid a pension in 1684—Visnich probably already engaged his father. The system worked well—for, despite the enormous distance separating the "seat of the crown" from the "felicitous port," Isfahan wrote Bandar Abbas every fortnight. The VOC at Bandar Abbas was thus well informed on prices at Isfahan. It could occasionally send products to the capital to break rings of merchants at Bandar Abbas who tried to force lower prices on the Company. This was a practice that was mightily resented by merchants at the latter place, if we are to believe Chardin, and probably caused the occasional attempts by *rahdari* posts to seize VOC merchandise as well, the officials being bribed by merchants. The *chapars* were, as we see, often Armenians. Hardly a cause for surprise: the Companies and the Portuguese were using the network of communications of Armenian traders.[85]

This was not only the case in Iran. The directors of the Company in Surat, Madras, Calcutta, or Chinsura also sat like spiders in the center of a large web of runners and regular correspondents, both Indian and Company personnel. Those correspondents linked the factory with a large number of out-and up-country stations and shops for the procurement of goods.[86]

Gujarati textiles were, especially in Broach district, woven in the villages surrounding the city, not in the towns themselves, for instance. Any transaction involving chintz would thus require lengthy negotiations in the hamlets, where the cloth was to be bought and apprised by representatives of the Company's textile-brokers, and this entailed a vast network of correspondents.[87] In view of the many chains tied up in the textile trade, the board of the VOC at Surat decided in 1693 to split the area of procurement into three parts: Ahmedabad, Broach, and Surat. Each could be reached within two days. So, if necessary, a servant of the VOC might visit a village and would not totally depend on the information provided by intermediaries.[88]

The Companies seem to have achieved a considerable intensification of the traffic in messages, and perhaps an overall drop in the costs involved in the procurement of news. It is, in any case, conspicuous that by 1690 a truly awesome mass of paper flowed both from Asia to Europe and between the various stations in Asia. The Gentlemen XVII were in 1692—with due justification!—complaining that the personnel in Malabar "seems set on sending us letters of truly disgusting length." This was an all-European trend, though, since Portuguese, Dutch, and English correspondences all began to increase to "disgusting lengths" by 1680.

The Europeans were but utilizing a network of Mughal runners and spies (*harkaras*), which had been a major investment of the empire. It may not be a coincidence that, parallel to this spiraling European paperwork, from about 1680 the Indian archives also begin to include masses of newsletters (*akhbarats*) generated by various chancelleries. The bureaucracies of the Mughal and the Safavid empires, as much as those of the Companies, were producing huge amounts of paper and were relying on the speedy conveyance of news. Even in Lucknow—only a provincial town—two or three *harkaras* were received daily at the chancellery carrying the bamboo sticks containing many important, and not so important, missives from Aurangabad. The avalanche of documents from the Deccan seriously overburdened the administration in Awadh, which still consisted of but a dozen scribes. Several important *farmans* had thus not been filed and were lost somewhere among heaps of scrap paper.[89]

Two further observations on this trade in news: First, messages were always better remitted overland than overseas, as the communications overseas were at the mercy of the treacherous winds. In the very urgent case of the English-Dutch war of 1653—when an English fleet was rumored to be heading from Bandar Abbas to Surat to relieve the hard-pressed English personnel there—the VOC in Persia sent this urgent message to Surat by a runner through Sind and Baluchistan rather than overseas. This was not a usual route: the poor *pattamar* was first robbed and subsequently lost his way in the desert.[90] But this was an exception. In general overland post was both speedy and reliable: despite the chaos in the Deccan in the nineties the VOC offices at Golconda and Surat used to send each other messages every fortnight, for example.[91]

Second, the collection of news was linked to certain nodal points of information and the flow of messages followed a number of well-established routes. F. Vallet, a French missionary traveling from St. Petersburg to Gilan in 1719, sent his messages through Moscow and from there to St. Petersburg. Arriving at Shamakhi, Vallet thought it better to send the letters to Tebriz and on to Constantinople. There were few postal ties between Shamakhi and Astrakhan.[92] Again, although it was possible to convey letters from Isfahan to Aleppo or to Smirna via Tebriz through the services of the Jesuits at Smirna, it was quicker, safer, and cheaper to send them through Baghdad with the Carmelites.[93]

This had momentous consequences for trade. The caravan trade to Iraq was pestered by insecurity. At Aleppo it was always uncertain whether the caravan from Baghdad might arrive in a week or three months and the prices of pepper or silk would fluctuate almost daily depending on the amounts one expected to receive.[94] Moreover, Aleppo was an expensive town, so the costs of waiting for the caravans to Basra or Isfahan might make up a substantial part of the merchant's expenditures on this trip.[95]

## Peddlers and Princes at Basra

Basra, the opposite terminus for the route across the Syrian desert, was a major center of trade as the connection between the Arabian seas and the routes to Anatolia. It was the hub of a thriving long-distance commerce characterized by unpredictable fluctuations, however. Like Aleppo, it was a true peddlers' market.

The profits on textiles could vary 30 to 60 percent from one year to another. Depending on the season and the dealer, the price of opium might differ from 32 to 36 reales, and for some kinds of textiles—for which there was a restricted demand—like *cassa* from Bengal, from 50 to 75 reales. Furthermore, even with those textiles for which there was theoretically a large demand, the market was segmented. There were as many as 12 different varieties of *bafta* for sale in Basra—produced in Gujarat, the Deccan, and the Coromandel Coast—and each of those varieties was sold in fairly restricted quantities. Thus the paramount advantage the Indian textile trade to the Middle East enjoyed was that the production in India could rapidly be adjusted to respond to shifts in demand. Prices in Basra could rise or fall by 30 percent within a month, depending on the number of merchants and on the amounts of currency they carried, which was expected to arrive on the *tanaqins* from Baghdad.[96]

Basically, these fluctuations of trade were caused by the limited availability of information. As Basra's trade depended on the sales in markets throughout the Middle East, demand and supply were impossible to predict. The silk and wool trade between Basra and Azerbaijan depended, for example, both on the demand from Turkey and the Levant and on exports to Russia from Azerbaijan. Again, both Basra and Mocha catered to the demand of the entire Ottoman empire—though the trade of Mocha was directed to Cairo and that of Basra to Istanbul. But there was a busy traffic between both. If large volumes of goods remained unsold in Yemen, these might quickly be sent on dhows to Basra. Indian and Persian merchants used to stock goods for trade within the Gulf at Kung too. If the prices were high at Basra, its market would be flooded with merchandise from both Kung and Mocha, which might cause its sudden collapse.[97]

The market was therefore a classic illustration of the "hog cycle." The first year, one variety of Gujarati textiles would fetch a good price at Basra. The next, everybody would invest in the textiles and prices would plummet. Since the amounts and prices of the dozens of different varieties that might be sold were unpredictable, the trade in Indian textiles in particular was a gamble; but prices followed a seesaw movement in the case of bulky products, like tin and iron, as well. Food prices, however, do not appear to show those fluctuations.

Added to those unpredictable commodity prices was the problem of the constant fluctuations of the amounts and kinds of money available at Basra. The currency in which a transaction was to be paid might not be procurable, or it might, but only at outrageous exchange rates. Currency by itself was not scarce in Basra. It made little sense, however, to export local Ottoman coins to India, as the heavy loss on these debased coins would devour any profit made on the voyage. But more profitable "trade coins" were only available in limited quantities. There were several (mainly Indian) bankers working at Basra but, constrained by the constant insecurity vexing the money market, they would rarely lend money for more than a month. That was never more than a few hundred reales and at exorbitant rates of 48–60 percent yearly.[98]

Theoretically, merchants might have forestalled such fluctuations through the formation of rings of buyers and sellers. But while peddlers departing for the adventurous journey to Basra from Mosul often pooled their merchandise together in partnership during the trip along the Euphrates, there is little that suggests those temporary associations persisted in the marketplace. Most merchants at Basra were typical peddlers. According to a letter from 1646, the merchants from Shiraz were the wealthiest: they possessed an average of 13,000 reales. The ordinary Arab and Turkish merchant at Basra could spend only 6,000 reales.[99] They would hide their purses under their cloaks and fetch the merchandise they had bought at Basra to Anatolia in a basket with fruit on top to dodge the myriad internal customs on expensive merchandise, which would total up to 10 percent ad valorem. They hiked from hamlet to hamlet, selling here a few pounds of spices, there an inch of cloth.

Another group was commissioners of shopkeepers at Istanbul, Bursa, and Edirne, who had signed a *commenda* contract enabling them to send an agent to Basra. Yet even the richest merchants had merely a few thousand reales to spend. And if rich Indian merchants would be represented in Basra they would deal through a host of small agents as well.[100]

The brokers would have to vouch for the creditworthiness of merchants, but they were merely small peddlers too. In any case, one would rarely be able to sell more than a few hundred pounds of pepper to a single trader. As soon as more was sold, prices would plummet. If one sold large amounts (say, 800 pounds of nutmeg or 2,000 pounds of pepper), the purchaser would first have to sell part of his goods to others in order to scrape together the cash to pay for the transaction at the contracted time. The normal way of selling goods in Basra (and in many other places in the Gulf, such as Bahrain, as well) was hence in *dastgardan:* installment puchases with a premium of 4–5 percent per month asked. When demanding immediate reimbursement, the purchaser would have to benefit from a 7 percent premium. This was obviously also a way of smoothing the effects of price fluctuation by spreading transactions over a prolonged period.[101]

Rather than asserting that this peddlers' market is typical of the trade throughout the Indian Ocean, though, one has to investigate the specific reasons for this setup. It would seem it was mainly caused by the ephemeral importance of long-distance trade for Basra itself, which was mainly a center for regional trade and commerce within the Ottoman empire.[102]

It appears the rich of the province of Basra—its wealthy urban notables and desert warlords—were little involved in the long-distance trade. The urban elite was heavily involved in the trade in dates and fish from Basra, grain and wood from Mosul and Baghdad, and this, according to the Ottoman tax registers, accounted for the bulk of Basra's customs revenues. The warlords of the Arabian deserts were mainly involved in the sale of horses from al-Hasha to the Ottoman army. This involved up to 3,000 horses yearly, large and frequently hugely profitable transactions, mostly monopolized by the sheikhs.[103] Only the risky long-distance trade was left to minute peddlers.

Another cause was that Basra, unlike Mocha, had no export product that made a substantial profit and could be sold in large quantities. Its major export was bullion, but the supply of this was unpredictable. It depended on the cash concealed under the caftans of merchants arriving from Smirna and Aleppo, on the circulation of money in Iraq itself, on the revenues demanded by the Ottoman court and the amount of money the Persian pilgrims brought to Iraq. That was a major factor, as these imports might amount to up to 2 million reales. But—

as witnessed by the golden domes of the sanctuaries of Iraq that were built in this period—much of this was given to shrines and scholars and did not enter circulation.[104]

The constant fluctuations of the Ottoman currency and the influx of bad (copper) money from al-Hasha and from Ardalan and Arabistan may well have ruined wealthy traders and landlords in Iraq who would have been willing to invest in foreign trade. With the decline of the spice trade in the 1630s the merchants of Baghdad were caught in a pincer movement: declining imports of currency from Aleppo along with increasing demands for bullion from Istanbul and from the Ottoman and Safavid armies in Iraq.

One has to imagine the market at Basra, then, "in the most tangible sense of the word: the market square on the beach, next to the gates of the city; the cramped streets of the town with their shops and warehouses; the bartering and haggling near the stock on the booths from man to man."[105] For van Leur this was a typical picture of the bazaar triumphant in Asia; one might see such scenes in Mukalla in 1936 and in Basra as much as in Mocha 300 years earlier. But the peddlers' market was only a particular segment of the bustling bazaar of Basra, akin to the modern option markets, where information is limited and there are few opportunities for buffer stock formation.

The bazaar, trading with the surroundings, on the other hand, was characterized by a system of traditional customs and relatively stable prices—customs in which the place where the trader established his booth was as precisely fixed as the discount he was prepared to accept.

## Yemen: The Coffee Revolution

When the investments, the supply, and the demand are all very uncertain, traders will not be inclined to experiment with different forms of organization and new products. Their ancient uses serve to defend merchants against risk. The setup of the Basra trade is one case, that of the Red Sea another. We know the organization of this trade in the twelfth century very well through the records of the Cairo *geniza*. Neither its organization nor the products imported showed basic changes from the eleventh to the eighteenth century.[106]

And yet in the early seventeenth century the agriculture and exports of Yemen underwent a veritable revolution with the booming cultivation of coffee. By 1640 coffee had replaced pepper as the major staple of the trade of Yemen, maybe of the Arabian seas at large.[107]

In 1687 Yemen produced, according to the VOC, about 20.7 million pounds of coffee. This was valued, using the Mocha price, at more than 4.6 million reales, a dazzling figure that tallies with Ottoman figures. Coffee had by 1640 become far and away the most important import in Egypt. In 1645 Mocha alone exported coffee valued at 1.5 million reales; by the end of the century this had mounted to 2.5 million reales. Yet Mocha was a less important exporter of coffee than Hodeida. Of this production, the bulk (about 17 million pounds) was sent to Egypt and from there to Istanbul in the great "coffee flotillas" linking the Bosporus with the Nile.[108]

The demand in Persia—this coffee trade was largely channeled through Muscat—seems to have rapidly increased too: Persia and Oman accounted for 200,000 pounds in 1642, 1 million in 1694. Those huge amounts of coffee were largely fetched by caravans traversing the Empty Quarter from Bait al-Faki to the Omani capital Naswa. This not only was a major income for the imams, but was doubly politically significant by virtue of being purely controlled by Omani merchants—quite different from the seaborne trade with its large Indian component. The other markets for coffee appear puny in comparison to those in the Middle East, but here too the demand was booming. Malabar accounted for 400,000 pounds of coffee in the 1690s, Surat for 300,000–400,000 pounds, and, of course, there was a rapidly expanding European demand which, up to 1686, was largely channeled through Cairo and from there mainly to Marseilles.[109]

This enormous growth of the coffee trade is striking for three reasons: first, it proves that the structure of consumer demand in the Arabian seas was not fixed and that agriculture in the region was able to cater to changes in demand in distant markets. The expansion of demand for tobacco is another case of this. As we shall see in chapter 7, there was a large trade in this American crop in the late seventeenth century. Second, it points to the existence of a huge internal market in the Ottoman empire, almost a world economy in itself, as Braudel has argued. The expanding trade in coffee was to some extent able to cushion the effects of the decline of the spice trade on the customs revenues of Ottoman Egypt, as Ottoman officials well recognized.[110]

Third, it points to the existence of a substantial "middle class" demand in the Middle East, with the consumption of coffee and tobacco spreading downward from the court to urban merchants, scholars, and manufacturers organized in the guilds. This not only applies to coffee and tobacco, of course. Many of the expensive Indian textiles sold in the Gulf were also meant for middle-class consumption, accounting for the constant shifts in fashion, as the taste of the middle-class consumers changed repeatedly and Indian textiles competed with European and Persian production.[111]

The ports of Yemen had mainly been entrepôts for Indian products in the sixteenth century whereas the merchants from the Ottoman empire, traveling to Arabia, were in the late seventeenth century primarily interested in the coffee trade. They would invest only part of their money in the speculative transit trade with India, Persia, and East Africa. When in 1677, for instance, due to an infestation of grasshoppers, the coffee crop largely failed, agents traveling to Arabia had to invest all their capital in coffee to comply with the orders of their Egyptian and Turkish chiefs, and the bazaar at Mocha collapsed. Often, merchants would barter products bought at Mocha for coffee at Bait al-Faki, which was more profitable than drawing bills of exchange on Mocha.[112]

The markets in the hinterland of Yemen—including the coffee markets of Bait al-Faki and Zabid; Taiṣ (a center for the metal trade), and Sa'na (mainly the focus for the consumption of the Zaidit court but also a center for the trade with horses)—had a different character than that of Mocha.[113] While the trade of Mocha essentially consisted of exchange of goods with bullion, the trade in the hinterland consisted of barter of commodities. Those markets were characterized by transparency, good faith, and rigid customs, as at Sa'na, where the *qazi* closely oversaw all transactions. If a merchant did not comply with maximum prices and the stipulations of a contract, he might reckon with very severe punishment. The place where a merchant was to sell his goods, the goods he was permitted to sell, and the maximum price allowed were tied to rigid schedules and guarded by superintendents of the market who were named by the court. The transactions in those towns were of much smaller scale and often more predictable than at Mocha. But it was a slow trade, obeying the rules of the caravan trade that we have been considering.

Indian merchants, established at Mocha, often sent *vakil*s to the mountains to sell their goods "to the common man." This peddling trade in the highlands, both in goods and in bullion, appears to have been largely controlled by the Jews of Yemen.[114] In 1644 merchant W. Alleman proposed that the VOC should send representatives to the highlands too. One could sell spices there, as these fetched a 30–45 percent higher profit in Sa'na than at Mocha. The gains would be partly consumed by the costs of bills drawn on Sa'na and by the high interest at Sa'na, normally 36–48 percent. But one might invest the proceeds in horses that could be sold at Surat or in coffee, which might be sold in Basra. Merchant W. van Oudermeulen was sent to Sa'na to investigate the commerce. He was less than enthusiastic.

> We have found this trade to be subject to innumerable dangers and fatigues for the merchants sit in the caravanserais or in the king's houses and sell their cloth or other merchandise by one or two pieces to the peasants and soldiers, to be paid months or days later with the fruits of the country.[115]

But the bulk market at Bait al-Faki was again very different from the peddlers' markets in the highlands. If the price of a product is declining and at the opportune moment one seller or purchaser is able to buy or sell, "the merchant can easily impose a market price and that with small quantities," as the VOC observed.[116] As K.N. Chaudhuri rightly remarks, the situation in the coffee market at Bait al-Faki is a good illustration of this rule.[117]

Although thousands of merchants were active on this market, by strategically withholding stocks rings were mostly able to fix the price of coffee. On the supply side, various Zaidit princes were active in Bait al-Faki and would sell coffee from their own plots using commissioners. On the demand side various rings were operating, which in some instances virtually controlled the price.

Syndicates of caravan merchants from Oman were in 1641 and 1642 only buying a fraction of the sales of Bait al-Faki—100,000 pounds—yet they were able to manipulate the price by coordinated purchases. The Ahmedabad *bhora* trader Sheikh Salla Bhai Showanji, who had acquired a fortune in the coffee trade, in 1698 proposed to the imam that he could farm the entire commerce for six years. But he was imprisoned on account of customs fraud before being able to carry out this scheme.[118]

Van Leur has given the classic description of the market in 1623, so we are well acquainted with the fluctuations in the trade of Mocha.[119] The trade of Mocha had a particular character, however, since Mocha was above all a free port. Customs there were much lower than at Hodeida and in Aden. As most offices in the port were farmed, the Zaidit imamate did not intervene in the setting of market prices (as was, for example, the case in Hodeida) nor had the town a powerful urban elite to tamper with the prices (as was the case in Aden).[120]

Yemen was an important market for a few products from the Gulf, Ethiopia, Madagascar, the Swahili Coast, and India: slaves, iron, rice, and sugar. But most goods—the Indian in particular—were, as at Basra, sold throughout the Ottoman Empire. Only a few hundred pounds of cloves were, for instance, marketed in Yemen; the rest was intended for Egypt, Ethiopia, Syria, and North Africa. The price was impossible to predict. How could one divine the demand for spices in a Syrian or Egyptian hamlet nine months after its purchase at Mocha? Supply could not adapt to demand, therefore, a result primarily of the limited access to information and also of the inability to stock goods.

Most traders at Mocha were in 1641 "agents and shopkeepers only" who had capital to spend of less than 3,000 reales.[121] Moreover, many hajjis were active at Mocha trying to recover some of their expenses by haggling for merchandise. Though some large merchants from Cairo operated on the market, several agents mostly represented them. For if it became known that some merchants had substantial capital to spend, prices would either soar or plummet. As at Basra, the price at Mocha showed stark monthly fluctuations depending upon rumors of how many goods would be received, and fluctuated as well from season to season. Textile prices might differ by 60 percent in one season. One had to buy small quantities slowly so as not to chase the prices upward by rapid purchases.[122]

Such trade was like a game of poker in which much depended on bluff, but not all traders were handed the same cards. A trader might, for example, be at an advantage when offering goods early in the season before the bulk of merchandise from India arrived. Many merchants thus hired warehouses and named local representatives—often *bania*s from Diu—to sell small lots of goods. A trader would be at an advantage too if he provided cheap and flexible credit. So a system of bills of exchange between Surat, Calicut, Cananore, Persia, and Mocha developed; it was much cheaper to furnish money thus than lending it at Mocha. To some extent a layer of intermediaries might therefore smooth the effect of fluctuations. But only powerful merchants could afford to do either of these two things.[123]

At the end of the seventeenth century the Mocha market was shifting in structure due to the increasing demand for coffee; the sale of merchandise was becoming a subsidiary activity to its purchase. By 1704 the VOC was selling its products to a single merchant—Mustafa Bakr, "whose commerce is both of great fame and great deeds." This merchant bought coffee on behalf of the Company in return for these goods. The EIC was selling to a ring of ten merchants.[124]

The structure of the market at Mocha was thus not fixed: the way in which trade was conducted evolved with the fluctuations of trade. To return to Braudel's metaphor: when money was accumulated through the coffee trade a second floor of monopoly was constructed on top of a (certainly persisting) ground level of peddling trade.

## Merchants and Marts of Gujarat

At Surat, Zwaardecroon wrote in 1703:

> The bazaar prices are diverse, for they differ not only from day to day but from hour to hour. Also they differ as to the merchant with whom one is dealing for one has here—as in other places—large dealers, maritime traders, small merchants, shopkeepers and many different kinds of hawkers. One merchant is able to sell one pound or less, another one maund, the third ten and the fourth 100 and so unto 1000 and 100,000. So one can well imagine the differences in the bazaar prices if they have to fetch a profit from one trader to the next.[125]

The hierarchical order of merchants described here, as Zwaardecroon well recognized, pretty much tallies with van der Kooy's model of the Amsterdam staple market. Trade was organized through a range of specialized merchants: import (or maritime) traders, "secondhand" merchants, and export dealers. It was by virtue of this hierarchic organization that Surat functioned as the staple market of the Arabian seas.

If Surat had such an important position in the trade of the Arabian seas, this was not because it had a significant manufacturing industry or because trade was drawn to the port by force. It was not on account of the availability of raw materials (though undoubtedly port and manufacturing industries at Surat profited from the cultivation of cotton in nearby Jambushir and in Malwa). It was not primarily because Mughal shipping was concentrated there, nor because custom dues were low. And it was certainly not because of its site. It was mainly because transaction costs there were cheapest.

For example, interest at Surat fluctuated approximately from about 10–16 percent yearly for the East India Companies to 24–38 percent for small caravan traders. (The risk incurred in lending to hawkers and the dangers of the road were reflected in the interest rates.)[126] These were to all appearances the lowest rents in the Arabian seas and, in fact, in the Indian Ocean. The VOC used to send money lent at Surat, in bar, to Chinsura since it would be far more expensive to borrow it at Hugly. The Dutch trade in Surat from 1667 onward can be characterized as "goods for bullion." The cash was sent to Hugly to finance the exchange of "bullion with goods."[127]

If interest rates were lower at Surat than elsewhere, this was not caused by an abundance of cash on the money market but rather by the presence of wealthy and creditworthy bankers. The risk discounted in the credit rate was lower than elsewhere. Furthermore, Surat was the focal point of information on the commercial conditions throughout the Arabian seas. When lending at Surat one was less plagued by uncertainty than elsewhere. Thus the rate at Agra and Ahmedabad was often 12–24 percent above that at Surat. It was 20–30 percent below that at Vengurla and 10 percent below that at Cochin. Interest rates responded to purely local conditions of demand and supply for bullion, loans to local authorities—mostly advances for the land revenue—and goods, and it is therefore difficult, if not impossible, to make sweeping statements on the movement of interest rates throughout the subcontinent.[128]

Again, in 1686 the VOC at Surat complained that both Vengurla and Cochin were shouldering Surat with the costs of supplying and repairing ships. But the costs of supplies were much lower in Kerala than at Surat. Rice cost 98 rupees for 500 pounds there; in Cochin it was only 40.[129] The point, however, was that specialized grain dealers, who had large stocks at their disposal, were able to deliver quickly at Surat—far more so than at Cochin, and certainly more than at Vengurla, where one would have to wait for weeks. Time was money too: the ships would not have to suffer the fixed costs incurred elsewhere. So, overall, grain was cheaper at Surat than at Cochin since the total cost involved in procuring it was lower.

### *Peddlers and Magnates*

At Surat, as anywhere else, there was small trade. The bazaar at Surat consisted of the small booths in the suburbs and around the caravanserais. This was a risky trade, for sales were subject to seasonal fluctuations. A commodity sold by a host of merchants—like sugar—could vary from 3 to 6 rupees per maund per day, "depending upon the quality and the daily supply."[130]

According to Schreuder, "The prices here rise and fall very swiftly for often a single rumor of the arrival of ships may cause a situation in which what was sold in the morning for 10 rupias can only be obtained in the evening for 7 or 8."[131] As Schreuder argued, the prices at the bazaar also differed between bulk and luxury goods. The latter showed appreciable variations from year to year

> any commitment and are imbued with a deep hatred for Christians. Therefore, if they have the slightest occasion to do so, they will try to weaken and possibly ruin and exterminate them.

Free trade could not be permitted since the "evil nature" of Asians might necessitate the use of force. But when free trade did prevail, other Europeans might obstruct retaliatory measures.

With the expression "evil nature," van Dam did not intend to imply the Asians were an "evil race" but rather that the law there was not based upon innate respect (*facultas*)—as Hugo de Groot would have voiced it—for "humanity." Humanity here was defined as a moral quality (*aptitudo*) whereby "an individual is competent to have or to do a certain thing justly."[16] For the Asian "nature" was corrupted by the lack of constitutional safeguards to liberty. Asians would only respect the brutal despotism of the ruler. As they did not recognize the innate respect for humanity, they could not be included within a system of international jurisdiction based on this.[17] Natural law, applying to all people (*ius inter gentes*),[18] could not be extended to Asian states. If these were not even minding their own subjects' interests, how could one expect them to consider the common interests of mankind, such as the common right enjoyed by people to trade with one another, for example?

Moreover, if the application of the "law of nations" (*ius gentium*) was to be extended to the territory of Asian states, this implied, in principle, that these would recognize the European system of states. The law of nations is, by definition, multilateral. But Asian states were not part of the European concert of nations.

The exception to this rule was Safavid Persia, which had signed legally valid treaties with England, Spain, Venice, the Holy Roman Empire, Poland, and the Dutch Republic. Treaties like the Persian-Dutch one of 1634 specified privileges of Persian subjects in the Netherlands and of Dutch subjects in Persia. These conventions are interesting in their own right and as a precedent for modern international law.[19] But their practical significance was small. It seems doubtful whether the Safavid state was able to enter into bilateral treaties along European lines with its neighbors in the Arabian seas. This would have implied that the law sanctioned the existence of the government of the other signatory states. For a Shiite state such would seem an odd admission.[20]

Treaties were probably perceived by the Safavid lawyers as temporary expedients, rather than permanent arrangements framed within an interlocking system of international treaties. The VOC—later on—did not particularly like being reminded of the existence of these arrangements either. The Company reasoned it was not bound to honor them. Freedom of movement was linked by the Safavid state to either the payment of 10 percent customs or to the procurement of silk from the treasury. These conditions on freedom were not implied in the treaty of 1634, the VOC in Persia argued.

Dissatisfied with this, Persia—after having consulted Batavia but not Gentlemen XVII—in 1645 used force to obtain freedom from customs by a blockade of Bandar Abbas and a (failed) attack on the fortress at Khism. When the Gentlemen XVII got word of this they were furious: "We understand the matters concerned quite well, even though we are not seated at Batavia," they wrote—underlining the word *Batavia*. The High Government of the Indies in Batavia apparently reasoned, Gentlemen XVII continued, that one could resort to force to sort out any trivial difference of opinion. "Too promptly one argues: we can not accept such conditions, ergo one may attack somebody without looking for any reason or justification. This is a stance we cannot vindicate to ourselves or to the world." The Persian point of view, that one was to pay customs or pack one's bags, was both reasonable in common sense and in law. "For might the king not argue: I am lord and master in my country. Either you will obey the law of the land or, if you do not want to, you may leave."[21]

This case prompted the Gentlemen XVII in 1650 to draw a General Instruction (*Generale instructie*) defining the legal status of the Company in Asia and the line of conduct that was to ensue.[22]

The *Generale instructie* distinguished three different areas of jurisdiction of the Company. First there were those where the Company enjoyed full sovereignty (the Moluccas). Second, there were regions where the Company had received certain prerogatives to exercise sovereignty over indigenous princes (Batavia, Ceylon, and later Kerala). And, lastly, there were lands where the Company did not enjoy any rights to exercise power and was but a humble merchant. In the latter case the Company was to trade peacefully and respect indigenous legal norms. This was as much a pragmatic as a moral position: except in the case of tyranny, when one has exhausted any alternative to resistance, one may not use violence against kings with a divine right to rule on their own territory. For in Calvinist thought God ordains the king.

What were the practical implications of this perspective for day-to-day policy? As Zwaardecroon wrote from Surat in 1702, where one traded in peace "one should behave with leniency, amiability and forbearance, though treated and abused by tyrants like a slave. For one always has to keep in mind the rule of old that one resides here as a merchant and not as a ruler. But one might wish that we were treated like a merchant too, for in that case it would be easier to adapt to the rules of the country!"[23]

One could reason, however, that if the Company was treated in an arbitrary manner it would have a right of resistance against tyranny. There was between the Gentlemen XVII and the High Government of the Indies at Batavia, the Board of Directors and the Presidencies of the EIC, the Conselho Ultramarino and the Conselho do Estado in Goa, a constant friction between two lines of thought.

There were those who argued that one could define on one's own what constituted tyranny in accordance with European legal norms. For if the Dutch, Portuguese, or English *natio*s was permitted preferential treatment, this implied

*The Gujarati Merchant as Capitalist*

Surat's great merchants might be termed by Bayly "portfolio capitalists." The term *portfolio* means that merchants spread their investments over a wide range of pursuits and partners, a form both of sharing profits and of spreading risks, which was, for reasons we appraised already, as common among princes as it was among peddlers.

This could mean spreading risks over a wide array of commercial pursuits. Let us consider a big example: Narain Das, who invested in many different branches of trade, and who turned to the VOC for help in recovering funds still due him from various merchants. At Golconda this amounted to 245,000 rupees; at Masulipatam to 125,000; in Siam 8,545; and in Bengal, finally, 26,500.[142]

Or it could mean dispersing risks over as many partners as feasible. Let us consider a very small example: Sadulla Tusa and Ahmad Tusa, two *bhora* peddlers, in 1677 signed a *respondentia* bill to transport piece-cloth in their sloop from Bassein to Surat. They had received this money from six different merchants, amounting to a sum of 1,000 rupees; the maximum from any one was 300 rupees. Their sloop sank. They were just poor people and not able to refund the money. Four of their lenders "who were powerful and vengeful" were not content with this settlement and appealed to the court at Bassein, which imposed a short term in prison on both.[143]

*Capitalist* is a more difficult term. There seems to be no reason to call Surat's merchants capitalists if one thinks about investments in production. Abdul Ghafur, among others, did have his own wharves. Yet, when buying textiles, Abdul Ghafur depended as much upon intermediaries, and was as much a victim of the market, as was any small peddler. But, because of the very scale of his transactions, procurements by merchants dealing with funds from Abdul Ghafur could influence the price of textiles. For these procurements could be larger than those of the EIC![144]

It is a moot question whether investments in land are, strictly speaking, productive investments. This involves the intricate problem of whether land rent and rural interest is productive capital. However that may be, there is evidence that in the seventeenth century Surat merchants were already acting as collectors of land revenues (as was common in the eighteenth).[145] For instance, the assistant broker of the VOC, Balav Das, became involved in a rather intricate quarrel with *girasias* who were demanding one-fourth of the revenue "of a few gardens and villages he owns." They planted a pole, with their demands nailed to it, next to his property, threatening to burn it down if he would not give in. This procedure seems to indicate that Balav Das was the collector—*mamlatdar*—for those estates.[146]

Yet the term *capitalist* makes perfect sense if thinking about sophisticated institutions for credit and insurance, rational bookkeeping, or ways to manipulate the market. Let us consider a concrete example to clarify the strategies used.

On 21 December 1692, the VOC offered 250 maunds of cloves, 100 nutmegs, and 75 bunches of mace for sale—estimated value 325,000 guilders, a massive sum. Broker Resik Das offered on account of an anonymous partner 117, 60, and 65 rupees per maund for the cloves, nutmeg, and mace provided that the Company would accept a 2 percent discount and that the merchant would be able to inspect the quality of the mace before the transaction. If he did not buy it, the Company would be permitted to sell it to another merchant. The VOC declined the offer. The buyer thereupon offered 107, 55, and 108 rupees. But the VOC had to decide within a week. Merchants heading for Hindustan, the main market for these products, had already packed their oxen and would depart in January. If the Company did not sell now, they would buy from Muhammad Sahid. This dealer had spices left from last year's sale and he would not hesitate to dump these if he got wind of the present transaction. The council of the VOC recognized that if they did not sell forthwith, there was a chance that no other dealers would appear. Muhammad Sahid would then easily be able to undersell them, as he now handled cloves at 119 rupees with a 1 percent discount for the loss of quality. His strategy was to control the market for two seasons. So, he would sell at a loss, 116 rupees, to obstruct competitors. The council resolved to sell the goods at the offered price.[147]

So in regard to the use of monopolist strategies, the capitalists of Amsterdam had nothing to teach their counterparts in India. Such practices, whereby traders could manipulate prices, characterized segmented monopolies. These might be found in some key sectors with high profits and a fairly predictable demand: most notably in banking, imperial finances, and trade with the court; in the commerce in metals, grain, and shipping; and in deals with the Companies. It was far from typical of all trade; the trade of the bazaar had a very different structure.

Yet one normally conducted long-distance trade by partnerships, either on a permanent or temporary basis. To portion out risk the merchants would normally pool their resources. Even in the case of the *khatri*, Kashmir or Pathan merchants, often very small traders, when dealing with the hinterland "everybody seeks to become a monopolist of goods before departing." Such partnerships were extensive concerns tying together merchant houses throughout India, as well as linking firms in India to *bania* firms operating in the Persian Gulf, Yemen, East Africa, Central Asia, and maybe Southeast Asia.

Consider the following humdrum example: Rauwel Naik, Saraswat, resident at Candal, signed a contract with the Portuguese: he would deliver 3,200 pounds of saltpeter to them. Therefore, he would name two brokers, Arjuna Naik and Baboji Naik—Saraswats too, resident at Goa. To procure the saltpeter he had drawn a bill of 2,000 xeraphins on Tulsi Das Lagi, *bania* from Ahmedabad. Tulsi Das, a powerful merchant prince, for a while the most important commissioner for the procurements of the Mughal army in Gujarat, who was probably the chief dealer of this combine, had entrusted an additional 3,500 xeraphins

behave very differently threatened with fire and sword than when listening to arguments without consequence." One ought not to be angered if rajahs were hesitating to honor commitments. If treaties were not even valid according to European norms, how should the rajahs be expected to comply with them?

## Companies and Courts

### *Merchants and Rulers: Malpractices and Corruption*

Shifting to a consideration of the policy of courts in the Arabian seas toward commercial matters and concerning trade with Europeans in particular, I could do no better than to quote T.B. Macaulay writing on the seventeenth century:[29]

> The most enlightened Englishmen looked on India with admiration. The most enlightened natives of India were scarcely aware England existed. . . . It was probably not known to one of the statesmen in the Durbar of Agra that there was near the setting sun a city of infidels called London, where a woman reigned and that she had given to an association of Frankish merchants the exclusive privilege of freighting ships to India. That this association would one day rule India . . . would have seemed to the wisest of European or Oriental politicians as impossible as that the inhabitants of our globe should found an Empire on Venus.

Indeed, why should the courts bother with such an obscure group of foreign merchants? One has to use a magnifying glass to gather any reference to traders, let alone to European traders, in official chronicles, an absence that is all the more puzzling if one knows that those same chronicles are mostly not altogether short on words.

To study the relation between states and merchants, historians have, therefore, often been prompted to take statements of travelers and Company accounts at face value. And when dealing with indigenous states these documents are full of complaints about "extortion," "bureaucratic interference," and "heavy taxation"—matters that traders are always bound to whine about, of course. Many writers have elaborated upon these complaints to argue that—to quote a very recent exposition of this very old view—"the agents of the Mughal government constituted the greatest source of political danger to the [merchant] community. For the officials of the Empire regarded the exaction of money, jewels and other valuable items from the trading population as a legitimate prerogative of rulership."[30]

It would be easy, too much so, to refute this argument by pointing out that all this oppression apparently did not hinder the accumulation of huge fortunes by the merchants of Surat or of New Julfa.[31] The very fact that the traders of Surat or Julfa are hardly noted in chronicles of the court would seem merely to indicate that they were little involved in the running of the realm. There were, obviously, no bureaucrats administering commerce.

Again, if there were occasional malpractices, in general Safavid and Mughal authorities mostly acted well within the constraints of law when committing what Europeans characterized as "abuses." Close examination of what the Companies considered "arbitrary acts of violence" reveals that such deeds were generally resorted to when merchants or Companies transgressed explicit limits on their freedom. These restrictions were for the most part expressly stipulated in the treaties or were seen as simple attempts to evade taxes.

Thus, to consider one case among many, the heavy additional imposts that the sultan of Bandar Abbas imposed in 1670 were labeled "despicable acts of tyranny" by the VOC. Zainal Khan, on the other hand, claimed these *avanias*—as they would have been called in the Levant—were merely his response to Dutch attempts to illegally fortify the factory and smuggle goods.[32]

Yet the evidence on corruption and administrative malpractice is too extensive to be entirely discounted. Traders and artisans in the Mughal empire or under the Safavids, the Zaidit imams, Bijapur, or the Marathas were indeed plagued by arbitrary impositions and had to bribe officials on a large scale.[33] In that respect, however, I would not vouch for the officials in Spain, France, or, as we shall see, England and Portugal either. As K.W. Swart has hinted in his study *The Sale of Office in the Seventeenth Century*, this practice and the widespread corruption it spawned both in Europe and in the Dar al-Islam may have had the same cause: the easy availability of cash—American silver.[34] In M. Weber's terms, this was the replacement of a "prebendal" by a "bureaucratic" administration.

Basically, both in Europe and in the Arabian seas the cornucopia of American bullion was emptied by the state in payments for a salaried bureaucracy and army. In either case officers, whether *noblesse de robe* in France or men of the pen—*ʿahl i-tajik*—in Iran, saw their position as their private fief rather than as a service to the public. They would resort to peculation to cover the inevitable fluctuations of income. Such oscillations might be caused by inflation, as in Persia in the second half of the seventeenth century, or, as in the Maratha Deccan, by fluctuations of the many local currencies. Or again, as in the Mughal empire, it might be caused by the resistance of local landholders to attempts to impose central authority and central taxation on them.[35]

Both Eastern and Western public functions were increasingly sold: thus, by 1670, in the Safavid empire most subordinate positions were sold. Under the Marathas in the eighteenth century the sale of office reached a unique pitch, but already in the seventeenth century Shivaji and Sjambaji had extensively resorted to selling positions. They were but following in the footsteps of the Deccan sultanates, where offices were also farmed on a large scale.[36]

Moreover, oriental bureaucracies were subject to their own "Parkinson's law." They were always attracting more people aspiring to office than they could

thus had to raise money to pay their tax farms. To do so openly, however, would be to draw disapproval upon oneself—for this might be tantamount to usury under Islamic law.

Apart from this second function, brokers also fulfilled a third one: to ascertain the creditworthiness of a merchant. A trader might not fulfill his contract and the broker would then have to bail him out. The calculation involved in assessing the creditworthiness of a firm was a complex one, entailing the size of the transactions as much as intangible factors like "suitable behavior," "harmony within the family," "proper honoring of debts to one's clients," and many others.

Credit ties had constantly to be reaffirmed by means of gifts, for example. If one had handed on *divali* a gold chain to but one partner, others might be affronted and demand one next year too. It was normal to provide gifts when closing a major deal. Many transactions also appear to have contained a percentage destined for gifts to Brahmins and the famous hospital for cows in Surat.[163] Of course it is tempting to consider such gifts and co-shares of religious institutions as belonging within the preserve of India's noneconomic man, *Homo politicus* or *Homo hierarchicus*, who strictly preserves rigid rules of caste and whose commercial conduct is always framed in ceremonies and ritual. And certainly the *bania*s were highly caste-and status-concious, yet gifts were equally based upon the very economic reasoning that lavish outlays on ceremony indicated the creditworthiness of a merchant.

So did marriage ceremonies, as marriage was obviously crucial to the survival of the family enterprise. Weddings of merchants at Surat were thus huge celebrations in which the entire town was afoot. Sometimes there were even casualties among the crawling masses of spectators, for generous distribution of alms often followed this revelry. Merchants appear to have heavily indebted themselves to pay for such lavish occasions. This was well-calculated behavior: was the merchant this short of cash reserves that he could not even fund a decent wedding?[164]

The calculation involved when ascertaining the creditworthiness of a merchant included his social and caste ranking as well. The *bhora* Muslim Abdul Ghafur, for instance, indulged in such displays as a suite of nautch girls, *sidhi* bodyguards, or a palatial residence—as was appropriate for the proper standing of a Mughal grandee and for the chief of the *bhora* community, the predecessor of the Agha Khan.[165] And justifiably so:

> This Abdul Gafour is very wealthy and disposes of all the funds of the king's *Gasie* [*qazi*]. Which is why this Gafour is more feared than anybody else is, even by the governor and grandees [*regenten*], and surely he could get such writs from the ecclesiastical judge of his majesty he might require.[166]

Such behavior would have been unbecoming for *bania* merchants, truly a *Lumpenbourgeoisie*. They were the wealthiest persons in Surat, Schreuder wrote, but "one would not judge from their appearance that they possess several tons of treasure. They can marvelously manage as if they were needy, and somebody who is not accustomed to their manners would not guess them to be merchants who would venture anything."[167]

Partly this was because rich merchants did not want to elicit the greed of rapacious Mughal officials, yet the *bania* merchant was, again, as much a *Homo economicus* as *Homo hierarchicus*—practicing ascetics. And, to be sure, the *bania* merchants of both Surat and Diu were very strict in their observance of ritual and of caste rules. Vicious captains of Diu might throw wealthy *bania* merchants in prison to extort money from them, and these would certainly starve to death there as they would absolutely refuse to eat food they had not cooked themselves.

There was thus always the possibility that the traders' good fortunes might be brusquely reversed, and the main aim of the firm was the survival of the family's credit in an environment of insecurity. There can be no doubt that the merchants of Surat were highly successful in this. The Rustamji family was in business for more than four generations; Sunder Das at least four; Celabi five.

Often the family firm would crash when entering its third generation. This applies to Vora's firm, which after the death of the venerable Virji Vora in 1665 became a bone of contention between his grandsons: Manek Sent Vora and Samar Sent Vora and their families. The association went almost bankrupt, though Virji Vora had left it with substantial reserves of capital. The grandsons exhausted this in endless suits over the inheritance. They finally seem to have settled on a compromise in 1675. The family's credit had meanwhile much diminished and they were forced to forsake less profitable activities, like shipping. Furthermore, the Vora brothers looked for some extra employment as brokers to the Compagnie des Indes.[168]

This was not only a difficult period for the Vora family. The entire merchant milieu of Surat appears to have suffered from a crisis in the sixties upon the looting of the town by Shivaji and subsequent Maratha incursions in southern Gujarat, which caused a state of panic in Surat.[169] Yet in Diu—ruined by parsimonious officials as much as by Muscati attacks—the merchants went through even harder times. We have the VOC writing in 1678 that most important traders had passed away and that, apart from the brokers, there were few merchants at Surat who were able to afford the Company's merchandise. Surat's merchants "are far greater in fame than they are in accomplishments now."[170] But by 1690 Surat's merchants had clearly recovered from this depression.

However, in the intervening period there appears to have occurred a shift in the kind of "portfolio investments" and in the composition of Surat's mercantile community. As to its composition: at the end of the seventeenth century, Persian, Turkish, and *bhora* shipowners played a far more important role than in the middle of the seventeenth century.

And as to the investment: portfolio investment may be divided into "horizon-

larger states: both the *colathiri* at Cananore and the *zamorin* were officially permitted by the Portuguese—and in their footsteps the VOC—to send two royal vessels to trade at Mocha. In reality this limit of two was soon transgressed, and Calicut operated an entire fleet.

*Ikkeri*

Officials of the Ikkeri *nayak* were engaged in seaborne trade in two directions. First, some of the coastal vessels used in the rice trade with Goa and Cochin were owned by officials. These were mainly the tax gatherers of Mangalore and Barcelore. Portuguese mercenaries dwelling at Barcelore often manned these crafts. Second, Ikkeri sent two or three ships yearly to Kung and Muscat, mainly loaded with rice; one generally brought horses in return.[45]

*Adilshah*

This case is well documented and merits a longer treatment. After the Portuguese-Adilshahi treaty of 1576, the Adilshah dynasty had been allotted the right to send two or three ships to Mocha and Hormuz yearly, which were to be given Portuguese navicerts. Royal goods would not have to pay customs dues. Bijapur would not transport prohibited goods aboard the royal ships—Christian slaves from Abyssinia and arms.[46]

Although the Estado had in the first half of the seventeenth century more pressing concerns than bickering with the Adilshahi empire, there was a great deal of resistance to this arrangement. Little respect was paid to the Portuguese prohibitions on "merchandise," which caused the Lusitanians to demur. Both Bassein and Goa protested that the Adilshah was stretching the terms of the treaty to the limit—and beyond. This led to several clashes where Adilshahi ships were seized and searched by the Portuguese authorities, only to be released from custody after Bijapuri protests. The growth of shipping at Dabhul and Rajapur, mostly with royal vessels, severely harmed the trade of Daman and Bassein, it was muttered there, particularly since lesser grandees, like the *faujdar* of Rajapur, and not just the grand vizier but lesser nobles in attendance at court too were claiming that privileges allotted to the Adilshah applied to them as well.[47] This is logical since many officials connected to the grand vizier, Mustafa Khan, *khan i-khanan* (1636–1645), for instance—the main shipowner on the Konkan Coast in that period, who operated more than seven ships—were immigrants from Persia or emancipated Ethiopian slaves with strong ties to Yemen, the Banadir Coast, and the Gulf.[48] Many officials in the Konkan ports were of such Sidhi stock and settlements of emancipated Ethiopian slaves, soldiering in the Bijapuri armies, may have shared in the revenue of harbors where there were powerful Sidhi communities. It was thus at Bassein and at Danda Rajapur (Gheria), which in the sixteenth and seventeenth centuries were places approaching "Ethiopian"—or rather African—city-states on the west coast that were ruled and mostly populated by the *Sidhi*s. The revenues of those ports were to be spent on arms and oared fighting ships for the Bijapuri campaigns in Sunda and Ahmadnagar. It was obviously important for Adilshah that trade increase. Despite the picturesque hosts that the Adilshahi sultanate could occasionally muster, the empire was continuously walking a financial tightrope. Since the bulk of land was assigned in fiefs, the income of the royal household from land was limited. But the incomes from Rajapur and Dabhul were partly the crown's, partly the grand vizier's revenues; it was important to tap this fountain of prosperity by operating ships and leasing the right to transport freight therein.[49]

In effect, the Portuguese were aiding the Adilshah with this policy. By treaty the Portuguese were to place a representative at Dabhul, who was to hand *cartazes* to ships from Dabhul. The Portuguese might sack ships heading to other ports, provided that half of the goods seized were handed to the Adilshah. Portuguese aid was an indispensable tool for developing the royal revenue, then. Nor was this only the case with the Adilshah: Nizamshah was also to receive half of the customs revenue of Chaul as tribute annually.[50]

### *Bhonsle Svaraj*

This older tradition of direct involvement of states in the Maratha Deccan with the maritime trade of the ports in the Konkan was pursued under the Marathas. L. Leendertsz, chief merchant of the VOC at Vengurla, put it thus:

> The countries, which Shivaji possesses, are poor: there is little trade there and few farmers. And they do not yield but half of the money he needs to pay for the garrisons and the 184 castles he presently possesses. [Therefore his revenue] mainly consists of those derived from the seashore; in particular the customs of a number of ports of which he is the proprietor. Otherwise he would be in severe trouble for the remainder of his income consists of poor land, planted with palms and some rice.[51]

This was certainly an exaggeration: the income from customs was only a tiny portion of the income of the kingdom. But customs revenues were of importance in the local context of the Konkan. For the conquest of the Konkan by the Bhonsles was a slow one: it only involved a few fortresses and market towns occupied by troops of the royal household. Most forts were not under the direct control of the Bhonsles; most revenue from the countryside collected by local landlords. Only in a few ports, Rajapur for instance, were taxes gathered directly by the Bhonsles. Hence the court strove to develop the revenue of those harbors. With such benefits one might engage mercenaries. And thus one might acquire a hold on the division of the land revenues, though only in the very long run.[52]

So, to attract trade, in 1664 the Bhonsles embarked upon an extensive program

(Hilversum, 1992). As is normal with such discussions, much of the bewilderment is probably due to the argument focusing on the "van Leur thesis" or "peddler thesis," which was never argued (in this form) by van Leur. For van Leur never denied the existence of great merchants in India. It is interesting (and symptomatic for the disciplinary walls separating the study of the Arabian seas) that van Leur's writings have had little to no discernible impact on East African studies, being discussed by Africanists dealing with wider issues of world trade, such as J. Goody's *The East in the West* (Cambridge, 1996), as "belonging" to Asian rather than African studies. This is odd, since every visitor to the continent can attest that peddlers are the pillar of the African markets. Instead, debates on African merchants are very much dominated by the "mode of production" theme, which did not play much of a role in Asian studies in turn.

3. Van Santen, "Verenigde Oost-Indische Compagnie," pp. 72–74; T. Bentley-Duncan, "Niels Steensgaard and the Europe-Asia Trade of the Early Seventeenth Century," *Journal of Modern History* 47 (3) (1975), pp. 512–19; M.A.P. Meilink-Roelofsz, "The Structure of Asian Trade: A Critical Appreciation of Steensgaard's *Asian Trade Revolution*," *Mare Luso-Indicum* 5 (1980), pp. 1–43; S. Subrahmanyam, *Portuguese Asia: A Political and Economic History* (London, 1990), pp. 241–44.

4. F. Braudel, *Capitalism and Material Life, 15th–18th Century,* 3 vols. (New York, 1984–86). Let me add, to be fair, that Braudel would not have agreed, as he considers this structure to be exclusively European. See his *Afterthoughts on Material Civilisation and Capitalism* (Baltimore, 1977), pp. 31, 55.

5. This point that has been expounded at length by French neo-Marxist economic anthropologists and much discussed in the literature on East Africa. A different articulation of the mode of production may entail a different economic rationality. Thus much of the long-distance trade among the polygamous Shona was really long-distance trade of women in exchange for cattle or cloth and commanded by the "rationality of alliance building" rather than cost-benefit calculations. Compare M. Godelier, *Rationalité et irrationalité en économie*, 2 vols. (Paris, 1969), pp. 140–91, and C. Meillassoux, *Terrains et théories* (Paris, 1977), p. 318. For a treatment of French neo-Marxist economic anthropology, see D. Seddon (ed.), *Relations of Production: Marxist Approaches to Social Anthropology* (London, 1978).

6. For a description of such small traders in Isfahan see N.A. Kuznetsovoi (ed.), *Chodzdenie kupča Fedoša Kotova v Persiu* (Moscow, 1958), p. 80.

7. E.A. Alpers and C. Ehrert, "Eastern Africa," in R. Gray (ed.), *The Cambridge History of Africa* (Cambridge, 1975), p. 531.

8. P. Chaunu, *Sevilla y América siglos XVI y XVII* (Seville, 1983), p. 325, has argued that the slack between supply and demand applies to all long-distance trade before the steam engine. This argument, however, ignores the role of stock formation and the price of information in the formation of prices; see G.A. Akerlof, "The Economics of Caste and of the Rat Race and Other Woeful Tales," in *An Economic Theorist's Book of Tales* (Cambridge, 1984), pp. 23–45.

9. Thus, for example, by P.W. Klein, "Kapitaal en stagnatie gedurende het Hollandse vroegkapitalisme," in A.M. Geurts (ed.), *Economische ontwikkeling en sociale emancipatie* (The Hague, 1977), p. 167.

10. C.A. Bayly, "Indian Merchants in a 'Traditional' Setting: Varanasi 1780–1830," in C.A. Dewey and A.G. Hopkins (eds.), *The Imperial Impact: Studies in the Economic History of India and Africa* (London, 1978), p. 186. The issue has not been investigated for Persian merchants. However, as trade in Safavid Persia was largely financed through

loans and bills of exchange, credit was clearly as important a consideration for Persian as for Indian merchants; see, for example, VOC/OB 1217, 24 June 1656, fo. 402.

11. *Hollands stapelmarkt en haar verval* (Amsterdam, 1931), p. 5 et seq.

12. As Fox has argued; see E.D. Genovese and L. Hochberg (eds.), *Geographic Perspectives in History* (London, 1989).

13. R. du Mans, *Estat de la Perse*, p. 214.

14. VOC/OB 1373, 26 May 1683, fo. 383 vo.; H. Dunlop, *Bronnen tot de geschiedenis van de Oost-Indische Compagnie in Perzië 1611–1638* (The Hague, *RGP*, 1936), p. 425; Geleynssen 204, "Invoices of merchandise received and sent"; see too VOC/OB 1611, "Memoir for F. Casteleyn," 31 May 1698, fo. 54.

15. There is as yet no fully satisfactory account of the Safavid economy in any Western European language; in Persian see M.A. Bastani-Parizi, *Siasat va eqtesad ʿasr i-Safavi* (Teheran, 1354), which is, obviously, very good on Persian sources but for Western sources almost exclusively relies on Chardin.

16. Geleynssen 246, "Expenses from Gamron to Spahan."

17. S.P. Blake, "The Structure of Monetary Exchange in North India," in J.F. Richards (ed.), *The Imperial Monetary System of Mughal India* (New Delhi, 1987), pp. 100–37; see also Subrahmanyam, *Political Economy*, p. 70; G.W. Skinner, "Marketing and Rural Structures in Rural China," *JAS* 24 (1964), pp. 195–229.

18. See T. Raychaudhuri, "Inland Trade," in I. Habib and T. Raychaudhuri (eds.), *The Cambridge Economic History of India*, 2 vols. (Cambridge, 1983–85), i, pp. 352–59; K.R. Hall, "Price-Making and Market Hierarchies in Early Medieval South India," *IESHR* 14 (2), pp. 207–30.

19. C.A. Bayly, *Rulers, Townsmen and Bazaars: North Indian Society in the Age of British Expansion* (Cambridge, 1983), p. 55; AHU, Índia, Cx. 37, 77, "Foral" of the Praças do Norte, ca. 1694.

20. ANTT, DRI, 35, 6 January 1635, fo. 203 vo.; but see mainly the Salcete diaries in BAC, A 501 and BAC, A 502, which list a number of petitions of shopkeepers and inventories of shops; Braudel, *Capitalism and Material Life*, ii, pp. 26–74.

21. See F. Perlin, "Of 'White Whale' and Countrymen in the Eighteenth Century Maratha Deccan: Extended Class-Relations, Rights and the Problem of Rural Autonomy Under the Ancien Régime," *Journal of Peasant Studies* 5 (2) (1978), pp. 211–13.

22. See, for example, VOC 1304, 15 May 1674, fo. 371, on the Thomas Christians in Vadakumkur: "wherever they live they build roads and establish permanent markets, to the convenience of the Malabars, who neither construct roads nor erect houses close together but instead live widely scattered in their gardens or plots."

23. VOC/OB 1307, 11 May 1676, fo. 675.

24. UBL, BPL, 83, "Transport and inventory of merchandise transferred by Nicolaas Overschie."

25. ARA, Coll. Geleynssen de Jong 251, "Inventory of merchandise, debts and further assets of the Company in Persia," 28 February 1643.

26. A.V. Chayanov, *On the Theory of Peasant Economies* (Delhi, 1987).

27. See two excellent close-up studies of peddlers and peddler communities along the caravan routes of central Asia: H.W. van Spengen, "Tibetan Borderlands: A Geo-Historical Analysis of Trade and Traders" (Academisch Proefschrift, Vrije Universiteit, Amsterdam, 1992); and the classic book by Owen Lattimore, *The Desert Road to Turkestan* (London, 1928).

28. N. Witsen, *Nord en Oost Tartarye*, 2 vols. (Amsterdam, 1672/1776), i, pp. 376–421.

products were often goods with clear military significance, too: horses, sulfur, powder, saltpeter, copper, and lead.

This applies to the monopoly of the Safavid empire in the silk trade with the VOC and the EIC as well—the most striking exception to the rule that the state hardly interfered in trade.[65] Emissary W. Bastinck had bothered Taqi more than enough with his interminable claims that the price of silk sold to the Dutch was to be lowered by two tomans, the grand vizier complained in 1643, for example. "Our friendship does not depend on the price of silk. This is but a merchant's affair; it is of no more value than straw. No, it is based on our grand alliance to strike a blow at our enemies."[66] To the court the prime concern was the grand alliance. This had to be munificently affirmed by giving presents to the court. The VOC should not bother the court with the price of presents or of silk; this should be left to the officials in charge—the *mustauwfa i-khass* in this case.

To the Safavid court the trade of the Company was a revenue matter of local importance, primarily an affair for local tax gatherers rather than for the department responsible for the administration of revenue (*divan*), and still less for the court. But—as the revenues of ports were mostly farmed—the *ali kapu* had, and could have had, but a very limited say in these matters. Affairs concerning the silk consigned to the VOC were handled as a rule by officials from the department of royal estates (*divan i-khass*) like the *mustauwfa i-khass*, the comptroller general of this department; the *nazir*, the treasurer general of the royal warehouses and workshops; and the "stick-keeper" responsible for visitors to the palace, the *icik agashi bashi*. Finally—to make the matter still more complex—during the reigns of Safi and Abbas I, the general accountant of the royal mint (the *sharaf bashi*), Mulaim Beg, was responsible for money received from the Company in return for silk.

These were all minor officials; the highest authority to whom Companies could appeal was the grand vizier, for the incomes from tax farms and the royal domains, from which most silk derived, were his responsibility. If, as was often the case with the VOC and the Portuguese, one desired to speak directly to the "head of state," or addressed letters to the shah, this was considered insolent behavior. It meant that humble traders put themselves on the pedestal of a king.[67] Representatives of European Companies were during audiences assigned the rank of minor Georgian chieftains who had rented some tax farms from the shah and occasionally made a fuss about it.

The same applied to the Mughal empire: here, too, the Europeans were seen as a *natio* among others, and at best as a band of rather unimportant allies—a band of no consequence on the coast. Their main task was to protect the interests of the maritime traders. The court might intervene if such interests were damaged, but rarely did so. The immunities granted to *natio*s had been allotted to allow merchants to carry on their own affairs. It would transgress the limit of competence of royal jurisdiction to intercede in any matter of minor importance. These were to be adjudicated through its proper customs among the *natio* itself.[68]

**Viceroys and Chieftains**

Let us now shift the focus from the court to local conditions. As Pearson has noted, there were different measures of involvement of officials in matters maritime and commercial.[69] On the west coast, or in the ports of the Red Sea and the Gulf, the incomes of officials directly depended on revenues gathered from customs. And not only did they rely on this. The customs of Surat, for example, were farmed. Portions of those incomes were assigned to expenses for "foodstuffs, weapons and *sepoys*" for the Mughal army operating in the Konkan. Local officials were thus bound to be keenly interested in trade. Their very survival depended on it.[70]

Grand seigneurs at court, the VOC at Surat noted in 1658, were a hard nut to crack; one should abstain, if possible, from dealing with them.[71] Local officials, however, were often financially involved in trade and would favor the Company's case. The Company thought they were easier to understand and more pliant, too. Even though they were corrupt, one could fathom their devious plots, whereas it was very hard to glean any precise insight into what was going on at court. The Companies—and the Portuguese—therefore rarely dealt directly with the ruler. They preferred to delegate affairs to Armenian or *bania* representatives whether in Golconda, Bijapur, the Mughal empire, Yemen, the Safavid empire, or Oman.[72]

Locally the Europeans could have a marked impact. There might arise markets and trade networks associated with a Company and often under European protection. Rings of merchants, who were closely tied to the local administration, were dealing with the Europeans too. European private traders began to deal in bulk products, which might infringe on tax revenues. And they recruited and trained soldiers and delivered arms. R. Frykenberg has assessed the impact of such developments on the local politics of India's east coast in the eighteenth century in an exemplary study.[73] What happened, Frykenberg argues, was that Indian magnates asked the EIC for help in the adjudication of various conflicts among themselves. Tussles occurred almost inevitably, for lengthy bargaining between various elite groups, between tax collectors and richer peasants, was always involved in the collection of the land revenue. Frykenberg calls this the "inner logic" of Indian politics. Such bargaining entailed the marshaling of military muscle as well.[74]

Thus an increase in local trade might well give rise to a tangled web of intrigue involving local potentates, mercenaries, and servants of the Company. They would coalesce to steal incomes of their overlords and carve out kingdoms of their own without the cognizance of any central authority. Such deals in the seventeenth century did not yet occur in the Mughal empire, certainly not at Surat, where the Europeans were completely at the empire's mercy. But they did eventuate in the more decentralized, and surely weaker, Bijapuri state, which bordered on the only territorial area under European control—the Portuguese

*to India* (London, 1924); P.H. Leupe, "Brievenvervoer over land naar Indië door de Verenigde Oost-Indische Compagnie in de zeventiende eeuw," *Bijdragen voor Vaderlandse Geschiedenis en Oudheidkunde*, Nieuwe Reeks 6 (1870), pp. 54–67.

80. AHU, Índia, Cx. 30, 99, 30 July 1676.

81. A.H. de Groot, *The Ottoman Empire and the Dutch Republic: A Study of Their Earliest Relations* (Leiden, Istanbul, 1978), p. 312; ARA, Coll. Geleynssen de Jong 247, "Register of outstanding debts."

82. BAC, A 499, 4 December 1676.

83. AHU, Índia, Cx. 27 bis, 97, 16 March 1667.

84. AHU, Índia, Cx. 37, 86, 2 December 1694.

85. Chardin, *Voyages*, v, p. 312; see W. Floor, "Commercial Conflicts Between Persia and the Netherlands" (University of Durham Centre for Islamic Studies Occasional Paper 37, Durham, 1988), p. 33; and for the costs of runners see, for example, Geleynssen 245, "Oncostenboek vanwege de uitgaven te Ispahan."

86. For the English courier service see J. Deloche, *La circulation*, i, p. 264–67; and E. Denison Love, *Vestiges of Old Madras 1640–1800,* 4 vols. (London, 1913; New York, 1968), ii, p. 100. Resik Das, the VOC's broker at Surat, also entertained regular courier services with Chinsura and with Calicut, which informed him when VOC ships were to arrive in Surat, allowing him to fix his price accordingly; see VOC/OB 1548, Surat resolution, 25 January 1695, fo. 179; VOC/OB 1512, 26 January 1693, fo. 24.

87. VOC/OB 1524, "Summary account of the trade of Broach," fo. 402.

88. VOC/OB 1548, Surat resolution, 19 June 1693, fo. 280 vo.; VOC/UB 916, 26 August 1689, fo. 602.

89. VOC/OB 1620, "Questionnaire to Birsiedas," fo. 301 vo.

90. VOC/UB 877, 19 September 1653, fo. 415; VOC/OB 3989, 23 April 1654, fo. 242 vo.

91. See VOC/OB 1475, "Register of letters received, and sent by ambassador Johan Bacherius."

92. ARU, Ancien archive de l'abbaye Port Royal, 3753, 21 February 1719; and 14 June 1719.

93. Geleynssen 287, 23 July 1646, fo. 405; and 27 August 1646, fo. 412; ARA, Legatiearchief Smirna A iii, "Appendices to my letter written from Tebriz to the Jesuit convent at Smirna."

94. Steensgaard, *Carracks Caravans and Companies*, pp. 42–56, but see Bruce Marshall's criticism, *The Beginnings of Western Economic Dominance in the Middle East: Mercantilism and the Islamic Economy in Aleppo 1600–1750* (New York, 1988), p. 56, which indicates that rather than speaking of Aleppo as a peddlers' market it is crucial which product one is considering and which group of merchants one is talking about.

95. Ajuda 46-X-17, "Nota delle persone."

96. See, for example, VOC/OB 1478, 26 September 1687, fo. 464 vo.; VOC/OB 1406, 28 August 1684, fo. 1254 vo.; VOC/OB 1379, 3 September 1683, fo. 993 vo.; VOC/OB 1408, Report by C. Soolmans (1684), Enclosure M, "Memoir of profits made on various trips to Bassora."

97. *English Factories* 1645–1650, p. 45; VOC/OB 1360, 4 March 1698 fo. 1877 vo.; VOC/OB 1307, "Note on the difference between the price of merchandise in Bassorah and Gamroon." Since most shipping to Basra was with Kung as intermediate station and entrepôt, the Portuguese crown thought Portuguese shares in the customs of Basra might well be cashiered at Kung instead of at Basra. BNL, Pombalina, Cód. 439, 26 January 1697, fo. 151.

98. See, for example, VOC/OB 1351, 1 September 1679, fo. 2582; VOC/OB 1355, 26 September 1681, fo. 439.

99. VOC/OB 1478, 6 August 1646, fo. 409.

100. VOC/OB 1373, 28 August 1683, fo. 996–97 vo.; J. Gentil de Silva, *Alguns documentos para o comércio da Índia de Portugal existentes na Bibliotheca Nacional de Madrid* (Lisbon, 1951), p. 45. On the organization of trade within the Ottoman empire, see R. Mantran, *Istanbul dans le second moitié du XVIIe siècle* (Paris, 1962); S. Farooqi, *Towns and Townsmen of Ottoman Anatolia: Trade, Crafts and Food Production in an Urban Setting 1520–1650* (Cambridge, 1983).

101. Risso, *Oman*, p. 201; Geleynssen 283, 4 October 1645, fo. 174; VOC/OB 1459, 20 December 1690, fo. 1016; VOC/UB 837, 6 September 1691, fo. 483.

102. This has been argued regarding Aleppo by A. Marcus, *The Middle East on the Eve of Modernity: Aleppo in the Eighteenth Century* (New York, 1989), p. 154.

103. R. Mantran, "Réglementations fiscaux ottomanes: Le sanjaq de Bassorah," *JESHO* 10 (2) (1977), pp. 224–77; BNL, FG, Cód. 28, fo. 14.

104. See, for example, Geleynssen 245, 4 October 1645, fo. 173; VOC/OB 1373, 29 May 1683, fo. 874–76 vo.; VOC/OB 1373, 26 May 1683, fo. 43.

105. Van Leur, *Enige beschouwingen*, p. 97.

106. S. Goitein, "From Aden to India: Specimens of India Traders of the Twelfth Century," *JESHO* 22 (1) (1980), pp. 43–66.

107. H. Becker, V. Hohfeld, and H. Kopf, *Kaffee aus Arabien. Der Bedeutungswandel eines Weltwirtschaftsgutes und seine siedlungsgeographische Konsequenz* (Wiesbaden, 1979), pp. 30–35.

108. R.S. Hattocx, *Coffee and Coffeehouse: The Origins of a Social Beverage in the Middle East* (Seattle, 1985); Mantran, *Istanbul dans le second moitié*, pp. 209–11; A. Raymond, *Marchands et commerçants du Caire au XVIIIe siècle*, 2 vols. (Damascus, 1973), i, p. 137, 147; Shaw, *Ottoman Egypt*, pp. 40–42; ARA, Legatiearchief Turkije i, fo. 29; VOC/OB 1598, "Report of Adriaan Verdonk on coffee," fo. 93; ARA, Coll. van Hoorn van Riebeeck 12, "Description of Mocha."

109. M. Rheda Bhacker, *Trade and Empire in Muscat and Zanzibar* (London, 1992), p. 15; VOC/OB 1409, fo. 1663 vo.; VOC/OB 1130, "Report by Pieter van den Broecke," fo. 167; VOC/OB 1152, "Short statement on trade with Mocha," fo. 425; VOC/OB 1355, 26 September 1681, fo. 438. It bears emphasis that the demand for coffee was segmented too. The lighter variety of coffee that was exported from Yemen to India, for example, could not be sold on the European and Middle Eastern market (VOC/UB 922, 3 August 1693, fo. 1432–33 vo.).

110. Braudel, *Capitalism and Material Civilisation,* iii, p. 467; S. Farooqi, "Coffee and Spices: Official Ottoman Reactions to Egyptian Trade in the Late Sixteenth Century," in *Festschrift für Andreas Tietzke.* Sonderheft wiener Zeitschrift für die Kunde des Morgenlandes, vol. 76 (Vienna, 1986), pp. 87–93.

111. See R. Matthee, "Coffee in Safavid Iran: Commerce and Consumption," *JESHO* 37 (1994), pp. 1–32

112. VOC/OB 1330, "Report by J. Wijns," fo. 957.

113. VOC/OB 1134, "Report by Wurffbain," fo. 169 vo.; VOC/OB 1605, 23 August 1698, fo. 1691 vo., see also Niebuhr, *Reise nach Arabien*, pp. 221–80.

114. VOC/OB 1152, fo. 424 vo., for the market regulations of Sa'na, which have been preserved in manuscript, see W. Dostal, "Der Markt von Sana," *Österreichische Akademie der Wissenschaften Sitzungberichte* 354 (Vienna, 1979), p. 21.

115. VOC/OB 1152, 10 January 1646, fo. 397–99.

116. Van Santen, "Verenigde Oost-Indische Compagnie," p. 70.
117. K.N. Chaudhuri, *The Trading World*, p. 379.
118. VOC/OB 1135, fo. 400; VOC/OB 1603, 23 August 1698, fo. 1682–84; for syndicates active in trade with Egypt, see also Raymond, *Marchands et commerçants*, i, pp. 302–6.
119. Van Leur, *Eenige opmerkingen*, p. 82; see also Meilink-Roelofs, *Asian Trade*, p. 325.
120. Van Santen, "Verenigde Oost-Indische Compagnie," p. 72; VOC/XVII, 16 April 1657, fo. 492; KITLV 10 b, "Report by Ryckloff van Goens," 18 October 1681, fo. 14.
121. VOC/OB 1134, "Report by Wurffbain," fo. 164.
122. P.H. Boxhall (ed.), "The Journal of a Mocha Coffee Merchant," *Journal of Arabian Studies* 1 (1974), p. 115; VOC/OB 1279, "Relation on the Mocha trade," fo. 463–66.
123. ARA, Coll. van Hoorn van Riebeeck 11, iii, 6 August 1701.
124. VOC 9115, "Report by J.J. Kettelaar," fo. 25; PRONI, D 654/31/15, 11 April 1724.
125. ARA, HRB 834, Memoir by Zwaardecroon, fo. 67.
126. VOC/OB 1649, 27 March 1701, fo. 267: the VOC had lent 300,000 rupees at a very unfavorable rate of 8 percent "and this only applies for us, the other nations have to pay a lot more"; see too VOC/OB 1364, 1 January 1681, fo. 316 vo.: the interest rate was 8–9 percent, the VOC paid 4–5 percent; for bills of exchange see *English Factories* 1655–1660, p. 18. So, contrary to Chaudhuri's opinion (*The Trading World*, p. 583), Indian moneylenders in the seventeenth century did behave, in principle, like modern-day *shroffs*.
127. V.B. Gupta, "The Dutch East India Company in Gujarat Trade, 1660–1700: A Study of Selected Aspects" (Ph.D. dissertation, New Delhi, 1991), p. 398; VOC/OB 1355, 30 January 1671, fo. 368.
128. As argued by Om Prakash, "Precious Metal Flows: Coinage and Prices in India in the 17th and Early 18th Century," in E.H.G. van Cauwenberge (ed.), *Money, Coins and Commerce: Essays in Monetary History of Asia and Europe* (Louvain, 1991), p. 65, though I should grant Om Prakash that, because of their close links with the Mughal central treasury (*khazana*), interest rates in Bengal and Surat can be used as global indicators of interest rates in the Mughal empire.
129. VOC/OB 1388, 16 June 1683, fo. 2157 vo.
130. VOC/OB 1659, Surat resolution, 23 January 1701, fo. 295.
131. ARA, KA, 8448, "Considerations Schreuder," fo. 314, 318.
132. A. Das Gupta, *Indian Merchants and the Decline*, p. 12.
133. For Yemen, see the freight lists in VOC 9115, Invoices of the *Oostersteyn*, and Geleynssen 102, "Notice on freight shipped in the *Valkenburg* to Surat," as an example.
134. BNL, FG, Cód. 864, fo. 110; ANTT, DRI, 44, Anonymous memorandum 1645, fo. 221.
135. See N.A. Toothi, *The Vaishnavas of Gujarat* (London, 1935), pp. 122–34.
136. ANTT, DRI, 44, fo. 221; AHU, Índia, Cx. 33 bis, 187, "A petition of the people of Diu," 1676.
137. So it was, for example, in the famous strike of 1669, for which see *English Factories* 1668–1669, pp. 190–92; VOC/OB 1270, 29 November 1669, fo. 854–55 vo.
138. VOC/OB 1364, 1 January 1681, fo. 2041; VOC/OB 1317, 16 June 1683, fo. 2145 vo.; VOC/OB 1495, Report by van Helsdingen, fo. 214–41 vo.

139. ARA, HRB, 838, Memoir by Schreuder, fo. 54–63; see A. Das Gupta, "The Merchants of Surat 1700–1750," in E. Leach and S.N. Mukherjee (eds.), *Elites in South Asia* (London, 1970), pp. 181–214.

140. K.H. Kamdar, "Virji Vora: The Profile of an Indian Businessman in the Seventeenth Century," *Journal of the Oriental Research Institute* 3 (4) (1979), pp. 96–107; and J.J. Modi, "Rustam Manock and the Persian Qisseh (History) of Rustam Manock: A Study," in *Asiatic Papers*, 4 vols. (Bombay, 1929), iv, pp. 101–321.

141. VOC/OB 1620, "Questionnaire," fo. 300 vo.; VOC/OB 1635, 22 December 1698, fo. 77.

142. VOC/OB 1259, Narain Das to Maatscuycker, 8 February 1666; VOC/RGGR 678, 23 January 1663.

143. BAC A 498, 9 July 1678, fo. 43.

144. VOC/OB 1635, Diary by Zwaardecroon, 23 January 1700, fo. 685 vo.; VOC/OB 1659, Surat resolution, 2 June 1701, fo. 405–6 vo.

145. R.D. Choksey, *Economic Life in the Bombay Gujarat* (Bombay, 1968), p. 27.

146. VOC/OB 1549, Surat diary, 7 September, fo. 522 vo. Samar Sen Vora also owned landed property in Khatragao close to Surat; VOC/OB 1649, Surat diary, 29 July, fo. 514.

147. VOC/OB 1548, Surat resolution, 10 May 1693, fo. 224.

148. AHU, Índia, Cx. 26, 64, "Copy of the saltpeter contract"; VOC/OB 1388, 31 March 1683, fo. 2163 vo.

149. VOC/OB 1475, Surat diary, 8 June 1687, fo. 393 vo.

150. VOC/OB 1611, 21 November 1697, fo. 68.

151. VOC/OB 1611, 16 November 1697, fo. 71.

152. VOC/OB 1545, Surat resolution, 29 February 1692, fo. 179.

153. AHU, Índia, Cx. 42, 2, "A petition of the Hindu and Moor people." Thus the extended family was a source of rather than a constraint to investment. See B.S. Cohn, *India: The Social Anthropology of a Civilization* (Englewood Cliffs, 1971), p. 50.

154. A. Das Gupta, *Indian Merchants*, p. 12, has emphasized the point and with due justification.

155. *Mémoires de François Martin* (A. Martineau, ed.), ii, p. 413; VOC/OB 1370, 8 December 1680, fo. 2396 vo.

156. J. Andersen and V. Iversen, "Orientalische Reisebeschreibung" (A. Olearius, ed.), *Deutsche Neudrucke Reihe: Barock* 27 (Tübingen, 1980), p. 213; VOC/OB 1246, "Extract Surat diary," fo. 764; see the inventory of the property of Surat's major banker in VOC/OB 1548, Surat diary, 26 November 1693, fo. 573: 15,000 reales in cash and more than 30,000 in gems and pearls.

157. On the Surat bankers, see G. Torri, "Trapped Inside the Colonial Order: The Hindu Bankers of Surat and their Business World During the Second Half of the Eighteenth Century," in G. Borsa (ed.), *Trade and Politics in the Indian Ocean: Historic and Contemporary Perspectives* (New Delhi, 1990), pp. 47–81.

158. ARA, HRB 838, Memoir by Schreuder, fo. 54.

159. M.L. Dantwale, *The Marketing of Raw Cotton in India* (London, 1928), p. 37, quoted in C.A. Bayly, *Rulers, Townsmen and Bazaars: North Indian Society in the Age of British Expansion* (Cambridge, 1983), p. 412; M.N. Pearson, "Brokers in Western Indian Port Cities: Their Role in Servicing Western Merchants," *MAS* 22 (3) (1988), pp. 455–72; VOC/OB 1567, Relation by van Helsdingen; VOC/OB 1567, "Response by me, Gelmer Vosburg, to the allegations of Mr. van Helsdingen," fo. 371 vo.

160. AHU, Índia, Cx. 34, 97, "Pareçer" Dom Fernando de Mascarenhas; ARA, HRB, 838, Report Schreuder, enclosure L, "Indications of the normal rate of rebate for merchandise."

161. VOC/OB 1383, 31 January 1684, fo. 683 vo.

162. VOC/OB 1333, 28 January 1679, fo. 646.

163. VOC/OB 1224, 23 April 1658, fo. 712, 714; ibid., 29 May 1657, fo. 741 vo.

164. Van Twist, *Generale Beschrijvinge*, p. 33; VOC/OB 1636, 5 August 1699, fo. 495 vo.; VOC/OB 1636, Deodati diary, 9 February, fo. 168 vo. On calculations involved in marriage and the search for partners among one group, closely linked to the commerce of Gujarat, see K. van Der Veen, "Huwelijk en hiërarchie bij de Ananvil Brahmanen van zuidelijk Gujarat" (*AZOA*-publikaties 12, Amsterdam, 1969), esp. p. 137.

165. VOC/OB 1548, Surat diary, 19 February 1693, fo. 410 vo.; and 17 March, fo. 441.

166. VOC/OB 1360, 23 February 1680, fo. 1820 vo.; see also Das Gupta, *Indian Merchants*, p. 77.

167. ARA, HRB 838, Memoir Schreuder, fo. 54.

168. *Mémoires de François Martin,* ii, pp. 387–89; L. Varadarajan, "The Brothers Bora and Virji Vora," *JESHO* 17 (1967), p. 224; VOC/OB 1204, 8 October 1674, fo. 429; VOC/OB 1370, 10 June 1681, fo. 2466; VOC/OB 1315, 20 January 1677, fo. 254; VOC/OB 1398, "Consultations on sales," fo. 556. On the Celabi family, see Modi, "Rustam Manock," pp. 258–64, and on the Celabis in the eighteenth century, see M. Tori, "In the Deep Blue Sea: Surat and Its Merchant Class During the Diarchic Era," *IESHR*, 19 (3) (1982), p. 272.

169. See, for example, ARA, St. Gen, Lias VOC, 5740 i, Report by A. Overbeeck, 20 August 1672.

170. VOC/OB 1323, 26 January 1678, fo. 399. See M.N. Pearson, "Shivaji and the Decline of the Mughal Empire," *JAS* 35, 2 (1976), p. 223.

171. See, for example, van Santen, "De Verenigde Oost-Indische Compagnie," p. 119; VOC/OB 1143, 7 May 1637, fo. 535; VOC/OB 1243, 5 June 1663, fo. 983; VOC/OB 1135, 15 April 1646, fo. 511 vo.; VOC/OB 1246, 29 March 1664, fo. 720–21.

172. See VOC/OB 1548, Surat resolution, 5 May 1693, fo. 334; VOC/UB 901, 20 August 1677, fo. 469; VOC/OB 1659, Surat resolution, 10 May 1701, fo. 375 vo.

173. VOC/OB 1620, "A memoir regarding funds," fo. 368–72.

174. See L. Subramanian, "Banias and British: The Role of Indigenous Credit in the Process of Imperial Expansion in Western India in the Second Half of the Eighteenth Century," *MAS* 21 (3) (1987), pp. 473–75; D. Haynes, "The Dynamics of Continuity in Indian Industry: *Jari* Manufacture in Surat 1900–1947," *IESHR* 23 (2) (1986), p. 131.

175. K.N. Chaudhuri, *Asia Before Europe: Economy and Civilisation of the Indian Ocean from the Rise of Islam to 1750* (Cambridge, 1990).

176. A. Udovitch, *Partnership and Profit in Medieval Islam* (Princeton, 1970).

# 6 The Tide of Trade: Man and Merchandise

According to N. Steensgaard, a basic shift occurred in Asian trade in the early seventeenth century that he sees as nothing less than a "trade revolution," and it was achieved by the Companies. The trade conducted by peddlers over the caravan routes from India to the Middle East and from there to Europe was redirected by the Companies around the Cape. This was—again according to Steensgaard—on the one hand effected by the use of monopolist practices that allowed the Companies to manipulate the price of products and thus oust their small competitors from the market. But the Asian merchants dealing with the Companies benefited as well: the Companies were able to reduce unpredictable fluctuations of the market. This was an innovation in the running of commerce: the Companies behaved, to use J. Schumpeter's term, like "creative monopolists."

On the other hand, the costs of protection were, in Steensgaard's view, internalized: protection rent was accounted for in the price of products sold by the Companies. This was quite different from the indigenous states, which merely secured protection rent on the caravan trade, and the same goes for the Estado da Índia, which only taxed, and hardly conducted, trade.

Although in the main I agree with Steensgaard's analysis, I do not see the use of monopsonic practices as the most important innovation of the VOC (and to some degree of its English competitor as well); rather, what seems most significant is its centralized conduct of trade and the consequent economy of scale. The VOC was able to manipulate stocks and plan production and supply for the long term, thus lowering the transaction cost per unit sold.

By utilizing their economies of scale the Companies were able to effect a marked expansion of the market for Asian goods in Europe and, to some extent, for new products in Asia. This was achieved by introducing new merchandise in the market (like coffee and tea in Europe, Japanese copper in India, Bengali silk in Japan) and by the centralized conduct of trade, both from Europe to Asia and within Asia. Moreover, the size and the continuity of the Companies' operations ensured they could raise vast amounts of capital. This implied, however, that they should capitalize on their economy of scale, and this could only be achieved if they were assured of a sizeable and predictable demand in Asia. Sales and purchases of the Companies (and of the Portuguese crown) thus tended to produce a duopoly. Indigenous intermediaries had to cushion the commercial risk.

Partly through those competitive advantages of the Companies over Asian merchants, products from the Arabian seas were replaced on European and some Asian markets by those produced elsewhere. This, for example, was the major factor involved in the disappearance of the transit trade in pepper from Kerala through the Red Sea and the Gulf to Europe from 1610 to 1640. This was replaced by exports of pepper from the Indonesian archipelago brought by the VOC, the EIC, and by a few minor players like the Danes, the Courteen Association, and the Portuguese crown. This may truly be styled a trade revolution since this venerable commerce dated back to dim antiquity, and in spite of all their efforts the Portuguese were unable to inhibit the trade with the Red Sea in the sixteenth century.[1]

Yet, as with any revolution, one may question the significance of this. As to the employment and quantities—but not the investments—involved, the pepper trade played but a minor role in the commerce of the Arabian seas. For, as one may already have observed in the first chapter, this commerce was not mainly in spices and luxury goods—"splendid but trifling," to use Gibbon's oft quoted words—but was mostly short-distance and in bulk goods. Bulk goods are here simply seen as products commanding a low price in relationship to their weight, luxury goods as fetching a high price relative to their weight and thus their transport price. Persian silk is hence a luxury good, Persian wheat and leather bulk goods. But silk employed thousands of weavers throughout Eurasia and was thus far from an insignificant product.

Of course, the term *bulk* is germane to proportions prevailing before the advent of the railway. The entire trade of the Indian Ocean would barely have filled one modern freighter, as Moreland would have emphasized—but then so would have the trade of the South Atlantic.[2] The commerce largely served the internal market, and seaborne trade was chiefly conducted within the Arabian seas; traffic with Europe derived from trade between India and the Middle East.

This even held true for Kerala. Clearly trade from Kerala was dominated by the pepper trade. It was "the bride around whom everybody dances," as the VOC put it.[3] And perhaps long-distance trade was more important to the economy of Kerala than to that of any other Indian region.[4] But to most inhabitants of Kerala the commerce in several other products was at least as important as pepper—even more so. The total trade of the East India Companies in Kerala in 1686 can be estimated at about 1 million guilders in value; the value of trade overland between Kerala and Konkunad then amounted to roughly 4 million guilders, that of seaborne trade with Gujarat and the Coromandel Coast to 3.5 million. And yet all this was of little value compared to the trade conducted within Kerala.[5]

There was rice, for instance, which was exported in substantial quantities (400,000–500,000 pounds yearly) from Cananore and Calicut to Muscat and in much smaller quantities to Gujarat. An abundance of rice was traded within Kerala too: largely via the internal waterways from Malabar to Travancore. Despite their fertile appearance, Travancore and Cochin were deficient in white rice and had to import this from Malabar, the Coromandel Coast, and primarily Canara. "This coast of Malabar is so short of provisions that if supplies from Canara, where these grow in abundance, could be intercepted, it could be subjugated without employing any other means." This was, the VOC thought, because the amount of water depended on the irregular rainfall on the Ghats. One year the seedlings might drown; the next there would be insufficient water.[6]

Then there was the arrack trade; the production of arrack nuts was estimated at 1.5 million pounds. in Canara and 3 million in Kerala, or about 100,000 guilders' value—not much money, but good for a lot of employment, as thousands of mostly female peddlers sold arrack.[7] Or one might mention the trade in coir and coconuts. Large quantities of those goods were exported to both Gujarat and the Gulf. The amounts involved are not totally certain but can be estimated at about 1 million pounds yearly in the late seventeenth century. Coir was the most important export from Cananore to Mocha. Yet this was but a small slice of a large cake of internal trade within Kerala. As regards both the volume of trade and the employment involved (but not its value and profit), the trade in arrack, coir, and coconuts far surpassed the pepper trade then.[8]

In addition, there were smithies for which more than 400,000 pounds of iron were imported from Coromandel.[9] And finally, there was a large textile industry in Kerala. Although piece-cloth from Travancore was occasionally exported to the Gulf, this industry mainly worked for the internal market. Kerala was a net importer of textiles—mainly from Bengal and the Coromandel Coast. Yet in the region from Tenagapatinnam to Cape Comorin alone were found more than 4,200 looms catering to the internal market.[10]

So in Kerala, as elsewhere, luxury goods were only a tiny portion of trade, both in total bulk and in value, and were quite marginal for employment; but those commodities were not only splendid—they were valuable too. Luxury goods generated the profits and might thus produce mercantile wealth, which could be invested in less profitable products and land and might attract trade in bulk goods. Moreover—as their value was expressed in gold and silver coin rather than in cowry or in lead—these luxury products were more easily taxed and generated customs revenues in cash. Hence the importance of the transit trade with pepper to the states in Kerala, including Calicut and Travancore. Most of the pepper that was shipped from their ports was produced outside of these kingdoms. To them the pepper trade engendered customs revenues in gold and with those coins they could hire an army of *nayyars*.[11]

## The Flux of Trade

If there was a decline of the transit trade between India, the Levant, and Europe, one might expect that commerce would decline; however, Om Prakash, K.N. Chaudhuri, and S. Arasaratnam are all positive that "the general trend of trade was one of expansion." "We can say this categorically," Arasaratnam affirms.[12]

What they are referring to when speaking about expansion is the shipping with Europe around the Cape, of course. We may allow for a decline of the average size of the ships used in the navigation between Asia and Europe in the course of the seventeenth century, for the galleons used by the Portuguese in the beginning measured up to 1,000 to 1,500 tons and most VOC and EIC vessels were much smaller than that (although the vessels used by the Compagnie des Indes were huge ships of 1,000 to 1,200 tons). Nevertheless, the increasing volume of European-Asian trade seems undeniable. In 1600 Lisbon might welcome three or four vessels annually from Goa and Cochin. In 1700 the Portuguese were receiving two ships yearly, the French (intermittently) two or three, London four or five, and Amsterdam (from Ceylon) six to eight. One may speak of an expansion of European shipping to the Arabian seas, then. Furthermore, figures on shipping of the Companies, which are often used as an indicator of shipping to and from Asia, do not convey the whole picture. At the end of the seventeenth century we would have to include interlopers and shipping to Madagascar and we would have to consider piracy too. An imponderable factor: pirates tended to fetch booty from the whole of Asia. But loot from the Arabian seas, sold in European and colonial markets, still constituted part of European demand.

J. Boyajian has argued against this expansion.[13] In his view the size of the Portuguese exports in the late sixteenth century has been seriously undervalued, as estimates so far only considered the trade of the crown and not that of private merchants. If considering the latter too, the total value of the imports from Asia on the European market declined in the seventeenth century from a peak around 1610, he argues. However—while we may safely skip the technical details of Boyajian's estimates, through noting that I am far from certain they are reliable—it may safely be doubted whether this is the case for the second half of the seventeenth century, although trade to Europe may temporarily have leveled off from 1620 to 1660.

But the demand for products like Indian piece-cloth was "increasing here, there and everywhere," as Gentlemen XVII put it in the final decades of the seventeenth century, while a demand for new goods, like coffee and tea, arose.[14] Bengal and Coromandel mainly supplied the piece-cloth, though: the demand for Gujarati piece-cloth, in Europe did not increase as markedly. And talking strictly about the Arabian seas rather than Asia, one may grant Bojayian two points.

First, the exports of some regions to Europe declined. This applies in particular to exports from Sind. At the beginning of the seventeenth century the Portuguese had exported Punjabi piece-cloth and occasionally saltpeter to Lisbon from Sind. Those exports had dwindled at the end of the seventeenth century. Shipments of piece-cloth from the Deccan to Europe also appear to have declined.[15]

Second, the VOC strove to pay for its exports from Surat, Vengurla, Mocha, and Persia by Asian commodities. And this was a very successful endeavor. Up to 1636 substantial amounts of bullion were sent to Surat to finance the procurement of Hindustani piece-cloth and indigo. But after 1665 the Dutch could export cash from Surat and Vengurla and still pay for purchases for the Netherlands with Asian products (from Vengurla the VOC mainly exported cotton yarn to Holland). In Persia likewise: even while investing parts of the proceeds in Persia in silk, the Company could still send silver from there. Exports of the Portuguese crown to Europe, on the other hand, were in the first half of the seventeenth century largely paid for by direct imports of bullion. Due to the growth of the European intra-Asian trade, the volume of imports from Europe to the Arabian seas—but not to Bengal or the Coromandel Coast—may have decreased in the second half of the seventeenth century.

The expansion of trade to Europe applied to two markets, which were mainly supplied through Western Europe but had a different route of access to the Arabian seas, as well. Let us consider Russia first. The Sund toll registers show a very rapid increase in the category "colonial commodities" (*kolonialværer*) after 1640, including both West Indian products and East Indian ones—like spices and a variety of Indian textiles, indigo, pepper, and silk (mainly Bengali silk). This trade was mostly directed to the Polish and Russian market.[16]

Both Russia and the Polish-Lithuanian commonwealth were also connected by overland routes, though. The overland trade via the Caucasus through Caffa on the Crimea to L'vov (L'viv/Lemberg) in Poland/Ukraine, which had prospered in the fourteenth and fifteenth centuries when L'vov was competing with Venice itself as terminus of Europe's oriental trade, was declining in the seventeenth century. However, L'vov still hosted a large Armenian community that dealt—mainly via Moscow in that period—with Persia too in products like silk and Indian cotton piece-cloth. From Poland products like carpets and Persian silk, and very occasionally Indian textiles, still regularly appeared in the fairs at Leipzig; via Caffa Persian silk was even occasionally fetched to Venice. The great age of Armenian trade with Persia overland via Poland seems to be situated before and beyond our period, however. It appears to be part of a redirection of Persian trade from the Gulf to the Caspian Sea that commenced about 1730.[17]

Most trade with Persia was conducted over the Volga and this trade was thriving. From the middle of the seventeenth century onward, Russian trade with India was also on the increase. Indian merchants arrived in Russia both from Central Asia and from the Caspian, as there was a large community of Indian merchants established at Tebriz and Shamakhi. Fifty-three Indian merchants and craftsmen were allotted the right to establish a settlement in the Moscow neighborhood Kitaigorod in 1663. There was an Indian settlement at Narva in 1690, and in 1702 more than 300 Indian merchants permanently resided at Astrakhan, selling mainly Bengali, Sindi, and Hindustani textiles.[18]

Indian textiles were also a significant good in the Russian empire's internal trade, both in Russian and in Siberian markets as at Tobol'sk and Tomsk, whence they were sold to Kashgar, and via the periodic markets at Lake Khalka to the Jungar steppes in outer Mongolia. It could be argued that the increasing consumption of Indian textiles in Russia explains the expansion of Indian settlements there too. The Indians had specialized knowledge of piece-cloth, which the Greeks, Tartars, Bukhariotes, and Armenians, who dominated trans-Eurasian trade throughout Russia, lacked. Most of the Hindustani textiles sold in Isfahan and Gilan were, according to the VOC, also destined for the Russian market, being taken there both by Russian merchants—for the Russians had permanent trading settlements in Gilan—and by Indian merchants.[19]

The other market was South America. Indian (principally Coromandel) textiles were important commodities traded at Cadiz. The invoices of ships employed in shipping with South America show a rapid increase in the export of textiles to America, which probably includes Indian textiles. Some of the Coromandel cloth received by the EIC was dispatched to Amsterdam partly for use in the slave trade, but most was sold at Cadiz.[20]

Yet Indian cloth was also shipped to South America via the Manila galleons. The total navigation of Manila—mainly its junk trade with China—expanded up to 1640 and then stagnated until 1690, according to Chaunu. But the demand for Indian products expanded.[21] Surat's trade with the Philippines thrived, particularly after 1660, when the Surat traders were seeking new commercial outlets as their traditional markets in Middle East were being "shipped to death." Manila was by 1680 annually touched by four or five capital ships from Surat owned by Abdul Ghafur and Muhammad Celabi. These brought freight from a host of smaller merchants, established at Surat and places like Goga and Cambay. To the Philippines, these ships mainly shipped textiles; to Surat, "incredibly white" sugar and tin, though not (as one might have expected) silver, if silver was taken from there to the Coromandel Coast.[22]

The largest increase in the trade to and from Europe occurred in Bengal.[23] This also benefited Surat's merchant houses. Gujarati firms established on the Hugly were often branches of firms from Surat and part of the profits may have been remitted in bills of exchange to Saurastra.

Despite a major setback in the nineties, it seems the trade in the Bay of Bengal expanded throughout the seventeenth century. To a large extent this was caused by the increase in the trade of the Companies there. Due to the increasing demand for piece-cloth from Europe, their operations were shifting from western to eastern India. While the trade with Bengal of the VOC only took off around 1640, by 1700 Bengal alone accounted for 33 percent of the value of the exports of the VOC to Europe; Surat then accounted for less than 10 percent, Persia for less than 3 percent.[24]

The most obvious area in the Arabian seas to profit from this booming trade in the Bay of Bengal was, obviously, neighboring Kerala. Although the VOC occasionally attempted to impede coastwise navigation between the Coromandel Coast and Coylan, by 1690 almost 80 small vessels were plying this route. Kerala's trade with Gujarat was then estimated at 3 million guilders' value, that with Coromandel at 2 million.[25] Those benefits only partly accrued to the traders of Kerala, however. The trade with the Coromandel Coast—both coastwise and overland—was mainly controlled by merchants from the Coromandel Coast. Direct trade between Kerala and Southeast Asia apparently collapsed in the second half of the seventeenth century.[26]

Surat did have a share in this expanding trade too. The major impetus for the growth of navigation between Surat and Southeast Asia was the expansion of Siamese trade. While in 1640 Surat was conducting little trade with Siam, by the late seventeenth century two ships were sailing from Surat to Siam yearly. These brought Indian textiles to Ayuthia and tin back. Ships of the Siamese king, partly freighted by the Persian *natio* there, also sailed directly to Bandar Abbas.[27]

The China trade suffered a decline during the toppling of the Ming dynasty and the Manchu invasion, but by 1690 Surat's vessels were regularly sailing to Canton. This expansion of shipping to East Asia partly resulted from a conscious policy of Surat's shipowners to conquer new markets. We find the governor of Surat inquiring with the VOC in 1640 whether one could obtain navicerts for China. Director P. Croocq sourly commented that "the Moors are growing more insolent daily." In 1674 Hodsia Minas of Surat requested from the Portuguese a permit to send one vessel to Macao annually. This was denied by the Portuguese, for if granted, "the whole commerce of China would be lost." But that was of little effect, for Armenian ships regularly sailed to Macao without formally applying for a permit.[28]

If these branches were growing, the picture of trade within the Arabian seas—particularly that between India and the Middle East—is not at all as rosy. According to D. de Couto, 12 to 14 big ships were yearly sailing to Yemen in 1590 and brought in goods to a value of 2 million rupees. The customs revenues that the Spanish crown could obtain, if all 42 vessels that departed yearly from Gujarat to the Middle East were diverted to Diu, was in 1626 estimated as 3.5 million xeraphins. In 1708 Grotenhuys estimated that the trade of 10 ships between Mocha and Surat was worth about 3 million rupees; that of 12 ships between Surat and Persia would have been about 2 million. These estimates point to stagnation at best.[29]

Although this source has its problems and is fragmentary, to say the least, the figures on Surat, Mocha, Bandar Abbas/Kung/Hormuz, Muscat, and Basra shipping compiled by the VOC are probably the best indicator (see Tables 6.1 and 6.2).

These point to a slowly growing trade until about 1660, a decline in Persia and stagnation in Yemen until 1690, and an expansion of trade with Yemen thereafter—albeit this expansion was primarily related to the growth of the coffee trade with Europe.

The Persian evidence, such as it is, is particularly hard to use as an indicator for trade to the Gulf. It leaves the important trade between Muscat on the one hand, Sind and the Konkani Coast on the other, out of account. The same applies for shipping between the Red Sea and Basra. The Surat figures show an increase from 1620 to 1650, a decline up to 1680, and an expansion thereafter. The figures on cargo have to be used with great caution, but these too indicate that trade was flourishing until about 1660 and declined thereafter.

Allowing for this insufficient material, I would say that the trend of trade within the Arabian seas is one of contraction from 1590 to 1620, recovery from 1620 to 1660, stagnation or decline from 1660 to 1690, and growth lasting roughly from 1690 to 1720.

The expansion of trade with Persia from 1620 to 1660 probably constituted a recovery from the dislocation caused by war and piracy in the Persian Gulf in the early seventeenth century. For example, Qais, it was noted in 1646, "was formerly—in the late sixteenth century—a fertile land, populated by Moors, but it has now been utterly devastated through the work of the armies of your majesty." And the growth of trade with Yemen from 1640 to 1660 might merely have been caused by its recuperation from the far more calamitous war between the Zaidit and Ottoman armies in the Tihama. This conflict virtually devastated the region and it aggravated its ancient scourge of piracy, since the Turks equipped corsairs to prey on shipping in the Red Sea.[30]

This directly influenced the trade of the Companies in two ways. First, in the first half of the seventeenth century we find both the VOC and the EIC conducting a busy trade in Hindustani textiles from Surat to Bandar Abbas. Profits on this trade began to decline from 1650 onward, and by 1664 both Companies ceased it. Profits amounted to about 40 percent in 1640—and to only 10 percent at the end of the seventeenth century. This is of some significance as Hindustani piece-cloth (trade along the overland route included) may have accounted for roughly half of the total amounts of textiles sold in Persia. There is no evidence that this decline was caused by an expansion of trade along the land routes; rather, I would argue, it was occasioned by increasing imports of European textiles from the Levant.

There was still demand for textiles from the Coromandel Coast, but the VOC in Persia complained in 1672:[31]

> The trade in piece-cloth from the Coromandel Coast and Bengal has of course in the last years been of little to no benefit and is now altogether stagnant [*die immers*

Table 6.1

**Ships Arriving at Muscat in 1672**

| Place of origin | Number |
|---|---|
| Sind | 16 |
| Malabar | 4 |
| Makran Coast | 4 |
| Karwar | 1 |
| Patan | 2 |
| Pate | 2 |
| Konkani ports | 14 |
| Mocha | 2 |
| Surat and Broach | 2 |
| Bhatkal, Barcelore, Mangalore | 27 |
| Maldives | 2 |
| Kung | 16 |

> *de laetste jaren van geen merite heeft gerendeerd, staet nu geheel in 't voetsand te geraecken*]. The reason is that here [Isfahan] and its surrounding villages there are woven large quantities of piece-cloth, which are more profitable to the common man than coarse *salempuri*. And both the cultivation of cotton and the workshops are advancing this so rapidly that it is virtually incredible. They have advanced this much with it that they surpass not only their quality but their color and fineness as well, which is why *sekelae*s and *rumal*s are also not vended.[32]

This growing production in Persia itself undoubtebly affected the demand in the Gulf, although it was mainly destined for the Russian market. For Russia—unlike India and Europe—bought large amounts of Persian silk and cotton textiles, largely produced in Tebriz, Shamaki, and Ardebil.[33]

In the second place, after 1660 the VOC ceased taking freight from Surat to Persia because this was by and large unprofitable—not only for the VOC but for all shipowners in Surat. Shipping between Persia and Gujarat was prospering in the 1650s, though profits were diminishing because too many ships were plying this route. But by 1663 they were dwindling and in 1677 this trade was said to be "completely shipped to death [*t' enemale dood gevaren*]."[34]

It is possible, of course, that there was an increase in navigation from ports in Sind, mostly conducted in small ships under 150 tons. But what meager evidence we have points in the opposite direction. Whereas merchants from Sind played an important role in Basra in 1654, for example, by 1700 references to them have disappeared completely.[35] This was partly, no doubt, because this commerce was shifting to Muscat and the Portuguese were forcefully diverting part of it to Kung. Yet Sindi trade to Mocha also showed a decline. The trade with the Konkan too collapsed after 1680.[36]

To all appearances, the period 1620–60 may be styled an age of prosperity. This age of plenty was ruefully interrupted by the great famine of 1630–34,

Table 6.2

**Ships Entering the Ports of Aden and Mocha, 1616–1705**

| Place of origin | Aden | Mocha | Aden | Mocha | Mocha | Mocha | Mocha | Mocha | Mocha | Mocha | Aden | Mocha | Mocha | Mocha | Mocha | Mocha |
|---|---|---|---|---|---|---|---|---|---|---|---|---|---|---|---|---|
| | 1616 | 1640 | 1640 | 1643 | 1645 | 1648 | 1658 | 1663 | 1673 | 1674 | 1676 | 1677 | 1687 | 1689 | 1700 | 1705 |
| Surat | 1 | 3 | | 6 | 5 | 4 | 1 | 8 | 6 | 8 | 8 | 8 | 9 | 6 | 10 | 3 |
| Diu | 7 | 3 | 1 | 4 | 3 | 2 | 3 | 1 | 3 | 2 | 2 | 2 | 2 | | | |
| Cambay | | | | 2 | 1 | | 2 | 2 | | | | | | | 3 | |
| Gujarat other | 1 | | | | 1 | | 2 | 2 | 1 | 2 | 1 | | | | 3 | 2 |
| Vengurla | | | | | 1 | | 1 | | 1 | 2 | 1 | | | | | |
| Dabhul | 2 | 2 | | | 1 | 1 | 2 | | | 1 | | | | | | |
| Chaul | 1 | | | 1 | 1 | 1 | 2 | | 1 | | | | 1 | | | |
| Rajapur | | | | | 1 | 1 | | | 3 | | 2 | | | | | |
| Konkan other | 1 | | | 2 | | 6 | | | | 2 | | 3 | | | | 1 |
| Calicut | 1 | | | | | | 1 | | | | | | 1 | 1 | 1 | 3 |
| Malabar other | 2 | 5 | 2 | | | 3 | | | 6 | 1 | 1 | 4 | 3 | 1 | 2 | 1 |
| Coromandel | | 1 | | | | | | | 1 | | | | | | | |

| | | | | | | | | | | | | | | | | |
|---|---|---|---|---|---|---|---|---|---|---|---|---|---|---|---|---|
| Bengal | | | | | | | | | | | | | 1 | | 1 | |
| Banten | | | | | 1 | | | | | | | | 1 | | | |
| Atjeh | 1 | 4 | | | | 2 | 1 | | | | | | | | | |
| Namana | | 2 | 3 | | | 1 | | | | 1 | | | 1 | 1 | | |
| Kathiawar | | N.A. | 7 | | 6 | | 8 | | | 1 | | 1 | | | 8 | |
| Basra | | | 4 | | 6 | | | | | | | | | | | |
| Gulf | | | | | 2 | 2 | | | | | | | | | | |
| Sind | 14 | | | 3 | | | | | | | | | | | | |
| Maldives | | | | | | | | | | 1 | 1 | | | | | |
| EIC | | | | | 3 | | 1 | | | 1 | | | 1 | | 1 | 4 |
| England private | | | | | | | | | | 2 | 2 | 2 | 1 | 2 | 2 | 5 |
| France | | | | | | | | | | | 1 | | | | | |
| Denmark | | | | | | | | | | | | | 2 | | | |
| Portugal | | | | | | | | | | | | | | | | 2 |
| Dutch (Batavia) | | 1 | | 1 | 1 | 1 | 1 | 1 | 1 | 1 | 1 | 2 | 2 | 3 | 3 | 4 |
| Total | 47 | 21 | 14 | 19 | 35 | 17 | 28 | 12 | 25 | 23 | 20 | 28 | 16 | 13 | 31 | 36 |

maybe the second greatest recorded famine in Indian history next to the 1943 famine, which in Gujarat alone may have caused up to 1 million deaths and which affected the whole west coast (even though Canara was hurt less severely). But the Gujarati manufacturing industry rapidly recovered from this disaster. That was partly because the Mughal emperor began to order huge amounts of textiles to be distributed among the poor of Mecca, maybe as some measure of relief. At Broach the governor had even stationed soldiers in the houses of weavers to force them to remain at work. Another factor was that there was a persistent demand for Hindustani and Gujarati piece-cloth in Persia and the Ottoman empire.[37]

The damage of the drought of 1659–63, which particularly hit Hindustan, could not be as easily repaired. This drought—despite being much less severe than that in 1630–34—was accompanied by the widespread dislocation of agricultural activities due to military movements during the succession struggle for the peacock throne in those years. Furthermore, it was also a time of monetary chaos because of a fall of the copper production in Rajasthan, partly caused by the war as well. This convulsion was concomitant with a long-term decline in profits on the trade in Bayana indigo and in textiles in Persia, caused by increasing supplies from the Levant. A sluggish global market thus aggravated the local effects of war and famine. This induced farmers previously cultivating cash crops like indigo to shift to the cultivation of food crops. Taxes, war's eternal twin, also hit the trade in Gujarat, which experienced a scarcity in 1660, if not of such severe proportions as in Hindustan.[38]

While harvests in the seventies were sufficient—though there were severe floods in Hindustan in 1674—the eighties was a grim decade, particularly in the Subah of Gujarat. It was a decade of meager harvests in Kathiawar, the Konkan, and Malwa too. Shortages could not be dealt with as usual by importing food from Malwa, for the cities in Gujarat were perpetually short of provisions. Throughout the eighties there were constant shortages and periodic starvation among both the urban poor and the peasants in southern Gujarat. The poor "are in such desperate straits as to be forced to choose a miserable death, others have to sell their children as slaves." This worsened the shortage in the cities, for the destitute were fleeing from the villages to urban slums.[39] The cycle of poor harvests afflicted the entire west coast. Bassein and Daman were in 1686 and 1687 also visited by starvation, which forced many Portuguese vassals to flee to the surrounding territory, or even sell their infants.[40]

The countryside of Goa was in 1683 flooded by bands of desperate people "who can not subsist on alms, and what is worst—as they are Christians—die of hunger without being administered the sacraments." The *misericórdia* was to gather this flock in secluded settlements in order that they not roam around. Those trying to escape were to be apprehended and punished.[41]

It is possible that cycles of starvation, as occurred in Gujarat in 1630–34 and in 1682–87, were related to short-term shifts in the monsoon. While northwestern India was suffering from drought in the latter period, the Coromandel Coast was afflicted by torrential rains and floods, which were said to have reached several meters in height. There might have been a long-term shift in climatic patterns involved too. During the lengthy discussions about whether one was to move the capital of the Estado da Índia from Goa to Marmagoa, it was pointed out that the climate at Goa had "much deteriorated." It was wetter than formerly, while the climate in Diu was drier than it used to be.[42]

Such climatic disturbances may be linked to longer-term changes in the climate, due either to the "little ice age," the Maunder minimum (a period of absence of sun spots that reached its peak in the 1680s), or, more likely, to the El Niño effect and volcanic activity. However, the effects of the little ice age or El Niño on the European, let alone the Indian and Persian, climate and ecology are far from clearly established.[43]

Moreover, as if drought did not suffice, in the eighties the Arabian seas were plagued by an epidemic. This may well have been the bubonic plague, which also ravaged southern Spain in this period and which is, of course, still endemic in Surat.[44] The bubonic plague probably originated in the Crimea, broke out in Istanbul around April 1686, swept through Tebriz, and reached Isfahan in the winter of 1686, to spread along the land route to Hindustan in summer 1687. Meanwhile it had also disseminated via the sea route to Gujarat in 1686. The summers of 1686 and 1687 were seasons of distress there. Hundreds were said to be dying at Surat daily, while at Burhanpur in 1686 the situation was disastrous: the town was completely depopulated by the plague. People were fleeing the cities, so the plague spread to the countryside and the refugees depleted the already meager stores of food in the villages. And the pandemic continued to ravage Burhanpur until 1693, while new outbreaks occurred in Ahmedabad and Broach.[45]

With due caution, the dim contours of a seventeenth-century crisis, extending from at least 1660 to 1690, may be discerned. This crisis extended to some extent to East Africa too. For, as we have seen already, the 1680s were a difficult, even dramatic, period in Mozambique and Zimbabwe as well.

Though this crisis was partly an agricultural one caused by meager harvests, there are also two human factors involved. First, the decline of the transit trade to the Levant certainly played a role in the Middle East. And second, there was the crushing weight of the state. The crisis of the seventeenth century, both in Europe and in the Arabian seas, partly arose because of the spiraling fiscal demands of the state, demands the economy could not support. Let us consider the burdens of warfare and taxation here.

In Iran the direct involvement of the state in the rural economy constantly increased under Abbas II. The amount of land directly taxed by the Safavid state reached its greatest extent with the annexation of Kart'li in 1654; so too did the royal demesne. Until 1664 more and more land was converted to *khass* either by the sequestration of land or by not renewing claims to military service grants (*tiyul*). Those revenues were collected by agents of the king—mostly tax farmers—and remitted to Isfahan after subtracting a substantial share for the tax farmers. The revenues demanded widely varied but might amount to 40 to 50 percent, still excluding a host of other taxes and dues. Those taxes were already a very severe burden on agriculture, yet they were worsened by a host of additional impositions, such as the dreaded forced labor dues.[46]

After 1664 this trend began to be reversed. This was partly to pay for Shah Sulaiman's succession to the throne, which was—to everybody's stupefaction—accomplished without the usual bloodshed. A remarkable feat, but one had to pay for it by generously allotting land and "gifts" to the nobility. The state was thus almost immediately in financial trouble.[47]

To pay this, collectorates were increasingly sold off or farmed. This hardly benefited the peasantry, for the tax farmers were not only corrupt but more unrelenting than the former "feudal" lords when collecting their dues. Moreover, the Safavid state increased the burden of taxation. This pulled good coins into the treasury. Provincial mints—not under the direct supervision of the court—profited by emitting a steady stream of false coins. The inflation caused the collapse of many a mercantile fortune, particularly of Jewish and Parsi merchants, who had often lent money to Safavid nobles. Many Persian traders withdrew from trade to the safe haven of investment in land.[48]

In India, to quote A. Barentszoon,

> the community is not burdened with exactions or levies but all revenues are derived from the land, whereto the farmers are handed oxen to plough and seeds. And they make a deal with the governor how much they will pay for each bigha or acre [*morgen*]. Most give half, which is most advantageous for, if the harvest would fail, they would be forced to sell wives and children.[49]

The historiography tends to support him. According to S. Moosvi's calculations, the Mughal state claimed roughly a 40 percent share of the harvest, with local *zamindar*s claiming another 20 percent. To move to a regional perspective: A. Cotta estimated in 1685 that Bicholim district in the Konkan was producing a total revenue of 25,000 pagodas: 15,000 of this was levied as tax by the Maratha kingdom, 3,000 absorbed by the local *desai*s. In other parts of the Konkan, too, about 60 percent of the total revenue was collected by the state, of which 20 percent was withheld by the local landholders. These are high figures—almost certainly too high—but one may well state that the levy of the land revenue tended to cream off a substantial portion of the agricultural production.[50]

This heavy fiscal burden was made even more unbearable by disturbances due to Aurengzeb's wars. There is in recent revisionist literature on the eighteenth century a tendency to diminish the disruptive impact of war on the Indian economy.[51] This is accurate, but only to an extent. No doubt warfare interrupted commerce, but "wars here are in general not fought this bitterly as to totally destroy trade, though they do impede it," as R. Lefer at Vengurla put it. And war not only caused destruction. It generated demand too. In seventeenth-century India war was a major industry, maybe even *the* major industry. The army created demand for horses, bullocks, arms, cloth, and grain as well as for the funds involved. Shivaji's army required more than 4,000 to 5,000 pack oxen and 7,000 to 8,000 porters. This involved expenses of several hundred thousand guilders. Shivaji was cajoling bankers throughout India to raise these funds.[52]

There is another side to this story, though. Such huge procurements for fleets and armies could also drive up the prices of foodstuffs and cause the people to starve while the dealers sent by the court to procure the grain made generous profits; so it was in Surat in 1683.[53] Moreover, moving armies often brought epidemics with them and they were often followed by hosts of marauders, by *banjara* caravans, grazing on the rice fields of the villages, and "coolie and bhil robbers," who served as porters and supplemented their niggardly pay with plunder. In the army's trail came columns of *begaris*, or forced laborers, who had to dig trenches, build campsites, and so forth. They were badly, or not at all, clothed and fed, and snatched what they were not given. And most importantly, as both the Maratha and the Mughal troops were increasingly irregularly paid, they began to harry as well.[54]

While Shivaji's "flying column," as the Dutch called it, was a well-disciplined army, fighting in the Deccan and the Konkan in the eighties and nineties had degenerated to skirmishes between ill-clothed, ill-paid, and ill-disciplined bands of mercenaries, followed by marauders.[55] Vengurla was looted no less than five times in the eighties; the entire population fled to the haven of the (fortified) Dutch factory. Other towns in the Konkan, like Candal and Punda, were not as fortunate. They were said to be utterly ruined by the constant fighting. The fighting devastated agriculture as well. The *havaldar* of Bicholim was in 1684, for example, begging the Portuguese to deliver rice to him to feed his family, "because of the general lack of foodstuffs there." One year later, fugitives from Candal who had fled the famine raging there swarmed Bardes. The situation in the Maratha Deccan was worse; entire districts were reportedly turning to waste. This is attested to by the Maratha sources as well, so that Perlin describes the period 1660–1700, with good reason, as "a dramatic crisis."[56]

The crisis in the hinterland caused a dramatic contraction of trade in the Konkan, particularly in the eighties. Vengurla was a flourishing port in the sixties. By 1686, Vengurla's shipping had almost disappeared and when the VOC, the only employer left, was evicted from its factory in 1693, the town dwindled to a heap of ruins overgrown by dense forest. The surrounding Candal district had become a virtual desert.[57]

All in all, we can speak of a crisis, then, in the second half of the seventeenth century, but with varying impacts on different areas. While the production of pepper declined in Kerala from 1630 to 1690, there is no evidence of meager harvests there.

And three areas were certainly prospering: Oman, Canara, and Madagascar. In Muscat, maritime trade as much as warfare was flourishing after 1660. This allowed the imam to build a substantial fortress in Naswa to assert his power over the unruly hinterland, and some of the profits of the booming trade at Muscat reached the hinterland too. The ruler and successful admirals established sugar cane plantations run with slave labor, and hired workers to dig new irrigation canals. Agriculture was booming. The production of sugar for export in Muscat rapidly expanded from 400,000 pounds in 1672 to up to 760,000 pounds at the end of the seventeenth century, for example. Sugar was mostly sold to Bahrain, Persia, and the Ottoman empire.

Was this prosperity of Oman also related to an increase of trade on the Mrima and the Banadir Coasts? This is possible—but it is very difficult to pin down due to the lack of any quantitative evidence. All I can say is this: On the one hand it is likely that the collapse of Portuguese control after 1654 at least did away with the attempts of Portuguese monopoly contractors to curtail the trade to the Gulf and Mozambique. On the other hand, while Surat still frequently received ships from Mogadishu in the 1650s, this direct shipping had completely disappeared by 1680 and the trade with East Africa there was now confined to one or two ships from Pate yearly; Diu's shipping as well showed no increase. Overall, the trade with India appears to have stagnated at best, but since that was only a very minor portion of the trade of the Mrima Coast it is very difficult to say anything definite about it.[58]

Canara produced a rice surplus of about 9 million pounds, of which about 6 million was exported overseas to Goa, the Gulf, and Gujarat, the remainder overland to the Deccan, partly as tribute of the Ikkeri rajah to the Adilshah, later to the Marathas. And "Canara is pretty much the granary of Persia and Arabia, the rice being sold in Muscat and fetched in small lots in barges to other ports" in the Gulf. Muscat yearly received about 300,000 pounds of rice from the Konkan and up to 2.4 million pounds from Canara. Most of this was consumed within the Gulf, but some was also used to feed the Omani garrisons in Pate and Zanzibar. As Canara rice fetched an 80 percent profit at Muscat and only 15 to 25 percent at Goa, it was generally much more enticing for the court merchants in Canara to sell it to the Muscatis than to the Portuguese.[59]

The kingdom of Ikkeri surely profited from the booming demand for foodstuffs from the Gulf and East Africa, from the Deccan and Gujarat during the bad harvests in 1659–61, and in the middle of the eighties. Though the scourge of war afflicted Canara too, these would appear to have been decades of prosperity for a Canara getting fat on famine. The bulk of the rice, sold at Mangalore and Barcelore, was bought on the marketplace by caravan and coastwise traders who bartered it for salt mainly, but also arms and bullion. However, the trade with the major partners of Canara—the Muscatis, the Portuguese at Goa, and the Dutch at Cochin—was held under tight control of the court of Ikkeri. It would appear this also applied to overland deliveries to the Mughal and Maratha armies.[60]

The prices of rice were mostly fixed by the court, mostly to be bartered for spices and copper in the Dutch case, salt from Bardes in the Portuguese, horses and silver in the Omani. The rice trade was controled by the "court merchants": Saraswat and Muslim merchants and moneylenders. They lent money to the central administration and were allowed to farm the customs and supervise the ports in return. But sometimes they might almost manage the very production of rice: they gave advances before the rice was planted to the peasants, who then had to deliver the crop to them. The Saraswat Malapa Malu was the most important trader. After the conquest of Onore and Barcelore, he yearly farmed their customs. As Malapa Malu handed vast sums of cash to the *nayak* of Ikkeri, he was in virtual control of the Canara rice trade from 1656 until his deposition from office in 1666.[61]

Yet, according to a report on Canara from 1657, the modest *rayyat* did not benefit from the booming trade of his rajah:

> According to the ancient customs the princes give out the entire country to the inhabitants for ten, twenty or even thirty years with leases which are this high that the tenants, after much labor and a reasonable crop, can hardly cover the barest of needs. And when they can not fully pay the said sums, because of a bad crop or other reasons, they are sentenced to harsh imprisonment, until they are bailed out by friends.[62]

While Gujarat and Kerala easily recovered from the depression and while Canara and Muscat thrived, the decline of trade from Sind was permanent. The former metropolis of Laribandar was in 1692 wrecked by a tidal wave and never rebuilt. The endless fields of ruins ringing Tatta from the early seventeenth century may be the visible remains of the "crisis of the seventeenth century" in the Arabian seas.[63]

Let us after this survey of the field now consider the trade in a number of "products." Aside from the weight of taxation and war, three further explanations for the listless pace of commerce in the second half of the seventeenth century might be adduced. One, war along the caravan routes, can be discounted. This is beyond the scope of this study, but basically as we saw already, trade—even along the long and dangerous silk route—was going on as before. To some extent too, Russia imposed a degree of stability on the northern steppe routes that had not been witnessed for centuries, as did the Safavid empire in Khorasan and Afghanistan. Second, as Steensgaard argues, the trade might have gone through a slump because of the disappearance of the pepper trade between the Levant and the west coast of India. This was certainly an important factor. And third, as I. Habib argues, the increasing exports of bullion around the Cape and into India might have caused inflation and a loss of purchasing power, which would have precipitated a decline of trade.[64]

## Bullion Trade

Those massive imports of bullion in India—which obsessed economists in the seventeenth century as much as historians nowadays—did not necessarily have to cause inflation, though, for there were vast stocks of precious metal in India already.[65] An increase in the imports of silver did not have an immediate impact upon the amount of money in circulation and thus on the price of commodities. The trade in precious metals was trade in just another kind of merchandise, superficial waves upon a placid ocean of silver, spelter, gold, and copper sunk in the countryside. As R. Lefer wrote to Batavia from Vengurla, precious metal was "simply the merchandise in which the exchangers are dealing. And the course of it varies when more or less silver and gold [coin] is imported."[66]

Likewise, Gentlemen XVII (the board of directors of the VOC) expressed their amazement that, while the quality of the Persian currency was deteriorating, this did not have an impact on the price of commodities.[67] The demand for, and the price of, the currencies that were imported was segmented too: it was not directly linked to the stock of commodities and hence did not directly influence the general level of prices. Nor did the exports of gold and silver to the Orient have to reflect any imbalance between the total stocks of silver relative to the commodities in circulation in Europe versus Asia, and hence a possible imbalance between economic growth in Asia versus Europe. Rather, the price of currencies was primarily related to the demand for other coins and secondarily to that for other metals—like gold, copper, tuttenag (an alloy of tin and copper), and spelter—and, to some extent, to quasi-currency like, in India, cowry shells and *badam* (an inedible almond).[68]

For Europe—whether around the Cape or via Yemen and the Persian Gulf—did not export silver or gold. It exported coins to Asia and in particular a special kind of coin, namely, "trading money" (*negotiepenningen,* as the Dutch called it), like Peruvian and Mexican reales or liondollars. These "trade coins" circulated over wide areas, were in high demand among merchants, and thus—as we have seen in the account of the Basra trade—commanded a considerable premium over coins that were only in local use. This accounts for the persistence of arbitrage profits in trade between Europe and Asia from the sixteenth right through to the nineteenth century.[69] The price ratios between the total stocks of silver available in Europe and in Asia ought to have equaled out with the export of silver from Europe to Asia. But since the demand for silver was segmented, profits could still be made on the export of some silver currencies, which fetched a premium relative to gold or copper currencies, to quasi-currencies, or to local currencies.

For, as in Europe in the same period, there were in the Middle East and India broadly three different circuits of, and therefore different markets for, money in the seventeenth century. There was purely local money (or perhaps, better, "privatized money," since the state had no monopoly on striking coins), as, for example, the mahmudi, which was only used in Gujarat; the Cochin fanam; or the ori, which only circulated in Gilan. After all, coins were not merely a means of circulation; they were also a powerful symbol of dynastic and regional identity. That was certainly the case in India, where traditionally Muslim potentates on their accession to the throne first had the *khutba* read and then had coins struck.

Then there was imperial money such as the abbasi in Iran or the rupee in India, in which the land revenues were expressed. And, finally, there was "trade money," which was mostly used for external trade and did not circulate internally. The price of each of these coins for different circuits was determined by its own supply and demand. It was hence prudent for small *shroffs* as much as for Aurengzeb's and Shivaji Bhonsle's treasury to keep a large stock of different coins at hand to purchase and sell these at the most opportune moment or to insure against fluctuations of the exchange rates.[70]

### *Sources of Supply*

There were in the seventeenth century four main sources for the supply of precious metals to the ports in the Arabian seas. We can be brief on the first source: Japanese, Southeast Asian, and Chinese gold. The VOC in the 1630s and 1640s had some Japanese gold minted at Surat.[71] The Estado imported some 80–90 marques of gold yearly from Macao, as (occasionally) did English private traders. If Atjeh and Palembang were major centers for the collection of the gold mined in Sumatra, and if the VOC mined some gold in Sillida, this was largely brought to Coromandel and Bengal; ships steering to Surat seldom brought gold there.[72]

Second, there was African gold: occasionally pilgrims brought gold from West Africa to Mecca. The pilgrimage of the king of Bornu in West Africa in 1670 is said to have upset the gold market in Mecca for years. The bulk of the Ethiopian gold was probably exported by caravans to Egypt. Production was estimated at about 600 marques yearly, of which about 40 to 50 were brought from Ethiopia over Massawa to Yemen, mainly Loheia—the terminus of the small *jilba* trade to the opposite shore. Most of this gold was probably used for circulation in Yemen. Ships from Mogadishu occasionally imported a few marques of gold from Ethiopia to Surat too.[73]

Then there was the gold trade of Mozambique and Mombasa, which, unlike the Ethiopian production, was by and large directed to India. The bulk of the gold mined in Mozambique was sent there, as in India one could obtain 100 percent profit on Mozambique gold and in Portugal—maybe—30 percent. Gold was by 1670 the major product dealt with in Goa: a trade that was largely monopolized by the Saraswat merchants there, who normally farmed the mint.[74]

After a long rise, during the decade 1672–82 the course of the gold mohur in the Mughal empire showed a decline relative to the silver rupee, the ratio between the two coins dropping from 1:12 to 1:10. The EIC attributed this decline to Aurengzeb throwing part of the gold, which had been hoarded by the notoriously avaricious Shah Jahan, on the market in order to pay for the shah's campaigns in the Deccan. Additionally—and more importantly—according to the VOC, the demand for gold was declining, since under Aurengzeb the land revenues were to be paid in silver *sicca* rupees only, no longer in gold coin. This explains the timing of the devaluation of the mohur in 1672 and the declining ratio of gold relative to silver.

However, more gold also seems to have become available on the subcontinent after a long period of relative scarcity.[75] There are probably two reasons. On the one hand, this may have been caused by the imports of gold by the VOC and the Compagnie des Indes on the Coromandel Coast and at Surat.[76] On the other hand, it was the period when the Mozambique gold trade showed an increase; new veins of gold had supposedly been discovered, and Portuguese merchant caravans were venturing further and further into the hinterland of Zimbabwe. Exports of gold, declared at the customs house of Mozambique, increased from about 600 marques in 1660 to 1,000 marques in 1676 and to 2,767 in 1679. What was declared was only a fraction of what really was exported, however, for most gold was smuggled. Even this was less than what might have been achieved, for the maximum production yearly realizable in Mozambique was estimated at 4,000 marques, or about 200,000 cruzados' value at the local rate.[77]

The amounts of gold brought to Mozambique, Angoche, and Querimba by Portuguese and Maravi traders were little affected by the falling price of this metal on the Indian market. For the sales of gold at Mozambique did not depend on its demand but on the supply of merchandise, and especially on the price of textiles in Cambay. Let us, to explain this, examine the gold trade in closer detail.

The gold produced in Mozambique was, wrote H. Hugo, "washed down when there is a little rainfall from furrows in the mountains and collected from the rivers, without anybody knowing—or caring to know—what is hidden in these mountains, which is allegedly something very big." Indeed, most of the gold circulating in Mozambique was gold dust sifted from the rivers.[78] But there were mines. In Mucaranga district the gold was generally mined in shallow shafts of a few palms' depth. In Manicca and in Chicanga gold was quarried by digging deep shafts, *lascas*, into the ground—very dangerous work. The "emperors" of Monomotappa and Torwa were using slaves, captives of war, for this work.[79] Yet its benefits were meager, for the gold veins occur in very thin layers near the surface.

**Map 5. Zambesi County**

It would be useless, Mozambique wrote Lisbon in 1696, to use slaves to work in the rivers. Too little gold was found to warrant the huge costs of feeding those slaves. For the peasant communities, the cost of labor in searching for gold, which was then sold to the Portuguese, was practically zero. For to the Shona agricultural communities the search was but a seasonal pursuit in addition to self-sufficient agriculture. The major problem involved in the Mozambique gold trade was thus not the costs of labor but those of transport.[80]

Since the Portuguese were, until the 1680s, hardly looking for gold themselves, one had to obtain it through the barter of Indian textiles with traders (in Querimba) and kings (in the Monomotappa *feiras*). Perhaps more gold could be obtained. But, on the one hand, the Monomotappa chiefs were extremely reluctant to permit the Portuguese to search for gold in their territory. For, as they rightly feared, a mass influx of *sertaneiros* would upset both the ecological and the political balance in the region. Maravi chiefs were even supposed to immediately execute anybody who might disclose the location of gold to the Portuguese. And, on the other hand, in Monomotappa one would trade as much gold as was needed to obtain a certain stock of Indian textiles—if more textiles were sold the result would only be that the exchange rate would drop and that less gold would be sold.[81]

There was a sizeable production of cotton and of textiles in Mozambique itself, so the Indian textiles served ceremonial rather than real utilitarian purposes.[82] The *feiras* were tightly scrutinized by supervisors of the Monomotappa, stipulating the rates for barter, with Indian textiles serving as unit of account and glass beads serving as the means of exchange in market transactions.[83] Indian fabrics, like *berauli* and *bairami* from Gujarat and the Deccan, thus served as a "reserve" currency in Monomotappa to measure either labor dues, the rates of barter on the *feiras*, or the ranking of chiefs, which were measured by the textiles they could afford. The Portuguese soldiers on the Zambesi were paid in piece-cloth rather than pennies. Both the Portuguese and the Monomotappa were thus eager to curtail imports in Mozambique in order to forestall inflation.[84]

The third source of precious metals was the supply of silver and gold brought by the East India Companies via the Cape. The quantities of Dutch and English exports are well known through the work of F. Gaastra and K.N. Chaudhuri.[85] These amounted to the bulk of European bullion exports to Asia as a whole in the second half of the seventeenth century. However, we are as yet not nearly as well informed on French exports of bullion, and these were an important factor in the Arabian seas. For, unlike the Dutch and the Portuguese, the French paid their trade there by the import of bullion.

Table 5.3 shows the distribution of money received by the VOC at Batavia: the bulk of it was destined for Bengal and the Coromandel Coast. The remainder was mainly spent on the Southeast Asian pepper trade—and only very small amounts were sent to China.[86] In spite of occasional remittances from Batavia and from Ceylon, the trade with Malabar was mainly financed by cash sent from Surat and Persia, partly obtained with the proceeds of pepper sold there. At the end of the seventeenth century, when more Malabar pepper was sold in the Netherlands, about 200,000 guilders in silver coin were imported yearly from Amsterdam via Ceylon.[87]

This paramount position of Bengal in the remittances of cash of the Companies also applied to the English trade, although Bombay occasionally received substantial quantities of bullion from England. On balance, in the second half of the seventeenth century bullion imports by the Companies only played a minor role in the Arabian seas. This was a different situation than at the beginning of the seventeenth century, however, when the Dutch, the English, and the Portuguese imported substantial amounts of bullion at Surat, Goa, and Cochin.

The fourth source of precious metals was supplies from the Levant brought through Persia and Yemen by Indian traders. At Surat these showed an increase

Table 6.3

**Remittances of Money Received in Batavia to Asian Offices by the VOC** (in "Asian guilders")

| Year | Bengal | Coromandel | Eastern Java | Banten | Amboina | Total |
|---|---|---|---|---|---|---|
| 1685 | 382,788 | 494,698 | 48,000 | 26,100 | 214,800 | 2,094,137 |
| 1686 | 221,268 | 231,311 | 9,000 | 254,700 | 168,000 | 1,811,089 |
| 1687 | 783,223 | 300,837 | | 302,615 | 219,000 | 2,770,799 |
| 1688 | 964,534 | 619,433 | 56,350 | 245,695 | | 3,208,031 |
| 1689 | 1,262,416 | 64,726 | 128,127 | 348,708 | 60,000 | 3,283,325 |
| 1690 | 498,188 | 36,901 | 195,944 | 214,347 | 96,000 | 1,734,627 |
| 1691 | 143,158 | 183,671 | 147,000 | 304,500 | 324,379 | 2,991,516 |
| 1692 | 1,216,844 | 310,518 | 115,327 | 399,833 | 120,000 | 3,308,135 |
| 1693 | 853,612 | 196,031 | 158,475 | 547,161 | 256,250 | 2,503,070 |
| 1694 | 1,441,756 | 346,469 | 101,700 | 457,021 | 244,593 | 3,614,662 |
| 1695 | 1,575,245 | 200,998 | 168,287 | 561,449 | 90,000 | 3,254,596 |
| 1696 | 1,711,688 | 841,638 | 121,200 | 675,980 | 18,000 | 4,131,686 |
| 1697 | 2,219,469 | | 110,845 | 409,532 | 300,006 | 3,703,001 |
| 1698 | 1,470,315 | | 205,575 | 603,600 | 150,000 | 3,119,190 |
| 1699 | 3,438,612 | 1,004,442 | 113,775 | 425,925 | 30,000 | 6,091,394 |
| 1700 | 3,462,031 | 1,180,249 | 170,700 | 649,634 | 300,003 | 6,102,087 |
| 1701 | 1,985,147 | 906,910 | 100,500 | 307,506 | 210,351 | 4,119,187 |
| 1702 | 2,309,226 | 1,335,172 | 263,317 | 457,796 | 301,024 | 5,361,047 |
| 1703 | 1,874,716 | 831,781 | 270,004 | 346,930 | 209,567 | 4,375,405 |
| 1704 | 1,833,454 | 348,632 | 360,137 | 416,617 | 154,500 | 4,016,088 |
| 1705 | 3,214,174 | 1,150,909 | 496,368 | 470,485 | 171,000 | 7,240,993 |
| 1706 | 2,583,973 | 1,043,860 | 387,677 | 462,236 | 180,000 | 5,822,125 |
| Sum | 35,445,837 | 10,629,186 | 3,728,308 | 8,888,370 | 3,817,473 | 84,656,190 |

from about 1.5 million rupees from Yemen and 1 million from Persia and Iraq in 1640 to 2 to 3 million yearly from Yemen at the end of the seventeenth century and 1 million from Persia, Iraq, and Oman. This did not exhaust the bullion exports from the Middle East: another 700,000 to 1 million guilders were exported annually from Yemen and Oman to Kerala. Ships from Canara also brought bullion on board, as did vessels from the Coromandel Coast and Bengal. And in the early eighteenth century Bengal may well have accounted for a major share of the exports of bullion from the Middle East, for country trade between Bengal and Yemen by and large consisted of the barter of bullion for sugar. There was a large flow of bullion overland through Kandahar from Persia to India too, although it is impossible to assess its size. At any rate, the amount of bullion coming to Bandar Abbas from Isfahan depended on the demand from the caravan traders in Isfahan, so that this would appear to have involved substantial amounts. The VOC, the EIC, the English country traders, and the Portuguese Gulf fleets were also exporting bullion from Persia and Yemen to India. One may well agree with the Carmelite friar Barnabás de San Theresa, then, who, observing the casks filled with coins embarked in Bandar

Abbas for India, noted that "it seems that all the money from the West Indies is coming to these East Indies" by way of Persia.[88]

We come now to a somewhat surprising conclusion: in spite of the growth of trade over the Cape, throughout the second half of the seventeenth century exports of bullion from Persia and Yemen to western India were larger than exports over the former route.[89] Despite the decline of the pepper trade, the exports of bullion from Persia and Yemen to India not only showed no decline but increased concurrently with the growth of exports around the Cape, though by 1660 more bullion was exported from the Red Sea and from Basra and less from Persia, where the state curtailed exports. Where did those quantities of bullion shipped from Persia, Iraq, and Yemen to India come from?

First, bullion was exported directly to the Levant by the Levant trade companies. The major exporter of bullion to the Levant was undoubtedly Marseilles. These exports are estimated at about 2.5 to 3 million guilders around 1670, generally directly consigned from Cadiz. This was to the chagrin of the central administration, which urged the Marseilles chamber of commerce to pay for its imports from the Levant by the export of textiles from the Languedoc, rather than in bullion.[90] The English Levant Company, on the other hand, was largely able to cover its imports from the Ottoman empire through the sale of English cloth. The English were interested in a fairly restricted range of products—silk, cotton, mohair, and raisins—and could often manage without substantial direct remittances of bullion.[91] The French traders on the other hand bought a far wider range of products, including Egyptian rice, grain from Asia Minor, dried fruits from the Greek islands, carpets, and coffee. This wider array of trade also involved more subsidies in bullion to support the exchange of goods.[92] The Dutch Smirna convoys in the eighties exported roughly 200,000 to 300,000 leeuwendaalders (i.e., 750,000–900,000 guilders) to Smirna from Amsterdam and Rotterdam.[93]

This evidence regarding the bullion exports from the various Levant Companies has to be used with caution, however. A large part of the trade with the Levant consisted of cabotage conducted from Genoa, Leghorn, and Venice. Dutch ships on their way to the Levant touched either at Leghorn or at Genoa to bring bullion on board. This was paid by bills of exchange drafted on Marseilles and Leghorn or directly on Amsterdam. Again, they might sell broadcloth, grain, fish, or leather at these ports and exchange the proceeds for bullion that could be taken to Smirna.[94] The English also dealt in that fashion. The statistics of the Levant Companies may not be a reliable guide to the true extent of English and Dutch bullion exports to the Levant, then, for an important part of the bullion exported was obtained from within the Mediterranean.

Moreover, the trade in the Levant was often financed through drafting bills of exchange on Leghorn. This occasionally involved further remittances of cash. And, as M. Morineau has noted,[95] in the late seventeenth century the bulk of Dutch—and to a lesser extent English—shipping consisted of freight trade: cotton, wool, silk, and pearls brought by Armenian, Sephardic, and Greek merchants—either to Leghorn or directly to London or Amsterdam, exchanged for silver.[96]

We have one crucial piece of evidence to suggest that, through these twisted highways and byways of commerce, bullion flows to the Levant may have increased in the seventeenth century. The reference here is to the accounts of the coinage of gold zeccini by the Venetian mint, which have been studied by U. Tucci.[97] The zeccino was the standard money of account in the trade of the Levant and was widely exported to Yemen, Persia, and, beyond, to India (although the *venetianen*, as the Dutch called them, appear to have largely disappeared from circulation in Persia at the end of the seventeenth century).[98] The zeccino thus provides a barometer of the amount of transactions conducted in the eastern Mediterranean. The accounts show a constant increase in the coinage throughout the seventeenth century, reaching a peak in the eighties.

All this adds up to a flow of bullion, both immense and complex, between the western and eastern Mediterranean that is far from perfectly understood and is beyond the compass of this study. This much seems certain: the Mediterranean had not stepped out of the limelight of the bullion trade, and the decline of the pepper trade cannot be explained via its lien to the bullion trade, as Braudel has argued.[99]

Second, about 100,000 to 200,000 guilders were sent yearly from Poland and Austria to the Ottoman empire. This was partly direct pay for merchandise received. In the Austrian case this was mainly Hungarian cattle and copper, in the Polish an array of goods—carpets, leather, textiles, copper, and fruit.[100] Partly too, silver was at a higher rate in the Ottoman province of Transylvania than in Poland and was thus a profitable export. Istanbul was in the 1640s flooded with phony akçes coined in Transylvania. This Transylvanian akçe was probably the "bad silver coin," flooding from Anatolia into Iraq and Persia, that was seen as a major cause of the Persian inflation.[101]

Third, the Crimean khanate was yearly sending huge tributes in bullion to Istanbul, while Russian merchants, sailing to the Bosporus, also used to fetch bullion. The trade of the Nogai steppes between the Volga River, the Crimea, and the Caucasus—if it was trade—largely consisted of spoils of war, slaves, and payments for the mercenaries of the Khans of the Crimea, who were partly recruited in the Caucasian domains of Imeretia, Circassia, and Karabagh.[102]

Though Kart'li exported some wine, silk, and fish, the principal export of this mountain realm was in the seventeenth century "services"—mercenaries, slaves, and indentured laborers. And Kart'li was apparently not doing the worst of it; the Safavid empire was an inexhaustible market for manpower and Russia was increasingly "importing" Georgian soldiers as well. Part of the remittances of those "guest laborers" landed in Kart'li in bar. The Tiflis mint was in the seventeenth century one of the busiest mints of the Safavid empire, though it mostly emitted debased silver and copper coins.[103]

Fourth, bullion was exported from Russia to Persia by way of Astrakhan. According to Herberstein, this amounted to about 1.5 million guilders in the mid-seventeenth century. The Astrakhan customs ledgers, which are available from 1737 onward, put the trade deficit far lower, though, at about 250,000 rubles or 750,000 guilders, with wild fluctuations. In the eighteenth century more manufactured products were exported from Russia to Persia than in the seventeenth, however, so the bullion flows to Persia may have decreased in the eighteenth century. Moreover, Russia also exported modest amounts of bullion to the Central Asian khanates, some of which may have ultimately landed in India.[104]

### *The Famine for Bullion in the Middle East*

With the disappearance of the pepper trade—a direct payment by Europe for goods received from the Middle East—the Ottoman and the Safavid empires were bound to have troubles with their balance of trade. The Ottoman empire largely paid for its deficit on the balance with India and Persia through a positive balance on the Levant trade, mainly obtained by the export of cotton. They were suffering from Indian competition, and later on American, however; the price of cotton was increasingly fixed on European exchanges and Ottoman production had to follow.[105]

As silk prices in Europe were falling and the transit trade to the Levant was in decline, this problem also came to the fore in Persia from 1640 onward. By 1640 the Persian economy apparently had a deficit on its balance of payments with India. This deficit could not be balanced by the transit trade with Indian textiles to the Ottoman empire and the exports of silk, cattle, and wool from Tebriz to Syria and Anatolia, large though this trade was, and of textiles, cotton, fruit, tobacco, silk, and carpets to Russia, even though this last commerce appears to have expanded. Furthermore, it seems as if the flow of diamonds, jewels, luxury cloth, and bullion remitted overseas by Persian immigrants in India—Golconda mainly, but Bijapur as well—to their homeland decreased after 1660. Those remittances may have been the most significant factor to even out the deficit of Persian trade to India in the early seventeenth century. The sums involved might amount to 2 million rupees yearly.[106]

India mainly, if not only, required bullion from Iran; other products exported either made minimal profits—like almonds and pistachios—or had a very restricted market, like carpets and ceremonial robes. Persia's most prestigious commodity, horses, was difficult to obtain for the average trader to the Gulf. To fetch horses out of the country, one needed a special permit from the *beglarbeg* of Shiraz and such permits were rarely, if ever, granted to traders. Additionally, only a few good steeds fetched a profit: seaborne horse trade between the Gulf and the West Coast was both a small commerce (perhaps 200–300 yearly) and a risky one. It seems likely that the horse trade between India and Iran was much more substantial in the sixteenth than in the seventeenth century, which may have contributed to Iran's worsening balance of payments.[107]

The effects of the deterioration of Iran's balance of payments first materialized in the trade with gold coins. For one could make a slight profit on gold in India, particularly, of course, in Kerala, where the currency was traditionally the gold fanam. There one obtained a 5 percent profit on gold ducats in 1674, and on the Coromandel Coast one made 6 percent.[108]

The Persian monetary system was nominally based on a gold standard. The golden abbasi was linked to the toman—the money of account—so that the Safavid empire strove to check the export of gold from the kingdom. In 1640 this was completely prohibited. The Safavid authorities tried to relax such regulations later on, but any permit to export gold was merely followed by new prohibitions. Traders exporting gold abbasi were even threatened with capital punishment. Yet both the Companies and the Indian merchants continued to smuggle gold from Persia. The ratio of gold to silver therefore showed a steady upward trend.[109]

Next, the problem began to occur with silver money too, which accounted for the bulk of the coins circulating in the empire. The price of silver currency was fixed to an official rate of exchange of the abbasi, for the payments of the land revenue had to be delivered in silver mahmudi haviz rated to the abbasi.[110]

Note, in parentheses, that this was a very different policy from that in the Ottoman Empire, where the land revenues were paid in a wide variety of currencies, for the Ottoman akçe showed wild fluctuations in value. Ottoman revenues were thus often paid in the money used for commerce: Iraq was in 1647 paying its revenues in reales, the major coin of trade there. This did contribute to the scarcity of cash there, however.[111]

Yet while the Safavid currency did remain at a steady rate, this policy of sticking to an official rate of exchange did lead—as students of centrally directed currency systems would predict—to a rampant black market. False or debased coins penetrated the Safavid empire from Oman, Georgia, Iraq, and Anatolia. And on the black market the ratio of Persian money to currencies in use on the world market—the Mexican real mainly—consistently dropped. By 1670 there were said to be no good reales current in Persia anymore. One had to settle for silver abbasi, for which one had to pay a 3 to 4 percent premium in 1670 and 6 to 7 percent in 1680.[112]

The Persian money market was thus subject to a twofold squeeze: good money was withdrawn from circulation through the payment of revenues on the one hand, by foreign trade on the other. Provincial mints—which were generally farmed by the provincial governors—profited by striking debased coins. The VOC argued that this monetary convulsion was the major cause for a stagnation of Persian trade in the second half of the seventeenth century. "Commerce here," as the VOC put it, "is like a river," leading bullion from the Levant through Persia to India, "and if one outlet is blocked the entire river will run dry."[113]

This stagnation was mainly blamed on the lack of good coins because of Sheikh Ali Khan's foolish policy of hoarding silver in the king's treasury instead of emitting more coins to stimulate the languishing commerce. However, this was not the whole explanation. The problem was rather that the profits on merchandise from Hindustan and Gujarat, sold in Persia, were declining. Thus the demand for bullion was increasing. The phenomenon was only too well known in Europe, which also experienced an era of clipped coins in this period: with a slack trade one tends to invest in tangible coin rather than in merchandise.[114]

The economy of Yemen was having fewer problems, apparently, but the bulk of transactions there were expressed in "petty, mostly low-value coins, the prices of which fluctuate day by day." There was no dearth of these, easily explainable by the expansion of the coffee trade and the consequent imports of low-value coins, minted in Syria and Egypt, to finance this trade. Albeit here too there was a severe scarcity of high-value coins directly imported from the Levant such as the rixdollar or the Mexican real, because of the burgeoning demand for these currencies from India. At the end of the seventeenth century one had to pay 10–12 percent in premiums to receive payments in those coins, on which one might make a slight profit in India.[115]

### *India: The Bottomless Sink*

Since the seventeenth century two possible explanations for the stream of bullion from Europe and the Middle East to the Indian subcontinent have been adduced. The constant flow of cash may be seen as a structure that stretches from Roman times to the present, for bullion was always more highly priced in India than in Europe and the Middle East. This higher price of bullion is mostly explained by the inclination of Indians to use silver and gold for adornments and "hoards."[116]

Indeed, as van Rheede noted on Kerala, "their attire and manner of clothing is not unlike that of girls for there is not a single man who does not wear wrought or minted gold on his body."[117] The sheer delight of Indians in gold and silver ornaments should not be discounted as a factor contributing to the flow of precious metals to the East. For why should Indians in the seventeenth century have perceived precious metals merely as a medium of exchange, as Kindleberger rightly wonders?[118]

Gold and silver adornments, as much as hoards, could be used as insurance against bad times too: to amass stockpiles was eminently rational in an uncertain monsoon climate. And, of course, the threat of war and taxes contributed to hoarding. The Surat council of the VOC noted in 1702, for example, that when rumors spread about the impending death of Aurengzeb everybody began to bury treasures.[119] In Surat the price of gold was said to depend "upon the amount of treasure requested by the Moorish nobles." Such treasures were amassed "to serve their children, for the king will surely declare himself to be their heir."[120]

Rather than stressing the higher price of bullion in the East, one could adduce instead that silver was exported to pay for procurement of goods. India needed few products from Europe and the Middle East, but both of these needed products from India. The two explanations need not be contradictory, of course. Particularly after the discovery of the American mines, one could argue that Europe exported silver since it enjoyed a comparative cost advantage in this product, allowing it to exchange silver economically with various Asian products.[121]

If bullion was simply exported to India because of an imbalance between Indian and European stocks and thus to gather arbitrage, was it profitable merchandise? It could be—certainly to Bengal, which accounted for the bulk of exports in the late seventeenth century. When minting rupees imprinted with the sign of the present year of Aurengzeb's reign (*sicca* rupees), the VOC fetched a 6 to 8 percent profit at Rajmahal. Silver was often first coined at Rajmahal and subsequently exported to other factories to pay for the procurement of goods.[122] It was, for example, proposed that Surat might convert its sales to bills of exchange, remit these to Bengal, and pay for its procurement in Gujarat with rupees minted at Rajmahal, which was much more advantageous than bringing silver to Surat. Again, the export by the VOC of gold was often very profitable. In 1641 one could obtain at Surat 10 percent profit on Japanese gold cobangs and at Masulipatam 9 percent. On Japanese and Chinese bar gold one could obtain 24 percent on the Coromandel Coast and in the Konkan, but only 3 percent in Surat. There was also a small profit to be made on the sale of silver Mexican reales in Goa. It was, therefore, profitable to take letters for loans raised in Portugal expressed in cruzados and convert them to reales in Goa.[123]

Was trade in bullion from Europe profitable for private traders too? Under pressure because of English concessions to Jewish traders, the VOC in 1686 permitted the Sephardic jewelers and bankers Abraham Pereira and Pedro Texeira to conduct commerce at Surat under the cover of the VOC. They were to trade in bullion received from Amsterdam and invest the proceeds in diamonds. Pereira and Texeira were soon in severe trouble. Counting additional charges of insurance, freight, customs, and mint dues, they took a loss of 2 to 3 percent on the import of reales, the most profitable currency. They might have suffered bankruptcy if the VOC personnel had not conducted private trade under the cover of these merchants.[124]

The picture of imports from Europe is thus a blurred one, but imports in India of bullion from the Middle East constituted an unprofitable commerce—sometimes a disastrous one. As we saw already, a heavy loss was suffered on the exports of bullion from Persia. Bullion from Yemen fetched meager profits at Surat too: 3 to 4 percent at most. Counting the expenses of coining, freight, and insurance, one took a loss on the exports of all currencies from the Middle East—and often a heavy one at that. Bullion was exported mainly to cashier the benefits of sales in Persia and to an extent Yemen. However, in some cases, as with exports of cash from Persia to Bengal, the 40 percent loss on silver abbasi devoured any profits on sales in Persia.[125]

And yet both the court of directors of the EIC and the High Government of the Indies insisted that the Persian factories invest their proceeds in bullion instead of more profitable products, like silk. For from 1640 onward this bullion could be invested on the Coromandel Coast and in Bengal in piece-cloth, which would fetch much higher profits in Europe than Persian silk.

The Companies imported bullion to the west coast of India not to make a profit there but to fuel the commodity trade, then. Theoretically European Companies might have financed their trade in the Arabian seas through the sale of European and colonial products. Indeed, the Estado largely financed its Asian trade by the sale of tobacco. The English and the French were selling European cloth at Surat too. Profits on this were meager (15 to 20 percent at most) and sales restricted. This cloth was mostly used for the fashion in the Islamic east of draping horses and elephants. Yet it would have been more profitable to export European cloth than bullion to Surat.[126]

But the bullion was mainly needed as collateral on the loans of the Companies: the trade of all Companies and of the Estado floated on the credit of Indian bankers. If the Compagnie des Indes did not receive bullion, its shaky credit would collapse and no one would be able to buy or sell anything. To the consternation of the directors, therefore, Surat continued to request cash. The directors would rather have financed the trade through selling tobacco, coral, cochineal, or, preferably, European textiles. Again, the VOC occasionally imported bullion in Surat when there was a danger of defaulting on its loans.[127]

Even though those European imports were small compared to those from the Middle East, they were often badly needed, for there were severe seasonal and periodic shortages of cash in Surat at the end of the seventeenth century. Thus in 1700, when insufficient money had been imported from the Middle East, interest rates rose from 12 percent to 24 percent; trade stagnated and bills of exchange were not available.[128] To obtain loans and honor their bills of exchange merchants therefore had to remit bullion from abroad. Bullion served as collateral not only for the traffic in bills within India but for that between India and the Middle East as well. It was usual for merchants operating from Kerala and Gujarat to draft bills on Mocha and Aden and for merchants from Surat to draft bills on Kung—the major center for banking within the Gulf. Yet this traffic in paper depended upon a steady flow of coin from the Middle East.[129]

A lack of bullion, in turn, hampered the collection of land revenue in Gujarat; rural credit rates would mount and so would the discount on bills of exchange drafted from Surat on Burhanpur or Ahmedabad to transfer the land revenues. For the land revenues and the incomes of nobles from their *mansab*s were largely remitted through bills too.

So, like the finances of the Companies, the finances of the Mughal state and those of myriad smaller states in Gujarat depended upon the credit furnished by

Indian bankers too. According to the director of the Compagnie des Indes, F. Martin, the prosperity of Surat was primarily generated by the presence of great bankers there, tied to *mansabdar*s at the court. From the European material we get some glimpses of wide-ranging banking operation connecting the merchants of Surat with the *shroffs* in the Deccan and northern India. These *shroffs* also cashed money for Mughal *mansabdar*s and soldiers. Bills of exchange drawn from Agra on respondents in Surat were not accepted in the small provincial town of Ujiain in 1690, for example. The market there was in turmoil due to scarcity of cash, as the VOC had to remit a sum of 200,000 rupees in bills to the Mughal army. Also, one major banker had gone bankrupt because his bills of exchange had not been honored by a *shroff* in the king's army.[130] Those bankers were in turn often connected to merchants trading for the Companies. Bahadur Khan, the *subehdar* of Gujarat, was still in debt for 550,000 rupees to his bankers in 1693. He was unable to repay, which forced him to resort to extortions. The main victim of his wrath was Varamali Das, son of the VOC's broker Balav Das, banker at Burhanpur, who still owed Bahadur Khan 100,000 rupees.[131]

The incomes to be received from a *mansab*, hoards, and various mobile assets like flocks of cattle and perhaps slaves were used as collateral for such loans. Take the debts of the *faujdar* of Broach, Mustafa Quli Khan, to the VOC, for instance. These were paid by assigning incomes from his service tenures (*jagir*) to a representative for paying the VOC. Or again, take the arrears of Muhammad Mirza Ardalani *Mir Musa* to the VOC, for which his *inam*-property in Bengal was used as security.[132] But to lend to the nobles was risky business, so the *shroffs* accompanying the court would often demand payment in cash instead of bills. And, according to A. Ali's meticulous examination of this problem, by the 1680s the average benefits from *mansab*s were on the decline as ever more newcomers in the administration aspired to a position. There were insufficient *mansab*s available to be partitioned among them. The Mughal nobility was facing a crisis of collateral.[133]

According to Potvlied, writing from the court at Aurangabad in 1701, the Mughal nobility was in desperate financial trouble. Interests on loans charged to *mansabdar*s had soared from 1 to 3 percent monthly. Small soldiers could hardly obtain cash; the rates for bills of exchange on Surat had mounted from 2 to 4 percent monthly and still more for bills drafted on the far-off estates of the nobility. Faced with this crisis of confidence in the value of the *mansab*s and thus the creditworthiness of the Mughal empire, the court resorted to drawing in more bullion from Surat and probably Bengal as well.[134]

In the eighties most coins minted at Surat were sent as cash in large caravans, accompanied by a mounted escort, to Golconda or Aurangabad. This was partly the land revenue of Gujarat, partly bullion remitted by bankers of *mansabdar*s to pay outstanding debts. Such funds would amount to 2 to 3 million rupees yearly.[135] This drain to the Deccan was said to be the prime cause of the constant scarcity of cash at Surat in the late seventeenth century. Now, the coinage of the mint at Surat accounts for about 25 percent of the total coinage of the Mughal empire in the period. The Deccan thus soaked up a substantial part of India's supply of bullion in the late seventeenth century.[136]

From Mughal sources we are able to make an informed guess as to the immediate destiny of the money disappearing in India's "bottomless sink." Most of the bullion received by the court and its *mansabdar*s was used to pay for outstanding debts, partly caused by the *mansab* crisis. It was also used to pay for an expensive administration that was to directly collect the revenues from land in the Deccan, drawn into the royal demesne by Aurengzeb. That demand from army and court caused a feverish commerce not only in silver in Golconda but in copper coins as well, in which the soldiers were paid. The copper sold by the VOC in Surat and Masulipatam, Gentlemen XVII thought, was mainly taken to Golconda.[137]

The impact of the import of bullion on the Indian economy should be viewed in a political context rather than one of price history or the growth in output. Whereas both the prices of foodstuffs and the sales of the VOC were expressed in *sicca* rupees in Surat and do show strong fluctuation, they show no clear increase, and the few wages we have show no definite trend to inflation either.[138] For the Indian market, the market of the imperial centers and not that of *ganj* or kasbah, was to a large extent a political one. The main cash crops traded were grain and rice for armies and courts; the army was probably the major employer in India, the remittance of the land revenue the largest of transactions. The imports of bullion are perhaps as much reflected in the huge size of (more or less available) military manpower in the countryside than in an increased production of textiles.[139]

This may apply not only to North India: most bullion and copper imported in Kerala was exported to Mysore. The drain of metals to Mysore increased markedly after 1650, when the Voydayar dynasty introduced a fixed rate of land revenue, which was to be paid in cash, and a standing army.[140]

The increase in Indian bullion imports was also reflected in the expansion of the Surat *sicca* rupee as money of account. This facilitated recruitment and internal trade throughout the subcontinent. For the "Indian market" did not really exist: it consisted of a vast array of linked small local markets. Thus, local coins were used in local circuits, while the *sicca* rupee was used for trade with other regions. In Goa in the late seventeenth century, for example, Portuguese transactions with the *subehdar* of Candal—procurement of rice and wages of soldiers—were paid in *sicca* rupees. Similarly, the trade with Bicholim was expressed in this coin. The xeraphin mainly played a role in internal circulation in Goa. At Daman most payments to the soldiers were done in mahmudi until 1686, when it was decided to replace this local Gujarati coin by rupees, for the mahmudi was wildly fluctuating but the rupee was at a steady rate.[141]

In Gujarat the silver *sicca* rupee was the money of account used for the land revenue "and always remains at the same rate," the VOC wrote. But the hun and the copper paisa showed continuous fluctuations depending on the amount of copper and gold for sale. Since the copper prices in Surat showed a falling trend, one may speak of an inflation of the copper paisa relative to the rupee.[142]

Again, coins minted at various provincial mints often had a lower silver content than *sicca* rupees, and the latter commanded a considerable premium over local coins. If one wanted to trade in Bayana in the late seventeenth century, one had to exchange one's *sicca* rupees in local currency. The exchange involved a considerable bonus. Such local rupees were worth only a fraction of the *sicca* rupee.[143]

This considerable difference between local coins and imperial coins is a form of inflation that put rural market centers at a disadvantage compared to major centers of trade. The land revenues had to be remitted in *sicca* rupees. Yet the premium on *sicca* rupees would also draw cash into the countryside. Through the medium of the Mughal *sicca* rupee, local economies were thus drawn into a larger network of recruitment and of supraregional, indeed international, markets. And—more importantly—the increasing use of rupees facilitated the extension of urban functions into the countryside.

While the imperial currency remained at a steady rate there was a multitude of local currencies too, some of which were clearly subject to inflation. And this occurred not only in Hindustan but in the Maratha Deccan as well. The bulk of the Maratha coinage in the period of Shivaji consisted of cheap, generally inferior copies of Bijapuri and Ahmadnagar golden huns ("pagoda samegris," as the VOC called these, or "padeshahi huns"—in Maratha documents—contrary to the "pagoda subehdaris" that were common in the Konkan). The Bijapur golden hun was worth 3⁴⁄₇ rupees and was at a steady and high rate, but the coins that were struck by the Marathas were worth only 2 rupees or less. The recourse to issuing debased and counterfeit coins was mainly occasioned by the constant financial problems facing the Bhonsles, the VOC argued. The hugely expensive hosts of Shivaji were paid in pagoda subehdaris and had to supplement their meager pay in false coins with plunder. Under Sjambaji there was even wider recourse to issuing debased currency.[144]

Parallel to this devaluation of the local currency there arose a nearly insatiable hunger for copper and tuttenag in the Maratha dominions. The copper was obtained from the VOC, tuttenag from the Portuguese. In 1678 Shivaji offered the VOC at Vengurla a contract in which he would buy more than 600,000 pounds of copper directly. Shivaji also tried to sign such a contract with the VOC's factory at Golconda. This copper and tuttenag was by and large intended for coinage. Timoji Nayak, Vengurla's broker, was to deliver all copper to the mint of the court at Panala, for which he would be paid a 25 percent provision. However, the VOC was loath to close this deal, as Shivaji was a notoriously bad debtor.[145]

Debased Maratha money—most of it copper but some silver coin as well—

was in the late seventeenth century flooding both Goa and southern Gujarat, chasing the good money away. At Goa this pull of Gresham's law in the 1690s caused a serious drain of gold são thomés, silver xeraphins, and first and foremost tuttenag bazarucos to Candal. Since the price of tuttenag was mounting because of the unquenchable demand from the Deccan, most bazarucos were withdrawn from circulation in Goa. Shops at Goa had to close down and the poor could not buy food.[146] And Mughal officials contributed their share to the inflation. The *subehdar* of Punda had in 1695 opened a new mint that was issuing counterfeit silver rupees. The *sicca* rupees were consequently immediately hoarded by the merchants. But the Portuguese were still charged the price of grain, which they procured from the mainland, in *sicca* rupees. It was decided to prohibit the import of this counterfeit coin. The *subehdar* protested. This prohibition would offend the Mughal emperor, he wrote. The Portuguese replied the emperor was probably unaware of the forgery committed by his vassal.[147]

As Steensgaard has argued, the main impact of the import of bullion should therefore be sought not in the context of its influence on prices or output, but rather in its impact on the fiscal structure.[148] The immediate consequence of imports of bullion would be a reallocation of the land revenue.

This would occur at Golconda under Mughal rule, for example, where indirectly taxed land was converted into crown revenue, or in the Maratha Deccan, where the sequestration of assigned revenues into crown lands or tax farms under Shivaji was accompanied by a massive demand for silver and copper to facilitate the remittances of those revenues[149] With copper, gold, and silver soaked into the treasury, there was in the Deccan a seemingly insatiable thirst for tuttenag to be used in petty transactions. The traders of Goa and Macao profited from the demand for lead that caused its scarcity in Goa throughout the seventeenth century.

The "Indian" economy is therefore presumably not the appropriate frame with which to approach the issue of whether India was suffering from inflation in the seventeenth century. The answer very much depends on which circuit and which segment of the money market one is talking about. The Mughal currency was not devalued and prices expressed in rupees do not show an inflationary trend.

Yet below the steady current of *sicca* rupees and pagoda samegris flowing to the seat of the Mughal court at Aurangabad or the Maratha treasury at Panala, there was a profusion of local circuits and the impact of the bullion imports varied from one local circuit to the next. In some circuits there was a definite trend toward both a deterioration of the quality of the money and inflation. This especially applied to the Deccan, the Konkan, southern Gujarat, and maybe the Doab, which were ravaged by war. And war and devaluation of the currency are always twins. The wide circulation of debased coins has been demonstrated by samples of the silver content of hoards from Hindustan as well.

Having considered bullion—nexus of trade and war—let us next examine the shifts in the overseas and caravan trade in three commodities: indigo, piece-cloth, and pepper. There occurred a revolutionary shift in the marketing of those three commodities, which, together with coffee, accounted for the bulk of the transit trade of the Arabian seas. This was not related to any structural deficiencies of the caravan trade and certainly not to turmoil along the caravan routes. The second half of the seventeenth century was actually a rather calm period along the caravan routes in Persia and from Persia to India.[150] The shift was mainly caused by the rise of new markets and new suppliers for the commodities produced in the Arabian seas and by a shift from merchandise originating in the Arabian seas to goods originating elsewhere.[151]

## Indigo: Commerce and Production

If the Companies were not successful in rerouting the silk trade overland, they were for a brief period in the 1640s very successful in redirecting the indigo trade from Hindustan. The EIC's and the VOC's procurement, shown in Table 6.4, then accounted for about half of the total production of Bayana indigo. This was a remarkable feat by any standard: without the use of violence and the benefit of easy access to information, the Companies were still able to oust the caravan traders who carried indigo overland to the Levant. This bulk procurement chased the Portuguese from the market as well. The sailors who each brought a few hundred pounds along in their luggage mainly conducted the Portuguese trade in indigo; they were unable to compete with the Companies.[152]

But this momentary predominance of the Companies did not last, and by 1647 the EIC abandoned the indigo trade. The cause of this was that various alternative suppliers were entering the market. Gentlemen XVII noted in 1645 that indigo obtained from Guatemala had hitherto been of inferior quality compared to Indian indigo. But it was now improving day by day and much cheaper. Later, indigo from the Caribbean began to enter the market as well, whereupon indigo cultivation spread rapidly through the tropics and subtropics: to Virginia, Bourbon, Mauritius, and Java. In view of this, Gentlemen XVII decided to curtail their procurement in Hindustan. The indigo trade went through a brief revival at the end of the seventeenth century, however. This was due to the disturbance of trade in the Caribbean during the nine years' war and, according to Gentlemen XVII, the deteriorating quality of the indigo imported from Guatemala. This in turn enticed the High Government of the Indies to start cultivating indigo on Java, further constricting the demand for Hindustani indigo.[153]

Meanwhile the caravan traders had seen their traditional market dwindle: this was most apparent in the Levant towns, which in the late sixteenth century were mainly supplied overland. In 1690 almost all indigo sold at Aleppo was derived from the Caribbean and Guatemala. Earlier the Italian market had disappeared, for Guatemalan indigo was largely destined for Italy, probably the major European market for indigo.[154]

**Map 6. Northwest India**

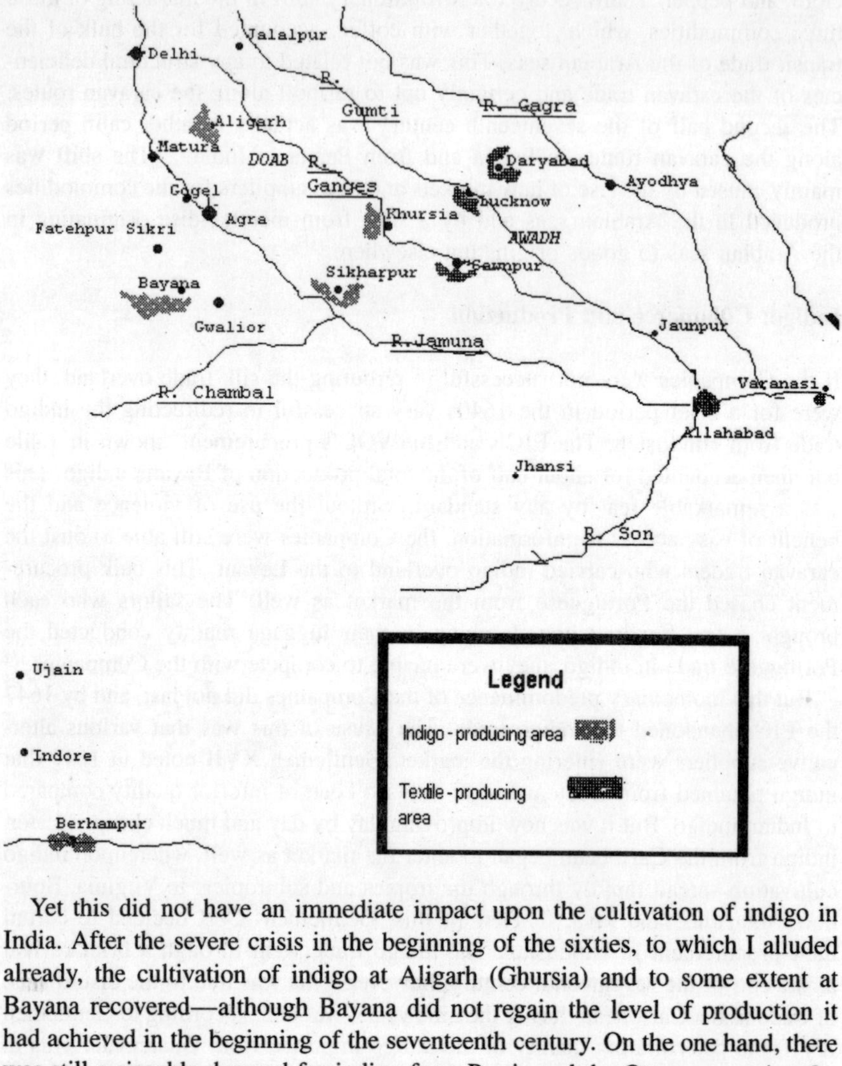


Yet this did not have an immediate impact upon the cultivation of indigo in India. After the severe crisis in the beginning of the sixties, to which I alluded already, the cultivation of indigo at Aligarh (Ghursia) and to some extent at Bayana recovered—although Bayana did not regain the level of production it had achieved in the beginning of the seventeenth century. On the one hand, there was still a sizeable demand for indigo from Persia and the Ottoman empire. On the other, in the increase of trade in piece-cloth to Europe the demand for indigo in India was expanding.[155]

There were four major areas of production for indigo in India: the Coromandel Coast; Sarkhej and Jambushir in Gujarat; Burhanpur in Malwa; and northwestern India—the Bayana tract and Alwar in Rajasthan and Aligarh. Most of this indigo was obviously destined for the Indian market: of the total estimated production

Table 6.4

**Exports of Indigo by the Dutch East India Company from Surat** (1621–1700, in lbs.)

| Year | Lbs. | Year | Lbs. |
|---|---|---|---|
| 1621 | 111,600 | 1661 | 57,404 |
| 1622 | N.A. | 1662 | 23,320 |
| 1623 | 150,700 | 1663 | 29,466 |
| 1624 | 124,000 | 1664 | None |
| 1625 | N.A. | 1665 | None |
| 1626 | 198,600 | 1666 | 110,000 |
| 1627 | 133,700 | 1667 | None |
| 1628 | 179,300 | 1668 | 32,211 |
| 1629 | 161,200 | 1669 | 104,724 |
| 1630 | None | 1670 | 180,518 |
| 1631 | 217,700 | 1671 | 427,824 |
| 1632 | 540,000 | 1672 | 133,072 |
| 1633 | 47,000 | 1673 | None |
| 1634 | 199,700 | 1674 | None |
| 1635 | 297,800 | 1675 | 166,782 |
| 1636 | 125,000 | 1676 | 50,032 |
| 1637 | 64,400 | 1677 | 50,032 |
| 1638 | 38,600 | 1678 | 30,104 |
| 1639 | 149,800 | 1679 | 60,080 |
| 1640 | 422,300 | 1680 | 60,192 |
| 1641 | 500,000 | 1681 | 50,160 |
| 1642 | 155,700 | 1682 | None |
| 1643 | 209,900 | 1683 | 55,176 |
| 1644 | 100,900 | 1684 | 79,883 |
| 1645 | 86,700 | 1685 | 81,928 |
| 1646 | 79,500 | 1686 | 110,320 |
| 1647 | 145,000 | 1687 | None |
| 1647 | N.A. | 1688 | 104,915 |
| 1649 | 180,000 | 1689 | 119,834 |
| 1650 | None | 1690 | 137,527 |
| 1651 | 25,400 | 1691 | 122,001 |
| 1652 | 103,500 | 1692 | 158,971 |
| 1752 | N.A. | 1693 | 189,226 |
| 1654 | None | 1694 | 249,205 |
| 1655 | 137,400 | 1695 | 102,275 |
| 1656 | 93,700 | 1696 | 181,080 |
| 1657 | 13,800 | 1697 | 316,710 |
| 1658 | N.A. | 1698 | None |
| 1659 | N.A. | 1699 | 70,015 |
| 1660 | N.A. | 1700 | 178,475 |

of India in 1690 of 3.5 million pounds, less than one-sixth was destined for export, whereas the production at Burhanpur, for example, was altogether destined for the internal market. In the late seventeenth century the production of Bayana indigo was also mainly destined for the internal market. Bayana's place in international trade was taken over by the Aligarh area, although Armenian and Uzbek traders had earlier already exported that indigo to Russia, Turkestan, and Persia.[156]

Basically, the Companies were able to achieve their dominant position on the indigo market because in this case they could fully use the advantages provided by their economies of scale. To understand this, we have to put the cultivation of indigo within the wider context of agricultural production in northern India.

To cultivate indigo is a risky decision for the cultivator: the crop ties down the land for three years and afterward the plot has to be left fallow, since indigo exhausts the soil. Again, indigo is highly sensitive to rainfall, its cultivation very much a gamble on the weather. As if this did not suffice, only the second year's indigo tended to fetch a profit; the indigo picked in the first and third years was mainly sold on the internal market and often at a loss.[157] Then there are outlays of capital involved: the farmer needed bowls to work the indigo, a well, and a warehouse to safely store it (though such facilities were often shared among various families). Furthermore, picking and drying indigo requires a large amount of labor, which cannot be provided by the family alone. And, finally, cultivating indigo requires a great deal of specialized equipment. Hence, indigo cultivation implies the existence of a great deal of agricultural capital—it is not a good that can be raised by mere toil of the peasant's family.[158]

Instead, indigo presupposed the tying in of individual households to a system of marketing and access to sources of labor recruitment. Due to the necessity of leaving the land fallow after three years, it also implies a mechanism for communal decision making. The resolution to make the step to the cultivation of indigo, or to a particular variety of indigo, was in generally taken collectively by assemblies of the peasants. This was the case at Sikharpur in 1697, when the farmers decided to start cultivating *nati* indigo for international trade instead of the *jauri* variety they had hitherto cultivated for the Indian market. This was not an easy decision to take, for they had to invest sizeable sums in digging wells, buying bowls, and hiring piece-labor.[159]

Because of these initial outlays, to procure the desired variety of indigo a potential buyer would have to invest a large sum of money as collateral to ensure that peasants would deliver indigo to him. If a Company decided to invest in indigo, they would thus have to invest in credit to the peasants as well. Up to 1645 the VOC had handed large amounts of credit to rich farmers in Bayana. In view of the risks involved in recovering such loans, the High Government of the Indies prohibited the factory at Agra from engaging in such practices and withdrew those loans forthwith. Yet, in spite of this prohibition, in 1686 the

VOC at Agra was again forced to hand substantial loans to a "large farmer" to entice him to cultivate indigo for the VOC alone.[160]

Transactions with indigo would thus involve a pyramid of credit. This stretched from major banking houses at Delhi or Agra through to an array of moneylenders at the local bazaars down to the peasant. Often, the *rayyat* was an unknown quantity to the purchaser, since the indigo was bought and delivered by middlemen: there were often up to five intermediaries between producer and buyer.[161]

So we have here peasant communities in a landlocked and remote region of Hindustan adjusting production and investing in equipment to cater to demand on the world market. We have, furthermore, an extensive rural credit system and, most remarkably, a market for free labor. For at both Aligarh and Bayana there is little evidence of the use of slaves or forced labor on plots cultivating indigo.[162]

Most cultivators of indigo were small peasants and most traders were only peddlers. And these accounted for an important share of production and sales, particularly for the indigo sent to Turkestan that was bought by Armenian and Uzbek peddlers in small lots. Those traders would plod from hut to hut to bargain a few pounds of indigo from the peasants in exchange for copper bracelets or a few inches of cotton cloth, as F. Pelsaert described it. However, such Armenian and Uzbek traders were often organized in rings and could coordinate their purchases and investments.[163]

But the small peasants were not the main sellers to the companies. In general the VOC and the EIC bought most indigo from the "chief farmers" (*hoofdbouwers*), after which smaller lots were bought from smaller suppliers. The price was negotiated in a contract between representatives of the Company and the assembled chief farmers. Those large farmers could then set the prices of the indigo delivered by the small farmers, as they were abreast of the market rate, and they often bought the small farmers' crops through advance buyers.[164]

These chief farmers were well aware of the state of the market in distant Lahore, Delhi, or Lucknow and were able to sell their indigo by representatives there if they were dissatisfied with the price offered by the Companies. In 1690 the chief farmers threatened the VOC, for instance, that if the Company would not accept their indigo, they would pay a merchant to take it to Lahore, where it could be bartered to the Uzbek merchants in exchange for horses, which were always in demand at the court.[165]

Furthermore, these chief farmers were connected to a web of moneylenders in the local kasbah. The local *shroffs* were in turn connected with dealers in places like Jaunpur, Cawnpur, Jahangirabad, and Jalalpur. Such traders were tied to branches of great merchant firms at Agra, Delhi, and Lucknow. The Companies certainly did not introduce such methods of marketing. The indigo farmers were apparently using the same bargaining techniques when negotiating with Armenian or Uzbek rings. And this was the same network of bankers that guaranteed the remittance of land revenues to Aurangabad or to the Rajput court of the Rathors of Jodhpur too.[166]

Now, this sophisticated trade and credit system does not tally with the traditional picture of the North Indian countryside as dominated by peasant smallholds, organized within the framework of household production and mainly producing for subsistence and to satisfy the land revenue. But maybe this image is a misleading one. One could suggest that already in the sixteenth century there was, aside from the peasant sector of the economy, another sector of commercialized large estates cultivating grain for the armies and cash crops for the caravan routes. I suspect such commercial estates were organized around the *madad i-ma'ash* grants or *soyurghal*s that were bestowed in large numbers by Shir Shah and Akbar upon minor officials and religious orders.[167] For the countryside of the Doab and northern Rajasthan was not the isolated backwater it may appear to modern eyes, which are used to perceiving ports alone as commercial outlets. It had long been the hub of caravan trade, a caravan trade that was accompanied by the spread of commercialized agriculture. And the countryside of Hindustan was dotted with rural bazaars and small market towns. In a ledger of 1687, relating to the costs of mustering a caravan from Lucknow to Agra, more than 40 such small kasbahs are mentioned as local centers both for the exchange of information and for the marketing of grain.[168]

R.C. Fox, dealing with the relation between market towns and countryside in North India in the late eighteenth century, has called such kasbahs "rurban."[169] The term implies that consumption and production for use of the elite—which in Europe and the Arab Middle East were mainly concentrated in the cities—were widespread in the countryside. Fox used the term mainly to refer to the family networks of Rajput, Jat, Pathan, or Mughal clans stretching from the rural market towns down to the smallest hamlet. Such clans lived in the countryside but they assembled regularly at the local kasbah. Bayana, probably a typical case, was described as "a Rajput place, full of warriors."[170]

This "rurban" nexus between town and countryside has both a political and an economic side. Bayana not only was the meeting place of the assemblies of Rajput warriors but also served as the site where one would be informed of the prices in Delhi and Agra and where one could recruit workers. "Laborers" might mean either musketeers or hands for the farm, but most were both, depending on the year and season.

As we can see from the Jodhpuri material laboriously gathered by Rana, "rebellious" clans (from the perspective of the Rathor dynasty) were in the late seventeenth century increasingly gaining a dominant hold on the countryside of Bayana.[171] They did this by evicting small peasants from their land and constraining sales of grain and cotton by small peasants in the local bazaars to their representatives. What mainly disturbed the Rathors was that those clans controlled sizeable resources of cash—which allowed them to entertain a redoubtable armed retinue. As well, this cash was withdrawn from the revenues delivered to Jodhpur, so the land revenue of the Rathors collected from Bayana was dwindling.

One may plausibly assume that those funds were obtained through the cultivation of indigo in Bayana. And indeed, both the Jodhpuri and the VOC evidence suggests there was a large and widening gap between the small peasants and the *hoofdbouwers* in Bayana district in the seventeenth century. The Rathor sources bewailed the heavy dues imposed upon the poor, small peasants by "rebelling landholders" who were almost certainly identical to the VOC's *hoofdbouwers.*

While the Jodhpuri documentation is mainly concerned with fiscal and military matters, the VOC material is mainly concerned with marketing. Small peasants could still sell their indigo to Armenian hawkers active along the caravan routes. But they were increasingly constrained to follow prices fixed by two or three major sellers of indigo. Indeed, the VOC material suggests that big farmers often forced peasants who had but 300–400 pounds of indigo for sale to vend it to contractors working for them. From the VOC sources we have the names of the major sellers of indigo in Bayana in 1637 (indigo entrepreneurs, as van Santen calls them)—all Muslim.[172] This seems to suggest that these entrepreneurs are the holders of small *madad i-ma'ash* grants. Apart from their role as large indigo cultivators, such *hoofdbouwers* fulfilled another function by linking the villages with the marketplace. And as with the *shroffs*, credit was generally first extended to the *hoofdbouwers,* who in turn extended it to the smaller cultivators. It also seems that they had at least some influence on the recruitment of soldiers in the villages. The *hoofdbouwers* generally provided the VOC with troops to guard its caravans.[173]

So in the case of indigo two basic conditions for the effective use of the huge resources of the companies in credit and purchasing power had been satisfied: supply was concentrated in a small area and deliveries were dominated by a limited group of suppliers. Yet the very character of the demand of the Companies tended to widen the gap between large landowners on the one hand, nobles and peasantry on the other, and these landowners might hire armed forces to defend their newly gathered wealth. Maybe the situation in Bayana is, then, a small case of what was beginning to happen in India at large. The Companies "created disorder" by the very nature of their trade.

## Textiles

### *India as Industrial Hub*

Those conditions that favored the Companies in the indigo trade did not, at first sight, exist in the textile trade or, indeed, in the case of most manufacturing industries in India. For, in principle, manufacturing could be found and founded throughout India.

"Another advantage of Hindustan is that it has unnumbered and endless workmen of any kind," the Mughal emperor Zahir ud Din Babar wrote, marveling at the incredible speed with which one could erect monuments in India.[174] The abundance of labor was striking in Kerala as well: "The commoners work everywhere in such endless numbers and at such low rates of pay that it is hardly worth mentioning."[175]

With such an abundance of labor one could put up a workshop anywhere, a situation that pretty much tallies with the theory of unlimited supply of labor expounded in a famous article by Lewis.[176] I would rather call it a quasi-unlimited supply of labor, however, meaning that large amounts of labor were used in agriculture or "services" that were only marginally productive.

There are two consequences to an unlimited supply of labor. First, there is a tendency to divide tasks whenever possible and to economize on equipment. For example, in 1667 the VOC tried to persuade its construction workers at Cochin to use bullock carts rather than pack oxen to carry stones. The oxen drivers, who saw their employment imperiled, protested. The VOC was finally driven to concede to their demand. Still, a bullock cart would have been far more economical than pack oxen, director Y. Goske complained.[177]

Second, the prime constraint on investment is not the price of the production factors—or to an extent the interest rate—but rather the costs of information and of transactions. The costs of machinery and labor were not a very important consideration; the problem for an Indian merchant was how to sell products.[178] Production thus followed the trader. The situation on the Coromandel Coast was described as follows in 1724:

> The Indians have very little property and the one who has somewhat higher income immediately establishes a workshop, where the ones who are even poorer go to work to earn a few paise for a bare living.[179]

One might, for example, encounter a substantial textile industry in the Maratha Deccan in the seventeenth century. There, such small towns as Karhad, Modal, Malwan, and Kolhapur were major suppliers of the "Bhaleghatte cloth" to the Portuguese: cheap cotton *dhoti* and *dobrada*s destined for the African market, both West Africa and Mozambique—or rather Dela Goa Bay. They also produced *dogeri,* which was taken by *khatri* merchants to Muscat and Persia. This is rather surprising if one remembers that in the late eighteenth century this region was considered a typical rural backwater. The Maratha *desh* would appear to have "deindustrialized" under the rule of the *peshwa.*[180]

Production thus arose and declined consecutive to the demand of the merchants who were serving as intermediaries between the weavers in the Maratha Deccan and the traders on the coast. For those textiles were obtained by the Portuguese private merchants through Indian intermediaries. "The trouble here [in Goa] is that everything we buy, we buy through middlemen," Antônio Mello e Castro warned the crown.

> To obtain cloth there are Hindu merchants who fetch it from the Baleghat, others who buy it on the opposite side and others who sell it here, so that when the Portuguese buy it, they do not even know the price for which it was purchased.[181]

There were exceptions to the rule that manufacturing industries were found and could be established throughout India. Some large cities—mostly ancient residencies of a court such as Golconda and Ahmedabad—boasted "guilds" of highly specialized craftsmen who tenaciously stuck to their location. Take the production of *paṭkalla* cloth at Ahmedabad, for instance, which was tightly controlled by a small group of weavers. These weavers were probably Jains, since to the consternation of the VOC they refused to touch paint in the monsoon period for fear that there might be mosquitoes in the paint. Nobody else possessed their skills, handed from generation to generation, and they could impose conditions upon the cloth merchants.[182]

Nor were they alone, for much of the highly specialized manufacturing of Ahmedabad—which ranged from the making of carts and ceremonial robes to that of poison—appears to have been organized along tight lines of caste, kin, and family, and clung to its location. The silk industry of Ahmedabad staunchly stuck to Ahmedabad in the eighties, while the weavers from the equally unruly Broach district were said to migrate in droves to Surat.[183]

But only a small part of India's manufacturing pursuits was in the hands of such tightly knit—and probably well-paid—specialist groups who were fabricating works of art. A very different case concerns a major, perhaps *the* major, textile exported from Surat: *bafta.* In the late seventeenth century the production of *bafta* involved three links. First, cotton delivered from Jambushir to Broach was handed to the weavers by advance merchants, generally commissioners of great traders. The amount and quality of *bafta* to be delivered by the weavers were precisely fixed in contracts. Weavers were often severely in debt to moneylenders, so they had few liberties to make anything else. They could abscond from a contract by fleeing, of course—and they did. Next the bales of cloth were taken to specialized workshops to be cut in pieces, and, finally, brought to Surat to be printed with stamps. Printing was a standardized procedure, as the amount of paint needed was precisely fixed. The printing was done by piece-laborers. This is almost a semi-industrial procedure. The production of *dhoti,* sailcloth, and other varieties of coarse textiles seems to have been organized in a similar way. Such textile production in bulk accounted for the lion's share of Surat's exports. The increasing use of stamps at the end of the seventeenth century may have fostered the growth of the manufacture of standardized products in Gujarat.[184]

This may be seen as a form of technological advance, if toward the more efficient use of labor rather than toward the input of more machinery. It was this advance in the division of labor that allowed urban manufacturing at Surat to still compete with rural manufacturing—and, indeed, manufacturing worldwide. For wages there appear to have been much higher than in rural Gujarat and Praças do Norte. At Tarapur, for example, casual laborers were paid only a fraction of what they received at Surat. Yet, although the manufacture of some coarse textiles, such as sailcloth, was moving to rural Bulsar district in the late seventeenth century, the manufacture of *bafta* stuck to its urban location.[185]

But such a standardization could not be achieved with the bulk of the silk manufactures and that of painted cotton cloth. There was a bewildering array of these, each of different size, color, and pattern: chintz, for instance, was divided into 35 different varieties.[186] The price of purchase and the price of sale of these various sorts differed widely. Such products were not fit for manufacture at a workshop.

### *Textiles: Demand, Markets and Purchase*

There were three segments of the market for textiles. That for long-distance trade had to be adjusted upward and downward very rapidly to cater to an ever-changing demand, both in Europe and in the Middle East. For, as any trader to the Levant knew, sales patterns in the Middle East repeatedly changed. It seems as if the expansion of demand for textiles from Bengal in Persia after 1670 was related to a change of fashion, for example.

The only exception to the rule of unpredictable demand, which meant that the trade in textiles could not be monopolized, was—for reasons we considered already—Mozambique, although the standard "currency" on the Zambesi, *bairami,* was manufactured both in the Deccan and in Sind, and *bafta* for Dela Goa Bay was manufactured at many different places. The issue for Portuguese merchants and officials seeking rent was therefore to monopolize the textile trade in its place of sale rather than its place of purchase, as we shall see in the next chapter.

This production for foreign markets was obviously only the top of a pyramid of production for the internal market. In the second segment, Indian internal trade, total demand was probably more predictable, but the quantities of supply for sale were unreliable since there was a host of manufacturers of the same product in different regions. Trade in textiles within India was thus quite risky. For this reason the VOC rarely sold Indian textiles in India.[187]

The exception to this rule was the third segment: the manufacture of textiles for the courts and for grandees, imitating the court, which did fetch steady, and high, profits but was concentrated in a few places like Agra, Ahmedabad, Bijapur, and Mysore. The substantial manufacturing industry in the last two places indeed entirely depended upon the court, although Bijapur was still a center for the production of turbans and shawls for the Maratha court in Poona in the eighteenth century.

Catering to such a segmented demand that is in the main erratic is also a familiar challenge to the modern fashion industry. The response nowadays is to move production from large factories to small workshops, closer to the clients. This point merits close attention. One may question the assumption that all of India's manufacturing pursuits might have led to production in factories (though it should be noted that there was a fairly smooth transition between proto-industry and industry in Ahmedabad). One needs both a demand for standardized products and a distribution system for standardized goods to centralize their production in big workshops. The essential advantage of Indian manufacturing was that production could be rapidly increased and decreased to respond to sudden shifts in demand.

Basically, because of the high degree of competitiveness of the internal market segment of India's textile manufacturing, the production for the external markets in both Europe and the Middle East could outclass manufacturing there too. But this very flexibility of the supply tended to perpetuate a highly segmented market structure for textiles within India, which overall was often not very conducive to production in factories or in large workshops.

In Gujarat the manufacture of cloth was a specialized activity for separate villages and families of weavers within the village. This specialization of manufacture ensured that a weaver would be closely tied to the intermediary merchants and that the product could only be sold in widely dispersed areas in small quantities. A weaver could hardly predict demand. Moreover, weavers were hesitant to make cloth of patterns different from what they normally manufactured for the Indian market in order to cater to European or Middle Eastern demand. They were "like donkeys who always trod the same path," the VOC complained; it was too expensive and risky for weavers to buy different looms and learn new patterns to adapt to recurrent and unpredictable changes in demand.[188]

This problem was taken care of by the advance buyers, who would hand an amount of money to the weaver, in return for which they were to receive textiles of a stipulated kind. The buyers, in turn, would deliver the piece-cloth to the purchaser. Such intermediaries essentially served as a buffer between the supply of textile and the shifting demand. Normally, the advance buyers also delivered raw materials (cotton, paint) to the weavers. The market price of textiles would, in Gujarat, depend on the cotton harvest.[189]

Now, a recurrent issue in the literature is the extent to which weavers depended upon those intermediaries. Were the weavers in Gujarat early proletarians? This is not a question to which one can give an unequivocal answer. In Gujarat the weavers were not employed by the advance buyers but, basically, they negotiated the price of textiles with the middlemen. The Indian advance buyers were thus not really "putting-out merchants" in the European sense, for the weavers generally bought the required raw materials themselves and owned their own looms. The strength of those two parties might depend on a number of factors: the relative skill of the weavers is one, demand another, the price and supply of raw materials yet another.

Primary materials would include food if the weavers were not employed in agriculture as well. In Hindustan weaving was mainly carried out during the monsoon and most weavers worked in agriculture during the harvest, as was the case on the Konkan Coast and in Kerala. In Gujarat, however, manufacturing textiles was a full-time pursuit in the cities as well as in villages with a significant manufacturing industry. According to Schreuder, one bought silk cloth in Gujarat in April. "For the silk is cheapest then and after the bad monsoon the weavers need money badly to buy grain."[190] Generally, if there was a rise of the prices of foodstuffs, wages and the price of textiles would tend to mount too. This trend might be upset by a decreasing demand, or by a fall in the interest rate or of the rate of silver relative to copper, however.[191]

In some cases weavers operated at an advantage in a sellers' market. It was thus at Broach in 1673 when the weavers of *tappachindi* were more or less at liberty to deliver textiles to the EIC or not. If the EIC did not accept the cloth, the weavers would walk to the VOC's factory, for both were trying to corner the market by buying large quantities of this fabric. But not all markets were sellers' markets, as K.N. Chaudhuri seems to argue.[192] Take the textile industry of Travancore in the 1690s, for example. This was a very different case from that of Broach. It was typically a buyers' market. The industry was working for a restricted and highly competitive internal market. The weavers of Travancore were competing with the same textiles, imported in Kerala from the Coromandel Coast. The merchants from there were mainly making a profit on the sale of pepper in Coromandel and would, if necessary, dump textiles to procure this. The weavers in Travancore were said to be fugitives from Tanjore, where they were vexed by outrageous taxes. Most of them were heavily in debt to *payyari* Brahmin moneylenders, often with debts stretching back for several generations. These "bonded laborers," as one would now call them, had to sweat practically without pay and would deliver their cloth as reimbursement of interests to the *shroff*s, who in turn apportioned them food. Since the latter systematically charged too much for those victuals, this tended to pull the weavers ever more into debt.[193]

Such impoverished migratory weavers were perhaps more the rule than the exception. A large part of the workforce employed in other branches of industry consisted of an itinerant labor force, paid and recruited by *mukaddami*s (akin to jobbers—*werkbazen,* as the Dutch called them) as well. In Agra in 1690 the VOC was unable to buy rugs, for example, for the *werkbazen* there either had died or followed the court to Aurangabad. They now had to "allot the work to poor little fellows who have to be kept working with the aid of soldiers." This quote tells us a lot about the *werkbazen,* upon whom the workers unilaterally depended. This dependence supports their comparison with the contemporary jobbers. The price of textiles contracted could vary from one jobber to another. The distinction between a jobber and a merchant was not a clear one. Some jobbers might gather considerable riches. Thus, Sham Das *mukaddami* and Magha Lal *mukaddami* were among the leading Diu merchants.[194]

### *"Proto-industrialization"?*

In sum, then, there was a growth in India of spatially spread production for distant markets where production was dominated by merchant capital. This growth of manufacture in the countryside for distant markets is a development bearing some resemblance to what some European economic historians have called "proto-industrialization." In an important article Perlin has pointed to this East-West parallel.[195] Certainly there is a correspondence here, which was produced by a similar structure of (quasi-) unlimited supply of labor and the dominance of merchant capital over production.[196]

However, one should be on one's guard about pushing the parallel too far. First, it is doubtful whether the Indian workforce was a "proletarian" population utterly devoid of contact with agricultural work, as is the main contention of the proto-industrialist school. Even in Gujarat—the area where there was the largest distance between rural and urban labor in India—weavers were said to have returned to agricultural work after the Maratha incursions in 1715.[197]

Elsewhere, textile production was clearly an adjunct to agricultural production. The manufacturing process was thus linked to the agricultural cycle. In Praças do Norte, for example, there were a few families of weavers in each village. These were mostly *curumbi*s: low-caste agricultural piece-laborers who were employed in weaving when they were not needed on the land. This textile production mainly catered to the consumption of the villages, the Portuguese landlords, and the army. But it amounted to a considerable production in total: according to the English, more than 5,000 pieces of taffeta were manufactured in Revbandar alone. The market was—and remained—small, however, since the Portuguese landlords preferred to wear Gujarati piece-cloth.[198]

This was rural manufacturing too. Yet it should not be perceived as proto-industrialization, for it did not represent an intermediary stage between production in the household and production in workshops. It was rather an evolutionary cul-de-sac. Since the worker largely toiled in agriculture, the cloth merchants could pay extremely low, or no, wages and engage or dismiss labor at will. Household production would then always be cheaper, and more flexible, than in a workshop because of the initial outlays involved in switching to production in the latter.[199]

A second reason to be cautious about the East-West parallel is that it is even more disputable whether manufacturing work caused a modification of the reproduction patterns and of the attitudes toward time and labor of these proletarians, accustoming them to work in factories. It seems doubtful too whether rural and urban manufacture in India disciplined the workers to working to the clock and alienated them from their products. Even in Surat, with its large rootless "proletariat," journeymen used in construction went home when they had earned sufficient money to eat. The VOC had to pay two "peons to encourage the workers to greater exertion."[200]

### *The Textile Trade: East India Companies and Indian Merchants*

Since textile purchases by the East India Companies for the European market have been very well studied, I will not deal with that topic at length. Suffice it to state that after 1660 the demand for Indian textiles in Europe was booming. But this mainly concerned textiles from the Coromandel Coast and Bengal. The exports of piece-cloth from Gujarat were not expanding as rapidly, and the share of textiles from the Arabian seas in exports to Europe was declining.

In general, in spite of some attempts to buy goods directly from the weavers or put up workshops, the Companies—and the Portuguese too—were forced to rely heavily on the services of middlemen. But because of the very size of their procurement the Companies, least of all the VOC, were unable to adjust their demand and supply—an issue to which we shall return in chapter 8. They were thus at a serious disadvantage compared to Indian merchants.

The VOC, for example, tried to sell Bengali textiles in Persia. Now, at first glance it had an excellent trump card in its hand, for one did not have to pay customs at Bandar Abbas. The VOC was allowed by the court not to pay customs provided that it bought an amount of silk from the royal treasury which was roughly equivalent to the value of its imports. But the VOC in Persia was, in this case, unable to compete with small caravan traders and unable to compete even with its own broker in Bandar Abbas, who sold at a price of 16 percent below that asked by the Company.[201]

Small traders, Persia explained, could evade customs; the Company could not—it was conspicuously present in Persia and could easily be punished. Moreover, transport costs were only 5 to 6 percent of total cost for the entire distance from Kasimbazar to Isfahan, "and therefore they prefer this road to that over sea." Furthermore, Indian merchants could travel to textile production areas, whereas the VOC used Indian middlemen to conduct purchases. "And they [the merchants] buy good qualities, in extremely small quantities, of equal or better yarn and always of a lower price than what is bought by the servants of the Company." For the peddlers' time was not money: merchants might remain in Hindustan for more than a year to buy good textiles. The traders were interested in limiting their drudgery and selling as much as possible rather than in obtaining the maximum profit. If a peddler dealing in Bengali or Hindustani textiles made 15 to 18 percent profit, "they think they have shot the parrot." Because of its massive overhead, however, the Company had to obtain 35 to 45 percent to see an investment as profitable.[202]

So, because of this arrangement of trade, those peddlers along the land routes from Multan to Kandahar, Mashed, and Isfahan, or from Multan to Kabul and from there to Balkh and Bukhara, were well able to survive the competition of the Companies and often profited from their trade. We have one list of the commodities involved that proves that seaborne trade was about equal to the caravan trade along the Kandahar route in 1636 and covered substantially the same commodities.[203]

We have very little information on the trade from Kandahar to Isfahan in the second half of the seventeenth century, but in 1639 this was still a substantial commerce: 2,500 camels arrived at Isfahan from India, carrying as much merchandise overland as overseas. Actually, the caravan and sea routes to Persia were complementary circuits: the traders of Ahmedabad, for example, would diversify risks by sending part of their merchandise through Kandahar overland, part overseas through Bandar Abbas. This trade consisted not only of cloth and indigo but of bulk goods like sugar as well. The caravan trade via Kandahar persisted at least until the eighteenth century and may partly have compensated for the decline of maritime trade to which I alluded earlier, though there is little evidence to definitely prove this.[204]

In the case of the commerce between Gujarat, the Punjab, and Central Asia, the Companies stimulated the caravan trade rather than impeded it. The VOC occasionally sold copper to Patan merchants, who brought this to Kabul and to Balkh. Again, even in the middle of the eighteenth century the trade of Bandar Abbas, particularly that in tin and Indian textiles, catered to the needs of Khiva in modern-day Uzbekistan too. The caravan and the Company trade were, to an extent, serving two different circuits. There was indeed a "trade revolution" in Asia, but it was not a struggle between caravans and companies.[205]

And the caravan trade to Central Asia flourished. There was a substantial textile industry in the Punjab, especially working for Central Asia. According to Codrington in 1634, Lahore was the main center for this commerce in northern India.[206] In the early eighteenth century this role was probably taken over by Delhi, but it was still a substantial trade.[207] Three thousand merchants yearly ventured from Lahore to Bukhara and from there to Khiva, according to a memorandum submitted to the expedition, which in 1734 was to construct Orenburg. This Russian fortress in the steppes was built partly to divert this trade.[208]

But the caravan traders to Persia were struggling with declining sales of textiles both there and in the Ottoman empire. This badly hurt the traffic over the caravan routes through the Makran, for example. In the early seventeenth century there was a fairly substantial caravan trade between the Coromandel Coast and Persia over Sind. In sum, the stretch from Masulipatam to Surat and then overland through Hyderabad to Kirman, Isfahan, Baghdad, and Aleppo would take five months. The products traded mainly consisted of Coromandel textiles and indigo. But, obviously, this was an expensive route and the stretch through the Makran was very dangerous. After 1640 this trade appears to have disappeared completely.[209]

By 1645 the markets in the Levant and in Italy were flooded with European and Indian piece-cloth sold by English and Dutch merchants, who were ruining their own market as much as they were spoiling that of the caravan merchants. The Board of Trade to the Mediterranean petitioned the Admiralty at Amsterdam in 1651 not to tax this trade more heavily and to better protect it. For what would become of all the vaunted profits of the East India trade if the demand for Indian textiles in Italy—still its major market—collapsed?[210] The argument proved shortsighted. If the Estates General still decided to impose a 1 percent tax, or *tanza*, on shipping to the Mediterranean, this did not spell the demise of the trade in Indian textiles. Far from it—by 1650 the demand for Indian cotton began to increase in northern Europe too. With the French entering the India trade, competition in the markets of the Levant between the English and Dutch, but especially between those two and the Marseilles traders, became well nigh murderous. The Frenchmen, in particular, were selling quantities of Indian and European textiles at Smirna and Aleppo, which by royal regulations they were not allowed to sell in France. Armenian traders brought Coromandel and European textiles sold in the Levant to Tebriz, where they ousted the products brought from India and the Gulf from the market.[211]

In Persia the profits on Coromandel and Bengali textiles did not show a decline. But it is possible that the disappearance of direct shipping by Persian traders and nobles, located on the Coromandel Coast, between the Coromandel Coast and Persia after 1660 was influenced by this fierce competition from the Levant.[212]

We end up with an apparent contradiction. In the microeconomic context of a single commodity, Bengali textiles, and a single route, Bengal to Persia, Indian traders were working far more efficiently and cheaply than Companies. But the macroeconomic picture is different. Because of their investments in bulk and economies of scale, the Companies could dominate the markets in Europe and increasingly in the Ottoman empire as well. By 1680 Western European traders dealing in Company products largely controlled the market for Indian textiles in the western parts of Persia and in the Ottoman empire. The Indian traders had seen much of their market slip away.

## Pepper from Kerala

Seen in a macroeconomic context, the Companies enjoyed comparative advantages: they could procure in bulk, they were able to plan ahead for the long term, and their purchases throughout Asia allowed them to substitute products from one area for those from another. However, such advantages might well turn to disadvantages in the microeconomic context of the trade in one product along one route. The most important example is pepper: the Companies indeed achieved a "trade revolution" in the exports to Europe. But in the case of the pepper trade to the Middle East and North India, the VOC was unable both to obstruct and to compete with the trade of Indian merchants. Thus, the VOC's conquest of Kerala was an unmitigated financial disaster.

### *Twilight of the Pepper Trade*

The essential problem facing the traders in Malabar was that in the seventeenth century Malabar was no longer the main supplier of pepper to the world market; Java and Sumatra were. Production in Sumatra and Java could be rapidly adjusted upward or downward, as there was plenty of land available there; thus it could conveniently be used to corner the pepper market. And production was already expanding in the sixteenth century in response to massive demand from China. There seems little doubt that in the sixteenth century China was the major market for pepper in the world.[213]

Consequently, when both the English and the Dutch invested heavily in the pepper trade and sent rapidly increasing shipments from the Indonesian archipelago to Europe to try to oust each other from the market, this caused an unprecedented drop in the price of pepper on the European market. "Nothing in living memory and no book ever told of such a low price and therefore these posessions [on the Malabar Coast] are a heavy burden on the Company indeed."[214] And the decline was only partly compensated for by increasing consumption in Europe. From the VOC's perspective—and the VOC was the major importer of pepper in Europe in the seventeenth century—pepper from Malabar was both more expensive than that from Sumatra and mostly inferior. It had a long way to go to Batavia and upon arrival there it was left to rot for half a year until the return fleets could leave. Although pepper was mostly sent by the fleets departing from Ceylon after 1674, it was still considered inferior to Sumatra pepper.[215]

To the declining demand in Europe were added ruinous ecological trends: the great drought in Kerala in 1632–34 was supposed to have ravaged the pepper plants. In Cochin the production had dropped to only one-third of its previous yield. It seems Kerala's production of pepper did not recover from this blow. The figures for the crops gathered in the second half of the seventeenth century were all much lower than those from the early seventeenth century.[216]

The possible negative consequences of those two shifts for the Portuguese communities in Kerala were, however, blunted by the rise of the port of Cochin after 1560. Cochin was the major center of *casado* trade on the West Coast by 1610. The income of the *capitania* was then mainly obtained through taxation of trade; one had to pay 3 to 5 percent anchor dues and 4 percent to the rajah, and ships had to sail in the Portuguese coastal flotillas. Van Rheede mused in 1675:

> The richness of Cochin was not derived from Malabar but from all of the Indies; both by being mart and staple of the Moorish, southern, eastern, Chinese and Japanese trade and being the abode of the richest merchants and their agents. This has made Malabar and her cities rich and renowned. But we have found, when conquering these places in a time when their fortunes were in decline, that fame widely differs from reality.[217]

In many ways the Portuguese trade from Malabar constituted a transfer of these earnings both in the form of an allowance to privately fetch pepper back home and by the arrangement that the community of Cochin might send its own ships to Lisbon. On these vessels the community might load such merchandise as it chose, if paying one-fifth of its value to the king.[218]

Nonetheless, by 1640 both the trade in pepper of the crown (as we shall see in the next chapter) and Portuguese private trade in Kerala were in desperate trouble. This was in part because the Dutch impeded the trade with cotton and opium from Bengal and hampered navigation to the Coromandel Coast and in part because the Portuguese crown prohibited the *casados* of Cochin from selling cinnamon or pepper to merchants from Bengal lest these products be sold to the Dutch. This was a vicious circle. The *câmera* of Cochin used to outfit vessels to guard the coastal fleets; with the declining incomes of the community the shipping of Cochin was increasingly imperiled by pirates too.[219] No doubt the senate of Cochin was exaggerating the plight of the community to receive favors from the crown, but the decline of Portuguese trade was real. It is, of course, an open question whether the decay of Indian (mainly *topaz*) shipping from Matancheri was equally marked.[220]

Not only Cochin but Lisbon as well had good reasons to be pessimistic about the prospects of pepper trade from Kerala. In the 1640s the Dutch, the Danes, the British, and the interlopers of the Courteen Association were dumping quantities of pepper on the markets in London and Amsterdam. The VOC was at all-out war with those competitors, dumping its pepper to oust them. "And so, if we are unable to sell pepper in the Indies," Gentlemen XVII wrote in 1649, "let the wagon roll along its path and we will see which competitor of the Company will drop out of its track first."[221]

That was probably the Portuguese crown. The avalanche of pepper harmed three other groups too: the Courteen Association, which was soon in severe trouble; the Danish Company, which defaulted on payments in 1650; and last but not least the caravan traders. But this policy of dumping was not primarily directed against the latter. It was mainly aimed against the English and first and foremost against the Danes since pepper of the Dansk Ostindiske Kompagni was largely sold in Amsterdam.[222]

Deliveries from the Persian Gulf to the Levant ceased after about 1630. The last reference to exports of pepper from the Red Sea to Europe is in 1642 when four Armenian merchants departed from Mocha to Alexandria "to bring the pepper to Europe on which they will, no doubt, earn a handsome profit."[223]

It is hard to disagree with Braudel's view, though, that at least some of the substantial quantities of spices sold to the Middle East at Jidda or Mocha may still have found their way to the Mediterranean.[224] In effect, in 1649 Gentlemen XVII were complaining that cloves brought via Mocha, Cairo, and Venice were spoiling the market in the Netherlands. Yet the trend of the spice trade between Asia and the Levant was a protracted decline. At the end of the seventeenth century cloves were even brought from Aleppo to Jidda.[225]

So when Rijkloff van Goens attacked Cochin in 1658 without having clear instructions to this effect from Gentlemen XVII, this pepper was not needed in the Netherlands at all. They received more than enough from Sumatra and Java. Gentlemen XVII had, in fact, just ordered a halt to the bartering of pepper in Calicut and Cananore. This was a trade that the VOC was conducting more to harass the Portuguese enemy than to make a profit, anyway. Whereas earlier the VOC had followed a policy of dumping in order to evict Danish and English "interlopers" from the trade of Sumatra and Java, after 1655 the board of the VOC (the *bewindhebbers*) decided to create a shortage in the market by buying as little pepper as possible. It should be just enough to "mind the old rule that it is always necessary to bar foreign traders from access to India."[226]

Since Malabar pepper was not needed in the Netherlands Rijkloff van Goens motivated his attack on Cochin by arguing that one could control the trade within Asia by gaining a foothold on the Malabar Coast. The Sumatra pepper could then be reserved for the Netherlands. In reality this was very much a justification in retrospect. Van Goens's driving vision was a chimerical design to establish a self-sufficient system of Dutch settlements along the Malabar Coast and in Ceylon. Malabar, with its countless toiling masses, would supply the Dutch colonists in Ceylon with provisions. And from the proceeds of the sales of Malabar pepper in Asia one could also pay for the export of pepper, or even of Ceylonese cinnamon, to the Netherlands.[227]

As the century advanced, van Goens's dream turned to a nightmare. In 1703 Zwaardecroon moaned: "We have gone through so much trouble to supply Malabar with cash and merchandise, yet everything has disappeared into a bottomless pit." Just like the Portuguese, the VOC was unable to obtain a monopoly on the pepper trade. War after war was waged, and yet "the Company will never ever attain anything with all this, unless there would be found some gold-mine, or a like precious matter, considered worthwhile for sitting constantly on the neck of the kings with a sword."[228] Kerala was the least profitable possession, constantly dragging the VOC into expensive conflicts with both princes and European powers. Before considering the reasons for this failure, however, let us first consider the pepper trade in detail.

### *Vicissitudes of the VOC's Pepper Trade*

In 1635 Cochin and Travancore were able to produce about 3.25 million pounds of pepper, Malabar about 1 million. In 1663 Travancore and Cochin produced 3 million pounds of pepper and Malabar 900,000 pounds. The cultivation of this plant depended on a number of factors, like rainfall, the prices on the world market, demand on the Indian market, and perhaps the price of labor. (The mountains of Kerala, where the pepper came from, were, unlike the coast, still sparsely settled "frontiers" in the seventeenth century.)[229] In 1687 only 1,006,007 pounds of pepper were sold, a historic low, but in 1690 2,300,912 pounds went to the coast alone, to which should be added about 2 million to the interior. Thus, while prices on the European market were low, from 1660 to 1690 about 3.5 million pounds of pepper were grown, and roughly half of that was taken to the Coromandel Coast and from there on to Bengal. After 1690 cultivation rapidly mounted, however, from 5.5 million pounds around 1690 to 6.5 million pounds in 1700.[230]

Cultivation of pepper could thus be rapidly adjusted upward and downward, though transport costs and the price of labor tended to put a ceiling on the maximum amount of pepper that could be cultivated. To these figures should be added the pepper production of Canara, Sunda, and southern Bijapur, estimated at 2 million pounds in 1664. The Canara pepper was mostly consumed on the Indian market; only one-third was intended for export, mainly to the Gulf.[231]

The bulk of the Kerala pepper was cultivated by "poor and miserable folk who are but rarely able to earn sufficient rice to eat and have to feed on carrots"; it was bought by intermediate traders. This was an unequal exchange since the *kainakarams* or "poor peasants" (*de arme landsman*), as the Dutch called them, received very low prices for the pepper. They were often forced to sell the entire crop to the middlemen on whom, due to accumulated debts, the peasants often completely depended. According to the VOC, this was the reason they received mainly unripe black pepper instead of the more profitable white pepper. The "poor peasants" picked the crop as quickly as possible in order to eliminate the debts still outstanding from last year. This was not a new problem, for the Portuguese had been facing the same difficulty.[232]

Intermediary traders brought pepper by canoe or pack oxen to one of the marts in the interior. Most of them worked on their own account, although some worked with money advanced by traders on the coast. The Company often complained about the unjustifiably high profits obtained by these intermediaries, estimated as 100 percent or more. Yet the merchants might not have ventured upon this risky trade without the lure of such gains. One might be robbed, or meet with unforeseen impositions by customs officials (for Kerala was full of internal customs stations); the peasant might default on payments; and the market might be glutted.[233] The pepper was then resold on a host of smaller markets, overarched by some major fairs, often associated with temples like that at Tirunavai: "there is held a fair there called *hastami*, where one can obtain whatever Malabar produces."[234]

Who were those traders? It would seem that the very strict regulations regarding pollution, which are found in Malayalam edicts of the period, were also very strictly adhered to. *Nambudiri* Brahmins were, for example, not even permitted to come near the shadow of an untouchable or venture beyond Kerala, and *nayyar*s and *nambudiri*s could not board a ship either.[235] Such restrictions certainly curtailed the participation of the elites of Kerala in trade since "they cannot enter many counties and villages for fear of being polluted."[236]

The Portuguese attempts to destruct their trade had certainly had an impact on the *mappila* Muslims.[237] In Travancore, Cochin, and Purakkad the Muslims were a rather impoverished community, mainly subsisting from peddling. But Malabar, where they were far more numerous and powerful, still contained many wealthy *deshi* and *paradeshi* merchants. There was the *mappila* Marakkar family of Calicut, for example, or the Turkish merchant Hadji Osman of Panani, who had six ships sailing to Yemen, Persia, and the Coromandel Coast. Hadji Osman was very likely the wealthiest merchant of Kerala.[238]

In Travancore—aside from the Thomas Christians—many merchants were *idayan*, "that is to say shepherds by caste." "For if they are lower castes" (untouchables) "one suffers from a lot of deprivations and is not permitted to come near persons of higher caste, and may not approach pagodas or the dwellings of kings."[239] Throughout Kerala many moneylenders were *payyari* Brahmins too. "One may say that they by and large control the pepper trade. They are Brahmins but they do not originate from Malabar but from the country of Carnataca. They are generally exchangers of gold and silver bullion who enjoy great liberty and benefices in the temples along the coast but not in the interior."[240]

As mentioned already, in Cochin the trade was dominated by Saraswats, "attracted there by the trade, which they first conducted with the Portuguese and later with the Dutch."[241] To quote Zwaardecroon in 1703 (who was certainly no friend of these "Konkani" Brahmins), "they are strangers in a strange land, and like the Jews they are involved in all kind of peddling trades and big business too." Albeit in Matancheri the Saraswats were courtiers rather than merchants: "They hate and despise the natives of the country and these detest them in turn. For they cannot suffer the opulence and domination of strangers, who are only interested in their own welfare, without any benefit to the people or country, where they come to dwell as foreigners."[242]

In view of those "dishonest profits" of the intermediaries, the VOC discussed whether they should attempt to concentrate the pepper trade in the entrepôts of Cochin and Coylan, or procure it where it was produced—mainly the districts of Tekumkur and Vadakumkur.[243] A proposal, put forward in 1664, to procure pepper in those foothills of the Ghats was turned down, however, since to do so would have subjected them to many hazards. The intermediaries sheltered the traders on the coast against risks and had thus an essential function to perform, however much the VOC might complain about them.[244]

Let us now consider the VOC's trade in pepper. The sale of pepper generally took place from the end of March until May. It was weighed in the warehouse in the presence of the *rajadores* and a Dutch merchant, balanced on scales, marked with Dutch weights, and packed in jute bags. The danger of being swindled was considerable, especially if dealing with small traders, as the merchants had to make up for the costs of sifting the pepper. They tried not only to put sand in the bags but to deliver pepper when still moist, with the concomitant risk of rot. A weight loss of 4 to 6 percent was generally thought acceptable but was often exceeded. In the VOC's accountancy system the costs of sifting pepper were booked under the expenses of the factory where this was done. Malabar thus often shipped its pepper unsifted so that these costs could be burdened on the factories in Persia and Surat—to the anger of those factories, of course.[245]

Whereas the Portuguese generally bought pepper in exchange for gold são thomés and the French and English paid in cash too, it was the VOC's policy to barter pepper for an array of merchandise (mainly copper, opium, steel, tin, and spices). One made a profit on merchandise, not much on bullion. In Canara, pepper was generally paid for in bullion and in Cananore until 1673 in merchandise, later in cash. In Cochin, Purakkad, Coylan, and Kayakulam pepper was exchanged for goods. The price of pepper was generally reckoned in rixdollars (the Levant and Mocha currency, as we observed), abbasis, or rupees. This was converted into merchandise and a quantity of pepper bartered for commodities. The deal was affirmed by signing a contract written in Malayalam and Dutch. The Dutch version was seen as valid, so merchants would be held responsible if contracts were forged.[246]

Confident that the demand for pepper on Asian markets would be limitless, the government of the Malabar Coast guaranteed until 1673 that all pepper offered would be purchased. The Dutch thus tried to oust the Portuguese, Muscati, and English competitors. In principle Gentlemen XVII welcomed the initiative, but they doubted whether pepper from the Malabar Coast would ever be cheaper than that from Sumatra. Indeed, Malabar's treasury proved unable to shoulder the burden. Sunda, Canara, Cananore, and Calicut pepper could not be sold in Persia, the intended market, and the VOC did not even try to sell it in Surat or Europe. Procurement of pepper was centralized in the "southern settlements" of Coylan, Purrakad, Kayakulam, and Cochin in 1673, and the purchases in Calicut and Cananore curtailed. This allowed the *zamorin* to sell his pepper to the English, Portuguese, and Muscati traders, although he had pledged to sell to the Dutch alone.[247]

Until 1689 Malabar was only permitted to send pepper to the Netherlands if the presidency had first complied with demands from the Asian factories. Proceeds from the sale of pepper in those factories (mainly in Persia and Surat) were to be sent in bullion to Malabar to cover the expenses of this presidency. From the revenues of sales in Kerala, Malabar was to remit bullion to Ceylon. This could then be used to pay the garrisons there.[248]

Predictably, this complicated scheme did not work smoothly. The bullion from Persia arrived either too late or not at all. And the mint at Matancheri, which was hired by the VOC from tax farmers of the rajah, was only too happy to coin prodigious quantities of fanams. The more coins struck, the more profit for the contractors. Thus, the price of the fanam fell relative to that of the são thomé, money of account at Cochin, and merchants and shopkeepers were unwilling to accept payments in fanams. Though, because of imports of bullion from the Red Sea, there was abundant cash at Cochin, the VOC was thus still short of means. To the anger of Ceylon and Batavia the presidency had to beg for ducats. If the presidency would not receive bullion, the Dutch credit would collapse, and the presidency might be unable to procure pepper.[249]

The shaky Dutch credit became a pressing concern after the foundation of the English factory at Tellichery in 1689 and the debut of the Danish trade to Kerala. Both paid cash and sold, according to the VOC, merchandise much cheaper than the Dutch. Demands for bullion from Malabar became ever more insistent, to which the High Government of the Indies had to comply.[250]

In Portuguese Cochin the pepper was predominantly bought from private traders, whose creditworthiness was guaranteed by the *rajadores*. The king levied a tax of 2 percent on the pepper brought to Cochin, and that pepper was sold on his behalf to the Estado. The ministers of the king similarly sold 1 percent. In addition, the pepper dealers paid a cash impost to the king.[251]

During pepper transactions of the VOC a ring of four to five merchants had to bail for its delivery. They were in principle completely responsible for it until delivered aboard ship. These intermediaries were almost certainly inherited by the Dutch from the Portuguese. Ganesha Parbhu, contractor of wood from Cochin to the Goa dockyard in 1638, may well be the father of the Dutch broker Nana Parbhu. Theoretically these intermediaries were highly useful to the Company, for one burdened those "merchants of the second hand" with the commercial risk. Yet the VOC complained that they profited from their monopoly position by bartering the merchandise far too cheaply. Often the VOC at Surat thus saw its sales of spices and copper imperiled by products from Cochin.[252]

It may be seriously doubted that the VOC paid too much for its pepper; in general its competitors paid more. It is true, however, that the Company effectively handed a monopoly over the market to its intermediaries: Saraswats in Cochin, the Azhi Raja and a ring of wealthy *mappila* merchants at Cananore. In order to ensure they would receive the pepper in time, the merchants pooled their money. Malabar was thus encouraged by Batavia to have the Saraswats unite in small commercial companies "like one finds on the Coromandel Coast."[253]

The presidency was hesitant to do so, for the Saraswats were not nearly as wealthy as the cloth merchants on the Coromandel Coast. Batavia overruled those objections, however—wrongly, as it turned out, for in 1694 Nanà Parbhu, the main contractor, went bankrupt, burdening the VOC with a debt of more than 500,000 guilders.[254]

But Ysbrand Goske had predicted as early as 1668 that the Company might stumble into a quagmire of debt when relying upon monopoly contractors. In his view, the magazines ought to be open to any trader who wanted to sell pepper to the Company—like the Portuguese had done. The Saraswat traders did not have a monopoly over the supplies of pepper "and indeed, the traders who come from outside to Cochin, when having no access to merchandise of the Company, seek a guarantee through selling the pepper more dearly or—when it is not accepted—take it elsewhere."[255]

But there were weighty reasons forcing the VOC to sell its products to intermediaries. The demand for the VOC's products on the coast was extremely limited, except for Egyptian and Bengali opium. The bulk of the other commodities—in particular copper, the major product sold in Kerala—was taken to the distant hinterland: Konkunad and especially Mysore. For Kerala had a deficit on its overseas trade with Gujarat and Canara and overland trade to Kokunad that had to be paid through the surpluses on trade with the Middle East and Europe.[256]

The "merchants of the second hand" protected the VOC against fluctuations on those markets in the interior. They provided buffer stocks of pepper too, allowing the Company to comply with the demand from the Netherlands in time. Hence, the other Companies were as much forced to rely on intermediaries as was the VOC; at Calicut, for instance, the English sold their products by and large to the Marakkar family.[257]

Now, as we saw in chapter 3, the VOC had signed contracts with the *perumal* of Cochin and the *signati* of Travancore that they were to deliver all pepper to the Company and expel all other traders. (To wit, the Dutch version of the treaties implied so.) The latter restriction never applied to those from Calicut and Cananore, who were permitted to take 100 *lasts* of pepper on their own vessels and were not obliged to evict foreign traders. The VOC was, hence, able to hand navicerts to Gujarati, Muscat, or Coromandel vessels requesting to trade in Cochin and Travancore. But they were strictly forbidden to trade in pepper.[258]

However, as Hustaert, van Goens's successor as commander on the Malabar Coast, noted in 1665:

> The said contracts only apply to the kings who have jurisdiction over the coast and do not apply to those in the interior . . . the kings are not endowed such power over their subjects as to be able to force them to deliver the pepper to the servants of the Company. For they think it is an iniquity that one enjoys no freedom of com-

> merce, and that the Rt. Hon. Company is allowed benefices that ought to be shared by all traders. And it is true that these contracts are to their disadvantage.[259]

The problem for both the VOC and the Estado was that the rajahs of Kerala had no power over the pepper crop. Part of the pepper delivered by the princes derived from the land of *kaimal*s—lesser princes of the royal blood. But such princes, like the ruler of Panani, were not at all willing to accommodate the VOC or the Portuguese and thus ruin their incomes. And most of the pepper delivered by the rajahs under the contracts was obtained through the taxation of trade. If the Estado or the VOC had tried to interrupt commerce, they would merely have cut their own veins, as the rajahs would then have been unable to deliver pepper to them.[260]

So if Batavia was urging the VOC at Cochin to interrupt the "smuggling" of pepper from Cochin to Gujarat, those in Gujarat were well aware that the Company was only chasing a mirage. On land it was impossible to control the maze of backwaters with a few dozen Dutch and a few hundred *lascarin* mercenaries: "a useless and frankly ridiculous pursuit." If this was already the case at Cochin, at Cananore the power of the VOC merely extended to 30 feet beyond the citadel.[261]

At sea, Cochin disposed of only four frigates to comb the extensive coastline. If one bay was blocked, "smugglers" would simply sail to the next one. Those "interlopers" were helped, furthermore, by the rajah of Badagara and by the Kunjalis, who were far too formidable a force to be challenged by Cochin. In any case prohibitions to sail could not be enforced at Surat. Navicerts written out at Surat usually stipulated that ships heading for Kerala were permitted to navigate to Calianpur to fetch coir, arrack, or wild cinnamon from the coast. There were some attempts to implement a total prohibition in the 1660s but in vain. For, as the VOC soon found, any attempt to seize ships from Gujarat in Cochin immediately led to troubles in Surat, where they were completely at the mercy of the Mughal empire. Besides, some of the Surat ships were well armed and could not be captured by the VOC's rowboats.[262]

There was precious little one could do against the Gujarati shipping. And whereas the VOC in Malabar tried in the 1680s to curtail this trade, their colleagues at Surat saw it as a source of revenue. They tried to hand out as many navicerts as possible—but these were only to Calianpur, of course; they would excuse themselves if Malabar protested. Malabar noted to its anger that a score of ships from Gujarat simply passed Cochin by to obtain pepper at Purakkad. The VOC's factories in Persia and Vengurla, in addition, aided the pepper trade to the Middle East by liberally handing navicerts to ships from Muscat to sail to Cananore. In 1694 about 2 million pounds of pepper were fetched from Kerala to Gujarat, "which dwarfs the amounts we are selling," the Gentlemen XVII grumbled.[263]

The issue of whether one was to use navicerts to curtail the shipping of arrack—an important export of the VOC from Ceylon—between Purakkad and the Coromandel Coast was a bone of contention between the presidencies of Ceylon and Kerala. It led to a very nasty personal conflict between Commander van Rheede at Cochin and van Goens at Colombo.[264] This forced the Gentlemen XVII, after much bickering between the two, to take the following position in 1681: it was not, they wrote, their intention to "constrain the kings to the pepper contracts." If, as van Goens desired, they followed a policy of force, they would finally end up occupying the entire Indian south coast. This was contrary to the most important maxim for the Company: "always keep one's household in order." For, and here we are back to the essence of the matter, sales of pepper from Malabar were not that crucially important to the Company as to justify massive expenses on fortresses and garrisons. The trade in arrack was even less significant; it was best to settle this matter amiably with the local princes.[265]

To summarize: the VOC very well succeeded in ruining the trade of Cochin by imposing a welter of restrictions on trade there, but certainly did not succeed in blocking the trade between Gujarat and Kerala, let alone Kerala and the Middle East.

### *The Survival of the Pepper Trade in the Middle East*

A true commercial fleet plying in 1663 between Yemen, Cananore, and Calicut transported at least 600,000 pounds of pepper to the Red Sea yearly. Again, in 1682 nine ships of the *zamorin* and three of his *kaimal*s took 140,000 pounds of pepper to Mocha and Gujarati and *paradeshi* ships fetched another 100,000 from Panani.[266]

As to the Gulf: by 1670 most of the pepper trade between Kerala, Sunda, and Canara on the one hand and the Persian Gulf on the other was arranged through a network of trade and war focused on Muscat. The Muscati *natio* at Cananore was in 1674, for example, sending three or four vessels to Muscat yearly or which brought about 200,000–300,000 pounds of pepper to the Arab Peninsula. Apart from this, the Azhi Raja equipped two vessels to Muscat too, which shipped pepper to and imported horses and dates from Muscat. These imports in Muscat were not intended for the poor hinterland of Oman, of course, but primarily for Persia. Traders from Lar and Shiraz had representatives at Muscat to buy the pepper. It was smuggled in tiny *tanaqin*s to inlets on the Persian shore. This was not only very much to the chagrin of the VOC but of the Safavid authorities as well. Nominal customs were charged there, since these anchorages were not under the direct control of the empire. This network of trade, which tied the *mappilas* to the merchants of the Arab Peninsula, may be called an anti-European, or rather anti-Christian, network. The *mappilas* of Calicut and the Azhi Raja had opposed the Portuguese with all their might. However, as we saw, the Azhi Raja cooperated as much with the Dutch as he opposed them.

After all, the Azhi Raja was the main creditor to the VOC in Cananore, so he had a vested interest in its prosperity![267]

Hence, as C.H. Wake already pointed out, substantial quantities of pepper were still reaching the Middle East, which can be estimated at 800,000 to 1 million pounds of pepper yearly. By comparison, the exports of pepper from Kerala to Yemen and Persia were estimated at 2 million pounds in 1605. The price of pepper in Yemen, Syria, and Egypt was still set by the supplies from Kerala—only if those faltered was pepper from Aleppo sold in Sa'na. In Wake's view the revival of the Mediterranean spice trade in the sixteenth century was mainly caused by the lure of this demand from the internal market in the Middle East.[268]

What caused the decline of the trade to Europe, if such large amounts were still shipped to the Middle East? The most important explanation is the increase in exports from the Archipelago, but there was also a conscious VOC policy of inhibiting exports to Europe. In the Arabian seas the VOC stuck to a policy whereby the price of spices was to be fixed in all other factories relative to the price offered at Surat. This price could mount to 10 percent below the rate in Amsterdam.[269] Products would then not be shipped to Europe. This policy was mainly followed to forestall trade via the Cape, but the Dutch interests in the Mediterranean played a role in the formulation of this policy as well.[270]

C. Verdonck pleaded in 1680 that the VOC's trade with Basra, which had not proven much of a success thus far, could be considerably larger than it was. Gentlemen XVII should desist from the policy of following the Surat price, he urged. Batavia immediately declined the proposal. Prices offered by the VOC at Basra should not harm the trade of Dutch merchants in the Levant. Verdonck had better keep in mind that immutable political maxim.[271]

Anyway, pepper and spices sold at Basra could not compete in Anatolia with those sold at Aleppo. The route over the Tigris was far more dangerous than that from Aleppo. The hawkers engaging in the former always had an additional 30–40 percent cost to reckon with, those from Aleppo maybe 10–15 percent. Moreover, Dutch merchants in the Levant worked with far more favorable conditions of sale than the VOC at Basra. They provided goods on long terms of delivery, were prepared to accept terms of payment extending for several months (whereas the VOC at Basra required cash), they were prepared to furnish cash, and they handed out presents with their goods. Basically, the VOC could not operate in a peddlers' market, whereas Dutch traders in the Levant could.[272]

The same conditions for trade also existed in the Red Sea. Customs dues from Mocha to Alexandria were high, but not prohibitively so—in 1696 about 10–14 percent if paid at the official rate. Most hawkers succeeded in paying far less. However, the main problem in the Red Sea trade was that pepper was several times resold and had to give a profit each time, and that Ottoman and Zaidit tax gatherers garnered their share of each transaction. Thus, pepper was sold at Aden at 60 rixdollars for 400 pounds; it was resold to the hajjis at Jidda for 120 rixdollars and vended at Alexandria for 200 rixdollars, not counting additional customs. From Loheia to Domvia the price of pepper would increase 300 percent. At these rates this pepper could not compete with sales by European merchants in the Levant.[273] Nor was this structure new to the seventeenth century. In the fifteenth already, according to Castanheda, pepper going from the foothills of the Ghats to Alexandria changed masters a dozen times.[274] As it had to give a profit every time it was resold, and since it was burdened with hefty customs at each intermediate station, it would be 300–400 percent more expensive at the end of its journey.[275]

Those "protection rents" did swallow most benefits of the trade; selling pepper in Persia, merchants might obtain 20 percent profit, in the Red Sea maybe 30 percent.[276] Trade with the merchants to the Cape should thus have been more enticing to the traders of Kerala than deals with Egyptian merchants. *Should* is the key word here—for there were other considerations than gain on pepper. The many chains involved in the trade also offered merchants a degree of protection against unforeseen fluctuations of the price. But the main reason was that the traders sold more products to the Middle East than pepper, such as iron, cowry shells, and coconuts, and often made a profit on the import of gold in Kerala. The Portuguese or Dutch did not offer a market for any of these products. And ships trading to the Red Sea often transported hajjis too, both a prestigious and a profitable traffic.[277]

Europeans might pester some merchants, might even evict some *paradeshi* traders from Kerala, but if they wanted to obtain pepper, they had to use precisely the same method of procurement as the other dealers. If they wanted to obtain a monopoly on production—the only way to wipe out the intermediaries—they would have to conquer the areas where pepper was produced. This would have been prohibitively expensive. Hence, they simply had to compete with the other traders, and these offered advantages, like credit and (in the case of Arab traders) prestige, with which neither the VOC nor the Portuguese could compete.[278]

It was most efficient, then, to pay for the procurements of pepper for the European market by taxing trade to the Middle East. And both the Dutch and the Portuguese reluctantly granted this point. By 1698 Cochin changed its policy. Whereas earlier the presidency had tried to prevent indigenous and English ships from using the Bay of Cochin, it now tried to entice them by offering lower customs. This yielded no small return. In the eighteenth century Cochin made a profit, enabling it to send more pepper to the Netherlands than it had earlier. This was mainly due to the taxation of booming trade from Matancheri, which thus "had its revenge"—a very tardy one—on the Europeans, in the opinion of Subrahmanyam.[279]

However, whether or not the peddlers took revenge on the Company later, there is no doubt that the VOC effected a true revolution in the trade with pepper. It was by and large successful in destroying the most famous and ancient trade of Asia, and it did so because it internalized the protection costs and was a creative monopolist; there is no doubt that in the case of the pepper trade to Europe Steensgaard is right.

## Madagascar and the Slave Trade

In the seventeenth century, the overseas demand for manpower from the Arabian seas boomed along with that for bulk products like indigo. We shall examine the trade with the Americas in detail in chapter 10. Here we shall deal with the conduct and context of the slave trade.[280]

The archipelagos of the southwestern Arabian seas—Madagascar, the Comoros, the Pate Archipelago, the Seychelles, and to an extent the Mascarenhas—were the junction of this traffic. The slave trade of the Swahili Coast, the Gulf, and the Red Sea here encountered that of the Atlantic.[281] The slave trades began to span a truly global circuit in the seventeenth century. Consider this rendering of the testimony of one Malagasy slave in 1614.

> When he was child, he had been taken captive during the war of Managara and sold at Mazalagem to an Arab named Abdalla, who took him to the island of Mayotte. From Mayotte his master took him to Arabia. He then took him back to Mayotte and from there to Mozambique. There, he sold him to one Francisco Belchior, with whom he had left the country on board of the Saint Valentine. This boat was captured by the English in the Bay of Sesimbra [in Portugal] and he was then taken to England. He then went to France and the Low Countries where he had gone on board a Dutch ship, which had taken him to the port of Santa Lucia [in Madagascar again].[282]

Though the origins of the slave trade from East Africa to the Middle East are hidden in the mist of far antiquity, demand for slaves from the Middle East was far from constant and appears to have flourished in the seventeenth century. In 1670 Arab ships from Pate, Khisn, Soccotra, and Muscat were fetching 3,000 to 4,000 slaves from Madagascar yearly, the Portuguese estimated, a trade far larger than that of the Europeans and larger than in the sixteenth century as well. However, since this mainly concerned men, rather than women of child-bearing age, this probably had little demographic effect on Madagascar since Malagasy society was polygamous. At Maselagache, too, Arab and Swahili merchants (mainly from Mogadishu and Brava) bought about 1,000 to 3,500 slaves yearly: substantial numbers even by the standards of the contemporary Atlantic slave trade. Most were apparently used on the Swahili Coast itself. But from Pate 400–500 slaves yearly were brought to Muscat and then sold to Persia and Basra too. Of these, 400 were normally bought by representatives of the imam; 100 were sold by representatives of merchants from Pate at Muscat.[283]

However, the traditional supplier of slaves to both the Middle East and India was Ethiopia—the male slaves serving as bodyguards and servants, the female slaves, who had light skin and faintly Caucasian features, for "reproductive purposes within the household" (in prudish modern academic jargon).[284] In Massawa, the VOC estimated in 1671, about 6,000 slaves were sold yearly, who were mainly taken to Jidda and Loheia in small *jilbas*. In Mocha about 2,000 slaves were auctioned yearly. They were outrageously expensive, however: 200 reales for a man and 150 for a woman. Besides, Muslims largely controlled the traffic and it was strictly prohibited to sell slaves to nonbelievers. Most slaves in Mocha were sold within Yemen itself. A few were also taken from Mocha to Egypt. About 200 slaves were sent from Mocha to Surat, Goga, and Dabhul. It appears as if this trade was monopolized by the Mughal and Adilshahi emperors.[285]

The increasing demand for slaves from Madagascar in Yemen and the Gulf was thus a simple economic matter. Ethiopian slaves were too expensive.[286] And although occasionally a few dozen slaves from India were sold in Yemen and a few hundred in Persia (with far more probably being sold over the land route to Central Asia), slaves from northwestern India were expensive too. A woman cost 48 guilders in 1642, a man up to 60. Since the supply depended upon disasters and the captives of war being sold off it was highly unpredictable as well. But most slaves in northern India were bonded laborers who could not simply be auctioned away since they were tied by debts. The Inquisition in Goa tried to combat this practice, as it often involved Christians becoming slaves of Hindu moneylenders. Instead, it was ordered that the *misericórdia* should refund those debts. But bonded labor was too deeply entrenched in Indian rural production to be conveniently abolished by decree.[287] Finally, there was a small flow of European slaves, but the Russian slaves, who were sold from the Crimea to Trebizond, were up to 50 times more expensive than those from Madagascar while the demand far exceeded the supply.[288]

For, as the bishop of Goa explained to the Portuguese crown in 1698—worried lest the Portuguese might trade in Christian Georgians and Russians—the number of such slaves in India was diminutive. There were no more than a few hundred slaves from Christendom on the whole west coast and they were so expensive that only the very wealthy—only the *subehdar* of Gujarat, for example—could afford a white slave. It is likely most were girls; in the Middle East Georgian beauties were considered the most prized treasure of the harem.[289]

But, fortunately for the less wealthy, African women, particularly the trim Somali beauties, were, at least in Yemen, a fair alternative.

> The Arabs have three or four women, as many as they desire or can entertain. But if a woman is tired of her husband she can easily raise her head up high, so he has to get rid of her. Thus, instead of getting married, many men stick to Abyssinian slaves: ugly black caffir-women who, for fear of being sold or rejected, have to obey their husband and master patiently.[290]

While this was common enough in Yemen, on the Swahili Coast such marriage or concubinage with slave girls did not merely have a sexual and economic importance—not to be underrated, as the business centered on the house and the house centered on women—but contributed to the acculturation of the Arabs too. The children, whether male or female, were raised in a purely African feminine environment.[291]

The new factor in Madagascar, however, was European demand. In the early seventeenth century Portuguese traders had dealt with Madagascar, buying a few dozen slaves there who were then sold to Portuguese Muscat. But in the beginning of the seventeenth century the Portuguese trade was mainly in rice, grain, turtle horn, and cattle, rather than in human beings. Those provisions were sent to Mozambique. The Portuguese were also short of wood for the construction of ships and for repair work on the Indiamen (ships in the East India trade) there. Wood for masts and bows of ships were then being fetched from the Ilha dos Lombos—probably St. Mary Island.[292]

And the European trade was with the return fleets too, both English and Dutch, which occasionally touched at Madagascar. In 1626 the VOC for the first time sent a vessel to Madagascar to explore whether slaves from there might be of use in Batavia. This was not a success, however. The trip was too long, too many perished, and slaves from Madagascar were more expensive than those from Bengal and the Coromandel Coast.[293]

But in the second half of the seventeenth century plantations were established in the seas surrounding Madagascar: by the Dutch at Mauritius and the Cape, by the French on Bourbon, and by the English on St. Helena. The demand for slaves rapidly increased.

By way of experiment, in 1658 the VOC sent two Indiamen to Angola and Guinea to buy "pieces" in the traditional circuit of the slave trade. But this was too complex a detour to be used more often. Also, van Goens rather fancifully argued, "as these two countries [Angola and the Cape] are linked the slaves will try to run away." The Dutch West Indian Company (WIC) viewed this trip as an infringement on its monopoly, as did the African Company too, by the way, when the EIC tried to procure slaves in Guinea for St. Helena. Although VOC ships occasionally still touched at Angola, São Thomé, and at Mina Castle on the Gold Coast to procure manioc there destined for Cape Town—and vessels of the EIC occasionally touched at São Thomé as well—they had to bring slaves from elsewhere. If permitted by Gentlemen XVII, though, Batavia would have liked to procure more slaves in Guinea and Angola since they were considered not to be as aggressive as people from Madagascar.[294]

The South African Khoisan (Hottentots) were not suitable as slaves. They fled and were thought too weak. And aside from any "humanitarian concerns" of the VOC—a favorite theme of older South African historiography—the Company could ill afford hazarding the critical exchange of cattle with the Khoisan by enslaving its partners. Other sources for Batavia, such as Arracan, New

Guinea, Bali, and the Malay Peninsula, were too remote from Cape Town and Mauritius. Besides, when the Cape commenced buying slaves at Madagascar in 1658, it killed two birds with one stone. Augustin Bay could also provide the Cape with rice, cattle, and salted meat, for as agriculture on the Cape was not yet very successful, inhabitants desperately needed provisions there. Malagasy cattle could be used to crossbreed with the Cape strain and the salted meat might be sent to Batavia. The plantations established on Mauritius needed many slaves too. From 1640 to 1644 this colony sent ships to Madagascar on its own, which returned to Mauritius with slaves and took ebony wood and slaves not needed there to Batavia. Later on, the Cape was to send some of its slaves to Mauritius.[295]

In 1671 the VOC started mining gold in Sillida, excessively harsh work in an area scorched by malaria. Workers perished in droves.[296] Batavia desperately required forced labor. As the king of Arracan had ceased sending expeditions to loot in Bengal, no slaves were obtainable there. New Guinean Bornean, Niasan, or Balinese slaves were thought too weak to suffer this excruciating labor.

Batavia then inquired whether Malabar could not send slaves, for—as we observed already—Malabar carried on a substantial slave trade. The VOC in Malabar sent a few dozen slaves to Ceylon yearly, where they cut sugar cane and labored in construction work. Malabar was short of funds, and wanted to preserve those for the pepper trade, however. The slaves were—Malabar wrote in 1686—fairly inexpensive: 20 to 30 guilders "a piece." But "they are by nature idle and weak and are unable to do heavy work, so they are of no use in the gold-mines."[297]

Madagascar remained the only option, for trading with Mozambique and the Mrima Coast was considered too risky. Slaves from Madagascar were "strong, robust and rudely built [*grof van leedenen*]" and could be used in heavy work. Additionally, in the beginning of the eighteenth century, Ceylon also began to buy slaves in Madagascar.[298]

Simultaneously, the Americans also began to procure slaves, and the EIC in the late seventeenth century bought human cargoes destined for its settlement in Bencoolen too, where they were used on the pepper plantations, and for St. Helena, where they were mainly intended for forced cultivation of grain for the Indiamen.[299]

Hence, the slave trade prospered. So much so, in fact, that VOC ships from Batavia, Cape Town, and Mauritius might even quarrel over their cargo. In 1672, the merchant from Cape Town at Maselagache could strike a deal with the "Americans" that one was to buy "pieces" at no more than 18 reales. But the captain of the ship from Batavia refused to cooperate: "Gentlemen—I need those bloody [*verdomde*] slaves, even if I should pay 20 reales, I am not going to return to Batavia without them."[300]

In Batavia, or in Pondicherry, which obtained its Malagasy slaves via Bourbon, slaves were mainly used as bodyguards, construction workers, or "bullies"—hands of the bailiff.[301] Although Malagasy slaves were more alienated from the Javanese environment than those from Sulawesi or Bali, yet not as likely to flee, they were still used for lack of an alternative. In Batavia Balinese slaves were far preferred for the household, for the Malagasy were considered "a lazy and torpid breed." And "when having arrived here, [they] do not healthily procreate but instead—to the marked damage and disadvantage of our citizens—perish."[302] Malagasy slaves were rarely sold to individuals, being used as chattel slaves by the Company. In both Batavia and Bencoolen the Malagasy slaves continued to form a community apart, for whom separate barracks had been cleared out, and there is no evidence of a flourishing community of Malagasy freemen in Batavia, though there were a few at Bencoolen.[303]

Slave owners in the Dutch West Indies—though obviously not later in Surinam—were renowned for their humane behavior toward slaves. In the East Indies, this might well have applied to Balinese domestic slaves—favorite sexual partners of the Dutch—but the VOC in Batavia, the Cape, or Mauritius certainly did not distinguish itself in regard to chattel slaves.[304] Wielding the whip was common for the slightest offense—absence, for example. A slave who had tried to flee several times was first "lashed with the cord," next hung on a rope "and left as prey to the birds."[305] Even more extreme was the casual brutality of the English toward the Malagasy slaves on St. Helena. There, a slave might be burned on the stake for mere theft.[306]

### *Arms and Kingdoms*[307]

The slave trade took place against the background of breathtaking scenic beauty. Coastal Madagascar consisted first of a row of dunes, then of an extensive tropical mangrove forest, and behind these fertile green fields. Sitting in a canoe that took him from Augustin Bay to the interior, Dirk Boogaart, dealer in slaves of the VOC's vessel *De Soldaat*, waxed quite lyrical on the magnificent landscape.

> If my body had not been so fatigued from the heat of the sun and the long walk, my eyes would not soon have tired of looking at so many magnificent views. Glens and inclines, hills, mountains and valleys are adorned with beautiful views of dense woods, flourishing farmland and green pastures. The fat earth only has to thank mother nature that it, more through her blessings than by work of any industrious farmer, yields more fruits than there are hands to pick. The lush pasture always offers green grass to eat and the cattle may play in it to their heart's desire: no lion, leopard, tiger or other devouring animals will threaten it, for there aren't any.[308]

This vision of Madagascar as the African Garden of Eden also held European chancelleries in thrall. In spite of the miserable failure of the French attempt to establish a new America on Madagascar such projects were never totally shelved, and the possibility of developing a flourishing colony on Madagascar with the proceeds of sales of provisions to the East Indiamen continued to haunt many an adventurer.[309]

And there was some justification for clinging to those dreams. The VOC had the cattle from Saldanha Bay weighed and found them to be the fattest in the Indian Ocean, weighing twice as much as Indian bullocks. But all those blessings were more than upset by the particularly deadly malaria endemic in coastal Madagascar. For all practical purposes, both the coast and the hinterland of Madagascar remained a forbidden paradise to European settlers and soldiers until the discovery of quinine.[310]

The hilly southern part of the Malagasy Coast had extensive grasslands, roamed by herdsmen, while the northern coast consisted of deep bays with many islands ringed by impenetrable tropical bogs: a dangerous, forbidding land for Europeans and Malagasy peasants alike.

Slaves became available in Madagascar due to a cycle of ever-increasing conflict, which is to some extent comparable with that in West Africa. On the southwestern and northeastern coast the Sakalava herdsmen—"lords of the muskets," as they were called by their neighbors—subdued peasant communities. Again, one wealthy household might obtain by force a predominant share of the community's cattle. Through the southern and northern migrations of the Sakalava from their ancestral lands in central-western Madagascar, more akin to mere plundering forays than to territorial conquests, arose the first two large kingdoms on the "island of the moon": Menabe and Boina—political constructions on a scale hitherto not known in Madagascar.[311]

Apart from monopolizing the cattle, the Sakalava kings would also monopolize the ancestral spirits, as men and especially women of the royal household were held to have special access to magic—a practice not confined to, but certainly much improved upon, by the Sakalava. As an element in gathering ritual predominance, they also instituted a very elaborate cult of the king, including the bath of the royal relics, still celebrated annually, and huge royal funerals often involving human sacrifices. Finally, daughters of allied households were adopted as concubines within the royal family—so royal families often contained hundreds of women. For, as elsewhere in Africa (as on Dela Goa Bay), in Madagascar too "wealth consists of women and livestock: the former are bartered for cattle and coral beads and who has most is the richest."[312]

Before the rise of the Sakalava, the Europeans encountered innumerable small chieftancies in coastal Madagascar, at best embryonic states—"there are so many that to enumerate them all would merely cause confusion," wrote the Portuguese.[313] An example is the Andreovola kingdom among the Mahafaly in Augustin Bay. The VOC called these small kings "captains" (probably a translation of *mpanjaka kely*, "small king," in the Augustin Bay dialect). The major kingdom there was that of Captain Manale (Andrianmanely in the Malafsay oral tradition), which arose in the 1640s, extending inland for a distance equivalent to three days' march. It was ruled by Manale's extended family and divided in fiefs for his three younger brothers—Diamanofotsy, Ratsimive, and Diamaranhetsy in Malafsay tradition. Their rank depended on their age. The household of the Andrevola clan consisted of a few hundred warriors, aside from innumerable women and domestic servers. The captains ruled their "loans" virtually independently. The Dutch noted that the members of the Andrevola clan could inflict capital punishment freely and would support each other only during war and during some major rituals. Indeed, according to the tradition, the four brothers hated and despised each other, leading to a civil war around 1663.[314]

When the VOC came there, Andrianmanely was already constantly at war with the founder of the Sakalava kingdom to the north, "Adrasia Sura" (Andrianamasira I in Sakalava oral tradition), who conquered his dominion around 1670. And indeed, Andrianamasira I had at his disposal more than 4,000 men and hundreds of firearms, while Andrianmanely's household was armed only with assegais, bows, and spears. Only Andrianmanely himself disposed of a firearm—obtained from the English Indiamen, according to tradition—which he used to administer "death by muzzle loader," or *tanga ampingaharatsa*, as it was known in the nineteenth century. This practice had succeeded the earlier practice of having convicts swim over a crocodile-invested river. There were myriad conflicts between the various households along the coast. In the middle of the seventeenth century these were relatively bloodless affairs. The two armed bands would face each other, swap insults, and a few chosen champions would stage a fight; if a few died, the loser would clear the field.[315]

But as the seventeenth century—"the age of troubles," as it was later known among the Imerina—advanced, conflicts involved ever more bloodshed. One now fought for spoils rather than for honor. Andrianmanely invited the VOC, for example, to "enter the field of war with him; the plunder, which is nothing but cattle [their only wealth], he would share with us, whatever it might be, equally." This invitation the VOC was glad to decline. Apart from cattle, the VOC also captured slaves. Merchant I. Blank met with various "kraals of reed, for their slaves who look after their cattle and do other work too." For "these three captains are no farmers; what they brought us, they obtained secondhand, but about 3 to 4 miles up-country there are villages where the inhabitants do nothing else but planting." Andrianmanely tried to expand the income of his kingdom by laying out plantations, run by chattel slaves, but Andrianamasira I immolated those plantations these time and time again.[316]

European slave traders exchanged their "pieces" mainly with arms, which gave rise to virtually constant war along the coast as much as in the interior.

> It was during Adrianjaka's rule that the Imerina conquered south Imerina and guns and powder. And Adrianjaka staged a great celebration for the entire people as he had found guns and powder, for that benefited the kingdom. Alas, there were merely fifty guns and thirty small barrels with powder!

Thus it was lamented in the *Tantara*, the oral tradition of the Hova—a unique source for many reasons, not the least of which is that it provides us with an African perspective on the slave trade.[317] And this perspective is from the "receiving edge," for the Hova were then the most commonly sold slaves rather than being slave traders themselves, as they were in the late eighteenth century.[318] And well might one grieve, for—according to C. de Swart, writing in 1654—one might chase 400 men with assegais away with a single musket.[319]

To put a very complex matter in a nutshell: power and prestige equaled firearms, and the kings went to war to sell captives; then, to obtain yet more arms, they sold off debt slaves and, finally, their own subjects.[320] When Adrianjaka had exhausted his stock of guns, he needed more to defend against his neighbors.

> The kings later on had many guns come. First, they sold captives in return for powder, flintlocks and rifles, and then they began to sell cattle too to obtain it. The people were abducted first, then the cattle. And those who were first fetched away from Imerina were those who were convicted.[321]

A grisly vicious circle of war and enslavement ensued: "The ones who had no means became slaves of others, parents sold their children; spouses who had no offspring, sold each other. One was sold; the other remained at home. And the home was empty," to quote the *Tantara* again.[322] Itinerant Sakalava and Antanoara traders would fetch these slaves from Imerina to the encampment along the coast, eventually to end up much, much further away.

*Malgachisants* (academic specialists in the study of Madagascar) like Kent, Berg, and Bloch—in line with the general trend in African studies in the sixties and seventies to stress the "autonomy" of African history—tended to diminish the importance of the arms trade in favor of "indigenous African" factors contributing to state formation.[323] That is partly true. Madagascar was—unlike Sofala or Dela Goa Bay, for example, where arms were traded only in small quantities—particularly receptive to firearms, and these were used there in internal warfare on a scale not witnessed anywhere else in East Africa. By 1720 the French from Mauritius were exporting literally thousands of muskets to Madagascar yearly and the Sakalava had an army of more than 5,000 musketeers.[324]

Thus, the muskets contributed to, but certainly did not cause, the rise of kingdoms on the red island. Did the greater productivity of the wet rice agriculture in Madagascar maybe allow for raising greater resources for war and a standing army, unlike elsewhere in East Africa? However that may be, the older trend of ignoring or slighting the external impact on state formation in Madagascar has recently been increasingly subjected to criticism—and rightly so.[325]

Not only were the Europeans much more involved in Madagascar than the *malgachisants* often used to think—for, as we shall see in chapter 10, piracy was not a single incident but a whole branch of commerce—but the "external" impact was not limited to Europeans alone. Nor were arms sales confined to the Europeans either, for the Muscati traders on the northwest coast also peddled arms—and in large numbers. The bulk sales of arms at Maselagache very likely played a very important role in the rise of the Sakalava, for example.[326] Finally, traders from Muscat and from the Comoros were also transporting Bantu warriors from the Swahili Coast, skilled with firearms, for use as mercenaries. There were sizeable communities of them on islands off the northwest coast in the early seventeenth century, where the Swahili communities formed their own tiny, independent city-states, scouring the shore for both cattle and slaves.[327]

On the Malagasy Coast no firearms or munitions were manufactured. This was probably more because the Europeans—and especially the Americans—had a cost advantage than because the Malagasy were unable to manufacture arms. By 1700 Malagasy traders used to check the quality of rifles by first taking them apart and then reassembling them.[328] Ammunition (powder, flint, etc.) was also normally included in the purchase price of arms. In the early stages of its Malagasy trade the VOC purchased its slaves with (quasi-) currency: bracelets, piece-cloth, and glass beads. Some were made in India, others specially made in Holland for the African slave trade.[329] But in the late seventeenth century, apart from small amounts of *bafta*, the only product that could still be exchanged for slaves was arms. Andriamandisoarivo, the king of the Boina state, known then to Europeans by his title of Maroserana, warned the Company in 1696 that he wanted to deal only in guns. If not, he would buy these from the Americans: "our trade, he said, would be of little advantage if we would not furnish guns in abundance."[330]

### Islam and Slavery

In northwestern Madagascar the Europeans were seen as just another branch of "people from across the sea" (*analoatra* or *orang behar* in the Malay rendering of the Dutch translator at Maselagache). The earlier *analoatra* were Swahili and Arab merchants, who had often been living there for several generations and had taken Malagasy wives. "The Malagasy people have no idea of the value of goods and therefore they cannot dispense with the services of the analoatra," as the nineteenth-century observer Bron de Vexela wrote—or rather they had not so much no idea as a different idea.[331] An economy oriented toward accumulating cattle and girls has a logic at variance with one accumulating money, and the *analoatra* stood at the interface of these two economic systems

The most striking case of the Islamic impact on Madagascar is the spread of Islamic practices and of Malagasy texts in Arab script (*sorabe*) among the Antemoro. According to de Swart, the Antemoro had been converted to Islam by the survivors from a Persian ship, wrecked on this shore in the early fifteenth century. Since the local inhabitants had never seen foreigners, they "were venerated by the inhabitants as if they were gods" and set up a kingdom there.

Overall, this seems quite plausible since the date would coincide with the establishment of the new Ibadi dynasty at Pate, whereupon many older families tracing their genealogy back to Shiraz had fled southward and may well have ended up in Madagascar.[332]

Another case is the growth of Hadramawti and Omani settlements on the Comoros. These were primarily built on the revenues from protection of trade in the narrow seas between the Swahili Coast and Madagascar in cattle, coconuts, livestock, and rice, but the slave trade was involved too.[333]

According to one memorandum on Anjuan, the island was a veritable terrestrial paradise, growing an abundance of foodstuffs and blessed not merely by nature, but with inhabitants who "have never known the scourge of war."[334] This might have been the case once, but in the early seventeenth century *ghazi* sultanates were established there, the elites mostly deriving from Suqutra and Yemen, and their dhows skulked along the Malagasy Coast on the lookout for booty and slaves. Anjuan, which probably obtained arms from both the Indiamen and Yemen, was a veritable entrepôt for the arms trade of the entire Swahili Coast. Muhammad Ibn as-Saltani Assani, sultan of Mombasa, procured muskets there upon revolting against the Portuguese in 1634, for example.[335]

"The slaves" who were sold at Anjuan "are generally people they have obtained from the Northwest Coast of Madagascar"—whether by barter or by ransack. These slaves from the northwest coast were supposedly more docile than those from the Augustin and Saldanha Bay area. H. Hugo thus counseled the High Government of the Indies to cease trading with the mainland and, like the English, to found a trading post at Anjuan. Slaves from there were largely sold to the Swahili Coast, Yemen, and the Gulf, though, and the Europeans were only marginally involved.[336]

On the islands off the northwest coast flourished yet another Islamic complex, hub of the trade with the Americas and Indonesia, which, though Malagasy in language, was in its customs more closely related to the Swahili Coast than to the mainland. The most important of these sultanates in the seventeenth century was Maselagache. This sultanate, centered on old Maselagache, appears to have been founded around 1520 and had already in the late sixteenth century assumed a dominant position in the commerce of the northwest coast. Although Maselagache was oriented toward Malindi—where much of its elite in the sixteenth century was said to derive from—this was also by the aid of the Portuguese at Angoche. There were a few *casados* there around 1600, some of them working as mercenaries. Because of its close tie with Angoche—to which Maselagache occasionally sent gifts—it was termed a vassal state by the Portuguese.[337]

In the beginning of the seventeenth century Maselagache moved from its old site to a new site on Antsoheribory Island. Parallel to this there appears to have been an influx of Malagasy warriors and merchants into the elite of Maselagache, and Maselagache was now Malagasy-instead of Swahili-speaking.[338]

The "city" of "new Maselagache" was in 1670 still only a tiny community of about 300 households.[339] But it was at the summit of its wealth and power. War sloops of the sultan had subjugated the mainland coast. The heads of the surrounding villages were kept hostage on Antsoheribory Island and had to kiss the hand of the sultan during his weekly audience. More important, they had to send yearly tribute of rice and slaves. The army consisted of about 3,000 men, mostly Arabs (and Swahili?) mercenaries, mustered with firearms "which they have obtained from the English." There were local auxiliaries, armed with assegais and spears, as well. These were much needed, for the aggressive Sakalava neighboring kingdom of Boina constantly threatened the sultanate and overran it in the beginning of the eighteenth century.

The seat of the sultan, Jani Khan, was located on Antsoheribory, while his eldest son controlled the "subjugated" mainland. There too were the palisades on an artificial hillock (*vahema*), where the slaves were imprisoned. They were brought there by slave traders via the streams linking the coast to the interior. But the trade on the northwest coast was mainly a trade in bulk goods: rice and vegetables. For the city-states along the littoral not only were chronically deficient in foodstuffs themselves, but were major emporia for the rice and cattle trade to Mozambique and the southern Mrima Coast too. Bulk goods could be cheaply fetched over the rivers, so that traders were not as burdened by transport costs as elsewhere in Africa. The *umland* of supply for the ports and inlets on the Malagasy Coast was thus both more extensive—up to 120 km—and the influence of port reached much deeper into the direct hinterland than was normal on the Swahili Coast.[340]

Traders from Antsoheribory bartered their bulk goods for iron and steel (mostly from Yemen), Persian copper, and textiles. Those goods come from India and from Pate as well, which had a substantial production of textiles for export, mainly being brought there over Angoche. The slave trade, however, was a royal monopoly. Three or four dhows would depart yearly to Muscat, Mogadishu, Khisn, and Aden.[341]

### *The Slave Trade*

The Malagasy slave trade was perhaps not as dangerous as that with Guinea. (I have not been able to trace cases of revolt on slave ships, for instance, though these did occur on other routes in the East Indies.) Yet it remained an extremely unpleasant business. And Madagascar was an eerie place, in spite of the grandiose scenery. Wrecks and bones, probably of French colonists, were strewn all over Antongil Bay, for example—hardly an encouraging sight for newcomers. The sailors in their camps on the shore were fearful of the putrid bogs infested by man-eating crocodiles; they shunned the gloomy tropical forests and loathed and distrusted the populace.[342] The landing parties, camping in ramshackle wooden huts, were stuck on the beach, rarely venturing one foot away from it. The crew of the *Jambi*, when the shape of Madagascar faded in the mists, spontaneously fell to its knees "to praise the Lord that he had at long last, delivered us from this ghastly country."[343]

Little was known about the waters surrounding the island of the moon: the bays were shallow and narrow, the water was full of dangerous reefs, the winds were unreliable, and there were no good maps. These dangers on departure made the long voyage across the Indian Ocean to Padang (the port of Sumatra's mines) directly, or through Colombo or Cochin as way stations, even more horrific. In April 1684, the brig *Hoogergeest* appeared at the roadstead of Cochin. It had departed from Augustin Bay to Padang in October but sailed into contrary winds. In January, with an already decimated cargo, it arrived at Suqutra and took on supplies there, but again lost its bearings. To the slaves the trip must have equaled an inferno: of the 274 with whom the *Hoogergeest* had left Madagascar only 131 survived the journey. They were so exhausted that several dozen more perished in the infirmary at Cochin.[344]

In regard to this, Gentlemen XVII in 1672 decided that they would give a premium to the captain for each slave delivered alive. But the expenses on each "piece" should also be pushed down, the profits of the trade being meager enough as they were. Captains, therefore, tried to curtail the expenses per slave, often allotting them barely enough food. The skippers tried to impose these expenses on the suppliers too. It was, for example, customary for the sellers of slaves in Augustin Bay to give them provisions for three months.[345]

Even without epidemics and "accidents," slaves perished because of sheer homesickness and misery. Malagasy slaves were notorious for jumping overboard on the high seas or for starving themselves to death. But frequently slaves simply passed away without any clear cause. Buy only slaves age 16 to 24, Batavia ordered, for the elderly, "bereft of kind, kin and fatherland, and fetched away in bondage for all eternity, when remembering their past life, immediately start to mourn, and die."[346]

From the logs of the slave ships one cannot learn a great deal about life on board. These are sober listings of mortality, winds, and degrees of latitude. Little is known about the customs on board too. Penalties probably differed little from those in use in the Atlantic slave trade, like "washing the feet" or lashing with the cat-o'-nine-tails or batons.[347] Seen from the sea, the eastern coast of Madagascar presented a monotonous site of empty beaches and jungle. Slave ships would search the coast very carefully, the crow's nest manned to scout for "evil islands" or reefs. In general, they did not have a clear destination; they had to look for a spot where slaves could cheaply be procured. These were long, drab days for the mariners. Sometimes they would throw out anchor and have a sloop with a bunch of armed sailors row ashore and survey the waterfront to look for footprints. Sometimes the voyage would lead them to deserted fishing villages, the inhabitants hiding in the jungle. Or they just gasped at smoldering ashes; buccaneers or other slavers had apparently torched these places.[348]

To stark boredom add stark terror—by 1690 the commerce became ever more dangerous, as buccaneers were everywhere, and sloops with armed Malagasy pirates were waiting for the unwary skippers too. Some captains were paid by the pirates to brief them when prey entered the inlets. The crews on the slave ships always had arms within reach. At night they would sleep on deck and guards were posted, in order that pirates would not suddenly board anchored ships. Remember the *Hoogergeest*: when part of its crew was ashore, the *Hoogergeest* was unexpectedly grappled by the crew of a privateer, which flew EIC colors.[349]

In these immense wastes humans were barely noticeable—sometimes the inhabitants would use smoke signals, or the slaver would fire the guns to make its presence known. The ships waited for the arrival of armed canoes loaded with fruits and rice, which the sailors would barter for piece-cloth, rings, and beads. Though money was known among the Sakalava and Imerina, it was rarely used in transactions. Only on the northwest coast were slaves paid for in reales. "They are very choosy when it comes to money; they only want it if it is of round shape, clearly stamped and weighty."[350] This was partly because the cash linked the northwest coast to the commercial circuit of the Mrima Coast. As well, money was bartered with the hinterland to be used as ornaments and funeral gifts there. Cash was occasionally used in trade within Madagascar. But the measurement for exchange was cattle, the medium beads rather than cash there.

Upon arrival the slave traders waited for the captains.

> Big and strong guys, almost nude like the Hottentots, but around their waist to their thighs they have a small woven piece of cloth, and they are rubbed in oil from their head to their toes. Like the last-mentioned Hottentots they speak bad English, so one can reasonably communicate with them.[351]

Spirits and arrack were handed to the captains—heady brew, so they invariably got drunk. Sometimes this became a drinking bout of Europeans and Malagasys together till the early hours. The reader can imagine the confusion. Yet the party really started when the women of the captains also joined in and drank even more vigorously than the males: everyone danced, chanted, chattered, and made love on board till daybreak.[352]

Upon disembarking, the slave merchant was then generally brought to the residence of the king. As this meant that the king would receive new firearms, slave traders were enthusiastically greeted. Andriamandisoarivo was in 1692 supposed to have hurled his assegai three times in the air for sheer joy. He had even learned some Dutch and greeted the VOC's merchant with a broken "*Goedendag*."[353]

There were toasts; the king often sacrificed a bull; sometimes he had the women of the household perform a welcome dance and talked business afterward. Sometimes slave traders were permitted to buy "pieces" from subordinate captains (only cattle could be procured freely). Other kings—like Andriamandisoarivo—controlled the entire trade. Anyway, slaves were always bought at a price fixed by the captains and kings. It was a protracted affair, and negotiations might take several weeks, demanding patience from both parties.

Various strategies of bargaining were in use: if the rates of exchange were "unfair," the slave traders would turn furious and leave the royal compound to stay elsewhere, refusing to freely distribute brandy or arrack to the royal household. The king in turn might say he did not consider beads or spirits merchandise, only rifles. These are useless without powder, which the Americans always handled—and so should the Dutch. Or the king would say that young males were no longer available at the stipulated price of 16 reales, only old men and females. If buying the "offal" for 10 reales, some healthy males were included with these "pieces" too. He might plead there were insufficient slaves in the slave barracks next to the royal kraal—the traders ought, please, to wait a few days, so the king might send heralds to the other captains to send their slaves. All these were mainly subterfuges to gain time: unlike the Americans, the Dutch and the EIC were in a hurry to catch the trade winds.[354]

Yet the stay of the slave traders was of direct use to the court. And Andriamandisoarivo well realized it. When J. Avery wanted to buy supplies, the king offered these at no cost: "look ye," D. Defoe has him saying, "I require nothing of you—all white men I look upon as my children. They helped me to conquer this country and all the cattle in it are at their service."[355]

The presence of European soldiers also intimidated unruly subjects and scared neighbors. Thus, the sultan of Maselagache requested that the Dutch and the "Americans" (colonial Americans, who were, strictly speaking, English) stage a parade. That would certainly frighten the Sakalava. They finally conceded to this demand; Dutch and Americans together "marched to the dwelling of the king in full armor and charged three times and swung their banners. Which the king looked at in great surprise while the inhabitants were gasping."[356]

Furthermore, these new *analoatra* pledged to the court their respect and donated status symbols. Andriamandisoarivo, in keeping with the normal procedure of both barter and politics between the *analoatra* and the kingdoms in Madagascar, requested whether in exchange for livestock and slaves his Dutch brothers might not present him with a blond girl. This logical proposal the Hollanders abhorred, of course. But they would submit it to Batavia, he was assured pro forma.[357]

The slave traders, on the other hand, could participate in all kinds of outdoor sports, like shooting parrots, which were quite an appetizing dish, merchant R. Deodati discovered to his amazement. We can reasonably assume too that the temporary wives allotted the slave traders did not merely clean the floors of their huts. The frequent use of ginzua scent, which Malagasys used as "a perfume to spread a pleasant smell in Venus' garden of lust," by the Europeans surely points in that direction.[358]

The slaves were generally loaded in canoes, guarded by European soldiers, and taken to the camp on the beach. A guard with dogs was posted and the slaves locked in chains. Generally some tried to escape, and once they had reached the surrounding jungle they could no longer be found. It was often arranged with neighboring villages that refugees were to be extradited, but few observed this. Should they be caught, the refugees were to be lashed.[359]

Bargaining was a specialized affair. The king generally first tried to burden the slavers with "refuse": sick or old men. If one accepted the first lot without protest, one would be delivered "dirt" ever after. If absolutely necessary, 10 or 20 "mediocre pieces" could be bought, but the buyers sought to purchase only healthy men. However, if slavers were buying men only and refusing the remainder, prices would mount. So some women and children might be purchased too. The women might also be useful for "breeding purposes" and to cook; if completely bereft of female companionship or of children, the men would feel even more dejected—and perish. Since the price of males was not dependent on their "quality," buyers had duly to appraise them by inspecting eyes, limbs, and teeth. Generally girls or boys under 12 were half the price of an adult man—2 reales less for a woman under 25 and 4 reales for one above that age. The age of a slave had to be gleaned from physical characteristics, as Malagasys often did not know precisely when they were born, where they were born, or how their name was spelled. For in Malagasy society, where personal identity was not fixed in any written records, such matters were of less significance than they were to Europeans.[360]

The location where slaves were bought depended not only on price but on other factors too. The VOC often fetched them from Augustin Bay, as they had an interpreter who spoke the local dialect. Again, cattle and rice were cheap there and rice served as ballast for ships heading to Cape Town, where it could sold at a profit. This would hardly be a consideration for American vessels, of course.[361]

With demand steadily increasing, the market became glutted—especially because of the American involvement, which was spoiling the trade, the VOC complained. At Maselagache, for example, "pieces" had become so expensive in the eighties that many slavers could not afford to deal there any longer and had to depart empty-handed. From about 12 reales a slave the price mounted to 18 or 20 reales apiece.[362] And—as mentioned—competition within the Arabian seas increased too. Europeans there were faced with well-organized rings of Muscati/Swahili merchants who would first take an option on all slaves arriving there and subsequently sell them to the others.

To mention another case: No European vessel had ever touched Mahajoamba Bay—east of Boina Bay—until a slave ship from Boston was accidentally grounded there in 1670. Slaves could be obtained there at the incredible rate of 2 reales apiece. Next year, slavers were crowding the bay, so prices mounted to 12 reales and more.[363]

The market was hence both unpredictable and easily congested: slave traders would ideally require a buffer of intermediaries, permanently established on the island, who could stock the "pieces" in order to forestall such a glut. To some extent the *analoatra* communities on the northwest coast fulfilled this function. In the seventeenth century this was still very much a concern apart, however; with the exception of the Portuguese *casados*, the *analoatra* were little connected to other Europeans. The buccaneers clearly were, but Cape Town, at least, was reluctant to collaborate with them.

The commissioner-general of Cape Town, J. Pitt, already was muttering in 1681 that the slaves from Madagascar were no good in comparison with those from Bali or Sulawesi: "They cost too much and too few arrive alive." He considered it better not to procure slaves for Sillida there. Moreover, due to their high price one was unable to sell slaves to families in Batavia and the returns from the Sillida mines did not compensate for the costs. Cape Town counseled Batavia in 1687 to cease the trade altogether. Only a 15 to 18 percent profit was made. This was not merely too little to warrant the risks involved, but was too little relative to the purchase price of the merchandise exchanged and the "debit" of mortality too. However, the VOC still persevered with the slave trade, mainly in order not to leave it entirely to the English.[364]

## Conclusion

So the slave trade was booming and had a massive impact on the political organization of the island. This was undoubtedly advantageous for merchants and kings. To some extent the Sakalava and later the Imerina "despotisms" in the eighteenth century were founded by exploiting the opportunities offered by foreign trade. These proceeds contributed to the construction of a state apparatus used to exploit the peasantry more thoroughly. Yet it would obviously be a stretch to ascribe the rise of even the Sakalava kingdoms on the coast—let alone of Imerina in the distant highlands—purely to external causes.

But, not least because of all these internal factors that we have been considering, Madagascar was drawn into the Atlantic economy. This was a process that, if perhaps more dramatic than elsewhere, was not so different from what was taking place in India—and in Kerala in particular. After all, the rise of wealthy, armed intermediaries—Saraswats and Thomas Christians in Cochin and Travancore, Swahili/Arab warrior-merchants on Boina Bay—and the rise of kingdoms around Augustin and Boina Bays, built on the proceeds of trade, was somewhat comparable to the consolidation of the kingdom of Cochin, or to that of Travancore in a slightly later period.

And, indeed, the simultaneous rise of Travancore and that of the Menabe kingdom show an uncanny resemblance. This concerns, for example, the clear impact of the arms trade, the role of foreign mercenaries, and attempts by the royal household to monopolize the slave and pepper trades and even their attempts to monopolize the performance of rituals to the royal household. Basically, in either case, the demand for taxable export goods rapidly increased while the exchange of slaves for weapons made warfare a profitable proposition—the economic boom of the late seventeenth and early eighteenth centuries was thus an "age of troubles" in Travancore as much as in Imerina. These two areas, seemingly so remote, were linked by a common world conjuncture.[365]

How, then, is one to define the trade in the Arabian seas in this period? Was it an era of crisis and stagnation or of dynamic growth? This depends entirely upon the perspective chosen. From the perspective of trade with Europe and its American colonies, this is an age of sustained growth. But we should be careful not to equate trends in trade with Europe with those within the Indian Ocean. This may be a flaw in much of the literature: exports to Europe are a good indicator of demand in Europe but not necessarily elsewhere.

Of course, it is tempting to make statements on population growth, output, or wage levels on an all-Indian, all-African, or all-Iranian level, but the available material simply does not allow this. It may be true in a very long-term perspective that crises such as those in the periods 1630–34, 1657–63, and the 1680s were but ripples in a pattern of steadily growing population and cultivated land in India—and perhaps Iran—from the sixteenth to the eighteenth century. But such a long-term trend of steady expansion could not smooth the immediate impact of short-term crises.[366]

The *moyen durée* does deserve attention, though, for assertions of immutable patterns or very long-run trends are often too readily made in an Indian context. From such supposed patterns are then derived uniquely "Indian" or "Asian" patterns, which are supposedly very different from "European" ones. Thus believes Gunder Frank, who argues that "the Asian economy" experienced a long, expansive cycle (or "A" phase) that began in 1400 and appears to have lasted into the eighteenth century but then turned into a "B" phase. Unlike in Western Europe, there were to Frank no signs of slow growth in the seventeenth century, though one is almost tempted to say there ought to have been.

If, on the other hand, the trade of the Arabian seas experienced a difficult period of slow and often interrupted growth, even stagnation, from 1660 to 1690, it would seem warranted to connect this with the pattern of European trade in the same period. For although the seventeenth century was perhaps not a period of dramatic contraction or mutation, as was originally argued by Hobsbawm in an article that set off a very long debate on the "seventeenth-century crisis in Europe," it was an age of slow, often interrupted, expansion throughout.[367]

To be sure, one should beware of carrying this argument too far. Hobsbawm originally argued that this "seventeenth-century crisis" was caused by a transition from the feudal to the capitalist mode of production. It would be fruitless, I suppose, to reenact this debate in an Indian, or Iranian, context. This would merely amount to a search for "germs of the capitalist mode of production" in India, which has been an (often rather pointless) pursuit of Indian and Soviet historians for decades.[368]

Nevertheless, two common factors in both Europe and the Arabian seas can be discerned. First, the seventeenth-century crisis can be seen as a crisis of the state. J.M. Goldstone argues for a "general cycle of state breakdown" throughout Eurasia during the 1640s. "The main trend was that population growth, in the context of relatively inflexible economic and social structures, led to changes in prices, shifts in resources, and increasing social demands with which the agrarian-bureaucratic states could not successfully cope."[369]

There are many problems with this argument. On the empirical level, it is problematic whether—as Goldstone argues—the Ottoman empire in any way "collapsed" in the 1640s and whether this supposed "crisis" can be linked to population growth at all. Another objection might be that in Persia and India this was actually a rather quiet period—so that states certainly did not break down "throughout Eurasia." The only real breakdown of authority in the Arabian seas occurred in the Ottoman *pashaliq* of Yemen and that was, of course, closely related to problems in the Ottoman empire.[370]

On a more theoretical level, Goldstone perhaps passes too lightly over the considerable autonomy of the early modern state vis-à-vis the economy. It is ironic that while Goldstone seeks to link the English civil war and the French Revolution to global economic change, the specialist literature on both has returned to seeing each as caused by a—very local—crisis of political legitimacy rather than by social or economic problems. This crisis was mainly triggered by the expansion of the fiscal demands of the state.[371]

Yet—departing from this "relative autonomy" of the state—one may save Goldstone's argument by turning it upside down. The problem was not that the state could not cope with an expanding economy, but rather the expanding state itself. The economy was only partly able to adjust to an increasing fiscal burden of the state and to the internecine warfare, which was in either case connected to the growth of a paid bureaucracy, standing armies, and the expansion of military empires.

Second, the seventeenth-century crisis can be seen as a readjustment of demand and supply on a global level. As Bruce Masters argues, one may speak of a revolution in the trade of the Arabian seas, but rather as a whisper than as a shout: a slow, often painful, process of adaptation—or subordination—of producers in the Arabian seas to a modern world economy increasingly dominated by Europeans.[372]

## Notes

1. There are literally scores of books on this topic. I would mention R. Ehrenberg, *Das Zeitalter der Fugger. Geldhandel und Creditverkehr im 16 Jahrhundert,* 2 vols.

(Frankfurt, 1896); A. Schulte, *Geschichte der grossen ravensbürger Handelsgesellschaft*, 3 vols. (Stuttgart, Berlin, 1936), ii, pp. 117–54; F. Braudel, *The Mediterranean and the Mediterranean World in the Age of Philip II* (S. Reynold, trans.), 2 vols. (New York, 1972), i, pp. 547–70; M.A.P. Meilink-Roelofs, *Asian Trade and European Influences in the Indonesian Archipelago Between 1500 and About 1630* (The Hague, 1962); D.H. Lach, *Asia in the Making of Europe*, 7 vols. so far (Chicago, 1965– ), i, pp. 98–142; V. Magalhães Godinho, *Os descobrimentos e a economia mundial*, 4 vols. (Lisbon, 1983–85), iii, pp. 7–171; N. Steensgaard, "European Shipping to Asia, 1497–1700," *Scandinavian Economic History Review* 18 (1970), pp 1–11.

2. W.H. Moreland, *India at the Death of Akbar: An Economic Study* (London, 1902), p. 237.

3. H.K. s'Jacob, "De VOC en de Malabarkust in de 17 e eeuw," in M.A.P. Meilink-Roelofs (ed.), *De VOC in Azië* (Bussum, 1976), p. 85.

4. S.B. Dale, *Islamic Society on the South Asian Frontier: The Mappilas of Malabar 1498–1922* (Oxford, 1980), p. 11, argues, therefore, that the states in Kerala resemble the city-states in Southeast Asia, built on the revenues from trade, rather than the territorial empires of the rest of India, primarily constructed on the proceeds of land revenue. Maybe so, though the importance of indirect incomes (succession dues, legal dues, etc.) from agriculture to the finances of the kingdoms in Kerala should not be underrated.

5. VOC/OB 1474, 14 March 1689, fo. 121.

6. F. Rodrigues Silveira, *Reformação da miliçia e governo da Índia Oriental* (B.N. Teensma, ed.) (Lisbon, 1996), p. 14; VOC/OB 1432, 17 December 1687, fo. 31; VOC/OB 1257, 10 October 1692, fo. 396; VOC/OB 1593, 10 December 1694, fo. 108.

7. VOC/OB 1474, 8 June 1689, fo. 223.

8. C.A. Innes, *Gazetteer of Malabar and Anjengo District*, 3 vols. (Madras, 1908), ii, p. 308; VOC/OB 1388, 31 March 1683, fo. 2031; VOC/OB 1360, "Report by Cornelis Huysman," 11 March 1680, fo. 1690; VOC/OB 1357, 10 October 1682, fo. 397.

9. Almeida Calado, *Libro em que se tratte muito por extenso*, pp. 60–62; VOC/OB 1280, 29 November 1671, fo. 602 vo. Of course the gold mines in Coorg district have always appealed more to the imagination, but this gold was mainly used for internal circulation and was hardly traded beyond Kerala. NAI, Foreign Miscellaneous 94, fo. 326.

10. J. Lockyer, *An Account* (London, 1711), p. 201; VOC/OB 1280, 29 November 1671, fo. 602 vo.; VOC/OB 1527, 10 October 1692, fo. 425 vo.; VOC/OB 1434, 17 December 1687, fo. 38 vo.

11. See, for example, VOC/OB 1434, 17 December 1687, fo. 79. For, although *nayyar* troops could be summoned by the rajah for one season, they had to be paid when deployed outside of their home province (*nadu*).

12. S. Arasaratnam, "India and the Indian Ocean in the Seventeenth Century," in Das Gupta and Pearson (eds.), *India and the Indian Ocean*, p. 123, and—reiterating Arasaratnam's view—J.F. Richards, "The Seventeenth Century Crisis in South Asia," *MAS* 24, no. 4 (1990), pp. 625–38.

13. Steensgaard, "European Shipping to Asia 1497–1700"; F. Kaeppelin, *Les Origines de l'Inde française. La Compagnie des Indes orientales et François Martin* (Paris, 1908), pp. 653–61; Boyajian, *Portuguese Trade in Asia.*

14. VOC/XVII 322, 30 August 1686, fo. 372 vo.

15. The problem here, of course, is to ascertain where the Portuguese exports were from; *chautar darriabadi* and *mir quli* were both exported from Surat and from Laribandar.

16. M. Hroch, "Die Rolle des zentraleuropäischen Handels im Ausgleich der Handelsbilanz zwischen Ost-und Westeuropa 1500–1650," in I. Bog (ed.), *Der Aussenhandel Ost-Mitteleuropas* (Cologne, Vienna, 1971), p. 12.

17. E. Schubert, *Einführung in die Grundprobleme der deutschen Geschichte im Spätmittelalter* (Darmstadt, 1992), p. 19; A. Ionissian (ed.), *Armjano-Russkie otnošenija v pervoi tretii XVIII veka* (*Sbornik, dokumentov*), 2 vols. (Erevan, 1964), ii, pp. 4–5, Document 2; J. Reinhold, *Polen/Litauen auf den leipziger Messen des 18 e Jahrhunderts* (Weimar, 1971). This shift of Persian trade to the north in the middle of the eighteenth century has been insufficiently studied for its effects on the Gulf, but see M.G. Abdullaev, *Politiceski, ekonomiceski i socialnogo istorija Azerbaidjana v XVIII v. i vsaimotnošenije ego s Rossijei* (Baku, 1976). The literature on the Armenian communities in Poland and Ukraine is both vast and inaccessible; see H.D. Andresyan, *Polonyali Simeon'un seyahatnâmesi* (Istanbul, 1964); J.R. Daskevic (ed.) *Ukrainsko-Armjanskie sviazi v XVII veke. Sbornik, dokumentov* (Kiev, 1966).

18. S. Dale, *Indian Merchants and Eurasian Trade 1600–1750* (Cambridge, 1994); A.I. Iuct, "Russko-vostocnaja torgovlija v XVII–XVIII v. i uctajnie v nei Indiskoi kupecestva," *Istorija SSR* 6 (1978), pp. 42–59; and on the merchant communities at Astrakhan, which were dominated by "Bukhariote" and "Tartar" merchants overall, see N.B. Golikova, *Astrakhanskoe voštanie 1706 g.* (Moscow, 1973), pp. 168–82. Identifiable Indian textiles in Russian customs ledgers would include *kankhani* (manufactured in Sind), the ubiquitous black *bafta* also from Sind, *churti* and white *bafta* from Bengal, and *daryabafta* and *sarbafta* from Hindustan.

19. VOC/UB 889, 13 September 1665, fo. 514.

20. VOC/XVII 319, 14 May 1667; A. García-Baquero González, *Andalucía y la carrera de Indias 1492–1824* (Seville, 1986), p. 97.

21. VOC/XVII 319, 14 May 1667; P. Chaunu, *Les Philippines et le Pacifique des ibériques* (Paris 1960).

22. VOC/OB 1406, 20 May 1684, fo. 956; VOC/OB 1549, 16 May 1694, fo. 189–192; Arasaratnam, *Merchants, Companies and Commerce on the Coromandel Coast, 1650–1740* (New Delhi, 1986) p. 302.

23. Om Prakash, *The Dutch East India Company and the Economy of Bengal* (Princeton, 1986), p. 201.

24. Ibid., p. 74; V.B. Gupta, "The Dutch East India Company in Gujarat Trade" (Ph.D. diss., Delhi School of Economics, 1991), p. 400. And, indeed, A. Reid, *Southeast Asia in the Age of Commerce*, ii, *Expansion and Crisis* (New Haven, 1993), p. 285, has argued that, while Company trade expanded, the trade of Southeast Asia as a whole declined.

25. VOC/OB 1474, 14 March 1689, fo. 6, 21; because of this larger trade with Gujarat, I think that, economically speaking, Kerala should be included in the Arabian seas and not in the South Indian subregion, as argued by Subrahmanyam. While trade between Kerala and Bengal was quite substantial at the beginning of the seventeenth century, it was small at its end. Was this a result of the crisis of the second half of the seventeenth century? Maybe. At any rate, by the end of the seventeenth century the region was receiving its opium from Egypt rather than from Bengal—opium being the main product imported from there (cf. Om Prakash, *The Dutch East India Company*, pp. 169–72).

26. In the early seventeenth century the ruler of Cochin conducted direct trade to Atjeh Bulhão according to Patto and A. da Silva Rago, *Documentos remettidos*, ii, p. 4; ANTT, DRI, 43, 1642, fo. 47.

27. See, for example, VOC/OB 1379, 6 March 1682, fo. 2666.

28. VOC/OB 1133, 19 May 1640, fo. 456; HAG, LM, 39, 30 July 1674, fo. 107; AHU, Índia, Cx. 29 bis, 186, 5 July 1674; together with a permit for China, Hodsia Minas also requested a permit for trade to Mombasa, which was granted to him. These attempts of the Portuguese to inhibit Armenian trade with China were to only limited avail, for at the end of the seventeenth century the Armenians mostly traded with China on English ships from Madras and Hugly.

29. ARA, HRB 834, Memoir by Jan Grootenhuys, 19 December 1708; Ajuda 51-VII-37, "Vossa majestade mandou me informar," fo. 128; M.N. Pearson, *Merchants and Rulers in Gujarat* (Berkeley, 1971), pp. 23–24, 101. Pearson argues that Gujarati trade must have grown on the base of the following assumptions: since the tax revenues of Surat were farmed—not directly collected—for 250.00 rupees, these revenues should therefore be at the Mughal custom rates of 2½% (10.000.000). Since Surat was the biggest port in Gujarat its trade should thus account for one-tenth of Gujarat's total trade. The total should be 100,000,000. However, this is not such a muddle as the argument presented by S. Subrahmanyam, *Portuguese Asia 1498–1700* (London, 1993), p. 176, and by Boyajian, *Portuguese Trade in Asia*, pp. 53–68. Assume, they say, that all seaborne trade in Asia went through the Portuguese settlements that the totals of customs revenues only refer to seaborne trade. Assume too that the sums for which a customs house was farmed are an accurate picture of the revenues collected and that everything collected was duly declared to the crown. Assuming all this, the customs revenues of the Portuguese factories can be multiplied by the "appropriate rates" to give us a value of total seaborne trade conducted in Asia. We have no figures of customs incomes after 1640 when—obviously—a large part of Asian trade was conducted outside of the Portuguese compass. Yet the figures after 1640 are much lower than before these, proving, Subrahmanyam and Boyajian assert, that Asian trade—and not merely Portuguese trade—declined after 1640.

30. M. Salim, *Al muʿarikhun al Yamaniyun fi'l ahd al-uthmani al-ʿahval* (Cairo, 1971), p. 76; ANTT, DRI 53, 1646, fo. 295, and 36, 20 January 1636, fo. 101.

31. VOC/OB 1343, "Advice by Reynier Cassembrood on Persian trade," fo. 602.

32. *Rumal* are coarse textiles from Bengal, mostly used for making handkerchiefs; *sekela* and *salempuri* were from the southern Coromandel Coast.

33. Ionissian, *Armjansko-Russkie otnošenija* ii, p. 24.

34. VOC/OB 1329, Report by Willem Volger, 1 June 1677, fo. 1486; VOC/OB 1294, 15 August 1655, fo. 708; VOC/UB 877, fo. 392.

35. VOC/UB 881, 5 September 1657, fo. 439.

36. On the Sind-Muscat connection see, for example, BAC, A 500, 3 December 1678; VOC/OB 1291, "Report Willemson," fo. 573.

37. W.H. Moreland, *From Akbar to Aurengzeb*, pp. 212–22; Van Santen, "Verenigde Oost-Indische Compagnie," pp. 175–77 (see list of unpublished papers in bibliography). Van Santen may be attributing too much Keynes to the Mughal empire, however; it was normal to order such large quantities of textiles for the poor at Mecca for reasons of court politics or prestige rather than strictly economic ones; see M.N. Pearson, *Pilgrimage to Mecca* (Princeton, 1996), p. 120.

38. VOC/OB 1233, 17 December 1661, fo. 115–17; VOC/OB 1236, 14 October 1660, fo. 22; VOC/OB 1240, 3 May 1662, fo. 986.

39. A. Muhammed Khan, *Mirat i-Ahmadi*, p. 286; VOC/OB 1434, 27 November 1687, fo. 284 vo.; VOC/OB 1425, 16 December 1686, fo. 172; VOC/OB 1434, Surat resolution, 8 May 1687, fo. 391, and Surat diary, 15 June 1686, fo. 464.

40. HAG 1376, Livro das provincias do Norte, "Alvará sobre as parçias," and "Regiment for Mello de Sampayo," 6 May 1686, fo. 13.

41. Note that the scarcity in Goa is also reflected in the sudden surge of the prices of grain there in the mid-eighties—T. de Souza, *Medieval Goa* (New Delhi, 1976), p. 216; AHU, Cód. 451, 1684, fo. 17; see also HAG, Petições despachadas para o conselho da fazenda, 1127, 7 September 1683, fo. 124; 29 October 1684, fo. 160 vo.

42. KITLV, H. 10 b, Report by Ryckloff van Goens, 18 October 1681; BNL, FG, Cód. 8538, 28 October 1688; Ajuda 50-V-37, doc. 349, "An advice why it is necessary to move the capital to Marmagoa"; ARA, St. Gen., Lias VOC, 5741 ii, Report by Robertus Padbrugge, 23 December 1689, fo. 6.

43. There is, however, some evidence on the Persian climate relative to the rise and fall of the level of the Caspian Sea and the (late) Aral Lake; V.V. Gumilev, *Rhitm Evrazii* (Moscow, 1992), p. 163; G. Utterström, "Climatic Fluctuation and Population Problems in Early Modern History," *Scandinavian Economic History Review*, 3 (1955), pp. 3–47; E. Le Roy Ladurie, *Histoire du climat depuis l'an mil,* 2 vols. (Paris, 1972); M.L. Parry, *Climatic Change, Agriculture and Settlement* (Dawson, 1978).

44. W.H. Mac Niell, *De pest in de geschiedenis* (Plagues and People) (Amsterdam, 1974), p. 177.

45. H. Maier-Lemgo (ed.), *Die Reisetagebücher Engelbert Kämpfer* (*Wiesbadener erdwissenschaftliche Forschungen* II) (Wiesbaden, 1968), pp. 125–27; ARA, LH, 29, 22 November 1686, fo. 548; VOC/OB 1490, fo. 163 vo.; VOC/OB 1425, 16 December 1686, fo. 235; VOC/OB 1455, 25 November 1687; VOC/OB 1529, Surat resolution, 9 January 1692, fo. 100 vo.; VOC/OB 1475, 27 October 1689, fo. 137 vo.; VOC/OB 1476, 31 December 1690, fo. 22; AHU, Índia, Cx. 38, 62, 28 February 1694.

46. Röhrborn, *Zentralverwaltung,* p. 42; K. Röhrborn, *Provinze und Zentralgewalt Persien im XVI und XVII Jahrhundert* (Berlin, Der Islam, *Beiheft* II), pp. 112–16; Papazian, *Agrarnie otnosenije*, pp. 165–72; Petruševski, *Ocerki po istorii*, pp. 98–107.

47. J. Chardin, *La Couronation de Suleiman, Roi présent du royaume de Perse* (facsimile reprint, Teheran, 1984); VOC/OB 1255, 30 November 1664, fo. 818; VOC/OB 1261, 12 July 1668, fo. 782.

48. R. Mathee, "Administrative Stability and Change in Late 17th Century Iran," *International Journal of Middle Eastern Studies* 26, no. 1 (1994), pp. 77–98; see VOC/OB 1278, 16 May 1670, fo. 1814 vo.; VOC/OB 1284, 26 August 1670, fo. 2278 vo. A. Keyvani, *Artisans and Guild Life During the Late Safavid Period* (Berlin, 1982), p. 227, argues that the general insecurity of mercantile property in Safavid Persia would largely have forestalled the acquisition of land by merchants. But there is plenty of evidence to the contrary; see, for example, VOC/OB 1370, 15 March 1681, fo. 2478, or Petrusevski, *Ocerki po istorii*, pp. 236–42.

49. ARA, St. Gen., Lias VOC, 5737 i, "Written report by Barentszoon."

50. S. Moosvi, *The Economy of the Mughal Empire c. 1595: A Statistical Study* (New Delhi, 1987), pp. 95–191; Ajuda, 51-VII-23, 10 February 1683, fo. 288 vo.

51. See C.A. Bayly, *Rulers, Townsmen and Bazaars* (Cambridge, 1983), pp. 68–73. For the traditional version of the impact of war in the time of Aurengzeb, see J. Sarkar, *A Short History of Aurengzeb* (Hyderabad, 1979), pp. 301–7.

52. VOC/OB 1243, 22 February 1665, fo. 1222.

53. VOC/OB 1388, 31 March 1683, fo. 2010–11 vo.

54. Ajuda 51-V-49, 30 September 1679, fo. 65; VOC/OB 1241, 10 October 1663, fo. 23 vo.; VOC/OB 1406, 11 April 1684, fo. 825.

55. ARA, St. Gen., Lias VOC, 5470 i, Report by Jacobus van Wayer, 11 December 1679: "*wonderlijke sprongen doet dese Sjuvaji met sijn vliegend leger.*"

56. F. Perlin, "Studies in Late Pre-colonial Indian Society and Economy" (Academisch Proefschrift, University of Leiden, 1984), ii, p. 27; Ajuda, 51-VII-23, 11 April 1684, fo. 390; 19 February 1685, fo. 533; VOC/OB 1549, Surat diary, 1 May 1694, fo. 492; VOC/OB 1474, "Report by accountant J. van Raets," fo. 328; VOC/OB 1461, "Relation relative to some terrifying events," fo. 1459 vo.; VOC/OB 1635, Diary H. Zwaardecroon, 1 December 1699, fo. 589–91; VOC/OB 1635, "Report by B. Ketel," 24 December 1699, fo. 556.

57. *Gaz.B.Pr.*, xii, p. 467; VOC/OB 1635, "Report by Ketel," fo. 556.

58. VOC/OB 1291, "Report Willemson," fo. 583; VOC/OB 1480, 16 March 1692, fo. 321 vo.; H.D. Ross, "Annals of Oman from Earliest Times to the Year 1728 A.D," *Journal of the Asiatic Society of Bengal,* 43 (1) (1874), p. 162; G. Bathurst, "Imamate and Maritime Trade," in D.K. Hopwood (ed.), *The Arab Peninsula* (London, 1972), p. 48; J.C. Wilkinson, *The Imamate Tradition of Oman* (Cambridge, 1987), pp. 220–23; Salih Ibn Raziq, *History of the Imams and Seyyids of Oman* (G.P. Badger ed.) (London, 1871), p. 56.

59. VOC/OB 1291, fo. 564; VOC/OB 1379, 1 May 1682, fo. 2352 vo.; VOC/OB 1279, "A discourse on Malabari trade to Mocha," fo. 467 vo.

60. HAG, Regimentos e instruções, 1423, "Instruction for Luís da Costa," 22 February 1658, fo. 9 vo.; and "Instruction for Faustono Borges de França," 28 December 1664, fo. 42 vo.

61. B.G. Shastri, *Studies in Indo-Portuguese History* (Bangalore, 1981), pp. 203–10; Subrahmanyam, "The Port of Basrur," p. 457; K.D. Swaminathan, *The Nayakas of Ikkeri* (Madras, 1957), p. 109; VOC/OB 1224, "Essay," fo. 77; HAG, Regimentos e instruções, 1423, "Regiment for Frey Francisco de Espinola," fo. 21 vo.

62. VOC/OB 1224, "An essay on the present state of the land Canarra," fo.75.

63. H. Cousins, "The Antiquities of Sind with Historical Outline," *Archaeological Survey of India,* XLVI, *Imperial Series* (Varanasi, 1975).

64. I. Habib, *The Agrarian System of Mughal India (1556–1707)* (London, 1963), pp. 392–94; see also A. Hasan, "The Silver Currency Output of the Mughal Empire and Prices in India During the 16th and 17th Century," *IESHR* 6 (1) (1969), pp. 85–116. Much criticism on either (see S. Subrahmanyam, "Precious Metal Flows and Prices in Western and Southern Asia, 1500–1750: Some Comparative and Conjunctural Aspects," in S. Subrahmanyam [ed.], *Money and the Market in India, 1100–1700* [Delhi, 1994], pp. 52–54) is due to a misunderstanding of the "Hamilton thesis": if there was an impact of imports of American silver on prices in India, we should expect this to occur mainly in the beginning of the seventeenth century (1590–1620). But the criticism of Habib and Hasan focuses essentially on the middle of the seventeenth century (1630–1650), when the volumes of silver imported in Seville were decreasing and the Portuguese were exporting less silver. So, as the evidence confirms, one would expect deflation or stable prices, rather than inflation.

65. A. Attman, *The Bullion Flow Between Europe and the East* (Acta Regiae societatis scientiarum et litterarum Gothenburgensis Humaniora 20) (Gotteburg, 1981), provides a good overview of the extensive literature on this topic.

66. VOC/OB 1295, "Report by Rombout Lefer," fo. 312.

67. VOC/XVII 321, 29 November 1683, fo. 140.

68. Thus it was, for example, in Cochin, where, according to the accounts in AHU,

Índia, Cx. 12, 12, cowries were commonly used in the 1630s to pay journeymen. In the late seventeenth century they were by and large paid in copper Dutch *schellingen*. This almost certainly reflected the large imports of copper by the VOC in the intervening period and hence an accrual of the total stock of money in Cochin.

69. D. Flynn, "The Microeconomics," in *World Silver*, p. 48.

70. M.T. Boyer-Xambeu, G. Deleplace, and L. Gillard, *Private Money and Public Currencies: The 16th Century Challenge* (Armonk, 1994), pp. 6–14; S.N. Sen, *Shiv Chatrapati* (Calcutta, 1920), p. 133–39; Y. Husain (ed.), *Selected Waqai of the Deccan* (Hyderabad, 1953), p. 37; Geleynssen 142, Appendix to Persia diaries: Reduction of the Persian coin.

71. Van Santen, "Verenigde Oost-Indische Compagnie," p. 35.

72. On the VOC's involvement in gold mining see P. Rueb, "Un mine d'or à Sumatra. Technologie saxon et méthodes indigènes au XVIIe siècle," *Archipel* 41 (1991), pp. 13–32. From 1703 onward some Brazilian gold was sent from Minas Gerais by Carreira da Índia ships, touching at Bahia, to Goa. It is as yet unclear how much, though: M.A.H. Fitzler, "Die Handelsgeselschaft Felix von Oldenburgs. Ein Beitrag zur Geschichte des Deutschtums im Portugal zur Zeitalter des Absolutismus," *Beiheft VSWG* 23 (1931), p. 231.

73. VOC/OB 1330, "Report by J. Wijns," fo. 1754; T. Walz, "Gold and Silver Exchanges Between Egypt and Sudan 16th–18th Century," in J.F. Richards (ed.), *Precious Metals in the Late Medieval and Early Modern World* (Durham, 1983), pp. 305–29.

74. Ajuda 51-VII-27, "Papel por Dom Sebastião de Magalhães"; AHU, Índia, Cx. 36, 51, "Auto da devaça tirado do juiz."

75. K.N. Chaudhuri, *The Trading World of Asia and the East India Company* (Cambridge, 1978), p. 179; S. Moosvi, "The Silver Influx, Money Supply and Revenue Extraction in Mughal India," *JESHO* 30 (1987), pp. 47–94; VOC/OB 1476, 12 August 1690, fo. 416–18; VOC/OB 1454, 27 November 1687, fo. 1331 vo.

76. I. Habib, "Prices and Monetary Structure," in *Cambridge Economic History of India*, i, p. 369.

77. Bragança Pereira, *Arquivo*, II, ii, p. 147; Theal, vi, pp. 452–62; Godinho, *Os descobrimentos*, i, p. 207; AHU, Moç. Cx. 1, 17, Memoir by Dom Jerónimo de Almeida; AHU, Moç, Cx. 3, 83, 23 February 1680. VOC estimates of imports of gold from Mozambique in Goa were as follows: 293 marques in 1661, 634 in 1663, 239 in 1664, 313 in 1665, 160 in 1668, 250 in 1669, and 430 in 1675; and from Mombasa 83 in 1663, 62 in 1664, and 194 in 1675. Note that these figures are all much lower than those of S.I.G. Mudenge, *A Political History of Munhumutapa* (Harare, 1988), p. 174, and would put Mozambique's and Mombasa's gold production at about half that of West Africa, which seems to tally with the observed historical record. If Mozambique had produced more gold, the Portuguese would certainly have started exporting it to Lisbon.

78. VOC/HB 4456, 14 April 1671; W.G.L. Randles, *L'Empire du Monomotapa du XV au XIXe siècle* (The Hague, 1975), pp. 78–79.

79. For a description of the remains of the *lascas*, see R. Summers, *Ancient Mining in Rhodesia* (Salisbury, 1969); J.F. Schofeld, "The Ancient Workings of South East Africa," *Native Affairs Department Annual* (Bulawayo) (1971) (3), p. 6; BNL, FG, Cód. 10.836, fo.15; AHU, Moç, 1, 100, "Treslado de certidão"; AHU, Moç. Cx. 3, 77, 22 June 1677.

80. Theal, *Records*, iii, pp. 458–69; Godinho, *Os descobrimentos*, i, pp. 184–87; ANTT, DRI, 39, "Brief testimony on the gold mines of Macaranga," fo. 251–54.

81. Mudenge, *Political History*, p. 170–74; Évora CV/2–7, "Discurso sobre a conquista," fo. 41–43 vo.; ANTT, DRI, 57, 11 January 1647, fo. 163–165.

82. Although, to be sure, this is a very controversial issue; see M.N. Pearson, *Port Cities and Intruders* (Baltimore and London, 1998), p. 123.

83. Such a "bead currency based on a cloth standard" was still normal in Ujijji on Lake Tanganyika in the nineteenth century; see B. Brown, "Muslim Influences on Trade and Politics in the Lake Tanganyika Region," *African Historical Studies* 4 (1971), p. 621.

84. This use of textiles as "cloth currency" has been well studied for western Africa; see P.D. Curtin, *Economic Change in Pre-Colonial Africa*, 2 vols. (Madison, 1975), i, pp. 237–40, AHU, Cód. 432, "Regimento das alfândegas," fo. 66.

85. F.S. Gaastra, "De Verenigde Oost-Indische Compagnie: de groei van een bedrijf. Geld tegen goederen. Een structurele verandering van het Nederlands-Aziatische handelsverkeer," *BMGN*, 89 (1976), pp. 249–72; K.N. Chaudhuri, "Treasure and Trade Balances: The East India Company's Export Trade 1660–1720," *EHR*, 16 (1968), pp. 480–502.

86. This merits special emphasis since it is so central to Gunder Frank's argument in *Reorient*, chapter 3 (following Flynn, TePaske, and Von Glahn), that China was the hub of the world's bullion trade. I suspect this is mainly a result of an elementary misunderstanding: namely, the idea that money sent to Southeast Asia *should* have ended up in China. But not only was most of the bullion sent to Southeast Asia destined for India, but Southeast Asia—especially Java and Sumatra—required large amounts of bullion itself. The VOC—and probably the EIC as well—actually sent far more bullion to Bencoolen and to Sumatra's west coast than to China in the late seventeenth century. Also, much of the bullion received in Manila was either a direct payment for troops and administration and would have remained there, or was taken to Southeast Asia and to India. The question should thus not be Why did China require silver? but Why did Asia as a whole require silver, gold, copper, tin, and spelter? And, given the comparative cost advantages Europeans enjoyed in the production of many of these metals, the communication problems, and the disparity between Europe's and Asia's population and total productive capacity, it is not that difficult to explain why these products were exported to Asia in bulk.

87. KITLV H 315 b, Note on cash remitted from Batavia.

88. V.B. Chick, *A Chronicle of the Carmelites* (London 1936), i, p. 360; VOC/OB 1224, 1 March 1658, fo. 800 vo.

89. A point already alluded to in Om Prakash and J. Krishnamurty, "Mugal Silver Currency—A Critique," *IESHR*, 7 (1) (1970), p. 143, and—surely from a very different vantage point—by F. Spooner, *The International Monetary Economy and Monetary Movements in France* (Cambridge, MA, 1982), p. 75.

90. M. Morineaux, *Incroyables gazettes et fabuleux métaux* (Paris, Cambridge, 1985), p. 307; P. Masson, *Histoire du commerce de Marseille* (Paris 1911; New York, 1967), p. 203; R. Paris, *Histoire du commerce de Marseille de 1660 à 1789. Le Levant* (Paris, 1953). On the structure of the Levant trade see also B. MacGowan, *Economic Life in Ottoman Turkey* (Paris, Cambridge, 1985), pp. 15–48.

91. R. Davis, "English Imports from the Middle East 1580–1780," in M.A. Coock (ed.), *Studies in the Economic History of the Middle East* (London, 1970), pp. 193–206; A.C. Wood, *A History of the Levant Company* (Oxford, 1935).

92. Masson, *Histoire*, p. 409; J.K. Heeringa et al. (eds.), *Bronnen tot de geschiedenis van den Levantschen handel*, 6 vols. (The Hague 1917–1967), iii, p. 460.

93. ARA, LH, 265, "Contant reekeninge wegens de lastgelden."

94. H. Wätjen, *Die Niederländer im Mittelmeergebiet zur Zeit ihrer höchste Machtsstellung* (Berlin, 1909), pp. 189–91; this is, however, mainly based on the *tanza* register in the ARA—see ARA, LH, 1, "Resolutieboek Directie," "Tanza op alle scheepen gaende naer de straat"; ARA, LH 267, "Rekeninge van 1 percent op alle scheepen gaende naer de straet in de jaren 1653, 1656, 1684, 1686"; ARA, LH 29, 6 May 1683, fo. 326–28.

95. "Naissance d'une domination: marchands européens et marchands du Levant au XVIII et XIXe siècle," *Cahiers de la Méditerranée* 1975, pp. 145–85.

96. See, for example, ARA, Legatiearchief Smirna, A ii, 18 November 1693, fo. 161–62 vo.; and in same, Smirna consultation, October 1693, fo. 347–49; ARA, LH, 29, 4 June 1682, fo. 233–34.

97. U. Tucci, "Le emissioni monetarie di Venezia e i movimenti internazionale dell'oro," in *Mercanti, navi e monete nel' cinquecento veneziano* (Bologna, 1981), pp. 275–316.

98. Thus, for example, Niebuhr, *Reise*, p. 218, "Man siehet in Yemen fast keine andere Goldmünzen als venetianische Dukaten, Zechini"; an important matter for the currency of Egypt and Yemen was based on a gold standard.

99. Braudel, *The Mediterranean*, i, p. 569. Rather, bullion did not attract goods, as Braudel argues, but quite the opposite: bullion was attracted to the eastern Mediterranean because of the busy traffic there—in grain, raisins, wool, or rice—which did certainly attract the pepper trade too.

100. M. Dan and S. Goldberg, "Le Commerce balkano-levantin de la Transylvanie au cours de la seconde moitié du XVI siècle et au début du XVII siècle," *Revue des études sud-est européennes* 5 (1967), pp. 97–106; A. Maczak, "Der polnische Getreideexport und das Problem der Handelsbilanz," in Hroch, *Der Aussenhandel Ostmitteleuropas*, p. 44; J.M. Malecki, "Die Wandlungen im krakauer und polnischen Handel zur zeit der Türkenkriege des 16 und 17 Jahhunderts," in O. Pickl (ed.), *Die wirtschaftliche Auswirkungen der Türkenkriege* (Graz, 1971), p. 145.

101. H. Sahillioglu, "The Role of International Monetary and Metal Movements in Ottoman Monetary History," in Richards (ed.), *Precious Metals*, p. 289; ARA, St. Gen., Lias Barbarije, 6904, 19 January 1644.

102. M. Fecner, *Torgovlija Russkogo gosudarst'va so stranami vostoka v XVI v.* (Moscow, 1956), pp. 116–24; V.A. Kostsekaev, *Nogaisko-Russkie otnošenija v XV–XVIII vv.* (Alma Ata, 1988), pp. 32–39.

103. A.M. Radzbali, "O mednom zekane v Sefevidskom gosudarst've (XVI–nacale XVIII v.)," in *Azerbaidjan tarikhine dair materiallar* 6 (Baku, 1963), p. 60; W.E.D. Allen, *A History of the Georgian People* (London, 1932), pp. 282–90.

104. A. Attman, *Den Rysska marknaden i det 1500-talets Baltiska politik* (Lund,1944), pp. 115–18; A. Kahan, *The Plow, the Hammer and the Knout: An Economic History of Eighteenth-Century Russia* (Chicago, 1985), p. 229.

105. See H. Inalcik, "Osmanli pamuklu pazari, Hindistan ve Inglitere: Pazar rekabetinde emek maliyetin rolü," *ÖDTU Gelisme Dergisi*, 2 (1979–80), pp. 1–65.

106. See in particular the report by A. Heusden on Golcunda in ARA, St. Gen., Lias VOC, 5737 i, 1651.

107. For the late sixteenth and early seventeenth century see Moosvi, *The Economy of the Mughal Empire*, pp. 373–79; and R.A. Allavi, "New Light on Mughal Cavalry," in *Medieval India: A Miscellany*, ii, Bombay, 1973, pp. 70–99.

108. VOC/OB 1467, "Check of Gamron accountancy," fo. 531–33 vo.; VOC/OB 1464, 11 July 1688, fo. 552.

109. H.L. Rabino di Borgomale, *The Coins and Seals of the Shahs of Iran 1500–1941* (Hertford, 1945), pp. 37–40; W. Hinz, "Die spätmittelalterichen Währungen im Bereich des Persischen Golfes," in C.E. Bosworth (ed.), *Iran and Islam: In Memory of the Late Vladimir Minorsky* (Edinburgh, 1971), p. 304; A. Hotz (ed.), *Journaal der reis van den gezant der O.I. Compagnie Johan Cunaeus naar Perzië* (Amsterdam, 1908), p. 48; VOC/OB 1236, 2 March 1661, fo. 312; VOC/OB 1603, 24 July 1699, fo. 1845–47 vo.; VOC/OB 1349, "Memoir by L. Bent," fo. 1712–13.

110. VOC/OB 1398, 13 October 1685, fo. 639–41 vo.

111. Sahilioglu, "Ottoman Monetary History," p. 287.

112. VOC/OB 1330, 12 August 1677, fo. 971; VOC/OB 1373, fo. 913–14; VOC/OB 1459, 29 April 1690, fo. 1041.

113. VOC/OB 1343, "Copy of a memoir on the present state of the Persian commerce," fo. 60; VOC/OB 1364, "Memoir for Justus van den Heuvel," fo. 368 vo. See, for example, Chick, *Chronicle*, ii, p. 776.

114. Thus, there was a relative lack of *some* coins, namely, coins for export, which explains why there is no evidence for a devaluation of the Safavid currency. See Dale, *Indian Merchants*, p. 27. In addition, the evidence largely comes from hoards, and hoarding—as a special form of saving—has two characteristics, limiting the usefulnes of hoards from the Safavid period as evidence. First, it is unlikely that people would hoard coins of low value, since these are better reserved for daily transactions and are unlikely to be accepted later on. Second, it is also likely that more is hoarded in periods of political instability; in periods of political stability with economic instability, such as the late Safavid period, one is more likely to invest in "safe" land. Thus, hoards from the late Safavid period are both few in number and tend to be confined to "safe" money, which was not devalued.

115. ARA, Coll. van Hoorn van Riebeeck 11 ii, "Specification of sales during the last two years in the town of Mocha."

116. See, for example, Braudel, *Mediterranean*, i, pp. 463–66.

117. VOC/OB 1308, 9 December 1675, fo. 734.

118. C.A. Kindleberger, *Spenders and Hoarders* (New York, 1992).

119. VOC/OB 1659, Surat resolution, 10 May 1701, fo. 365 vo.

120. VOC/OB 1625, 22 November 1698, fo. 6.

121. Klein, "De wereldhandel in edele metalen," p. 196.

122. VOC/UB 871, 7 August 1647, fo. 388.

123. Geleynssen 211, 11 July 1641; Geleynssen 177, 9 August 1641; AHU, Índia, Cx. 11, 148, 3 April 1635.

124. VOC/OB 1454, 27 November 1687, fo. 1331 vo.; VOC/XVII 323, 27 August 1694.

125. VOC/OB 1459, 20 December 1690, fo. 1017; VOC/OB 1464, 6 July 1689, fo. 531 vo.; VOC/UB, 17 August 1688, fo. 1094.

126. VOC/OB 1383, 31 March 1683, fo. 2005 vo.; VOC/XVII 322, October 1686, fo. 391.

127. J.J. Brenning, "Silver in Seventeenth Century Surat: Monetary Circulation and the Price Revolution in Mughal India," in Richards (ed.), *Precious Metals*, p. 481; *English Factories* 1678–1684, p. 151; Kaeppelin, *La Compagnie des Indes*, pp. 175–84, 496; VOC/OB 1549, Surat diary, 24 August 1695, fo. 520 vo.

128. VOC/OB 1649, 20 March 1701, fo. 250–51.

129. VOC/OB 1383, 4 September 1684, fo. 707; VOC/OB 1285, 16 October 1673, fo. 383.

130. F. Martin in Kaeppelin, *La Compagnie des Indes*, p. 42. See van Santen, "Verenigde Oost-Indische Compagnie," p. 257; and I. Habib, "Banking in Mughal India," in T. Raychaudhuri (ed.), *Contributions to Indian Economic History,* 2 vols. (Calcutta, 1960), i, pp. 10–11.

131. VOC/OB 1548, Surat diary, 4 June 1693, fo. 485.

132. VOC/OB 1652, 15 October 1701, fo. 942; Van Dam, *Beschrijvinge*, II, iii, pp. 8–11; VOC/OB 1279, 12 December 1670, fo. 181 vo.; compare on mir Musa in general, S. Subrahmanyam, *Political Economy of Trade* (Cambridge, 1990), pp. 322–27.

133. M. Athar Ali, *The Mughal Nobility Under Aurengzeb* (London, 1966); see K.I. Leonard, "The 'Great Firm' Theory of the Mughal Empire," *Comparative Studies in Society and History* 21 (2) (1979), pp. 151–61, whose argument that the finances of the Mughal empire were not only based upon assignments of the land revenue but also upon the operations of banking houses I would support. This argument does not invalidate J.F. Richards's contention ("Mughal State Finance and the Premodern World Economy," *Comparative Studies in Society and History* 23, 2, [1981], pp. 285–308) that the Mughal empire was largely financed by the land revenue until at least the 1680s, without the need to draw in finances from bankers, because the scope of banking operations expanded and began to include bankers in Golcunda to finance Aurengzeb's campaigns in the Deccan.

134. VOC/OB 1652, 17 May 1701, fo. 948.

135. VOC/OB 1383, "Summary of Surat diary," 30 October 1683; VOC/OB 1388, Surat diary, 23 August 1684; VOC/OB 1529, Surat diary, 4 November 1694, fo. 520 vo.; BNL, FG, Cód. 864, fo. 48 vo. But earlier a major portion of the coins minted at Surat was sent to the court—see VOC/OB 1130, 30 December 1638, fo. 1195.

136. Brenning, "Silver in Seventeenth Century Surat," p. 486; and, according to S. Moosvi's samples of hoards in the United Provinces, the output of the mints of the Mughal empire, and particulary that of Surat, peaked in the eighties of the seventeenth century, a contention VOC material seems to support; VOC/OB 1409, Surat diary, 1 November 1684, fo. 1631; VOC/OB 1425, Surat diary, 11 June 1686, fo. 353; VOC/OB 1635, 14 November 1700, fo. 145.

137. J.F. Richards, *Mughal Administration in Golconda 1687–1724* (Oxford, 1975), p. 125; and in that volume, "Mughal State Finances," pp. 301–4. VOC/XVII 322, 30 September 1689, fo. 542 vo.

138. See van Santen, "Verenigde Oost-Indische Compagnie," p. 103; Gupta, "The Dutch East India Company in Gujarat," pp. 316–18.

139. See Kolff, "An Armed Peasantry," p. 16; and D.E. Streusand, *The Formation of the Mughal Empire* (New Delhi, 1989), p. 40.

140. Wilkes, *Historical Sketches*, ii, p. 54; VOC/OB 1308, 9 December 1675, fo. 734; VOC/OB 1527, 10 October 1692, fo. 416 vo.

141. AHU, Índia, Cx. 34, 10, 23 March 1686; thus, the mahmudi was, contrary to the *communis opinio* among scholars, still in circulation in southern Gujarat in the 1680s—it is likely the coinage of the mahmudi ceased after the Maratha takeover at Ramnagar.

142. Van Santen, "Verenigde Oost-Indische Compagnie," pp. 105–12; VOC/OB 1548, 7 January 1694, fo. 13 vo.

143. VOC/OB 1475, "Invoice *van Spijck*"; VOC/OB 1476, "Invoice *Moercarspel*," fo. 363; 4 May 1691, fo. 276 vo.; 26 July 1690, fo. 276 vo; VOC/OB 1476, 25 October 1687, fo. 313 vo.

144. F. Perlin, "Money-Use in Late Pre-Colonial India," p. 263; VOC/OB 1370, 25 March 1681, fo. 2118; VOC/OB 1379, 1 May 1682, fo. 2344 vo. At the end of the

seventeenth century, though, with the subsiding of the constant warfare in the Konkan, the area increasingly settled on the Belgaum rupee as money of account.

145. VOC/OB 1333, 14 December 1678, fo. 456 vo.; VOC/OB 1329, 17 March 1677, fo. 1331 vo.; VOC/OB 1379, 1 May 1682, fo. 2350 vo.

146. A.P.S. Teixeira de Aragão, *Descrição geral e histórica das moedas cunhadas em nome dos reis, regentes e governadores de Portugal*, 3 vols. (Lisbon, 1874–83), iii, p. 352 AHU, India, Cx. 34.; HAG, LM, 54, 24 January 1690, fo. 9; AHU, Índia, Cx. 34, 80, 24 January 1688; 128, "Propositions on bazarucos."

147. AHU, Índia, Cx. 39 bis, 66, 11 September 1697.

148. N. Steensgaard, "Commodities, Bullion and Services in Inter-Continental Transactions Before 1790," in H. Pohl (ed.), *The European Discovery of the World and Its Economic Effects on Pre-Industrial Society* (Stuttgart, 1990), p. 22.

149. Wink, *Land and Sovereignty Under the Eighteenth Century Maratha Suaraj* (Cambridge, 1989), p. 269.

150. The conflict on Kandahar and occasional forays of Uzbeki and Turkmenian robbers in Khorasan are the exception, yet this violence was common along the overland roads and did not hamper trade for very long.

151. See M. Rossabi, "The 'Decline' of the Central Asian Caravan-Trade," in J.D. Tracy (ed.), *The Rise of Merchant Empire*, 2 vols. (Cambridge, 1990), i, pp. 360–63.

152. Van Santen, "Verenigde Oost-Indische Compagnie," pp. 133. For the Portuguese trade in indigo see AHU, Índia, Cx. 15, 87, 10 December 1645; for the overland trade in indigo, see for example Geleynssen 161, 13 March 1641; 23 November 1641.

153. VOC/XVII 317, 22 September 1648, fo. 114; VOC/XVII 323, 27 August 1694; L.G. Fuentes, *El comercio español con América* (Seville, 1980), pp. 330–2; Chaudhuri, *The Trading World*, p. 330–33; Nachtegaal, "Rijden op een Hollandse Tijger," pp. 177–80. Indigo was cultivated by the VOC at Java after an unsuccessful attempt to plant it at Cape Town.

154. For the indigo trade to Aleppo see in particular GAA, 5060, Coll. Koopmansboeken 154, Anonymous ledgerbook, ca. 1690, containing shipments of indigo both bought from the VOC at Amsterdam to Aleppo, from the Compagnie des Indes from Nantes to Aleppo and Leghorn and from Cadiz to Aleppo and Leghorn; ARA, LH 161 ii, "Tariffà di mercandizie"; VOC 359, "Memoir to the ministers and assistant-ministers."

155. VOC/OB 1241, 22 November 1663, fo. 594; VOC/OB 1434, 31 October 1687, fo. 537 vo.

156. Habib, *Agrarian System*, p. 42; Moreland, *Akbar to Aurengzeb*, pp. 107–9; J.N. Sarkar, *Studies in Economic Life in Mughal India* (Delhi, 1975), pp. 138–47; AHU, Casa da Índia, Cx. 1, "Pauta que fêz o doutor Rodriguês Botelho" (1635); VOC/OB 1246, 29 March 1664, fo. 712; VOC/OB 1476, 25 October 1690, fo. 315; VOC/OB 1620, 9 August 1696, fo. 286.

157. VOC/OB 1273, "Memoir for Andries Bonde," fo. 1802.

158. Habib, *Agrarian System*, p. 46. On the method of preparing indigo in Bayana see F. Pelsaert, *De geschriften van F. Pelsaert over Mughal India. Kroniek en remonstrantie* (H.W. van Santen and D.H.A. Kolff, eds.) (The Hague, *WLV*, 1979), pp. 183–87; and see too the memoir of P. van Henninck on the indigo production in Sarkhej (VOC/OB 1575, "Provisional notices regarding the cultivation and preparation of indigo in Sarkhej"), partly reproduced in van Dam, *Beschrijvinge*, ii, ii, pp. 81–87. It would seem this memorandum was used by the VOC to instruct Javanese peasants in the cultivation of this crop.

159. VOC/OB 1620, 1 July 1697, fo. 289 vo.

160. Van Santen, "De Verenigde Oost-Indische Compagnie," pp. 151–62; VOC/OB 1425, 16 December 1686, fo. 166.

161. VOC/OB 1408, Report by Cornelis Soolmans, fo. 785 vo.

162. See the declarations for payments to laborers in VOC/OB 1470, "Invoice *van Spijk*."

163. Pelsaert, *Kroniek en Remonstrantie*, p. 262; VOC/OB 1649, "Translation of a letter by 17 Armenian merchants," fo. 234–36.

164. VOC/OB 1388, 31 March 1683, fo. 2041 vo.

165. VOC/OB 1475, 26 July 1690, fo. 278 vo.

166. G.D. Sharma (ed.), *Vakil Reports Maharajganj* (New Delhi, 1986), p. 36; VOC/OB 1261, 20 November 1667, fo. 735; VOC/OB 1475, 16 July 1690, fo. 377; VOC/OB 1364, 13 January 1681, fo. 1683 vo.

167. M. Alam, *The Crisis of Empire in Mughal North India: Awadh and the Punjab 1707–1748* (Delhi, 1986), pp. 90–126.

168. VOC/OB 1475, "Passage-and road-dues between Lukhnow and Agra"; H.K. Naqvi, *Urbanisation and Urban Centres in Upper India 1556–1803* (Bombay, 1968). For those who can read Japanese, compare on the markets in the Bayana district H. Nagashima, "Indigo Production and Circulation in North India during the 17th Century: A Study of the Bayana Tract," *The Shirin* 63 (4) (1980), pp. 527–60.

169. R.C. Fox, *King, Clan, Raja and Rule: State-Hinterland Relations in Pre-Colonial India* (Berkeley, 1973).

170. VOC/OB 1549, 16 May 1694, fo. 212 vo.

171. R.P. Rana, "Agrarian Revolts in Northern India During the Late 17th and Early 18th Century," *IESHR*, 18 (3, 4) (1981), pp. 287–326.

172. Van Santen, "Verenigde Oost Indische Compagnie," p. 137; VOC/OB 1379, 16 March 1682, fo. 2474 vo; VOC/OB 1388, 31 March 1683, fo. 2014.

173. See VOC/OB 1475, 26 July 1690, fo. 272 vo.; and in same, "Invoice *Huis Ter Spyck*"; VOC/OB 1649, 30 January 1701, fo. 566.

174. A.S. Beveridge (ed. and trans.), *Babur Nama (Memoirs of Babur)* (London, 1922; Delhi, 1979), p. 550.

175. VOC/OB 1259, 18 May 1667, fo. 77.

176. W.A. Lewis, "Economic Development with Unlimited Supply of Labour," in A.N. Agarawal and S.P. Singh (eds.), *The Economics of Underdevelopment: A Series of Articles and Papers* (London, 1958), pp. 400–49.

177. VOC/OB 1264, 10 March 1667, fo. 565 vo.

178. This is one problem with the argument of P. Parthasarathi, "Rethinking Wages and Competiveness in the Eighteenth Century: Britain and South India," *Past and Present* 158 (1998), pp. 79–110. On the basis of a very few selected figures on wages, and although the contemporary qualitative evidence overwhelmingly suggests that many weavers were very poor, he still concludes these few wages must have presented a much higher real purchasing power than in England. This is in turn explained by a supposed higher productivity of South Indian agriculture. And this again is held to explain the comparative advantages all Indian textiles enjoyed on the world market. Parthasarathi ignores the possibility that wages may not have been a very important component of the prices of textiles, as compared to transport costs, transaction costs, raw material costs, and so forth. He does not separate in any way wages of weavers by regions or clarify what section of the market the weavers were working for. Nor, in fact, is he willing to consider the very clear indications in the sources of frequent famines and relatively widespread malnutrition in South India, which belies the whole argument of South India's

high productivity as compared to England. I guess for the moment Parthasarathi's argument is therefore at best not proven.

179. UBL, BPL, 623, "A brief statement on the present state of the East-India Company" (1724) (anonymous), fo. 367.

180. VOC/OB 1671, "Memoir for Rombout Lefer," fo. 1751; A. Ahmad, *Indo-Portuguese Trade* (New Delhi, 1991), p. 95; AHU, Índia, Cx. 42, 3, "Carregação na nao que deús salve *Nossa Senhora da Conceição*"; according to ARA, HRB, 836, "Notion of Surat's customs," Aurangabad, Bijapur, and Tallegao in 1754 carried on a substantial trade in white and bleached cotton piece-cloth with Surat, as well as in shawls and turbans, receiving other piece-cloth in return. However, Puna, Satara, and Khed mainly specialized in rice, paint, and cotton.

181. AHU, Índia, Cx. 27, 28, 28 January 1666.

182. VOC/OB 1635, 14 November 1700, fo. 33.

183. VOC/OB 1406, 20 May 1684, fo. 962 vo.

184. ARA, HRB, 834, Memoir Zwaardecroon, fo. 34–38; VOC/OB, 1659, Surat Resolution, 6 July 1699, fo. 171–72 vo.; cf. R.P. Schwartz, *Printing on Cotton at Ahmadabad, India, in 1678* (Ahmedabad, 1969).

185. HRB, 836, "Notice on merchandise received"; ARA, K.A. 8448, "Considerations Schreuder"; see K.N. Chaudhuri, *The Trading World*, pp. 238–39, 272–75.

186. See J. Irwin and K.B. Brett, *Origins of Chintz* (London, 1970).

187. See, for example, A.I. Chicerov, *India: Economic Development 16th to 18th Century: Outline History of Crafts and Industry* (Moscow, 1971), pp. 130–37.

188. VOC/OB 1598, 30 April 1697, fo. 127.

189. See, for example, VOC/OB 1625, 17 July 1699, fo. 11–12.

190. Van Santen, "Verenigde Oost-Indische Compagnie," pp. 177–95; ARA, Coll. Hoppe K.A. 8448, "Considerations Schreuder" paragraph 318.

191. VOC/OB 1259, 19 July 1666, fo. 3182; VOC/XVII 332, 15 March 1671.

192. Chaudhuri, *The Trading World*, p. 257.

193. VOC/OB 1280, 29 November 1671, fo. 602 vo.; and in same "Report by Laurens Pyl," fo. 634 vo.; VOC/OB 1527, 19 February 1692, fo. 539. See also D. Kumar, *Land and Caste in South India: Agricultural Labour in the Madras Presidency During the Nineteenth Century* (Cambridge, 1965), p. 88 et seq.

194. AHU, Índia, Cx. 14, 110, "Petição do povo infiel" (1642); VOC/OB 1475, 19 August 1689, fo. 286; and in same, 26 July 1689, fo. 280 vo.; VOC/OB 1620, Report Ketting, fo. 198 vo.

195. F. Perlin, "Proto-Industrialisation and Pre-Colonial South Asia," *Past and Present* 98 (1983), pp. 30–95.

196. See, for example, P. Kriedte, H. Medick, and J. Schlumböhm, *Industrialisierung vor der Industrialisierung* (Göttingen, 1977).

197. Chaudhuri, *The Trading World*, p. 268.

198. Bocarro, "Livro," i, p. 55; A. de Bragança Pereira, *Notas para a história dos portugueses em Damão* (Bastora, 1936), p. 213; BNL, FG, Cód. 10.405, "Discurso apologético," and 46, 60; AHU, Índia, Cx. 38, 77, *Foral* of the Praças do Norte; Bruce, *Annals*, ii, p. 241.

199. One might agree with K. Pomeranz (*The Great Divergence: Europe, China and the Making of the Modern World* [Princeton, 2000], p. 207) that "proto-industrialization" throughout Eurasia itself was a dead-end alley, not leading to industrialization anywhere—but in that case, it was "proto" to what?

200. VOC/OB 1578, 15 August 1693, fo. 143.

201. VOC/OB 1251, "Specification of goods bought by Keval Ram"; VOC/OB 1253, 6 June 1665, fo. 1507.

202. VOC/OB 1373, 26 May 1683, fo. 904–6; VOC/OB 1133, 4 December 1639, fo. 408 vo.

203. Dunlop, *Bronnen*, p. 499.

204. VOC/OB 1132, 20 April 1639, fo. 688 vo.; and in same, 24 December 1639, fo. 524.

205. Chaudhuri, *Trade and Civilisation*, p. 169.

206. *English Factories* 1637–1641, pp. 141–44.

207. The important Armenian community by and large ran its trade from there—AHU, Índia, Cx. 33 bis, 178.

208. A.A. Antonova (ed.), *Russko-Indiskie otnošenija XVIII v.* (Moscow, 1968), p. 76.

209. Van Santen, "Verenigde Oost-Indische Compagnie," p. 65; ARA, Coll. Sweers/Manis 5, "Description of various kingdoms from Golconda right up to Aleppo"; ANTT, Con. d. Gr., Cx., II E, "Advertençia sobre o comérçio de seda," fo. 452.

210. VOC/UB 871, 7 August 1647, fo. 386; ARA, LH, 74, Remonstrantieboek Directie, 14 February 1651, fo. 24.

211. A. Rachmani, *Azerbaidjan v kontse XVI i XVII v.* (Baku, 1974), pp. 176–83; VOC/XVII 319, 5 April 1672; ARA, Legatiearchief Smirna A iii, 14 December 1695, fo. 61 vo.; and in same, "Copy of my letter" etc., fo. 74 vo; VOC/OB 1642, 22 November 1701, fo. 1584.

212. S. Subrahmanyam, "Persians, Pilgrims and Portuguese: The Travails of Masulipatam Shipping in the Western Indian Ocean 1590–1665," *MAS* 22 (3) (1988), pp. 528–30; VOC/OB 1416, 9 April 1685, fo. 1675 vo.; another factor was probably the increase in country trade, since the English often fetched freight—apparently from the nobles at Golcunda—to the ports in the Gulf (*Generale Missiven*, iv, p. 729).

213. Godinho, *Os descobrimentos*, ii, pp. 197–201; J. Bastin, *The Changing Pattern of the Early South-East Asian Spice Trade* (Kuala Lumpur, 1956).

214. ARA, St. Gen., Lias VOC, 5740 ii, "Report by Gysbert Strandwyck."

215. Glaman, *Dutch Asiatic Trade*, pp. 76–83; W.A. Horst, "De peperhandel van de Vereenigde Oost Indische Compagnie," *Bijdragen voor Vaderlandsche Geschiedenis en Oudheidkunde* 8 (3), (1941), pp. 95–101 See ARA, St. Gen., Lias VOC, 5470 ii, Report by Gysbert Strandwyck.

216. ANTT, DRI, 33, 18 February 1636, fo. 246; AHU, Índia, Cx. 13, 10, 8 January 1638—even if discounting the fantastic figures given by Francisco da Costa ("Relatório sobre o tratto da pimenta por Francisco da Costa," in *Documentação ultramarina portuguêsa*, iii, p. 351), which would put the production around 1620 above 10 million pounds.

217. VOC/OB 1398, 9 December 1675, fo. 731.

218. Subrahmanyam, *Political Economy*, pp. 210–25; ANTT, DRI, 48, 8 March 1643, fo. 246 vo.

219. AHU, Índia, Cx. 11 bis, 203, 6 January 1635; AHU, Índia, Cx. 11, 40, 22 February 1633.

220. ANTT, DRI, 37, 6 November 1636, fo. 247; S. Subrahmanyam, "Cochin in Decline 1600–1650: Myth and Manipulation in the Estado da Índia," in R. Ptak (ed.), *Portuguese Asia: Aspects in History and Economy* (Stuttgart, 1987), p. 186. For the Portuguese, *Saraswat* and *mappila* merchants of Matancherri conducted a thriving trade with Jidda, Khisn, Shir, Suqutra, and Mocha under "Moorish" cover as well as a busy

commerce with the Maldives and with Gujarat. Matancherri was a major staple for cowry shells, which Portuguese Indians often fetched to Portugal too; VOC/OB 1210, "Brief representation," fo. 72; Bulhão Pato, *Documetos Remettidos*, ii, p. 12.

221. VOC/XVII 317, 23 September 1649, fo. 142 vo.

222. For Danish sales in Amsterdam see ARA, St. Gen., Lias VOC 5736 ii, "Copy of a contract between W. Leyel and Raimond de Smidt, Jacob Six and Cornelis Simonsz (1638)."

223. Meilink-Roelofs, *Asian Trade*, p. 386.

224. Braudel, *Material Civilisation and Capitalism*, iii, p. 487.

225. VOC/XVII 317, 23 September 1649, fo. 154; VOC/OB 1603, 23 August 1698, fo. 1693.

226. VOC/XVII 318, 18 April 1658, fo. 33; 5 September 1659, fo. 197; VOC/HB 4455, 18 March 1658.

227. H.K. s'Jacob, *De Nederlanders in Kerala* (The Hague, 1976), p. lxvii; K.W. Gunewardena, "A New Netherlands in Ceylon: Dutch Attempts to Found a Colony During Their First Quarter Century of Power in Ceylon," *Ceylon Journal of Historical and Social Studies* 2 (1959), pp. 203–44. There are two excellent biographies of van Goens, neither of which, alas, extends to after 1660: J. Aalbers, *Rykloff Volckertsz van Goens. Commisaris en Veldoverste van de Oost-Indische Compagnie en zijn arbeidsveld in Indië 1653/1654 en 1657/1658* (Groningen, 1916); and J. Ottow, *Rijckloff Volckertsz. van Goens. De carrière van een diplomaat* (Utrecht, 1955).

228. VOC/OB 1593, 10 December 1697, fo. 32.

229. P. van der Werff, "Frontier Poverty: Labour Household Strategies and Limited Economic Circulation in the Foothills of Kerala, India" (Academisch Proefschrift, Gemeenteuniversiteit Amsterdam, 1987), pp. 20–25.

230. ANTT, DRI, 41, 9 August 1638, fo. 23; VOC/OB 1308, 9 December 1675, fo. 733 vo.; VOC/OB 1364, 27 November 1687, fo. 289; VOC/OB 1361, 6 May 1680, fo. 521; VOC/OB 1474, 14 March 1689, fo. 4; VOC/OB 1448, 17 February 1700, fo. 396 vo.

231. VOC/OB 1255, 6 August 1667, fo. 892; s'Jacob, *Nederlanders*, p. 75.

232. A. Das Gupta, *Malabar in Asian Trade*, p. 23; Disney, *A decadênçia*, p. 44; VOC/OB 1528, 27 April 1693, fo. 26–30; VOC/OB 1256, 30 May 1666, fo. 306; AHU, Índia, Cx. 11, 34, 20 February 1635.

233. VOC/OB 1256, 18 May 1667, fo. 82 vo.; VOC/OB 1474, 14 March 1689, fo. 6, 21.

234. ARA Coll. Aanwinsten 1856, "Malabars Woordenboek."

235. BNL, FG, Cód. 301, fo. 3.

236. BNL, FG, Cód. 301, fo. 3 vo.; see S. Bayly, "Hindu Kingship and the Origins of Community: Religion, State and Society in Kerala," *MAS* 18 (2) (1984), pp. 177–213. For some examples of strict rules prohibiting close contact between castes, see, for example, *Travancore Archaeological Series*, vii, p. 28. To mention another example, Ravi Varma said to van Goens that he was permitted "neither to eat nor even to do anything on board a vessel" (VOC/OB 1307, Diary of Ryckloff van Goens, 8 March). Note too that, contrary to the claims of some authors, Europeans in the seventeenth century were well aware of the existence of both *varna* and *jati*.

237. See Dale, *Islamic Society*, p. 13–34; and Miller, *Mappila Muslims*, p. 75.

238. VOC/OB 1256, 16 May 1667, fo. 91; VOC/OB 1474, "Memoir of the chief of Coylan," fo. 417–22 vo. Hadji Osman protected the English at Panani against the VOC,

for unlike the Dutch, the English very much dealt through the network of trade of the *mappilas*.

239. A.N. Thurston, *The Castes and Tribes of the Madras Presidency*, 7 vols. (Madras, 1909–13), iv, pp. 352–66; VOC/OB 1273, 16 May, fo. 1279.

240. ARA, Coll. Aanwinsten 1856, "Malabars woordenboek."

241. Canter Vischer, *Malabarse Brieven*, p. 389.

242. VOC/OB 1652, "A brief relation on pepper by H. Zwaardecroon," fo. 814; M.N. Purosthama, "Saraswats in History with Special Reference to Kerala," *Journal of Kerala Studies* 4 (1) (1977), pp. 75–78; Canter Vischer, *Malabarse brieven*, pp. 388–91; K.P. Padmanabha Menon, *History of Kerala*, 3 vols. (Ernakulam, 1924–37), iii, pp. 609–33.

243. VOC/OB 1254, 15 April 1665, fo.1100 vo.; VOC/OB 1256, 18 June 1667, fo. 312.

244. VOC/OB 1256, 17 January 1667, fo. 14 vo.

245. VOC/OB 1593, fo. pp. 335–41; VOC/OB 1474, 10 August 1690, fo. 146 vo. For the organization of pepper transactions under the Portuguese see Disney, *A decadênçia*, pp. 54–60.

246. VOC/OB 1280, 29 November 1671, fo. 561; VOC/OB 1256, 17 January 1667, fo. 15.

247. VOC/XVII 318, 5 September 1659, fo. 197; VOC/OB 1270, 16 February 1670, fo. 938; VOC/OB 1474, 14 March 1689, fo. 105.

248. VOC/OB 1264, 10 March 1667, fo. 564.

249. VOC/OB 1280, 29 November 1671, fo. 561; VOC/OB 1474, 10 August 1690, fo. 146.

250. K.N. Kurup, "Telicherry Factory: A Case Study in British Colonialism," in *Aspects of Kerala History and Culture* (Trivandrum, 1977), pp. 50–60; J. Brønstedt (ed.), *Vore Gamle Tropenkolonier*, 2 vols., i, *Dansk Ostindien* (Copenhagen, 1967), p. 112; VOC/OB 1559, 25 October 1693, fo. 234; VOC/OB 1665, 5 April 1702, fo. 234.

251. Da Costa, "Relatório," pp. 309–11; but see mainly (for da Costa appears not to be entirely reliable) AHU, Índia, Cx. 23, 89, and AHU, Índia, Cx. 12, 12 (these are the accounts of the first Portuguese East India Company).

252. AHU, Índia, Cx. 13, 2; VOC/UB 932, 16 July 1694, fo.1254; see also H.K. s'Jacob, "State Formation and the Role of Portfolio Investors in Cochin 1663–1700," *Itinerário* 18 (2) (1994), p. 85.

253. VOC/OB 1360, 11 March 1680, fo. 1691 vo.; for the joint-stock Companies of Coromandel see J. Brenning, "Joint-Stock Companies of Coromandel," in Kling and Pearson (eds.), *The Age of Partnership*, pp. 71–94; Arasaratnam, *Merchants, Companies*, pp. 240–47. The discussion on these joint-stock companies on the Coromandel Coast would profit from comparisons with contemporary joint-stock companies among other Indian merchants, such as the Mazanes association in Diu.

254. H.K. s'Jacob, "Nana Parbhu: The Dutch and a Konkani Merchant," in L. Blussé (ed.), "All of One Company: The Biographical Approach to VOC History," *Itinerário*, Special Issue 7 (1986), pp. 92–102.

255. VOC/OB 1268, 12 March 1668, fo. 1095.

256. Baldaeus, *Nauwekeurige Beschrijvinge,* p. 101; VOC/OB 1329, 22 May 1677, fo. 1409; VOC/OB 1355, 24 December 1680, fo. 274.

257. *English Factories* 1670–1677, p. 341.

258. Heeres, *Corpus Diplomaticum*, ii, pp. 323, 270, 261, 207, iii, p. 287, 267, 229.

259. VOC/OB 1245, "Extract from the essay by the Hon. Rijckloff van Goens with marginal notes by Hustaert."

260. See, for example, KITLV, H. 49, "Malabar's interest"; and VOC/OB 1434, 13 December 1679, fo. 461.

261. VOC/OB 1333, 14 December 1678, fo. 454.

262. VOC/OB 1370, 25 March 1681, fo. 2076; VOC/OB 1270, 16 February 1670, fo. 939 vo.; VOC/OB 1329, 17 March 1677, fo. 1411 vo.; VOC/OB 1360, 23 February 1680, fo. 1791–93: Nor did the VOC's "overwhelming weaponry" frighten English interlopers a great deal. See, for instance, the case of the *Scipio Africanus*, who bought pepper in Cochin from the *rajadores* there without the Dutch being able to do much about it (VOC/OB 1396, fo. 665).

263. VOC/OB 1343, 18 October 1679, fo. 425; VOC/XVII 323, 27 August 1694.

264. s'Jacob, *Nederlanders*, pp. lxx–ii.

265. VOC/XVII 321, 8 June 1682, fo. 64 vo.

266. VOC/OB 1383, fo. 678 vo.; VOC/OB 1379, 1 May 1682, fo. 2364.

267. AHU, Índia, Cx. 29 bis, 171, Anonymous memorandum 1673; VOC/OB 1261, 12 July 1668, fo. 775; ARA, HRB, 876, "Instruction for Huybert de Lairesse"; VOC/OB 1279, 21 June 1671, fo. 1019 vo. The traders from Kerala at Muscat threatened they would boycott the town if the imam permitted the Dutch to trade there, a threat that to all appearences was taken quite seriously by its *vali;* see VOC/OB 1295, 5 January 1673, fo. 479 vo. VOC 1527, "Extract on money due by the Company at Cananore."

268. C.H. Wake, "The Changing Pattern of Europe's Pepper and Spice Imports," *Journal of European Economic History* 47 (3) (1975), pp. 512–19; ANTT, SV, 14, 15 March 1605, fo. 163; Geleynssen 287, 20 October 1645, fo. 234.

269. Glamann, *Dutch Asiatic Trade*, p. 104.

270. See, for example, VOC/XVII 318, 5 September 1659, fo. 200.

271. VOC/UB, 21 October 1682, fo. 1203–4 vo.; VOC/OB 1279, "A memoir on what could be sold at Basra," fo. 461; see also VOC/UB 876, 17 September 1652, fo. 661 vo.

272. VOC/OB 1379, 2 October 1681, fo. 2634–5; VOC/OB 1373, 28 August 1683, fo. 996.

273. VOC/OB 1625, fo. 123, 127, 131; VOC/OB 1279, fo. 462.

274. A passage commented upon in details in A. Sergio's classic, *Breve interpretação de história de Portugal* (Lisbon, 1975), pp. 42–44.

275. See in this respect the considerations of Julião de Campos Barros in AHU, Índia, Cx. 11 bis, 203.

276. VOC/OB 1150, "Note on what profits might be earned on cargoes sold"; Geleynssen 319, 17 September 1642.

277. ANTT, SV, 14, 15 March 1605, fo. 163; A.H. Lybyer ("The Ottoman Turks and the Routes of Oriental Trade," *English Historical Review* 30 [4] [1915], pp. 585–87) already made the point for the opposite end of the Levant trade that it continued because it involved far more products than only pepper, but this is oddly still an ignored position. Most of the literature instead focuses on political and military reasons for the Portuguese failure to control the pepper trade. See for the traditional military-political position, for example, G. Bouchon, "Sixteenth Century Malabar," in Pearson and Das Gupta (eds.), *India and the Indian Ocean*, p. 182.

278. See the lament of the Spanish king in ANTT, SV, 14, 15 March 1605 fo. 163 vo.

279. See Das Gupta, *Malabar in Asian Trade*; S. Subrahmanyam, "Cochin in Decline," p. 186.

280. Both sources and literature on this topic are rather scarce relative to the massive amounts available for the Atlantic slave trade; however, see J.C. Armstrong, "Madagascar

and the Slave Trade in the Seventeenth Century," *Omaly sy Anio* 23/24 (1986), pp. 211–35; and G. Campbell, "Madagascar and the Slave Trade 1810–1895," in same, pp. 279–311.

281. See M. Mollat, "Les Contacts historiques de l'Afrique et de Madagascar avec l'Asie du Sud et du Sud-est et le rôle de l'Océan Indien," *Archipel* 21 (1981), p. 40.

282. *COACM*, ii, p. 194.

283. AHU, Moç., Cx. 2, 102, "Petition to Luís de Mendonça Furtado, the protector of the people of Mozambique"; VOC/OB 1291, Report Willemsen, fo. 565; VOC/OB 1323, 12 February 1678, fo. 676; Theal, iii, p. 497; for the nineteenth-century destination of slaves compare R. Austen, "The 19th Century Islamic Slave Trade from East Africa (Swahili and Red Sea Coast): A Tentative Census," in W.G. Clarence Smith (ed.), *The Economics of the Indian Ocean Slave Trade in the Nineteenth Century* (London, 1989), p. 26

284. See, for example, A.G.B. Fisher and H.J. Fisher, *Slavery and Muslim Society in Africa* (New York, 1971), p. 116. And slaves were used for "reproductive purposes" outside of the household, for in Yemen African slave girls were normally used as prostitutes.

285. VOC/OB 1625, "Report by N. Welters," fo. 159–61; VOC/OB 1209, "Memoir of bania and Moorish ships arriving at Surat 1654–1655," fo. 456–459; C.G. Brouwer, "Die Madagascar 'Connection': Holländische Beiträge zur Erforschung der Yemenitische Sklavengeschichte," *Orientations: A Multidisciplinary Annual of the Dutch Association for Middle Eastern and Islamic Studies* (1992), pp. 56–86.

286. In the nineteenth century Ethiopian slaves were still more than twice as expensive as slaves from Zanzibar; F. Cooper, *Plantation Slavery on the East Coast of Africa* (New Haven, 1977), p. 35.

287. J. Pinto, *Slavery in Portuguese India* (Bombay, 1992); Wycki, *O Livro*, p. 297.

288. N.A. Smirnov, *Politika Rossii na Kavkaze v XVI–XIX vekac* (Moscow, 1958), p. 20.

289. AHU, Índia, Cx. 40, 28, 12 December 1696.

290. ARA, Coll. van Hoorn van Riebeeck 12, "Description of Mocha."

291. C.M. Eastman, "Wạnawaka, Watumwa na Wageni: African Cultural Influences in the Formation of the Northern Swahili," Paper presented to 29th annual meeting of the African Studies Association, Madison, 30 October–2 November 1986, p. 20.

292. Leitão, *Os dois descobrimentos*; ANTT, DRI, 57, Suit against Julio Moniz, fo. 318.

293. *Generale Missiven*, i, p. 450.

294. J.C. Vrijmans, *Slavenhalers en slavenhandel* (Kampen, 1937), p. 106; Van Dam, *Beschrijvinge*, I, ii, p. 652; *Dagregister*, 1656, p. 292; *Generale Missiven*, iv, p. 747; VOC/OB 3993, "Diary of the *Hasselt*," fo. 751–92; VOC/RXVII 220, 3 February 1670; 19 October 1676.

295. R. Elphick, *Kraal and Castle: Khoikoi and the Founding of White South Africa* (London, 1977); A.J. Böeseken, *De Nederlandse commissarisen aan de Kaap 1657–1700* (The Hague, 1938), pp. 63–65; VOC/OB 3997, "Instruction for the *Waterhoen*," fo. 911–14 vo.; VOC/XVII 317, 16 August 1646, fo. 57 vo.; VOC/OB 1432, "Regiments for sailing to Madagascar," fo. 428.

296. E. Hesse, *Goldbergwerke auf der Küste Sumatras* (S.C. Honoré Nabré ed.) (The Hague, 1931).

297. VOC/OB 1434, 30 April 1687, fo. 817 vo.; Van Dam, *Beschrijvinge*, I, ii, pp. 658–60.

298. S. Pieters (ed. and trans.), *Memoir of Zwaardecroon* (Colombo, 1911), p. 21; VOC/RXVII 215, 11 August 1692.

299. Bruce, *Annals*, iii, p. 165; *Gazetteer Bombay*, ii, pp. 255–57; Holden Furber, *Bombay Presidency in the Mid-Eighteenth Century* (Bombay, 1967), p. 6; J. Bastin, *The British in Western Sumatra* (London, 1965), pp. 88–91.

300. VOC/OB 4013, "Diary *Voorhouten*," 10 August 1686.

301. VOC/OB 4026, "Rolle des servants de Pondicherry."

302. VOC/RGGR 664, 11 September 1642.

303. Slaves were occasionally fetched by their proud owners from Batavia to the Netherlands, a practice prohibited by the Gentlemen XVII since witnessing that actual slavery offended the sensitivities of the Dutch population. But it is uncertain whether this also concerned Malagasy slaves—VOC/XVII 321, 6 April 1685, fo. 233.

304. Lequin, "Het personeel," i, pp. 177–80; N. Worden, *Slavery in Dutch South Africa* (Cambridge, 1985), p. 117; R. Ross, *Cape of Torments: Slavery and Resistance in South Africa* (London, 1983).

305. VOC/CR 9292, 15 September 1681.

306. H.P. Janish (ed.), *Selections from St. Helena Records* (St. Helena, 1885), pp. 53, 75.

307. An earlier version of this paragraph appeared as "Slaving on the Malagasy Coast," in S. Evers and M. Spindler (eds.), *Civilisations de Madagascar: Flux et reflux des influences* (Leiden, 1995), pp. 137–57.

308. VOC 10811, Diary of the *Soldaat*, 19 December 1696.

309. Not only in the seventeenth but also in the eighteenth century, for which see P. Cultru, *Madagascar au XVIIIème siècle. Benyowski* (Paris, 1936).

310. D. Feraud, *Du paludisme à Madagascar* (Montpelier, 1887).

311. H. Deschamps, *Histoire de Madagascar* (Paris, 1959), pp. 106–9; the Sakalava court at Boina is described in VOC 10811, "Diary of the *Soldaat*," 21 January 1696.

312. J. de Buqoi on the Tongas, Theal, vi, p. 434; C. Meillassoux, *Femmes, greniers et capitaux* (Paris, 1975). On the importance of the barter of women to Sakalava politics, see S. Godefroit, "Reflexions sur la nation de royauté sacré à Madagascar. L'exemple du Sakalava de Menabe," *Studia Africana* 9 (1998), pp. 159–73; R. Jaovelo Dzao, "Funérailles royales chez les Sakalaves du nord de Madagascar," *Omaly sy anio* 25 (1987), pp. 9–19.

313. Leitão, *Os dois descobrimentos*, p. 201.

314. VOC/OB 3998, Diary Blanck, 16 July 1664; Étienne de Flacourt also described this state, *COACM*, ix, pp. 125–32; A. Grandidier, *Histoire politique et coloniale de Madagascar*, iii, *Histoire des peuples autre que les Merinas* (Paris, 1915), pp. 77–84.

315. VOC/OB 3998, Diary Blanck, 18, 21 July 1664, see Mondain, *Histoire des tribus de l'Imoro*, pp. 133–45.

316. VOC/OB 3998, Diary Blanck, 18 July, 20 July 1668.

317. R. Challet (ed. and trans.), *Histoire des Rois. Tantaran'ny adriana*, 3 vols. (Antananarivo, 1972–74), i, p. 461.

318. See Leitão, *Os dois descobrimentos*, p. 297: "e tocam de branco se acham alguns" [in Masalagache in 1613] "que são trazidos do reino de Uva, que é o sertão e mais interior a terra e vêm a vender a Mazalagacem aos mouros de costa de Melinde."

319. VOC/OB 1237, Report de Swart, fo. 280.

320. The impact of firearms on African society is a very controversial issue in the literature; see, for example, R. Beachy, "The Arms Trade in East Africa in the Late Nineteenth Century," *JAH* 3 (1962), pp. 451–67; G. White, "The Impact of Fire-Arms

on Africa: An Introduction," *JAH* 18 (2) (1977), pp. 173–84; and R. Kea, "Firearms and Warfare on the Slave and Gold Coast from the Sixteenth to the Nineteenth Century," *JAH* 12 (2) (1971), pp. 185–213.

321. *Tantara*, i, p. 655.

322. Ibid., i, p. 557.

323. Kent, *Early States*, pp. 27–29; C.C. Berg, "The Sacrev Musket: Tactics, Technology and Power in Eighteenth Century Madagascar," *Comparative Studies in Society and History* 27 (2) (1985), pp. 261–79, and according to Bloch, "the slave trade mode of production" is a separate way of organizing society that does not arise because of any external pressure—M. Bloch, "Mode of Production and Slavery in Madagascar: Two Case Studies," in J.L. Watson, *African and Asian Systems of Slavery* (Oxford, 1980), pp. 100–34. But the consensus amongt the *malgachisants* is now that Madagascar did not have a "slave trade mode of production" since the overwhelming bulk of the Malagasy peasantry (more than 80 percent, Campbell estimates) was free, though of subordinate (*fanompoana*) status. Slave labor in the nineteenth century appears to have been confined to domestic work, some plantations, producing goods for export, and to notoriously unruly communities. Slavery would thus appear to have been rather a "mode of dominance" than a "mode of production" (see L. Mosca, "La schiavitu e la sua abolizione nel Madagascar," *Africa: Instituto Italiano per l'Africa e l'Oriente* 52 [4] [1997], pp. 497–535).

324. Gray and Marks, "Southern Africa and Madagascar," p. 463.

325. G. Campbell, "The Structure of Trade in Madagascar 1750–1823," *IJAHS* 26 (1) (1993), pp. 111–48.

326. AHU, Moç., Cx. 2, 102, "Petition to Luís de Mendonça Furtado."

327. Leitão, *Os dois descobrimentos*, p. 219; and Kent, *Early States*, p. 198.

328. COACM, v., p. 84.

329. Ibid. These Dutch beads have been found in substantial quantities in Antongil Bay. W. van der Sleen, *A Handbook on Beads* (Liege, 1967), pp. 80–90.

330. VOC 10811, "Diary *Soldaat*," 16 December 1696; For among the Sakalava the king is given a new name after his death, with the old name then being taboo.

331. J. Bron de Vexela, "Voyage à Madagascar et aux Comores," *Revue d'Orient*, ix (1846), p. 331, quoted in Verin, *History of Civilisation*, p. 398.

332. VOC/OB 1237, Report de Swart 662, fo. 273, Allen, *Swahili Origins*, p. 203; see also Mondain, *L'histoire*, p. 185; and Kent, *Early States*, p. 90.

333. Martin, *Comores*, i, p. 35; Martin, "Arab Migrations," p. 198.

334. VOC/OB 4021, "Brief relation of Anjuani," fo. 655.

335. M.D.D. Newitt, "The Comoro Islands in Indian Ocean Trade Before the 19th Century," *Cahiers d'Études Africaines* 23 (1983), pp. 139–65; G. Shepperd, "The Comorians and East African Slave Trade," in Watson (ed.), *African and Asian Systems*, pp. 73–89; ANTT, DRI, 40, 23 August 1637, fo. 263 vo.; and in same, 14 April 1637, fo. 257. On the revolt of 1634 in Mombasa see C.S.P. Freeman Grenville, *The Mombasa Rising Against the Portuguese 1634: From Sworn Evidence* (London, 1980).

336. ANTT, DRI, 40, loc. cit.; VOC/HB 4456, 14 April 1671.

337. Verin, *History of Civilisation*, pp. 96–103.

338. Leitão, *Os dois descobrimentos*, p. 309, 288.

339. VOC/OB 4022, "Brief description of Maselagache"; see also P. van Dam, *Beschrijvinge*, I, ii, p. 605; *COACM*, ii, pp. 325–28.

340. See Drury, *Madagascar*, pp. 277–85; Leitão, *Os dois descobrimentos*, p. 234.

341. Leitão, *Os dois descobrimentos*, p. 205; Pearson, *Port Cities and Intruders*, p. 123; ANTT, DRI, 40, 23 August 1637, fo. 263 vo.

342. See the map of southern Madagascar in ARA, Kaartenzaal, De Graaf 9, where an insert reads, "This area is dangerous because of crocodiles."

343. VOC/OB 4023, "Diary *Jambi*," 6 October.

344. VOC/OB 1396, 18 May 1684, fo. 714.

345. VOC/RXVII 220, 19 September 1685; Van Dam, *Beschrijvinge*, I, ii, p. 659; VOC/OB 4022, "Instructions *Westerwijk*," fo. 4087.

346. VOC/OB 4022, "Instruction *Westerwijck*," fo. 487.

347. See J. Postma, *The Dutch Participation in the Slave Trade: Slaving on the Guinea Coast* (Cambridge, 1981), pp. 227–58.

348. VOC/OB 4018, "Diary of James Barry regarding a trip in the *Philips* from New York to Madagascar," 27 April 1687; VOC/OB 4013, "Diary of the *Voorhouten*," 18–20 June 1676; VOC/OB 4022, "Diary of Barlow," 12 July, 13 July.

349. VOC/OB 4043, "Declaration of Jan Caen," fo. 822–24 vo.

350. VOC/OB 4012, "Diary *Voorhouten*," 14 June 1676.

351. VOC/OB 4022, "Diary *Jambi*," 25 August 1686.

352. VOC 10125, "Diary *Ter Aa*," 25 August 1705.

353. VOC 10812, "Diary *Ter Aa*," 25 August 1705.

354. VOC 10811, "Diary *Soldaat*," 18 January 1696; VOC 10812, "Diary *Ter Aa*," 29 August 1705, see too Deschamps, *Histoire des peuples autre que les Merina*, p. 46.

355. D. Defoe, *A General History of the Robberies and Murders of the Most Notorious Pirates of the English Nation* (M. Schlumhorn ed.) (Columbia, 1972), p. 529.

356. VOC/OB 4012, "Diary *Voorhouten*," 9 August 1676.

357. VOC/OB 4023, "Diary *Jambi*," 8 August 1686.

358. VOC/OB 4018, "Diary James Bary," 15 July 1682; VOC/OB 4023, "Diary *Jambi*," 17 August 1686.

359. VOC 10812, "Diary *Ter Aa*," 27 August 1705.

360. VOC/OB 4023, "Diary *Jambi*," 29 August 1686.

361. VOC/OB 4023, "Diary *Jan en Marie*," 1705 fo. 859.

362. VOC/OB 4017, "Diary *Sillida*," 3 August 1682; VOC 10811, "Diary *Soldaat*," 17 December 1696.

363. VOC/OB 4009, "Diary *De Pijl*," 30 December 1672; *Dagregister* 1681, p. 59.

364. VOC/OB 4029, 18 April 1687, fo. 35; Van Dam, *Beschrijvinge*, I, ii, p. 666; Worden, *Slavery*, pp. 46, 158.

365. See M. De Lannoy, *The Kulasekhara Perumals of Travancore: History and State Formations in Travancore from 1671 to 1758* (Leiden, 1997).

366. See, for example, the cautious assertion of I. Habib ("Population," in *Cambridge Economic History of India*) that India's population might have grown by 0.45 percent yearly in the seventeenth century. Subrahmanyam denies this, arguing that as the European population was growing more rapidly, Indian population should have grown more rapidly too. Yet—as we saw—Indian agriculture was subject to severe ancien-régime-type food crises, which in this monsoon climate may have been worse than in Europe. For Europe, see W. Abel, *Massenarmut und Hungerkrisen im vorindustriellen Europa* (Hamburg, 1974). And, in fact, there is plenty of evidence for devastating famines on the Coromandel Coast in the period covered by Subrahmanyam; see J. Schurhammer, *Die zeitgenössische Quellen zur Geschichte portugiesisch Asien und seine Nachbahrstaaten zur Zeit des heiligen Franz Xaviers* (Freiburg, 1956), p. 354, or ARA, St. Gen.,

Lias VOC, 5739 i, Report by Jacobus Cauw, 22 December 1666. Such famines probably held the growth of the population in check.

367. See the essays collected in T. Ashton (ed.), *Crisis in Europe 1550–1650* (London, 1964); and G. Parker and L. Smith (eds.), *The General Crisis of the Seventeenth Century* (London, 1978).

368. See the capable, but not entirely fair, discussion in Subrahmanyam, *Political Economy*, p. 3.

369. *Revolutions and Rebellions in the Early Modern World* (Berkeley, 1991), p. 459.

370. G.M. Udalova, *Yemen v period pervogo osmanskogo zavoevanija* (Moscow, 1988). On the issue of the "crisis of the Ottoman empire," see my "Braudel, the Ottoman Empire and the Mediterranean," paper read at 6th conference of the World History Association, Pamplona, 1996. On the somewhat careless ease with which many historians are able to discern "crises" in Islam, see, for example, Risso, *Merchants and Faith*, p. 67, who argues that a "crisis" involving the "breakdown of order" in Islam apparently lasted from the 1590s up to 1723. Either Islam was, thus, always in crisis, or Risso mistakes the normal political bargaining with use of force in Islam for a "breakdown of order."

371. See G. Lewis, *The French Revolution: Rethinking the Debate* (London, 1993), p. 110.

372. *The Beginnings of Western Economic Dominance*, p. 216.

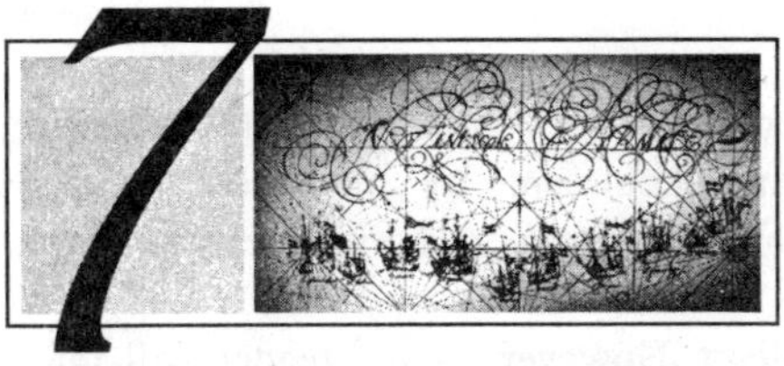

# 7 O Estado da Índia

## European Trade to Asia: General Remarks

Even though the Europeans were allotted privileges exempting them from the law of the realm by indigenous states, such concessions were to be affirmed by the regular display of military prowess. The way in which the Europeans cashed "protection rent" is thus a crucial issue when studying the history of the Europeans in the Arabian seas. No doubt, one may criticize Steensgaard's theory on the "internalization of protection costs" by the Companies on points of detail, but the brunt of this argument has well withstood criticism.[1] The VOC, the EIC, and, to an extent, the Compagnie des Indes included their overhead costs—armies, navies, and administrations—in the costs of products sold in Europe. This was not the case for the Portuguese.

Like most other writers, Steensgaard perceives the chartered Companies as trade organizations. That is, however, only partly true. In Europe the Companies were merchants; in Asia they were states. The Companies were endowed with a monopoly of force and legitimacy within the area covered by their charter. The trade with Europe was based on the state in Asia, but the Company as a state and tax gatherer and the Company as a merchant did not have the same interests.

The state conducted trade by a bureaucratic arrangement, particularly in the case of the VOC. This arrangement was based on "rational" calculation in the sense of M. Weber, estimating profit and loss at the main office, preferably by assessing expenditure and returns in advance. And the VOC may well be called a rational bureaucracy according to Weber's definition. The officials were not to use their office for personal enrichment, had a clearly delimited competence, were responsible for neatly defined tasks, and were named according to their merit.[2]

What was the background of this bureaucratic arrangement? In the seventeenth century the emergent national states had to exploit the resources of world trade for their own benefit: they had to create institutions to protect trade and production on the one hand, and to generate revenues by excises and the farming of taxes on the other. States tried to attract commerce by the use of force and to centralize and control commerce by a system of monopolies run by a bureaucracy.

This policy may be called mercantilism. However, as the reader will infer from the cautious "may," a considerable amount of terminological bewilderment surrounds this word. This particularly relates to two points: First, is this mercantilism an "ism"—a consistent doctrine—or was it rather a series of impromptu arrangements? And second, does the term not suggest a larger leverage of the state in Europe than it really had? One may use the word but with due caution.[3]

Under mercantilism I understand a loose set of notions and a practice. The basic notion is that the advantages of commerce should accrue to one's own nation. The total amount of trade and production of manufactured products will always remain relatively constant, it was assumed, for both are based on the stock of precious metal in circulation, and the ratio of precious metal to the total amount of economic activity will remain the same, it was argued. Hence, an injection of more bullion will only lead to inflation, a decrease of the amount to deflation. Since gains are by definition unequally divided among countries, a country may hand trade and production to state monopolies in order to further its industry and commerce, and it may heavily tax the commerce of the competitors. The practice—only slightly linked to the doctrine—was a system of monopolies, imposts, and tax farms to exploit the benefits of trade and manufacture.

The East India Companies, an essential part of the mercantilist system—in many ways its crowning institutional achievement—may be seen as institutions to bridle and tax commerce to the benefit of the dominant elites of the state and to the disadvantage of merchants not connected to the elite. But while they were committed to the aim of effecting far-reaching bureaucratic control, they were particularly apt to be embroiled in conflicts with interlopers and tussles between the directors of the Companies and their personnel. One may well extend the term "institutionalized corruption"—which Steensgaard reserves for the Estado—to the institutions of the Companies as well.

To explain this tense relationship between the Companies or the Estado and their own servants we may refer to the theories of J. van Klaveren on the links between corruption and mercantilism.[4] We are best served by a broad definition: Corruption is the exploitation of public revenues by civil servants for their own use. Officials, van Klaveren argues, conceived offices as a service sold to their customers—somebody needing some benefit from the state—and they did so for a fixed fee, as they enjoyed a monopoly on this service. In neoclassical terms, the officials were "seeking rent." Mercantilism may then be perceived as but corruption or "rent seeking" writ large: a system of regulations "to transfer benefits to the dominant groups of the state. All fiscal concerns were characterized by a preoccupation with tribute to allow such a transference."[5]

As among any band of pirates—as we shall see—the division of loot depended on a system of loyalty. One was rewarded with the possibility of gathering perquisites for one's own use, rather than a salary. Yet one was supposed to abide by rigid bureaucratic criteria that prohibited or inhibited private enrichment.

In their search for rent obtained from monopolies there is little to distinguish the Companies from the Portuguese.[6] The Estado da Índia was as much a rent-seeking society as were the Companies. But in the Portuguese case it was private entrepreneurs that were seeking rent, rather than a centralized organization.

The state might therefore languish while its own officials swallowed its incomes, and this was certainly the case in Portugal. For, seen from the perspective of the central authorities, the conditions in the Portuguese colonies were downright disastrous. The Conselho Ultramarino was moved to write in 1673:

> Reviewing the lamentable condition we are in, the councilors are reminded of those crofters who by the whim of fortune are allotted a small stretch of ground, plant their seeds and if their land is ruined have to move to another patch of soil which can feed them.[7]

Yet, miraculously, the Portuguese empire did not totter and fall but continued to exist, if much reduced in geographic compass. Often, perhaps too often, it has been demonstrated why the Estado lost the fight with the Companies. There is nothing very mysterious about this. After the restoration of the Portuguese monarchy Portugal had to fight much more powerful adversaries. The monarchy was struggling with a chronic lack of funds. It was enmeshed in a bitter conflict with Spain; mercenaries had to be hired abroad, (war) ships bought in England and the Netherlands. Because of deficient production in Portugal and Madeira, large amounts of grain had to be purchased in the Baltic and England. Not surprisingly, the problem facing the Portuguese exchequer was that throughout the seventeenth century the Portuguese balance of payments was negative. This, as the Portuguese diplomat and economist Duarte Ribeiro de Machedo argued, had fatal consequences. "Since we need foreign products the foreigners can determine the price of our merchandise."[8]

The foreigners did not need Portuguese products, Ribeiro de Machedo observed, so any attempt to raise the price of products would either result in a drastic drop in imports or the substitution of Portuguese goods by those produced elsewhere. And indeed, the two major sources of revenue of the crown—the salt of Setubal and Brazilian sugar—were suffering from foreign competition from France and Spain and from the Caribbean, respectively. Yet they were forced to sell those products cheaply. For if they did not do so, "the conquests will be lost, which are only preserved because of their sale." The colonies thus did not benefit but burdened the Portuguese economy, Ribeiro de Machedo argued. It was necessary to sell colonial products to obtain at least some benefits from the colonies and not possible to impose tariffs on imports, as this would scare away the purchasers of colonial products. Therefore, the country was flooded by cheap manufactured goods that crushed domestic manufacture.

As has often been argued, the Portuguese position was hence typically that of what I. Wallerstein would label a "semi-peripheral country." Portugal was able to impose low monopoly prices on the producers of sugar in Brazil—or earlier, to some extent, in India—but did not control the final market for those products. Thus, the more cheaply they sold them the less these products were worth compared to the imports; the more expensively they sold them the larger the possibility other and cheaper suppliers would enter the market.[9]

Discussions on Portuguese foreign trade in the second half of the seventeenth century would inevitably focus on Brazilian sugar rather than on Indian products. The focus of Portuguese trade shifted from the Indian Ocean to the South Atlantic with the loss of the monopoly on the trade via the Cape. There is an ongoing debate about the precise date of this shift. Personally, I would opt for the mid-twenties, after the fall of Hormuz.[10] But whatever the date, when after 1663 an East Indiaman dropped anchor at Belém together with 80 or 90 ships from Brazil, the Indiaman would be worth commenting upon, since this had become a rare sight indeed.

"The cause is that the people who make such a journey obtain this little profit. And, therefore, economists say that if the kingdom was to rely upon the self-interest of traders it would lose more than it would gain," commented A. Paixão, author of the tract "Monstrosities of Time and Providence" (*Monstruosidades do tempo e da fortuna*) in 1680: a libel most appropriately titled for the gloomy atmosphere of the times.[11] But the modest size of trade with Portugal does not justify the common reference to the Estado da Índia after 1663 as being "in decay." In histories of Portugal, India in the seventeenth century is mostly considered in a few lines, while taking pride of place in the historiography on the sixteenth.[12]

For after all, in spite of its reduced trade with Portugal, in our period the Estado was still a great power in the Arabian seas. The Portuguese still owned major centers of trade like Bassein, Goa, and Daman. Goa and the Praças do Norte were the only European territorial possessions in the Arabian seas. And there were still the huge conquests in Mozambique, of course. It is indeed ironic that while everybody—then and now—considered the seventeenth century its "period of decline," the Portuguese empire in the Arabian seas reached its greatest territorial extent ever. The common perspective on the seventeenth century as a century of decline has also obscured the fact that after 1663 Portuguese private trade within Asia revived. In the seventeenth century the Estado was, rather than decadent, simply different from the Portuguese empire in the sixteenth century. This is so mainly in two ways:

First, the Estado changed, as A.R. Disney has noted, after the Persian conquest of Hormuz from a society of warriors and sailors to one of peasants and landlords.[13] This not only applies to Mozambique; in India as well the incomes of nobles, government, and church shifted from imposts on trade to taxes levied on peasant communities. For instance, in 1684 the Maratha armies had occupied "all the villages" in Bardes, Salcete, and most of the Bassein countryside "and we have lost all our incomes," the Conselho Ultramarino bewailed—maritime customs were not worth consideration, it seems.[14] Furthermore, the intra-Asian trade of the Estado shifted from trade in exotic goods like cinnamon and nutmeg to agrarian bulk products like wood, rice, and arrack, mainly obtained from the territorial possessions.

While trade—with the metropolis in particular—declined, the territorial possessions in India increased in size. By 1690 the territory of the Estado covered about 6,800 square miles, of which 2,400 were located in Goa. From 1684 to 1688 new territory in Praças do Norte was conquered (near the Serra de Agacerim) and Nagar Haveli near Daman. Not only did the Portuguese thus acquire the passes leading from the sea to the Deccan, but a sizeable agrarian population, which may be estimated at 30,000 people, was added to Portuguese territory as well.[15]

Second, as we shall see below, the Estado became a virtually independent economic and political system, which developed almost apart from the home country. Portuguese trade networks became interwoven with those of Indian, Arab, and other European merchants.

## The Portuguese Administrative System

The Estado is sometimes seen as a "feudal" organization—contrary to the "capitalist" Companies. This is true in many respects. Basic institutions of the Estado were framed on feudal law, such as *foros* and *prazos*. However, one often implies with the word *feudal* that Portuguese (or *a fortiori* Iberian) expansion was an "earlier" or "less articulate" form of European expansion than was northwest European expansion. This is somewhat beside the point, as is rightly emphasized by A.P. Meilink-Roelofs.[16] The use of the terminology of feudal law by the Portuguese does not exclude the capitalist calculation of profit and loss but rather implied it: fiefs were generally bought and sold. The terminology in which Portuguese institutional arrangements were couched has a somewhat archaic, feudal hue as compared to the Companies, but this should not obscure the fact that the content of this institutional language was capitalist and modern.

In view of the confusion reigning supreme during the Habsburg period, when the responsibility for Indian affairs appertained to several overlapping councils, in 1643 all overseas possessions were brought under the supervision of the Conselho Ultramarino. This council offered written advice to the king, which was generally heeded. Matters concerning the nomination of personnel and legislation in the colonies were entrusted to the Conselho Ultramarino. However, the Admiralty was responsible for escorting Indiamen from the Azores to Lisbon to guard them against the Barbary pirates. The East India House (Casa da India), which resorted under the Conselho da Fazenda, was responsible for fitting out sails and the trade in monopoly products of the crown. Private goods and bills of exchange had to be cleared at the Casa da Índia. In the Habsburg period the Casa da Índia still conducted an extensive trade in monopoly products of the crown. But at the end of the seventeenth century it was merely a branch of customs, which taxed goods received from the Orient.[17]

This conciliar system might lead to lengthy arguments between different councils, mainly between the Conselho da Fazenda and Conselho Ultramarino. It might lead to lengthy administrative delays too. Yet the system was simpler in practice than it was on paper, for most important decisions were taken by a group of mutually related councilors. And various persons with long experience in Asia—like the Count of Alvor and Antônio Pães de Sande—had an important, probably decisive, say in decisions taken by the Conselho Ultramarino. All too often, though, advice from Portugal arrived in India late or never, due more to communication problems than to bureaucratic inertia or incapacity.

India and Brazil were both ruled by a viceroy, named by the crown for a three-year term. In general the crown took the merits of aspirants to office well into consideration. Some viceroys, like the Counts of Linhares and of Alvor, can certainly be termed great administrators—even prospective conquistadors—if in the wrong period.[18]

Two administrative councils assisted the viceroy. In the first place was the council of state (Conselho do Estado)—in principle the supreme administrative institution in Portuguese Asia. In this body the archbishop of Goa, the chancellor of the exchequer (*vedor da fazenda*), the chief justice, the grand inquisitor, the mayor of Goa, the captain of the Indiamen, and a number of councilors were normally seated. The king appointed the counsellors.[19] Yet all too often this council of state was a lion's den since the various nobles represented ferociously combated each other. It was not very sensible for a viceroy to ignore the urgent advice of the Conselho do Estado since all factions would then turn against him. This was experienced, for instance, by the Count of Óbidos, who was deposed by the Conselho do Estado in 1654 for contempt.[20]

Many viceroys regarded the sessions of the Conselho do Estado as a pain in the neck, to be avoided if possible. To take decisions took a long, long time since these had to be handed down from the Conselho do Estado to the chancellery and the Conselho da Fazenda. And, with so many persons involved, the secrets of state were discussed in every inn and alley.[21]

After 1670 the Council of State was hence assembled only on pressing occasions or to deliberate on confidential draft laws (*pareceres*) remitted by the crown to India. The viceroys exercised an increasingly absolute rule, and hardly consulted with the church or the nobles.[22] For all that, viceroys came and went and Goa's administration was still run by a small band of old India hands and the church: "*vicerei vão e vem, padre jesuita sempre tem*," as the saying went in Brazil.

In the second place there was the Conselho da Fazenda, which generally was also presided over by the viceroy. This council was in principle responsible for tax farms, investments of crown funds, and payment of personnel. The treasury (Casa dos Contos), which fell under the responsibility of the Conselho da Fazenda, was responsible for current financial affairs and the "budget." This was not really a budget in modern terms, however. The military and fiscal administrations on the one hand and the commercial administration on the other were separated in the Portuguese empire. The financial administration was split between the captain (*capitão*) and the chief merchant (*feitor*). The former was responsible for taxes gathered in India, the latter for the trade of the crown.

The Estado was supposed to be self-supporting. The trade with India conducted by the crown differed from the finances of India. To conduct this trade the crown sent an amount of cash or goods from the kingdom (the *cabedal do reino*) that was to be invested in precisely designated goods. The viceroy was not allowed to touch the *cabedal*, although all too often he would snatch this treasure to cover some expense. There was no attempt to overhaul this system in the seventeenth century, even though no lesser a person than the chairman of the Conselho Ultramarino thought it was the most "harmful and scandalous arrangement I have ever come across." For the survival of the Estado might hinge on the *cabedal*.[23]

Beginning in 1642 private traders were allowed complete freedom to fetch goods from and to Portugal. This did not initially include cinnamon from Ceylon, which the crown wanted to restrict to a monopoly trade. This restraint was repealed perforce in 1667 when the Portuguese had lost Ceylon. Officers, captains, and sailors were also allowed quite liberal concessions to freely take goods along from and to India in their liberty chests, if paying customs.[24]

Like the VOC and the EIC, the Portuguese distinguished factories (*feitorias*) and "presidencies," called *commandementen* by the VOC, *presidências* or *capitanias* by the Portuguese. At small *feitorias* like, in our period, Kung and Querimba, and in an earlier period, San Thomé, there was a merchant who cashed customs revenues and a scribe taking care of administrative matters. The *capitanias* had a military administration too.

In the presidencies—Praças do Norte, Goa, and earlier Ceylon (Mozambique was a presidency in effect but was styled a *capitania*)—there was a separate administration for the collection of land revenues. These territories were subdivided into "collectorates," known as *tanahdarias*.[25]

The high court, or *relaçao*, resided in Goa and handled the higher jurisdiction. At the out-stations it was exercised by justices of the peace (*ouvidores*), who in principle were responsible to the *relação* at Goa and not to any *capitão* on the spot; but this was so on paper, hardly in practice. In Goa justice was mostly spoken by the viceroy since judges were ill or absent. At the out-stations, even in Mozambique, there were mostly no *ouvidores*. Rough soldiers who tended to indiscriminately impose severe penalties for any triviality generally administered jurisdiction there. The *relação* was responsible in turn to the high court at Lisbon (the *desembargadores do paço*), which, on paper again, nominated the judges.[26]

In principle the Conselho Ultramarino named all other functionaries. Since there were generally more applicants than profitable positions this led to all kind of ingenious forgeries of the testimony to one's record of service. It also meant one might be placed on waiting lists for many years. When some official's term of office expired he was allowed to name three candidates for his succession. In return, the candidates would award him a donation. As the number of applicants for office increased, the sums of money involved in these *renuncias* increased as well. This system led to interminable suits, scandals, "and arguments with the use of firearms which causes ruin, loss of capital, discredit of persons, destruction of houses and families and, inexorably, loss of lives."[27]

In the Habsburg period it became usual to farm a baffling array of administrative positions, contracts for the delivery of goods, and all revenues of the crown for a span of three years. This *renda* system has often been criticized in the literature and, admittedly, invited misuse. Yet in favor of this system one could say that the crown could administer Asia more cheaply with *rendas* than it could have done with a centralized system. Moreover, the farmer also had to shoulder the risks involved in the revenues sold to him.[28]

Goa had in 1535 been awarded the privileges of Lisbon. The estates of Goa were allowed to elect a town council (*senado da câmera*), aldermen (*vereadores*), and a sheriff. The third estate was represented by the guild masters (*procuradores dos mesteres*). During the course of the seventeenth century other cities received such communal rights too, generally framed on those of Goa: Daman in 1634, Bassein in 1659, and Chaul in 1660.

In those towns of the north all citizens could have a say during the seating of the *senado da câmera*. That was merely a jamboree, the captain of Daman judged; there were very few sensible voices in the *senado* and these would be lost in the noise. Finally, there was—after the loss of Colombo, Tuticorin, and Cochin—the peculiar "freetown" of Macao, where the communal institutions were of far greater importance than was the viceroy, let alone the very remote king of Portugal.[29]

Those municipal institutions were extended to the countryside as well. There existed in northern Portugal a long tradition of municipalities (*vilhas*), often mere hamlets, ruled by a rural assembly and using part of their land as common lands. Such villages were founded by way of royal charter.[30] This Portuguese arrangement was adapted to Indian conditions to include the indigenous *panchayats* at Bardes and Salcete, who were allotted the right to name their own rural *câmera*. These *câmeras* were of paramount importance in the division of land and labor there.[31]

We will briefly have to consider the organization of the church, for the number of priests in Goa often surpassed the number of laymen there—and not only there. In Chaul there were in 1664 50 monks and 45 Portuguese laymen. They were not just defenders of the faith by argument, however. Soldiers often put on the habit to escape from military duties. Many viceroys complained about this. The Count of Alvor told the crown not to worry: the pristine men of the church had not forgotten their old craft and were often more bloodthirsty warriors than professional soldiers.[32]

Bishops of the Asian dioceses were nominated by the Portuguese crown (the *padroado*), and the orders resorted under this *padroado*. In return the crown paid the mission. The entire arrangement was very much to the displeasure of the missionary society of the Vatican, the Sacra Congregatione de Propaganda Fide. Therefore, after 1626 the curia named itinerant bishops who could ordain priests without consulting the "Catholic king." Goa mounted a militant campaign to obstruct them. However, after the concordat between Portugal and the Holy See in 1665 the Estado was forced to aid the missionaries sent by the Vatican, though very reluctantly.[33]

The archbishop of Goa was shepherd of the largest ecclesiastical province: the whole of Asia. Under this see were the diocese of Cochin, of Cranganore (or *sierra*—the mission among the Thomas-Christians), of Ethiopia (without fixed seat, as the bishop of Ethiopia in exile at Goa lived until 1663), of San Thomé, Malacca, and Macao (and later of Peking and Nanking). In the diocese of Goa the archbishop supervised the parishes in converted Salcete and Bardes and the still largely Hindu Praças do Norte. In both areas parochial churches and chapters were funded from the revenues of the temples, demolished in 1540. The cathedral and the missionaries, on the other hand, were paid for from the treasury.[34]

In Goa was situated the tribunal of the Inquisition too. In India the Inquisition mainly watched over the converts and, of course, Jews and new Christians. Some inquisitors exercised a true reign of terror over their province. Yet the grand inquisitor of Goa occasionally also acted as spokesman for his flock of poor Indian Christians and protected them against abuses of the worldly authorities. On balance, the Inquisition probably was a baneful influence on the Portuguese empire, however. For example, in 1674 when the inquisitors wanted to inspect Bassein, the viceroy beseeched the crown to prevent this, as it would cause panic there, if not among the Hindus, then among the converts, who in fear might turn Hindu again. The crown might contend it needed to support the Inquisition in India, "a land where there is so much heathendom and idolatry." Yet the viceroy had good reason to distrust the Inquisition, "which time after time far transgresses the boundaries of its jurisdiction."[35]

The Inquisition enjoyed the right to confiscate the property of deceased "heathens" in order to teach their children the faith. To implement this measure the Inquisition had a separate functionary: the *pai dos christãos*. But both the viceroy and the Hindu community staunchly resisted the strict implementation of this regulation. It could only be enforced when the deceased had no relatives to the third degree, and there was a host of exceptions. Goa would, Viceroy Caetano de Mello e Castro wrote the crown in 1703, soon decay if they implemented what had been stipulated by law. Most of Goa's trade was in the hands of these same heathens and they would certainly flee.[36]

Ecclesiastical authors often wrote that the men of the church were true patriots, rather than *fidalgos* who were only minding their own interest.[37] This was not untrue. The church was organized in a more bureaucratic fashion than the state. Unlike the state as well, it had a clear structure of power and punishment. Monks thus often handled important affairs. "They are the only persons here to whom you can entrust confidential missions," the viceroy argued.[38]

The Portuguese church also linked the various elements of the Luso-Indian *natio*—even where the troops had cleared the field. A good example is the situation in the diocese *sierra*, which—as noted—was plagued by a schism between "Catholic" Thomas Christians and "orthodox" Thomas Christians. The VOC did everything in its power to have the Thomas Christians placed under the authority of the see of Antioch, but outside of Cochin the bishop of Goa won this contest. The VOC with due respect commented: "The Portuguese are often more successful amongst the natives with five or six popes than we are with one or two hundred soldiers."[39]

**Trade with Portugal**

Goa's port did not offer a flourishing sight after 1663. According to the Portuguese themselves, Asian ships rarely touched Goa since they were chased away by the hefty 6 to 7 percent customs demanded. Only three Indiamen at most arrived every year from Lisbon at Goa. According to viceroy Caetano de Mello e Castro, not a single ship was anchored on the Mandovi in 1702.[40] Moreover, these vessels were also smaller than the giant galleons that the crown sent to Asia in the beginning of the seventeenth century. The nadir of the *carreira* came in the seventies, when only a very few ships reached Lisbon—though the crown still bravely tried to carry on a modest shipping with India. Thereafter the navigation began to revive but both the volume of shipping and the amount of goods carried were much, much lower than at the beginning of the seventeenth century (Table 7.1).[41]

According to G. Barlaeus, the Dutch ambassador in Lisbon, the East Indiamen were in 1670 "well chalked below the waterline" and, therefore, often more seaworthy ships than French or English Indiamen. They carried more guns than the other vessels too. But because of this, their capacity for cargo was small and they could carry no more than 400 men. Ships had begun to "shrink" from 1640 onward. The big galleons had too deep a draft to be safely unloaded under the guns of Aguado. The crown had better build smaller ships, Goa recommended.[42]

In the beginning of the seventeenth century the *carreira da Índia* ships were primarily intended as passenger vessels, carrying both soldiers and their liberty

Table 7.1

**Ships Departing from Portugal to India**

| Year | Ships | Year | Ships | Year | Ships | Year | Ships |
|---|---|---|---|---|---|---|---|
| 1600 | 6[1] | 1626 | 4 | 1652 | 4 | 1678 | 5 |
| 1601 | 4 | 1627 | 7[13] | 1653 | 2 | 1679 | 2[33] |
| 1602 | 6 | 1628 | 3[14] | 1654 | 3 | 1680 | 2 |
| 1603 | 5 | 1629 | 9[15] | 1655 | 4 | 1681 | 3 |
| 1604 | 5[2] | 1630 | 5[16] | 1656 | 2 | 1682 | 1 |
| 1605 | 3[3] | 1631 | None | 1657 | 4[22] | 1683 | 2 |
| 1606 | 8[4] | 1632 | 3 | 1658 | 2 | 1684 | 2 |
| 1607 | 7[5] | 1633 | 3 | 1659 | 1 | 1685 | 4 |
| 1608 | 14[6] | 1634 | 3 | 1660 | 3[23] | 1686 | 1 |
| 1609 | 10 | 1635 | 2. | 1661 | 1[24] | 1687 | 1 |
| 1610 | 5 | 1636 | 2 | 1662 | None | 1688 | 1 |
| 1611 | 7 | 1637 | 2 | 1663 | 2 | 1689 | 1 |
| 1612 | 3 | 1638 | 2[17] | 1664 | 2[25] | 1690 | 2 |
| 1613 | 7[7] | 1639 | None | 1665 | 2 | 1691 | 2 |
| 1614 | 7[8] | 1640 | 5 | 1666 | 4[26] | 1692 | 2 |
| 1615 | 4 | 1641 | 2 | 1667 | 1 | 1693 | 1 |
| 1616 | 3 | 1642 | 4[18] | 1668 | 1 | 1694 | 3 |
| 1617 | 6 | 1643 | 2 | 1669 | 1 | 1695 | 2 |
| 1618 | 5 | 1644 | 6[19] | 1670 | 5[27] | 1696 | 2 |
| 1619 | 9[9] | 1645 | 5 | 1671 | 2[28] | 1697 | 2 |
| 1620 | 4[10] | 1646 | 2 | 1672 | 4[29] | 1698 | 2 |
| 1621 | 10 | 1647 | 4 | 1673 | 2[30] | 1699 | 3 |
| 1622 | 8[11] | 1648 | 2[20] | 1674 | 2 | 1700 | 1 |
| 1623 | 8[12] | 1649 | 2[21] | 1675 | 1 | 1701 | 3[34] |
| 1624 | 8 | 1650 | 6 | 1676 | 2[31] | 1702 | 3 |
| 1625 | 2 | 1651 | 3 | 1677 | 2[32] | 1703 | 4 |

*Notes:* [1]Four ships arrived at Goa; one sunk, one destined to Cochin; [2]One sunk, one destined to Cochin; [3]Destined for Malacca; [4]One returned to Portugal without reaching Goa; three more ships unable to depart from Lisbon; [5]One sunk, one taken by the Dutch; [6]Five sunk, two back to Portugal, one taken by English and one destined for Hormuz; [7]Five galleons, two small patashes, to dispatch messages; [8]Two sunk, two destined to Mozambique; [9]Five galleons of fleet of Ruy Freyre de Andrade to Hormuz of which one lost, one lost of the other ships; [10]One lost, one back to Portugal; [11]One lost, one back to Portugal; [12]Two sunk; [13]Two carracks, one patash, four galleons, one to Malacca, one to Cochin; [14]Two back to Portugal; [15]One patash, two sunk; [16]One sunk, two back to Portugal and again departed next year; [17]One galleon, one small *navetta;* [18]Two galleons, two patash; [19]Three galleons of which one lost, two patash, one *navetta;* [20]One back to Portugal; [21]One sunk; [22]One patash; [23]One patash, one sunk; [24]One small ship, to accompany two English ships, heading from Lisbon to Bombay, with Portuguese freight; [25]One stranded in Bahia; [26]One back to Portugal; [27]One sunk; [28]One patash; [29]One patash; [30]One patash; [31]One patash; [32]One galleon to Goa, one patash to Mozambique; [33]One to Mozambique; [34]One ship sent from Bahia, to fetch cargo back to Portugal.

chests, which accounts for their huge size. The proportions then often prevailed over the quality of the ship, particularly during the war with the VOC, when the crown sent any available keel to India.[43] This was one cause of the catastrophic losses to shipwreck from 1640 to 1659, which worsened the financial plight of the Estado. Other causes of shipwreck were overloading, ignoring the regulations on times for sailing (since illegal trade was conducted in transitional ports), and bad seamanship. To Boxer, the authority on the matter, the last was the most important cause and this applied not only to the sailors but to their officers as well.

The right to succeed to the position of commodore (*capitão-mor*) for the *carreira* was sold. The money involved could amount to more than 25,000 guilders. Since a *capitão-mor* was allowed to take a large number of "creatures" along—each of whom could fetch a number of liberty chests—the potential benefits well rewarded the investment. Obviously, however, many a good but poor captain could not furnish such sums.[44]

Let us consider the structure of imports and exports of Goa in closer detail.[45] These show appreciable differences between the Portuguese on the one hand and the Dutch, French, Danish, and English Companies on the other. Basically, Portuguese trade with Europe differed from that of the Companies as it mainly consisted of investment of individual merchants, who had obtained their funds from taxes and private trade. If Steensgaard therefore emphasizes that Portuguese trade with Europe was not so much oriented to obtaining a profit in Europe as to cashiering profits made in Asia, he is certainly right.[46]

### *Exports*

As was the case in other European countries, the Portuguese suffered from a lack of export products from the motherland to the Orient, except silver. During the Habsburg period this could be easily obtained: part of the silver arriving at Seville could be assigned to Lisbon. But after 1640 the Portuguese had to rely on smuggling between Portugal and Spain—occasionally between Brazil and the Rio de la Plata—and mainly on the services of Antwerp and Amsterdam bankers. Those three erratic sources of supply hardly sufficed to quell the demand for silver from Brazil and the metropolis, let alone that from India. On this account the crown did everything in its power to curtail exports of silver to India. It had some success: whereas in the beginning of the seventeenth century Portugal still exported substantial amounts of silver (150,000–160,000 cruzados), at the end of the seventeenth century this had diminished to about 30,000 cruzados only. The want of silver precipitated the frantic but vain search for silver veins in Mozambique too.[47]

With other products from Portugal one could hardly stow the hold. One sometimes exported mercury and coral. The latter was obtained from the new-Christian and Sephardic merchants at Leghorn who largely controlled the commerce. It was bought from the Brazil Company too, exchanged by the consul of this Company for brazilwood at Pisa. The English, and the French in particular, also exported coral. It appears the Portuguese trade had difficulty surviving cutthroat French competition.[48]

When Japan, with the closing of its borders, had been eliminated as a source of supply, the Estado was provided with copper from the kingdom and—within

Asia—from Siam. Dutch traders in Lisbon mainly sold copper.[49] Particularly during the war with the VOC, but later too, iron, gunpowder, and arms were shipped from Lisbon to the Mandovi, a trade in arms that took a predominant share of exports during the grim fifties. This constituted another massive problem for the crown since in the Habsburg period arms were generally procured in Spain.[50] These exports of arms tended to devour the already meager profits on sales in Portugal.

The lion's share of exports from the kingdom was not so much intended for commerce as for the use of the Portuguese communities, however. This applied especially to exports by private traders to Asia: vinegar, olive oil, candles, knives, furniture, reams of paper, Douro and Madeira wines. The wine was traded to the English and the Dutch at Bombay and Surat; Madeira was the most popular drink among Europeans in Asia. Paper was traded to the Marathas—in quantity. This was an indispensable European contribution to the rise of bureaucracies in India.[51]

Whereas Portuguese products were not a major export to Asia, Brazilian products such as sugar, leather, and especially tobacco became ever more important. Tobacco had been processed in Portugal already and was used as snuff in India and Mozambique, but not on the Mrima Coast since Mombasa had a special *renda* for *tabaco do fumo*. The royal monopoly on pounding and selling tobacco (Estanco do Tabaco) was one of the major incomes of the crown at home. In Goa the sale was farmed to monopoly contractors who could, if required, enforce the Estanco by force. This was necessary, for many officials were illegally selling tobacco as well.[52] The trade in tobacco became to the major income of the crown in India: its value soared from 26,666 xeraphins in 1674 to 101,500 xeraphins in 1681. The return cargoes were by then mostly paid for through the proceeds from the Estanco do Tabaco, and the board of the Estanco—the Junta do Tabaco—largely supervised the India trade. So the investments in the *cabedal do reino* were increasingly part of a triangular trade between Salvador da Bahia, Lisbon, and Goa.[53]

The crown tried to reserve the benefits of this trade to itself—a hopeless fight because, quite typically for the Portuguese reason of state, possibilities for elites to evade it were created simultaneously with the monopoly. Some nobles had, for example, been allotted an exemption from the Estanco do Tabaco, which they utilized to smuggle tobacco.[54]

To avoid smuggling to and within Brazil, the crown prohibited ships of the *carreira da Índia* to anchor in Brazilian ports on the trip to India. During the journey home, vessels were supposed to head directly for the Azores and wait for naval escorts there without touching Bahia. Those regulations for sailing were largely futile. East Indiamen normally touched at Bahia on the journey home for a refit. The precious oriental cargo was normally divided there among the ships carrying sugar from Salvador to avert the risk of shipwreck.[55]

Though ships from India might have a refit at Bahia, the inhabitants of India were not to participate in the Brazilian trade. In 1665 the *senado da câmera* of Goa supplicated the crown for the right to send ships to Luanda and Pernambuco. That was the only potentially profitable traffic left, except that of Mozambique, "and that is reserved by the captains of that fortress for themselves alone." No, the Conselho Ultramarin countered, they could not afford to squander the trade of Portugal with Brazil and Angola, which partly consisted of Indian textiles.[56]

As the merchants of Bahia owned a large fleet, which cruised throughout the Atlantic, it was more significant that the inhabitants of Brazil were not permitted to trade with India either. Brazilian ships could have exchanged tobacco for slaves at Madagascar, gold for slaves in Mozambique, or sugar and tobacco for slaves from Africa and textiles from India—as they did in the nineteenth century. It was therefore proposed in 1701 that one should allow the merchants of Bahia to send three ships to India.[57] But the Junta do Tabaco demurred:

> It would be harmful to entice traders from America to Asia, for the remote areas remain obedient if they have to obtain everything they need from Portugal. So, it is not good if they are going to look for what they now receive from the kingdom themselves. For, surely, their obedience is assured by their dependence.[58]

Despite these prohibitions, Brazilian merchants did try to trade in the Arabian seas. In 1669 the *nao Santa Theresa* and in 1685 the *São Antônio* (400 tons) were sent from Bahia to Mozambique. The supercargo of the second ship went to considerable length to market his goods: he not only conducted trade on Mozambique island but visited the market at Tete to vend tobacco and sugar as well.[59] But what was one to purchase there? Mozambique gold fetched a meager 10 percent profit in Brazil and the experience in the trade with Guinea had taught the Conselho do Estado in 1704 that "if ships remain at sea for longer than thirty days almost all slaves will die, for illnesses will then erupt."[60] Quite true: for some reason, the Portuguese ships suffered much heavier mortality on the last two weeks of the stretch from Benin to Rio de Janeiro than did ships that spent a comparable time sailing to the West Indies.[61]

Neither were the sales very successful. The sugar sold in Mozambique mostly came from Bassein and the tobacco from Bengal, which was preferred to the sweeter Brazilian variety. It is likely that already in the seventeenth century the Yao merchants sold this tobacco to the interior, with the cultivation of tobacco taking off in the eighteenth century, whereas in Zimbabwe the cultivation of tobacco began around the middle of the seventeenth. Finally, tobacco was planted in quantity in Dela Goa Bay in the eighteenth century, "but because of its high content of tar [*syne vettigheid*] it is not very fit for smoking."[62]

The Brazilians did not have much success elsewhere either. There was certainly demand for tobacco in Persia and Goa. Most of it was produced locally, though it was imported from Bengal as well. The Brazilian brand was considered too sweet in India, however, and it lost its flavor during the long trip from Pernambuco.[63] Finally, sugar had long been exported from the Estado da Índia. There was definitely a market for sugar in Persia. At Bassein there were four sugar mills (*engenhos*), which refined sugar cane produced in the Praças.[64] This production partly catered to demand from the Gulf, though the bulk was sent to Gujarat and to Mozambique. In 1699 a Brazilian ship loaded with sugar anchored in front of Kung. Sugar was not in demand and it had to be taken all the way to Isfahan, where it was finally sold at a loss.[65]

While direct trade between Mozambique and Bahia was unsuccessful and Brazilian traders proved reluctant to invest money in direct trade with India, there did develop a flourishing illegal trade on the Indiamen between Goa and Bahia in which the entire merchant community of Goa and Bahia, the two viceroys included, was involved. The advice frigates, fast ships that were specially dispatched to convey important messages to Portugal, were only loaded with cargoes destined for Brazil. Indiamen also touched at Luanda, where Indian textiles were unloaded to be exchanged for slaves and ivory.[66]

The crown might bemoan "the major damage to our incomes" arising from this illicit trade, but there was little they could do about it. There was always some subterfuge about how a captain might lose the trade winds and "was therefore forced to set course for Bahia." Once at Bahia, sailors and captains could sell the Indian textiles stowed in their liberty chests, which fetched better prices there than at Lisbon, in exchange for tobacco and sugar.[67]

In 1674 the Conselho Ultramarino saw no alternative but to permit this trade. The only apparent way to attract sailors on board the East Indiamen was to allow them a profitable trade at Bahia. As goods were now smuggled anyway, the treasury would do better to reap some profit. But when staying at Bahia the Indiamen repeatedly missed the trade winds. The crews suffered severe mortality from the lengthy detour—which cost the crown dearly in pensions—and products often arrived too late in the season at Lisbon. Therefore, the traders of Goa dispatched goods on board English rather than Portuguese vessels.[68]

As Portuguese trade increasingly focused on Brazil, the Estado da Índia was shifting to a subsidiary branch of the Brazil trade. This was not only because the deficit on the trade with the *carreira da Índia* had to be financed by the benefits from Brazil, but for three other reasons as well.

First, as is well known from the literature, already during the Habsburg period many of the leading (new-Christian) merchant families of the *carreira da Índia*—like the Lopes de Veigas, the Brandãos, or the Roíz de Lisboas—had correspondents in and dealings with Brazil. Brazilian profits were invested in the India trade—often under severe pressure of the crown, for the former was far less hazardous than the latter.[69] This topic has still to be explored for old-Christian merchants and for the second half of the seventeenth century. But, to mention one example, the major trader of the *carreira da Índia* in the seventies,

Manuel da Gama de Padoa, was director of the Brazil Company and a major dealer with Angola as well.[70]

Second—and this is a topic that certainly merits more research—some Portuguese noble families owned property in Portugal, Brazil, and India, and traded both on the *carreira da Índia* and the *carreira do Brasil.*[71] Such *fidalgos mercadores,* for example, were the Noronha/Mem de Sá family, proprietors of the large sugar plant at Sergipe. Returned from Goa, the Count of Linhares and his wife, Dona Inez de Noronha, were still busily trading with India in precious stones and furniture.[72]

And finally, the vassals of the Portuguese crown in Goa were involved in deals with Brazil too. For example, Luís Mendonça de Furtado, Francisco de Lima, and Diego de Fonesca had in 1671 concluded a partnership: their agent Manuel de Castro was to sell Coromandel and Gujarati textiles to the governor of Mozambique. This was to be bartered with slaves and gold. Part of the proceeds was allotted to the governor and the scribe of the customs—a bribe, apparently, in order that they seclude competitors from the market. With these profits one would draft bills of exchange on Brazil. These bills were to be invested in sugar in Bahia, which would be dispatched to Portugal.[73]

***Imports***

In the beginning of the seventeenth century the bulk of the exports of the *cabedal do reino* consisted of pepper and cinnamon. These products were mainly sold to a few monopoly contractors. They surely made inordinate profits, yet, basically, the problem facing the Portuguese crown in the cinnamon and pepper trade was its position in the semi-periphery. The *vedor da fazenda* of Goa was in 1643 marveling at the incredible amounts of cinnamon the Dutch were exporting from Ceylon: more than 350,000 pounds. The crown had, when it still enjoyed a monopoly, the greatest of difficulties in selling 100,000 pounds in Lisbon. Apparently the Dutch market and Dutch demand were limitless. If the Portuguese could succeed in selling such quantities, and for such a high price, this would suffice to pay for all their ships and sailors.[74]

As mentioned already, the pepper trade of the Portuguese crown was severely damaged by the price war between the Companies in the 1640s. In 1639 already—and worse was still to come—the contractor only wanted to buy pepper if he was granted a knighthood. The crown agreed there was no demand for pepper whatsoever. Yet bartering pepper for a knighthood could "have very bad consequences in the future."[75]

When the supplies from Java and Sumatra had faltered, pepper was mainly obtained from Canara and to a lesser extent from Kerala: the period from 1620 to 1640 was the golden age of Portuguese purchases in Canara. This pepper was contracted with the *nayak* and mainly bartered for copper and lead. With the English establishment on the coast, Virabanda Nayak requested ever higher prices, however.[76] So the Portuguese lost their dominant position on this market while, meanwhile, increasing amounts of pepper were fetched overland from Kerala and Canara to the Konkan, a trade that had increased strongly in the thirties as the prices of pepper soared "because of the recent great drought" in Kerala. To some extent, this shift of the trade from sea to land benefited the Portuguese. The deliveries of pepper from Canara to Goa overland were handed to a monopoly contractor: Rama Keni. The Portuguese would then not have to transport it from Barcelore with the consequent risks.[77]

Yet the Portuguese *feitor* at Bhatkal in Canara in 1643 was hardly to be envied.[78] English procurement there (mainly for private trade) had raised prices from 18 to 28 pagodas the bahar in the last four years. In the pepper-producing lands par excellence, Mount Eli and Calicut, the VOC had driven up prices from 20 pagodas to 32. The English establishment at Rajabad in 1637 and the collapse of the control of Portuguese flotillas over the Konkan Coast had pushed up prices in the pepper markets in the interior of Bijapur—Atroli and Banda—too. There, traders were prepared to pay up to 36 pagodas. Merchants from Malabar would rather barter their pepper to the (Muslim) merchants from Bijapur for Coromandel and Gujarati textiles, saltpeter, and cotton than receive bad Portuguese são thomés in return for it. One could actually procure pepper more cheaply overland than buy it at Barcelore or at Onore.[79]

Even in Cochin itself the Portuguese pepper trade was obstructed by its competitors. There the *rajadores* were colluding with the VOC to barter economical Dutch merchandise for pepper. And most exasperating of all was that the Portuguese officials were furtively selling cinnamon and pepper to the English, the Danish, and the Dutch as well. In 1645, when a truce had just been signed with the Dutch, the crown yearned to recommence the war to punish the VOC for such smuggling. There was apparently no way the crown could compete with the contraband of its own officials or punish them.[80]

In 1654 the cinnamon trade had disappeared and the pepper trade with Malabar had dwindled. When the VOC conquered Cochin and signed its monopoly contracts with the rajahs, Cochin disappeared as a supplier of pepper. The Estado had to depend upon coastwise shipping between Travancore, Rajapur, and Karwar and Goa, and on the supplies from Tanore, Canara, and Sunda.

Canara and Sunda produced more than sufficient pepper to fulfill the orders from Lisbon, but the Estado was struggling with rival English and Muscati traders there. In Sunda the Compagnie des Indes was added to the already long list of competitors in 1672. The French were a very serious threat, for they disposed of far more ample funds than the Portuguese (or the Muscatis). They tried to sign monopoly contracts with the rajah of Sunda. Fortunately for the Lusitanians, however, the Compagnie des Indes was not successful. King and merchants seriously doubted whether the French were creditworthy, as they insisted on paying for their transactions with bills drafted on the factory at Surat and were unwilling to hand over cash.[81]

As mentioned, the bulk of Canara's production was sent overland to Malwa and Gujarat. The remainder was bought by contractors of the court and sold to the European traders. Because of their virtual monopoly over the supply of pepper to the Portuguese, the contractors appointed by the court of Ikkeri were in the enviable position of being able to impose the harshest of conditions on them. The *feitor* at Barcelore was in 1670 burdened with a pepper contract: he was to purchase 100,000 pounds of pepper for the exorbitant price of 40 pagodas the bahar, twice that paid by the VOC at Cochin. Part of it had to be paid in são thomés, part bartered for textiles, ivory, and salt. However, this duopoly in Canara gave some advantage to the Portuguese crown as well, which explains the important role of Canara in the Portuguese purchases. The contractors had to guarantee both the timely delivery of pepper and its quality. Canara pepper might have been more expensive than pepper from Malabar, but supplies were more predictable. And it was often better too.[82]

At Tanore the flotillas of the Estado bartered Egyptian opium obtained from Diu and gold coins for pepper. On account of Portuguese private traders, three to four frigates sailed to Tanore in the 1690s, which sometimes bought pepper with money supplied by the Junta do Tabaco. Occasionally ships of the *zamorin* brought pepper to Goa too. Albeit, the captains maintained, this trade was forbidden by the VOC and the Portuguese were charged much higher prices than those paid by the Companies. Indeed, the pepper imported in Lisbon from London was at the end of the seventeenth century cheaper than pepper that the Junta do Tabaco brought from Calicut.[83]

Traditionally, the trade in pepper outside of Cochin was cloaked as a tribute in pepper of the rajahs in Kerala to the Estado in return for armed support. This was mainly disguising trade in the garb of the warrior, but it was not entirely a sham. The Portuguese were to help the kings with guns and powder in settling conflicts among themselves. Thus the *zamorin* warned the viceroy in 1640 that he would not sell pepper to the Portuguese if they would not lend a hand in the war against the *colathiri.*[84]

The pattern after 1663 was still similar. At Cananore the Azhi Raja handed a sum of pepper to the fleet of the Estado, which was supposed "to guard him against Muscat depredations." This was not merely a pretext: the Muscatis were no gentlemen. But the Portuguese admiral in 1664 threatened to pillage the town if Cananore would not pay this racket. At Calicut too, with which the Estado conducted a small trade war in 1682, the Portuguese still requested pepper in return for military support.[85]

This pepper could not compete with that sold by the East India Companies, however. By 1670 the bulk of the pepper sold at Lisbon came from London and Amsterdam.[86] The crown had to look for a cheaper alternative to purchases in India. It therefore tried cultivating spices in Brazil and requested tendrils and cultivators. The cultivation of cinnamon in the Jeronimo convent of Pernambuco was a success. That of pepper was not, since orders to send tendrils to Brazil had to be repeated several times.[87]

With the pepper trade of the Portuguese succumbing to that of its competitors, saltpeter and diamonds assumed its place. In 1617 the crown had already ordered Goa "to send henceforward as much saltpeter to the kingdom as possible, for it is needed to make powder here."[88]

In the 1630s the saltpeter was bartered with the *nayak* of Madure in exchange for elephants from Ceylon. This trade was not just a duopoly there. In Goa saltpeter sold to the king was delivered by a single contractor, Deva Nayak, who had to bail for the deliveries. Monopoly contractors also delivered saltpeter from Bengal.[89]

In 1694, "because of the great demand, caused by the present wars in Europe," the *cabedal* was split: part was, on account of King Pedro, to be spent on saltpeter; part, on behalf of Queen Mary of Savoy, on diamonds. The saltpeter was partly obtained from *banjara* traders from the Deccan. Goa would rather have procured it from Bengal, however, through a monopoly contract with Francisco de Carvalho, merchant at Macao. The supplies from the "Balleghat" were too unreliable. Again, the crown was searching for a cheaper alternative. In 1700 the crown requested the viceroy to search for *canarins* who could put up the manufacture of saltpeter in Maranhão. There were none to be found at Goa, the viceroy replied, but one might summon them from Bengal.[90]

The trade in diamonds between Bijapur, the staple market for diamonds in western India, Surat, and Goa was in 1637 taken care of by a dozen *bania* merchant houses, established in the Bijapur suburb of Shahpur. To them the trade with Goa was but a subsidiary branch of a more important trade in rubies and emeralds with the Bijapuri court. The contracts for diamonds were negotiated behind closed doors between the Conselho da Fazenda and those *bania* rings.[91] It was a sellers' market: the Portuguese had little leeway in these negotiations, for they had to purchase the diamonds quickly. Everything had to be done in the utmost secrecy too: as soon as information on the quantity requested by the crown leaked out, the prices would soar. Hence the important position of the broker of the crown, Moqua Gitta—"a Gujarati Brahmin." He was in 1639 even granted a knighthood. Since the Compagnie des Indes and French private merchants often bought diamonds with the aid of the Jewish traders established at Goa, Goa remained a major center of the diamond trade on the West Coast.[92]

However, with growing competition from Madras, the Portuguese diamond trade was in trouble in the 1680s. The basic problem faced by the Junta do Tabaco, when investing the proceeds of tobacco in diamonds, was the massive fluctuation in price. One year it might make a 50–60 percent profit and the next suffer a 30 percent loss. Moreover, when trying to vend large quantities, the price in Lisbon would plummet. Thus in 1687 all diamonds were assigned to

João Nunes de Costa, the representative of the crown in Amsterdam, who was slowly to sell them in small batches. In 1686 the diamonds received were so bad that the Junta do Tabaco considered sending them back to India. The king ordered the officials to buy either saltpeter or pepper from the proceeds of the tobacco "because of the small profit on diamonds."[93]

But for the Portuguese private traders investing in diamonds, the main consideration was not to obtain a profit—rather, diamonds were a reimbursement of funds obtained from land revenues and offices. We have one complete list of gems remitted from Goa to Lisbon in 1636. Although a portion of these diamonds was destined for the great diamond merchants, the bulk constituted remittances of small sums obtained from offices. One bizalho of diamonds, with a value of 1,300 pardaos, was sent to José de Couto, widow of the historian Diego de Couto for example.[94] One could smuggle these diamonds through customs without paying duties at Lisbon or Goa.[95] At the end of the seventeenth century, however—because of the declining profits made on diamonds—Portuguese remittances to and from India increasingly appear to have been financed by bills of exchange.

This was rare in the beginning of the century. The Portuguese then mostly remitted Asian gains home in goods. This Portuguese private trade appears to show a pattern of investments comparable to that of the Companies. In some products the Portuguese private trade was the forerunner of the investment of the companies. Portuguese merchants first traded Coromandel and Bengal textiles via the Cape, for instance. Though products from Malacca like spices, lacquer, and sandalwood still played a significant role in the private trade to Portugal in the thirties, diamonds and textiles from India took an increasingly prominent place.[96]

The most important markets for the piece-cloth from the Deccan, Sind, and Gujarat were Angola, Brazil, and especially Guinea, to which mainly coarse textiles (like *mouri* and *guingan*) were exported. The demand for Indian textiles "for the exchange at El Mina" fluctuated with the Portuguese slave and gold trade. In the 1630s the orders for textile were commensurate to the amounts the farmers of this trade thought they might sell.[97]

Moreover, cotton yarn and cotton were also exported from Kolhapur to the kingdom. With the increasing difficulties experienced in fetching goods from the Deccan in the seventies, the private trade to the kingdom moved to the Coromandel Coast and to Bengal—for both textiles and other products. But this trade was increasingly carried out by the English country traders, who supplied the Portuguese too. Products from Macao were also traded—silk, cloth, and porcelain.[98]

These private traders to Portugal were often severely in debt to Indian bankers. Around 1700 it was said that "while everybody in Goa is poor, these heathens alone are growing more opulent daily." Portuguese functionaries in India were serving as brokers for the remittances of diamonds by Indian traders to Portugal;

these diamonds were sold by the representatives of the officials. This was a most undesirable trend, it was judged in Portugal: "The Hindus are becoming masters of all secrets of our commerce." It was not an entirely new trend, however, for during the Habsburg period the short-lived Companhia do Comércio had already specialized in fetching *bania* freight to Lisbon.[99]

In the very readable tract *Arte de furtar* (The Fine Art of Theft) it was remarked that *carreira da Índia* ships often sank because they were, on the point of departure, quickly stowed with the contraband of sailors that was not registered in the customs house.[100] It seems a reasonable deduction: the main income for the mariners came from smuggling goods in their liberty chests to Lisbon. This was hard to trace, as the mariners during their brief stay in Goa would take care not to incriminate each other. Lisbon was hard-pressed to check the goods of the mariners when the ships were unloaded, particularly diamonds, which could easily be hidden under an overcoat. And officials in Portugal, like the chatelaine of Cascais, were only too willing to assist smugglers. Goa should check the vessels when disembarking, Lisbon urged.[101]

But there was little Goa could do either, it was pleaded there: "The minor officials of the customs are native blacks, willing to sell an entire ship for a sixpence." Furthermore, clerics often exploited their right to exemptions from customs to conduct smuggle.[102]

It is doubtful whether the mariners' trade between Portugal and Asia was very profitable. Sailors bringing private goods were useful for defrauding customs and serving as a buffer for the merchants of Lisbon. The tars were generally in severe debt. They had to sell their goods in a hurry and at any price: the Lisbon traders could buy these goods for a trifle. Merchants often preferred to have freight sent in that way, rather than do it themselves.[103]

## A Poor State with Rich Citizens

### *Financial Troubles*

The Estado mainly differed from the VOC in that most of its incomes were farmed; it was thus structurally weaker than the VOC since most of its reserves were not used by the state. Yet, mainly because of this, the Estado da Índia constituted the exchequer's dream. Portuguese budget calculations, *orçamentos*, as a matter of principle always assigned one source of revenue to cover one particular expense. The balance would thus always appear positive. This has occasioned a long debate among scholars on whether the Estado was running at a profit or at a loss.[104] Pedro Baretto de Resende noted in 1635, for example, that on the negative side the balance did not account for unforeseen expenses like the ransom paid for freeing the patriarch of Ethiopia from an Ottoman prison. However, on the positive side, the incomes from the sales of concessionary voyages to Manila and China were not stated in the accounts either. In spite of more than twelve years' hard work he was still utterly unable to say whether the Estado da Índia was showing a profit or a loss.[105]

Macao had a separate accountancy, which did not figure on the *orçamentos* of Goa, nor did Timor's. Functionaries there were not paid and had to subsist on trading. The *orçamento* of the Estado da Índia of 1688 stated laconically about the incomes of all settlements but Goa: "they are not declared for they are uncertain." In 1648 the viceroy thought it was better not to include Mozambique in the accounts, for everything was embezzled there anyway. The viceroy could really only rely on the money obtained from farming the *alfândega* of Goa, customs stations on its border, salt and tobacco farms, and a few agrarian revenues from Bardes and Salcete.[106]

This rather meager income of roughly 100,000 xeraphins would have to suffice to pay a top-heavy bureaucracy on which, the crown complained in 1658, "one continues to make superfluous and fantastic expenses."[107] Small wonder the Estado lived from hand to mouth. Until about 1635 it was able to manage, for better or worse. But after 1635, with dramatically mounting costs because of the war with the VOC, benefits from *rendas* were showing an equally serious drop.[108]

It will not be necessary to trace the long and rather depressing story of the various desperate attempts to supplicate for or extort funds from *moradores,* church, and *misericórdia* in the first half of the seventeenth century here. The financial collapse followed in 1651. After new loans had been exacted by Viceroys Mascarenhas and Óbidos, the means of the community and of the church were exhausted in 1656. The *alfândegas* and *rendas* were the sole income of the state, Óbidos warned the king, and both were declining very rapidly. If these collapsed, the state could not rely on voluntary contributions for long.[109]

Óbidos was deposed in 1654, an act prompted to no small extent by precisely these contributions; Óbidos was spending them without the approval of the Conselho do Estado.[110] The Conselho Ultramarino thought this was merely a sign of discontent with a single individual. The vassals in the Orient were as loyal to the king as ever before. One just needed to send an able successor to settle affairs at Goa. Unfortunately Óbidos's successor, the Count of Sarzedas, died almost immediately upon his arrival in Goa.[111] Since the Conselho Ultramarino was unable to settle on a new viceroy, this led to chaos at Goa. The governors, who—pending news from Lisbon—were uncertain whether they were allowed to steer the ship of state, spent their time playing cards, drinking, and quarreling. There was no government left and every *fidalgo* considered himself the summit of authority.[112]

In view of the steep drop in incomes, in 1657 the diet established a "common treasure" in which the tithe and the incomes of *rendas* would be pooled to pay the expenses of the state. It was a total failure. Church and *gaokar*s, jointly and stubbornly, resisted this attempt, with due justification: while Cochin and Sofala were crying for succor, ships were rotting away on the Mandovi and soldiers were starving. If money was expended to such effect, there was little reason to contribute. One had to send soldiers to the villages to extort money, which worsened the anarchy. The diet (*junta do povo*) convened in 1661 to demand a new entreaty lamented it had not a penny left. Goa would be lost during a Dutch attack, which was expected sooner rather than later.[113] In 1665 another direct levy of one bazaruco per year for every house was introduced, to pay the Dutch republic an indemnity, but this was a failure too. Salcete and Bardes did contribute a reasonable sum but Praças do Norte contributed nothing at all. And Goa claimed it would collect as much as tallied with the liberty of the town—it was very little indeed.[114]

The new viceroy, Antônio de Mello e Castro, tried to effect a financial recovery. He was only partly successful. The crown had told poor Mello e Castro that there was a "need for major reforms" but had not allotted him the means to bring about those reforms.[115] If corruption was not uprooted, the viceroy nevertheless succeeded in restoring at least the semblance of justice. Writs and settlement registers could no longer be stolen or forged at will. The court of justice functioned again whereas in the fifties its activities had virtually ceased. Some evildoers were at least exposed; a few were even punished.[116]

After 1680 the accounts, as shown in Table 7.2, revealed that the Estado even made a small profit, but emergencies again pulled it into the abyss, as it did not dispose of any reserve. During the war with the Marathas in 1683, the viceroy had to plead with the diet for a loan of 200,000 xeraphins. This was completely insufficient. To save Goa the Count of Alvor was finally compelled to auction the church silver.[117]

With these accumulated debts the Estado was after 1685 once again in deep trouble: according to Governor A. de Costa, the Estado had to receive at least 60,000 xeraphins from Portugal yearly to stay out of financial trouble. But the crown resisted such special pleading: the Estado was to take care of its own finances. Consequently, when Oman besieged Mombasa the Estado again had to convene a diet to ask for a loan of 400,000 xeraphins, which once more proved utterly insufficient.[118]

It does not follow from this grim tale that the Portuguese empire was in decay, for its inhabitants still conducted a flourishing trade. This capital was mainly invested in positions. That raised the sums paid for office, but mostly without benefit to the crown. The king, for example, remarked that so many *rendas* were sold illicitly that "no viceroy and governor can inhibit the indulgence in such abuses, if this prohibited traffic continues in such fashion."[119]

Again, the value of a *capitania* did not depend upon what was paid to the crown for a nomination. One paid much more to the patron who had taken care of the *renúncia* to a captaincy. Such a nomination was mostly a private deal, but one might go as far as to auction *renúncias* in the marketplace.[120] Money handed in this way had to be regained in the best case by private trade, in the worst by robbery.

Table 7.2

**Incomes and Expenses of the Estado da Índia, 1682 and 1686** (in xeraphins)

| | 1682 | | 1686 | |
|---|---|---|---|---|
| | Income | Expenses | Income | Expenses |
| Goa | 359,579 | 211,485 | 356,310 | 551,735 |
| Chaul | 19,579 | 25,515 | 45,347 | 44,730 |
| Bassein | 161,274 | 75,853 | 171,920 | 107,164 |
| Manora | 4,872 | 5,961 | 4,806 | 5,900 |
| Daman | 89,240 | 49,168 | 102,980 | 41,168 |
| Diu | 30,773 | 54,130 | 92,240 | 65,610 |
| Mombasa | 21,110 | 255,154 | 34,200 | 24,579 |
| Anjidiva | — | — | 1,889 | 6,359 |
| Mangalore | 1,397 | 1,065 | 4,165 | 1,839 |
| Kung | 44,000 | 6,339 | 44,000 | 6,359 |
| Total | 731,824 | 684,670 | 857,857 | 855,443 |

The Portuguese term for the ensuing abuse of office was not *corruption* but *irregularities* (*descaminhos*). Somebody who had been allowed the tenure of an office might well seek gain for himself and his family. If he profited from an office, this would raise the sums involved. Besides, officials were supposed to pay all kinds of expenses associated with their position themselves. Viceroy Conde de Aveiras, for example, when arriving in India, had to hire troops and equip warships but pay them from his own purse. "This entire state presently runs on my own credit," he complained. If an official had to pay the kingdom's expenses, he might as well dispose of its funds too.[121]

Yet one had the moral duty to spare the needy, women, and children, to look after one's clients, and to not push self-enrichment to a point where the defense, the incomes, and the good name of crown and ecclesia would suffer irreparable damage. And this, sadly, occurred all too often in Portuguese India. If there was already something rotten in the state of India in the late sixteenth century—when Couto wrote his venomous pamphlet *Soldado prático*—there seems little doubt of the putridity during the war with the Dutch. Most factories became less profitable while the demand for office remained equal or increased. As trade became ever more hazardous, the demand for secure administrative tenures multiplied and so did extortion, as officials tried to have their initial investment in a position pay off.[122]

The many rotten apples in the bin of Portuguese officialdom ought not obscure the fact that there was still many a decent and honest man in Portuguese Asia. "There are, here in India, a great many scribblers around who are always trying to censure anything you do," Conde de Aveiras muttered to the king. The ubiquitous complaints (*queixas*) about malpractice filling the Portuguese files have to be taken with a grain of salt. It was in the nature of the Portuguese system of checks and balances to produce them, be it because of the welter of *juntas* suspiciously scrutinizing each other's doings or because every official was, after his term of office, required to submit to an inquest (*residência*) regarding his demeanor.[123]

### *Elites: The Church*

Nevertheless, both the nobility and the church enriched themselves to the detriment of the state. That money was swallowed in vast amounts by the monasteries was, according to many viceroys, the principal cause for its lack.[124]

This issue was, inevitably in the Habsburg empire, submitted to a *junta* in 1636—hardly an impartial one: it consisted entirely of clerics. His majesty had probably been wrongly informed, the bishop of Cochin summarized their not very surprising conclusion. Most of them were "poor and destitute" and needed every penny to pay the mission. Nonsense, Viceroy Pedro da Silva responded; if the clergy was that indigent, where did all the money to raise so many sumptuous churches come from?[125]

"While your majesty has not a single ship in India, the Jesuits have an entire fleet," said da Silva, and they had hired a private army so nobody would trespass on their ports. Some fathers would lead their *lascarins,* muskets in hands.[126] However, the Jesuits were not the worst. A particularly obnoxious case was the trade of the Dominicans in Goa itself. On Divar Island the friars had put up a separate customs station and warehouses adjacent to those of the crown. These stations had attracted the bulk of Goa's trade across the *passos secos.* The friars had even mustered an armed band to guard those stations, which repeatedly fought the *lascarins* of the crown. There were many other cases like this. The Jesuits were leading an exemplary life, the Count of Alvor noted, but the other orders were apparently more preoccupied with the wallets of the natives than with their souls. The crown might well announce that the property of the monasteries would be forfeited if they dealt with such profane matters, but this was to little avail.[127]

On the other hand, without those investments of the church, Portuguese trade might not have been conducted at all, certainly not at the end of the seventeenth century. Because, as Canter Vischer wrote of Goa, "for the Portuguese *fidalgos* it would be a disgrace to conduct trade but the Jesuits pride themselves on it and they are the major traders there."[128]

But only a portion of the incomes of the monasteries at Goa and in Praças do Norte was gathered through commerce. The ownership of land was a far more important source of revenue. Although the crown fixed a ceiling to ecclesiastical landed property, ever more land fell under the regular church. The crown was worried about this for several reasons. The more land devoted to feeding monks, the less available for troops and horsemen. Church property was generally exempt from taxation and, not least important, if too many Portuguese chose to live in celibacy, their community would not procreate.[129]

Since in the second half of the seventeenth century *casados* and *fidalgos* invested heavily in estates, more and more land was bestowed on the church by legacies. One may consider as an example the property of the Carmelite missionaries that had been accumulated after 1620. It included more than eight palm groves in Goa alone, with a value of more than 20,000 xeraphins, and more property in Praças. But those large properties notwithstanding, "the monastery is still showing a loss of 1745 xeraphins yearly." Most of this estate had been acquired when Portuguese landowners had bestowed land on the Carmelites for reading masses for the deceased. Much land had fallen to the church as a bail when monks took care of transactions too. This property of the Carmelites was illegally acquired, for because of its quarrel with the *propaganda fide* the crown had never given a permit for the construction of this particular monastery.[130]

Both in Praças do Norte and in Goa ecclesiastical property consisted, apart from the domain of the church (the confiscated temple lands in Bardes and Salcete), of a welter of rights on land, seigneurial dues, and taxes on the marketing of everything from vinnegar to cattle. The cash obtained might vary from thousands to one xeraphin. By assembling dues and landed property the monasteries aimed to become self-sufficient and invest those revenues in buildings and good works. Thus the orders were normally nearly breaking even or operating at a loss.[131]

But the peasants did not always crowd to church lands because the monks were good masters. The Augustinians in Bardes, in particular, were accused of being more devoted to shepherding riches than their flock. "There are many monks of this order in the churches in Bardes who to judge from the way they administer their office, will be brought straight to hell," the archbishop of Goa sputtered. In the Praças the Indians had little choice anyway since most peasants on those estates were serfs.[132]

And, as the sumptuous churches built in this period testify, if the state did not prosper, the orders certainly did—financially too. The boom in building did not extend—as we saw—to the cathedral or to the parochial churches, which were in severe financial difficulties. The chapter of the cathedral of Cochin, paid from the customs of this town, was in such dire trouble that it had to be closed in 1644.[133]

To be fair, one should add that part of these incomes were invested in loans to the state. In 1664 the Jesuits wrote the crown that they had lent more than 35,500 xeraphins. Their college had recently burned down, but since all funds they had advanced to the king had "evaporated" somehow, they were unable to rebuild it.[134]

### *Elites: The Nobles*

In 1686 the nobility of Goa consisted of 106 families.[135] Forty-three had arrived from Portugal. The majority of the *reinois* were born in Lisbon but some towns in northern and eastern Portugal were represented too. Of the Indian natives 26 were from Goa, the others from Daman and Bassein. There were four families from Cochin: the last scions of an independent nobility, which had constituted a competitor to Goa's aristocracy in the beginning of the seventeenth century. The average income of a noble in Goa from various rights and dues amounted to about 15,000 xeraphins yearly. The richest group was the Bassein nobles. By way of comparison, a viceroy was paid 24,463 xeraphins yearly, a judge 1,583, a skilled laborer 80, and an unskilled worker 40.

What were these aristocrats spending their money on? Francisco de Siqueira Fária, *fidalgo,* in 1698 possessed the incomes from four villages in Daman.[136] He had spent those revenues on four houses: one in Daman, one in Goa, and two villas in Goa and Daman. Apart from this, Fária had acquired the revenues from several rice fields and gardens in Goa. He owed a number of slaves and was busily involved in the slave trade with Mozambique. About 50,000 xeraphins had been partly invested with Indian bankers and shopkeepers, partly entrusted in bottomry to various Portuguese traders. Another 30,500 were invested in treasure: boxes with pearls, diamonds, robes, ornaments, and statues.

J.H. van Linschoten in the late sixteenth century mocked the empty pomp of Goa's *fidalgos.* Portuguese sumptuary laws wherein, for example, the excessive use of palanquins or of black bodyguards was forbidden certainly confirm this picture.[137] But such indulgence in pageantry did not exclude the calculation of benefit. Splendor was a way to demonstrate credit. Investments in gold or silver treasures were also meant as security for obtaining funds to buy tax farms or conduct trade.

But nobles mainly invested in land. Such investments were preferably, if possible, made in Portugal but if not, in India. These investments in land in Asia undoubtedly constituted a reaction to the Dutch and English encroachment on the Portuguese monopoly of trade to Europe and to their depredations on Portuguese private trade. However, they can also be related to a quest for "rooted property" (*bens de raíz*), as the Portuguese called it. Such "rooted property" could be used as collateral on loans and as a last resort if all investments failed. For intra-Asian trade was a gamble: for every *fidalgo* returning home rich, there were as many "who die overburdened by debt. And all possessions of their wives are then auctioned by their creditors and by the exchequer of your majesty," as the *senado da câmera* of Goa emphasized.[138] In 1678, for example, Dom Francisco de Castro, *moço fidalgo,* was unable to pay his arrears to the farmer of the *renda do tabaco* of Mahim, Narain Sinay. Since he had no "rooted property" to pay, "he has become a hunted man, who is nowhere safe; not even in Bombay, where he has fled, and where the infidels have succeeded in tracking him down as well."[139]

The fountain of prosperity for the nobility was *conquista*—often rather pillage than conquest. We have impartial testimony from the crown itself: the Portuguese ought to bravely face the Muscati enemy, but no—"the main occupation of the *armadas* is robbing the ships of friendly kings with fake pretexts."[140] Much of the warfare conducted by the Estado was *guerre de course.* Commanders would look upon their right to exercise violence as a tax farm, which they were totally free to exploit. Such violence was often counterproductive since the prospect for booty might prevail over the interests of the state. "The prime reason why we have lost so much has mainly been the excesses of the captains, rather than the arms of the enemy," the viceroy wrote in 1681.[141]

It is often argued that the Estado da Índia faced a choice between peaceful commerce and conquest in the late sixteenth century. For the state, "fighting and trading are more opposed than North and South Pole,"[142] wrote one Portuguese author. But this was not so for the *fidalgos mercadores* who constituted its ruling class. Their commerce depended on both the funds and the exploitation of the right to protection generated by war and piracy.

For, all the profound legal justifications notwithstanding, the Portuguese navicerts or *cartazes* were really simply letters of marque, safeguarding ships from being robbed. Normally, any ship without a *cartaz* was liable to be plundered by captain and crew of a Portuguese vessel, with only one-fifth of the proceeds benefiting the crown. In 1636 Goa still mustered a fleet of 25 *sanguiceis adventureiros:* corsairs, largely fitted out by private entrepreneurs.[143]

Although I doubt this, in the sixteenth century the *cartazes* might have been used by the Portuguese as an instrument of a consistent policy to redirect trade, as some writers argue.[144] In the seventeenth century, anyhow, *cartazes* had two functions.

First, they were a way for the viceroy and his retinue to earn money—"protection rent," plain and simple. The right to issue *cartazes* was therefore centralized in Goa in 1672, to the anger of the captain at Diu and the governor of Surat. Yet this was somewhat justified, for individual captains used navicerts to scramble for money as well, often to the detriment of the state. At Diu, for example, ships of its inhabitants were normally exempt from paying *cartazes,* so the captains went to all lengths to have traders move to Surat to earn more themselves.

Second, the *cartazes* were used to impede trade on routes that had been reserved for concessionary voyages. This did not merely benefit the Portuguese traders. Probably the most outspoken advocates for rigidly curtailing the issue of *cartazes* to the inhabitants of Portuguese territory alone were the *bania*s of Diu and the rajah of Cochin.[145]

### *Elites: Indigenous Merchants*

#### *India*

The great Portuguese historian Manuel Severim da Fária in 1634 briefly considered writing a chronicle of Portuguese India—but in an optimistic mode: small wonder he did not pursue this idea very long. The wise Viceroy Linhares had 2,000 Brahmins baptized but he had to pay for it himself, da Fária recounted. "For many ministers did not want these Hindus to be converted; they are rich and most of the royal *rendas* are run on their account."[146] Modern research has abundantly confirmed their insight.[147]

Those merchants financed both the state and the *fidalgos,* for Portuguese captains were as inextricably tied to their Gujarati or Parsi brokers and moneylenders as were the Dutch or English merchants. These *shroffs* were funding both their private and their official expenses. The personal broker of Francisco Lobo de Silveira, second Count of Sarzedas, governor of Bassein, used to be Magha Mehta. This Parsi trader handled his benefits from office, which Silveira had invested in the trade with rice from Bassein to Surat and Goa. Magha Mehta had in 1677 withdrawn from business "and has transferred his credit upon his eldest son." To run his affairs as much as to pay his soldiers and seven servants, the count of Sarzedas was in dire need of funds. But "there are presently no loans available which would be of any service to your highness," he was assured. "For there is a general shortage of funds this year"; "these lands are almost unpopulated and Bombay is full of our people."[148]

The Indian role differed from one settlement to another. At Diu and, to a lesser extent, Chaul and Daman, the trade was largely controlled by Indians. We shall discuss the Parek family's involvement in the customs of Diu later on. After 1680 these were farmed by Hodsia Minas, an Armenian tycoon resident at Surat—but *católico,* it was stressed to Lisbon. Alvor tried to lure Hodsia Minas to Diu with his ships and small barges, his extended family, and clients. That would be a much-needed boost to Diu's trade. Hodsia Minas demanded complete exemption from all customs and fines for *cartazes* in return. If not allowed this very humble request, "your most obedient and subservient of slaves" threatened the king of Portugal that the trade of Diu would be completely ruined.[149]

Daman, again, was a center of Parsi traders who leased several revenues of the fortress. These Parsis traded horses from the Deccan and dealt with slaves from Mozambique in Surat—to the severe embarrassment of Goa since some were baptized.[150]

The bulk of the population of these towns was Hindu. At Christian Goa, non-Christian merchants were more isolated from the Catholic population and lived in the segregated quarter of Nossa Senhora do Monte (Pearson compares it to a ghetto). There were two groups of traders there. First, the *banias*: shipowners and bankers to traders. And, second, the *chatins* (as the Portuguese called them), or Saraswat Brahmins: gold traders, moneylenders, and merchants to the interior. The Saraswat capital in Goa was mainly invested in land revenues and in farming taxes of the state.[151]

Partly, this paramount role of Indian bankers in Portuguese finances resulted from wise policy of the Conselho da Fazenda. Portuguese tax farmers, who stayed only a few years in India—like those running the Estanco do Tabaco—

were often apt to slaughter the goose that lays the golden eggs by squeezing the peasant communities like a lemon. The other way round, Saraswats also seem to have had a preference for investment in a secure portfolio like the *renda do katvali* (i.e., the income for small fines) or the farm on the sale of betel rather than investing in trade.[152] The Conselho da Fazenda tried to reserve *rendas* for the Christian inhabitants of the Estado. Nonetheless, Hindus from the mainland also invested in *rendas*, so money fled the Estado's territory and was spent in Punda on Hindu "ceremonies [*romarias*] and gifts to, or for, the embellishment of temples, or in sumptuous new buildings for said temples."[153]

In the sphere of state finances, just like with the *cabedal do reino*, we encounter a tendency toward duopoly. In 1698 half of all the *rendas* of Goa were leased, and then subcontracted to a host of other investors, by the brothers Narsana and Vitoji Sinay, Hindu Saraswats. Through their monopoly over most *rendas* the brothers had succeeded in raising their value three- or fourfold. They were creditworthy merchants: bankers were soon eager to lend to them. The brothers Sinay were granted the hereditary position of "chief tax farmer" (*rendeiro-mor)* in 1697 by virtue of their "singular services to this state." They were also allowed to pass to and from from Goa to the mainland "without being searched or touched by any Hindu" at the customs stations.[154]

The Portuguese capital bordered the rural districts of Bardes and Salcete—almost an alien environment. "The *canarins* [Goa's Indian Christians] hate us and they will never allow us access to their villages," chancellor Francisco Cabral de Almeida wrote. This had fatal consequences, he argued. Since there was no possibility for investments in land and one had to rely on the transient incomes from commerce, a stable aristocracy was unable to take root at Goa.[155]

In 1519 the major *gaokar* clans of Bardes and Salcete administered a solemn oath to Albuquerque. The Portuguese had promised that they would respect to all eternity the rights to the use of the land by the ones who had first tilled the soil: the *gaokar*s. The *gaokar*s were to allot the labor in the fields. On the other hand, the *gaokar*s would pay rent to the king of Portugal. Lands could not be alienated or sold without paying a premium to the king and these were not to be acquired by Portuguese. The Portuguese crown scrupulously adhered to this stipulation.[156]

This arrangement was, to pursue Almeida's argument, mostly defended by pointing out that the people of the villages had a say in the *câmeras* of Bardes and Salcete and that the *gaokar*s protected the poor peasants. Yet the small peasants were exploited by the *gaokar*s who forced labor dues on them and evicted the poor from their lands.[157] While the *câmeras* in Bardes were supposed to speak for the humble tiller, they really represented only three wealthy families. Since decisions of the rural *câmeras* were taken by general approval, a powerful *gaokar* could block any decision that was to his disadvantage. One could as well assign land to Portuguese soldiers, Almeida concluded. The Conselho Ultramarino agreed in principle, but said that if this was done, "there will be a great revolt."[158]

The situation in Praças do Norte was considerably more complex than that in Goa. The *praças* were allotted in fiefs during a long period stretching from 1576 to 1596. Afterward, lands were subject to a complicated process of subinfeudation. Families might die out—naming wardens of their possessions to whom in due course devolved the use of the property—or families might have acquired land beyond the limits of their original possessions. It had become very hard to figure out who was the precise owner of land, since by 1640 the ancient *tombos* had little relation to reality. Thus the system of land revenue differed appreciably from area to area, from hamlet to hamlet.[159]

In Bombay, where the reclamation of land and the laying of dikes took place under the leadership of Portuguese *foreiros*, a manorial system developed. A large part of Bombay island was property of the family of Garcia de Orta. The inhabitants owed them dues either in cash or in labor. But in the rural districts near Daman—which were already densely settled when the Portuguese took over—taxes were levied by the village heads (*desai*s) or village accountants (*pattakar*s). They had to turn over one-sixth of land revenue to the *foreiros* in some villages, one-fifth in others. In the borderlands of Praças do Norte villages had to entertain a number of armed men and horses but were liberated from taxes. In the surroundings of fortresses villages had been allotted to the strongholds: the inhabitants had to guard the walls, deliver provisions, and perform manorial labor to repair the walls. They were freed from taxes, however. Some of these labor dues were in the seventeenth century commuted to taxes in cash, as were the duties to entertain horsemen.[160]

Yet the Praças do Norte still were a "frontier, close to powerful enemies." *Foreiros* depended on Indian forces to defend their territory. Troops were drafted from the villages, but these merely consisted of a few lame steeds and a handful of bumpkins with rusty helmets and broken lances.[161] Manpower had to be obtained through contractors and mainly from Mughal territory.

Essoji Raja, the main military contractor, had acquired in 1683 the right to levy taxes in 38 hamlets. The largest estates were in the Praças do Norte, for which he had to pay dues of 4,000 xeraphins. This was merely the land for supporting his wives and children, however—he had more land in Mughal territory. Essoji was pestered by the surrounding Portuguese *foreiros:* they had dammed his canals and grazed their cattle on his rice fields. So Essoji Raja was finally driven to rebel. His lands were confiscated, divided into several fiefs, and leased to a host of Portuguese investors, all much poorer than this military entrepreneur.[162]

Next to the *gaokar*s or the *desai*s stood the interpreters, who were always Indians ("since the Portuguese are loath to learn another language") and mostly Brahmin. Their office was generally hereditary. Both in Goa and in the North it was usual that the land revenue was divided between the village head and the village scribe (*kulkarni* in Goa), generally a Saraswat Brahmin. The Conselho da Fazenda required that villages be able to demonstrate their right to the use of the soil by showing an attest in writing. The *kulkarnis* were indispensable for this, "since they are devious and smart, change the charters, customs and uses," as the *gaokars* of Bardes complained in 1680.[163]

The Saraswat Brahmins were indispensable for the administration of the Estado da Índia too. Brahmins, who knew Portuguese, controlled the lower echelons of the administration and the rural courts as well. By 1670 such Brahmin clans, who generally had relatives across the Maratha border, ran most tribunals. That was only logical, for in civil cases in Praças do Norte, and probably in cases involving Hindus in Goa as well, the *shastras* were in force—not Portuguese legislation. All the same, the Conselho Ultramarino was unwilling to man the *relação* with Brahmins. Christians could not be subject to a "heathen" judge, as this conflicted with ecclesiastical law, while "the [Christian] natives are good for nothing."[164]

### *East Africa*

Let us now take a look at East Africa. The community of ex-criminal "Manuels" in Mombasa was hardly popular on the Mrima Coast. As they saying went,

> *Enda Manoel, ututukizije*
> *Enda, na sulubu uyititizje*
>
> [Go away, Manuel, you have made us hate you. Go away and carry your cross with you][165]

Yet the Portuguese commercial and political "empire" in both Mombasa and Mozambique was erected upon the foundation of Arab and Swahili trade, and for the coastwise navigation pretty much depended on it. Thus—as we saw already—in the case of the barter with Sofala and Dela Goa Bay from Mozambique, which was largely financed and arranged by the Swahili and *canarin* merchants in Mozambique, to a very large extent this whole commerce may be seen as just a continuation of the pre-existing pattern of coastwise trade on which a Portuguese "protection enterprise" was grafted.[166] And, it could be added, there was a "protection enterprise" of the missionaries as well: the Dominicans were heavily involved in the gold and ivory trade with Sofala and took care to protect their flock as well as their merchandise with arms as much as with prayer.[167] Due to the decline of trade at Mozambique and the shift of the commerce northward to Kilwa and Querimba—which we have been considering—it was even proposed the Portuguese should move the main *feitoria* for buying ivory there.[168] This ivory was bought from rings of Swahili traders who in turn ob-

**Map 7. East Africa**

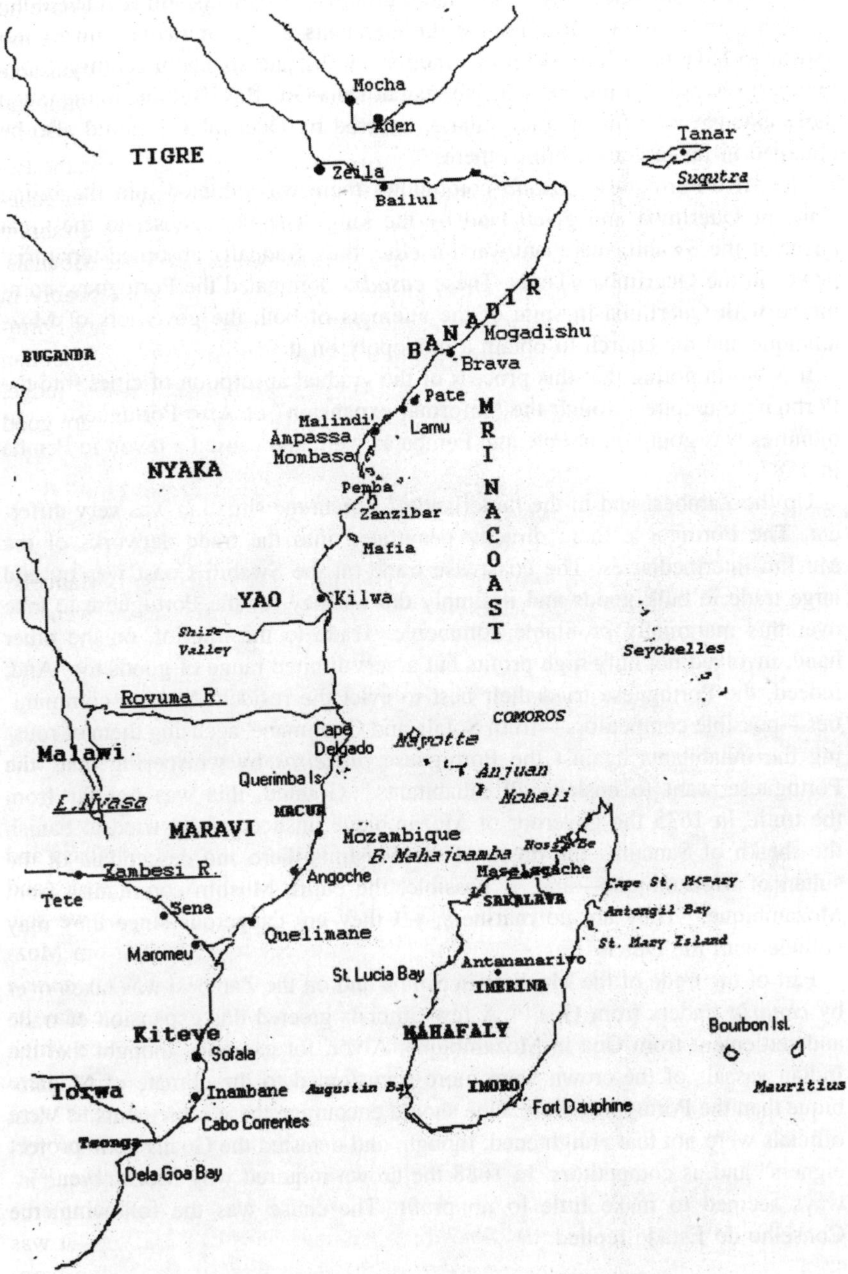

tained it via the Yao merchant/nomads. This was largely through a relay system. For, unlike at Dela Goa Bay, where large groups of elephants still roamed along the coast, in northern Mozambique the elephants in the immediate hinterland appear to have been hunted into extinction by the late sixteenth century. Ivory in Querimba was far more expensive than at Dela Goa Bay. But due to the much more extensive circuit of trade inland, covered by Querimba, it could also be obtained in far larger quantities there.[169]

The Afro-Portuguese *casado* community there was adopted into the ruling clans of Querimba and given land by the king. The Portuguese, to the great anger of the Swahili merchant/warrior elite, thus gradually absorbed territorial power in the Querimba islands. These *casados* dominated the Portuguese commerce with Querimba in spite of the attempts of both the governors of Mozambique and the church to obtain a monopoly on it.[170]

It is worth noting that this process of the gradual absorption of cities into the Portuguese empire through the "informal expansion" of Afro-Portuguese communities was going on at Pate and Pemba as well, and caused a revolt in Pemba in 1587.[171]

Up the Zambesi and in the hinterland of Sofala the situation was very different. The Portuguese there directly penetrated into the trade networks of the Muslim intermediaries. The coastwise trade on the Swahili Coast was by and large trade in bulk goods and it simply did not pay for the Portuguese to take over this marginally profitable commerce. Trade to the interior, on the other hand, involved not only high profits but a very limited range of goods too. And, indeed, the Portuguese tried their best to evict the resident Muslim communities—possible competitors—from Sofala and Quelimane, accusing them of rousing the inhabitants against the Portuguese *prazeiros* by whispering that "the Portuguese want to enslave all inhabitants." Granted, this was not far from the truth. In 1635 the governor of Mozambique unsuccessfully tried to banish the sheikh of Sanculi—the imam of the Muslims there and descendant of the sultan of Mozambique—and, if possible, the entire Muslim community from Mozambique. "They are no mariners, yet they are dangerous since they may collude with the Dutch."[172]

Part of the trade of the Muslims in Sofala and on the Zambesi was taken over by *canarin* traders from Goa.[173] A few officials greeted this expansion of trade and settlement from Goa in Mozambique. Alvor, for example, thought that the Indian vassals of the crown were more accustomed to the climate of Mozambique than the Portuguese were. One should encourage these settlements.[174] Most officials were not that enlightened, though, and detested the Goans both as "foreigners" and as competitors. In 1688 the crown inquired why Mozambique always seemed to make little to no profit. The cause was the following, the Conselho do Estado replied:

> The natives of this state are our main opponent, as experience has shown. For, as soon as the *canarins* have arrived at Cuama, they start to trade in gold. Until now,

> we have been unable to forestall this, for these merchants are more numerous and cunning than we are. And should we prohibit this several customs houses would have no incomes whatsoever.[175]

As the sole possibility to inhibit this destructive competition of the *canarin* traders, the crown proposed to hand the trade to a monopoly company of traders from Goa. Otherwise, mutual competition between Indian peddlers at Tete and Sena would result in a surfeit of Indian textiles for sale. Because of the peculiar structure of the gold trade—which we have been considering—this might severely damage the Portuguese gold trade and ruin the revenue from the customs. Besides, as the *canarins* did not fund mercenary armies, the "conquests" in the hinterland were at peril too.

To the Conselho do Estado this still appeared insufficient. It was even suggested that the Estado evict all Indian traders from Mozambique and prohibit Indian traders from joining caravans heading from Sena to the *feiras* by threat of capital punishment, lest they divulge the secrets of this traffic. Henceforth *canarin* traders apprehended on any ship heading to Mozambique were to be locked in chains.

These measures were not implemented nor could they have been. For the *canarins* connected both the Swahili and the Portuguese merchants to the banking and trade circuit of the Deccan and Gujarat, where ivory and gold were sold. The peddlers to the Zambesi or Sofala were the humble infantries of Goa's rich Saraswats and the *bania*s from Diu. And as the price of ivory in India wildly fluctuated, the *bania*s from Diu functioned as an indispensable "second hand" between the traders working in Mozambique and the Indian market.[176]

There was no practical way to inhibit Indian trade to Mozambique from Diu either. As the piece-cloth trade to the Zambesi depended upon regular supplies of *bafta* and *berauli* from Diu, it was decided participation should be limited in order that unhampered trade not cause a drop in the rates of barter. In 1688 the viceroy conceded to a petition of the *mahajan,* the assembly of the *bania* traders of Diu, to establish a company to conduct this trade. This association was to outfit two or three keels yearly from Diu to Mombasa and Malindi. In return the *bania*s were to hand over lump sums to finance the war against Muscat. After the monopoly of this Mazanes association had been suspended in 1693, it was revived in 1701. Not only was the Mazanes association to gather funds from the merchants at Diu, but traders from Surat and Cambay might invest in it too.[177]

## Monopolists and Smugglers

### *Private Trade: Private Monopoly*

The officials of the Estado were not likely to welcome Indian competition since they normally invested their incomes in private trade. And so did the viceroy. Any viceroy, it was argued in 1656, who arrived in India normally carried a huge retinue of bastard sons and favorites in his trail. Those fellows would rapidly buy positions that would cost them five or six times their nominal value. To finance these huge initial outlays they would have to borrow heavily from Gujarati or Saraswat bankers. Such money they would strive to recover at all costs in order that the bankers not doubt their creditworthiness or that of their successors. And indeed, the Portuguese were not considered creditworthy; the moneylenders were normally charging 25–30 percent yearly, three or four times more than they would charge the VOC. The Portuguese would have to lease ships and take up bottomry to rapidly make a fortune. At the end of their term of office they would normally be in a frenzy to repay those debts and would have to resort to extortion.[178]

However, only part of the initial capital to invest in private trade was derived from India. Portuguese nobles, before departing for India, normally entrusted their estates to an attorney. This *procurador* would convert part of the revenues of their incomes in Portugal (or in Brazil) into bills of exchange or—more rarely—into bullion, which could be invested in office, land, or trade.[179]

The viceroys were generally wealthy nobles; they had excellent opportunities to obtain credit and conduct private trade, and many repatriated with considerable riches. They, or their families, were often major shipowners. This, for example, applied to Mello e Castro, who owned more than six ships. His possessions, when returning to Portugal, were valued at more than 1 million reales—to Paixão a refutation of all fairy tales about the impoverishment of India.[180]

The Conselho da Fazenda considered in 1639 that it had proven to be a waste of resources to have intra-Asian trade conducted by the crown. Virtually all profits of voyages in Asia were absorbed by the costs of running factories and of personnel to conduct shipping. Therefore, to tap the potential benefits from intra-Asian trade, the crown had in the second half of the sixteenth century instituted an intricate system of concessionary voyages. Ideally, the concessionaire was to pay a lump sum to the crown, in return for which he was to enjoy the monopoly on a voyage. A concessionary voyage was private property and could be used as such.[181]

This system was expanded to cover an array of expenses until, in the first half of the seventeenth century, it encompassed the bulk of long-distance trade from the Portuguese settlements. Concessions were generally sold to cover some unforeseen expense. These ranged from repairing the walls of San Thomé to the construction of an altar for the cathedral of Cranganore, and from the support of infants in need to that of the (apparently also penurious) queen of Spain. Faced with ever higher prices of the concessionary voyages, those fortunate enough to have been allowed one waged as bitter—and as fruitless—a battle against "private trade" as did the VOC. One should really guard against jumbling this monopoly trade and the various smugglers on the margin of the Portuguese empire together to prove that Portuguese private trade was free trade. Portuguese private trade was only "free" for a small group of monopolists.[182]

"Interlopers," who disposed of neither the initial capital nor the connections to purchase a concessionary voyage nor shares in it, were forced to seek their fortunes outside the pale of the Estado. These communities of smugglers were rejoined by deserters and fugitive criminals "who live without God, without King, and without Law" (*sem Deus, sem Rey, sem Ley*). It is probably no coincidence that the Portuguese settlements that provided the majority of Portuguese *lançado* communities—Malacca, Mombasa, Sofala, Mozambique, the Moluccas, and Ceylon—were all penal colonies at one time or another.[183] Thus one would find everywhere outside of the territory of the Estado da Índia a Portuguese *natio* with obscure origins. According to many in Goa, most Portuguese in Bengal were fugitive cutthroats, for example, although their valor had demonstrated they were true Portuguese, it was conceded. These Portuguese communities have been quite well researched for the Bay of Bengal and East Asia.[184]

Such communities appear as a mirror image—a "shadow-empire," G.D. Winius calls it—of the "official" Portuguese empire. They seem relatively free of racial prejudice; they were willing to adapt to life in the Indies; they provided technological help to the inhabitants; contrary to the monopolist companies, they were devoted to free trade—the ideal development agency workers, one would nearly conclude from the literature. But were these *casados* or *lançados* really "Portuguese"—except for a token Christian name, and perhaps religion? King João IV proposed the giving of alms to the poor white *casados* of Goa. Not necessary, the viceroy replied. There were but 50 of them and of this lot most were "mulattos and mestizos."[185]

Converts to Roman Catholicism considered themselves members of the Portuguese *natio*. National belonging was not attributive but descriptive. It does seem rather far-fetched to call communities such as the *topazes* in Cochin, the *muzungos* in Sofala, or the ephemeral community of freebooters on the Hugly and in Arracan a "shadow empire" or an "improvised empire." Although they might sometimes have a Portuguese name or wave the Portuguese flag, links with the empire were far too weak. It is more accurate to call them the Portuguese *natio*.[186]

Apart from deserters, converts, and fugitives, many of the communities making up the Portuguese *natio* beyond the pale of the Estado probably stemmed from Portuguese slaves. Goa's traders were busily selling their Indian Catholic brethren to the Coromandel Coast, for example, mostly to Islamic grandees. "They often lose the faith then, since they are not yet very steadfast in it," the crown protested. There was little one could do about this, but the crown advised using the utmost restraint in selling them to Muslims. Again, the Portuguese community at Surat was mostly made up of refugee Catholic serfs from Praças do Norte.[187]

Such Portuguese private traders in the Arabian seas often had close familial links with Indians and Africans and can well be compared, as emphasized by both van Leur and Steensgaard, with Indian or Swahili peddlers. And, indeed, as we have seen in the case of Sofala, they *were* African but for a Portuguese name.

Nevertheless, magnates like Ferdinand Kron in the early seventeenth century or João de Prado, Goa's most important trader in the 1660s, were certainly no peddlers.[188] The latter possessed four ships and capital of more than 600,000 xeraphins. João de Prado was mainly involved in a very different branch of commerce than most private traders, however—the trade with the Philippines and with Macao. This entailed both huge investments and huge risks. It was not a trade that could be conducted by men of modest means.[189]

We will consider three cases more closely to further clarify the character of Portuguese private trade: two cases where private trade was tightly linked to such military might as the Estado could muster, and one case of peaceful settlement. The first case, in particular, may prove to be surprising since in the literature it is often supposed that the Portuguese controlled and taxed—or at least looted—the trade of this area.

### *Plunder and Trade Along the Mrima Coast*

Although the Portuguese crown claimed paramountcy over the Mrima Coast, this Portuguese rule was never more than a flimsily thin veneer. Philip Carstenszoon, commodore of a VOC fleet cruising off Mogadishu in 1634, wrote that Mombasa "mainly served to preserve Christianity and for the pomp and majesty of the king, rather than to fetch profits. For the customs, obtained by the king from . . . [imports] and exports (being ivory, ambergris, rice and millet) are not by far as important as the costs of fortifications and garrisons."[190]

The main income of Mombasa consisted of benefits obtained from selling navicerts to the small crafts plying the coast, far from a cornucopia. Other revenues, like the tribute handed by the sultan of Pemba, Sio, and Pate to the Portuguese crown, hardly sufficed to cover expenses, consisting of a merely symbolic 150 xeraphins each. Hence, although those tributary sultans were supposed to muster and pay for the grandiloquently styled *armada* of small dhows (*parangues*) with which the Portuguese tried to tax coastwise navigation as well, Mombasa booked a deficit of 10,000 xeraphins yearly. And "illegal" private benefits connected to the position of captain did not compensate for the official losses, so that Mombasa was not a field for more or less condoned patronage of the Goa nobility like Mozambique—and earlier San Thomé.[191]

According to Carstenszoon, the Portuguese had established themselves along the coast in search of gold, and they met many Ethiopian traders there, with whose help they hoped to exterminate Islam along the coast. "And so, after some years, a drove of Portuguese and mestizos have established themselves southward in the places Qilva, Maoursi, Monfia and Quarimba." They navigated there with small vessels from Diu, Daman, and Chaul loaded with coarse (Deccani) piece-cloth like *robalho*, *teada*, and *boralha* exchanged for millet and ivory. And when they had finished fortifying Mombasa, "aided, and with the consent of, the captain of the castle occasionally armed men would make forays to the mainland to catch slaves; which, after some voyages had well succeeded, they looked upon as their prerogative."[192]

Carstenszoon's view is largely confirmed by Portuguese documents. Partly, Portuguese expansion on the Mrima Coast consisted of more or less permitted robbery: raids, kidnapping of slaves, and plundering of the Swahili towns with or without the consent of the authorities at Mombasa, Mozambique, or Goa. Thus, the sultan of the small principality of Sio in the Lamu Archipelago complained that, without the central administration's being aware of it, the Portuguese "convert our vassals to Christianity and they next auction them or they seize them without endorsement from their lords and proprietors." The slaves were mostly sold to the Gulf, although Mombasa occasionally sent 100 to 200 slaves to Goa too. Most slaves auctioned at Mombasa were simply bought from the mainland, though, bartered for textiles. For the Muzungulos were "continuously at war and they sell each other as slaves." Such would imply that the circuit of the Portuguese slave trade in the seventeenth century was largely confined to the immediate hinterland of Mombasa.[193]

There was "institutionalized robbery" besides. In the third year of their tenure normally the governors of Mozambique paid a so-called ceremonial visit to the subordinate kings, such as at Kilwa and Querimba. This was little more than a pretext for extorting protection money from these cities. And the governors of Mombasa did the same in Pemba and Ampassa. Though this was not permitted by Goa, with ransack running into the hundred thousands of cruzados, it was not the least appetizing perquisite of office.[194]

Parties might get a permit from the governor of Mombasa to plunder "enemy" towns too. The conquest of Pate in 1686 started as a private expedition of Mombasa's governor, João Nunes de Portugal, who, in collaboration with neighboring princes, had outfitted three ships to go looting on his own account. The proceeds of this were to be divided between the sultan of Ampassa, a Muzungulo chief, a consortium of Arab merchants from Mombasa, and—last but not least—João Nunes de Portugal himself. Alvor—as we saw already—was hardly overjoyed with this local initiative: it was blunt insubordination.[195]

But Portuguese expansion mainly consisted of the more or less peaceful dissemination of Afro-Portuguese *casado* communities along the coast. Goa had little control over the Portuguese *natio* there. It would either recognize a *casado* as its *feitor*—as at Malindi and Pate, where the Portuguese had bought a right to a share of the customs—or it would, as it did in Pemba, bestow fiefs upon the *casados*. Granted such a fief, the *casados* were then free to conduct trade, and might attract other settlers as they saw fit. At Malindi the sultan legally was considered a vassal of the Portuguese king, and was then given the right to grant lands and offices in the town to his Afro-Portuguese subfeudatories.[196]

Sometimes the *casados* were adopted within the ruling lineages of towns;

they could establish plantations and enjoy the benefit thereof. At Angoche as much as at Querimba, the Portuguese *casados* had either bought or gradually absorbed most offices of the towns. And the Portuguese had also obtained plots of land both on Pemba island and on the mainland, as well as some offices there.[197]

Those *casados* on the Mrima Coast consisted of a few dozen families at most, who on the southern Swahili Coast were concentrated at Angoche and on the northern at Zanzibar. Apparently the inhabitants of Mombasa moved there after 1620. By 1635 Mombasa was said to be almost depopulated. This was partly linked to the Portuguese extortions but also to the war in Yemen since the commerce of Mombasa was tightly connected to that of the Red Sea. And it was probably also related to the migration of Gala tribes southward, which made the coast north of Mombasa very dangerous.[198]

Zanzibar, wrote *ouvidor* Pedro Álvarez Pereira in 1630, "is the gathering place for all soldiers who flee from Mombasa and Mozambique." It was a rowdy band of freebooters "who serve nothing good, merely violating, robbing and assaulting everyone who passes this island and defrauding the customs of Mombasa. For they know of no justice and behave as if they would like that all the fortresses of your majesty would be uninhabited." Álvarez Pereira dragged two fugitive assassins to Mombasa but finally had to acquiesce, not prosecuting the others.[199]

Some *casados* had actually adopted the "Moorish faith"; most lived at least with Swahili or Arab wives. This stout-hearted people mainly subsisted from coastwise trade along the Mrima Coast (with textiles and slaves) and by soldiering on behalf of the Swahili cities. A few commanded small private armies of several hundred African mercenaries and slaves, and mustered several *parangais*. The church was the *traité d'union* between Goa and this remote settlement. The Augustinian friar at Zanzibar, apparently paid by the community, would remit the revenues from the Coast to Goa and probably to Portugal. The *casados* themselves entertained but few contacts with Goa. Most trade with India was carried on through Diu and Chaul. The *casados*, however, largely dealt with their fellow *casados* at Muscat and in the sultanate of Khisn.[200]

Most traffic along the Swahili Coast was conducted between the towns themselves and with the Gulf. For in the seventeenth century already the trade with the Gulf and the Red Sea was typically one in bulk goods (fish, grain, or fruit), whereas that with India consisted of luxury goods. And while the trade with the Persian Gulf normally showed a positive balance, so that East Africa imported bullion from the Gulf, Mexican reales were exported to India. That was in modest quantities, but given the small size of the stock of bullion on the Mrima Coast, this probably constituted a severe drain on its economy. The former commerce both eluded the Portuguese control and fetched benefits too meager to make taxation of it pay. Before 1640 Pate was, for example, sending two or three ships owned by the aristocracy of the town to Muscat and Yemen yearly.

It also had a fleet of some 40 dhows connecting it with the other Swahili towns. The Swahili traders and the small resident Indian community there by and large operated these vessels. The Portuguese at Mombasa were not involved at all.[201]

As an example of the kind of commerce that *was* conducted under the Portuguese flag, consider two small ships heading for Muscat from Malindi captured by the VOC near Mogadishu in 1634. The *São Antônio* had a crew of 10 Portuguese, 1 Englishman, 4 women, and 54 mestizos and slaves, and the *Nossa Senhora da Luz* had 4 Portuguese, 3 black women, and 49 mestizos. On board were carried slaves, rice, millet, and beans (*gur*).[202]

Such commerce—very much a peddlers' trade—was conducted by the Portuguese in close collaboration with the Arab and Swahili merchants. The frigate *Nossa Senhora dos Milagres* of João Nunes de Portugal, for example, was freighted by himself; a certain Estevão Pinto, *casado* of Mombasa; the king of Mombasa; the sultan of Ampassa; and the harbor master of the former town, one "Xa de Benga." It was to fetch piece-cloth to Zanzibar from Mombasa until João Nunes de Portugal seized it for use in his raid on Pate.[203]

And in Zanzibar, indeed, the Portuguese and Arabs were largely indistinguishable. More frequent in other settlements was that the Portuguese were dealing through or on behalf of Indian merchants. In many ways the typical relationship between the European merchant and the indigenous broker was reversed on the Mrima Coast. Here, the Indian merchants were often wealthy but young and inexperienced and needed a Portuguese *casado* to guide them through the intricacies of trade and politics on this alien continent.[204]

The main branch of trade to the Mrima Coast in which the Portuguese authorities were involved was that from Diu. This was in 1688 carried out in small vessels of 100 to 140 tons that would conduct barter from one Swahili harbor to the next, exchanging steel and Cambay textiles with tortoiseshell, ivory, gold, and ambergris. However, the governor of Diu merely handed navicerts to these vessels; they were Indian owned, freighted, and manned. As we saw, one did try to reserve the benefits to the inhabitants of Diu, but many merchants of Diu were mere agents of traders in Cambay. It was but a small trade, fetching minimal profits. One could earn about 50 percent benefit on the sale of Cambay piece-cloth on the Coast, but the hefty premium charged for bottomry in India of up to 30 percent tended to devour this profit. One shipwreck could ruin the entire trade. Money to invest was hard to obtain, therefore, which further reduced the size of the trade.[205]

By 1656, with the incursions of Ja'ariba fleets on the Mrima Coast and repeated Muscati attacks on Zanzibar and Mombasa, even this illusion of Portuguese control collapsed. Ships from Pemba and Kilwa still were provided with Portuguese navicerts, but the other ports did not accept them any longer. It seems as if ships from Portuguese merchants now had often to be provided with *cartazes* from Muscat instead.[206]

So the Portuguese did not destroy the trade of the Mrima and the Banadir

Coast, nor that with India—as has long been recognized in the literature—and maybe interrupted but certainly did not destroy that with the Persian Gulf and the Red Sea. The Portuguese never interrupted Khisn's, Suqutra's, and Mogadishu's trade with either—nor was that of Zeila and Bailul much affected. The captains of Mombasa were accused of handing navicerts to ships of Arab and Swahili traders who sold wood to the "Turks" of Zeila. The crown prohibited it—on the rather drastic penalty of death—but to little avail. Despite the enmity between Turks and Portuguese, Bailul and Zeila still conducted a busy traffic in their frail dhows with both the Swahili Coast and Madagascar. This direct commerce from the Red Sea appears to have declined in the second half of the seventeenth century, however, probably due to Muscati attempts to constrict it to Muscat.[207]

Yet even before the rise of Muscat, the Portuguese hold on the Mrima Coast was fragile at best for a number of reasons. First, and perhaps fatally, Mombasa was—particularly given the exodus from the island in 1630, which halved the number of the inhabitants of the area—chronically short of foodstuffs. The king of Pemba was to deliver the millet and cattle it needed as his annual levy (*parea*). This generally did not suffice and Mombasa had to buy much of its foodstuffs at Chaul.[208]

Second, as we saw already, the Portuguese did not control the roads to the interior, and had to negotiate supplies of gold and ivory with the merchants and chiefs on the mainland.[209]

And third, there were some ports linked to the Ottoman empire in the Red Sea, Mogadishu in particular, which never recognized the Portuguese control.[210] After the fall of Hormuz and Muscat the Portuguese did not control the routes to the Gulf, another source of demand for slaves, either. The *casados* at Zanzibar had to reach some understanding with the Ja'ariba imamate to sell slaves and wood. This entailed quite substantial concessions: the *casados* at Zanzibar were accused of selling arms, slaves, and metal to Pate. The *sultana* of Pate in turn fetched this to Mogadishu and Muscat.[211]

But then, though the Ja'ariba imamate and the Portuguese both perceived their war as a crusade, on the Mrima Coast local alliances did not square with religion. At Pate and Malindi there were both anti- and pro-Muscati factions, but since Pate was controlled by a force of Arab mercenaries there was little space for political maneuvers. Lamu sided with Muscat, as it wanted to restore its old sovereignty over Mombasa; Pemba sided with the Portuguese because of long-standing feuds with Pate, and Ampassa was also staunchly allied to the Portuguese.[212]

The reasons for this lay partly embedded in the factional politics of the Swahili towns, but were economic as well. For the customs revenues of these ports mainly depended on the ivory and gold trade. The Portuguese often had more favorable conditions to offer than Muscat. Most of the leading Muzungulo families favored the Portuguese cause, therefore. The Muscati invasion of Mombasa was triggered by the anger of those neighboring kings, it was explained later, who had secretly promised the Ja'ariba army their support. They had always been allotted the right to freely conduct commerce with other ports of the coast without paying for navicerts. And they had been allowed a high and steady price for ivory too if they were willing to sell this to the Portuguese. However, the new Junta do Comércio had tried to bridle the free trade of Mozambique and had radically lowered the agreed price of ivory. It had also tried to constrict the ivory trade to Mombasa by restricting the number of navicerts handed out.[213]

Fourth, the Portuguese at Mombasa were suffering from a chronic lack of both manpower and ships. This became particularly acute when the link with Muscat, which had earlier mostly supplied these, was severed. Only mercenaries from Muscat, Suqutra, and Khisn would be of any real use in Mombasa, for its climate was probably the worst-suited for Europeans in the entire Arabian seas, it was argued. It was normal that half the garrison was in sick bay. True, the hirelings sent to Mombasa were later mostly Indians (from Baluchistan and Kathiawar in particular) and "kaffirs, armed with bows and arrows" from Mozambique, but they too were decimated by the plagues.

This shortage of keels and hands really hurt—in 1662 Diu would have liked to sign a proposal by a group of merchants at Surat, headed by Hodsia Minas. They would lend ships and arms to the Portuguese at Mombasa. The Surat traders should then be allowed navicerts to trade anywhere along the Swahili Coast. Goa prohibited this though, since it feared direct trade from Surat would harm the commerce of Chaul and Diu, but it had no succor to offer in return. Instead Goa now turned to the *foreiros* of Bassein and Daman, enticing them to build small dhows for privateering on the Mrima Coast. They were glad to oblige, as were, we shall see, the buccaneers. Thus, in the late seventeenth century the Portuguese presence on the Coast increasingly devolved to a mere privateering enterprise and Mombasa to a local Mrima variant of St. Mary. But then, of course, Portuguese Mombasa had to a large extent been a sea rovers' lair all along.[214]

### *Trade and Plunder in the Persian Gulf*

The second case of Portuguese private trade we will be considering concerns the Portuguese trade with the Persian Gulf after the fall of Hormuz. The Portuguese then still controlled a chain of fortresses along the Omani coast, which were laid out in the 1580s for protection against Ottoman incursions into the Arabian seas and Muscat.

The loss of Hormuz did not lead so much to the destruction of the Portuguese trade network in the Persian Gulf as to its restructuring. Whereas Portuguese private traders from Diu had been active in the Gulf in the sixteenth century and the Hormuz *casados* had engaged in (semi-illegal) trade with Basra, the

Portuguese administration of Hormuz conducted little commerce. Rather, it scared the merchants away with its perpetual extortions.[215]

After the eruption of the war between the Ja'ariba imams and the Estado in 1636, exports to Muscat consisted almost exclusively of weapons and warriors for the conduct of a dragging, petty war. Surrounded by the date plantations stood Portuguese strongholds, often, like Dobhia, but a gunshot from fortified villages that were under Ja'ariba sheikhs. The Lusitanian strongholds were, ideally, commanded by some minor Portuguese *fidalgo* assisted by small bands of *lascarins* and auxiliary forces of allied sheikhs.[216] The latter were to assemble yearly at Muscat where the Portuguese would allot them a 40 percent share of the customs revenues. Yet, according to Resende, many of the small fortresses contained not a single Portuguese soldier. There, Baluchi *lascarins* and Arabs from al-Batinah were conducting a fierce struggle with Arabs from the mountains: the familiar face of Omani politics with a Portuguese hat on.[217]

Some of the villages of al-Batinah were assigned to the fortresses and had to provide for armed support, some were assigned to the commanders of strongholds. They received one-fourth of the dates collected as their due, which they could sell to Persia and Sind. When fighting would erupt with the neighboring Ja'ariba hamlets the Portuguese would sneak into the mountains and date groves to loot a village, capture some slaves, or merely grab goats. This was the private war of the commanders of the strongholds. Goa wasted little attention on it. They rather reserved their forces for the far more immediate concern of the war with the VOC.[218]

Small wonder that stronghold after stronghold passed into Ja'ariba hands, practically unnoticed by Goa. Though Goa prided itself on the staunch loyalty of the sheikhs and its Baluchi mercenaries, the governor of Muscat noted more realistically that the Portuguese had as many enemies inside the fortress as outside.[219] The fighting finally climaxed in the "bloody or rather bloody stupid [*bloedig ofte liever bloodig*] loss," the Dutch giggled, of Muscat to the Ja'ariba troops in 1650. They had succeeded in penetrating Muscat's land defenses: one of the gates was open, be it through treason or neglect. Although the loss of Muscat was blamed on "criminal negligence and irresponsibility" of the governor, it was Goa's fault too, having allotted insufficient support to Muscat.[220]

Potentially Muscat was a profitable post—its customs, its horse trade, and the loot produced by the fortress along the Omani Coast could well compensate for its expenses.[221] But the war devoured those benefits. Muscat ran at a loss. Especially since it was chronically deficient in foodstuffs, Goa had to send grain there, paid for from the treasury. The meager revenues of Muscat were sent, partly in bullion, partly in horses, dates, and fruit, to Diu and Chaul. The *casados* of Goa were hardly interested in the trade to the Gulf. But Chaul had a vital interest in it: "it is as much as its warehouse." Goa's administration yearly sent two or three frigates to escort the ships of Portuguese traders from Sind and Diu to Muscat and to the Shatt al-Arab.[222]

Most trade at Muscat was conducted by the small *casado* community (about 150 persons), many of whom were refugees from Hormuz, and by the Jewish traders there. The *casados* also traded with Mogadishu, Suqutra, Malindi, and Mombasa, exchanging fruit and textiles from India and al-Hasha for slaves, grain, wood, and camphor. From Yemen they imported *urz*—a reeking body lotion that was yet very prized in Arabia—and coffee, which were bartered for Persian silk, camelots (decorative and expensive pieces of textile), carpets, and Indian textiles. Muscat's *casados* dealt with Sind and Basra too. This was done in small dhows, built at as-Shir and Muscat and manned with black slaves, Arabs, and *lascarins*.[223]

Trade and plunder were hardly distinguishable in the maritime zone of the lower Gulf. The Portuguese yearly sent a fleet of *tanaqins* to Bahrain and Qatar, Persian possessions, to claim one-fourth of the revenue of Bahrain and hand navicerts to the pearl fleets. The incomes of the small fortress of Curiat mainly depended on those revenues. The sultans of Bahrain and of Qatif were bitter enemies, so the Portuguese at Muscat assisted the latter with soldiers and war *tanaqins* to loot the pearl fleets from Bahrain. A cruel guerrilla war was waged between those two sheikhdoms, the Portuguese chatelaines, and the Safavid empire, which encouraged *nakhila* corsairs to prey on Portuguese shipping. "If you come across any ship," the commander of the fleet to Bahrain was instructed, "you should order them to strike their sails and you shall burn their crafts."[224]

However, Muscat's customs mainly depended on the trade between Basra and the West Coast. Indian ships would pay customs dues at Muscat and be assigned to the Gulf flotillas—20 to 30 small ships guarded by 2 or 3 Portuguese frigates and armed *tanaqins*, which were mustered locally and manned by Baluchi mercenaries. Apart from Indian textiles, the Gulf flotillas fetched pepper from Malabar to Basra as well. The trade with pepper to the Gulf was formally forbidden, but Goa was unable to do much about it: this stealthy trade was the main revenue of the admirals of the Gulf fleet. But it was a hazardous trade because of the risk of shipwreck and the danger from the *nakhila* pirates.[225]

A Portuguese flotilla had assisted the pasha of Basra in repelling a Persian attempt to invade Basra in 1624: the Portuguese were allotted a share in the customs of Basra, freedom from toll, and from the capitation tax as a reward. Besides those special circumstances, the pasha of Basra and the *capitão* of Muscat were in need of each other: Muscat needed wood from Anatolia, Basra grain from Khism, Qais, and Bandar Rig, and the Portuguese could interrupt that trade. A small Portuguese *natio* had settled along the Euphrates, consisting during its heyday around 1630 of about thousand persons. They lived in a separate neighborhood and financed a small Augustinian convent. Most of them were Indian Christians and Jacobinian Christians converted to Catholicism, intermediaries for the Sindi and Diu merchants. The Jacobite Christians conducted a busy coastwise trade within the Gulf too.[226]

With the loss of Muscat this Portuguese shipping to the Gulf dwindled. However, the link to the Gulf was still vital to the Estado, as it was its only available Asian source of silver. The merchants from Diu still occasionally sent ships to Kung and Basra. But the Portuguese trade in the Gulf was too dangerous. It appears to have merged therefore with Indian shipping or to have used the English cover. There is also some evidence to suggest that by 1670 there was a community of Portuguese renegades at Muscat, some of them former slaves who were not liable for ransom.[227]

If the Portuguese communities in the Persian Gulf were merely lingering on, such was certainly not the case for the *banias*, especially for the Sindhi community at Muscat. Most revenues of Muscat were farmed, as were the sugar plantations in the interior. The imamate depended upon the Indian traders, who could raise funds for such farms. The commerce of Muscat was controlled by a ring of Indian merchants, associated with the admirals of the Ja'ariba war fleets and urban notables. There were two Indian communities there—residents from the Portuguese period, mostly Kaphol *banias* from Diu (the wealthiest merchants there), and newcomers, often *mappilas* from Kerala. The former were permitted various exemptions from taxes.[228]

Apart from the Indians, the other beneficiary of the fall of Muscat was ironically Goa itself. Whereas the fortresses in the Gulf operated at a loss, the war with Muscat was—until at least 1680—profitable, fetching a 50 to 60 percent profit for the contractors of the warships. That was obtained by confiscating ships, plundering the al-Batinah coast and, first and foremost, from the Portuguese share of the customs of Kung. This was, after 1663, practically the only cash that was instantly available to pay the mercenaries and fleets; everything else had already been assigned to cover some expense. Thus, there was considerable interest to invest in the Gulf fleets in Goa. Merchants sometimes offered to equip ships on their own account to further this very Christian cause.[229]

### The Portuguese in Sind

The Portuguese *natio* in Sind was one of the richest Portuguese communities in Asia, but its trace is lost in the late seventeenth century. Portuguese *casados* appear to have settled in Sind in about 1560. They were following the caravan routes. Tatta was then the nodal point of the overland routes linking Hormuz to Gujarat. Italian merchants were apparently already established at Tatta in the fifteenth century.

After the Mughal conquest of Sind the Portuguese were allotted a *farman* to settle there in 1584. They were to pay 3 percent customs and were freed of other imposts. Horses could be imported free of charge. In return, the Portuguese were to hand three *cartazes* to ships of the Mughal emperor.[230] Goa rarely sent ships directly to Sind. Products like pepper, cinnamon, and ivory were exported there via Diu and Chaul; on the other hand, a ship of 250 to 500 tons was sent yearly from Sind to Goa. Those vessels were, together with "the great ships from Armagon," the biggest in use in the Portuguese intra-Asian trade. They were loaded at Laribandar with grain, horses, and Punjabi textiles. Ships from Mozambique sailed occasionally, ships from Mombasa regularly, to Laribandar to sell ivory there.[231]

As mentioned, textiles from Punjab were an important export commodity to Portugal in the early seventeenth century—mainly for the trade with Angola. These were exported from Chaul to the Gulf and from Chaul to Mozambique as well, occasionally directly from Laribandar. Sind also produced salt-peter. Such were the commercial incentives for the Portuguese, partly refugees from Hormuz, to settle on the mouth of the Indus. Most of the private trade of the captains of Hormuz, and later on of Muscat, was also conducted with Laribandar.[232]

Goa was little interested in putting up an administrative structure. The Portuguese *natio* governed itself, probably through the communal gathering of the *natio*, which the Portuguese normally styled a *senado da câmera*. Its "mayor" was recognized by Goa as a *feitor*, but he was not paid. At Laribandar the Portuguese lived in an autonomous neighborhood—a community of about 300 persons, by and large *topazes*. At Tatta the 66 Portuguese families paid for a small Carmelite church. Again, they were mainly *topazes*. There were in 1638 only five Portuguese merchants established at Tatta and only the Ruíz de Fraia family were wealthy traders. In Laribandar one could find a small Augustinian mission post, supported by the dimes of the Portuguese *natio*. But the mission in due course paid for itself, since the friars dabbled in trade with Muscat and the Swahili Coast. The Portuguese settlers farmed part of the customs revenues of Laribandar, so they enjoyed considerable influence there. This allowed them to hamper both Dutch and English attempts to establish a factory at Laribandar.[233]

Let us consider an example of the kind of trade conducted from Sind. The frigate *Bom Jesús da Vitória* was heading from Sind to Basra when captured by the VOC in 1653. This very Portuguese-named ship measured 240 tons and was armed with 34 guns, a vessel of considerable size; most sails used in the trade between Sind and Basra were much smaller. Such vessels were largely constructed at Laribandar, although Sindi merchants appear to have occasionally bought them at Surat and Chaul too. It was loaded with goods of a consortium, consisting of two Sindi *casados*, three *bania* merchants, and one "Moorish" trader. The crew consisted of 8 white Portuguese, 10 mestizos, and 40 "Moorish lascarins," "all very poor fellows," and 7 blacks, slaves of the Portuguese. On board could be found—besides ammunition, clothes, and a few carpets—textiles, 122,280 pounds of white rice, and 221,670 pounds of brown rice. The white rice was sold by the VOC with a 7 percent profit at Bandar Abbas, the brown with 8 percent; the Punjabi piece-cloth was vended at 7 to 20 percent profits. It was a fairly normal cargo, the Basra port registers indicate. Thus, the trade from Sind was common coastwise navigation, and the members of the Portuguese *natio* there were mostly peddlers engaged in this.[234]

The heyday of Portuguese trade from Sind was the early seventeenth century, but until the forties more than 30 vessels sailed from Sind to Basra. The trade collapsed after 1660. We do not know what happened to the Portuguese at Sind after 1660. Obviously they were suffering from the Muscati corsairs, and—as mentioned already—the trade from Sind appears to have slumped in the second half of the seventeenth century. However, the main mission of the Gulf fleet was still to conduct ships from Laribandar to Basra and Kung, which they had to await at Diu. Some trade was still conducted then, but not a very profitable or very large one. Sindi textiles fetched profits of a mere 10 to 20 percent at Basra and Bandar Abbas, really insufficient to warrant the risks involved. The Portuguese at Laribandar, always closely related to the Armenian and *bania* community, merged into the Indian merchants. Whereas the Portuguese trade network disappeared after 1660, the Sindi trade network remained intact. Those merchants still conducted trade with Goa too.[235]

What these three cases may teach us is that van Leur and, more recently, Pearson are partly right if they argue that the Portuguese fitted into "traditional Asian trade" and did not bring about major changes in the structure of that trade.[236] Rather than plundering indigenous merchants, the Portuguese collaborated with them. Through the flowering of Islamic sultanates like Pate, Maselagache, Zanzibar, or Anjuan, the Portuguese even played an unintentional part in the propagation of the so much maledicted Islam.

However, this private trade was closely linked to the military and administrative might of the Estado and in some areas the use of force to further the interest of merchants may have been an innovation. More importantly, the Portuguese private trade contributed to the formation of states in some stateless societies, or more precisely to the formation of systems of power and allegiance linked to the control of trade routes: it was thus on Maselagache and on the Comoros. The word *state* suggests rather more than one should imagine.

The most striking case of this was, as we have seen already, found in the *prazos* of Mozambique, where private traders and renegades founded something resembling a state themselves—very much to the displeasure of both Goa and the Portuguese crown, which throughout the seventeenth century engaged in somewhat clumsy efforts to discipline its vassals in Mozambique.

## Muddling Through the Second Half of the Seventeenth Century

### *The Failure of Reform*

Notwithstanding all the woes visiting the Portuguese, the Conselho Ultramarino considered in 1670 that—by the grace of the Lord—Portugal still possessed one huge conquest alone: Mozambique. Yet, although Mozambique was potentially one of the richest areas of the entire Portuguese empire, its revenues were consumed locally or flowed to Goa without benefit for Portugal or Brazil. And Goa squandered those revenues, as Lisbon protested throughout the seventeenth century, by allotting the monopoly right to trade there to the minions of the viceroy and to its ruling elite.

Mozambique occasionally sent a few tusks of ivory to Portugal, but this commerce was largely conducted via Goa and most ivory was sold there. For the profits obtained on Mozambique ivory—largely used for making bracelets—were higher in India than in Portugal and Brazil. Prices of ivory at Surat—the main market for ivory—were unsteady, however, since the Companies, the Siamese king, and Indian merchants from Siam also shipped ivory. And even though it was of lesser quality than the East African "soft" ivory, it was shipped there in larger quantities.[237]

From Goa, two or three large (250 to 300 tons) vessels were yearly sent to Mozambique and one to three to Mombasa. From Diu and Chaul departed one to three big ships to Mozambique. These were loaded with coarse Gujarati, Deccani, and Sindi textiles (*bafta* and *mouri*), rice, and iron.[238]

The trade between the Zambesi and Goa resembled on a small scale the relationship of dependency found between the Brazilian colonies and the metropolis. The exports of Goa to Mozambique largely consisted of goods like wine, furniture, casks, and so forth, for the use of the Portuguese community, and arms, nominally intended for the garrisons. But, I should add, although the sale of weapons to "hostile natives," like the Maravis, was formally prohibited, these were still an important commodity exchanged for ivory and gold in the interior.[239] Products like pearl beads, iron, and copper were also destined for exchange on the marts up the Zambesi. Mozambique produced mainly coarse sorghum. Wheat for Mozambique's islands, other food befitting a Portuguese dish (like white rice), fruits, and arrack for the Zambesi were imported from Goa and Madagascar.[240]

Until 1670 the trade to the interior was run as a tax farm by the captains of Mozambique. In return for paying 40,300 xeraphins for a three-year lease of the fortress, which included the obligation to feed and pay the garrison, captains were also allotted a monopoly on the trade in Indian piece-cloth between Mozambique and the hinterland.[241]

Many officials in both Lisbon and Goa constantly inveighed against this. Normally most gold brought to Mozambique had to be sold to the governor, with the Jesuits there normally also grabbing their share. This monopoly scared both the Maravi intermediary merchants and the *prazeiro* dealers away from Mozambique. The captains also curtailed shipping by the inhabitants by allotting this right to only a few inhabitants in return for considerable bribes.[242]

Although, as argued above, the misconduct of the governors was not the main cause of the decline of Mozambique, there was reason to blame it on this. Some managed to return as millionaires from this godforsaken place, like Francisco de Lima. He had earned more than 1 million cruzados there through practices ranging from forging testaments or demanding payment for nonexistent soldiers down to simple burglary. And such reprehensible conduct was, alas, rather the norm than the exception.[243]

One had to obtain a concession for the trade to Mozambique and Mombasa. Such permits were only handed to Goa traders, generally creatures of the viceroy. These monopolists, Lisbon accused Goa, charged inflated prices for their products at Mozambique. In turn the governor—coalescing with those very same creatures—had a monopoly on the sale of those goods. He could either sell them to the tiny resident Portuguese merchant community on the island or, mostly, his Indian brokers in Sena or Tete would sell the goods.

The governor handed out concessions at Mozambique to barter these products at Dela Goa Bay or Querimba as well. But the *prazeiro* traders as well as the Yao and Maravi merchants were charged rigged prices for Indian textiles sold by the governor. They, in turn, tried to profit by selling debased gold at Mozambique and Querimba. A concessionaire could make 300 to 400 percent profit on selling textiles at Querimba. But the governor of Mozambique and his minions pocketed everything.[244]

Lisbon was by 1670 fed up with an arrangement whereby the fabulous wealth of the Cuama accrued to one wealthy *fidalgo* who—returning to Goa—"might then spend it on the poor soldiers he has to feed; an embassy he might be offered; politics in Goa; or dimes to the *misericórdia*" instead of on the interest of the state. The motherland should exert itself to develop this colony—rich, yet neglected. It was decided, therefore, this abominable monopoly of the governors on the trade was to be abolished and that the motherland would henceforward take charge of the trade of Mozambique.[245]

A bill decreeing liberty of trade to Mozambique was promulgated in 1672, but the traders of Lisbon were not interested. The crown tried to entice merchants to invest in a ship that was to sail to Mozambique on their account. Nobody wanted to entrust any cargo to it. After three months the crown was still unable to get any cargo together and it was forced to dispatch the ship on its own account.[246]

Once again it appeared as if private initiative was unwilling to hazard money on matters of common interest of the kingdom if these were too risky. The merchants being uninterested in free trade, the only way out would be to allot them monopoly profits. The crown thus resolved in 1675 to allot the exploitation of Mozambique to a monopoly run by officials named by the crown. This institution, the Estanco, was to pay the garrison at Mozambique and was, in return, allowed the revenues from the gold trade. This might give a direly needed impetus to commerce. In 1677 three ships were sent directly from Lisbon to Mozambique with troops and materials to strengthen the fortress and with miners to scout for gold and silver deposits.[247]

Moreover, the crown had also been assured its conquests were in peril as long as the white population there consisted of but a few hundred among millions of Africans. There would be space for 300,000 settlers. For even the smallest estate in Mozambique had the size of a European kingdom. Obviously "it will take some time before settled agriculture takes root," but the crown intended to force Goa, Tete, and Sena to deliver foodstuffs to the settlers in the meantime, as these were now merely squandered.[248]

The Conselho Ultramarino agreed. They could ship peasants from the island of Fayal on the Azores who had offered to migrate to the colonies to Mozambique. They had been told that they were to be taken to Maranhão, but Mozambique and Brazil were both in the tropics anyway, so what would be the difference? In 1677 500 Portuguese peasants were thus sent to Cuama, whether voluntarily (as the crown was told) or involuntarily: as the Dutch ambassador observed, "people were lifted from their bed in the middle of the night and dragged to the ships in chains."[249]

The settlers were destined to a cruel fate. The lands on the lower Zambesi where they were marooned are lands with poor soil, not fit for the cultivation of grain with the plow. The harvests therefore failed. Though the colonists were starving, Goa was unable to send supplies in time. And it was perhaps unwilling to as well since this did not fetch a profit for the viceroy or for his creatures. The settlers thus had to buy provisions in Madagascar at hugely inflated prices. Malaria and cattle plagues ravaged the settlement too. The crown tried to stem the dissemination of all that bad news at home, but without much success, so that, inevitably, there was little enthusiasm in Portugal to migrate after 1680.[250]

The remaining settlers fled to Sena, establishing themselves—as we saw—as mercenaries, cattle thieves, or peddlers, which was perhaps better anyway. The *senado da camêra* in Mozambique wrote: "The colonists who have been sent here have been of no use whatsoever—except perhaps for burdening the exchequer and for greatly discrediting the Portuguese nation."[251]

The effort to establish a settlement proved a burden the Cuama Estanco was unable to shoulder. On paper the Estanco obtained a 50 percent profit and sent goods with a value of 24,511 (Mozambique) cruzados to Goa yearly. Yet the goods remitted to Goa were burdened with the hefty 30 to 40 percent demanded for insuring the cargoes and were therefore way too expensive, so that the Estanco was running at a tiny profit without having to pay for a colony in addition. This did not exhaust its problems. In 1687 the viceroy seized most of its investment capital and divided it among the merchants of Goa to finance the expedition to Pate, which was an utter failure on top of that.

Moreover, its own superintendents were utilizing the ships to conduct private trade in collaboration with the captains of Diu and Daman instead of handing goods to the Estanco. In 1680 it had accumulated a debt of 30,000 cruzados and was utterly unable to pay. The next year the crown decided, therefore, to abolish the monopoly and allow the inhabitants of Goa and Mozambique to sail wherever they wanted, although they had to pay 20 percent customs at Quelimane or Mozambique to the Estanco. The draft legislation to that effect was forwarded to Goa to be discussed by the Conselho do Estado.[252]

Viceroy Mendonça Furtado, when receiving this *parecer*, was reluctant to call the Conselho do Estado together at all. The whole nobility was interested in this trade, the viceroy warned the crown, and it would immediately block any proposal to free it.[253]

As the viceroy had feared, the Conselho do Estado unilaterally and bluntly refused to implement the law. The Conselho do Estado adduced that the amount of goods sold at Mozambique was quite small and that the market was very limited. Mozambique needed very few products from outside. Competition between various traders would therefore only lead to falling prices. With free trade nobody would dare to conduct it, for the "natives" were whimsical and ferocious: someone daring to deal with such savages ought to be rewarded richly.[254]

The Conselho Ultramarino wavered: perhaps this was not such a good idea after all. But King Pedro I remained adamant that "one is not to change the resolutions that have been taken already."[255]

Goa continued to object, however. And with good reason apparently, for the amount of gold received at Mozambique began to decline from 1685 onward. This was blamed on foreign and *canarin* competition. The exchange rate of gold to textiles was hence falling.[256] Goa pleaded that the trade not only of Mozambique but of the whole of Asia should be closed completely. It was to be allowed to be a monopoly company instead, "which is now the only way possible for redeeming the Estado." This company was to pay for two or three ships to be outfitted for Goa yearly and was to finance the fortresses along the coast of Mozambique.[257]

After long insistence by Goa, Lisbon complied. The trade between Goa and Mozambique, between Goa, Bengal, and Malabar, and the sandalwood trade with Timor was to be arranged through the Junta do Comércio on the basis of joint stock. Though this scheme was obviously inspired by the Dutch and English example, it was framed on the setup of the Brazil Company, which had proven a great success.[258]

The crown was to participate for 86,000 cruzados, the Goa merchants for 40,000, and those of Lisbon for 50,000 yearly. The Company was to be granted a charter for twelve years and the crown to receive one-third of the benefits. The participants could name independent merchants, and the inhabitants of Mozambique should sell gold and ivory to the Junta do Comércio alone. Moreover, the sandalwood trade with Timor was to be reserved for the Junta do Comércio. All other branches of trade—like that between Portugal and India—were still open to private traders. The Casa da Índia was, henceforward, to be run by the merchants: the king would only name an official to collect freight dues.[259]

In Lisbon the crown resorted to a dramatic gesture to gather the sums required. All merchants of Lisbon were solemnly summoned by the Count of Alvor to the palace and requested to contribute as much as they could afford. They promised to, but only in symbolic amounts. The crown had hoped to collect at least 200,000 cruzados but was barely able to gather 80,000 in all and even that with great difficulty. Thus it had to drop its magnificent scheme of constructing 22 vessels for trade with Asia; a bare 2 were all that could be afforded. It was hoped Goa could remit funds to Lisbon, though.[260]

But in the Estado da Índia the results proved even more disappointing. There they were scarcely able to scrape 60,000 cruzados together, mostly derived from the viceroy himself, who was forced to invest in the Company by the crown. Merchants were unwilling to donate a single penny. There was plenty of money around in Goa, viceroy Count of Villa Verde argued. "But the spirit of us, Portuguese, is like that of musicians who always make a fuss if they are requested to play a tune and when they have started to play it is even harder to persuade them to stop playing."[261]

Of the other settlements, Diu, Daman, and Bassein were unwilling or unable to contribute anything. And Macao immediately refused to participate at all. Thus, the Junta do Comércio was in arrears for 200,000 cruzados in 1699. It could not finance any ship to Asia, so the crown had to pay again. And it was unable as well to commit any badly needed funds to the defense of either the settlements on the Zambesi or those of Mombasa.[262]

Aside from this, the Junta do Comércio also proved singularly inept at handling commerce. Its own servants smuggled goods or sold wares imported by the Company and pocketed the receipts. Besides, the traders of Diu were obdurately not observing the Junta's monopoly and continued to send ships to Mozambique themselves.[263]

The crown was buried under complaints. The *casados* of Mozambique were complaining that their cloth trade was monopolized by the company: "we are so destitute now that we have to pawn the earrings of our wives." The incomes from this trade alone allowed them to pay African mercenaries. The Portuguese soldiers were perishing or fleeing, since their only remuneration was bartering cloth. Chaul was whining that the Company had stopped sending ships from there: "we are all dying from hunger." Goa lamented that the insufficient shipping, sent by the Junta do Comércio, caused the loss of Mombasa. The servants of the Junta, in contrast, were complaining about everybody else: the merchants of Goa continued to dodge the Junta's monopoly, whereas at the customs the Company's goods were valued at inflated prices, stolen, or seized by officials.[264]

There were dissident voices, aside from the general chorus of discontent, as we shall see. Actually, the Junta do Comércio was not doing all too badly. From 1695 to 1698 it made a profit of 63 percent.[265]

But the crown was finally moved to concede to the complaints. The Junta do Comércio had been established at the behest of the inhabitants of India. As they judged this was, after all, not in their own interest, the Junta do Comércio was abolished after 1700. The crown now reverted to the older scheme of opening the trade with Mozambique to all Portuguese traders—provided they would pay customs to a revived Cuama Estanco, which was not to conduct trade itself. Parallel to this—as we saw already—the crown also tried to curtail the Indian trade to Mozambique from Diu by re-establishing the Mazanes company there. For, even more than before, the trade of Mozambique was conducted by Portuguese working on behalf of Indian bankers.

### A Crisis in the European Trade and a Flourishing Asian Trade

Indeed, the Estado da Índia itself had an increasingly "creole" character in the second half of the seventeenth century. Portuguese *casados* gradually merged into Indian communities as far as their social status, habits, and customs, but not their language and religion—the primary distinction of a *natio*. Both in settlements taken over by a Company from the Portuguese—like Cochin and Bombay—and in new settlements like Chinsura, Madras, Batavia, or Calcutta, the Luso-Indian *topazes* and mestizos controlled an important part of the small and retail trade and of the "service sector": anything from prostitution to soldiering.[266]

Portuguese intra-Asian trade increasingly merged with trade of Asian merchants too. At Surat in the late seventeenth century the average trader of the Portuguese *natio* was usually a huckster with a few bottles of arrack or a small shopkeeper rather than a rich shipowner. It was almost impossible as well to distinguish between the small oared vessels of the *armado dos remos*, fetching agricultural products from Goa and Bassein, and Indian vessels. Furthermore, many *bania*s would register ships as Portuguese to pay lower customs. Most of these *bania* merchants, and VOC personnel indulging in private trade, used the Portuguese flag merely as one of convenience.[267]

Hence, as to its prestige, the Portuguese empire in the Arabian seas had indeed sadly declined: at the end of the century the shield of Aviz was no longer feared. Rather, it was the cheapest flag available. Indian ships generally sailed with neither Portuguese flag nor safe conducts. Though the Portuguese king might still style himself "lord of navigation in the East," in 1688 the total revenue raised from navicerts was worth a ridiculous 176 xeraphins.[268]

And in spite of all the attempts to revive the trade, Lisbon's merchants had written off the Asian trade. In 1641, for example, the newly restored Portuguese crown had to beg the Lisbon merchants to fetch pepper to the Tague on their own account. They refused, pleading there was insufficient capital in Lisbon to venture on such risky commerce. One hoped the Goa merchants would fulfill their patriotic duty and fit out an Indiaman, but with equally disappointing results.[269]

As conceived from Lisbon, Goa was a relic from the sixteenth century, albeit one that cost the taxpayer dearly. In the 1630s the Casa da Índia reaped a benefit of 406,640 cruzados a year; the cost of sending ships to India trade amounted to more than a million. With the bulk of these incomes already expended on providing succor to Brazil, that to India had to be funded through contributions of the Portuguese communities. In 1641, again, the crown had consigned 17,783,991 milreis from customs to pay for the India fleets—insufficient by far, for 6,570,157 was demanded by the communities.[270]

No doubt the crown was facing a critical situation then, yet to all appearances India was costing the Portuguese taxpayer dearly throughout the seventeenth century. In 1670 the crown was approximately expending 200,000 cruzados more than was being received from the India trade. In 1688 the ships to India cost the crown 149,000 cruzados, while incomes of the Casa da Índia (and Guinea) amounted to a mere 68,000. At the end of the century the crown still sustained a loss of some 200,000 cruzados yearly, it was estimated. Since, then, the India trade represented the major expense of the king without much benefit to show in return, it was but logical that the crown held this trade under tight control.[271]

One might say the Portuguese administration was emotionally attached to the Estado da Índia, however. His majesty was not prepared to cede this India, "for which so much Portuguese blood has been shed."[272] Such a tendency to hold on to unprofitable colonial possessions for "sentimental reasons" may well be an entrenched characteristic of Portuguese colonialism, but other motives played a part too. The English pressured the Portuguese crown not to hand over any stronghold to a potential enemy.[273] And India was a field for patronage. Boxer rightly argues that the Estado da Índia mainly existed in the seventeenth century by virtue of being a nice site for the "outdoor leisure of the upper classes"—very different from industrious but dull Brazil.[274]

Yet the complaints of the officials in India about the sorrowful state they were in were often but thinly disguised attempts to beg for subsidies from Portugal. The crown was hesitant to send this. India was to pay its own expenses. In turn, it would strive to paint its predicament in the darkest possible colors: to regularly receive bullion served to show the creditworthiness of merchants. Although some Portuguese settlements were languishing in the second half of the seventeenth century, not the entire picture is gloomy. The Portuguese settlement at Timor, for example, was able to "muddle through," although it received little military and financial aid from Goa.[275]

Goa's administration was little interested in Macao too. After the fall of Malacca most trade of this place was no longer conducted with the Estado but with English country traders and with Batavia. From the official documentation one would gather that the trade of Macao was on the verge of expiring and that horrifying poverty afflicted the *casados* there. As G.B. Souza has pointed out, this is very questionable.[276] Shipping with Batavia offered new opportunities for Macao's traders. In view of Macao's constant complaints about it, the concessionary voyages with which the crown had hitherto tried to harness this navigation were abolished in 1670.

The Macao trade was probably the second most important branch of Goa's seaborne commerce, after the gold trade with Mozambique. After 1670, the community of Macao sent yearly a large vessel of up to 300 tons to Goa. Goa's traders yearly sent two or three vessels to Macao, Diu's one or two. The trade with Macao had a peculiar structure. Goa hardly disposed of products that could be sold there. Hence, the vessels to Macao were loaded with ballast like salt and iron, though at the end of the seventeenth century cotton, indigo, and saltpeter were exported too. They would return, however, with fabulous riches: gold, silk, velvet, benzoic, tuttenag, and sugar. The deficit was probably covered with bills drafted by the Macao *misericórdia* on that of Goa.

This trade was pretty much the private domain of the viceroy and the Goa nobility, to the anger of the *casados* of Goa and Chaul. Those of Chaul repeatedly petitioned the viceroy to be allowed a share in this trade, but to no avail. In Diu as well the trade was virtually a demesne of the governor and of the Jesuits there—their main revenue of office. The considerable sums needed to load these ships were mainly "donated" by the *bania* and Armenian communities at Surat and the tuttenag and gold from Macao taken there. The Jesuits were really but brokers for Indian merchants.[277]

The second half of the seventeenth century was certainly not a golden age for Goa's trade, but it was not an iron one either. Apart from more than 60 small vessels used in the trade with Gujarat, Goa's fleet in 1668 comprised 25 ships exceeding 120 tons, which were used in intra-Asian trade. Moreover, there were at least 100 crafts for coastwise navigation with Canara. This would still make Goa's fleet the second largest of the Arabian seas, after that of Surat.[278]

Although the conquest of Macassar in 1668—the bridgehead of Portuguese private trade in the Indonesian archipelago—was a blow for Goa's trade with Southeast Asia, the Lusitanians were never entirely evicted from the archipelago. After the foundation of Batavia there still was a Portuguese *natio* at Banten, Macassar, Jambi, and Palembang. Goa's and San Thomé's *casados* entertained close relations with these communities. Goa's traders also sent regularly small patashes loaded with Gujarati textiles and diamonds to the archipelago and to Pegu (Burma). Moreover, in the sixties a busy private trade flourished with Atjeh. There Indian textiles, diamonds, silver, coral, and wheat were bartered with gold, tin, sandalwood, ivory, and pepper. Obviously, this was very much to the dislike of the VOC—but the Company was unable to impede those dealings.[279]

A new branch of commerce, which developed in the sixties, was the Siamese trade with Goa. It was partly conducted by the Siamese king, partly by ministers, like the famous Greek mercenary Christopher Phaulkon. Such contacts were entertained in the cloak of diplomatic missions and the mutual exchange of gifts. After several Siamese ambassadors had visited Goa in 1666, 1672, and 1683, Goa sent an embassy to Ayuthia in 1683. To negotiate an agreement on free trade, two Siamese ambassadors were sent to Portugal in 1686 but they and their suite disappeared in the waves near Mauritius. Portuguese trade with Southeast

Asia was, hence, certainly made a great deal more difficult by the VOC, but not completely eradicated.[280]

Yet the long-distance trade of the Estado was not as large at the end as at the beginning of the seventeenth century, and it declined still further in the eighties. In 1698 the trade of Goa with Mozambique amounted to 120,000 cruzados and was run at 35 percent profit in the eighties, later 20 percent; that with China amounted to 500,000 xeraphins and was run at about 50 percent; and that with Bengal was worth 25,000 xeraphins at 40 percent profit.[281] But the Portuguese coastwise trade was growing.

In the sixteenth century the Estado da Índia may be conceived as a "commercial and naval network"—as L.F. Thomaz put it—that distributed the trade in bullion and luxury goods. Looking at the commerce between Goa and Diu, for example, we see that Goa functioned in the first half of the seventeenth century mainly as entrepôt. From there to Diu were sent luxury goods that did not derive from Goa but from all over Asia. These were exchanged at Diu for indigo, cotton, and textiles from Saurastra and grain, butter, and cattle from Kathiawar.[282]

By 1670, however, the Estado was mainly a territorial power: the commerce of its entrepôts was derived from its domain. Goods traded by the Portuguese in Gujarat were largely coming from Goa and Praças do Norte: coconuts, coir, and especially arrack. The trade from Praças do Norte with Gujarat was far more substantial than that conducted from Goa. From *Praças* was yearly dispatched a fleet of 40–60 small vessels. These mainly exported agricultural products: rice, grain, and sugar. In return Surat sent manufactured goods like paint, glue, incense, ironware, and soap. This trade was worth about 300,000 to 500,000 rupees yearly. Surat, too, delivered spices and indigo to Goa and *Praças*. The *bandar-i mobarak* by 1700 depended for a number of products, especially for wood, on the Portuguese possessions.[283]

This important role of products from agriculture and forestry in the trade with Gujarat, and of salt in that with Canara, reflects a shift of the Estado from a "sailor" to a "landlord" society. It is reflected in the revenue figures of the Estado too. With the declining incomes and subsequent loss of Cochin, Daman and especially Bassein became its financial linchpin.

Considering that only a tiny portion of the revenues of Bassein were collected by the administration and a much larger share in Goa, the Praças do Norte were by 1670 the most significant Portuguese possession in Asia. Whereas the finances of the "northern quarters," of Daman in particular, were around 1620 largely derived from taxation of Indian shipping by 1670, land revenues had become far more important. The fortune of cities in the northern quarters depended upon the amount of disposable land.

In Diu, mostly important as a customs station for shipping to the Gulf of Cambay, incomes dwindled from 200,000 xeraphins around 1620 to only 40,000 in 1700. Apart from the trade with Mozambique and Yemen, these revenues were around 1700 mainly obtained from the farming of palm groves on the island. Some revenues were also derived from the taxation of trade in agrarian products from Kathiawar—mainly exchanged for salt and tobacco—and from imposts on fishing in the Gulf of Cambay. One had to compete for the latter benefits with the neighboring villages of *koli* fishermen and pirates who were repeatedly sacked by Portuguese vessels. For this "commerce" Diu mustered a fleet of 30 to 40 sloops.[284]

Whereas the customs station was in decline, the population and prosperity of Bassein were increasing. It was mainly a regional center of trade and the locus for the conspicuous consumption of landlords in the Praças do Norte. In view of the growing population of Bassein, in 1656 a request was submitted to build five new parochial churches in the area. As to its prosperity, in 1676 it was noted that the value of some *foros* had increased five or six times, without benefit for the administration. Rates were still at the late sixteenth-century level. The land should be partitioned in small fiefs—as small as possible—A. Cotta pleaded. The prospect of earning a piece of land in Praças do Norte was the only reward open for soldiers of merit.[285] This put increasing pressure upon the system of landed property. While it was forbidden to sell or infeudate *foros*, in effect this was done at will. In the course of time some *foreiros* accumulated ever more land. By 1670 there were but two powerful landholders left in Bassein: Dom Rodriques de Castro and Gaspar Paim de Mello. They could defy any order of the viceroy since they had a private army. These potentates exercised a reign of terror over both the Indian peasants and the poor Portuguese; they stole their cattle and imposed labor dues or arbitrary levies. One might complain with the captain of Bassein but he would not consider any grievance, as he was scared of those *foreiros* too. Poor Francisco Carvalho was robbed by Pascoal de Machedo of most of his property, yet he did not dare to protest. If he did, "he will send some kaffirs with chains and bamboo canes." And if he would not do so, his clients would, "for he is very powerful in this city of Bassein and he has many friends and relatives who are *fidalgos*." Such armed gangs, led by Portuguese landlords, terrorized the peasants too: "they will violate their houses, rape their daughters and commit adultery with their wives."[286]

The status of the *abunhados* appears to have evolved from serfdom to slavery. They were unilaterally tied to a master; a serf who had tried to run away from his master could be flogged, often to death. The Portuguese masters were busily abducting each other's slaves, which led to endless feuds among various families.[287] *Abunhados* often tried to flee from this oppressive environment; the Portuguese had to make special arrangements with the neighboring kings that serfs were to be returned to their territory. For every refugee, the rajah of Ramnagar was to pay a fine of 300 pardaos, the captain of Daman proposed—twice the value of a serf's life. The Inquisition demurred, however; this amounted to selling Portuguese subjects to a heathen.[288]

### *Toward Integration*

Such trade as was left was increasingly conducted in close collaboration with the other members of the European *natio*. English and French intra-Asian trade were constructed upon the foundation of Portuguese networks of trade. This was particularly significant in Mozambique, where in the late seventeenth century an important shift began to occur. On the one hand, Mozambique changed from a largely Portuguese preserve to a hub of multinational smuggling, and on the other, the demand shifted from mainly gold and ivory to slaves.

It has been argued this was a fatal shift as the slave trade caused a drain of manpower from Mozambique. But this was probably only the case from the late eighteenth century onward, with the demand for manpower for Mauritius and Brazil increasing to several thousand, instead of the few hundred slaves exported in the seventeenth. In the seventeenth century slave trade from Mozambique was a typical peddlers' affair, with dozens of small Portuguese merchants each taking one to five slaves in order to sell them "piecewise" on the slave market of Goa—a very different structure from the slave trade of the VOC or even of the Americans, as we saw. For Mozambique this was surely a blessing, for these procurements were simply too small to have any impact on its population.[289]

Foreign traders, who wanted to buy slaves at Mozambique theoretically needed a permit from the Estanco, but this could easily be obtained in return for a small bribe. Hence, VOC vessels heading to and from Madagascar after 1676 regularly touched at Mozambique island to fetch supplies and merchandise. If one, at first, mainly dealt in ivory, bartered for textiles and cash, in 1705 the Company also bought slaves there.[290] Contrary to the wild scramble for slaves in Madagascar, the trade in Mozambique was fairly tightly controlled; interlopers and buccaneers thus in general preferred to procure human cargo in Madagascar. One had to buy slaves from the governor of Mozambique for monopoly prices fixed by the governor in consultation with the abbot of the Jesuit monastery.[291]

It was, of course, almost inevitable that the Estado da Índia was closely linked to the Catholic compatriots of the Compagnie des Indes, even though the haughty Frenchmen, who treated their fellow Catholics as "natives," appear to have been far from popular at Goa. In Surat at the end of the century the French and the Portuguese were using the same broker, Rustamji, and probably the same network of Indian purchasers. Bills of the Compagnie des Indes were often honored in Goa; bullion for the Compagnie at Surat was often sent on board of Portuguese flotillas.[292]

The servants of the Compagnie des Indes used to send diamonds to cash the profits from private trade on board Portuguese homeward bound ships. Jewish bankers and jewelers, established at Goa, would take care of the diamond trade of the French East India Company too and were involved in its important coral trade. Their vessels being obviously at risk from the Dutch and English during the war of the Spanish succession, French cargoes were often sent to Surat—

from Bengal, for example—on Portuguese sails. The VOC insinuated, if this was exaggerated, that Portuguese trade with Bengal at the end of the seventeenth century was financed and run by the Compagnie des Indes.[293] Little is known about French relationships with Mozambique before 1700. It seems probable that French pirates and interlopers regularly touched there. The French commenced buying slaves for Bourbon there in 1678. At the end of the seventeenth century Breton interlopers apparently regularly sailed to Mozambique with a commission from the *colons* at Bourbon to take human cargo there. Bourbon was supplied with slaves from Mozambique, either bartered or sacked by British interlopers and pirates. Finally, French Indiamen also regularly touched at Mozambique.[294] For both the EIC and the Dansk Ostindiske Kompagni the Dutch-Portuguese conflict smelled like profit. There ensued various forms of smuggling, linking the Portuguese *casados* with English and Danish private traders. This caused the VOC great concern. The Dutch sent a steady stream of letters to Madras and Tranquebar, protesting against the English and Danish help to the Portuguese.

And the Dutch-Portuguese war was certainly a boon for the trade of Tranquebar. *Casado* firms established at Tuticorin would put up subsidiaries there, to register freight as Danish. "Danish" private traders supplied Malacca, besieged by the VOC, with arms and supplies. The Danish office at Banten served as a station where cargoes dispatched to the Philippines from the Coromandel Coast could be "cleansed," considered neutral Danish property. D. Pessaert, the Danish director, in 1637 proposed that Tranquebar would furnish all Portuguese fortresses on the Coromandel Coast and Ceylon with supplies and ammunition. The Estado should be happy with this proposal, Pessaert wrote; the king of Spain might not realize it but the Dutch ridiculed the Portuguese "and dare to say that they will wipe their shoes on this Portuguese nation." This rather realistic proposal was rebuked by the Conselho do Estado: the Danes were too weak to be of any use. Instead, the Habsburg crown dallied with an unrealistic scheme to station a Portuguese garrison at Tranquebar.[295]

"*Cum heriticis fide non est observanda*, and so we believe that not love to us but hatred to the Hollanders hath in policy humbled them," T. Methwold observed on the English-Spanish truce of 1635.[296] The EIC founded a factory at Goa, which soon proved to be a very profitable settlement. The English would buy cinnamon at Goa, for example, bartered for iron, (Cornwall) tin, lead, and copper—unprofitable merchandise from England—and, above all, arms. The VOC's blockade of Goa proved a boost to the English. The Portuguese handed precious cinnamon "and the English barter this for worthless trinkets [*brincos*], worth nothing in the customs," Pedro da Silva muttered. The commodores of the VOC's fleets, blockading Goa, had received orders from Batavia to search English vessels, which tried to enter the Mandovi, and confiscate non-English merchandise. But what was really English freight? One may safely assume the

VOC's commanders would not be all too precise in their search if handed a few coins.[297] The servants of the English Company would in the forties send two to three ships to Goa from Surat, Banten, and Madras stowed with copper, tin, iron, and textiles. Some vessels carried more than 500,000 guilders' value. As the Portuguese during the fifties often fetched pepper from Malabar to Goa under the English flag, they could never have complied with the orders of the crown without the (questionable) benefit of English support. Cochin remitted pepper to Portugal by English ships in 1642. But, obviously, the "English ally" had himself well paid for such aid: the *feitores* sold them cinnamon for 30 xeraphins, whereas the crown had to pay 34.[298]

Such ties, forged during the blockade of Goa, remained intact after the cessation of the Dutch-Portuguese hostilities. Goa's wealthy merchants, such as João de Prado and Manuel de Fonsequa, conducted a triangular trade between Goa, Madras, and the Philippines. Most profitable was this smuggling—for trade with the Philippines was only permitted by the Spanish crown to Portuguese subjects. They would send ships from Goa first to Porto Novo to obtain a Portuguese free-conduct for the Philippines, and next to Madras to take in English merchandise registered as Portuguese. The Lusitanians would also buy sugar, saltpeter, textiles, and powder from Bengal at Madras, shipped to Goa aboard English vessels. In return, the English received bullion and Sunda pepper.[299] To smuggle goods to Lisbon from London one normally used English Indiamen as well. A notorious case, eliciting anger from Governor Pães de Sande, irritation from the VOC at Vengurla, and wonder of the Abbé Carré, was that of the *Gloucester*, which, while anchored at Anjidiva Island near Goa, was surreptitiously stowed with saltpeter and "unbelievable numbers of diamonds" from Goa. "It has been going on like this for three years now; this will utterly ruin us," Pães de Sande commented.[300]

In 1673 the Portuguese were permitted to establish factories in English territory.[301] The crown thereupon nominated a *feitor*, one Álvaro Casallo, at Madras. Casallo not only bought textiles and saltpeter brought by English merchants from Bengal, but also had warships constructed at Madras.[302]

### *Strangers on the East African Coast*

English Indiamen often anchored at Mozambique when they could not reach their preferred way stations at Saldanha Bay or Anjuan, where the English homeward-bound vessels generally stocked supplies. After the Portuguese-English alliance, English ships were officially allowed to take in some supplies and water at Mozambique but not to conduct barter there. Yet, during their stay on the island, English skippers often smuggled some ambergris and ivory on board exchanged for Indian textiles.[303] From 1640 onward, English country trade vessels sailed regularly to the Swahili Coast and to Mozambique too. During the heyday of this trade in the fifties two ships, rented by director Merry and companions at Surat, sailed every year to Malindi, Querimba, and Angoche in order to exchange textiles for ivory and ambergris.[304]

As the EIC had little interest in the trade, one would not have to fear trouble with the Company. Merry's counterpart, Captain Manuel de Sousa, prohibited the *casados* from trade with Merry's ship, the *Assade Merchant*, which—on its way to Nossi Bé to rescue the colonists there—anchored off Mozambique in 1651. And then Sousa bought the English piece-cloth himself to sell it to his Portuguese subjects. If he would not buy piece-cloth, Sousa explained, the English might proceed to Sofala or Inambane, and "since the kaffirs"—regrettably—"buy and sell only to those who have most and cheapest cloth," such insolent consumer behavior might ruin the Portuguese trade.[305]

Sousa was not altogether wrong, though, for it was certainly true that no ships had come from Goa and Portugal, and one therefore had better trade with the English. It is doubtful whether settlements, such as the band of Afro-Portuguese merchants and the single Jesuit friar on the outpost at Dela Goa Bay, could have subsisted without "smuggling"—selling provisions and slaves to Indiamen and buccaneers.[306] Although Gentlemen XVII requested Surat to send a ship to Malindi to investigate this commerce, Surat hesitated to do so. Only a 10 to 20 percent profit could be obtained on Indian textiles on the Swahili Coast, 10 to 20 percent on African ivory in Surat, director van Gent warned the Netherlands. He was right: it was not a very profitable trade. After 1663, when the EIC unleashed the trade, allowing it to go to more enticing destinations, the English country trade on the Mrima Coast declined. It did not disappear entirely, though. Harris, governor of Bombay, sent a ship to Mombasa in 1669. Director Annesley at Surat in the 1680s regularly sent his vessel to Pate to buy ivory.[307]

But while this traffic declined, a direct link between the American colonies and Mozambique developed. From Madagascar American vessels would sail to Mozambique and probably Malindi and Querimba too. If this commerce with "interlopers" was formally prohibited by Lisbon, church and Cuama Estanco were having no objections colluding with them. In 1675, when the Bostonian smuggler Thomas Edwards touched Mozambique, "the governor was very polite and assured me the English were as free to buy the slaves as their own nation." And indeed Edwards procured his human cargo there.[308]

In 1684 the Americans had three commissioners living at Mozambique; accused of giving tips to pirates, they were sent to Goa and hanged in 1686. They could have welcomed several countrymen at Mozambique—and admittedly on the gallows too. The *Voorhouten* encountered the *Bristol* at Maselagache, coming from Bridgetown to fetch slaves for Barbados in Madagascar. As Arab traders had bought most slaves there, the English had proceeded to Mozambique, purchasing 170 slaves there. Two months later the *Society* from New York arrived, as well as a vessel from Barbados; they had just come from Mozambique, where they had obtained letters of marque from the governor to prey on Muscati ships.[309]

By 1690 a small triangular trade had arisen between the American colonies, England (and probably Scotland), the Caribbean, and Mozambique. Tiny crafts from Britain, often no more than 100 tons, would provision at Madagascar and then set sail to Cabo Correntes, Dela Goa, or Inambane Bay. This trade had to be well covered up in order that the Royal African Company not get wind of it. For the trade in African goods, such as ivory and slaves, was in principle a monopoly of that Company. Therefore, even sailors recruited by the interlopers sailing from Portsmouth to Mozambique were kept completely in the dark as to their true destination. They might be told they were heading for some innocent harbor like Cadiz rather than to the remote shores of East Africa.[310] The trade in ivory was slow business. The interlopers normally put a band of freebooters ashore. They would receive pay and merchandise: beads and rum, but mainly firearms. Thus provided, they would part on lengthy journeys to the interior to buy ivory piecemeal. Such wanderings often took more than a year and might take them right into the interior of present-day Natal. "Where they met a hospitable people"—the Zulus, apparently—"both men and women competed with each other to give them food and drink and offer their houses for shelter." They would be taken on board by interloper vessels at designated spots on the African shore again, with such ivory as they might have gathered and, surely, some tall tales to tell.[311]

## Conclusion

Let me summarize this chapter by addressing two different problems discussed in the literature.

The first concerns whether the Estado was feudal and traditional or capitalist and modern. V.M. Godinho sees the Portuguese empire as a petrified institutional system within the context of a dynamically expanding trade.[312] The benefits of trade were drained off by investment in office and corruption—hardly any formation of productive capital took place. Thomaz and G.B. Souza have rather emphasized the dynamic Portuguese private trade, developing aside from the parasitic military/administrative apparatus.[313] In fact, there is no real contradiction between private trade and investment in office. "Since men have become merchants, whereas in olden times they were soldiers, they are looking for gain rather than honor," whether through perquisites or trade, Antônio de Mello e Castro argued.[314]

It is not merely a question of mentality: Gonçalves de Câmera Coutinho contemplated the issue in 1698.[315] Earlier everybody had been requiring that one should establish a company because they expected immediate short-term benefits on the monopoly, he noted. Now that one had established such a company and profits turned out to be a little bit disappointing, everybody was equally loudly screaming for its abolition. Yet, just as a seedling does not immediately grow to a forest, you cannot expect a company to instantly bring a profit. The system could fetch high returns for state and citizens alike but not in the short run. Whereas the VOC had long carried on without profit, and could entrust funds to long-term projects, Portuguese officials and traders promptly withdrew their funds.

The prime cause for the woes visiting the Estado, Câmera Coutinho argued further, was not the excessive interference of the crown in trade but rather the excessive claims of the inhabitants to constitutional liberties. Truly, man seeks freedom, yet any body politic is subject to political and, indeed, economic laws. Such laws are imposed upon the polity by the common consent of the people and in the public interest, the king may impose regulations that curtail the liberty of individuals. But in the Estado da Índia everybody was out to gather personal gain under a banner of liberty and scorned the interest of both the state and of his fellow man.

Thus, any collective enterprise was immediately ruined by private greed. The officials of the Junta do comérçio would charge far too high prices, for example; were not interested in selling goods; or would use the merchandise received for their own trade. Instead of serving the public good, they would force merchants to sell goods to them and use their office to extort entreaties from Indian merchants.

The Estado's officials were thus calculating entrepreneurs who saw their office as a source for personal gain that might be used to raise funds for commerce—or might not.

This leads us to a second discussion. Was the VOC different from or more efficient than the Portuguese? Boyajian and Subrahmanyam have argued that the VOC—as a monopolist—tried to curtail trade, whereas the Portuguese were devoted to a free trade that they conducted far more efficiently than the Company.[316]

Since trade and revenue of the Estado was run by beneficia allotted to private persons it is really of little use to ask whether it was "more efficient" than the VOC. As to the accountancy for example: some Portuguese *feitores* running an *estanco*, like those of the Cuama *junta*, used double bookkeeping.[317] But it was no use to do so for the central administration. The benefits obtained on *rendas* could not be predicted in advance: in spite of its many flaws, the VOC's accountancy allowed it to gather a picture of the commercial operation as a whole. Portuguese *orçamentos* did not—and as a matter of principle.

Again, there might be a lot of capital circulating in the Portuguese empire, but could this be used for long-term outlays, as with the VOC, which was willing to sacrifice immediate profits to long-term ones? The viceroy, the count of Villaverde, pleaded there was more than sufficient capital to invest in a merchant company, yet the Conselho do estado, assembled to deliberate on this topic, disagreed. Goa's merchants had invested their funds by and large in *respondentia* bills. There were few Portuguese merchants or officials who had any proper sources of income from trade—everything was run on loans. They needed immediate benefits to repay their outlays and were unable to invest in a *junta*, which might only provide long-term gains.

It is very difficult to make any sweeping statement regarding Portuguese private trade: as we observed, it is necessary to distinguish between the trade carried out by authorization of the central authorities and "smugglers" on the margin of the system. The *casados* in Sind and on the Swahili Coast cooperated with indigenous merchants and closely resembled them. The commerce conducted under the aegis of the Portuguese administration is quite a different proposition though: this was as much a "rent-seeking enterprise" as the VOC. When faced with any form of serious competition the private traders would immediately claim protection by the state. Yet, whereas this kind of private trade thrived on coercion and monopoly, these very same merchants were unwilling to shoulder the costs of fleets and fortresses necessary to enforce this.

Thus, the Estado da Índia was not behaving differently from the VOC, but monopoly worked to the advantage of beneficiaries and not the central organization. Rent might then be plowed back into the metropolitan economy or be invested in office.[318] Since the VOC constituted an overall monopoly, it could better plan ahead than could Portuguese private traders and could seek overall benefit instead of immediate gain. The VOC was, thus, a more rational organization than the Estado da Índia. But this is not to argue that the Portuguese merchants were inefficient, only that they were different.

## Notes

1. See, for example, Subrahmanyam, *The Political Economy*, p. 223; and Meilink-Roelofs, "The Structure of Trade," pp. 1–43.

2. M. Weber, *Wirtschaft und Gesellschaft: Grundriss der verstehende Soziologie,* 2 vols. (Cologne, Bonn, 1964), ii, pp. 739–71, though, admittedly, the VOC officials were badly deficient in "thoroughgoing professional schooling," which constitutes an additional criterion defining a modern bureaucracy for Weber.

3. The classic work on the doctrine and practice of mercantilism is of course that of E. Heckscher, *Der Merkantilismus*, 2 vols. (Jena, 1932); more recent contributions would include D.C. Coleman (ed.), *Revisions in Mercantilism* (London, 1969), and R.B. Ekelund and R.D. Tollison, *Mercantilism as a Rent-Seeking Society* (College Station, 1981), to which I obviously owe a great deal.

4. J. van Klaveren, "Die historische Erscheinung der Korruption in ihrer Zusammenhang mit der Staats-und Gesellschaftstruktur betrachtet," *VSWG* 54 (1957), pp. 289–324; and "Fiskalismus, Merkantilismus und Korruption. Drei Aspekte der Sozial-und Wirtschaftspolitik des Ancien régime," *VSWG* 55 (1958), pp. 443–504.

5. F.J. Falcon, *Mercantilismo e transição* (São Paulo, 1981), p. 58; see also F. Novais, *Estrutura e dinâmica do sistema colonial* (Lisbon, n.d.).

6. This is as opposed to Boyajian's argument (*Portuguese Trade*, p. 275) that the Portuguese embraced free trade whereas the Dutch were monopolists.

7. AHU, Moç. Cx. 3, 9, 9 August 1673.

8. BAC, Mss. Vermelho 281, "Discurso político do Doutor Duarte Ribeiro de Machedo," fo. 6 (this tract has been published in his *Obras Inéditas* [Lisbon, 1817]). There is a large literature on the *restoração*: see A. França, *Portugal na época da restoração* (São Paulo, 1951); and V.M. Godinho, "1580 e a restoração," in *Ensaios*, 3 vols. (Lisbon, 1969), ii, pp. 257–90; for the later period—which is very inadequately studied—see C.A. Hanson, *Economy and Society in Baroque Portugal* (London, 1981).

9. S. Sideri, *Profit and Power: Informal Colonialism in Anglo-Portuguese Relations* (Rotterdam, 1970), p. 24; C.A. Hanson, "The Luso-Brazilian 'Renovation' and the South Atlantic Economy," *Review* 6 (4) (1983), pp. 475–521.

10. This has first been expounded in a classic essay by L. de Azevedo, *Épocas de Portugal econômico* (Lisbon, 1947/1978).

11. D. Peres (ed.), *Monstruosidades do tempo e da fortuna*, 4 vols., (Porto, 1938), iv, p. 17.

12. Thus it is, for example, in J.V. Serrão, *História de Portugal V: Époqua do asolutismo* (Lisbon, 1979); and in A. Saraiva (ed.), *História de Portugal*, 9 vols. vi, *A restoração* (Lisbon, 1979–82). Both Subrahmanyam, *Portuguese Asia*, and M.N. Pearson, *The Portuguese in India*, in *New Cambridge History of India*, First Series, vol. 1 (Cambridge, 1987), term the seventeenth and eighteenth centuries *terra incognita*, although Subrahmanyam (probably as much enchanted with round figures as the present author) carries the story up to 1700.

13. A.R. Disney, "The Portuguese Empire in India ca. 1550–1650: Some Suggestions for a Less Seaborne, More Land-Based Approach to Its Socio-Economic History," in Correia-Alfonso (ed.), *Indo-Portuguese History*, pp. 148–62.

14. AHU, Índia, Cx. 33, 1, 24 January 1684.

15. Bragança Pereira, "História das relações," pp. 235–38; AHU, Índia, Cx. 33, 102, December 1685; HAG, LM, 47, 24 January 1683, fo. 127; HAG, LM, 51 bis, 24 June 1686, fo. 207 vo.

16. Meilink-Roelofs, "The Structure of Trade," pp. 9–27.

17. AHU, Cód. 169, "Regimento do conselho ultramarino," fo. 1–12; AHU, Casa da Índia, Cx. 1, "Regimento da saída da mercandiçia." We badly need studies on the makeup of the Conselho Ultramarino, but see the useful notes in M. Caetano, *O conselho ultramarino: Esboço da sua história* (Lisbon, 1967). There are, likewise, few studies on the metropolitan side of the administration of the Portuguese colonies in the second half of the seventeenth century either, but see G. Salgado et al. (eds.), *Fiscais e meirinhos. A administração no Brazil colonial* (Rio de Janeiro, 1985).

18. F. Martins, *Os vicereis da Índia* (Lisbon, 1935); see too C.R. Boxer, *A Índia Portuguêsa em meados do século XVII* (Portuguese India in the Mid-Seventeenth Century) (Lisbon, 1981), p. 23. As various viceroys of India have been viceroy of Brazil too, see also R. Bardwell, "The Governors of Portugal's South Atlantic Empire in the Seventeenth Century: Social Background, Qualifications, Selections and Rewards," (Ph.D. dissertation, University of California at Santa Barbara, 1974). Contemporaries all agreed on the capability of Francisco de Távora, Count of Alvor, "whose unique virtues and zeal to serve your majesty are still increasing day by day" (AHU, Índia, Cx. 23, 113, 7 October 1683). By contrast, the other famous viceroy of this period—Francisco de Noronha, Count of Linhares—was a very controversial figure, not least because of

his feud with the clergy: "If the Count of Linhares, who is this rich and powerful[,] departed from here this poor and miserable this will suffice for your majesty to grasp how much work he has accomplished" (ANTT, DRI, 44, 15 March 1636, fo. 163 vo.).

19. AHU, Índia, Cx. 37, 82, 27 November 1694.

20. See G.D. Winius, *The Fatal History of Portuguese Ceylon: Transition to Dutch Rule* (Gainesville, 1977), pp. 131–41.

21. See the complaints of Mello e Castro in AHU, Índia, Cx. 26, 119, 4 December 1662.

22. See the accusations of Henriques Jaques de Magalhães against Câmera Coutinho in AHU, Índia, Cx. 43, 10, 29 December 1699.

23. AHU, Índia, Cód. 212, 16 March 1675, fo. 8.

24. ANTT, DRI, 50, fo. 80; ANTT, DRI, 44, 9 April 1644, fo. 152.

25. For the organization of the collection of land revenues in Goa see de Souza, *Medieval Goa*, part 2; for Ceylon see T. Abeyasinge, *Portuguese Rule in Ceylon* (Colombo, 1966), pp. 100–166.

26. ANTT, DRI, 35, 29 August 1638, fo. 186 vo. The Conselho Ultramarino almost habitually complained about the understaffing of the courts of justices, the main cause for the "lack of justice," one argued; see, for example, AHU, Cód. 212, 11 September 1696, fo. 252–56 vo.; C.R. Gonçalves Pereira, *História da administração de justícia no Estado da Índia*, 2 vols. (Lisbon, 1964–65); AHU, Índia, Cx. 39, 30, 28 February 1697; on Portuguese jurisdiction in the *ultramar* in general, compare S.B. Schwartz, *Sovereignty and Society in Colonial Brazil: The High Court of Bahia and Its Judges 1609–1757* (Berkeley, 1973), pp. 10–24.

27. G.D. Winius, *The Black Legend of Portuguese India: Diogo do Couto, His Contemporaries and the "Soldado Prático"* (New Delhi, 1985), AHU, Índia, Cx. 29 bis, 208, 4 December 1674.

28. See I.I.A. Thompson, *War and Society in Habsburg Spain 1580–1640* (London, 1986).

29. Boxer, *Portuguese Society in the Tropics*, pp. 12–41; BAC, A 58, 25 April 1677, fo. 207; HAG, LM, 35, 4 February 1656, fo. 126; AHU, Índia, Cx. 24, 108, 23 August 1658; ANTT, DRI, 58, 1648, fo. 54.

30. See H.B. Moreno, *Os municípios portuguêses nos séculos XIII a XVI* (Lisbon, 1986).

31. For a concrete case, see for example, ANTT, DRI, 60, 10 March 1649, fo. 156–59 vo.; and in same, "Treslado da vista que se-derão passar na câmera."

32. AHU, Índia, Cx. 33 bis; 133, 24 January 1686.

33. Thekkedath, *History of Christianity*, p. 414; J. Wycki, "Unbewältigte Probleme in Indien, Ceylon und Burma," in *Sacra Congregatione de Propaganda Fide: Memoria Rerum*, 2 vols. (Rome, Freiburg, 1972), ii, pp. 547–72.

34. J.F. da Costa, "The Demolition of the Temples on the Island of Goa in 1540 and the Disposition of the Temple Lands," *Neues Zeitschrift für Missionswissenschaft* 18 (1962), pp. 161–71; for the struggle against "paganism" in Goa see Souza, *Medieval Goa*, pp. 260–62, and in Bassein see Garçia, *Archivo*, pp. 661–64.

35. AHU, Índia, Cx. 38, 11, 21 March 1693, and 20 October 1694; A. Baião, *A inquisição de Goa*, 2 vols. (Lisbon, 1930, 1945); A.K. Priolkar, *The Goa Inquisition* (Bombay, 1961).

36. Wycki, *O livro*, pp. 216–19; relative to Bassein, Pães de Sande warned the king that if the Inquisition were introduced there, "the Moors and gentiles of your majesty's

lands will sell their goods and property, and the lands of your majesty will soon become depopulated" (HAG, LM, 40, 3 December 1674).

37. A good example of such patriotic writings is F. de Queiroz, *Vida do venerável irmão Basto* (Lisbon, 1687).

38. Boxer, *A Índia*, p. 36.

39. VOC/OB 1256, 18 May 1667, fo. 1223; Thekkedath, *History of Christianity*, pp. 91–120; Bow, *Indian Christians*, p. 109; F.E. Keay, *A History of the Syrian Church in India* (New Delhi, 1960), pp. 59–61; for the VOC's view on this schism see VOC/OB 1304, 15 May 1673, fo. 364–73.

40. HAG, LM, 75, 8 January 1703, but Caetano de Mello e Castro wanted to incite the crown to lower the customs dues, so he may have been exaggerating.

41. See G.J. Ames, 'The Carreira da India 1668–1682: Maritime Enterprise and the Quest for Stability in Portugal's Asian Empire," *Journal of European Economic History* 20 (1) (1991), pp. 7–27; and for *carreira da Índia* ships touching the Azores, see also T. Bentley Duncan, *Atlantic Islands: Madeira, the Azores and the Cape Verdes in Seventeenth-Century Commerce and Navigation* (Chicago, 1972), p. 126.

42. ARA, St. Gen., Lias Portugal, 7013 ii, 17 December 1669, and 7 April 1670; AHU, Índia, Cx. 42, 148, ca. 1626. Most ships used in the *carreira da Índia* in the seventeenth century have been described in A.M. Esparteiro, *Três séculos no mar. Ementa histórica das naos portuguêses*, 2 vols. (Lisbon, 1974, 1975).

43. Évora, CV/2–7, "As cauzas porque as naos chegaram a demasiada grandezza," fo. 76–78; ANTT, DRI, 56, "Memorial para ver alguns advertencias da Índia," fo. 76.

44. Boxer, *A Índia*, pp. 39–57; T.R. Duffy, *Shipwreck and Empire: Portuguese Maritime Disaster in an Age of Decline* (Cambridge, MA, 1965); AHU, Índia, Cx. 23, 146, "Renúncias que tirerão os tabeliães"; AHU, Índia, Cx. 37, 10, 10 February 1694; AHU, Índia, Cx. 11, 145, 31 March 1635, and 115, 26 March 1635; India also constantly complained about a lack of skilled mariners—see, for example, ANTT, DRI, 61, 11 January 1649, fo. 47.

45. This is mainly based on the following sources: the correspondence of the Dutch embassy in Lisbon (in ARA, St. Gen., Lias Portugal), which lists all incoming ships from India and Brazil; the correspondence of Vengurla in VOC, Overgekomen Brieven; Ahmad, *Indo-Portuguese Trade; Documentação ultramarina portuguêsa*, vol. 4; Rau (ed.), "Arquivo geral da alfândega de Lisboa, Livro das Cartas Gerais," pp. 5–34; HAG, Feitoria Geral, 14.593, "Conta dos cabedães que veirão do Reino," fo. 13–34; J.R. de Amaral Lapa, "O Brasil e a navegação portuguêsa para a ásia" *Estudos históricos* (Marilla, 1968), pp. 110–73.

46. Steensgaard, *Carracks*, p. 92.

47. AHU, Índia, Cx. 13 bis, 134, 31 December 1638; Boxer, *The Portuguese Seaborne Empire*, p. 379; Ajuda 51-VII-23, fo. 205–9 vo.

48. F. Mauro, *Le Portugal et l'Atlantique au XVII siàcle* (Paris, 1960), p. 143; Disney, *A decadência*, p. 162; Yogev, *Diamonds and Coral*, p. 106; *English Factories* 1646–1650, p. 36; ANTT, DRI, 53, 22 December 1646, fo. 477. On the Jewish coral trade in Leghorn see also GAA, PA 334, Archive of the Portuguese Israelite synagogue, 858, Anonymous ledgerbook of a coral trader in Leghorn (in Ladino), ca. 1670.

49. ARA, St. Gen., Lias Portugal, 7010 i, 18 November 1641.

50. See AHU, Reino, Mç. 10, 1 April 1639.

51. BAC, A 497, 11 February 1678, fo. 102; HAG, LM, 52, "Rendimento geral," mentions a separate *renda* on the sale of *papel veneçiano* to the mainland, for example.

52. ANTT, J.d.T., Mç. 1, 19 October 1674 and 14 March 1676.

53. VOC/OB 1343, 5 November 1681, fo. 2403; for the tobacco trade of Bahia see P. Verger, *Flux et réflux de la traite des nègres entre le Golfe de Bénin et Bahia de Todos os Santos du xviie au xixe siècle* (Paris, 1968), pp. 48–52.

54. ANTT, J.d.T., Mç. 2, 22 February 1684.

55. Amaral Lapa, "O Brasil," pp. 125–34; Boxer, *Portuguese Seaborne Empire*, p. 219. The crown regularly prohibited exports of tobacco from Portugal to India by private traders—see HAG, LM, 49, 29 March 1684. One could be punished with imprisonment for smuggling tobacco, ARA, St. Gen., Lias Portugal, 7015 i, 9 October 1685.

56. AHU, Índia, Cx. 26 bis, 134, 26 March 1665.

57. Ajuda 51-VII-26, 19 October 1700, fo. 16, and 18 March 1701, fo. 21.

58. HAG, LM, 73, 28 February 1704, fo. 164.

59. V. Rau and G. Gomes, *Os manuscritos do arquivo da Casa de Cadaval respeitante ao Brasil*, 2 vols. (Coimbra, 1953, 1956), i, p. 237; AHU, Índia, Cx. 29, 112, 21 January 1670; VOC/OB 4012, 10 March 1686.

60. HAG, LM, 72, fo. 802 vo.

61. R.L. Stein, *The French Slave Trade in the Eighteenth Century: An Old Régime Business* (Madison, 1979), p. 97; on the food rations and way of life of Portuguese slave ships heading from Mozambique to Goa and Brazil, see Theal, vi, pp. 468–69.

62. Koponen, *People and Production*, p. 108; Beach, *The Shona*, p. 134; Theal, vi, p. 433

63. Ajuda 51-VII-24, 2 December 1700, fo. 135; ANTT, J.d.T., Mç. 1, 14 March 1676.

64. AHU, Índia, Cx. 38, 77, "Foral" of Praças do Norte.

65. HAG, LM, 72, fo. 420; VOC/OB 1261, 26 January 1665, fo. 737 vo.

66. VOC/UB 862, 9 November 1638, fo. 544; ARA, St. Gen., Lias Portugal, 7010 i, 5 November 1686; and 22 October 1686; AHU, Índia, Cx. 10, 59, 12 December 1633.

67. See the complaints of Mello e Castro in AHU, Índia, Cx. 26, 140, 8 January 1663.

68. A. Iria, *Da navegação portuguêsa no índico no século XVII (Documentos do arquivo histórico ultramarino)* (Lisbon, 1963), p. 37; C.R. Boxer, "The Principal Ports of Call in the Carreira da Índia," in *From Lisbon to Goa: Studies in Portuguese Trade and Navigation* (London, 1984), chapter 2, p. 48; AHU, Índia, Cx. 30, 8 February 1675; AHU, Cód. 53, 2 March 1672, and 2 January 1675; HAG, 1425, Livro dos regimentos e instruções, 23 November 1692, fo. 18.

69. AHU, Índia, Cx. 13 bis, 109, "O provedor . . ."; AHU, Índia, Cx. 13, 24, 26 January 1638; Boyajian, *Portuguese Trade with Asia*, passim; J. Gonçalves Salvador, *Os cristãos novos e o comércio na Atlântico meridional* (São Paulo, 1978).

70. Ajuda, 54-X-19, "Rol da fazenda"; D.G. Smith, "The Mercantile Class of Portugal and Brazil in the Seventeenth Century: A Socio-Economic Survey of the Merchants of Lisbon and Bahia" (Ph.D. dissertation, University of Texas at Austin, 1975), pp. 45 et seq.

71. Along the lines of V. Rau's study of the Timorese nobleman/trader Antônio Coelho Guerreiro's *Livro de razão* in "Nobreza portuguêsa e fortunas ultramarinas no século XVII," *Revista Portuguêsa da História* 8 (1961), pp. 1–55.

72. AHU, Índia, Cx. 14, 157, 16 February 1647; documents on the Brazilian connections of the Noronha/De Sá family can be found in ANTT, Cartório das Jesuitas, Mç. 10–14; another apparent case is the Marquise of Niza, who also owned land in both

Portugal and in India—see ARA, Coll. Aitzema 92. The Marquise of Niza was also one of the most significant merchants in the India trade in the seventies: Ajuda 54-X-19, "Rol da fazenda."

73. Ajuda 51-V-49, fo. 79; AHU, Bahia, Cx. 20, 2449.

74. AHU, Índia, Cx. 15, 103, 27 December 1643.

75. AHU, Índia, Cx. 13 bis, 188, 10 December 1639, and enclosures.

76. Disney, *A decadência,* p. 45; Godinho, *Os descobrimentos,* iii, p. 45; Ahmad, *Indo-Portuguese Trade,* pp. 76–85; ANTT, DRI, 40, 5 October 1637, fo. 99.

77. Meilink-Roelofs, *Vestiging,* pp. 73–7; ANTT, DRI, 40, 20 August 1637, fo. 138; ANTT, DRI, 44, 27 March 1638, fo. 156.

78. Geleynssen 319, 22 October 1642.

79. See Ahmad, *Indo-Portuguese Trade,* p. 85; ANTT, DRI, 40, 5 October 1637, fo. 116; VOC/OB 1166, 9 October 1647, fo. 790 vo.; VOC/OB 1162, 15 April 1646, fo. 511 vo.; Geleynssen 319, 22 October 1642.

80. AHU, Índia, Cx. 17, 5, 5 October 1644, and 7 October 1644; ANTT, DRI, 56, 13 March 1645, fo. 125.

81. VOC/OB 1286, 13 June 1668, fo. 1122; VOC/OB 1246, 23 February 1664, fo. 1408; HAG, LM, 42, 22 October 1667, fo. 92, and 29 January 1668, fo. 14; VOC/OB 1277, 14 August 1670, fo. 1688 vo; VOC/OB 1248, 2 April 1671, fo. 2156.

82. AHU, Índia, Cx. 42, 51; VOC 1278, 28 April 1670, fo. 534; VOC 1361, "Report by D. Jonktys," fo. 521.

83. VOC/OB 1379, 31 December 1681, fo. 2404; ANTT, J.d.T., Mç 3, 22 March 1686.

84. ANTT, DRI, 47, 6 November 1640, fo. 90; see S. Subrahmanyam, "The *Kagemusa* Effect: The Portuguese, Firearms and the State in Early-Modern South India," *Moyen Orient et Océan Indien* 4 (1987), pp. 249–62.

85. On Portuguese relations with Cananore, see the bundle of documents in VOC/OB 1336, fo. 464–504; and AHU, Índia, Cx. 26 bis, 224, 14 December 1665; on Calicut see AHU, Índia, Cx. 32, 106, "Capitulations of Peace."

86. AHU, Índia, Cx. 29 bis, 162, 12 February 1674; BAC, Vermelho 281, "Discurso político," fo. 2 vo.

87. J.R. de Amaral Lapa, *O Brasil e as drogas do Oriente* (Amaril, 1973); L.F. de Almeida, "Acclimatação de plantas do Oriente no Brasil durante os séculos XVII e XVIII," *Revista Portuguêsa da História,* 15 (1976), pp. 339–81.

88. ANTT, SV, 18, 7 March 1617, fo. 264.

89. ANTT, DRI, 32, 28 March 1635, fo. 156, 172; and 36, 6 March 1636, fo. 202, 218, 234; 40, fo. 343–45.

90. ARA, St. Gen., Lias Portugal, 7016 i, 19 November 1697; AHU, Índia, Cx. 33 bis, 125, 24 January 1686; Ajuda, 51-VII-24, fo. 13; Ajuda 51-VII-39, fo. 15, 11.

91. VOC 1122, "Report van Twist," fo. 499; Ajuda 51-VII-23, 21 January 1685, fo. 511, and 22 January 1685, fo. 511.

92. ANTT, DRI, 46, 14 January 1639, fo. 63; ANTT, J.d.T., Mç. 3, 9 March 1686; Yogev, *Diamonds and Coral,* p. 65; Ajuda 51-VII-23, 10 May 1683, fo. 115; VOC/OB 1409, "André Souras de Sourat à Antonio et Diego Marsin, marchands, joualiers de Paris," fo. 183.

93. ANTT, J.d.T., Mç. 3, 14 March 1689 and 3 March 1687; ANTT, J.d.T., Mç. 2, 14 January 1684 and 13 November 1683.

94. AHU, Índia, Cx. 12, 19, "Treslado das diligençias."

95. ANTT, DRI, 56, 6 April 1645, fo. 165, "Todas ditas coizas de pedraria e amber,

há que se-descaminharem e não vierem registadas da Índia e assi da moeda, ouro e prata que deste reino sair seja tudo perdido pera mina fazenda." According to the Dutch ambassador less than half of the diamonds fetched to Lisbon were declared at customs.

96. AHU, Índia, Cx. 11 bis, 193, 6 November 1635; ANTT, DRI, 35, "Alcançá da fazenda," fo. 344–47.

97. AHU, Índia, Cx. 13, 66, "As sortes de roupas."

98. BNL, Pombalina, Cód. 439, 5 December 1697, fo. 42; AHU, Índia, Cx. 26 bis, 213, 1665; for the textile trade with Portugal see GAA, PA, 1, Burlamachi Papers, 739, 13 December 1681; the cultivation of cotton in Brazil only became important in the eighteenth century—see R. Simonson, *História econômica do Brasil* (São Paulo, 1957), p. 369.

99. Ajuda 51-VII-25, fo. 264–66; ANTT, DRI, 32, 24 February 1635, fo. 96.

100. J. Ribeiro (ed.) *Arte de Furtar* (Rio de Janeiro, 1907), iv, p. 218.

101. AHU, Reino, Mç. 8, 28 September 1635; Ajuda 51-VII-25, fo. 23.

102. Ajuda 51-VII-25, 20 March 1699, fo. 23. and 15 March 1699, fo. 73; AHU, Índia, Cx. 22 bis, 16, 30 January 1654; AHU, Índia, Cx. 40, 12, 13 January 1698.

103. Ajuda 51-VII-25, 20 March 1699, fo. 23; AHU, Índia, Cx. 26, 140, 8 January 1663; ANTT, DRI, 43, October 1638, fo. 154.

104. A. Rodrigues Monteiro, *Do orçamento português* (Lisbon, 1921), quoted by A. de Oliveira, *Poder e oposição política em Portugal no período filipino* (Lisbon, 1990), p. 77; V.M. Godinho, *Les Finances de l'état portugais des Indes* (Paris, 1982); Disney, *A decadência,* pp. 63–72; A. Farinho de Carvalho, *Diogo do Couto. O soldado prático e a India* (Lisbon, 1979), pp. 124–42; A.T. de Matos, "The Financial Situation of the State of India in the Philippine Period," in de Souza (ed.), *Indo-Portuguese History,* p. 97.

105. BNL, FG, Cód. 1783, "Livro das receitas," fo. 112–13.

106. BNL, FG, Cód. 8538, "Relação dos rendimentos"; BNL, Pombalina, Cód. 439, 2 January 1698, fo. 4; ANTT, DRI, 55, 7 December 1646, fo. 382.

107. HAG, LM, 36, 26 March 1658, fo. 400; there are many other complaints of the crown on the overburdened bureaucracy of Goa—see Garçia, *Archivo,* p. 301, or HAG, Livro Verde, 2950, fo. 28.

108. ANTT, DRI, 61, 1650, fo. 380–83.

109. ANTT, DRI, 56, 4 March 1653, fo. 489; AHU, Índia, Cx. 24, 43, "Treslado do assento," February 1653; Ferreira Martins, *História da misericórdia,* iii, pp. 286–89.

110. See VOC/OB 3989, 21 February 1654, fo. 136–40.

111. AHU, Cód. 15, 28 February 1654, fo. 132.

112. AHU, Índia, Cx. 24, 159, 2 December 1660; HAG, LM, 37, 6 April 1662, fo. 125.

113. Pissurlencar, *Assentos,* iii, p. 629; HAG, LM, 36, 23 January 1659, fo. 353; VOC/OB 1224, 14 May 1657, fo. 54; VOC/OB 1246, 28 February 1664, fo. 1438 vo.; AHU, Índia, Cx. 24, 78, 3 November 1657; AHU, Índia, Cx. 24 bis, 123.

114. AHU, Índia, Cx. 26, 137, 5 January 1665.

115. HAG, LM, 37, 5 February 1663, fo. 115.

116. G.J. Ames, "The Estado da Índia 1662–1684: Strategies and Priorities in Europe and the East," *Studia* 48 (1989), pp. 234–36; Bragança Pereira, "Os Portugueses em Baçaim," pp. 164–67; AHU, Índia, Cx. 27 bis, 177, 27 November 1668.

117. ANTT, J.d.T., Mç. 4, 19 September 1692; AHU, India, Cx. 34, 88, 24 January 1688.

118. HAG, LM, 52, 24 January 1687, fo. 19, and 2 March 1687, fo. 21; ARA, St.

Gen., Lias VOC, 5471 i, Report by C. Hartsink; AHU, Índia, Cx. 38, 62, 28 February 1694, and enclosures thereto.

119. HAG, LM, 37, 8 January 1662, fo. 104.

120. AHU, Índia, Cx. 34, 5, 22 January 1687.

121. ANTT, DRI, 47, 26 November 1640, fo. 74, and 20 January 1641, fo. 83; M.N. Pearson, "Corruption and Corsairs in Sixteenth Century Western India," in *Coastal Western India,* p. 24, argues that to speak about "corruption" in the early seventeenth century is an anachronism. True, the word *corrupção* was not used by the Portuguese, but "clean hands" (*limpezza de mão*), the standard expression used for good conduct during a *devassa,* covers more or less the same meaning.

122. See Winius, *The Black Legend,* p. 112.

123. ANTT, Mss. da livrária, 699, "Alvará," 27 February 1622; BAC, A 58, 12 September, fo. 39; AHU, Índia, Cx. 15, 65, 6 December 1643.

124. Thus, for instance, Linhares's troubles with the church. See A.R. Disney, "The Viceroy Linhares in Goa," in Guerreiro and Albuquerque (eds.), *IIo seminário,* p. 235.

125. ANTT, DRI, 35, "Pareçer dos prelados e religiosos sobre a matéria que se tratou na junta," fo. 163–254; ANTT, DRI, 41, 3 September 1638, fo. 105–6.

126. AHU, Índia, Cx. 28, 6, 1 March 1669.

127. AHU, Índia, Cx. 33, 24 January 1686; ANTT, Con. d. Gr., Cx. III, E, 15 March 1687, fo. 143.

128. *Malabarse Brieven,* p. 71. See G.B. Souza, *A sobrevivência do império. Os portugueses na China (1630–1754)* (Lisbon, 1991), p. 52; and now in particular J. Borges, *The Economics of the Goa Jesuits* (New Delhi, 1996).

129. AHU, Índia, Cx. 14, 47, 2 December 1641, fo. 7.

130. HAG, LM, 75, "A relation by Father Francisco de Sá, vicar of the Carmelite friars"; AHU, Índia, Cx. 30 bis, 24 March 1679.

131. HAG, LM, 51 B, "List of incomes of the Franciscans." This topic is for Goa well documented in the HAG, Papeis dos conventos extintos-series; Borges, *The Economy,* pp. 125–30; see also J.R. de Amancio Grácias, "Bens pensionadas de Goa," in *O Oriente português* (Nova séria), 4, (1936), pp. 26–38; BAC, Mss. Vermelho, 34, fo. 120.

132. AHU, Índia, Cx. 40, 28. The monasteries had no objections to owning slaves and serfs, who were often badly treated by the monks, all too frequently causing Christian serfs to flee from the estates of the church, often to Maratha territory. See, for example, BAC, A 497, 15 February 1676, fo. 137.

133. AHU, Índia, Cx. 17, 45, 7 December 1644.

134. AHU, Índia, Cx. 26, 35, 24 June 1664.

135. AHU, Índia, Cx. 31 bis, 179, "A list of *fidalgos* who reside in this state." Alas, this document is severely damaged by water and partly illegible.

136. AHU, Índia Cx. 41, 63.

137. J.H. van Linschoten, *Itinerario ofte schipvaart* (J. Kern and H. Terpstra, eds.), 2 vols. (The Hague, *WLV,* 1903), i, pp. 144–45; Laval, *Voyages,* ii, p. 82; for comments see Steensgaard, *Carracks,* p. 85, and Winius, *Fatal History,* p. 55; prohibitions on luxury can for example be found in HAG, Livro Azul, 8784, "Alvará," 23 April 1624, fo. 2; Bragança Pereira, *Arquivo português oriental,* i, 3, lxxix; Garcia, *Archivo,* p. 627, 633.

138. AHU, Índia, Cx. 14, 57, 1641, fo. 9.

139. BAC, A 500, 15 December 1678.

140. HAG, LM, 46 bis, "Regiment for Francisco de Távora," 24 March 1684, paragraph 4; M.D.D. Newitt, "Plunder and the Reward of Office in the Portuguese Empire,"

in M. Duffy (ed.), *The Military Revolution and the State 1500–1800* (Exeter, 1980), pp. 10–25.

141. HAG, LM, 44, 23 January 1681, fo. 43.

142. V. Magalhães Godinho, *Os descobrimentos,* i, p. 56.

143. Évora, CXV/1–39, "Treslado do assento," fo. 35–36; Steensgaard, *Carracks,* p. 89; BNL, FG, Cód. 1783, "Livro das receitas e depezas."

144. Thus, for example, Braudel, *Mediterrenean,* i, p. 545.

145. AHU, Cód. 53, 5 March 1649, fo. 2; AHU, Índia, Cx. 28 bis, 181, 6 March 1671; AHU, India, Cx. 17, 63, 24 December 1644; AHU, Índia, Cx. 42, 90, ca. 1643.

146. BNL, FG, Cód. 7640, "Breve relação," fo. 63.

147. G.V. Scammel, "The Pillars of Empire: Indigenous Assistance and the Survival of the Estado da Índia," *MAS* 22 (2) (1988), pp. 473–89; Pearson, "Banias and Brahmins"; T.R. de Souza, "Glimpses of Hindu Dominance of Goan Economy in the Seventeenth Century," *Indica* 12 (1975), pp. 27–35.

148. BAC, A 496, 4 January 1678, fo. 132; BAC, A 499, "Depezas das 461 pardaos da feitoria que consta no recibo atraz."

149. AHU, Índia Cx. 33, 110, 30 December 1689.

150. HAG, Petições despachadas para o conselho da fazenda, 1184, 10 April 1683, fo. 87; HAG, Livro da provinçia do Norte, 1376, "Alvará sobre as Parçias."

151. HAG, Arrematações das rendas, Mss. no. 656 and 2600; for seaborne trade of *banias* from Goa, see in particular VOC/OB 1266, 20 August 1668, fo. 851 (a list of Indian ships departing from Goa).

152. HAG, LM, 59, 17 March 1697, fo. 166; F. Nery Xavier, *Bosquejo histórico das communidades das ilhas de Goa, de Bardes e de Salcete,* 2 vols. in one (Nova Goa, 1853/Bastora, 1905), ii, p. 137.

153. HAG, LM, 53, 22 December 1686; Baião, *A inquisição de Goa,* i, p. 103; VOC/OB 1240, 31 May 1662, fo. 670.

154. AHU, India, Cx. 40, 31, 15 February 1698; Ajuda 54-XIII-15, no. 115, "Lista da importancia das rendas reais."

155. AHU, Índia, Cx. 30, 146, 20 January 1676.

156. F. Nery Xavier, *Defensa dos direitos das Gão-carias, Gão-càres e seus privilégios* (Nova Goa, 1858), p. 13; Évora, CXV/1–39, 23 February 1681, fo. 353.

157. See also AHU, Índia, Cx. 37, 24, September 1693.

158. AHU, Índia, Cx. 30, 146, 19 March 1677.

159. Bragança Pereira, "Os Portugueses em Baçaim," pp. 165–67; Évora CXV/1–39, 5 December 1668, fo. 416; HAG, LM, 44, 13 January 1680, fo. 73–78; AHU, Índia, Cx. 28 bis, 203, 17 July 1671.

160. F.N. Malabari, *Bombay in the Making* (London, 1910), pp. 364–431; J.R. de Lima Felner (ed.), *Subsídios para a história da Índia portuguêsa* (Lisbon, 1868), ii, pp. 5–9; J. Aubin, "Le Orçamento do Estado da Índia de Antônio de Abreu," *Studia* 4 (1959), pp. 187–208; P.P.S. Pissurlencar (ed.), *Regimentos das fortalezas da Índia* (Bastora, 1951), pp. 411–25.

161. BAC, A 496, 3 December 1677, fo. 13 vo.

162. BAC, A 496, 12 December 1677, fo. 54; AHU, Índia, Cx. 23, 108, 27 October 1682; HAG, LM, 51 bis, 16 March 1689, fo. 23, 84; HAG, LM, 49, 4 January 1683, fo. 23; HAG, LM, 46 bis, 12 January 1681.

163. HAG, LM, 46 bis, 19 February 1681, and enclosure, "Petition of the Bardes *câmera* to the Viceroy"; AHU, Índia, Cx. 24, 45, 8 March 1657.

164. HAG, LM, 34, 1679, fo. 42; AHU, Índia, Cx. 19 bis, 144, "Petition of Brahmin fathers to king"; Aubin, "Orçamento," p. 187; Garcia, *Archivo,* p. 367, 560.

165. Middleton, *World of the Swahili,* p. 47.

166. Compare A. Rita Ferreira, *Fixação portuguêsa e história pre-colonial de Moçambique* (Lisbon, 1986).

167. W. Rea, *The Economics of the Zambesi Mission 1580–1795* (Rome, 1976).

168. HAG, LM, 49, 20 December 1685, fo. 329. VOC shipping lists from Vengurla—which include private imports from Mombasa and Mozambique, as the ivory trade was not included within the crown monopoly—provide a clue on the comparative order of magnitude of the ivory trade from Kilwa and Mombasa. In 1661, two ships fetched 47 bahar from Mombasa and, in 1662, 20 bahar from Mombasa, 180 picol from Mozambique; in 1663 486 quintal from Mombasa, 186 from Mozambique; in 1664 800 bahar from Mombasa, 98 quintal from Mozambique; in 1664 880 bahar from Mombasa, 93 bahar from Mozambique; and in 1668 100 bahar from Mombasa, none from Mozambique; and in 1675 110 bahar from Mombasa. Finally, according to Évora CV/1–17, "Sobre a conservaçao da Índia," fo. 14, Pate, the main port for the trade in ivory around 1680, could export at most 1,200 bahar, leaving us with an estimated maximum production of about 1,500 bahar of ivory for the Mrima Coast and much less for Mozambique. A figure of 110,000 pounds in the same period is quoted in E.A. Thorbahn, "The Precolonial Ivory Trade of East Africa: Reconstruction of a Human–Elephant Ecosystem" (Ph.D. dissertation, University of London, 1971). However, Thorbahn bases this on estimates of what the Portuguese thought *might* be exported, which in the Portuguese case often widely differs from what really was exported.

169. Theal, vi, p. 433: "de bossen en de velden"—on Dela Goa Bay—"syn voorsien van allerlei wild: leeuwen, tygers, eliphanten, renosters, elanden, gemsen, herten, wolven en wilde ezels." Newitt, *History of Mozambique,* p. 179; VOC/OB 4013, Diary "*Voorhouten,*" 26 September 1674

170. Newitt, *History of Mozambique,* pp. 189–91; D. Hafkin, "Politics and Trade in Northern Mozambique in the Late Eighteenth and Early Nineteenth Century" (Ph.D. dissertation, Indiana University 1974), pp. 22–45; AHU, Índia, Cx. 10, 69, 27 February 1633; AHU, Índia, Cx. 29, 5, "As despoçições annexas são os sequintes"; HAG, LM, 44, 28 June 1680; HAG, LM, 46 bis, 9 January 1681 and enclosures.

171. Couto, *Da Ásia,* Dec. XI, Cap. 8.

172. AHU, Índia Cx. 12, 76, 8 November 1636; Theal, iv, p. 267.

173. C.A. Hromnik, "Canarins in the Rios de Cuama," *Journal of African Studies* 6 (1) (1979), pp. 27–37; L.F. Dias Antunes, "The Trade Activities of the *Banyans* in Mozambique: Private Indian Dynamics in the Portuguese State Economy 1686–1777," in K.S. Mathew (ed.), *Mariners, Merchants and Oceans: Studies in Maritime History* (New Delhi, 1995), pp. 301–31. Note that, *contra* Antunes, *canarins* in Mozambique generally refers to Indian Christians from Goa—not to Hindu *banias*, which in my impression were not present in significant numbers in Mozambique in the seventeenth century.

174. AHU, Cód. 212, 28 December 1683, fo. 144 vo.

175. HAG, LM, 55 bis, 2 December 1690, fo. 173 vo.

176. A.A. de Andrade, *Relações de Moçambique settecentista* (Lisbon, 1956), pp. 132, 156; M. Lobato, "Relações commerciais entre a Índia e a costa africana nos séculos XVI e XVII: O papel do Guzerate no comércio de Moçambique," in *Portuguese India and Its Northern Provinces: Proceedings of the 7th International Seminar on Indo-Portuguese History* (Lisbon, 1995), p. 169. Also, HAG, LM, 39, 14 March 1675, fo. 279, and 27 January 1676, fo. 281.

177. E.A. Alpers, "Gujarat and the Trade of East Africa," *IJAHS,* 9 (1) (1976), p. 40; F. Hoppe, *Portugiesisch Ost-Afrika zur Zeit des Mârques de Pombal* (Berlin, 1965), pp. 117–24; HAG, LM, 70, 15 December 1696, fo. 149; Ajuda 51-VII-54, 20 March 1698, fo. 1; BAC, A 513, 15 December 1696, fo. 60.

178. Ajuda 50-V-38, fo. 162.

179. Such was, for example, the case with Viceroys Luís de Mendonça Furtado, Ajuda 51-V-49, fo. 45, and Gonçalves de Câmera Coutinho; Évora, CIX/1–13, "Tombo de fazenda de Antônio Luís Gonçalves de Câmera Coutinho."

180. Boxer, *A Índia,* p. 54; for the fortunes amassed by the count of Aveiras, see A.R. Disney, "Goa in the Seventeenth Century," in Newitt, *The First Portuguese Empire,* p. 93; A. Paixão, *Monstruosidades,* ii, p. 102.

181. AHU, Cód. 210, 7 February 1639, fo. 15 vo. See Subrahmanyam, *Political Economy,* pp. 162–64.

182. AHU, Índia, Cx. 22, 51, 22 February 1655; ANTT, DRI, 48, 18 March 1641, fo. 60; ANTT, DRI, 61, 20 December 1651, fo. 316.

183. Coates, *Degredados e orfãs,* pp. 131–34; ANTT, DRI, 35, 6 January 1635, fo. 236; BAC, A 96, 18 February 1622, fo. 76 vo.; and in same, 1618, fo. 34; see in particular AHU, Índia, Cx. 29 bis, 174, Anonymous memorandum 1673. Such would imply one should translate *lançado* with "outlaw" rather than with "settler" or "deserter."

184. BAC, A 96, 1618, fo. 34; M.A. Lima Cruz, "Exiles and Renegades in Early Sixteenth Century Portuguese Asia," *IESHR* 23 (3) (1986), pp. 249–62; L. Felipe Thomaz, "Les Portugais dans les mers de l'Archipel au XVIe siècle," *Archipel* 18 (1979), pp. 105–25; G.D. Winius, "The 'Shadow-Empire' of Goa in the Bay of Bengal," *Itinerário* 7 (2) (1983), pp. 83–101; S. Subrahmanyam, "Staying On: The Portuguese on the Coromandel Coast in the Late Seventeenth Century," *IESHR,* 22 (4) (1985), pp. 455–63.

185. ANTT, DRI, 56, 12 January 1646, fo. 411.

186. S. Subrahmanyam, *Improvising Empire: Portuguese Trade and Settlement on the Bay of Bengal 1500–1700* (Delhi, 1990).

187. AHU, Cód. 451, 9 March 1684, fo. 9; BAC, A 53, July 1677, fo. 268. At Cochin most slaves were Roman Catholic and spoke Portuguese too; they may well have considered themselves "vassals" of the Portuguese king—see VOC/OB 1364, "Inventory of the estate of Jacob Chardavere."

188. On Ferdinand Kron and the pepper contracts of the Fuggers, see: H. Kellenbenz, "Les Frères Fugger et le marché international du poivre autour de 1600," *Annales ESC,* 11 (1) (1956), p. 15; and "Le Front hispano-portugais contre l'Inde et le rôle d'une agence de renseignement au service des marchands allemands et flamands," in *Océan Indien et Méditerranée* (Lisbon, 1962), pp. 263–90. Invoices of goods send by Ferdinand Kron to Portugal can be found in UBL/BPL, 876, "Liber Mercatorum Francisco de Gama Barros."

189. VOC/OB 1273, 27 March 1669, fo. 1772; AHU, Índia 34 bis, 205, May 1663; AHU, Índia, Cx. 27, 24, 28 January 1666; AHU, Cód 53, 15 December 1668, fo. 321.

190. VOC/OB 1133, "Report by W. Carstensz. on the cruise for the carracks from Lisbon," fo. 217.

191. Godinho, *Les Finances,* p. 75; Bocarro, *Livro,* i, p. 43; Pissurlencar, *Regimentos,* p. 193; AHU, Índia, Cx. 10, 24, 12 April 1632; ANTT, DRI, 40, "Copia dos apontamentos que Francisco de Seixas tirou com o Rey de Patta."

192. J. Strandes, *Die Portugiesenzeit deutsch und englisch Ost Afrikas* (Berlin, 1899), is in my view the definitive work on the political history of the Portuguese on this coast as seen from the Portuguese documentation; see also the essays collected by A.C. Ogot (ed.), *Zamani* (Nairobi, 1975).

193. AHU, Índia, Cx. 14 bis, 178, "Inquiry into the complaints of the king of Sio and Patta"; BNL, FG, Cód. 485, fo. 25.

194. Garcia, *Archivo da relação,* p. 586; VOC/OB 4009, "Short report by Hubert Hugo," fo. 264; Newitt, "Plunder and the Reward of Office," p. 26.

195. BNL, FG, Cód. 8538, "Copy of a letter by João Nunes de Portugal on the fall of Pate."

196. ANTT, SV, 14, 10 March 1601, fo. 195; Bulhão Patto, *Documentos remettidos,* iv, pp. 87, 247, 249.

197. M.D.D. Newitt, "The Southern Swahili Coast in the First Century of Portuguese Expansion," *Azania* 13 (1978), p. 114; Martin, *The History of Malindi,* p. 54; Bulhão Patto, *Documentos remettidos,* iv, p. 87.

198. BNL, FG, Cód. 1783, "Livro das receitas e depezas," fo. 18; R. Wilding, *The Shorefolk: Aspects of the Early Development of Swahili Culture* (Fort Jesus, 1987), pp. 99–107.

199. AHU, Moç., Cx. 1, 66, "Information of Pedro Alvarez Pereira."

200. A. dos Campos, *Os Portugueses em Zanzibar e Pemba* (Bastora, 1936); HAG, Papeis dos conventos extintos, 3033, fo. 62; Bulhão Patto, *Documentos remettidos,* iii, p. 12.

201. HRB 838, "Note on merchandise"; AHU, Índia, Cx. 14 bis, 178, "Inquiry into the complaints."

202. VOC/OB 1113, "Report Carstensz.," fo. 214.

203. AHU, Índia, Cx. 29 bis, 184, "Treslado da devaça sobre o ambar"; BNL, FG, Cód. 8538, "Copy of a letter."

204. AHU, Índia, Cx. 29 bis, 184, "Treslado da devaça sobre o ambar," which contains a list of *bania*s resident at Mombasa in 1638, with place of origin, age, and members of family.

205. Bulhão Patto, *Documentos remettidos,* iv, p. 51; Strandes, *Die Portugiesenzeit,* p. 230; VOC/OB 1490, 10 October 1690, fo. 173 vo.; BAC, A 513, 16 December 1696, fo. 89; see also *Assentos,* ii, p. 124—Bassein and Chaul had to provide ships for the reconquest of Mombasa "since this is entirely their trade."

206. VOC/OB 1279, 22 January 1672, fo. 993; BNL, FG, Cód. 10.836, 16 August 1676, fo. 97; ANTT, DRI, 32, 28 March 1635, fo. 132; HAG, LM, 41, 16 August, 1676; ANTT, DRI, 56, 28 January 1653, fo. 466 vo.

207. *COACM,* ii, p. 312; Ajuda 50-v-37, fo. 72 vo; BAC, A 96, 21 March 1619; Brouwer, *Al-Mukha,* p. 340; see for Mogadishu's trade with Surat VOC/OB 1209, "Memoir of various ships arriving here," 29 May 1654: three ships from Mogadishu, carrying 18,700 pounds of ivory, 220 slaves, 136 pounds of tortoise shell, and 1,530 pounds of mire.

208. BNL, FG 1783, "Livro de Receitas."

209. ANTT, Con. d. Gr. Cx. III, 5, "Rendimentos e depezas."

210. On Mogadishu see Schurhammer, *Franciscus Xavier,* II, i, pp. 135–38; and E. Cerulli, *Somalia: Scritii varii e inediti,* 2 vols. (Rome, 1957), i, pp. 333–38.

211. HAG, LM, 41, 16 August 1676; VOC/OB 1291, "Report Willemson," fo. 583.

212. On the intricate factional politics of Mombasa see F.J. Berg, "Mombasa Under the Busaidi Sultanate: The City and Its Hinterland in the Nineteenth Century," (Ph.D. diss., University of Wisconsin, 1971), pp. 69–76; BNL, FG, Cód. 584, "História de Mombaça," fo. 10; HAG, LM 52, 1687, fo. 262–67.

213. BNL, FG, Cód. 584, "História de Mombaça," fo. 12, 22, 34.

214. HAG, LM, 30, 27 September 1652, fo. 381; ARA, St. Gen., Lias VOC, 5738 ii, Report by Herman Klencke, 6 August 1663; ANTT, Con. d. Gr, Cx. III, 5, "Rendimento e depezas"; HAG, LM, 37, 6 February 1663, fo. 119; HAG, LM 30, 3 August 1652, fo. 384.

215. See Steensgaard, *Carracks,* p. 95; and L. Cordeiro (ed.), *Como se perdeu Hormuz (Processo inédito do século XVII)* (Lisbon, 1896), p. 210.

216. A. de Bragança Pereira, *Notas sobre as fortalezas da Sofala, Moçambique, Mombaça, Mascatte, Sohar e outras de Árabia e Diu* (Bastora, 1938); ANTT, DRI, 33, 8 March 1636, fo. 258.

217. ANTT, DRI, 47, 17 November 1640, fo. 19 vo; AHU, Índia, Cx. 22, 12, 18 December 1650; AHU, Índia, Cx. 10, 32, Petition by Alvares Pinto de Fonseca; BNL, FG, Cód. 1783, "Livro das receitas e depezas," fo. 35; see Wilkinson, *Oman,* pp. 16–25.

218. Bocarro, *Livro,* i, pp. 81–87; G. Leyte (ed.), *Comentários do grande capitão Ruy Freyre de Andrade* (Lisbon, 1940), pp. 241–45; *Documentação ultramarina portugêsa,* i, p. 213; Bragança Pereira, *Notas,* p. 327; Bulhão Patto, *Documentos remettidos,* iv, pp. 321–33; AHU, India, Cx. 24, 75, "Papeis do serviçio" of Alvares Pinto de Alfonso.

219. ANTT, DRI, 59, 11 September 1648, fo. 68; and 7 December 1648, fo. 74 vo.

220. AHU, Índia, Cx. 20, 47, 9 October 1648. For the fall of Muscat see Pissurlencar, *Assentos,* iii, p. 519 et seq.; AHU, Índia, 22, 13, 20 December 1650. The crown had ordered the viceroy to impeach the officials guilty for the loss of Muscat, but he continued to hesitate with this until 1656, when the "culprits" had either repatriated or died (HAG, LM, 31, 7 February 1653, fo. 74; HAG, LM, 35, 26 January 1656, fo. 116).

221. W.F. Sinclair (ed.), *The Journey of Pedro Teixeira from India to Italy by Land, with His Chronicles of the Kings of Hormuz* (London, *WHS,* 1901), p. 239; ANTT, DRI, 58, 2 April 1650, fo. 95.

222. AHU, Cód. 218, fo. 15; VOC/OB 1143, 4 June 1643, fo. 684–85 vo.; AHU, Índia, Cx. 10, 33, 8 January 1633; AHU, Índia, Cx. 18, 44, 19 November 1646; VOC/OB 1444, "Diary kept in the offensive fleet," 20 January 1643, fo. 159, and fo. 432 vo.; *Diário do terceiro conde de Linhares Vice-rei da Índia,* 2 vols. (Lisbon 1937, 1943), ii, p. 177; *Assentos,* i, p. 101.

223. VOC/OB 1113, Report Carstensz., fo. 218–20; ANTT, DRI, 35, 1635, fo. 60–61 vo.; Resende, fo. 316–18; Ajuda 50-V-38, "Relação de alguns coizas accontencidas (1634)," fo. 143.

224. AHU, Índia, Cx. 19, 5, "Papeis de serviçio de Dom Gonçalco de Silveira": Instruction for Dom Gonçalco de Silveira 1628: "se tomar alguns embarcações lhes mandera tomar as cabezzas, queimando as embarcações"; Geleynssen 99, 20 January 1646; ANTT, DRI 59, 30 November 1648, fo. 93 vo.; Bulhão Patto, *Documentos Remettidos,* iv, p. 59.

225. ARA Coll. Sweers/Manis 9, Brief relation by Becher, fo. 122; *Assentos,* ii, p. 180; AHU, Índia, Cx. 19, 5, "Papeis do serviçio," "Alvará" 1623; ANTT, DRI, 32, 3 January 1635, fo. 35; ANTT, DRI, 33, 3 February 1635, fo. 35; Linhares, *Diário,* ii, p. 180.

226. Bocarro, "Livro do estado," i, p. 83; C.R. Boxer, "Anglo-Portuguese Rivalry in the Persian Gulf 1615–1633," in E. Prestage (ed.), *Chapters in Anglo-Portuguese Relations* (Watford, 1935), p. 129; Chick, *A Chronicle,* ii, pp. 1125–7; AHU, Índia, Cx. 19, 5, "Papeis do serviçio": Letter by pasha of Basra 15 January 1629; and in same, *Farman* by Ali, the governor of Basra; ANTT, DRI, 35, "Pareçer" by the provincial of the augustinian mission; ANTT, DRI, 55, 11 April 1645, fo. 290, 294.

227. *Assentos,* iv, p. 154.

228. C.H. Allen, "The Indian Merchant Community of Mascat," *Bulletin of the School of Oriental and African Studies* 44 (1) (1981), p. 41; Reda Baker, *Trade and Empire,* p. 12, citing two (nineteenth-century?) Omani chronicles, reports they were granted these preferential tariffs because one of them had helped the Ja'ariba troops to penetrate Muscat—this seems very much to be an ex post facto fabrication, though. VOC/OB 1291, "Report by Willemson," fo. 562; VOC/OB 1285, 16 July 1672, fo. 383.

229. BNL, FG, Cód. 10.836, 24 January 1676, fo. 79; BAC, A 513, 15 December 1696, fo. 30; VOC/OB 1255, 26 January 1677, fo. 1033, and 30 March 1677, fo. 1038; VOC/OB 1273, 27 March 1669, fo. 1771 vo.

230. Couto, *Da Ásia,* Dec. VII, book 3, ch. xiv; Resende, fo. 55; ANTT, DRI, 31 January 1646, fo. 48 vo.

231. ANTT, DRI, 37, 23 November 1636, fo. 57, and 28 March 1636, fo. 275.

232. BNL, FG. Cód. 580, fo. 11; Pissurlencar, *Assentos,* iii, p. 505; Geleynssen 157, 6 March 1641; *Documentação ultramarina portuguêsa,* i, p. 218; AHU, Cx. 10, 81, 24 February 1634.

233. Geleynssen 157, 21 June 1641; *English Factories* 1637–1641, p. 248; *English Factories* 1634–1636, pp. 122–25; Resende, fo. 57; *Boletim* 2 (5–7), 1964, p. 143; Sîlva Correia, *História da colonização,* iii, p. 320; Bulhão Patto, *Documentos remettidos,* ii, p. 219; Bocarro, "Livro," i, p. 65; ANTT, DRI, "Copia das propostas que o Mir Xârife fêz," fo. 49.

234. VOC/OB 3989, "An inventory of two captured frigates"; see too the rather derogatory remarks of T. Best on the Portuguese trade in the Gulf in *English Factories* 1650–1654, p. 64.

235. VOC/UB 880, 26 September 1656, fo. 427.

236. Pearson, "The Sixteenth Century," in Pearson and Das Gupta (eds.), *India and the Indian Ocean,* p. 90.

237. On the intricate system for dividing ivory into different qualities at Kilwa—following that at Diu—see Alpers, *Ivory and Slaves,* p. 138.

238. HAG, Feitoria de Moçambique, 2324, fo. 12–17; see too HAG, LM, 72, *Proposta* Domingues Doreiro d'Oliveira, fo. 24; HAG, LM, 31, 28 January 1653, fo. 59.

239. AHU, Moç., Cx. 1, 63, 16 January 1632.

240. Ajuda 50-V-37, fo. 383–84; HAG, Feitoria de Moçambique, fo. 12–14; VOC/OB 1444, "Diary of the offensive fleet," fo. 163 vo. (this is an inventory of the frigate *Nossa Senhora do Rosário* heading to Mozambique from Goa); HAG, LM, 75, 20 December 1694, fo. 30.

241. ANTT, DRI, 35, "Treslado do contracto que fêz Dom Phelipe Mascarenhas," fo. 125–27.

242. Garçia, *Archivo,* p. 586; Newitt, "Plunder," p. 26; VOC/OB 4012, "Diary of T. Edwards," fo. 773, 27 June; VOC/OB 4012, "A brief summary of the report by commander H. Hugo," fo. 264; AHU, Moç., Cx. 3, 5, 8 June 1671.

243. AHU, Índia, Cx. 25, 28, "Appontamentos que Martinho Velho Baretto offereceu."

244. HAG, Feitoria de Moçambique 2324, fo. 5; M.B. de Araujo, *O ciclo Moçambicano. Subsidio para a história de Moçambique (1498–1752)* (Coimbra, 1992), p. 203.

245. Ajuda 50-V-37, fo. 385; AHU, Índia, Cx. 28, 94, 17 October 1669.

246. ARA, St. Gen., Lias Portugal, 7013 ii, 19 January 1672.

247. Ames, "The Estado da Índia"; A. Bolleo, "O Regimento para o novo comércio de Moçambique de 1673," *Studia* 3 (1959), pp. 153–74.

248. AHU, Índia, Cx. 28, 94, Anonymous memorandum 1669.

249. AHU, Índia, Cx. 29, 155, 28 September 1674; AHU, Moç. Cx. 3, 16, 5 April 1677; ARA, St. Gen., Lias Portugal, 7017 i, 28 September 1677.

250. BNL, FG, Cód., 10.836, 11 July 1676, fo. 103–5; AHU, Cód. 1221, 30 August 1680, fo. 99 vo.; HAG, LM, 44, "Os cazados que vierão de Sena e atraz."

251. AHU, Moç., Cx. 3, 99, 3 July 1682; see also Axelson, *Portuguese,* pp. 144–54; however (according to HAG, LM, 44, "Os cazados que vierão de Sena"), in 1680 there were 58 colonists still alive in Sena; 20 had died from 1676 onward.

252. AHU, Índia, Cx. 33, 38, 23 February 1680, and 88, 9 August 1680, and 99; AHU, Cód. 212, 9 August 1680, fo. 95–96 vo.

253. HAG, LM, 44, 3 December 1679, fo. 64.

254. HAG, LM, 44, 12 September 1679, fo. 4–25.

255. AHU, Cód. 1221, 7 September 1681, fo. 114 (marginal note by King Pedro).

256. AHU, Índia, Cx. 34, 142, 29 October 1688.

257. AHU, Índia, 34 bis, 156, 22 January 1684.

258. On the Brazil Company see G. de Freitas, "A companhia geral do comércio do Brazil," *Revista de História* (São Paulo, 1951).

259. Ajuda 51-VII-34, fo. 70–77, AHU, Casa da Índia, Cx. 1, "Regimento da saída da mercandiçia da Índia."

260. ARA, St. Gen., Lias Portugal, 7015 ii, 5 April 1689; BNL, Pombalina, Cód. 439, 15 March 1697, fo. 210, and 14 March 1697, 4 January 1698, fo. 211, 14 January 1698, fo. 225; AHU, Índia, Cx. 35, 95, "Copy of the conditions demanded by the merchants of this state for the foundation of a company of trade."

261. BAC, A 512, 8 December 1693, fo. 38.

262. AHU, Índia, Cx. 37, 52, *Pareçeres* relative to the trade Company; Ajuda 51-VII-34, 16 March 1697, fo. 75 vo.

263. Ajuda 50-V-37, fo. 488; AHU, Índia, Cx. 38, 24, 24 March 1695.

264. Ajuda 51-VII-34, fo. 7, fo. 42 vo.

265. Ajuda 51-VII-34, 12 December 1698, fo. 5.

266. On the Coromandel Coast see Subrahmanyam, "Staying On," p. 463; for the Portuguese colony in Madras also see Love, *Vestiges,* i, p. 423; and see in particular HAG, LM, 47, fo. 127–29, which contains an appeal to restore the walls and church of San Thomé at the cost of the Portuguese community at Madras, which then consisted of 47 families. For the Portuguese in Tranquebar see K. Larsen, *De Dansk-Ostindiske Kolonier Historie (Trankebar)* (Copenhagen, 1907), p. 59; and for Bengal see Bowrey, *A Geographical Account,* pp. 191–4l. For the *mardijker,* or Portuguese-speaking community, in Batavia see Taylor, *Smeltkroes Batavia,* p. 71, and J. de Haan, "De laatste der Mardijkers," *BTLV* 73 (1917), pp. 219–25; for the community of Portuguese slaves in Batavia see J. de Haan, *Oud Batavia,* 2 vols. (Bandung, 1922/1935), i, p. 421. Domestic slaves of VOC personnel were already before the conquest of Cochin often derived from Kerala, and sometimes even from Goa—see VOC/CR 9285, 22 February 1655; VOC/CR, 9287, 8 June 1657.

267. G.B. Souza, *A sobrevivência,* pp. 210–13; VOC/OB 1479, 14 May 1690, fo. 50.

268. ANTT, Con. d. Gr. Cx. III, E, "Rendimentos e depezas."

269. AHU, Índia, Cx. 14, 45, 10 February 1641.

270. Oliveira, *Poder e opposição,* pp. 89–95; AHU, Reino, Mç. 10, 27 October 1635; AHU, Índia, Cx. 14 bis, 172, "Consignações das naos da Índia," 15 April 1643.

271. Ajuda 51-VII-27, fo. 11; Évora, CXIII/2–28, "Rendimento das cazas dos direitos reais."

272. BNL, FG, Cód. 10.836, 15 March 1676, fo. 83.

273. This was the reason to turn down a French proposal to purchase Daman from the Portuguese king, according to Barlaeus, ARA, St. Gen., Lias Portugal, 7013 i, 9 September 1669.

274. Boxer, *A Índia,* p. 57.

275. H. Leitão, *Os portugueses em Solor e Timor de 1512 a 1702* (Lisbon, 1948).

276. G.B. Souza, *A sobrevivência,* pp. 201–67.

277. Boxer, *A Índia,* p. 72; HAG, LM, 71, 15 December 1698, fo. 4; VOC/OB 1413, Malacca diary, 22 December 1684; 8 July 1685; HAG, Petições despachadas para o conselho da fazenda, 1128, 27 April 1683, 11 May 1685, fo. 36 vo.; VOC/OB 1403, Extract from Malacca diary, 15 July 1684; VOC/OB 1369, List of ships touching here (Malacca), 15 July 1681; and see the inventories of two Portuguese ships from Macao captured by the VOC in VOC/RGGR 661, 1 December 1637 and 10 July 1638; AHU, Índia, Cx. 33, 109, 30 December 1685.

278. VOC/OB 1266, 20 August 1668, fo. 669–71.

279. Souza, *A sobrevivência,* pp. 111–38; C.R. Boxer, *Francisco Veira de Figueiredo: A Portuguese Merchant Adventurer in South East Asia* (The Hague, 1967); *Dagregister* 1661, pp. 265–67; Cummins, *Travels and Controversies of Navarette,* i, p. 119; VOC/OB 1259, 31 January 1668, fo. 2977; VOC/OB 1264, 18 May 1667, fo. 593–94 vo.; VOC/OB 1255, 10 March 1667, fo. 1055; VOC/UB 893, 26 September 1669, fo. 729.

280. On Christopher Phaulkon see J. van Goor, *Kooplieden, predikanten en bestuurders overzee. Beeldvorming en plaatsbepaling in een vreemde wereld* (Utrecht, 1982), pp. 52–62; *Dagregister* 1678, p. 21; *Generale Missiven,* v, p. 42; ARA, St. Gen., Lias Portugal, 7015 i, 22 October 1686; HAG, LM, 51, "Relação da embaixada que o Sr. Vice-Rey mandasse fazêr para o reino de Sião."

281. Ajuda 51-VII-34, 2 December 1698, fo. 3.

282. "Uma rede commercial e maritíma," wrote L. Felipe Thomaz in "Estrutura politica e administrativa do Estado da Índia no século XVI," in Guerreiro and Albuquerque (eds.), *IIo Seminário Internacional,* pp. 515–16. For the organization and equipment of the coastal fleet to Bassein, see HAG, Correspondênçia de Baçaim, 1249, which almost completely deals with the coastal fleet sent there in 1640.

283. HAG, Livro das provinçias do Norte, 1367, 6 May 1686, fo. 12; ARA, HRB, 826, "A note regarding woodwork in Surat"; AHU, Índia, Cx. 20, 102, 2 March 1649; ANTT, DRI, 57, 15 November 1646, fo. 125; AHU, Índia, Cx. 30, 93, 27 February 1671, 22 September 1676.

284. M.N. Pearson, "Indian Seafarers in the Sixteenth Century," in *Coastal Western India,* p. 131; HAG, LM, 42, 22 December 1663; HAG, Registro de feitoria de Diu, 7962, "Enforma que o Feitor de Diu fêz"; HAG, LM, 71, "Declaration of the incomes of Diu"; BAC, A 513, 15 December 1696, fo. 57.

285. ANTT, Con. d. Gr. Cx. III, E, "Receitas e depezas"; HAG, LM, 31, 27 January 1653, fo. 104; HAG, LM, 44, 12 January 1680, fo. 93; AHU, Índia, 35, 38, 20 January 1690.

286. BAC, A 497, 11 February 1678, fo. 115; AHU, Índia, Cx. 28, 12, 4 February 1669; AHU, Índia, Cx. 33, 98, 24 January 1676.

287. AHU, Índia, Cx. 37, 65, 22 November 1694.

288. AHU, Índia, Cx. 32, 10, "Capitulations of peace with the *rey Chauthai*"; AHU, Índia, Cx. 38, 37, 8 December 1695.

289. HAG, Feitoria Geral 14, 953, "Inventory of merchandise and slaves in the frigate *Nossa Senhora dos Milagros*"; Beach, *The Shona,* p. 195.

290. VOC 10812, "Diary of *Ter Aa,*" 6 December 1705.

291. VOC 10812, "Diary of *Ter Has*"; J.M. Filliot, *La Traite des esclaves vers les Mascareignes au XVIIIème siècle* (Tanarive, 1971), p. 168.

292. P.P.S. Pissurlencar, *Agentes da diplomacia portuguêsa no Oriente (Hindus, Moslims e Parcias)* (Bastora, 1964), pp. 415–45.

293. VOC/OB 1571, 30 January 1696, fo. 302.

294. Filliot, *La Traite,* pp. 160–65; J. Capela and E. Medeiros, *O tráfico de escravos de Moçambique para as Ilhas do Índico 1720–1920* (Maputo, 1987), pp. 1–124; AHU, Moç., Cx. 2, 78, 23 December 1679.

295. *Assentos,* ii, p. 214; HAG, Livro do segredo, 1416, 4 October 1639, fo. 30–32; ANTT, DRI, 40, 21 September 1637, fo. 375; ANTT, DRI, 50, 28 November 1643, fo. 36; VOC/XVII 316, 14 March 1639, fo. 258 vo.; VOC/RGGR 662, 11 May 1639; VOC/RGGR 664, 28 September 1640; AHU, Cód. 1221, 8 March 1655, fo. 250.

296. *English Factories* 1634–1636, p. 94.

297. C.R. Boxer, "The General of the Galleons and the Anglo-Portuguese Truce Celebrated at Goa in January 1635," *Ethnos* 1 (1935), pp. 27–32; Disney, *A decadência,* p. 185; *English Factories* 1645–1650, p. 15; ANTT, DRI, 37, 15 December 1637, fo. 411 vo., and 4 March 1637, fo. 481.

298. HAG, 1164, "Assento Conselho da fazenda" (Goa), 11 January 1644; VOC/UB 882, "Instruction for Adriaen Roothaas," fo. 349; ANTT, DRI, 44, 20 November 1642, fo. 69; ANTT, DRI, 56, 13 March 1645, fo. 47.

299. See, for example, VOC/OB, 26 April 1670, fo. 1752; for English trade to the Philippines under Portuguese cover see S.D. Quaisòn, *English "Country-Trade" with the Philippines 1644–1765* (Quezon City, 1966), p. 35 et seq.

300. AHU, Índia, Cx. 28, 108, 30 January 1670; C.H. Fawcett (ed. and trans.), *The Travels of Abbé Carré in Asia and the Middle East,* 3 vols. (London, *WHS,* 1947), i, p. 88. Nor did this smuggling elude Dutch attention: VOC/OB 1278, 26 April 1670, fo. 152.

301. AHU, Índia, Cx. 29 bis, 174, "Proposition of the Rt. Hon. Luís de Mendonça Furtado to Mr. Gerauld Aungier."

302. HAG, Petições despachadas para o conselho da fazenda, 1129, 11 May 1685, fo. 36 vo.; HAG, Feitoria Geral, 14593, fo. 127–32 vo., "Register of letters of Alvaro Casallo."

303. HAG, LM, 31, 22 March 1653, fo. 203; *English Factories* 1651–1654, pp. 144, 184; Theal, iv, p. 332; J.R. Jensen (ed.), *The Journal of Nicholas Buckridge* (Minneapolis, 1973), p. 125.

304. AHU, Moç, Cx. 1, 104, 22 September 1654.

305. G.S.P. Freeman Grenville (ed.), *The East African Coast: Selected Sources from the First to the Early Nineteenth Century* (Oxford, 1966), p. 187; M. Newitt, "The East India Company in the West Indian Ocean in the Early Seventeenth Century," *Journal of Imperial and Commonwealth History* 14 (1986), pp. 5–33; Theal, iv, p. 325; HAG, LM, 31, 20 July 1653, fo. 208–10; *English Factories* 1651–1654, p. 71.

306. Bragança Pereira, *Arquivo,* II, I, 2, pp. 237–41; Lobato, *Quatro Estúdios,* p. 33 ff.; VOC/OB 4023, Cape Town Diary, 23 April 1685; HAG, LM, 52, fo. 5, and *Assento da Junta Geral de Moçambique,* 6 August 1686, fo. 4.

307. VOC/OB 1215, 24 April 1656, fo. 561–63; see van Dam, *Beschryvinge,* II, iii, p. 53; AHU, Índia, Cx. 28, 158, 25 January 1670.

308. VOC/OB 4012, "Diary of Thomas Edwards," fo. 773, 27 June; see Smith, "Dela Goa Bay," p. 271.

309. VOC/OB 1382, 20 October 1682, fo. 376; VOC 4029, Diary of the *Noord,* 19 March; VOC 4012, Diary of the *Voorhouten,* fo. 688, 25 June.

310. VOC/OB 4023, "Relation of Hendrick Wilkinson," fo. 114 vo.; AHU, Índia, Cx. 35, 36, 24 January 1690; BNL, FG, Cód. 8538, 24 January 1687, Enclosure 1 and 2.

311. VOC/OB 4023, "A relation by John Crixton," fo. 116 vo.

312. V.M. Godinho, *Os descobrimentos,* i, p. 62.

313. Souza, *A sobrevivência;* L.F. Thomaz, "Les Portugais," p. 124. Contrary to the argument of A.R. Disney, "Contrasting Models of Empire," in A.R. Duttra (ed.), *The Portuguese and the Pacific* (Santa Barbara, 1995), pp. 26–38, we have had ample occasion to observe that the two developed side by side throughout the Estado da Índia; there is no "formal" expansion in the Arabian seas versus an "informal" expansion in the Bay of Bengal and the South China Seas, although, obviously, formal expansion had more weight in the Arabian seas.

314. AHU, Índia, Cx. 26, 119, 4 December 1662.

315. Ajuda 51-VII-34, 2 December 1698, fo. 2–5.

316. Boyajian, *Portuguese Trade in Asia,* pp. 106–27.

317. AHU, Moç., Cx. 3, 80, "Carta corrente das entradas e saídas dos resgates que se fêz nos portos do contratto."

318. I am mainly following F. Novais's (*Estrutura e dinâmica)* argument here.

# 8

# The Verenigde Oost-Indische Compagnie

As we have seen, the contrast between the VOC and the Estado, the Dutch Republic and Portugal, may be conceived as that between center and semi-periphery, where Brazil and the West Indies might be conceived as the periphery. The vast flows of capital at the VOC's disposal, to be poured into hazardous trading ventures, can partly be explained by the prosperity of the Republic and by its role as the central money market in Europe. Again, the Portuguese habitually complained that the Dutch had at their disposal an "infinite number" of ships.

But within the Portuguese economy a large amount of treasure was available too, Portuguese economists insisted. Yet however much the crown tried to woo private traders to invest in Asia, they were not interested—and with good reason. They had to insure their goods at 35 percent, send commissioners to the region, and pay heavy imposts for fortresses and troops. Private traders simply could not afford this. The only way to trade with Asia was by means of a company, therefore, as Portuguese economists often argued. A company should be willing to shoulder the costs of fortresses and administration, though, and be free from interference by the state. Traders were not likely to invest when the state did not guarantee they would be allowed the returns from their investments. Quite the contrary was normally the case in Portugal, however, as military exigencies often forced the crown to cover immediate expenses by seizing traders' goods.[1]

The VOC, on the other hand, always staunchly resisted attempts by the Estates General to control its cargoes. During the war with England in 1653 it did provide a loan of 300,000 guilders to the Estates General but resolutely refused pleas of the Estates General that they be allowed to sell part of the cargo. This would risk the trust of merchants in the Company, the *bewindhebber*s adduced.

The records of the Haagsch Besoigne—a committee instituted in 1656 to prepare for the meetings of the Gentlemen XVII and to handle dealings with the Estates General—prove that the VOC negotiated with the Estates General on an equal footing.[2] The Estates General could not as bluntly require concessions from the VOC as could King Pedro II or the Sun King, or as easily change its charter as could the Portuguese king.

The VOC consisted of seven "chambers" (Amsterdam, Delft, Flushing, Hoorn, Middelburg, Enkhuizen, and Rotterdam), each of which equipped its own ships, sold parcels of goods, and hired its own personnel. Although in practice the Amsterdam chamber was far and away the most important, there was a considerable amount of rivalry between Amsterdam and Zeeland (Middelburg/Vlissingen). The chambers were represented on the board of the VOC, Gentlemen XVII, which convened for a month each year for a term of four years in Amsterdam, two in Vlissingen. Gentlemen XVII were responsible for demands from Asia, the construction of ships, and allotting of goods to the various chambers; personnel were generally hired by the chambers.

Obviously, there was an intimate tie between Gentlemen XVII and the *regenten* presiding over matters of state of the Dutch Republic. Via the nomination to the board of the regional chambers the directors of the VOC were related to the municipalities as well. This particularly applies to the minor seats of the Noorderkwartier, where there were often lengthy quarrels on nominations to the board of Enkhuizen and Hoorn. The seat of Delft in the Gentlemen XVII was the stake of a maze of communal intrigues as well. Yet despite this, contentious issues, such as the representation of the shareholders of the Company in Gentlemen XVII or the access to sales of the Company—which among the English led to open conflict—were mostly settled by deferring them to "secret" committees or, during conflicts within Gentlemen XVII, by amiably cloaking them from both the public and the Estates General. Amiably, for the *regenten* represented on the board of the VOC were a small and closely interrelated group. Anyway, the Estates General were told, if the VOC made huge profits, was there anything to bother about?

As the same circle ruled both the VOC and the provinces of Holland and Zeeland, conflicts between Company and state rarely occurred. The VOC was a chartered Company, though: in principle it followed its own policy in regard to nomination to office, its rate of pay, and political issues. Apart from presenting every ten years a balance sheet of transactions to the Estates General and an amount of money to get the charter renewed (the *tien jaarlijkse rekening*), naming one *bewindhebber* on behalf of the Stadholder, and regularly giving an overview of its affairs to a committee of the Estates General dealing with colonial affairs, the VOC had few direct obligations to the Estates General. A major difference with England and France was that, in return for delivering a lump sum to the Admiralty for import dues (the *convooi en licentiegeld*), the Dutch Admiralty did not intervene in affairs east of the Cape (aside from incidental cases where the VOC lent ships to the Admiralty or where the navy sometimes provided a convoy to the VOC's return fleets in European waters).

The importance of the VOC was, in its own view, that it benefited the welfare of the state and of the people of the Republic by trade, not by martial glory.

And indeed, with the VOC paying handsome dividends after 1660, there was little public dispute anymore over the status of the VOC. Such criticism as was voiced was mostly confined to confidential meetings of the Gentlemen XVII and rarely reached the Estates General.

In this chapter we shall first look at the way in which the VOC viewed trade in Asia. We shall see that the free exchange that the VOC was said to be defending was in fact relegated to an intricate system of bureaucratically controlled commerce. This allowed the VOC to profit from its economy of scale. The VOC was thus able to effect a major commercial innovation in trade with and within Asia—planning purchases and sales for the long term—but it had to pay a high price for this. Faced with competitors who were not burdened by the costs and delays of its cumbersome central administration, the VOC had to oust them with force.

While the VOC in Europe was a trade organization, in Asia the VOC should rather be seen as a bureaucratic state in view of the objectives it at least strove to achieve. These would include its monopoly on violence, nomination of personnel because of proven adequacy to their task, thoroughly defined schedules of tasks to be accomplished, and the duty of all levels to conform to explicit criteria of behavior. Yet as primarily a tax gatherer, this VOC state in Asia had very different interests than the Company as a trade organization in Europe.

## The Company as King

The Company was truly like "a sovereign king in its own lands," an anonymous pamphlet of 1644 boasted.[3] Which petty German prince reigned over so many rich territories? How many European kingdoms could muster such a powerful fleet? Which European king had treasures worth more than 40 million guilders?

Juridically too, it is well justified to call the VOC in Asia a state: it could sign treaties, wage wars, or appoint personnel in the area covered by its charter. Based upon this legal title the VOC brushed aside any local prerogatives and the governor-general and the High Council (Hoge Regering) of the Indies exercised an absolute rule. Free cities—as existed under Portuguese, English, and French sway—were alien to the VOC's arrangements. When the Dutch conquered Portuguese municipalities like Cochin, Colombo, and Tuticorin, they were submitted to rigid control. The Council of the Indies named (based on nomination by the citizens) urban functionaries in Batavia and Colombo like the aldermen or the sergeants of the urban militia.

The court of justice enjoyed little power and little prestige too. Judges were named by the High Council of the Indies and not by the High Court at home, as was the case with all other Europeans. More importantly, as a rule one could not appeal to the metropolitan high court, as among the English, the French, and the Portuguese. This did not improve the quality of the law provided. Because of the lack of legal knowledge among the personnel in Asia, Gentlemen

XVII decided in 1698 to name the Batavia Court of Justice (Schepenenbank) directly from the Netherlands.[4]

The Gentlemen XVII even designated parsons, after a nomination by the provincial councils (*classis*) of the Dutch Reformed Church. The vicars were expected to support the policy of the Company; sermons that the Company did not like were censored by the High Council of the Indies.[5] Again, all correspondence to and from Asia fell under the rubric "secret of the Company." It had to be handed to the postmaster and was liable to censorship.[6] No other Company disposed of such far-reaching powers.

The VOC in Asia can thus be perceived as a bureaucratic and absolutist state that—unlike states in Europe—did not have to take ancient privileges into account. In principle, the VOC strove to achieve the greatest possible efficiency of its organization.

A case in point is the army. Most European states (and the Estado) mustered military forces paid and recruited by private entrepreneurs. In most European forces the soldiers had to look after their own dress and arms and somehow figure out how to earn a living between campaigns. The VOC maintained a standing army, paid and supplied by the Company, that had to buy clothes from its stores. There are thus few cases of soldiers of VOC garrisons running shops, or of the quartermaster selling provisions to the soldiers—normal practices in Europe and with the Portuguese and English in Asia.[7]

In Europe one qualified most often by patronage or descent rather than ability. There were no precise regulations of the rates of pay and there was a vast circuit of formally disavowed prerequisites of office. In the VOC, on the contrary, one was promoted according to merit. Everybody was paid according to fixed scales. Gathering of spoils from office was strictly prohibited, as was private trade. And, indeed—whatever inconsistencies the Company might have displayed in living up to its own norms—as Boxer has often pointed out, most Dutch personnel were chosen not because of birth but because of merit.

Whereas in Europe the tasks that an official had to carry out were rarely fixed, in the VOC these were minutely circumscribed. All levels of the administration were required to hand in detailed financial statements and specify precisely what work they were doing when. It was also expected that the merchants of the Company would be able to predict the gain on an investment in advance and provide figures.[8]

It is this urge to account for expenses and possible profits in advance that explains the enormous quantity of figures in Dutch sources. The Portuguese, for example, were not interested in submitting lists of the number of ships arriving at Goa to the administration in Lisbon, let alone in registering their cargo. These incomes were farmed—so why bother? Meanwhile the VOC at Vengurla spent a great deal of money and effort to obtain precisely these figures from its spies "A" (the Saraswat secretary of the viceroy) and "B."[9]

It is easy, too much so, to criticize the shortcomings of the VOC's bookkeeping: Masulipatam's ledgers were in 1710, for example, certainly not exemplary—partly to conceal private trade there. Yet they compared quite favorably with Madras's accountancy, in which whole runs of those ledgers were lost, eaten by ants, and anyway, the balances were wrong.[10]

The military and commercial successes of the VOC are to be explained by a superior organization rather than by superiority in numbers over the Portuguese or the English. As Francisco de Silveira noted, "to save the body it is sometimes necessary to risk, even to cut off members"; by trying to hold on to everything, the Portuguese forces were weak everywhere.[11] The VOC was able to concentrate overwhelming forces at the opponent's weak points. Again, it was able to invest huge amounts of capital in a single product whereby it could manipulate its price. As we saw, the VOC was thus able to oust the caravan trade in pepper.

But such rationalization had a shadow side too. We may consider the opinion of an outsider in this respect. The Portuguese Viceroy Conde de Alvor reacted furiously in 1684 to the proposal of the crown to establish an East India Company.[12] He was glad, he wrote, that he now was finally able to dislodge this stubborn, stupid superstition that an East India Company was the best way to trade with the Indies. No doubt, the East India Companies had enjoyed prodigious successes, but these might have been achieved as well if the crown had allotted sufficient funds to the Indies. One ought to consider the way the companies were really organized. Then one would see that all (but of course Alvor was mainly thinking about the VOC) were in decline and—optimistic indeed!—would endure for only a few years longer.

A small clique of wealthy traders controlled the Companies, whereas trade carried out by the state benefited the taxpayer. Hence, most citizens were not interested in the Company. This was a true predicament in Asia, since the personnel there did not have the slightest interest in the welfare of the Companies, and "everybody trades on his own account." The Companies had built a huge system of fortresses and strongholds. Most were only built to enhance the prestige of the servants. They had conquered areas and forced monopoly contracts upon Asian princes. In the course of time these had turned from a blessing to a burden. But it was impossible to get rid of them, for this would harm the "respect" of the Companies, and cause their shares to fall in price.

Alvor was not the only one voicing such a view, for in the same period the VOC was also criticized by van Beuningen, whose "proposals for a general reversal of policy" (*het generale redres*) were duly considered by the Gentlemen XVII in the eighties. Gaastra has examined these discussions at length, so it is not necessary to dwell on them here.[13]

The *bewindhebbers* thus realized that Asia was not functioning as well as it ought to. But if the Company was to function better, more prescriptions and more intricate procedures for control were needed too. That was virtually impossible without reaching a point of diminishing returns. Take the complicated account keeping of the Company: the *bewindhebbers* have often been accused of stupidity for failing to adjust this system. The Gentlemen XVII were, for example, unable to say anything definite on the precise incomes and expenses of factories, as sales of products from one factory were listed on the books of another. They were unable as well to say whether operations in Asia ran at a loss or a profit, as the costs of shipping to, and the sales in, the Netherlands were not on the books of the Asian accounts.[14]

But there existed a bureaucratic convention in Asia that stunted attempts to overhaul the system. P. Ketting had received orders from Batavia to have the system of accountancy used at Surat correspond to that at Batavia. This was a daunting task, Ketting soon found out. During the busy months the accounts were often four to five months in arrears. Nobody knew how many pieces of cloth went into a single package. Some goods were reckoned in pounds, others in bags or bundles, and this had been the practice for decades. Just to figure out how much the goods bought for the Netherlands had cost "was an appalling chore, involving toil day and night. And what is worst, because of these reasons, I am not even sure whether the account remitted is completely free of error."[15]

One should be wary of overemphasizing such deficiencies too: all's well that ends well. Both the balance sheet provided by Batavia (Table 8.1) and the extensive independent calculations by J. Hudde, *bewindhebber* and brilliant mathematician, indicated that the Company in Asia as a whole made a profit—even if a slender one—throughout the period that concerns us.[16] Furthermore, the Company was able to adapt to the shifting demand in Europe. And, indeed, to an extent it dominated the expanding markets for Asian commodities to Europe. Even if the Company lost ground to English competition, it was still the major shipping concern within Asia. Hence, Gaastra rightly contests the view of earlier Dutch historians that the period 1650–1700 constitutes an "afterglow" of the Company's prosperity.[17]

Now, apparently there was a contradiction between the idea of free trade underwritten by the Company in Europe and the bureaucratic control, based on force, that it exercised in the area covered by its charter. Such an apparent *contradictio in terminis* was, however, defended by two arguments: first, the argument that European law could not be applied to Asian despotism and that, of necessity, one was to trade with "money in one hand and a sword in the

Table 8.1

**Total Profits and Losses of Dutch East India Company in Asia** (in guilders)

| Decade | Profit | Loss |
|---|---|---|
| 1654–1663 | 45,471,220 | 43,465,636 |
| 1664–1673 | 68,599,667 | 51,365,481 |
| 1674–1683 | 64,424,609 | 58,717,976 |
| 1684–1693 | 61,824,420 | 69,760,694 |
| Total | 240,319,916 | 223,309,787 |

other," as the English put it; second, the mercantilist line of reasoning that there is a fair share of prosperity, which one has to redivide. But how should that be done? There were very different views on this.

## *Freedom of Trade, Freedom of the Sea*

In pamphlets directed against the Company, it was often suggested that the whole system of chartered Companies went contrary to everything useful and desirable. The tightly reasoned tracts of Willem Usselincx are a good example, but such ideas can also be found in a manifesto directed against the VOC in 1644 by the Australian Company—which was to conduct trade with the Pacific.[18]

Basically, Usselincx's ideas are as follows: The market should be freely accessible to all. The market is ruled by profit. Thus monopolist practices, of states as much as merchants, distort the market and inhibit free and equitable commerce that could benefit all. Usselincx saw the Companies as political and military instruments: government should only establish them if other states tried to restrain its freedom. As soon as this restraint had been forestalled, the state should confine itself to creating favorable conditions for free trade of individual merchants. If a Company had achieved its original design—opening the market to all dealers—it ought to be abolished. For a monopoly was objectionable in principle and free trade would attract settlers too.

These ideas might well apply to America, the *bewindhebbers* would object, but the situation in Asia was very different.[19] Though free trade was undoubtedly desirable in principle, it could not be realized in practice. Not only was one dealing with the Portuguese, a hereditary enemy, but the feeling of justice in Asia was very different from that in European countries. Traders were compelled to assume the function of a sovereign power, for free and equitable international trade could only be conducted on the basis of a law of nations. Such a foundation was not present in Asia. The Company therefore had to be allotted sovereign rights by the Estates General and there could only be one Company.

For trade with Asia, moreover, enormous initial investments were required. Individual traders would not be able to raise such sums, so they had to be united in a partnership. This needed to be a chartered one, as the merchants would only benefit on their initial outlays if obtaining a monopoly. And it had to be a company based on shares, so that everybody—including persons who were not able to personally conduct trade—could invest in it.

The Gentlemen XVII defended the Company as a special institution to conduct trade with Asia, but well agreed with the dogma of free trade current in the Dutch Republic. The Haagsch Besoigne and the Gentlemen XVII rarely fixed explicit norms of conduct. And even when they did recognize these, they often deviated from them in the daily running of trade. Yet, in general, they appear to have stuck to a number of principles.

The involvement of bodies of government or princes with the trade of the

VOC was undesirable and illegitimate—illegitimate, for politics and trade were two separate spheres that should be kept apart; undesirable, since political considerations might jeopardize the capable conduct of trade. In Asia the Gentlemen XVII in general were opposed to direct transactions with officials. In the China trade, for example, individuals were to deal with officials only as long as the Celestial Empire would not permit free trade, for officials can never be keen merchants.

Monopolization of a product by one merchant or a ring of merchants was disadvantageous to the Company and its partners—not only because the monopolist would fix the price, but also because the benefits of commerce should accrue to all. And one had to behave "in mercantile fashion [*koopmansstijl*]." One should outwit one's competitor, but not by the use of advance knowledge or force. The Company's servants ought not to allow advantages to one trader, even if offered a higher price. Furthermore, they ought to give all merchants equal chances when freighting or purchasing goods.

These were noble principles and I think the VOC went to considerable length to implement them. But such principles were modeled on European notions. In the Arabian seas, to obtain a profit was not the sole aim of the merchant; profit was always related to the desire to uphold one's credit with associates. However, the Gentlemen XVII insisted that sales be made purely dependent upon the price offered: intrigues were disapproved of, though occasionally necessary.

That the VOC on the one hand lauded such principles, yet on the other tried to curb trade and shipping in Asia with the use of force is merely a contradiction if the VOC is perceived as a trade organization. Indeed it was in Europe, but in Asia the VOC was a state.

As a state the Company claimed the right to *mare clausum*, not only in the waters of the Archipelago but on the west coast, too—even if the latter claim was more apparent than real. The right to issue navicerts and, more importantly, their use to constrain shipping were the most controversial consequence of the Company's monopoly. It starkly contrasted to the *mare liberum*, which the Dutch Republic upheld in Europe with the sword and the pen. Therefore, the Company had often to draft defenses to vindicate this right against independent skippers to the Indies, against Indian or Armenian shipowners, or against the English representatives.

It was a hotly contested issue between those two governments throughout the seventeenth century. After the conquest of Banten in 1684 the Estates General had, they moaned, once again to put up with those interminable English complaints against the alleged arbitrary seizure of English property by the VOC. And this came after a long series of previous disputes: the "Amboina massacre," the damage claimed by the EIC from the VOC in 1656, the incident of the seizure of the English *Bon Adventure Merchant* by the Dutch off the Malabar Coast in 1663, and the disputes between the VOC and the EIC after the conquest of Macassar in 1670.[20]

The Gentlemen XVII responded to all these protests in 1681 in a long letter, which signaled to some extent a retreat from the past policy that all ships in Asia were required to carry a navicert from the VOC, European ones included.[21] The *bewindhebbers* argued that the VOC was entitled to curb shipping to places included in the first category of the *generale instructie* (where it exercised sovereign power), to places in the second category (with which it had signed exclusive contracts), and to places with which it was at war. This concerned European vessels to which European law applied. Vessels with a European navicert or European flag were seen as "indigenous ships." All "Moorish" or "indigenous" keels could, by force of the *mare clausum* in Asia, be refused access to all harbors—even where the Company did not enjoy special prerogatives. Ships without a passport could be confiscated.

How did this come about? Originally, the Portuguese had arrogated the superior power at sea in Asia, the Gentleman XVII wrote. They refused to tolerate shipping if ships had not received a *cartaz* from the Portuguese crown. This right to issue navicerts had "devolved upon the Company" when it conquered the Portuguese possessions. Furthermore, one also claimed this on the ground that the VOC, like the Portuguese, supposedly protected ships against corsairs. When granting navicerts, the Company enjoyed arbitrary powers. The principle "free ship is free freight," which was applied by the Dutch Republic in Europe, was not applicable in Asia. For those who gave out navicerts were legally not proprietors of the ships. In Europe one could seize enemy cargo aboard a neutral vessel as well. If the ship or its cargo belonged to an enemy, it could be confiscated. Hence, the Company enjoyed the right to halt ships, even if they had a navicert of another nation.

The memorandum of van Dam from 1669, to which I alluded earlier, shows how they managed to defend *mare clausum* by invoking arguments originally developed to vindicate *mare liberum*.[22] The VOC did not have a warrant, the English ambassador adduced, to curtail English trade within Asia. According to the navigation treaties signed between the Dutch Republic and England, both—if paying customs dues—were permitted to trade on each other's territory and that of third parties. However, van Dam reasoned that these English reproaches were not well founded in law. Treaties between the two countries, van Dam argued, did not apply to Asia, in particular in those kingdoms with whom the VOC had signed exclusive treaties.

> For by the force of such exclusive contracts one is allowed to act against the nation, with whom one has signed such a treaty. And also within its territory against the ones who infringe on this within said territory, particularly when one is authorized to do so by that nation or its government.

Hence, legally, the VOC was entitled to confiscate pepper from vessels trading with the Malabar Coast but not arrack or cinnamon. There was considerable disagreement between the Gentlemen XVII over the extent to which the pepper contracts constrained the rajahs to deliver pepper to the Company alone, however, and over whether the VOC was thus authorized to constrain shipping. As we saw, they judged it best to be rather lenient on this score.

The "abundance which one nation has in goods, lacking in another nation, ensures there is a right of mutual commerce between countries," van Dam pursued his argument, invoking Grotius. This entitled nations to conduct trade, mutually and with third parties, to the benefit of either. Yet freedom of trade is not a natural right, for trade is only necessary "to satisfy the wants of the needy." From the "humanity of relations" between people it ensues in general that one has to comply with requests for free trade, as long as this does not harm oneself. "But the same humanity does not permit that one should allow somebody else to use one's own property if he could, under the pretext of conducting commerce—without the need for doing so—make the trade of the one who allowed it fruitless."

It is true that one cannot inhibit the trade of "free and independent" people. But if people in Asia were independent, the English would not have to claim a covenant to trade with them from the Dutch. Asia legally held the status of a colony. The English did not permit the Dutch free trade with the New Netherlands or Virginia either. "In both Indies this has never been permitted amongst European nations."

There is a clear difference between this line of reasoning and that of the Spanish and Portuguese legal scholars. In the tract "De Iusto Imperio Asiatico Lusitanorum" of de Freitas, the thesis was defended that the right to free trade was not linked to treaties and the *ius gentium* to Christianity.[23] In heathen lands Spain and Portugal represented the Christian *imperium:* the right to rule in order to propagate the faith. They enjoyed this *imperium* because of a papal bull, and because the Portuguese enjoyed usufruct by having discovered the road to India. Furthermore, they protected indigenous trade and therefore enjoyed the right to regulate it. The Asian waters were *mare clausum:* any ship without a navicert of the Portuguese crown was an enemy vessel, while a ship with a safe conduct was legally neutral. It could still be searched, and cargo originating from hostile territory could be seized.

As we saw, the VOC defended the view that Asian nations were aware of natural law, not linked to Christianity. The VOC would thus have to respect indigenous laws. The passport system was, therefore, defended through a very different line of argument, which one might call mercantilist.

There was a limited amount of wealth in the world that was unequally divided, for countries are by definition uneven in resources. Commerce always being a zero-sum game, it is but justified if one seeks to exploit one's colonies to one's own benefit and exclude other traders. Giving out navicerts was in the Dutch case part and parcel of an overall economic policy, whereas in the Portuguese—and English—case it was purely dictated by the interests of individual tax farmers or captains.

In practical terms this engendered a relentless drive to implement this monopoly. The VOC tried after the conquest of Malacca to inhibit Indian sails taking the route to the Indonesian Archipelago, thereby hampering its sale of Indian textiles. They had long enough "been playing the good Dutchman," Batavia argued in 1647. The right to control this shipping had after the conquest "devolved" upon the Company; if the Portuguese had used force, so ought the Dutch.[24]

A successful implementation of this policy, however, depended on two conditions. It would have required that the VOC withstand possible retaliations by Indian states. And there should have been no alternative ports and routes to Malacca and the Malacca Strait. In reality, neither of these two conditions was satisfied.

At Surat, the VOC's attempt to prohibit trade to Malacca soon led to trouble with Governor Mir Musa, who arranged the sack of the factory by "mutinous troops" in 1647. The VOC finally decided to initiate a naval blockade of Surat to force the prohibition on the empire. This did not impress the Mughal authorities a great deal, though. For even if the VOC seized two of Nur Begam's ships, it was too late in the season to inflict more damage upon the trade of the *bandar-i mobarak*. J. Tacq was in 1650 sent to Delhi to negotiate a settlement with the court. Alone, very far away from the ship's artillery, Tacq was finally pressed to sign a treaty in which the VOC was to provide at least six navicerts to Malacca.[25]

Again, in 1684, when the VOC in Persia tried to curtail Gujarati shipping, the governor threatened the VOC in Surat with retaliation if passports were not handed out. The small traders would still pay for navicerts but the great dealers certainly would use their *vakil*s at court to forestall even this. Yes, the VOC might be brave and refuse them, Surat's council reasoned, but the Company totally at the mercy of the Mughal empire. And what would be the use of it? The English offered to take all Indian freight on board their ships anyway.[26]

In regard to the second condition: it would require too that the VOC control the entire coastline of the archipelago, which was far from the case. At least three ports openly challenged the Company's "overwhelming weaponry": Macassar, Banten, and—last but not least—Atjeh.[27] Apart from receiving Indian ships these three ports also conducted extensive trade: Atjeh carried on with shipping throughout the Bay of Bengal, and occasionally sent ships for the hajj to Jidda and to Muscat. However, though Atjeh was a nagging nuisance, the major threat to the VOC's monopoly was the direct shipping of ṣultan Abu al Fatah of Banten. By 1680 Banten possessed at least a dozen vessels; some were more than 600 tons. Banten then sent two or three ships to Surat, three or four to Mocha, and one or two to Muscat. These crafts shipped pepper in direct defiance of the VOC. "The shipping of the Moors is positively a cancer for the Rt. Hon. Company," director D. Parve at Surat stressed, for the problem was that the VOC could not compete with Asian ships in intra-Asian trade.[28] It was the same in the trade in piece-cloth between Surat and Java. As Haagsch Besoigne argued:

> It is obvious that the Company sails with large and heavily manned bottoms and has to as well, particularly in wartime. So, she cannot suffer Moorish competition. For in their shipping, and in particular their trade with piece-cloth, they are subject to much lower costs than we are.[29]

This open challenge to the VOC offered by Banten finally prompted the Company "high and mighty" to declare war on Banten, which was conquered in 1683.[30]

The VOC meanwhile had to concede that it would continue to suffer competition by new "interloper" ports or of increased shipping to Atjeh. So together with the stick of military retaliation it would have to offer the carrot of easier access to Batavia and Malacca. Instead of trying to obliterate Indian shipping to the archipelago it had better attract it by stipulating favorable conditions in the navicerts. This would benefit the incomes of Batavia and Malacca—a reasonable concession, for by 1700 Johore and Bencoolen began to emerge as new competitors to Batavia and Malacca. The policy of the VOC to thwart Indian shipping to Indonesia had thus only been partly successful. And some pleaded that "the shipping of the Moors and Indian nations has now increased to such a preposterous extent that it seems to fill all seas of the Indies."[31]

The Gentlemen XVII did not agree with the latter position, however. The Indian shipping to the archipelago was indeed declining, they noted in 1687. That was mainly because of the smaller demand for Indian textiles on Java, which they blamed on the recent wars on the island. Furthermore, in this case, the private trade of the Dutch was a blessing in disguise because Indian traders had difficulties competing with them.[32]

The VOC's policy of curtailing Indian shipping was not without effects, however, but different ones from those envisaged by the VOC. Comparing the situation of the trade from the Arabian seas to the archipelago in 1640 with that in 1700, one would note that direct Indonesian trade between the Indonesian Archipelago and the Arabian seas had dwindled to very little. Shipping to the Arabian seas from Banten had disappeared, and navigation from Atjeh was in decline. Indian trade was moving from Macassar and Banten to Batavia, the Philippines, and Siam. By 1700 Batavia was receiving significant benefits from direct trade with ships from Surat. And there was a momentous rise of English country trade in the Malay Archipelago. In the long run one of the main beneficiaries of the VOC's monopoly was the English.[33]

So while the VOC's policy of curtailing trade to benefit its monopoly could be realized in a small area like the Moluccas—where the VOC by and large succeeded in limiting shipping to regional trade alone—this was virtually impossible in larger areas, like Java or Ceylon.[34] On Ceylon the VOC faced insurmountable problems in implementing a monopoly of trade. The island depended upon the Coromandel Coast for supplies of grain and textiles.[35] If the VOC had severed all communications between the Coromandel Coast and Ceylon, it would have had to take over practically the entire retail trade on the island against unforeseeable costs.

### *Monopoly and Free Trade*

This led to a debate between advocates of free trade and those who favored a strict implementation of the monopoly in Ceylon.[36] Some argued the VOC should maintain its monopoly through the use of force. No doubt, if the VOC were to prohibit the grain trade with Coromandel, it would have to conduct the trade itself. But this would lead to an increase in agricultural prices, prompting the main "loafers" who roamed the island to look for a regular job. Due to cheap imports of rice from the Coromandel Coast by Indian traders, it was now more lucrative to seek employment with the VOC rather than lay hand to plow. If the VOC guaranteed high agricultural prices on Ceylon, farming would become a profitable pursuit. The peasants would receive sufficient cash to switch to the cultivation of other grains. Furthermore, it would enable the Company to trade in bulk goods, which in the long run promised higher returns than commerce in spices. With higher incomes from agriculture, inhabitants would be able to buy more products of the Company and manufacture would flourish.

On the other hand there were functionaries who argued that the VOC should only trade in the monopoly products (cinnamon and opium) and permit trade in all other goods. The VOC would in that case have much lower expenses, which would allow for trimming the budget deficit with which Ceylon was struggling at present. Because of the lower food prices the inhabitants would have more money to spend. This would attract dwellers in the hinterland to come and live along the coast. It would lead to greater prosperity among the inhabitants of Ceylon, so they could spend this money on Dutch luxury products. It would foster the demand for Coromandel textiles too. This would guarantee a market for the products of weavers who wanted to settle under the protection of the Company. The VOC would thus be able to obtain products for export to the Netherlands and Insulinde more cheaply.

Although the monopoly system has found very few defenders, it did have some undeniable benefits. The insurance against risk by the formation of a monopoly led to a marked increase of trade between Europe and Asia and the commerce of the Companies within Asia. This could lead to commercial innovation: the introduction in the market of new products, for instance, or the exploitation of new trade routes. In Asia this applied to the trade in Japanese copper to Surat for example, the demand for which strongly expanded. There are other cases, like the sale of sugar in the Middle East, which in Persia (and after 1700 Yemen) accounted for the major share of the VOC's trade.[37]

By the use of its monopoly the Company was also able to make investments involving high risks, on a large scale, and backed by monopoly prices and force. The idea here was to control the entire line from consumer to producer. The monopoly would eliminate imperfections in the market and benefit the consumer by making supplies large and predictable, whereas the producer would benefit by the expansion of production.

A case in point is the cultivation of sugar in the surroundings (*ommelanden*) of Batavia. J.K. de Jonge, a writer to be taken very seriously, has sharply criticized the Company for buying the sugar at a guaranteed price. As it was too low, most sugar plantations ran at a loss. This was the "logic of the small grocer," de Jonge argues.[38] But one may wonder whether sugar production would ever have developed without the protective cover of this system.

According to the High Government of the Indies in 1661, the sugar that was fabricated in the *ommelanden* could hardly be sold in the Netherlands, due to the murderous competition of the sugar from Barbados. They ordered, therefore, that the VOC in Persia—the major Asian market for that commodity—was to increase its sales of Javanese sugar to 1.5 million pounds. Persia had hitherto mainly obtained sugar from southern China or the plantations on Taiwan. To comply with the immediate need for the product after the loss of Formosa, Persia could for the time being order its sugar from Bengal. But, in the longer run, most of it would have to come from Batavia. The High Government wanted to expand the acreage in the *ommelanden*. One now had to rely too much on foodstuffs from the unruly neighbor state of Mataram. Grains, however, were not profitable enough to induce the Dutch and Chinese colonists to bring the wild forests of the *ommelanden* under cultivation. The Council wanted to allow poor Dutchmen a decent living as yeomen too. Sugar would be a good alternative. By selling this substance to the Company the colonists would be able to finance clearings and irrigation works. They could then also cultivate rice there. Capital generated through the sugar trade might be invested in this.[39]

The Dutch factories in Persia were far from satisfied with the Javanese sugar, however, and wanted to get rid of that burden in 1664. In 1675 the VOC in Persia once again tried to sell Javanese sugar, but the profits were far below those on Bengal sugar. In 1689 Persia was nevertheless prohibited from ordering any more sugar from Bengal. It did not follow this prescription. It was argued at Bandar Abbas that sales of Bengali sugar would not depress the price of Javanese sugar. It was of a much coarser grain than Javanese sugar and apparently more suitable for its use in sweets among the Persians. Java also delivered insufficient brown sugar, Persia adduced.

Batavia promised it would strive to cover this shortage; however, Persia should not order sugar from elsewhere, so as not to damage the cultivation of sugar in Batavia. If necessary, Batavia should accept low profits. As Persia was the single most important market for Javanese sugar, one may then well say its cultivation could not have expanded without the systematic protection of the

Company and its procurement at a guaranteed price. To achieve such long-term objectives the Company was willing to shoulder losses for considerable periods.[40]

But developing cash crop cultivation under the loving care of a body of greedy monopolists was surely no guarantee of good government or general prosperity. A case in point is the depressing story of the VOC's settlement at Mauritius.[41]

This settlement was originally intended for cutting ebony. As the lumberjacks of the VOC cut down the primeval ebony forests that covered the island, and set the jungle aflame, the topsoil was washed away. Crops like indigo or sugar would not flourish. To be sure, Gentlemen XVII were aware of this threat, since they prescribed that the lumberjacks plant new seedlings, but to no avail.

Again, lacking a population of natural predators, the island was suffering under plagues of biblical proportions: first rats and then wild boars devoured the harvests. Inhabitants were struggling with a scourge of wild mongrels too. The island was also repeatedly devastated by typhoons that wrecked construction there.

With the opportunities for agriculture exhausted, efforts were made to develop the island as a slaughterhouse for the Cape; the grass was green and the cows fatter than they were anywhere else in the Indies. The company tried to rear wild goats too, which in turn added to the exhaustion of the soil. The classic case of the "econocide" on Mauritius is, of course, the depletion of the supply of wild fowl—the famous dodo was to be slaughtered, salted, and exported to the Cape.[42]

As if those natural disasters were not sufficient, the island was suffering under mismanagement of its human resources as well. Slaves fled to the forest, which forced the Company to mount expensive forays against these maroons, who would retaliate by burning the crops. This occurred despite the insistence of Gentlemen XVII that a deal be struck with the maroons. They were to enjoy liberty if they returned new refugees to their owners.[43]

And finally, the VOC's servants at the factory were constantly involved in quarrels amongst themselves and with the Huguenot settlers. All this human misery was compounded by the eruption of a smallpox epidemic on the island.

Such sadness and waste, exclaimed the governor of Mauritius, J. Lamotius, in 1687, and all of this against the background of such breathtakingly beautiful nature![44] Preferring Mauritius to Cape Town as a way station, Lamotius bewailed its undue neglect by the VOC, which he blamed on its mismanagement by the government of Cape Town.

But there was system behind the neglect. To the government of the Cape the colony on the island was merely established to cut ebony. Everything but expenses connected to this was seen as bothersome costs by Cape Town. The reserves of the Cape were already hard pressed—why, then, still allot them to another settlement? The Cape was not interested in developing other resources on Mauritius except cattle and ebony; agriculture might devolve to a competitor.

The Cape hence systematically exhausted the supplies that the Gentlemen XVII had sent for both the Cape and Mauritius, and Mauritius thus suffered a constant lack of money, labor, shipping, iron, and copper—well nigh everything.[45]

When the supplies of ebony were exhausted, there were no other profitable pursuits due to the lack of resources and shipping. Thus the Huguenot and Waldensian colonists on the islands languished. In 1693, there were only 12 families alive on the island; the rest had fled to Cape Town or perished. A suit brought against Lamotius by the settlers, in which he was accused of deeds I had better not relate lest I spoil the reader's appetite, gives an image of the general impoverishment of the colony and of the dreadful tyranny exercised by the merchant in chief.[46]

With its high monopoly prices, the VOC often made the substitution of products or their introduction into the market a profitable proposition. Let us consider an Asian example. After the VOC had made exports of cinnamon from Ceylon impossible, the demand in north India and the Middle East shifted to wild cinnamon (*cassia ligna*), which grew in the foothills of the Ghats in Kerala. "The Moors, now that they cannot obtain expensive spices, have to accommodate themselves in a different fashion." If *cassia ligna* had less flavor than Ceylonese cinnamon, it was much cheaper. Exports of *cassia ligna* increased from about 200,000 pounds in 1670 to 800,000 at the end of the century. Profits on this were too meager to enable the VOC to deal in it. The Company was unable to lower the price of cinnamon in India, however: it might have incurred the risk that cinnamon would be re-exported to Europe.[47]

Malabar thereupon decided the VOC should "extirpate" the *cassia ligna* plants. The forests where this grew would be leased from the rajah of Cochin. Raiding parties were to be dispatched into the jungle to cut the *cassia ligna* plants and prepare oil from them, which would be sold to the rajah. But while Dutch patrols were cutting down the *cassia ligna* bushes in one forest, the local inhabitants were fervently at work in the next to plant new ones. No doubt too, many a sergeant would casually "forget" bushes when offered a few pennies. Moreover, the VOC did not control the mountainous regions of Coorg, where most *cassia ligna* grew. The VOC saw the prospects of its cinnamon trade within Asia dwindle without being able to do much about it.[48]

However, when procuring bulk goods, like spices, copper, tin, or even Guinea piece-cloth, the VOC was at an advantage over its competitors because of the very scale of its trade. In the last case, for example, one could attract weavers to work exclusively for the Company by guaranteeing them a market. Furthermore, it might take years for weavers to adapt their looms and learn the skills needed to comply with the highly specialized demand for luxury cloth in Europe. Long-term contracts were the norm—and only the Companies could afford to sign these. After 1690 Gentlemen XVII emphasized, therefore, that it should mainly deal in those textiles the marketing and production of which could be controlled by the Company, or buy at factories that were too rémote for competitors. The personnel on the Coromandel Coast was also instructed to obtain undisputed territorial possession of the factories there, so that weavers could be attracted to work exclusively for the Company.[49]

Hand in hand with the scale of its operations came the advantage that the VOC also extensively participated in intra-Asian trade. Part of the procurements could thus be financed by the sale of Asian commodities. But to engage in intra-Asian trade involved a balancing act. The structure of intra-Asian trade was often compared to a giant clock.[50] If everything went according to plan, the various branches of trade could finance each other. Profits obtained could be expended on cargoes to the Netherlands, so the Gentlemen XVII would not have to send bullion. And this certainly was what the *bewindhebbers* aimed at. Indeed, it seems intra-Asian trade was a profitable proposition for most of the seventeenth century.

If there were problems with the exports of cash from Japan, these were partly compensated for by increasing exports of bullion from Surat and Persia in the second half of the seventeenth century. Malabar excepted, all factories in the Arabian seas made a profit. So did Japan. The VOC to a very large extent succeeded in covering the exports from the southern Coromandel Coast through sales at Masulipatam and Golconda. And if Hugly's exports far surpassed its sales, net sales of Bengal still showed a rapid increase. True, most factories in the archipelago ran at a loss, particularly Macassar and Java's east coast, but these losses were explicable by these places' proximity to Batavia and their military significance. Batavia's losses could be explained by its position as capital of the Indies. Ceylon's losses were far less acceptable, as were those of Malabar. Yet, on balance, the VOC made a profit on Ceylon too, when adding in the proceeds of cinnamon sold in the Netherlands.[51]

There were clouds on the horizon, however. Asia needed ever more cash to pay for the exports of piece-cloth to the Netherlands after 1676.[52] This could not be provided through intra-Asian trade. In itself this was not much of a problem—it would have been unreasonable for the *bewindhebbers* to expect Asia to completely finance the procurements for the Netherlands. But only part of the cash brought from the Netherlands was used to buy goods for intra-Asian trade; it also had to be used to cover the rampant costs of Batavia and Ceylon. Intra-Asian trade was increasingly conducted for its own sake without ulterior benefits for the Netherlands. Batavia was constantly requesting more bullion from the Netherlands and other factories to cover its expenses and backlogs. One could try to recoup these costs through intra-Asian trade, but this would entail the establishment of new factories, incurring new costs.[53]

The factories should try to enlarge intra-Asian trade and exports to the Netherlands. It was impossible to do these two things simultaneously, however. Faced with stiff competition from the EIC and English interlopers, Batavia would have to economize in order to conduct a profitable trade. Batavia did not bother about this, Gentleman XVII complained, but instead only burdened them with requests for more ducats.

***The Merchant-Warrior at Work***[54]

The factories, which were territorial possessions, approximately broke even or ran at a loss, even when the sales in the Netherlands of products exported by these establishments were taken into account (to wit, Batavia, Macassar, and Malabar). To be sure, Amboina, Ternate, Banda, and Java's east coast also showed losses on the Asian account but were profitable when adding in the proceeds of sales in Holland. The VOC needed expensive garrisons and an administration there. Massive remittances of cash were required between those possessions and the "commercial settlements." But in the long run, disbursements for fortresses and territorial administrations were so large that these could not be covered through intra-Asian trade.[55]

The Gentlemen XVII to a large extent blamed prodigality and private trade by servants for what was really caused by the expansion of the VOC to a territorial state. Some *bewindhebbers*, like Hudde, were clearly aware of this too. Hence Hudde argued that one should really book the losses made by Malabar on Ceylon's account, since Malabar was not a commercial settlement but a military bulwark for Ceylon.

P. van Hoorn, councilor of the Indies, was also well aware. Indeed, as he noted in 1676, the Company was no longer primarily a trader; instead it was a "large and powerful state" and "such things have on the one hand an inborn impetus and desire to conserve themselves; to constantly fear decline; to shy away from any change which might be harmful; and to embrace, on the other hand, anything which may strengthen them."[56]

So, as van Hoorn argued, there was an innate tension between the VOC as a trade organization and the VOC as a state seeking revenues and security, by military force when necessary. And such a pursuit might obstruct the conduct of trade, in Java as much as Ceylon and last but not least in Kerala.

Malabar was surely no profitable directorate, but as Zwaardecroon wrote:

> The respect of the Rt. Hon. Company cannot be neglected. First and foremost since initially one has given oneself such a bearing of being considered among the kings as lord supreme of the whole of Malabar. And so we have to exact revenge for shame and scorn, and cannot suffer damage and disrepute—which, too, would conflict with the law of nature.[57]

What after all, Gentlemen XVII wondered in 1677, had been the commercial benefit of all these bulwarks and fortresses on the Malabar Coast? When the high and mighty Company had but a single small warehouse in Kayakulam it had easily obtained as much pepper as was gathered with all this military might now.[58]

But although schemes were unfolded in 1683 to at least reduce the size of the citadel and garrisons in Cochin and Cananore and demolish the fortresses in Coylan and Cranganore, new fortifications were constantly being built. "Commerce in these lands with its many chiefs and which are deeply divided entirely depends on the awe the Hon. Company inspires," Cochin adduced in explanation.[59] When Colombo had been conquered the company needed to secure a forward bulwark in Tuticorin. And when Tuticorin had been subdued the VOC was threatened from Cochin. Once Cochin had been taken and fortified at vast expense, the VOC needed to secure the strategic node of the traffic to Cochin but to this end needed the forward bulwarks of Cochin, Cranganore, and Cananore in turn.[60]

But Cranganore sucked the VOC into the fatal "inner logic of Indian politics." Lands of the Anchi Kaimal around Cranganore had fallen to the Dutch by escheat in 1666, though the *kaimal*s there were "liegemen" of the *zamorin*. This was a constant challenge to the *zamorin,* who repeatedly sent raiding parties to assert his rights over the Anchi Kaimal by burning some houses, ravaging a few fields, or taking some hostages. Such normal skirmishes were then blown up by the VOC's ally, the Perumal of Cochin, to a full-fledged military threat.[61]

For the puppet king Kerala Varma, although despised by the VOC as an imbecile perpetually immersed in nonsensical Hindu rituals—"he is like a log which has been laying in the water for too long and won't burn very well," van Rheede disdainfully noted—cunningly exploited his very weakness.[62] Had he not been coronated by van Goens with a crown bearing the VOC's emblem? Was the Company then not wont to protect its vassal at all costs?[63]

Kerala Varma, and in particular his very capable successor Ravi Varma, thus utilized the Company's military support and its financial subsidies to assert their own power over defiant or rebellious princes. Several of them—like the Anchi Kaimal and the rajah of Parur—had supported the rival royal lineage (the Vettatu *tanazava*) of Cochin in the civil war there, which had brought them to power.

The VOC's aid was exploited for state building too. For instance, they substituted for their often unreliable *nayyar* and *nambudiri* officials Saraswat ones who were more dependent on the Cochin court and in order to brush aside the prerogatives of allied kings and *kaimal*s to name *rajadores*.[64] And, obviously, the rajahs of Cochin imposed new taxes on the inhabitants. Those heavy and mostly unprecedented taxes led, for instance, in 1684 to the refusal of untouchable *pulyar* workers, who gathered wild cinnamon, to pay them. Only the VOC understood this as a rebellion, though; the *pulyar* had an established right to refuse to pay illegal impositions, but it was violently repressed by the VOC's forces at the behest of the Perumal.[65]

Hence, to quote Zwaardecroon:

> [O]ne does not request aid from the Company because somebody is really offended, is really threatened, or is really in peril of suffering notable damage but to further one's interests of money and power, be it rightfully or wrongfully. Because they well know there's no bigger advantage than being reputed as having the Company on one's side. And so one uses the Company in Malabar as a bully among the indigenous princes. And those of Cochin can manage this skillfully in particular, thus acting on the Rt. Hon. Company's wallet.[66]

It was in the best interest of the Perumal that the Company live in a constant state of "cold war" with its neighbors, as this would ensure continued Dutch support.

But it was not only in his interest. Van Rheede said in his apology to Gentlemen XVII from 1676 regarding his conduct of policy in Cochin that the diplomacy of Rijkloff van Goens was needlessly tough.[67] Both the wars with Candy and with the *zamorin* could have been avoided if van Goens had not tried to impose unacceptable demands on them. Van Goens, by building fortifications and establishing garrisons everywhere, sought to establish territorial control over both Kerala and Ceylon. To seek some justification for that policy he tried to provoke both Candy and Calicut into declaring war on the Company. For all this was approved neither by the High Government, which van Goens ignored as being hostile to him personally and not grasping the conundrum of the man "on the spot," nor by Gentlemen XVII.[68]

And the supposed threat emanating from the neighbors was sufficient cause for the local commanders to impose a virtually constant state of military emergency, to assert their own power, and to safely conduct their own private trade. Corporal Joost Seggenaar complained to the Haagsch Besoigne (in the rendering of the Haagsch Besoigne) that:

> The lofty schemes of van Goens have utterly spoiled the country. Who dares to contradict him is considered his enemy and he himself says that if anybody has other thoughts and plans than him he is not considered his friend. He, Seggenaar, states that when he found out how things are really carried out there [Ceylon] he did not want to stay there any longer, and that he had to serve the Company as if he was a slave. Occasionally he sent letters to Mr. van Goens contradicting some plans of his but his excellency kept all these letters, refusing to send them on to anybody.[69]

## Power, Patronage, Private Trade

So the interests of the state clashed with those of the merchant, and when they did, the state would generally prevail—not only by pursuing revenue and security to the detriment of trade, but also because, like most administrations in the seventeenth century, the state was largely based upon a system of patronage.

This patronage in turn was oiled by the benefits gathered from private trade—just as among the English and the Portuguese. The officials of the Company regarded their office as a source for personal gain and the advancement of their kin rather than a service to their masters. "Institutionalized corruption" was as much entrenched within the VOC as in the Estado or England's "Old Corruption."

### *Patronage*

As was often remarked in the libels (handbills) directed against the Company in the eighteenth century, the power of high-placed servants in Asia increased in parallel with the ever more involved system of bureaucratic control.[70]

This was in itself harmless enough; working through patronage and factions is often smoother than observing prescribed bureaucratic procedure. The problem was particularly urgent in the out-stations, where all decisions had to be taken by the "political council"—involving all merchants, assistant merchants, bookkeepers, and captains of ships. Resolutions had to be underwritten by all those people. In Ketting's view concerning Surat—one of the factories notorious for constant bickering between director and council—no one in the council dared to make any important decision, for this would put his career on the line. This often paralyzed the council, so the directors had to make decisions alone. If they made a wrong one, they would be blamed afterward. On the other hand, incompetent councilors would request a say in any trivial matter "if the respect they imagine they are due is not complied with." A score of unimportant affairs were delayed for months, obstructing any major decisions.[71]

This often prompted directors to take decisions on their own and correspond directly with the governor-general, without considering the opinion of either the council or Gentlemen XVII. Either procedure would have signified indefinite postponement. J. de Buquoi did this in Surat, for example, when he decided to recommence the trade with Mocha in 1684 to the anger of Gentlemen XVII, who had not been consulted.[72]

Yet this power of high-ranking employees would only have benefited the VOC if its servants were paragons: they were not, far from it. This was clearly proven, if any proof was needed, by independent attorney van Helsdingen's investigation of the situation in Surat. Asia was in his view one big mess: everybody scorned orders from the Netherlands—not to the disadvantage "of the ministers of the Company, but surely to that of society in general."[73] The servants were knaves and cheats, stealing the pennies of widows and orphanages who had invested all their savings in the Company. Riffraff ruled supreme. On the out-stations one was dealing with "scurvy" servants—all of them common thieves. In Surat in 1689 the council consisted of director G. Vosburg, an "avaricious" and "greedy" man, and his cronies: merchants L. Schorer, J. van de Berg, and K. de Haan.

Every major decision was made in private deals between this cabal and broker Sundar Das.[74]

Vosburg was closely linked to L. Janszoon Pijl, governor of the Coromandel Coast, whose private trade at Surat was handled by Vosburg. Through Pijl's connections, Vosburg entertained close relations with Governor-General van Oudhoorn. Van de Berg was apparently also benefiting from links with the wealthy and mighty in Batavia. For, although he was dismissed on explicit orders from the Gentlemen XVII, he was promptly exonerated, promoted from merchant to chief merchant, and sent back to Surat.[75]

After long insistence by van Helsdingen, it was decided by Commissioner van Rheede to sack Vosburg. However, the Council of the Indies, without any inquest, promptly named Vosburg director of Malacca despite his behavior. But that was easy to comprehend, van Helsdingen insinuated; wasn't Vosburg a relative of P. van Hoorn, who was married to the daughter of Governor-General van Oudhoorn? W. Valckenier, brother of the Amsterdam alderman C. Valckenier, was married to van Oudhoorn's sister, and because of that was promoted to the position of councilor of the Indies. This triumvirate exercised monarchical power in the Indies. "They can advance their minions and ruin the ones whom they dislike for the slightest dereliction."[76] The power of this claque extended not only to the Council of the Indies but to the High Court of the Indies as well—so somebody they might abhor could count on severe punishment.

True, such were common practices in small Dutch towns as well, van Helsdingen conceded, but the *regenten* there "have nothing like the power of a governor-general."[77] As the saying among both Dutch and English had it, "first self, then Company," and pleasing a powerful patron was a more immediate concern than serving the Company.

In Gentlemen XVII's view Batavia's bureaucracy largely functioned as an engine of patronage. Of the 125 servants nominally employed in the accountancy in 1677, "the majority is idle or without a present occupation, which costs the Hon. Company a lot of money without any benefit."[78] For those in power mainly employed incompetents, who could hardly write, to provide jobs for their favorites. Batavia was suffering from a surplus of personnel, Gentlemen XVII complained, idling their days away waiting for a profitable posting. One such posting was Bengal: "the common saying there—Batavia—is: 'Bengal is gain for all' [*Bengalen daar valt wat te halen*]."[79]

This scramble for wealth was said in the eighteenth century to have wrecked the VOC, the initials of which were facetiously said to stand for *Vergaan Onder Corruptie*. And indeed, while one had to take an oath to be a trustworthy servant of the Company, when departing to the Indies this was no great concern to the majority. One did not leave for the Indies to eat hay, as P. Nuyts put it.[80] And as Schreuder noted, "from his pay and perquisites the director has to scratch a living; he has to manage soberly indeed, if he wants to have a few pennies left for his retirement."[81]

But those constant laments about insufficient pay emanating from Asia—and, granted, high-ranking personnel of the Dutch Company were not paid as well as English personnel—were caused, according to Gentlemen XVII, by the prodigious consumption of their servants there; this was also the prevailing opinion in Holland. These views of Gentlemen XVII, mostly staunch Calvinists, were only stiffened by the generally disapproving sermons of the *predikanten* in Asia on the licentiousness there.[82]

No doubt, servants of the VOC often indulged in considerable pomp, yet a cultural difference was involved too. In Batavia Ketting was renowned for his sober living, he noted, but at Surat, "in these countries (where I have never been before) I had to look through different eyes and speak a different tongue. Everybody I encountered told me how important the display of worldly splendor was for the interest of the Company."[83] The director represented the *natio* to Indian spectators and merchants alike, and if he looked like a pauper, the *natio* could not be creditworthy either. Ketting had to fund this pomp from his own pocket. And how was one to finance that but by private trade and corruption?[84]

This was certainly putting the finger on a sore spot: the average VOC employee had to "have nimble fingers" (*moest den hand reppen*) if he wanted to save a trifle for his retirement. Simple theft rarely occurred among VOC personnel. Commonplace, on the contrary, was "creative bookkeeping," opportunities for which obviously increased the further the factory was located from Batavia. One should not underrate the extent to which the main office controlled the out-stations. Bandar Abbas, for example, chided Isfahan in 1646 for the "excessive costs" of keeping two "woolly cats."[85] But still, factories like Agra, Ahmedabad, Basra, Broach, Cananore, Cranganore, Isfahan, or Panani were so remote that they could not be properly checked. Their accountancy often resembled a smokescreen for illegal deals. So one set out to have a jolly good time on an out-station. In 1686, for instance, the *shahbandar* of Bandar Abbas muttered about van de Heuvel, the envoy to the Persian court:

> I do not know what the Hon. Mr. van de Heuvel is doing at Isfahan. I believe he sleeps the whole day. Yet he has delicious roasted game, good wine and beautiful girls there, as well as healthy air, while we, here, have to muddle through in such a miserable way.[86]

In general, chances of being caught were slight, even though van de Heuvel did manage to get in trouble. But his impeachment dragged on for more than fifteen years and the alleged malpractices were never firmly proven.

The servants also displayed an impressive creativity in finding loopholes in the bookkeeping. There were, for example, manipulations with the course of money. Van de Heuvel, for one, counted the exchange rate of low-alloy Abbas; from the Tiflis mint to the course of higher alloy Tolpur Abbasis from the mint of Isfahan and pocketed the differential.[87] Another possibility was overrating *laccage* (the loss of weight of a good during its transport). Although Batavia generally checked this, very little could be proven if this was tampered with. There were myriad other possibilities: entering the price of quality goods for low-quality stuff, overestimating the purchase price or the price of sale, and so forth.

While such were simple cases of swindling, graft becomes a much more complicated issue when considering relations with indigenous states. The VOC often had a more rigid conception of what constituted "private" versus "public" domain than Indian or Persian nobles. They also often perceived taxes as *peshkash*—gifts or tribute. Since Surat's accountancy showed a constant increase in "gifts" to the Surat *divan*, correlated with an increase of trade, Gentlemen XVII inquired of its director, Ketting, whether one could not economize on this or request gifts in return. Ketting wrote that he had had a "healthy laugh about this."[88] The governor gave out worthless baubles in return for the expensive presents (horses, swords, honorary robes, etc.) of the VOC. These tokens really represented an additional tax on the increasing incomes of the VOC. The increase in *peshkash* and extortion may well be related to the growth of private trade, which was also not paid at customs.[89]

Furthermore, "presents" were—as mentioned—also important to assert the credit of a merchant. It might be unclear whether Indian merchants, in giving a gift, were expecting a service from a minister of the Company or one of the VOC. If Resik Das sent a box with gems to Antoinette van Oudhoorn, was that merely a token to the governor-general's wife or was it in order that van Oudhoorn cover up illicit dealings?[90]

But cultural differences can be invoked only to a certain point. Most bribes were seen as bribes in an Asian context too.[91] And the VOC was well aware of this, for they distinguished "presents," normal working expenses for trade, from "extraordinary presents," generally known as graft to any mortal but bookkeepers.[92]

For example, the supervisor for visitors to the palace (*mehmandar bashi*) was in the Safavid administrative system allotted a 1–2 percent share as his legitimate spoil of all presents handed to the court. In 1692, however, the *mehmandar bashi* requested 15 percent from Ambassador van Leene. If not allowed this sum, he would refuse the VOC access to the court. This was plainly corruption within the Persian system of norms as well. Van Leene refused to pay. Yet the VOC had earlier never protested the 2 percent payment, which had always figured under the heading "gifts" in the accountancy. And, in effect, the VOC was not alone in objecting: the sultan of Mazendaran protested against these practices to Shah Sulaiman too.[93] Such practices were illegal in both European administrative systems and Asian ones.

This might result in the Company's servants' bribing local officials to obtain influence there, to further their own interests. This was quite common in the

Dutch factories of Vengurla and Canara as well as to all appearances in the small factories in Kerala.[94]

Let us consider one case of many. In 1652 Vengurla was stormed by troops of Samnaji Pandit, the governor of Candal. C. Bacheracht, director, blamed this on the "malevolent motions" of Grand Vizier Fatah Khan; he was forced to move the factory to the *peta* of Salse, some miles from Vengurla.[95] According to P. Andrieszoon—who was sent by Batavia to investigate the matter—this was a very smelly affair indeed.[96]

Bacheracht had now for some time been handing money to the brokers Krishna and Narsana Vai so they would buy pepper on his private account. The brokers would sell it in Gujarat under their name. Part of these funds were used by the brothers to obtain the position of *desai* of Vengurla; they had invested it in bribes to Fatah Khan and to forge an alliance with the *desai* of Candal. But Samnaji Pandit, was in the way of this coterie. So they decided to assassinate him. On a dark night their cutthroats ambushed Samnaji Pandit who, unfortunately for the brokers, managed to escape to Bijapur. He invoked the help of Fatah Khan. Krishna fled to Goa; Fatah Khan took Narsana into custody. This was very necessary too: Bacheracht had meanwhile hired assassins to silence them.

In the meantime Bacheracht had become entangled in a conflict with Samnaji Pandit; he had refused to hand over to the latter assets of the Vais he had seized. Samnaji Pandit subsequently had the factory sacked. Fatah Khan knew he had better keep these two gamecocks apart, and assigned a different place of settlement to Bacheracht. Why not invoke armed support from the VOC to sort the matter out? Fatah Khan appears to have wondered. The grand vizier received Andrieszoon very well at Bijapur, and offered him the position of *desai* of Vengurla. Andrieszoon preferred to live to see another day than to accept that dubious blessing. Next, the brothers Vai (Krishna had been extradited by the Portuguese) were brought before Andrieszoon, who magnanimously granted them pardon. Fatah Khan assured Andrieszoon that he would have had them strangled otherwise—no doubt to cover his part in the affair.

### *Private Trade*

Besides the general spirit of slothfulness (the *Jan Salie-geest)* supposedly pervading Dutch society after 1650, the illegal private trade of the Dutch servants is often seen as the main cause of the decline of the VOC.[97]

And truly the highway to fortune for Dutch as much as for English and Portuguese officials was private trade, whether or not it was prohibited. Now, obviously, the opportunities for such deals differed from factory to factory. Malacca excepted, most factories in the archipelago were probably too close to Batavia to offer many prospects for private trade. There was a large amount of smuggling of diamonds and tea to the Netherlands in the liberty chests that servants were allowed to bring to Europe. But, barring those two goods, the private trade of its servants did not seriously impinge upon the commerce of the VOC to Europe.[98] The importance of private trade mainly comes to the fore when considering the *westerkwartieren* (Bengal and the settlements in India and Persia) as well as when considering Japan, where this problem has been well studied.[99]

Amazingly, there is no lack of material on this stealthy trade. Two lists of private trade were compiled: one by van Helsdingen covering private trade at Surat from 1672 to 1694, another by Deodati covering 1698 to 1702.[100] A petition directed against the "falsehoods" Deodati raised against other servants was sent to the Netherlands simultaneously. Deodati had privately traded goods pass his inspection, provided that 1 percent of their value was paid to him; those who did met pay might be denounced.[101] It is not very surprising one was this well informed: private trade was only "smuggling" to some extent. Goods were generally neatly cleared at the local customs stations, when these were owned by the Mughal empire—as at Surat and Hugly—or farmed by the Company—as at Pulicat and Sadraspatnam. Goods might be seized if smuggled. So, once unloaded, they ceased being contraband and locally one had quite an accurate picture of the amount of private trade carried on.

According to van Helsdingen, private trade at Surat amounted to about 10 percent of the total trade of the VOC at Surat. Since he could not trace transactions of captains of ships and those handled in *commenda* with Indian merchants, this was rather a conservative estimate. For, by way of comparison, at Pulicat private trade in textiles of the Company's servants surpassed that of the Company after 1672. In the 1680s one-third to one-fourth of all cargo space involved in the VOC's shipping to the Coromandel Coast was used for private trade, according to the Gentlemen XVII.[102] If this conjecture was correct, it would make Dutch private trade from the Coromandel Coast larger in volume than Danish or Portuguese trade. The Dutch private trade was far from a marginal factor, therefore—on the contrary, the Dutch personnel were, all limitations and prohibitions notwithstanding, a major force in the trade of the Indian Ocean. Moreover, although it obviously mainly involved products of small volume, occasionally even saltpeter was traded on the private account.

This business was dominated by a number of great magnates who entertained a network of patronage throughout Asia. Such networks also extended to the Netherlands and probably to England as well. Private trade was built upon patronage. One could only conduct it under the cover of a mighty patron. The business of the wife of the governor of the Coromandel Coast, A. Paviljoen, worth 2,353 guilders, was, for example, quite a different affair than that of "the *topaz* Anthony"—worth 1 guilder—or that of the "master-smith"—worth 2 guilders.[103] Through such affairs, coupled with political power and patronage, arose "great families" controlling both the private trade and the politics of the Oost-Indische Compagnie.

The best example is Governor-General C.J. Speelman himself. Speelman left a huge fortune, valued at 325,000 rixdollars. He could never have acquired this by licit means, the Council of the Indies suspected.[104] And indeed, Speelman was engaged in private trade throughout his career. In the fifties, for example, when he was chief accountant at Batavia—responsible for preventing private trade—his family in the Netherlands sent him amber, coral, and jewels, which he exchanged for textiles, tea, and jewels. Speelman collaborated with free-burghers like Pieter Moerbeeke, who handled Speelman's trade in textiles at Surat and with officials like merchant Arnold Goossens on the Malabar Coast, who purchased pepper on Speelman's account. His partners included the director of Malacca as well, who handled his transactions in tin. To keep these dealings well covered Speelman had most of the trade carried on in the name of his in-laws, and in particular in the name of his wife, P. Wonderaers. Although Speelman was convicted of private trade by the Batavia court of criminal justice in 1655, this did not hamper his career at all.[105]

Governor-General Speelman was a large conglomerate—as befits a governor-general. But it was not above Speelman's rank to grab a few pennies from any hawker who might cross his path.[106] His operations included a banking branch from which Speelman had lent 17,000 guilders to the king of Ternate. Next there was an agroindustrial branch: a sugar mill, shares in another manufacture, and a large number of domestic and agrarian serfs. There was a commercial branch too: under many fake names Speelman had dealings with Chinese, Armenian, "Moorish," and Portuguese traders throughout the Archipelago and, no doubt, with the English too (although this last set of dealings does not figure among Speelman's assets). Furthermore, there was a Dutch branch comprising bills on the Netherlands and presumably on England too. And finally there was the construction branch: Speelman possessed at least three pieces of land, two houses in town, and various estates in the country. Certainly, although this would merit further research, the average high-ranking VOC servant did not return home a pauper. The assets of van Goens, the "haughtiest and most arrogant bird of prey [*de hofvaardigste en laetdunckentse grijpvogel*] in the entire Indies," as he was locally known, in Asia alone amounted to more than 45,000 guilders—no trifle.

And, as van Helsdingen pointed out, since the court of justice was controlled by these grand families, it was not very sensible to denounce private trade to the governor-general. Although the officials constantly professed to be combating private trade by any means, this was a futile claim. If director De Keyser at Surat had indulged in private trade, Ketting was unable to prove anything.

> One fools around with the names of owners and nakhudas here like a magician, so it is hard to find out. I think that if Mr. De Keyser would have conducted private

trade, he would have dealt under a Portuguese name with *banias*, and would have transported goods in indigenous sloops.[107]

The officials interpreted the prohibition of private trade, according to Ketting, as meaning that no commerce was to be conducted "with such ships, such goods and in such quantities as would harm the trade of the Company. But it would certainly not be the intention of the Rt. Hon. Gentlemen XVII to prefer and favor Moors and heathens to them."[108] It seems this view was generally shared among servants of the VOC.

There was something to this view. At Surat, for example, Dutch private goods were sold in small consignments at the bazaar. Their sale did not immediately hamper the bulk transactions of the VOC, except in the case of tin. Private trade was primarily conducted in goods of marginal importance to the sales of the Company: tortoiseshell, opium, and pewter. As to the tin and pepper sold by the private traders, the VOC—with its bulk transactions—was the price setter. The quantities sold by private trade followed the price on the bazaar and were sold by the brokers of the Dutch merchants there. Private goods were mainly brought aboard ships rented by the officials and to a lesser extent aboard vessels engaged in intra-Asian shipping. Since sails earmarked to depart for the Netherlands were more tightly controlled and did not touch at intermediate stations, private trade did not immediately obstruct the traffic with the home country either.

Thus, though Gentlemen XVII urged the High Government of the Indies to take on abuses in Bengal, Japan, Surat, and Coromandel, in practice little was done to punish the culprits. If higher personnel were occasionally ensnared, Batavia's attorney general usually let mercy prevail over equity. By 1680 Gentlemen XVII were at last fed up with this malpractice. They probably did not have any objections in principle against some private trade, but such wheeling and dealing "has now become such a cancer, that it is almost seen as normal." Thus, they concluded that it seriously obstructed trade to the Netherlands. In Bengal it was now the rule rather than the exception, they complained, that goods, urgently needed in Amsterdam, were hurled ashore and left to rot while private goods were loaded: all ships, sailing to Batavia, were crammed with them. In Batavia opium and piece-cloth were smuggled in such quantities from Bengal and Coromandel that products of the VOC could not be sold.[109]

To uproot those abuses once and for all the Gentlemen XVII decided in 1687 to send van Rheede as a special extraordinary commissioner (*extraordinair commissaris*) to Asia to take command of the *westerkwartieren*. The Gentlemen XVII also sent "independent attorneys" along to serve as permanent controllers on their behalf.[110]

This mission of van Rheede was, to put it mildly, not very successful. To quote an outsider, the French director at Surat, J. Pillavoine,

> The Dutch are deeply disturbed by the rigorous orders which have been given to the commissioner, named van Rheede, which he executes in the factories with an amount of force which comes close to tyranny, and with which justice has nothing to do. Those at Batavia, as sovereign power, are not in favor of his mission. So, he is not aided and they hope that he will fail in all his enterprises—and they have refused to allot him help, with the pretext that they have barely sufficient people to sustain themselves at Batavia.[111]

Not only Batavia but most personnel under the governor-general as well turned against the independent attorneys, who first reported to van Rheede and after his death in 1695 directly to the Gentlemen XVII. As could have been predicted, bedlam resulted in Surat and Coromandel. One could appeal to two different authorities and this led to intense mutual distrust.[112]

With the arrival of independent attorney (*fiscaal*) van Helsdingen at Surat, this factory became well nigh ungovernable. After Gentlemen XVII fired Vosburg (in 1691), van Helsdingen ran the factory for half a year. On Batavia's insistence van Ommen was named as co-director. Van Helsdingen seems to have hoped he would be able to intimidate young van Ommen. He immediately tackled him with bland accusations of earlier misbehavior, hoping a frightened van Ommen might then recognize van Helsdingen as his superior. Van Ommen became furious instead, so a nasty feud ensued between the two. The gentlemen lost no opportunity to cast slurs at each other. Van Helsdingen and his hangers-on opposed any decision of van Ommen's. The latter imposed house arrest upon the independent attorney, who took revenge by showering the Gentlemen XVII with accusations.[113]

Batavia intervened by naming De Keyser as director (1694). Van Helsdingen thought that De Keyser—a close acquaintance of van Oudhoorn's—had been sent in order to cover up facts that might incriminate the High Council of the Indies. Van Helsdingen bluntly refused to obey. Meetings of the council turned into bouts of screaming and cursing. De Keyser prohibited the independent attorney entrance to the main building and access to the letters of Surat. Van Helsdingen thereupon exclaimed that he would accept any anonymous accusation against De Keyser. The latter (rightly) considered that van Helsdingen wanted to ruin him, whereas van Helsdingen suspected (whether or not on solid grounds) that De Keyser was plotting to have him assassinated.[114]

At the behest of Gentlemen XVII, Batavia next sent P. de Rhoo, chief bookkeeper of Batavia, to Surat so that he might allay these conflicts. De Rhoo, however, died after six months under mysterious circumstances. Van Helsdingen accused the broker of having poisoned de Rhoo, perhaps with the privity of De Keyser. This altogether unheard-of accusation was sent in a secret letter to the Gentlemen XVII, who decided that Batavia should inquire into the case. Van Oudhoorn and the council were understandably enraged, yet decided to send Ketting as commissioner to Batavia.[115]

Ketting finally dismissed the allegation due to lack of proof, but to what extent was he unprejudiced?[116] When the commissioner arrived at Surat in 1696 the Gentlemen XVII hoped—wrongly, as it turned out—that Ketting would certainly put an end to the chaos in Surat. They decided to allow van Helsdingen to repatriate honorably. His file was far from closed, however, since van Helsdingen immediately became embroiled in a quarrel with Gentlemen XVII.[117]

Deodati was named as the next independent attorney on the recommendation of Ketting. But Deodati virtually immediately quarreled with Ketting, who, Deodati wrote, was nothing but a drunken fool. And after Ketting's death his successor, Zwaardecroon, and Deodati were again instantly at loggerheads.

When the Gentlemen XVII decided in 1706 not to name any more independent attorneys they admitted in effect to having lost the struggle for control of the East Indies. Efforts to control Batavia from the Netherlands would but lead to turmoil. Asia would henceforth set its own rules of conduct, which the Gentlemen XVII might endorse or loudly disapprove of; that was about it.

## Monopolists and Middlemen in Surat

The way the VOC operated on the market also hinged on the tangled web of patronage. The Company largely dealt through brokers, closely tied to the Company; the prices offered to and the amounts sold by the Company depended upon the creditworthiness of the broker. Both in Kerala, as we saw already, and in Surat there ensued a duopoly: through the support of the Company, merchants could obtain a dominant position in the segment of the market where its products were sold.

Yet dealing with the merchants in Surat, Pillavoine wrote, "*c'est comme entretenir des loups, qui vous mangent,*" but the French as much as the VOC had to rely on them since they were a buffer that sheltered them against price fluctuations.[118] Nonetheless, with its spice trade the VOC was in a monopoly position; it might theoretically have asked any price it wished. There were a number of constraints to the monopoly, however.[119]

As we saw already, if the VOC sold goods for a much higher price at Surat than elsewhere, these would be shipped there. The price offered at Surat therefore served as a guideline for those in Kerala, Persia, Golconda, and Vengurla. In addition, the VOC sold goods by way of package deals. The price of the other products sold was linked to that of spices. In 1693 the Company tried to abolish this system. Spices were then certainly sold for a better price, but the VOC remained stuck with the far less profitable tortoiseshell.[120] Presumably, the VOC could merely have sold spices, but most products sold at Surat consisted of bulk goods, fetching lower profits but marketed in large quantities. These accounted for the lion's share of Surat's proceeds, and the first and foremost was copper. But the Company did not enjoy a monopoly in this product; the French and the English sold it too, so the market for this metal was more unpredictable than that for spices. If selling spices, the merchant was assured of a profit—but windfalls were obtained on copper, not on spices.[121] In addition, the VOC needed credit to finance its purchases. It was often necessary to sell products rapidly in order to get cash, so the VOC was at the mercy of its creditors.[122]

In economic terms the VOC enjoyed a segmented monopoly: it sold a packet of products, for some of which it could ask a monopoly price. The price demanded was constrained by that of the other products, however. The purchaser of goods could enjoy a monopoly position in one commodity but if he tried to maximize his profits, others might enter the market—monopolist competition, economists would call this. Theory predicts that both parties would be interested in making deals. This would result in rigid prices occasionally interrupted by sudden bouts of price wars.[123] And, indeed, as is obvious from Table 8.2, the pattern of prices and sales of the VOC at Surat shows a fairly steady pattern in which an even increase was interrupted by sudden increases and decreases related to price wars.

In theory the VOC could choose between various methods of marketing. It was possible to transport the goods to Ahmedabad or Agra but this ceased in 1630. Bills of exchange could better finance the trade of those settlements; the road was long and arduous and these markets were more unpredictable than Surat.[124] It was also possible to establish a shop or have the goods vended in the bazaar by trusted *banias*. This would have been a cumbersome affair indeed, since the small purchasers could not afford to buy the substantial quantities offered by the VOC at once and the goods would have to be stored with the danger of rot. Moreover, shopkeepers were linked by credit with big merchants. If a small shopkeeper tried to usurp the virtual monopoly of the great merchants over the VOC's products, his credit might be withdrawn. Most other merchants would be afraid to deal with him, as would his clients, since the credit he allowed them would be shaky too. The bulk goods—tin, lead, and copper—could not be sold to shopkeepers. These were purchased by commissioners of the mint and the army and those agents were reluctant to make major deals with untrustworthy small hawkers. They needed prompt delivery, if necessary at high prices.[125]

Hence, in 1658 the "Japanese system" was introduced, which continued in use throughout the seventeenth century.[126] All merchants might, on a request by the broker, send a sealed letter to the council. It was preferable for these offers to be made under the merchant's proper name. At the end of the century, however, one could also make an offer anonymously, or in the name of the broker. This was common practice at Surat: a great many persons traded who were not really supposed to. In theory, the Company would duly take any bid into consideration, and would not tell the merchants how many other buyers were interested.

This was mere theory; it was a secret, extensively exposed by both Volger and van Helsdingen, that prices were fixed in a tête-tête between director and broker while enjoying refreshments in the garden of the Company several days before the council assembled.[127] The broker thereupon set the prices and invited a few friends to play competitor. When the council had assembled, time was spent joking and gossiping. Every offer was duly noted in the "resolution book" and then deposited in the wastepaper basket. The director sold the goods to the broker with a 2 percent benefit for himself and 1 percent for the council. And indeed, looking at Table 8.2, it is obvious that the VOC was constantly selling to the same people—two or at most three syndicates.

Until 1667 the VOC was selling to Virji Vora either through intermediaries or directly. As G. Pelgrom put it, "the trouble is that our creditors are our purchasers as well." They were heavily in debt to Virji Vora and to Shanti Das Jagarawath (the *nagarseth* of Ahmedabad) and had to sell products to them or else they would not be able to raise the huge sums needed for the purchases of the Company. For textiles were ordered in a different season than that in which goods were sold, and to pay for the purchases of cloth it was necessary to borrow money to cover the expenses in the interim period.

When Virji Vora and Said Beg died, broker Kisen Das saw a golden opportunity to push prospective competitors aside. After 1679 Calian Sen and Samar Sen Vora tried to take over the VOC trade again—to naught, since Kisen Das was backed by director Boogaart, whose private trade he financed.[128]

This was an important change in the pattern of the trade. Vora was far from a compradore. But Kisen Das owed virtually his entire fortune to the VOC. Sundar Das, Kisen Das's father, had apparently been serving the VOC since its first establishment at Surat. Kisen Das's grandsons, Resik Das and Sundar Das, were virtually raised in the factory. Most of such independent commerce as the house conducted was sponsored by the servants of the Company and closely intertwined with their private trade. Examples include taking bills on Malabar, the trade in indigo, and the commerce of Balav Das, who—before being Zwaardecroon's broker—also acted as personal broker to the VOC personnel at Agra and earlier at Broach, where he was "not only Mr. van Ommen's broker but also his supplier of warm [women's] flesh."[129]

Commissioner Soolmans argued that there was no alternative to selling to the brokers, since other merchants could not raise the capital required.[130] This sounds like mere subterfuge for not trying to sell, however. Some great bankers or shipowners might have amassed sufficient resources. But in keeping with the growing specialization of Surat's trade, a small circle of merchants increasingly controlled the segment of the market served by the Company's products. They were subsidized by the Companies and if necessary seen through temporary difficulties by them.

This was a trend apparently extending to the monopoly Companies in general, not only to the VOC. According to Zwaardecroon, the Manek family, the English

Table 8.2

**Purchasers and Prices of Cloves, Mace, and Nutmeg Sold by the VOC in Surat, 1671–1697** (in rupees per maund)

| | Cloves | | Mace | | Nutmeg | |
|---|---|---|---|---|---|---|
| Year | Purchaser | Ru | Purchaser | Ru | Purchaser | Ru |
| 1671 | Mirza Musem | 117 | Mirza Musem | 120 | Mirza Musem | 34 |
| 1672 | Manek Vora | 122 | Manek Vora | 122 | Manek Vora | 40 |
| 1673 | Manek Vora | 125 | Manek Vora | 122 | Manek Vora | 35 |
| 1674 | Sew Das | 120 | Sew Das | 118 | Sew Das | 30 |
| 1675 | Kisen Das | 116 | Kisen Das | 116 | Kisen Das | 32 |
| 1676 | Kisen Das | 113 | | | | |
| 1677 | Kisen Das | 113 | Kisen Das | 105 | Kisen Das | 27 |
| 1678 | Kisen Das | 112 | Kisen Das | 103 | Kisen Das | 23 |
| 1679 | Kisen Das | 114 | Kisen Das | 118 | Kisen Das | 46 |
| 1680 | Manek Vora | 119 | Manek Vora | 115 | Manek Vora | 34 |
| 1681 | Kisen Das | 120 | Kisen Das | 123 | Kisen Das | 37 |
| 1682 | Samar Vora | 122 | Samar Vora | 125 | Kisen Das | 30 |
| 1683 | Sew Das | 122 | Sew Das | 126 | Sew Das | 38 |
| 1684 | Sew Das | 120 | Sew Das | 124 | | |
| 1685 | Sew Das | 109 | Sew Das | 120 | Sew Das | 108 |
| 1686 | | | Sew Das | 112 | Sew Das | 86 |
| 1687 | Sew Das | 109 | Kisen Das | 115 | Sew Das | 67 |
| 1688 | Resik Das | 109 | Resik Das | 112 | Sew Das | 50 |
| 1689 | Samar Vora | 118 | Samar Vora | 116 | Samar Vora | 42 |
| 1690 | Govind Das | 125 | Govind Das | 121 | Govind Das | 49 |
| 1691 | Mahmed Sahid | 122 | M. Sahid | 121 | Mahmed Sahid | 47 |
| 1692 | Various | 115 | | | Various | 47 |
| 1693 | Mahmed Sahid | 108 | Varma Sen | 125 | Mahmed Sahid | 55 |
| 1694 | Govind Das | 109 | Govind Das | 120 | Govind Das | 52 |
| 1695 | Govind Das | 107 | | | Govind Das | 53 |
| 1696 | Govind Das | 110 | Gopal Das | 150 | Govind Das | 60 |
| 1697 | Mahmed Sahid | 108 | M. Sahid | 160 | Mahmed Sahid | 54 |

brokers in the eighteenth century, had been a bunch of rather obscure hawkers until Rustamji Manek was named by the Compagnie des Indes as bazaar broker.[131] Admiral Barbosa de Machedo next catapulted Rustamji to chief representative of the Portuguese nation at Surat, probably since Rustamji took care of the admiral's private trade. Whereas Rustamji had remained "a very poor man" in his last assignment, this new one was a treasure trove. Rustamji could earn rich rewards from brokerage when selling the right to use the Portuguese flag and permits to Dutch, French, and Indian traders. He also controlled the traffic in bills between the Portuguese possessions and Surat and benefited from his position as official correspondent to the viceroy. He had ample advance knowledge of how many ships were to arrive at Surat, as he probably had already served English interlopers with navicerts and permits. Rustamji was named broker to the English Company in 1698. He was, after the merger of the East India Company and the English Company, taken over, together with the stock of the English Company, by the Joint East India Company in 1704.[132]

There were weighty reasons for Indian merchants to cooperate: the Europeans occasionally provided armed support to merchants dealing on their behalf, for example. More important, the Companies were a secure investment—thus, the interest charged the EIC and the VOC fell throughout the seventeenth century. G. Pelgrom boasted in 1656 that he would have no difficulty collecting 2 million rupees in a month at a 10.5 percent rate, and one could easily have repeated this later on.[133] For the Companies could not go bankrupt, as they proved through the occasional imports of cash that served to confirm their creditworthiness. In the unsettled conditions of the seventeenth-century crisis merchants crowded to lend money to the Company. This was, of course, even more the case during the turmoil of the eighteenth century.

Was this situation, whereby sales were controlled by a tiny circle of indigenous merchants, disadvantageous to the Company, and did the VOC sell as much in Surat as it would theoretically be able to? One group of servants, including J. de Buqoi[134] at Surat and P. van Dam in the Netherlands, thought the spice monopoly adversely affected demand in India.[135] The common man, "who is here, as anywhere else in the world, the major part of mankind," was no longer able to afford spices, de Buqoi reasoned.[136] After 1662 the Company had virtually doubled the price. The Indians had virtually ceased to chew on betel leaves with pepper and cinnamon, and instead had shifted to other narcotics like *pan* and *bang*. If the VOC insisted on selling at an inordinate rate of profit, one had to sell to a tiny ring of merchants, serving the court and the wealthy, while spices could no longer be sold in the bazaar. Van Dam also reasoned that the demand for spices in India had declined since the sixteenth century. Demand for expensive Sumatra and Java pepper had virtually disappeared, for example, while the consumer now bought Canara pepper.

Others, including Commissioner Soolmans and Director P. de Witt, argued that the strong rise of the prices of spices did not ensue in a markedly receding demand. Even more spices were sold after 1660 than previously, so the elasticity of price and demand was apparently high. Of course, the virtual duopoly over VOC sales was abominable—yet, considering the minimal profits made by these intermediaries, it was reasonable they would be compensated for this by enjoying a monopoly. Essentially, P. de Vos considered in 1703, the VOC could not sell large quantities of spices, ask a high price, and then insist that goods not be sold to a ring.[137] The broker would always keep large quantities of spices at hand to sell two to three months before the new consignment of spices arrived at Surat, in order to effect a drop in price. The Dutch either had to sell diminutive quantities at a high price or vend the goods elsewhere—for example, at Mocha. Or the Company could sell at a price lower than that of the broker and thus make it impossible to undercut the Company. However, in that case, the VOC would incur the risk that the English would buy up all the spices and take them to Europe. Since neither of the two alternatives was really feasible, the VOC would have to work through a ring, however much this conflicted with its avowed principles.

A reasonable contention, it seems—in Surat one reckoned with a difference of only 10 percent between the wholesale and the bazaar values of goods. Given additional costs, such as rebate and weighing-house taxes, the profit on a transaction with the VOC was for an intermediary only reckoned at 4–5 percent. However, this was certain profit—and on transactions of several millions in value, this was no trifling gain.[138]

As an explanation for the expansion of sales at Surat, I would advance that in the seventeenth century the area covered by the Surat market expanded. Products from there were in the late seventeenth century sold in Sind, Agra, and fetched to Isfahan and probably to Central Asia. Since the merchants of the "second hand" to which products were sold sheltered the market from unpredictable price fluctuations, the demand did not primarily build upon the supply and the price asked by the Company, but rather upon the expanding demand in the interior.[139]

## Conclusion

There was a considerable gap between theory and practice in the VOC. Though the VOC argued that it should offer all indigenous merchants an equal chance, it was in fact working through rings. Again, though the VOC proposed to be, and to some extent was, a meritocracy, its administrative system worked through a system of patronage to a much greater degree than it was willing to acknowledge. The trouble—as F. Lequin has remarked—was that, to some extent, the true Asian setup resembled that of the Dutch Republic itself.[140] Was not the polity of the Republic built on patronage, on local privileges? And were not the *bewindhebbers* themselves named by patrons?

The lower personnel in the Indies thought to quote from the pamphlet "The East Indian Chat" (*Het Oost-Indische praetje*):

> Why, then, should those who have newly arrived here not carry on in the same vein as their masters do? For one believes—here in the Indies—on the one hand, that things are fishy amongst the *bewindhebbers* themselves too. But they, on the other hand, continue to pester their employees with infeasible ordinances, so that they are forced to have nimble fingers if they ever want to return home.[141]

To those servants the monopolies instituted by the mercantilist state were merely an elaborate device to rob millions for the benefit of the elite, so why should they not be permitted some petty embezzlement? Although the VOC tried, and with considerable success, to have intra-Asian trade conducted by the monopoly organization and to proscribe private gain from office, many merchants of the VOC were still known to "shake more fruits from the tree of plenty than its leaseholder." "To own is to own, but to grab is a fine art." "The peasant well knows how the gentleman has gathered his money." Thus went some of the proverbs (as quoted in "The East Indian Chat") current in the Indies. *Bewindhebbers* and other ranking personnel were knaves and cheats themselves, so the rank and file could hardly be blamed if they were stealing from their masters.

And their English compatriots would have fully agreed with those proverbs: the EIC, too, was a "bunch of knaves, cheats and a Company of base, quarrelling people." In the English case too, it was after 1680 hardly possible to rule Asia from Europe. Both the EIC's and the VOC's business were then controlled by congeries of their powerful servants, and in both cases these disposed of an extensive network of private trade. But England's "Old Corruption" was better prepared to accommodate the shameless quest for self-enrichment of its servants. English private trade was thus both more extensive and the English were able to take greater risks than Dutch private traders could.

Yet even though these may appear—retrospectively—as positive aspects, the English were struggling with a massive problem of smuggling and with constant constitutional entanglements in Parliament. Thus, even at the end of the century, compared with the solid VOC, the EIC appeared a much more fragile organization.

One has to guard against weighing the respective merits of the Dutch and English organizations with the benefit of hindsight: the EIC eventually survived longer than the VOC and was perhaps more successful in the long run. Yet on its jubilee in 1702 the VOC had good reason to congratulate itself. The French were virtually driven from the seas, the Portuguese mere peddlers, while the English were absorbed in a bitter struggle between two contending Companies. And the VOC's success was to no small extent achieved because of the secrecy of its affairs and its decentralization at home—either of which could with hindsight appear as weaknesses. The VOC still ran a hugely profitable business far overshadowing that of the EIC, mainly because of its monopoly system—as unwieldy as it might seem to outsiders and contemporary historians.

Hence, if—with hindsight again—one wishes to look for a period of "incipient decay" of the VOC, it will not be found in the second half of the seventeenth century. Clouds might have appeared on the horizon, but they were on the horizon still. Such difficulties as were facing the Company were very much a result of its success.

## Notes

1. Ajuda, 50-V-37, "Enformação," fo. 385–89; Évora CV/1-7, "Sobre a conservação da India," fo. 1–42. We badly need studies on the differences and similarities between Spanish/Portuguese and English/Dutch companies, but see G.D. Winius, "Two Lusitanian

Variations on a Dutch Theme: Portuguese Companies in Times of Crisis," in Blussé and Gaastra (eds.), *Companies and Trade,* pp. 119–35.

2. See the instructions for the Haagsch Besoigne in KITLV, H. 604.

3. *Aenwysinge dat men van de West- en Oost-Indische Compagnie een Compagnie dient te maecken. Mitsgaders twintig consideratiën op de trafycque, scheepvaart ende commerciën deser landen* (The Hague, 1644) (Knuttel, 5117).

4. J. van der Kan, *Uit de rechtsgeschiedenis der Oost-Indische Compagnie,* 2 vols. (Batavia, 1930, 1935), ii, p. 4; F.W. Stapel, "Bijdragen tot de geschiedenis der rechtspraak bij de VOC," *BTLV* 89 (1932), pp. 42–45.

5. See J. Mooy, *Geschiedenis van de Protestantse kerk in Nederlandsch-Indië,* vol. 1 (only one published), *Van de stichting der Oost-Indische Compagnie tot het optreden der Gouverneur-Generall Antonio van Diemen* (Weltevreden, 1927), p. 329 et seq.; Boxer, *Dutch Seaborne Empire,* p. 150.

6. VOC/RGGR 668, 29 July 1645; VOC/RGGR 674, 23 July 1653. See Lequin, "Het personeel," i, p. 165. On the policy of secrecy in the Netherlands see M.A.P. Meilink-Roelofs, "Van geheim tot openbaar" (Inaugural lecture, Leiden, 1970), p. 25.

7. For one case see VOC/CR 9286, 9 January 1652.

8. VOC 359, "Memoir regarding the issues the officers will have to consider when drafting reports to the *bewindhebbers.*"

9. VOC/OB 1278, "Memoir for A. Lefebvre," fo. 1755, though, granted, merchant Robert Lindsay was little impressed by the quality of the information received from Goa, "being merely street rumours."

10. VOC/XVII 323, 27 August 1694; *Records of Ft. St. George: Despatches to England* (Madras, 1919), 1711–1714, p. 32.

11. Silveira, *Reformação da milícia,* p. 186; see also, for example, J. Wycki (ed.), "Duas relações sobre a situação da Índia portuguêsa nos anos 1568 e 1569," *Studia,* 8 (1961), pp. 185–93.

12. HAG, LM, 51 bis, 28 January 1686, fo. 74.

13. *Bewind en beleid bij de VOC* (Zutphen, 1989).

14. This is a very well studied topic, starting from the classic study by W.F. Mansveld, *Rechtsvorm en geldelijk beheer bij de Oost-Indische compagnie* (Amsterdam, 1922), esp. p. 103. His very skeptical view on the Company's finances—an impenetrable labyrinth largely due to the Company's institutional setup—has by and large been supported by J. Steur, *Herstel of ondergang. De voorstellen tot redres van de VOC* (Utrecht, 1984), p. 193, who uses modern techniques of bookkeeping to show that the VOC also floundered because of its inefficient account keeping. However, J.P. de Korte, *De jaarlijkse financiële verantwoording in de Verenigde Oost-Indische Compagnie* (Leiden, 1984), and L.D. Westera, "Boekhouding en management bij de Verenigde Oostindische Compagnie," *Economisch-historische jaarboek* 55 (1992), pp. 75–105, take a much more positive view of the Company's bookkeeping, stressing that Gentlemen XVII were well abreast of what was happening in the Company.

15. VOC/OB 1582, 25 December 1696, fo. 81. For a study of the somewhat similar problems of another factory, see P.W. Klein, "Japanse rendementen in de achttiende eeuw: Innovatie en inertie," *Economisch-historische jaarboek* 47 (1984), pp. 195–204. Not, of course, that Ketting had a very high opinion of the personnel on the accountancy in Surat. "Those who are here are mostly drunks, can badly write and lack any knowledge. And those who have any capacity speak, if some position may fall to somebody else, immediately of being released from their position," (VOC/OB 1582, December 1696, fo. 82)

16. F.W. Stapel, "Johannes Hudde over de balansen van de Verenigde Oost-Indische Compagnie," *Economisch-historische jaarboek* 13 (1927).

17. Gaastra, *Bewind en beleid,* p. 275.

18. ARA, St. Gen., Lias VOC, 5737 i, 19 March 1644; ARA, St. Gen., Lias Portugal, 7010 ii, 15 October 1644; on W. Usselincx, see C. Ligtenberg, *Willem Usselincx* (Utrecht, 1914); O. van Rees, *Geschiedenis der staatshuishoudkunde in Nederland tot het einde der achttiende eeuw,* 2 vols. (Utrecht, 1856, 1868), vol. ii; and H. Laspreyes, *Geschichte der volkswirtschaftliche Anschauungen der Niederländer und ihre Literatur zur Zeit der Republik* (Leipzig, 1863; Nieuwkoop, 1961), pp. 80–99.

19. *Lof der Oost-Indische Compagnie ende den edelachtbaren Heeren Bewindhebbers van dien* (Leiden, 1645) (Knuttel 5358); ARA, St. Gen., Lias VOC, 5737 i, 16 September 1643.

20. *Berigt van den bewindhebbers van de Oost-Indische Compagnie op 't subject van de klagten bij de heer Shekelton, extraordinaris envooy van den koning van Engeland gedaen* (Amsterdam, 1685) (Knuttel, 12615); N. Japikse, *De diplomatieke verwikkelingen tussen de Republiek en Engeland van 1660 tot 1665* (Leiden, 1900), pp. 92–104; C.H. Wilson, *Profit and Power: A Study of England and the Dutch Wars* (London, 1957), p. 119; K.G. Feiling, *British Foreign Policy 1660–1672* (London, 1930/1968), pp. 78–110.

21. VOC/XVII 320, 20 January 1680; see also the summary in Gaastra, *Bewind en beleid,* p. 133.

22. ARA, St. Gen., Lias VOC, 5738 i, 19 March 1669.

23. S. de Freitas, *Do justo império asiático dos portugueses* (S. Leite, ed. and trans.), 2 vols. (Lisbon, 1980).

24. P.A. Tiele, *Bouwstoffen voor de geschiedenis van de Nederlanders in den Maleischen archipel,* 3 vols. (The Hague, 1886–95), iii, p. 145; VOC/UB 871, 30 October 1647, fo. 472.

25. M. Vink, "Passes and Protection Rights: The Dutch East India Company as a Redistributive Enterprise in Malacca 1641–1662," *Moyen Orient et Océan Indien,* 7 (1990), pp. 73–101; Van Santen, "Verenigde Oost-Indische Compagnie," pp. 19–25.

26. VOC/OB 1409, Surat Diary, 31 October 1684, fo. 1643–49.

27. I. Takeshi, "The World of Adat Aceh: A Historical Study of the Sultanate of Aceh" (Ph.D. dissertation, Australian National University, Canberra, 1984).

28. VOC/OB 1349, 8 April 1679, fo. 612.

29. VOC/HB 4457, 26 April 1679, fo. 479.

30. Gaastra, *Bewind en beleid,* pp. 140–43.

31. ARA, Coll. van Hoorn van Riebeeck 11 c, "Considerations regarding the general letter"; for a somewhat later period see D.D. Lewis, "The Dutch East India Company and the Straits of Malacca" (Ph.D. disseration, Australian National University, Canberra 1970); and R. Vos, "Koopman en koning. De VOC en de Maleise tinhandel" (Academisch proefschrift, Utrecht, 1990).

32. VOC/XVII 322, 10 November 1687, fo. 446 vo.

33. D.K. Bassett, "British 'Country Trade' and Local Trade Networks in the Thay and Malay States ca. 1680–1770," *MAS* 23 (4) (1989), pp. 631–35; S. Arasaratnam, "The Coromandel Southeast Asia Trade 1650–1740: Challenges and Adaptation of a Commercial System," *Journal of Asian History* 18 (1984), pp. 113–35; see also, for example, VOC/OB 1765, "Questionnaire to Jean Le Bon" (concerns an attempt of a British "interloper" to establish trade with the Moluccas in 1702), *Records of Ft. St. George: Despatches to England 1711–1714,* p. 44.

34. G.J. Knaap, *Kruidnagelen en christenen. De Verenigde Oost-Indische Compagnie en de bevolking van Ambon 1656–1696* (Dordrecht, 1987).

35. S. Arasaratnam, *Dutch Power in Ceylon 1659–1676* (Amsterdam, 1958), p. 160; and "Dutch Monopoly Policy in Ceylon and Its Effects on the Indo-Ceylon Trade," *IESHR* 4 (2) (1967), pp. 119–30.

36. S. Arasaratnam, "Monopoly and Free Trade in Dutch-Asian Commercial Policy," *Journal of Southeast Asian History* (1973), pp. 1–15; *Memoir of Rycklof van Goens* (J. Reimes, ed. and trans.) (Colombo, 1932), p. 43; VOC/OB 1251, 28 December 1665, fo. 537–41 vo.

37. In fact, the Gentlemen XVII tried to diversify supply to Persia by also inducing Malabar and Ceylon to establish sugar plantations. Furthermore, they also tried to expand the cultivation of silk in Ceylon. (VOC/XVII 319, 22 August 1668).

38. De Jonge, *Opkomst,* vii, p. cxxxi; see Blussé, *Strange Company,* p. 91.

39. VOC/UB 887, 15 June 1664, fo. 504–6.

40. Om Prakash, *Dutch East India Company,* p. 176; VOC/OB 1490, 19 October 1694, fo. 878–81; ARA, Coll. Hoppe K.A. 8492, "Extract from a letter of the Governor-General to François Tacq."

41. See P. Morree, *A Concise History of Dutch Mauritius: A Fruitful and Healthy Land* (London, 1998); and A. Toussaint, *Histoire de l'Île Maurice* (Paris, 1973); neither of which entirely replaces the old study of A. Pitot, *'T eyland Mauritius. Esquisse historique* (Port Louis, 1905).

42. VOC/XVII 320, 13 March 1672; S. Drescher, *Econocide: British Slavery in the Age of Abolition* (Pittsburg, 1977).

43. VOC/XVII 317, 15 April 1654, fo. 334.

44. And surely Lamotius had some right to speak here, for—although something of a gentleman gangster—Lamotius was also a very capable amateur botanist. Cf. R.N. Grove, *Green Imperialism: Colonial Expansion, Tropical Island Edens and the Origins of Environmentalism 1600–1860* (Cambridge, 1995), p. 105

45. Pitot, *'T eyland Mauritius,* p. 235; VOC/HB 4459, 11 June 1693.

46. K.N. Liebrand (ed.), *Précis of the Archives of Cape of Good Hope,* 6 vols. (Cape Town, 1896–1906), ii, pp. 10–14; VOC/OB 1457, "Trial of Johan Lamotius, formerly chief-merchant of Mauritius," fo. 485–95.

47. VOC/OB 1593, 29 November 1671, fo. 604; Van Dam, *Beschrijvinge,* III, ii, p. 327.

48. VOC/OB 1474, "Report by Isaac van der Dielen," fo. 175 vo.; VOC/OB 1527, 22 February 1693 fo. 51 vo; VOC/OB 1448, 17 January 1689, fo. 376–79 vo.; VOC/OB 1593, 10 December 1697, fo. 19.

49. VOC/XVII 323, 31 June 1698; VOC/XVII 321, 8 October 1685 fo. 284–85; VOC/XVII 319, 5 April 1672.

50. VOC/XVII 317, 12 April 1643, fo. 7.

51. See ARA, Coll. Hudde 14 (33), "Net profit and losses of all factories 1670–1692." Compare also the complaints of Gentlemen XVII (VOC/XVII 320, 28 September 1675) on the huge amounts of bills of exchange that Ceylon was drawing on the factories on the Coromandel Coast, Persia, and Surat, "from which those trading stations, of which the profits have to come, markedly suffer."

52. F. Gaastra, "The Shifting Balance of Trade of the Dutch East India," in Blussé and Gaastra, *Companies and Trade,* p. 63.

53. Gaastra, *Bewind en beleid,* p. 16.

54. G.D. Winius and M.P.M. Vink, *The Merchant-Warrior Pacified: The VOC (the Dutch East India Company) and Its Changing Political Economy in India* (New Delhi, 1991)

55. Gaastra, *Bewind en beleid,* pp. 216–21; C.R. Boxer, "On the Eighteenth Century as a Category in Indonesian History: A Reconsideration of J.C. van Leur," *Documentatieblad 18 e eeuw,*" 41/42 (1979), p. 9; VOC/XVII 320, 28 September 1675. Batavia, for example, adduced it took a loss because of the war against Banten, but even after a category in the accounts of the Indies had been reserved for "expenses in the war against Banten" Batavia continued taking losses (ARA, Coll. Hudde 10, "General demonstration of profit and losses on the office Batavia").

56. VOC/OB 1297, "Preparatory considerations by Pieter van Hoorn (1676)," fo. 696 vo.

57. VOC/OB 1593, 10 December 1697, fo. 19.

58. VOC/XVII 320, 11 May 1677; see also van Dam, *Beschrijvinge,* II, ii, p. 287.

59. VOC/OB 1369, "Considerations on withdrawing factories from the Malabar Coast"; VOC/OB 1571, 29 February 1695, fo. 713 vo.: "*de commercie in deese veelhoofdige en verdeelde landen is t' eenemaale afhanckelyck van 's Comp.'s agtbaarheid.*"

60. See, for example, ARA, St. Gen. 5738 ii, Report by P. Van Dam; and VOC/OB 1280, 29 November 1671, fo. 580.

61. VOC/OB 1280, 29 November 1671, fo. 584; VOC/OB 1527, 22 February 1693, fo. 195, and in same, "Treaty with the king *Zamorin,*" fo. 301–2.

62. VOC/OB, "Diary by Rijckloff van Goens," 1 March 1677.

63. Roelofs, *Vestiging,* p. 353.

64. See s' Jacob, *The Rajas of Cochin;* and for example, VOC/OB 1474, 13 January 1691, fo. 753.

65. K.N. Pillai, *Studies in Kerala History* (Trivandrum, 1978), p. 360–62; VOC/OB 1396, 18 November 1684, fo. 699–705; VOC/OB 1474 13 January 1693, fo. 563–65.

66. VOC/OB 10 December 1697, fo. 101 vo.

67. ARA, HRB, 543, "Notes on the present state and commerce of Malabar and Ceylon," fo. 14, 81.

68. VOC/OB 1293, 10 September 1662, fo. 1514–16; and see also van Goens's justification in ARA, Coll. van Goens 6, "Authentic biographical sketch of the life of Rijckloff van Goens by van Goens Jr.," fo. 4.

69. VOC/HB 4457, 12 April 1677, fo. 171. See also van Dam, *Beschrijvinge,* III, ii, p. 351.

70. G.J. Schutte, *De Nederlandse patriotten en de koloniën: een onderzoek naar hun denkbeelden en optreden* (Groningen, 1974), pp. 32–42.

71. VOC/OB 1620, Report Ketting, fo. 140.

72. VOC/RXVII 224, 1 October 1686; VOC/XVII 322, 12 June 1683, fo. 386; VOC/XVII 323, 7 September 1696.

73. VOC/OB 1512, 22 December 1692, fo. 11 vo.

74. VOC/OB 1495, Report by P. van Helsdingen, fo. 189.

75. VOC/OB 1495, Report by van Helsdingen, fo. 193; VOC/OB 1567, "Response by me, Gelmer Vosburg," fo. 360–65.

76. VOC/OB 1497, 22 December 1692, fo. 34 vo.

77. VOC/OB 1567, "Statement by Pieter van Helsdingen."

78. VOC/XVII 320, 18 October 1677.

79. UBL/BPL, 623, fo. 343.

80. Boxer, *Dutch Seaborne Empire,* p. 58; Van Dam, *Beschryvinge,* III, i, p. 395.

81. ARA, HRB, 838, Memoir Schreuder, fo. 328.

82. For example, VOC/XVII 322, 27 June 1691, fo. 638: "De pracht en overdaed nootsaeckt de ministers en suppoosten veel sijdegangen te gaen tot verval dier kosten"; see De Haan, *Oud Batavia,* ii, p. 217; Van Dam, *Beschryvinge,* III, i, p. 455; *Plakaatboek,* ii, p.111; iii, p. 47.

83. VOC/OB 1598, 30 December 1696, fo. 65.

84. VOC/OB 1598, 30 December 1696, fo. 48 vo.; for Dutch pageantry in Surat see Kolff and van Santen, *De geschriften van Francisco Pelsaert,* pp. 25, 30; and van Santen, "Verenigde Oost-Indische Compagnie," p. 11.

85. Geleynssen 102, 2 November 1645.

86. VOC/OB 1564, "Papers concerning J. van den Heuvel," fo. 1442.

87. VOC/OB 1542, "Statement on Persian accounts"; VOC/XVII 323, 1692.

88. VOC/OB 1611, Report Ketting, fo. 333 vo.

89. Gupta, "Dutch East India Company," p. 56; see for example, VOC/OB 1636, 9 March 1700, fo. 57.

90. VOC/OB 1567, "Response by me, Gelmer Vosburg," fo. 360 vo.

91. B. Stein, "Does Culture Make Practice Perfect?" in *All the King's Mana: Papers on Medieval South Indian History* (Madras, 1984), pp. 90–117.

92. See, for example, VOC/OB 1611, Report Ketting, fo. 332–37; among the bribes one would probably have to include the bottles of spirits with which the VOC habitually regaled wrathful Mughal officials and which did not figure among the "extraordinary presents."

93. VOC/OB 1476, "Diary of events during the embassy," fo. 377, 379; see Minorsky, *Tadhikarat,* p. 93, and Hotz, *Cunaeus,* p. 161.

94. For the abuses in Vengurla, see Aalders, *Rijkloff van Goens,* pp. 73, 101; VOC/OB 1224, 3 May 1658, fo. 408 vo.

95. VOC/OB 3989, 21 February 1654, fo. 314.

96. VOC/OB 3989, fo. 325–29 vo.

97. H. Terpstra, *De Nederlanders in Voor-Indië* (Amsterdam, 1947), pp. 155–169; Boxer, *Dutch Seaborne Empire,* p. 226; Lequin, "Het personeel," i, pp. 84–86.

98. VOC/XVII 321, 6 April 1685; see too van Dam, *Beschrijvinge,* II, i, p. 375.

99. Y. Nagazumi, "From Company to Individual Company Servants. Dutch Trade to Japan in the Eighteenth Century" (unpublished paper, Leiden, 1993); O. Nachod, *Die Beziehungen der niederländischen ostindischen Kompagnie zur Japan im siebzehnte Jahrhundert* (Leipzig, 1897), pp. 180–84.

100. VOC/OB 1459, "Summary of private merchandise arrived here," fo. 19–23; and in same, "Summary of all goods arrived here on private accounts."

101. VOC/OB 1649, 16 March 1701, fo. 488.

102. VOC/OB 1459, "Summary"; Van Dam, *Beschrijvinge,* III, ii, p. 139; VOC/OB 1450, "Merchandise according to the Palicat price sold here to private merchants," fo. 1170, 1175; and in same, "Merchandise with their price sold to individual servants," fo. 1190; VOC/XVII 322, 8 June 1688, fo. 62 vo.

103. VOC/OB 1450, "Extracts regarding private trade," fo. 1090.

104. Gaastra, *Bewind en beleid,* p. 314; F. Stapel, "Cornelis Janszoon Speelman," *BTLV* 94 (1936), pp. 1–122.

105. VOC/CR 9288, 20 March 1655.

106. GAR, Weeskamerarchief, 18, "Total accounts and exhaustive exposition regarding properties left by the late Cornelis Janszoon Speelman."

107. VOC/OB 1620, Report Ketting, fo. 204.

108. VOC/OB 1620, Report Ketting, fo. 208.

109. Om Prakash, *Dutch East India Company,* pp. 83–89; VOC/XVII 322, 16 November 1687, fo. 565–67; and in same, 30 September 1689, fo. 547–49; ARU, Coll. Huydecooper 621, "Writ by Hendrick Adriaenszoon van Rheede, Hugly," 15 February 1690.

110. F.S. Gaastra, "The Independent Fiscaals of the VOC," in L. Blussé, *All of One Company,* pp. 92–102; P.H.J. Veth, "H.A. van Rheede tot Drakensteyn," *De Gids* 4 (1887), pp. 120–55; Van Dam, *Beschrijvinge,* III, i, p. 136.

111. VOC/OB 1490, 10 October 1690, fo. 168 vo.

112. *Van Dam, Beschrijvinge,* III, i, p. 142.

113. Ibid., ii, p. 132. Ketting's judgment on this case, which fills many thousand folio pages in the VOC archive, was probably the least clouded by rage; see VOC/OB 1620, fo. 135–87.

114. VOC/OB 1567, "Account of van Helsdingen"; VOC/OB 1571, February 1695, fo. 246–70.

115. VOC/UB 926, "Instruction for Paulus de Rhoo," 15 July 1695, fo. 1085–1116.

116. VOC/OB 1620, "Sketch of the illness and death of the commissioner De Rhoo"; and in same, Report Ketting, fo. 208–11.

117. Van Dam, *Beschrijvinge,* II, ii, p. 174; VOC/XVII 323, 7 September 1696.

118. VOC/OB 1490, 9 October 1689, fo. 744.

119. Compare Om Prakash, "Restrictive Trading Regimes: VOC and the Asian Spice Trade in the 17th Century," in R. Ptak and D. Rothermund (eds.), *Emporia, Commodities and Entrepreneurs in Asian Maritime Trade ca. 1400–1750* (Stuttgart, 1991), pp. 120–26.

120. VOC/OB 1548, Surat resolution, 8 September 1693, fo. 337–43.

121. See, for example, VOC/OB 1507, Surat resolution, fo. 229–35; VOC/UB 837, 16 July 1694, fo. 1302.

122. See, for example, VOC/OB 1548, Surat resolution, 25 January 1693, fo. 183 vo.

123. J. Robinson, *The Economics of Imperfect Competition* (London, 1956).

124. Van Santen, "Verenigde Oost-Indische Compagnie," p. 43; University Library Utrecht, mss. 1313, "Thorough description of Surat by D. van Rheede" (1754), fo. 24.

125. VOC/OB 1659, Surat resolution, 9 May 1697, fo. 126.

126. VOC/UB 882, 21 September 1658, fo. 467, see also van Dam, *Beschryvinge,* II, iii, pp. 25–32.

127. VOC/OB 1479, 28 February 1690, fo. 47 vo.; VOC/OB 1620, Report Ketting, fo. 183 vo.; VOC/OB 1279, 27 January 1674, fo. 220–23 vo.

128. VOC/OB 1297, 2 May 1674, fo. 515–17.

129. VOC/OB 1529, Surat resolution, fo. 262–65; VOC/OB 1512, 26 January 1693, fo. 71; VOC/OB 1649, 20 January 1701, fo. 216 vo.; VOC/OB 1612, 16 January 1693, fo. 174; VOC/OB 1168, "Notice of how much director Arent Barentszoon has handed." Neither had the English a very favorable view on Resik Das: Das Gupta, *Indian Merchants,* p. 133.

130. VOC/OB 1408, "Report by commissioner Soolmans," fo. 777 vo.

131. VOC/OB 1635, 10 November 1700, fo. 289.

132. On Rustamji as English broker see Das Gupta, *Indian Merchants,* p. 81; D.L. White, "Parsis in the Commercial World of Western India," *IESHR* 24 (2) (1987), pp. 198–201; C. Das, *The Norris Embassy to Aurengzeb* (Calcutta, 1947), pp. 210–15; and on his Portuguese connections see Modi, "Rostam," pp. 143–48; P.P.S. Pissurlencar, *Portuguese Documents on Rustamji* (Bastóra, 1936), pp. xxxii; BNL, Pombalina, Cód. 439, 14 January 1698, fo. 340.

133. Van Santen, "Verenigde Oost-Indische Compagnie," p. 119.
134. VOC/OB 1425, 6 May 1686, fo. 228 vo.
135. Van Dam, *Beschrijvinge,* III, iii, pp. 40–45.
136. VOC/OB 1425, 16 December 1686, fo. 2228 vo.
137. ARA, Coll. van Ghesel 198, "Concept memoir on putting the price of spices at Surat at a fixed standard," 1703.
138. VOC/UB 922, 3 August 1692, fo. 1424–26.
139. For the marketing of Surat merchandise in North India see VOC/OB 1661, "Specification of goods available in Agra"; and the complaints of Isfahan that goods from Surat which were only 4 percent more expensive than in Agra were spoiling its market in VOC/OB 1220, 6 May 1656, fo. 712 vo.
140. "Het personeel," i, p. 93.
141. *Oost-Indisch praetje voorgevallen op Batavia tusschen vier Nederlanders* (Amsterdam [?] 1684), unpaged (Knuttel, 8756); Blussé considers this libel to be published in Batavia but since it contains allegations against both the High Government of the Indies and Gentlemen XVII, this seems unlikely.
142. Ibid.

9

# The Affairs of the English

However logical, indeed inevitable, the comparison, it is not at all easy to compare Dutch and English expansion in the Arabian seas.[1] Superficially the two great monopoly Companies, VOC and EIC, had a great deal in common. Both were chartered joint-stock Companies, independent organizations to which certain extra-territorial rights had been allotted. Hence, no other institutions interfered in their affairs, such as the navy or other companies that benefited from their trade; the board of directors of each was responsible to the shareholders and not to the minister of finance. All of this contrasted markedly with the Compagnie des Indes.

Nonetheless, there are major differences between the two. These differences concern two points: the internalization of protection cost and the degree of bureaucratic control over trade.

As to the first point: officially, in the VOC the Company alone dealt in protection whereas among the EIC the personnel did so too. And as to the second point: the EIC was not intending to achieve a monopoly from production to sale, and was organized in a less rigidly bureaucratic fashion than the VOC.

## EIC and VOC in Comparison

The national chartered Companies, the EIC and the VOC, can certainly be perceived as mercantilist institutions (as, of course, can the Compagnie des Indes).[2] Both were instruments of the state to tax traders and foster commercial interests. They served as collateral during loans of the state, in attracting investments in institutions connected to the state, and in institutionally separating national economic interests from international trading concerns.[3]

In some respects the English link to the state was more intimate than was the Dutch. As we saw, the VOC's position was never put to serious questioning in the Estates General. The EIC, on the other hand, was often but a pawn in parliamentary intrigues and in relations between court and Parliament. No doubt, too, the disturbances in England in the seventeenth century had a deeply adverse effect on the trade of the East India Company.

This vulnerability of the EIC to conflict in Parliament clearly came to the fore in 1698. Parliament then approved a loan with the right to conduct trade with Asia as collateral. The EIC could subscribe to this, but so could the rival "English Company trading to the East Indies." Parliament was not overly fond of the EIC, given its ancient royalist leanings. Moreover, it had always been closely linked to the old ring of London's Merchant Adventurers, as its full name indicated: The Company of London Merchants Trading to the East Indies.[4] Whereas most other Companies, the Levant Company principally, were increasingly opened to new investors during the restoration, the East India Company remained a closed organization. The Levant traders largely financed the new English Company and the wine merchants were involved too, for both had long resented the restriction of the oriental trade to the Merchant Adventurers. Jewish and Armenian merchants also supported the English Company.[5]

The Board of Directors instructed its servants to destroy this competitor by any means available. And the relationship between the two Companies was acrimonious indeed. To the common commercial strife were added personal feuds, as among the scions of the Pitt family, and political differences between Whigs and Tories.

At Surat, for example, the factories of the two Companies were in an open state of war—each accusing the other to the Mughal authorities of paying corsairs and selling loot. This feud harmed the entire European *natio*, however, not just the English. Again, the two Companies frantically sought to out-price each other. So the English were the laughingstock of the *banias*, "who do not want to deal anymore with this band of buffoons [*hansworsten*]."[6]

But the Board of the EIC kept its stiff upper lip throughout all this turmoil: "if the rest of the world laughs at the pain the two companies took to ruin each other, they can't help it because they are on good grounds and had a charter."[7]

As to the conflict between crown and Parliament, the crown was far from hesitant in trying to fork its favorites into positions of authority in the administration of the Company—though these were often interlopers on the Company's monopoly, like the London/Vlissingen trader W. Courteen. If the EIC tried to resist such practices, the crown might grant separate charters, as it did to Courteen.

Again, the charter of the VOC provided that it would enjoy a monopoly of power within the area covered by its charter. The rights of the EIC to construct fortresses, to strike coinage, and more such royal prerogatives were granted to the EIC by separate charters, which were not included in that of the Company. The EIC had to conduct separate negotiations to obtain them. And often these could only be obtained after lending substantial sums to the exchequer. The monarchy also reserved certain prerogatives in Asia, which were bestowed on the Company by allowance and could be withdrawn. The VOC possesed such rights *de jure*. This especially applied in Bombay, formally a crown colony leased by the East India Company.

Of course, the monopoly enjoyed by the VOC did not go uncontested, but after the grant of its charter in 1602, the charter was reaffirmed every ten years by the Estates General and hence the monopoly was officially endorsed by the central metropolitan authorities. On the other hand, the permanent charter allotted in 1657 to the East India Company was not formally endorsed by parliamentary act. Hence, the EIC could not adduce valid grounds for limiting interlopers' access to Asian markets and confiscating their properties. It could be, and was, sued at the Privy Council in that case. This might involve lengthy and expensive suits, so the Court of Directors often winked at interlopers.[8]

This can be put in a wider context: First, the East India Company represented vested authority in an age in which Englishmen were questioning the very foundations of sovereignty, as I. Bruce Watson emphasizes.[9] If the English civil war and the Glorious Revolution led to little overt conflict in the East (very much contrary to the West) Indies, it did encourage merchants of the outposts and personnel in Asia to question the right of the Board of Directors to curtail their liberty. This particularly applied during the Glorious Revolution, when the directors were supposed to be inclined toward the Royalist cause, their charter being granted by James II.[10]

Second, Englishmen never questioned the right of individuals to free trade: to English observers its curtailment by the VOC was a monstrosity, inconcievable for free Englishmen. And the EIC was not established as an instrument of war with the Portuguese, like the VOC. It was not a military and political but only a commercial body. If, as in the Dutch case, individual directors of the EIC were deeply involved in communal politics, the fairly direct intervention of communal councils in the nomination of the *bewindhebbers* does not appear to have a counterpart in England. The Board of Directors of the EIC was elected by, and responsible to, the shareholders' assembly. Gentlemen XVII, on the other hand, enjoyed a marked degree of independence from their shareholders (the *participanten*). These shareholders were partly derived from the gentry, partly from the London merchants. Parliament and boroughs had little direct influence. If one desired a say in the EIC one had to buy stock. With Parliament blocking proposals to enlarge the stock capital of the EIC, and the right to deal in stock curtailed by parliamentary act too, the Company was run by a tiny merchant elite with little direct interference from the state.[11]

The VOC was intended from its very beginning to be an instrument of national policy and a permanent enterprise.. The EIC, on the contrary, was but one of many commercial enterprises of the Merchant Adventurers. If one perceives the Dutch Voorcompagnieën as investments in a single commercial voyage, one may say that the English persevered far longer with this than did the Dutch, though with the important difference that the English always departed from London, not from several ports. The EIC, therefore, originally did not dispose of a permanent joint stock. Until 1636 stock was issued on a single trip and dividends paid per voyage. Such an investment expired after three or four years.

When this "separate stock" was amalgamated in a "joint stock" in 1656, the EIC still clung to some arrangements from the preceding period. The English system was (as was the case with the French and the Danish) less continuous than the Dutch enterprise. The trade with Asia was seen as a series of individual commercial voyages from and to Asia. The VOC thus split its accountancy system between revenues obtained by the regional chambers in the Dutch Republic and the Asian account, while the EIC did not.[12]

Unlike the Compagnie des Indes, the Portuguese crown, and the VOC, the EIC did not construct ships itself but leased them from consortia of shipowners (or ship husbands). They were sometimes directors of the Company, but the shipping interest was a group separate from the Company. Such vessels were insured separately, whereas VOC ships were collectively insured. This was probably a key reason why the English were less prone to institute a convoy system than was the VOC. If the VOC lost a ship, the Company would thenceforth be charged a higher insurance premium.[13]

Different from the VOC too—but like the Compagnie des Indes—departing fleets were seen as individual commercial voyages. Ships were provided with a supercargo who had to look after purchases and sales of merchandise. One did not differentiate between the trade with Europe and the trade in Asia. If an English ship, for instance, made a voyage within Asia to fetch freight, the returns were booked on the accountancy of the voyage. Among the Dutch, on the other hand, these were charged to either the central accounts of Batavia or those of the factory concerned.

The Court of Directors named the English personnel on the basis of a recommendation by an official of the Company or a stockholder. There was generally a host of candidates for a single position. So, the EIC appears to have engaged fewer foreigners than did the Dutch. Captains were examined for nautical skills, personnel ashore for skills in accounting and writing. The Dutch did not do this formally. But more important than any formal qualification was that in the EIC individuals had to pay a very high bail for a recommendation, sums that appear to have increased throughout the century. And personnel were generally selected on the basis of such a recommendation. Individuals were sent for a four-year period as "writer" to Asia, and later advanced to assistant, merchant, and chief merchant. Anyone who was so fortunate as to survive—no mean accomplishment—would be automatically promoted to a higher rank and salary. However, obtaining a profitable position too meant obtaining another recommendation, and this was an expensive affair. This was not so among the Dutch. Although many a candidate probably gave a few pennies to a *bewindhebber* of a regional chamber for a position, it was never a formally acknowledged system.[14]

So this was institutionalized corruption *avant la lettre*. But then, England's administrative system was generally styled "Old Corruption" too. As E.P. Thompson put it, it was "a sophisticated system of brigandage which, though conducted upon so gigantic a scale, was bound to congeal into something resembling an estate"—or a Company, one might add.[15] The personnel in Asia were forthrightly corrupt. But London was little concerned about this as long as they "christened the Company's child first"—sent profitable merchandise to England. No doubt the skinning of the soldiers by their own officers did lead to Keigwin's rebellion at Bombay in 1683. Differences over who would reach the trough first led to prolonged quarrels among the personnel as well; such infighting was as acrimonious as among the VOC servants. And this occurred both within the factories and between the boards of the presidencies, like between Madras and Bengal, or, in the 1670s, between the officials at Madras and those at Bombay.

"I employ the cursedest villain that ever was in the world, and see him cheat me before my face, but then he is a most dextrous, indefatigable fellow in business, which makes me such amends, that I can afford to bear with it."[16] Thus wrote T. Pitt of his Indian servants, a view the directors would undoubtedly have echoed regarding theirs. For the Company's personnel dextrously promoted its private trade rather than that of the Company—private trade from Surat to Persia, for example, "has raised some of your servants to great fortunes," J. Blackman asserted—but reduced others to beggary.[17] Until 1666 private trade was officially forbidden but, Blackman alleged, the servants earned far too little to induce them to desist from it. Anyway, the Company was unable to forestall it. They were unable to thoroughly search ships in intra-Asian trade or seize cargoes. The English servants commonly peddled the flag to Indian ships as well. "These flags are really mostly employed to dodge the customs the Company raises on imported merchandise," the VOC thought. Unlike the *bewindhebbers* the Board of Directors gradually came to terms with the inevitable, and permitted free trade within Asia.[18]

And with its institutionalized system of patronage the EIC allowed ample leeway for private trade. Bails were obviously to be repaid by subsequent earnings. This was partly to the advantage of the Company, for funds gathered thus were invested in loans of the Company. Therefore, it disposed of ample financial means in Asia to engage mercenaries, invest in goods, or lease taxes and farm ports.

Hence, in spite of the many abuses and the profuse possibilities thereto, which only began to concern the public in the eighteenth century, the corruptibility of the servants did not do notable harm to the English. The communities (including the assembly of the planters at St. Helena) and courts of justices enjoyed considerable autonomy and could declare the worst misappropriations to Parliament or the Privy Council. Furthermore, the administrative apparatus was decentralized so that each presidency's greed kept the others in balance. If Madras tried to favor its own personnel, for instance by keeping the right to trade in China to its own, this would duly lead to protest by Calcutta.[19]

Even more importantly, perquisites from office were invested in trade. English servants invested on the stock exchanges or in banks in Asia or bought land. What accumulated was English capital, not the number of positions, for the Court of Directors kept a tight reign upon the number of offices created. And, indeed, compared to its French or Dutch counterparts the English Company was undermanned.

Due to this very English policy of benign neglect the English created administrative institutions by custom and precedent rather than formally instituting them. The Dutch, the Portuguese, and the French possessed a hierarchical structure of government *de forma*, the English only *de facto*. For, unlike the VOC, the EIC did not look upon Europe and Asia as two different branches of the Company's operations. The staff in Asia was supposed merely to take care of purchases and sales for Europe. There was thus no centralized board of government in Asia like the High Government of the Indies or, to an extent, the Conseil Souvereign at Pondicherry. Furthermore, unlike the VOC (but like the Compagnie des Indes) the EIC regarded itself as a trade organization. Completely unlike the VOC too, the EIC did not have extensive territorial possessions, and those few colonies (Bombay and St. Helena) were seen as a liability rather than an asset.[20] But lest one argue that the EIC was truly an "empire of trade"—not a merchant warrior like the VOC—one has to add the important and partly separate position of the army.

For, as S.G. Webb has asserted, the British empire was in both the seventeenth and the eighteenth centuries not only a commercial but also a military enterprise.[21] Its colonies comprised both the familiar trade settlements, operated by chartered companies, and a very different—and often overlooked—"Ulster model" of garrison towns controlled by military governors appointed by the crown. Webb's model of military settlements from which some commerce might be conducted may be contrasted to the older model of British expansion by merchants and companies.

And, to some extent, this applies to Asia as well: there was a separate army of the crown in the East Indies that was not subordinate to the interest of the Company. Some settlements—Bombay, St. Helena, and Bencoolen—were garrisons with a demand dictated by military exigencies rather than commercial ones. And, once garrisons of the crown and a naval establishment were stationed at Bombay and St. Helena, military exigencies tended to develop an impetus of their own. The troops had to be supplied at any cost, which involved extensive participation in coastwise navigation to fetch those stores. They had to be defended against the French and pirates as well. This implied the extension of the Admiralty's jurisdiction to the dominion of the EIC and increasing activity of the Royal Navy in eastern seas at the turn of the seventeenth century.

Yet trade had always been linked to the use of force. Servants of the Company would, when entangled in conflicts with local authorities, plead for the use of the military means of the Company. This could already be said for the blockade of Surat in 1612 or that of Aden in 1610. The latter is an interesting case. It was not instituted by the directors, and arose out of a purely local quarrel between the English director and the sultan of Aden.[22] And a pattern of spiraling demands for military support with the growth of trade can be demonstrated for the entire course of the century, evolving from local quarrels right up to the war with the Mughal empire. Privileges bestowed on the EIC would also benefit private traders—often not the case with the VOC. If the English traders benefited from their possession of free conducts or *dastak*s, they used, or rather abused, a right forcibly extorted by the Company's arms.[23]

This was not acknowledged by the Board of Directors until the end of the seventeenth century. The servants, the EIC reasoned, were mere merchants. The administrative and political arrangement was subordinate to the trade. Yet by 1700 there arose a territorial structure of rule. This was never formally instituted; it had evolved more or less accidentally. It is, therefore, not easy to compare the VOC's administrative structure with that of the English. Decisions were in the EIC's case taken not by administrative bodies with a firmly established competence but rather by informal dealings and improvised committees. This was the case in Europe as well. The tangled web of committees operating the EIC in the eighteenth century (committee of correspondence, committee of shipping, private trade, etc.) had been improvised from informal meetings of the directors rather than formally established.[24]

The English distinguished three presidencies: Bengal, Madras, and Bombay. These were administered by the president in council, who was named by nomination by the board of a settlement, by the Board of Directors of the EIC. Factories resorting under the presidencies enjoyed a considerable degree of autonomy.

Since the EIC had, as mentioned, no formal institutions of government, the judiciary also arose gradually. Initially the director administered justice. Upon the acquisition of Bombay the English were faced with the problem of having to rule over the Portuguese and Indian communities there. Thus, three courts of justice were established, presided over by a member of the board of the presidency. Very different from the Dutch, the English based their administrative practices upon presumed local self-government. They did so partly since it was cheaper, partly to hush up the protests of the Portuguese communities living under English law.[25]

Hence, the community could elect the bailiffs and civil cases were tried on the basis of their customary law. As in the Dutch case, the Board of Directors named parsons. The EIC did not do any missionary work. By creating institutions by precedent it was easier for the English to integrate Indian institutions within their administrative system than it was for the Dutch, who in Ceylon, for example, judged cases according to modified Roman law.[26] I should add, though, that at Cochin cases involving Christians under the jurisdiction of the Company were also brought before the rajah's court, "advised" by the Dutch, and not before the board of the Company. This arrangement was roughly comparable to the English *mofusil* courts.

However, after the largely unsuccessful war with the Mughal empire, there was a shift in this policy of benign neglect. So far London had financed the fortresses and troops in the presidencies, scantily and grudgingly, but now the Board of Directors concluded the presidencies should seek their own incomes—by customs and land revenues. For the land revenue was "a well-grounded revenue," as the president of the Board, J. Childe, wrote, quite unlike the unpredictable income from intra-Asian trade. "The sure foundation for a large and well-grounded English dominion in India for all times to come," Childe stressed in a famous—and in retrospect, ominous—phrase.[27]

This was by then a major income from the VOC too, and Childe indeed exhorted the Board of Directors to learn from the "wise Dutch."[28] Yet in the English case this revenue was to be obtained through the taxation of private trade, whereas the VOC often forestalled the trade of its subjects. This might cause a decline of its tax revenue.

## The Rise of English Country Trade

The profits on the English private trade and the sale of offices were invested in an English credit circuit in Asia, in which Indian bankers invested as well. To be sure, the growth of English banking in India in the seventeenth and especially the eighteenth centuries can partly be explained by the improvement of techniques of credit and trade, like the advancements in the use of bills of exchange negotiable to third parties, and of insurance.

But there were among the other Europeans—except the French in the eighteenth century—no institutions comparable to the English agency houses. These were commercial and banking houses, generally based on joint-stock capital, that dealt in bills and in monetary transactions, or organized commercial voyages. They were taking care of money from legacies or invested by departing merchants of the EIC. This system of obtaining funds was one of the main instruments for the expansion of British trade and shipping in the second half of the eighteenth century, which—with due cause—is often styled the "era of the agency house."[29]

By way of comparison: in the late seventeenth century it was common that inheritances of Portuguese traders were to be used for trade in Asia, and Portuguese *moradores* often named agents to invest such funds in merchandise.[30] However, the development of such practices was curtailed by the role of both the church and the *misericórdia*. Portuguese subjects were required by law until 1685 to deposit estates in the *misericórdia*. The Santa Casa received a 2 percent benefit. The *provedores* as a rule tended to invest this in commerce—not always to the best effect, for they often gambled away entire inheritances. This virtually blocked the rise of agency houses in the Estado. The system was abolished later on, but the church was still a major competitor to private bankers.[31]

Again, banking at Batavia was predominantly controlled by servants of the Company, and to a lesser extent by the Chinese; the Company tended to cream off investments by systematically offering higher interests.

From such funds the English financed a flourishing private trade: a "country trade" that may surely be perceived as paramount to the rise of the British empire in Asia. Holden Furber, P.J. Marshall, and other writers have demonstrated how in the eighteenth century English country trade came to dominate shipping in the Indian Ocean, and how the ever-inflating demands for protecting the interest of the country traders dragged the British state along in a colonial enterprise.[32]

In the seventeenth century the English private trade was less sizeable than the intra-Asian trade of the VOC. But, unlike the latter, it was involved in direct competition with Indian traders. Hence, English country trade often had a more profound impact upon the shipping in the Indian Ocean than the intra-Asian trade of the VOC.

In general, one can say that the VOC after 1656 desisted from conducting intra-Asian trade over short distances, such as between Surat and Bandar Abbas, Vengurla, or Mocha. Fetching goods instead of carrying freight over such short distances, Gentlemen XVII argued, "has only been a burden for the Company and a boost for private trade." The EIC retreated from these branches of traffic after 1660 too. But English private traders specifically devoted themselves to this.[33]

Moreover, the VOC mainly dealt in products on which a high profit could assuredly be obtained. The VOC also sold Indian commodities, like textiles and sugar, in the Arabian seas. But the backbone of its commerce in the seventeenth century—not in the eighteenth, but that is a different story—was formed by monopoly goods, in which it alone traded, such as Japanese copper, Banka tin, Javanese (earlier Taiwanese) sugar, sandalwood, Javanese pepper, and, of course, spices. Thus the English private traders and the Dutch were to an extent covering a different segment of the market.

For the English sold products that competed directly with Indian traders, like Siamese tin, Philippine or Bengali sugar in Surat, Canara and Malabar pepper, and Indian textiles in Persia. On some routes (as in shipping to the Philippines) they gradually forced Indian traders out of the market. Investments of merchants under English protection penetrated the bulk goods trade of the Arabian seas too.

Two causes for the rapid expansion of the country trade in the eighteenth century already played a role in the seventeenth. First, one could freely establish oneself in settlements controlled by the EIC. Through the liberty one enjoyed there, coupled with the protection of the EIC, Madras rapidly evolved from a hamlet to a major trade center, for example.

But there was a high price tag attached to this protection; only a very few wealthy merchants could afford English support. According to the Count of Villa Verde, customs were 6 percent at Madras plus anchor dues; in Masulipatam and Cuddalore, which were under close supervision by Mughal authorities, 5 percent; but at the free ports of San Thomé and Porto Novo only 2 percent.[34] "This is a major attraction to merchants." Finally, at the VOC port of Negapatnam customs were 10 percent. Moreover, the customs of Madras were farmed, and tax farmers often tried to squeeze merchants—to such an extent that in 1719 the inhabitants were said to have fled Madras in droves.[35] There was a clear niche for free ports, then. Even English traders might register ship and freight in "interloper ports" like San Thomé, which were spared the "benefit" of the EIC's protection.

In view of this, S. Arasaratnam has argued that the growth of Madras in the seventeenth century has been overrated and that the protection of the Company was hardly a factor involved in this growth. Officials of the EIC hence as much oppressed the inhabitants of Madras as did those in Mughal ports—proof, if any was necessary, that corruption was a common problem in the seventeenth century.[36]

Yet the High Government of the Indies, certainly an unbiased source, also registered its amazement at the rapid expansion of Madras in 1687.[37] There seems to be no reason to question the English boasts about the flourishing trade conducted by Madras then.[38] For settling in free ports was risky—given the unsettled political conditions on the coast. And—whatever the taxes there—Madras still contrasted favorably with both Tuticorin and Pulicat, controlled by the VOC. There most of the population was deserting the towns, partly to Madras, mainly since they were not only vexed by customs and heavy taxation but harassed by erratic prohibitions to trade in, or even to manufacture goods as well.[39]

A second cause for the rapid expansion of trade was that the EIC permitted every servant to engage in trade within Asia. The navigation to Europe was reserved for the Company but passengers and crew on the Indiamen might take some goods to and from Asia. Armenian and Jewish dealers were allotted special permits to take goods along on English ships to and from Asia as well. This was confirmed by treaty between the Armenian *natio* resident at London and the EIC.

In contrast to this, the VOC in 1687 permitted Jewish merchants to fetch goods to Asia. A comparable request of the Armenians in Amsterdam was considered by Gentlemen XVII in 1699 but turned down. The Armenians demanded that a ship be specially chartered to sail to Hugly and Persia to fetch merchandise. This entailed unacceptable risks. And one feared too, rightly, that these merchants mainly fetched private goods of VOC servants to the Netherlands.[40]

Since K.N. Chaudhuri has treated the trade of the EIC with Europe in exhaustive detail I will not dwell on this theme. One should, however, keep its expansion after 1662 in mind. The trade of the EIC between India—and after 1686 China—and London increased more rapidly than that with Amsterdam.

As mentioned, the English ships, unlike those of the VOC and of the Portuguese, and like the French, did not depart to Europe in convoys from a central rendezvous (like Goa, or Batavia and Gale) but mostly directly from the anchorages where ships were loaded. In order to safeguard shipping the crown regularly sent squadrons of the navy to Asia, whereas Bombay in 1674 bought two frigates to protect English coastal trade.[41]

### *English Shipping and Shipbuilding*

A puzzling question in the literature on country trade is whether English vessels had certain advantages over Asian ships.[42]

In general, country vessels had a minimum of crew and a maximum of cargo. Ships of the Compagnie des Indes, by contrast, were often manned by wartime crews, and with good reason: French ships had to run the gauntlet of British corsairs. Ships of the EIC, apart from the necessary crew, also had troops and servants aboard. Gentlemen XVII insisted that a ship engaged in intra-Asian trade should have a maximum crew of 50 men for frigates and 90 for the largest flutes: but they often carried twice as many. Batavia discussed the matter but did not agree with the *bewindhebbers'* criticism. The ships should have sufficient crew to defend themselves against pirates and to bring cargo rapidly on board (especially necessary in the trade with Cambodia and Sima and in the wood trade), as well as to do repair work to the keels at their place of destination.[43]

As evinced by Tables 9.1 and 9.2, country trade ships also had smaller crews than Indian ships. Surat's vessels generally had more crew than European ones, for instance. These sails often were passenger ships, carrying pilgrims and mercenaries instead of merchandise: the large Mughal vessels had a 150- to 170-man crew and 300 to 400 passengers. Moreover, the sailors of these ships were allowed to take some freight along, "to benefit their family," which they could sell at the destination. As sailors were largely remunerated thus, there was no need to economize on the strength of the crew.[44]

In addition, *nakhuda*s of Indian ships were men of dignity. They were wont to take a large number of retainers along, even if this did not benefit the effective compliance with tasks aboard.[45]

Basically, the major advantage enjoyed by the shipping of the country traders was that they benefited both from the advantages of the Companies and of Asian shipping. As Haagsch Besoigne summarized the letters from Malacca:

Table 9.1

**English Ships Touching at Malacca, 1677–1699**

| Place of departure | Year | Ships | Crew | Guns | Size in tons |
|---|---|---|---|---|---|
| Madras | 1677 | 3 | | | |
| Persia | 1677 | 1 | | | |
| Surat | 1677 | 1 | | | |
| Madras | 1681 | 2 | 43 | 12 | 190 |
| Surat | 1681 | 2 | 60 | 12 | 350 |
| Bombay | 1681 | 1 | 50 | 12 | 200 |
| Atjeh | 1684 | 1 | 21 | 14 | 100 |
| Bengal | 1684 | 2 | 34 | 11 | 300 |
| Surat | 1684 | 1 | 40 | 12 | 340 |
| Madras | 1685 | 2 | 43 | 8 | 240 |
| England | 1685 | 2 | 42 | 18 | 450 |
| Masulipatam | 1685 | 1 | 28 | 10 | 200 |
| Bengal | 1685 | 1 | 30 | 4 | 120 |
| Surat | 1685 | 1 | 60 | 14 | 360 |
| Balasore | 1686 | 2 | 25 | 13 | 320 |
| Visiaganapatnam | 1686 | 1 | 25 | 6 | 120 |
| Madras | 1686 | 4 | 38 | 20 | 232 |
| England and Bencoolen | 1686 | 1 | 25 | 12 | 140 |
| Bengal | 1687 | 2 | 30 | 8 | 180 |
| Surat | 1687 | 3 | 45 | 10 | 250 |
| Surat | 1695 | 3 | 65 | 13 | 300 |
| Madras | 1695 | 4 | 40 | 17 | 230 |
| Bombay | 1695 | 1 | 50 | 25 | 180 |
| Johore | 1696 | 2 | 20 | 4 | 70 |
| Surat | 1696 | 3 | 26 | 12 | 156 |
| Madras | 1696 | 3 | 52 | 18 | 360 |
| Atjeh | 1696 | 1 | 17 | | 24 |
| Atjeh | 1697 | 2 | 31 | 17 | 130 |
| Surat | 1697 | 1 | 60 | 12 | 250 |
| Madras | 1697 | 4 | 32 | 8 | 90 |
| Surat | 1699 | 1 | 60 | 28 | 250 |
| England | 1699 | 1 | 40 | 16 | 340 |
| Pulicat | 1699 | 1 | 160 | 13 | 300 |
| Madras | 1699 | 1 | 46 | 14 | 180 |
| Atjeh | 1699 | 1 | 30 | 6 | 100 |

| Total ships | Average crew size | Average no. guns | Average size |
|---|---|---|---|
| 63 | 43 | 13 | 220 |

Table 9.2

**Indian Ships Touching at Malacca, 1677–1696**

| Place of departure | Year | Ships | Crew | Guns | Size in tons |
|---|---|---|---|---|---|
| Mocha | 1677 | 1 | | | |
| Balasore | 1677 | 1 | | | |
| Cuddalore | 1677 | 1 | | | |
| Surat | 1681 | 1 | 38 | 4 | 200 |
| Porto Novo | 1681 | 1 | 100 | 3 | 200 |
| Tranquebar | 1681 | 1 | 40 | 4 | 400 |
| Surat | 1683 | 1 | 90 | 15 | 400 |
| Hugly | 1683 | 2 | 90 | 9 | 450 |
| Madras | 1683 | 1 | 40 | 7 | 200 |
| Hugly | 1684 | 1 | | | |
| Balasore | 1684 | 2 | 83 | 6 | 400 |
| Pulicat | 1686 | 1 | 80 | 14 | 250 |
| Hugly | 1686 | 1 | 70 | 4 | 250 |
| Surat | 1686 | 4 | 90 | 13 | 300 |
| Madras | 1686 | 2 | 90 | 8 | |
| Porto Novo | 1687 | 2 | 85 | 0 | 220 |
| Tranquebar | 1687 | 1 | 60 | 4 | 400 |
| Balasore | 1687 | 1 | 70 | 4 | 200 |
| Cuddalore | 1694 | 2 | 60 | 3 | 150 |
| Surat | 1694 | 4 | 32 | 12 | 360 |
| Madras | 1694 | 1 | 45 | 5 | 486 |
| Pulicat | 1695 | 1 | 70 | 0 | 100 |
| Surat | 1695 | 2 | 50 | 12 | 400 |
| Surat | 1696 | 4 | 85 | 16 | 400 |
| Pulicat | 1696 | 1 | 70 | 0 | 100 |
| Cuddalore | 1696 | 1 | 100 | 3 | 130 |

| | | Total ships | Average crew size | Average no. guns | Average size |
|---|---|---|---|---|---|
| | | 41 | 70 | 7 | 280 |

> As regards the English, one has to remember that in the Indies they are considered as little different from the Moors. For theirs are not Company ships but mostly ships of private traders, who live at Madraspatam under their jurisdiction. They are generally manned with indigenous sailors and mariners.[46]

Neither the VOC's nor the Compagnie des Indes' ships enjoyed the advantages of Indian shipping. The VOC experienced a certain aversion to leaving the good care of its expensive bottoms to Indian mariners, for instance. They were often insufficiently trained and were thought lazy.[47] Apart from this, fear of mutiny may have played a role too. And this was with some justification, for there are cases of mutinies of Indonesian sailors on record.[48] Ships of the Compagnie des Indes rarely had Asian crews on board either.

English ships engaging in country trade, on the other hand, were largely manned by *lascarins*, an English helmsman, supercargo, boatswain, and a few British sailors. Since a *lascarin* was paid much less than a European sailor, and generally took his own food and clothes along, it was advantageous to man ships with Indians. Taking bottomry insured against risks.

Furthermore, intra-Asian shipping of the VOC was linked to a tight seasonal pattern, basically dependent upon the rhythm of the return fleet. One had to have ships and goods ready in a timely way. By contrast, country trade vessels could tramp from one port to another to look for profitable cargoes or transactions, typical of Indian coastwise navigation. In the Gulf, for example, empty vessels of the VOC anchored at Bandar Abbas could not proceed to Kung or to Muscat, as the English normally did, to fetch some freight because the cargo of silk, awaited from Isfahan, had to be delivered to Batavia on time.[49]

What costs were normally involved in intra-Asian trade? To rent a ship in Surat for a voyage to Basra of 300 tons and with a 45-man crew consisting of Indian sailors would require 15,000 rupees in 1683. The crew cost in total 4,000—partly paid before the trip, partly after its completion. The profit of the trip was estimated at 6,000 rupees. Insurance of the cargo would cost another 600 rupees. Net profit would, thus, average 23 percent—too low a percentage to tempt the VOC to undertake such a voyage.

Again, in 1682 it would cost 13,000 rupees to rent a vessel of 500 tons for a trip to Mocha. This could be manned with Indian sailors for 3,000 rupees. The insurance of the ship would come to about 700 rupees and the additional costs at Mocha to 1,400. The profit of the trip would be about 5,000 rupees; on freight one might gain about 5,000.[50] So, if the profit on some routes of intra-Asian trade with Indian ships—like the trip from China to Madras—was considerable, the average benefit of voyages within the Arabian seas might be estimated at 30–40 percent at most. This was far too little for the Company.

The difference between the shipping of the Companies and that of country traders was one between two different institutional systems. Through the large scale of their procurement the Companies generally sustained higher expenditures than private traders did. The Companies therefore required high profits to see any investment as rewarding. But the economy of scale of the Companies could also lower the overhead costs. Thus, for example, at Pulicat the VOC bought piece-cloth at a 35 percent higher rate than the country traders did. But—unlike the country traders, who paid cash—the VOC bartered this cloth for Asian merchandise and in order to sell substantial quantities of goods they had to pay a higher price for textiles.[51]

Where did the ships for use in the country trade in the seventeenth century derive from? Some Indiamen were, after being used for a considerable time in intra-Asian trade, sold to country traders. But after 1674 the EIC mainly confined its activities to sailing between London and Asia. The Indiamen were sent directly to their destination, loaded, and sent back to England. For some Asian routes old Indiamen were used, particularly those routes with a considerable danger of piracy, like the stretch from Surat to China, for which heavily armed vessels were needed. Most sails used in intra-Asian shipping were not built in England, however.

The English sometimes bought ships of other European powers in Asia. In the forties W. Geleynssen—then director of Persia—thought his English counterpart was mainly using old Portuguese ships to carry on his affairs in Asia. The English country traders occasionally bought ships at Manila too. On the other hand, the Portuguese now and then bought English vessels too—as did the Spanish in Manila.[52]

As far as I can track the matter down (neither Bruce Watson nor Coates deals with it at any length) the development of English shipping in Asia can be summarized as follows: Until about 1654 the EIC servants used Indiamen for intra-Asian shipping, which remained for several seasons in Asia.[53] This was mainly financed by freighting cargo of Indian merchants.[54] But English trade was outnumbered and outclassed by the VOC's competition, and it spawned constant conflict between the Board of Directors and the personnel in Asia on how to use of the holds of the expensive Indiamen. Most of the supposed Indian freight consisted of goods used for the private trade of the servants, whereas London did have to pay for those ships.

When private trade was officially allowed in 1663, Indiamen were mainly used in shipping to England and to fetch bullion, servants, and troops to the factories. Intra-Asian shipping and trade was done in Indian vessels, leased by the English or provided with the colors. After 1674 the EIC concentrated on trade with Europe (and later between India and China) while the personnel now began to construct sails on the subcontinent itself.

These crafts were initially mainly built at Narsapur and Madapullam on the Coromandel Coast, where there was an ancient tradition of ship construction. Later on, the English also had ships built on the Hugly, and occasionally bought and manufactured them at Surat.[55] G. Aungier, the governor of Bombay, explained:

> We doe find many reasons inducing us to build the shipping in this country, where tymber, iron worke, carpenters are very cheape. The building farre more substantial than in England, and more proper for these parts, in regard they will require noe sheeting and chalking more than the decks.[56]

Were ships built in India cheaper than ships constructed in Europe, then? The answer to this question depends upon which country one is talking about and which use of the ships one is considering.

Galleons built at Goa would in the 1630s cost about 35,000 to 40,000 xeraphins, those built at Cochin only 25,000. This was less than half of the price of Lisbon. However, the difference in price was offset by the time involved when building a ship in India: it might take up to two years, and at Bassein three and more. In addition, steel, iron, and wood were delivered to the crown by monopoly contractors who charged inflated prices and often delivered inferior quality. This, surely, was a further cause for the terrible rate of loss to shipwreck visiting the Portuguese.[57]

The VOC, on the other hand, repeatedly tried to construct vessels of up to 300 tons at Pulicat and Negapatam. These were intended to fetch goods between the factories. Gentlemen XVII soon ordered the Coromandel Coast to cease such construction: in 1692 it was even prohibited to build ships in Asia larger than 180 tons at all. This was partly intended to forestall competition with the shipbuilding in the Netherlands and partly because vessels constructed on the Coromandel Coast proved to be more expensive than vessels built at home. Gentlemen XVII were not especially enthusiastic about the rope made on the Coromandel Coast, and the quality of steel and metalwork forged there, as it was considered too brittle for use in repairing return ships.[58]

What has been said here for Coromandel applies to other parts of India too. Although the Portuguese had constructed *carreira da Índia* vessels at Cochin, the VOC used the wharves there merely for repairs—occasionally to build small sails engaged in coastwise shipping. But this was costlier than in Java, for wood from Java or from Pegu (Burma) was much cheaper. Even in the nineteenth century, ships built on the Hugly were still more expensive than those constructed on the Tames or in Rangoon.[59]

But due to the use of teakwood and the chalk with which they were sheēted Indian ships lasted longer than European ones. Whereas even in the nineteenth century, Indiamen could withstand tropical heat for five or six years at best, ships built at Surat or Bassein "will last in these seas for fifteen or even unto twenty-five years."[60] That Indian ships needed fewer repairs than European ones was not a very important consideration for the intra-Asian trade of the VOC. Since the repair of ships was booked on the accountancy of the Netherlands, vessels were free in Asia. But it was an important matter for the English traders. In the long run English country trade had, thus, a more advantageous cost structure than Dutch intra-Asian trade.[61]

If British ships were mostly built in India, did English vessels enjoy the advantage of heavier armament, or were they better constructed than those of indigenous traders? The latter seems improbable, for Indian vessels constructed at Surat were, at the end of the seventeenth century, precise copies of those built in the European manner. "If their models were as fine as those of the English, of whom they especially prefer the imitation, there would be no exaggeration in averring that they build incomparably the best ships in the world," E. Gosse pointed out.[62]

C.N. Parkinson has argued that Indian vessels were built to look like European vessels, since pirates were rather bound to respect European sails than *grabs* or *bombaras*.[63] This seems a good argument: more recent authors often tend to overlook the importance of the threat of piracy to shipping and shipbuilding in the Arabian seas. Piracy was as much an everyday risk to be reckoned with as a storm.

And when assaulting a European vessel one could count on retaliation by the European navies, or by the VOC. This did not make country trade immune to attacks by corsairs, but it was safer to load cargo on European than on indigenous ships. At Surat in 1701 skippers engaged in country trade could ask 2 percent more freight than the average shipowner and 1 percent more than Abdul Ghafur's captains could.[64]

That was perhaps because Abdul Ghafur's vessels were as well provided with guns as were vessels of the Company and Abdul Ghafur would fine or punish sailors who had not given a good account of themselves. But if these big vessels had as many guns as European sails, this does not imply that they were as well defended. To tie and move the guns appears to have been a problem on Indian keels. A. Das Gupta also argues there was insufficient space on these often overloaded and overmanned crafts for the ammunition trolleys to pass freely.[65] This is possible. The ships from Basra were indeed carrying many "Moorish women with their husbands and infinite treasures," but not every vessel was overcrowded. The inferior quality of Indian rope may have contributed to this too. More importantly, Indian steel tended to break when subjected to heavy stress.[66] For example, according to G. Willemsen, the guns of Muscati ships were more a peril to the sailors than to the enemy since they regularly exploded. And this concerns Muscat—the only Asian fleet that in the seventeenth century engaged a European naval power in combat on the open sea. Whatever the main cause, large Indian ships were often easily disabled by much smaller and less well gunned buccaneers.[67]

### ***Privileges to the Company as Private Benefits***

Thus, both at sea and ashore the country trade benefited from the protection of the EIC. At sea a country trade vessel was secured by the EIC without having to pay for a navicert. Obviously too, a vessel flying the Union Jack was less likely to be seized by the VOC, the Danes, or the Portuguese—a risk not to be taken lightly when sailing to Malacca, for example. On land the Companies benefited from various advantages of which the average Asian merchant did not dispose. This was no minor benefit at Bandar Abbas, for example, where EIC ships did not have to pay the hefty customs, only consulate dues of 4 percent when smuggling the goods under a British name.[68]

But also where this was not expressly stipulated, the Companies often paid lower customs than Indian traders did. For instance, at Mocha in 1700 the Companies and the country traders paid 3 percent customs; freight cost Abdul Ghafur 1 percent, other Muslims 2 percent, and other traders 6 percent. The Europeans and traders from Kerala could, however, have goods weighed on their own scales. Since customs officials often tampered with the weights to gain a few pennies, this entailed a 1–2 percent advantage.[69]

Important, too, was that goods bought in the interior by English private traders were protected by the Company. In Bengal and Persia the Company granted free permits (*dastaks*) to fetch goods without paying customs to Kasimbazar or Isfahan. English traders sold such *dastaks* to Indian traders, both in Bengal and in Persia, where this constituted a major income of the factory. The Persian broker sold *dastaks* as well, which embroiled the English factory in lengthy disputes with the court. Likewise, *dastaks* were widely used in the trade in Awadh and the Doab. Here too, the English sold such concessions to Armenian traders. If only because of such advantages, it was a profitable proposition to register one's freight as English.[70]

It would thus seem attractive to subscribe to the theory of the "creative poverty" of the English, which has been proposed by D.K. Basset.[71] By this is meant that the English had to seize any minor advantage of trade, as they disposed of far less capital than the VOC. The possession of the monopoly products, on which some profit was always obtained, had made the VOC "lazy." But although one can support this argument until 1657 the English were thereafter, if perhaps creative, certainly not indigent. Not only private trade, and that of the EIC with Europe, increased but also England's trade in general, by which vast reserves of capital were accumulated in the City of London.

And through the clientele system of the directors, country trade was linked to the city. To mention some examples from the nineties: T. Pitt, president of Madras, had outfitted four ships on his account to sail between Madras, the Philippines, and Bengal; from Bengal via Madras to Mocha; and from Madras to Anjengo and Surat. Pitt was linked with various important families in the city and the American colonies. E. Yale, with whom he was closely collaborating, had not only invested in diamonds, an estate, art, and an endowment of a seminary (named after him), but also the stock exchange. Yale's uncle in London was, during their absence in Asia, taking care of the interests of both. Pitt participated in trade with other servants of the EIC throughout Asia, like J. Gayer at Telicherry and W. Hedges at Calcutta. Gayer entertained his proper network in turn. A. Hamilton, free skipper, worked for Gayer, for instance. With funds provided to him by the former he navigated between Surat and Manila, and from Telicherry to Muscat.[72]

One could not successfully conduct trade in Asia without reliance on Europe. As evinced by the proceedings of the court of Madras, which have been examined in detail by Arasaratnam,[73] English businessmen were linked by their Indian counterparts to the credit of their employer. The personnel of the Company was seen as the *vakil* of their king in England, and—as mentioned—a *vakil* disposed of considerable freedom of action. Private traders involved in suits with Indian merchants could at least count on the judicial support of the EIC. This was no minor advantage since the Europeans had often been allotted prerogatives in the recovery of debts over other nations. But sometimes the Company's treasure at Madras also supported the private transactions of servants there.

If this was already the case at Madras, which was under fairly tight scrutiny by England, it was more so at Surat and Bombay. There, director G. Oxenden overtly used bullion from the Company's treasury to invest in his own shipping. This was an abuse Oxenden was ready to acknowledge. It was better that trade was carried on by Mr. Oxenden than that there was no English trade at all. Portions of the EIC cargoes were bought at Surat through the proceeds of Mr. Oxenden's deals. The credit enjoyed by the EIC provided English country traders with highly effective collateral. Therefore, English traders could often pay lower interest rates than Indian merchants.[74]

The causes for the success of the country trade can be sought in the combination of the very effective protection provided by the EIC (and the admiralty) and its creditworthiness. The EIC did not burden its servants' private trade with protection rent but discounted it in the price of goods sold in Europe and the payments to the shareholders of the Company. This became the rule after the abolition of the separate stock, when dividends were curtailed to account for the costs of the establishments in Asia—not much to the pleasure of the shareholders, one might imagine.[75]

As to the commercial practices in use, English country trade did not differ very much from trade habitual among Dutch free burghers or Portuguese *casados*. But, although the Portuguese influence is undeniable, the English were not just doing what the Portuguese had done before them. The East India Company to a larger extent protected English mercantile communities more than Portugal protected the *casados*. This was not only the case along the Coromandel Coast, where the Estado had only a factory, no military contingent. In Gujarat as well there is little proof that the Portuguese crown directly intervened to support the *casados* in Cambay, whereas English country traders at Surat were living under the EIC's protection.[76] The English also differed from the Portuguese in the much more intricate organization of their trade; to be sure, this reflects the further development of legislation on joint stock promulgated in the seventeenth century.

In the Bay of Bengal a romantic breed of English free captains was active who on their own account engaged in trade and piracy. This was small traffic—piracy rather than commerce—but it constituted a persistent nuisance to the Dutch.[77]

Much more significant were those captains who were sailing on their own ships with the backing of the EIC and financed by its servants. The English generally invested in single voyages through temporary partnerships (ventures or investments) instituted for the course of a single trip. Generally there were two or three major participants in a venture and others might invest. In Madras those shares were put up for public auction and Portuguese, *chettiar*, or Danish merchants might make a bid too.[78]

In smaller settlements, like Telicherry, Anjengo, or Surat, investments were cozily agreed on in the local tavern—as we observed. But here too foreign traders were permitted to participate, unofficially. Of course, the main investors were higher servants of the EIC but practically every Englishman in the Orient spent some pennies, though that was not always in everybody's best interest. The good skipper E. Barlow, for instance, lost all his hard-earned savings and resolved that he henceforth might do better to leave trading to merchants.[79]

Permanent trading cooperation on the base of written engagements was exceptional in the seventeenth century—of course, given the harrowing mortality among Europeans in Asia. Ventures were generally arranged in Asia. But in some cases a few preliminary arrangements were already made in Plymouth on how to collaborate in Asia.[80]

Keels were in the possession not only of their captains but of landlubbers too. Since they possessed the most capital, the directors of the presidencies owned the lion's share of the sails. Aungier already possessed three bottoms and his successors at Bombay, like G. Waite, invested large sums in both leasing and buying ships. Waite owned at least five, which he mainly used in the trade with Madras, Surat, and Bombay, Mocha, and Persia. But then, the directors of Bombay were usually discontented with their tough life and meager salaries and were always begging for another assignment. One ought to be allowed a trifling reward when eking out such a dogged existence.[81]

Apparently, life at Madras was not a bit easier. The directors there too wheeled and dealed. That would include fellows like Yale, "king of the interlopers," and Thomas "Diamond" Pitt, the founder of that illustrious family. Personnel along the Hugly had also busily traded—and intrigued with interlopers. But only upon the rapid growth of Calcutta as a free port after 1710, attracting a great deal of Indian capital, did Hugly's country trade begin to eclipse that of Madras.[82]

To support those operations there arose an intricate system of finances and services that was the kernel of the rise of the agency houses in the eighteenth century. First, there was the position of the supercargo in intra-Asian voyages. Supercargoes were mostly former servants, permanently established in Asia. They would, in return for a payment on commission of 5 percent of the proceeds, invest the participants' money in profitable products on the destination of a voyage. They also mediated in the investment of funds. At the end of the seventeenth century there were thus in several EIC settlements (like Surat, Madras, Bencoolen, and Calicut) resident English merchants acting as financial consultants to the English servants.

Second, English merchants often collaborated with mercenaries who would take care of the transactions of English merchants and provide them with information. Free merchant B. Franklin, for example, in 1685 sold goods brought to Mocha by English merchants to the imam at Sa'na. Such intermediaries were not always Englishmen. In 1695 two Italian merchants, who had come overland from the Levant, established themselves at Bombay to engage in maritime trade.[83]

And third, some English servants devoted themselves to insuring ships and supplying funds for bottomry. The tariffs charged for bottomry in Madras would vary, according to Lockyer, from 15 percent for a trip from Madras to Surat, to 30 percent for a voyage to Manila.[84] By comparison, in Goa the percentage charged for a trip to Bengal was 30 percent, to Manila 40 percent, and to Mozambique 35 percent. The lower rates charged by the English obviously constituted an incentive for Portuguese traders to entrust goods to them.[85] In Surat, however, hub of insurance and banking in India, percentages were often lower. One could even insure a cargo destined to Europe for 20 percent there. This may have contributed to the continued vitality of Indian shipping from Surat in the seventeenth century.[86]

As to obtaining capital: according to Lockyer, one should try to become a legatee of as many servants as possible when accepting a position at Bandar Abbas.[87] Roughly half of the servants there would succumb within two years. One might leave this settlement either wealthy or in a coffin. Again, English ladies could not board ships but they might invest their pennies in a venture. To Lockyer the trade of Madras was mainly financed by such plucky females. The profits would be remitted in cash or bills to Europe.[88]

Entrusting money to a commissioner to be spent on private trade upon leaving Asia or earthly existence was prohibited to VOC servants. However, in Surat this was common practice among them as well, under the cover of *bania* merchants. Moreover, Dutch traders also invested such funds with English private merchants.[89]

Let us now, just as we did with the Portuguese, consider a number of regional cases to highlight the character of English private trade.

### *The Rise of Bombay*

"When Bombay was granted to the King of England," Luís de Mendonça Furtado wrote in 1676,

> it seemed at the time one gave them nothing. And now it is the most prosperous port of the entire north and the commerce of all fortresses of your highness has much diminished as the English have attracted everybody by allowing them to freely rule themselves according to Hindu or Muslim law.[90]

Aside from granting liberty, Aungier thought, it would be a good idea to attract trade by allotting military protection to Indian merchants. "The greater force you maintain on the island for its defence the more encouragement you give to merchants of all nations on condition they entrust their estates and family and ships there."[91]

At first, Bombay was indeed favored by fortune. The attack of Shivaji on Surat harmed Surat a great deal. This was so much so that the son of Hodsia Said Beg proposed that the EIC move to Bombay in 1665. This did not materialize but the *nagarseth* of Diu, Sam Das Parek, did transfer to the future *urbs prima* in India in 1672. The Parek family had possessed this position for several generations and had long farmed the customs. As kin and retainers moved too, this was a severe blow to Diu. To the traders of Diu this was as much occasioned by the constant attempts of the captains of Diu to engross all traffic there as by Muscati attacks.[92]

Diu and Chaul were not the only Portuguese settlements under the spell of Bombay. "The Portuguese lands," the representative of the Portuguese crown accused the EIC in 1678, "are becoming unpopulated, for all the vassals of his highness are leaving his royal service. And in Bombay they are assembling the minute people who used to frequent his lands, and mariners who used to serve on his majesty's fleets."[93] He argued that the EIC should hand over all Portuguese subjects who sought refuge in Bombay. Goa did not insist on this very much, though. "Bombay's money is accepted in Goa too," went the comment in Bassein.[94]

The migration to Bombay was especially furthered by the chaos prevailing in the Konkan after 1670. It was a mixed blessing; this also seriously hampered Bombay's connections with the interior. This was one factor in the temporary decline of its trade in the 1680s.[95]

The English succeeded as well in concentrating the rice trade of the surroundings at the Bombay staple. The fight for the rice from Tana was the background of the continuous disputes between the Portuguese *alfândegas* in Tana and the Jesuit and Augustinian friars there on the one hand, the English customs stations on the other hand. The *alfândegas* claimed the English used preferential tariffs, if not sheer force, to attract peddlers with rice from Tana to Bombay. English private traders then sold this to Surat. Furthermore the English also tried to obtain on a monopoly on the extraction of salt at Mahim and on its sale, traditionally a right of the Jesuit monastery at Parel.[96]

Bombay also succeeded in attracting part of the regional trade in foodstuffs to the island. In this barren place one needed lots of provisions, so the presidency handed advance payments to English and Indian private traders to procure rice in Barcelore and Mangalore. This was partly exchanged for bullion, partly for salt. But this rice often did not arrive at Bombay, being sold to Muscat or Surat. The presidency subsidized the rice trade and had it protected by the navy, however. By 1700 the English country traders, and the EIC, which regularly sent vessels there for supplying the garrison at Bombay, had ousted the VOC from the market of Barcelore, and later on the Portuguese from the bazaar of Mangalore.[97]

Banking was paramount to the rise of Bombay, an issue rather neglected in the extensive literature on the city. It was the policy of the EIC to stimulate the traffic in bills between Surat and Bombay by stipulating that goods that were sold by the EIC in Surat should be paid at Bombay.[98] This was no small advantage for English private traders too, as the government of the presidency would provide a bail for them if bills could not be cashed at Surat. The EIC demanded lower customs on the imports of bullion than did the Mughal authorities at Surat (1 percent against 1.5 percent). This cash was often transported on board the vessels of the navy from Bombay to Surat too. It was therefore attractive for Indian merchants to send bullion from Yemen to Bombay, draft bills on Surat, and to remit the bar coin in small amounts to Surat. In the longer run this could attract trade as well: shipping may have moved from Surat to Bombay in the 1730s because of the low rate of insurance, bottomry, and exchange there.[99]

Already in the seventies Bombay's private traders engaged in a busy traffic between Bombay, Chaul, Poona, and Satara in rice, grain, and textiles from Bombay, Salcete, and Europe. It was exchanged for cotton, coconuts, and wheat from the Maratha-Deccan. The brokers of the Maratha governors in the surroundings, who were responsible for supplying the Maratha army as well, did most of this trade in provisions. As Bombay needed the wheat in order not to become utterly dependent on the Portuguese, they sent various missions to Satara to deal with Shivaji. The Board considered that this trade in grain fetched but meager profits. It was important for the personnel, however, as was the trade in cotton, which one might send from Bombay to Persia.[100] Thus the interests of English private traders tangled with those of Maratha merchants and gentry. The first of these tried to sign all kinds of monopoly contracts with them to sell the grain, at prices amounting to usury, to the presidency. T. Pitt had at the beginning of his career as assistant merchant pursued such affairs. And after his departure he appeared not to have rendered money he had borrowed from the Maratha *subehdar* of Chaul. This caused a great deal of trouble to the Board afterward.[101]

None the less, in spite of its magnificent bay, Bombay was not a very good location for a major entrepôt. "The island," Schreuder wrote, "is sandy and barren, it hardly produces more than a few vegetables" and some coconuts, while the English never succeeded in attracting many weavers there.[102] Cotton was received too irregularly from the hinterland to supply the weavers and one may well suspect that rapacious officials of the Company tried exploiting them. Unlike Madras and Calcutta Bombay was not a good location to purchase merchandise intended for Europe; for this one had to sail to Surat. As befits a trade Company, London constantly complained that Bombay submitted impressive expense sheets but had little merchandise to show in return. Those who did not toy with the idea of razing the settlement altogether at least grouched that it was far too costly. So Bombay was (and was to remain) primarily of military importance, a garrison town welded to the need of the army.[103]

### *Sugar and Country Trade in Persia*

For reasons we have explored already, the EIC after 1660 abandoned the direct trade in silk between England and Persia. The servants at the factory there had to subsist largely on smuggling and the sale of licences for shipping. The VOC in Persia until 1680 considered the English as annoying interlopers on its virtual monopoly rather than as serious competitors.[104]

After the opening of the private trade with the Hugly, however, the English sugar trade with Persia began to grow rapidly. Profits on the sugar from Birbhum district could be most appetizing—up to 60 percent—but were unsteady as these depended on the VOC's supplies and on imports from Muscat.[105]

Yet by 1688 the English had become the major importer of this sweetener after the VOC. Though the EIC also sent ships from Surat, Hugly, and England to Bandar Abbas, private trade had by 1687 surpassed the trade of the Company. At Bandar Abbas the English then had become the second largest traders in sugar, after the VOC, with sales amounting to 200,000–400,000 pounds, while those of the VOC amounted to 600,000–800,000 pounds yearly, and at Kung the English played a substantial role too.[106]

Furthermore—and this to the great anger of the Gentlemen XVII—the English traders were also seriously threatening the Dutch trade with Bengali and Coromandel textiles to Persia. For, whereas the Dutch were unwilling to trade goods at less than 40 percent profit, the country traders seemed to be content with 25 percent, even with 5–6 percent freight and insurance discounted. The VOC would never be able to compete with such low rates of profit. The problem, the *bewindhebbers* thought, was that the VOC had to procure textiles at interest rates of 14 percent from its advance buyers, as cloth for Europe could only be obtained thus. Procurements for Persia were but a very small part of those bulk investments.[107]

The servants of the EIC were not doing too badly from this. Lockyer warned prospective investors for the officials:

> All privaie trade has been so long engrossed by the Company's servants that they really think they have a right to it at their own rates. The agent at Isphahan is concerned one-third and the rest of the factors in Persia the other third of all investments. So that there's scarcely an Englishman in the place, who will give a true account of the value of goods, against his own interest.[108]

From 1692 onward the VOC's Gombroon shipping lists record the size and armament of English ships from Bengal touching at Bandar Abbas. It leaves one with a picture of small but well-armed sails, manned with *lascarins* and probably built on the Hugly. What is striking by comparison is the light armament of the ships from Bombay. But the EIC enjoyed an advantage over Indian traders, since the navy often protected the keels from Bombay. Furthermore, the English could show their flag without any hesitation. Indian vessels were not thus blessed. The hitherto important Armenian shipping from the Hugly to Persia was virtually annihilated by 1700 by Danish corsairs and Muscati fleets waiting for them near Larak, for example.[109]

For this reason, as much as the English manipulations with *dastak*s, it was highly profitable for Indian merchants to collaborate with the English, both in Persia and on the Hugly. English cargoes, particularly those of the EIC's vessels, largely consisted of freight. In 1702 the *Colchester* was even completely stowed with goods of one Armenian merchant from Cassimbazaar, Hodsia Pir Amin. Indeed, the British at Surat and Bombay conducted little trade with Persia. Proceeds on this traffic were obtained through the sale of flags, or by fetching freight.[110] Such profits were invested "in vast quantities of pearls and other treasure," and Lockyer considered English ships sailing from Persia to Surat "to be the richest vessels in that part of the world."[111]

The main competitors to the trade that Bombay and Surat merchants conducted to the Gulf with rice, wheat, coconuts, and, after 1697, pepper, were found in the Praças do Norte. But Portuguese ships had to sail in the convoys of the Gulf flotillas; this effectively barred them from tramping within the Gulf, and they ran the gauntlet of Muscati corsairs. The rice brought on the English vessels was partly derived from Portuguese territory. The English bartered this for textiles from Coromandel. In fact, the Portuguese-Muscati wars were a double boost to English trade. These eliminated a competitor and, after undertaking a trip to the Gulf, old vessels from Bombay or new sails from Surat were often sold to the Muscati fleets.[112]

### *The Rise of Country Trade in Yemen*

During the lean years of the trade with Mocha from 1656 until 1687, when both the VOC and the EIC had raised their settlements there, and only incidentally sent ships to Mocha—mainly to provide for bullion—the trade of English servants was mostly conducted under Asian cover. The English rented Asian ships too. Keels from the king of Banten, or from Atjeh, often disposed of English navicerts, or had English freight and sailors on board—a challenge to the VOC, of course.[113]

After the official opening of the trade on Mocha to private traders in 1682 the involvement of English traders in this commerce increased rapidly whether openly, in collaboration with Dutch free burghers or on ships of the Dansk Ostindiske Kompagni. For coffee—which accounted for the bulk of English private trade between Mocha, Anjengo, and Surat—was one of the products that officially could only be purchased and sold by the EIC. The sudden boom in demand for coffee after 1685, to which London reacted faster than Amsterdam or Lorient by sending ships directly from England, provided the English personnel with a major advantage.[114] The EIC arranged with the English cloth traders that it would sell varieties of cloth woven for Aleppo, which commanded a ready market in Mocha. Since the English had lengthy experience with the sale of European cloth in the Middle East, unlike the VOC, this expansion of the coffee trade markedly benefited the English.[115] Besides, English private traders succeeded in finding a highly profitable commodity to market at Mocha: Bengali sugar. By 1710, while trade with England stabilized and then declined, ships from Calcutta were ever more conspicuous at Mocha.[116]

The EIC, by imports of bullion from Europe, disposed of quantities of ready money that could easily be used to provide capital to English private traders, contrary to the VOC (and the French). Hence, the private traders enjoyed a great deal of credit, unlike Dutch free burghers, and VOC servants operating ships on their own account from Cochin and Surat. They had to raise capital at the unreliable capital market in Mocha and the merchants of Surat and Cochin were hesitant to entrust funds to them.

And according to R. Cowan, a man from Ulster, who was initially merchant and later governor of Bombay, the English servants there minded their own business first and only then that of the Company. They often used funds received from England to buy coffee on behalf of the EIC for their private trade. Mocha was a dreadful place, "the worst in the whole of the Indies," yet one had to pay quite a high bail for a nomination there. "Mocha is a nasty coffee-roaster," Cowan contemplated, "but no matter for that—there's profit to be gained and that's the great idol of our age."[117]

### A Portent of Change: Surat

At Surat, too, there was a profit to be gained. If the trade with England grew fast, country trade grew faster.[118] In the development of the country trade there three changes occurred that can be termed structural shifts and are in many respects exemplary for English country trade in India: the English role in coastal shipping increased, navigation to China increased, and the English succeeded in exploiting the commerce with Bengal.

Around 1650 trade with Surat was dominated by shipping between England and Gujarat. Within Asia voyages were undertaken by Indiamen—nominally to take care of the connections between the factories and finance this by fetching freight, especially to Bandar Abbas where the English enjoyed lower customs. In fact, the ships largely carried private goods. Director Methwold, his successor Merry, and their rings were openly using the Indiamen for their own affairs. The Board of Directors did grumble, but—as H. Furber has underlined—it is doubtful whether English trade would have survived the commotion of the civil war without Methwold and his successors running their own trade in the name of that of the Company.[119] Ships mainly sailed from Surat to Bandar Abbas to Basra back to Surat and from there to Rajapur, with the occasional excursion from Surat to Laribandar and on to Basra and Surat, or from Mocha (onetime Massawa) to Surat and finally from Surat to Malindi to Rajapur and then back to Surat.

Still, such was small trade; very small, in fact. Antônio de Mello e Castro wrote in 1666 that "the English have in this Orient no forces, and no wars. They are merely living under the penumbra of the armies of your Majesty." And yet, while the Dutch "are lords over the seas, the English are masters over the wealth of the Orient." And that was precisely since they had no forces—the English were neutral conveyors of goods.[120]

By 1700 this had changed completely. On the one hand Indiamen now mainly sailed from England to Surat or from England to Persia, Mocha, and back to the Downs. (Bombay functioned mainly as an intermediate port.) Indiamen coming from other Asian harbors often touched at Surat (or Bombay) to take on provisions, but—the important exception of the China trade apart—the EIC had withdrawn from intra-Asian commerce.

On the other hand there was now an impressive fleet of country trade vessels. First, an important coastal trade between Bombay, Telicherry or Anjengo, and Surat had developed. Many *zambuccas* (up to 20 yearly were touching at Surat) or even small *houris* were provided with flags and navicerts by the governor of Bombay and loaded with bulk goods like coconuts, rice, rope, and arrack. As the diaries the VOC kept at Surat and Cochin generally do not register the proprietors of ships, one cannot state with any certainty who owned these crafts. It seems, however, as if the brokers of the EIC at Bombay and Surat had their own ships and that at least crafts from small ports in the Konkan—like Rajapur and Karwar—happily accepted English flags and passes. The main income of the servants of Karwar (an unprofitable factory) was its sale.[121]

This "English" coastwise navigation mainly concerns crafts that were loaded by English-Indian consortia, had an English boatswain and captain on board with a *lascarin* crew, and were built in Surat and Karwar. There may well be a link between the navy of Bombay preying on Indian shipping during the war with the Mughal empire from 1689 to 1692 and the rapid growth of Bombay's coastwise trade afterward. Indian traders had been sufficiently intimidated. Thus, English capital penetrated the vast bulk-good trade on the west coast.[122] This English coastwise trade appears to have surpassed Portuguese coastwise navigation by 1700, and was second only to Indian commerce. And the trend was toward a further increase: by 1750 the bulk of coastwise trade to Surat was under English protection.

We also observe the flourishing of English trade with Bengal in opium, silk, sugar, and textiles. This seaborne trade had partly displaced the overland trade, as mentioned already. The competitive freight offered by the English was but a minor factor in the shift. English country trade, which toward 1730 had surpassed the trade of the Companies from Surat, was, however, mainly built on this trade with Bengal.[123] While the VOC remained a major competitor, the country trade pushed all others out of the market. The Portuguese did not conduct a sizeable trade between the Hugly and Surat. In fact, Portuguese trade with the Hugly was largely erected with English support. The French trade only emerged during and through F. Dupleix's involvement.[124] And most remarkably the English also ousted Indian competition. Indian merchants thus still asserted a dominant position in the areas where they had traditionally traded—like the Gulf, Yemen, and Kerala. But English trade was paramount in new branches like Bengal and China.

After the shift in the center of gravity of commerce from Indonesia to India by 1650, by 1700 a new shift was discernible: the hub of intra-Asian trade was increasingly located in China. The growth of the country trade immediately preceded that of the trade with tea to Europe. I think that the English Company and country trade also seized a head start in this trade. Contrary to the Danish, Swedish, or Oostende competitors—and to an extent the French—they could partly finance this tea trade by selling Asian goods, such as cotton and opium (from Egypt and Malwa). And they could pay for it with funds raised in India. This was already the case in the seventeenth century, since English country traders sold those products from very early on.[125]

When the trade with Canton was opened by the Chinese authorities in 1683 wares from the Middle Kingdom rapidly turned up in Surat on board EIC and country-trade vessels. The Company was involved, as this long and dangerous stretch required large, heavily gunned vessels. One could obtain bullion for the China trade from the sale of European commodities at Surat and Bombay: iron to Indian merchants, wine and textiles to Europeans. The export of silver to China may be the key to the periodic scarcity of bullion in Surat in the late seventeenth century.[126]

Bombay and Madras were the first ports from which the English attempted intra-Asian voyages to China. Country-trade vessels from China or the Philippines with tea, porcelain, or Chinese sugar on board appeared in Persia in 1692 and at Mocha in 1698. The vessels from Persia and Yemen fetched bullion to China; those from Surat brought cotton, textiles, opium, and cash. This was a very profitable trade, in which the Compagnie des Indes participated from 1697 as well, as did, as we saw already, keels from Surat's merchants. In addition, fleets of sloops (*frotta dos remos*) from Goa also fetched commodities from Macao (like tortoiseshell, tuttenag, and copper) to Surat.

Such was the dawning of a new commercial age and an ominous portent for the VOC's trade at Surat. For the opening of the China trade would damage Dutch commerce in monopoly products, and not only those from China and Tonkin. It also infringed on the trade with Japan. Many Chinese junks sailed from Canton to Nagasaki. These would vend the Japanese bar copper to the

English. The China trade obviously hurt Dutch trade in Japanese porcelain as well, and was a bad omen for the commerce in Javanese sugar, for Chinese sugar was cheaper than Javanese.[127]

## Conclusion

In summary, let us review this causes of the remarkable success of English private trade, not only compared to the Dutch and the French, but also relative to Portuguese and most importantly Indian competitors.

First, one should allow that, contrary to what P.J. Marshall argues, the English did have some technological advantages. The armament of English ships was superior to that of Indian ships, and their naval stores in general were better, for Indian dockyards often bought these.[128] It seems that the use of the telescope and the compass, which were rarely used on Indian vessels, better maps, and cartographic techniques—like measurement by degrees—enabled English ships to sail new routes that were generally shunned by Indian vessels.

Second, the English used the services of Portuguese merchants and mariners as well as those of Indian sailors and soldiers. This was to their mutual benefit: to an Indian merchant contacts with the EIC servants would offer the same advantages as dealings with the VOC. Indian merchants and, on the Coromandel Coast, Portuguese *casados* served as a buffer for English traders. The relation between those merchants and the English should in the seventeenth century certainly still be styled partnership rather than subjugation. But some merchant houses, like Rustamji's, began to slide into the position of compradores for the English, as their sales and provisioning of purchasing power depended on English funds.

Third, as Bruce Watson has rightly pointed out, violence and the threat of it played an important role in English trade in general, and private trade in particular.[129] If English servants dealt in *dastak*s, they traded in protection. This "protection rent" was paid by the Company's customers and shareholders while its servants were only partly burdened with its costs.[130]

Fourth, the advantage enjoyed by the English country trade was basically that it could benefit from the advantages of both European and Asian shipping.

In addition to all these grounds, which have been mentioned in the literature before, one may point to two further causes for English success. Fifth, there is the English capacity to unify different legal traditions within a single practice, and the relatively loose reign of the Company. Since the English allowed them to function under their own legal norms, it was far more attractive for the *chettiar* or Armenian *natio*s to settle under English jurisdiction than under that of the Dutch, or look for shelter at Bombay instead of Bassein, where there was always the threat of the Inquisition.

The sixth is that the English trade network in Asia was closely connected by the patronage of the EIC's servants with that in the Atlantic. The growth of trade in the Atlantic stimulated that with Asia and vice versa.

## Notes

1. I received Om Prakash, *European Commercial Enterprises in Precolonial India* (Cambridge, 1998), too late to consider in this text. Useful earlier texts would include Holden Furber, *Rival Empires*, pp. 186–201; L. Blussé, "The Run to the Coast: Comparative Notes on Early Dutch and English Expansion and State Formation in Asia," *Itinerário* 12 (1) (1988), pp. 195–215; and M.A.P. Meilink-Roelofs, "Een vergelijkend onderzoek naar de Nederlandse en Engelse koloniale instellingen" *BMGN* 91 (1976), pp. 196–217.

2. P.J. Thomas, *Mercantilism and the East India Trade* (London, 1926). While there are few comparisons between the EIC and the VOC, on the comparison between the Compagnie des Indes and the EIC we have L. Dermigny, *L'Europe et la Chine. Le commerce à Canton au XVIIIème siècle*, 3 vols. (Paris, 1964).

3. The classic account is, of course, C.W. Scott, *Constitution and Finance of English, Scottish and Irish Joint-Stock Companies*, 3 vols. (London, 1903–7).

4. T.K. Rabb, *Investment in Empire: Merchant and Gentry Investment in the Expansion of England* (Cambridge, MA, 1967), p. 47.

5. Hunter, *History of British India*, ii, pp. 288–327; A.S. Khan, *The East India Trade in the Seventeenth Century in Its Political and Economic Aspect* (Oxford, 1932; New Delhi, 1971), p. 208; Bruce, *Annals*, ii, p. 476; for Jewish investments in the English company see, for example, GAA, P.A., 334, Archives of the Portuguese-Israelite Synagogue, 862, Anonymous Ledger book, fo. 32, "*Por via de Simeon de Costa Athias por acções da Companhia nova das Índias Orientais em Londres voltou f. 2334.*"

6. ARA, HRB, 834, Memoir Zwaardecroon, fo. 151; VOC/OB 1636, 14 December 1700, fo. 43 vo.; Das, *The Norris Embassy*, pp. 215–28.

7. Bruce, *Annals*, III, p. 257.

8. See E.L. Saxe, "Fortune's Tangled Web: Trading Networks of English Merchants in Eastern India" (Ph.D. dissertation, Yale University, 1979).

9. I. Bruce Watson, *Foundations for Empire: British Private Trade in India 1659–1760* (New Delhi, 1984).

10. K.N. Chaudhuri and J.I. Israel, "The East India Company and the Revolution of 1688–1689," in, J.I. Israel (ed.), *The Anglo-Dutch Moment: Essays on the Glorious Revolution and Its World Impact* (Cambridge, 1991), p. 435.

11. A.A. Sherman, "Commerce, Colonies and Competition: Special Interest Groups and English Commercial and Colonial Policy 1660–1673" (Ph.D. dissertation, Yale University, 1973), p. 47.

12. Chaudhuri, *The English East India Company: The Study of an Early Joint Stock Company* (London, 1965), pp. 125–34; Hunter, *British India*, ii, p. 45.

13. Chaudhuri, *The English East India Company*, pp. 85–95; see also L. Sutherland, *A London Merchant 1695–1774* (Oxford, 1933). However, it should be added that the French Company often leased ships and the Portuguese crown leased advice frigates and *de jure* leased ships to the Portuguese East India Company and later to the Junta do Comércio.

14. *The Laws or Standing Orders of the East India Company* (London, 1621; Farnborough, 1968), p. 11; Bruce, *Annals*, ii, p. 347; *Court Minutes* 1674–1676, p. 248; for the eighteenth century see Lequin, "Het personeel," i, p. 63.

15. E.P. Thompson, "The Peculiarities of the English," in *The Poverty of Theory and Other Essays* (London, 1978), pp. 48–49.

16. Bruce Watson, *Foundations*, p. 162.

17. *English Factories* 1651–1654, p. 107.

18. *Court Minutes* 1662–1667, p. 159; VOC/OB 1224, 16 March 1657.

19. This "mutual counterbalance" of greed was brilliantly analyzed in E. Burke, *Works*, 8 vols. (London, 1854–57), vi, *Speeches in the Trial of Warren Hastings*, pp. 23–30; Bruce Watson, *Foundations*, p. 125.

20. See *Court Minutes* 1674–1676, pp. 322–24; Bruce, *Annals*, iii, pp. 352–54.

21. S.G. Webb, *The Governors-General. The English Army and the Definition of Empire* (Chapel Hill, 1979).

22. *Cal. St. Pap. Colonial Series East Indies 1513–1616*, pp. 210–16; I. Bruce Watson, "The Establishment of English Commerce in North-Western India in the Seventeenth Century," *IESHR* 11 (2) (1978), pp. 54–64.

23. I. Bruce Watson, "Fortifications and the Idea of 'Force' in Early English East India Company Relations with India," *Past and Present* 88 (1976), pp. 70–87.

24. A. Auber, *An Analysis of the Constitution of the East India Company* (London, 1826), pp. 228–55.

25. C.H. Fawcett, *The First Century of British Justice in India* (Oxford, 1934; Aalen, 1979); Malabari, *Bombay*, pp. 146–82.

26. See L. Hovy, *Ceylonees Plakaatboek: Plakkaten en andere wetten uitgevaardigd door het Nederlands bestuur op Ceylon 1638–1796* (Hilversum, 1991), 2 vols.

27. K.C. Birdwood, *Report on the Old Records Preserved in the India Office* (London, 1861), p. 65.

28. Bruce, *Annals*, iii, p. 78.

29. L. Dermigny, *L'Europe et la Chine*, ii, p. 875.

30. For an example, see BNL, Pombalina, Cód. 520, fo. 133A.

31. AHU, Índia, Cx. 33 bis, 180, "Enformação do custo entre Antônio de Gama Padoa e Francisco de Pinto Teixeira"; AHU, Índia, Cx. 33, 99, Documents relative to endowments.

32. *John Company at Work* (Cambridge, MA, 1948); P.J. Marshall, "British Expansion," pp. 28–43.

33. *Court Minutes* 1663–1666, p. 153; VOC/XVII 316, 13 October 1656; VOC/UB 881, 5 September 1657, fo. 441, 442; VOC/UB 883, 22 September 1659, fo. 769; VOC/XVII 321, 8 October 1685.

34. HAG, LM, 69, appendix, 15 October 1696, fo. 13.

35. BNL, Pombalina, Cód. 525, fo. 71.

36. Arasaratnam, *Merchants, Companies*, p. 200.

37. *Generale Missiven*, iv, p. 621.

38. See Love, *Vestiges*, i, pp. 430–42; and *Historical Manuscript Commission* xiiith report *MSS of J.B. Fortescue* (London, 1892-), i, p. 45; and see, finally, also BNL, FG, Cód. 8548, fo. 170. In spite of its bad roadstead, Madras, rather than San Thomé, was now "*porto de frequentajaõ de todas as nações*."

39. VOC/XVII 323, 27 August 1694.

40. V. Baladounian, "Armenian Trade with the English East India Company," *Journal of European Economic History* 15 (1) (1987), pp. 157–63; R.W. Ferrier, "The Armenians and the English East India Company in Persia in the 17th and Early 18th Century," *EHR* 26 (1) (1973), p. 56; VOC/OB 1635, "Translation of a Gujarati," fo. 818–20 vo.; VOC/UB, 3 November 1699, fo. 1022 vo.; VOC/XVII 234, 6 March 1699; 19 February 1700.

41. French ships generally sailed in fleets to Europe, however, so only little time was

gained. C.R. Low, *History of the Indian Navy*, 2 vols. (London, 1877), i, p. 65; *English Factories* 1670–1677, p. 40.

42. For P.J. Marshall has in his *British in Bengal in the Eighteenth Century* (Oxford, 1976), p. 60, considered every possible advantage of English shipping relative to Indian and refuted every single one of them.

43. VOC/XVII 318, 23 December 1662, fo. 576 vo.; VOC/UB 678, "Brief notice on the reasons why Company vessels are generally overcrowded," fo. 223–26.

44. VOC/OB 1659, Surat resolution, 15 March 1701, fo. 333 vo.; A. Das Gupta, *Indian Merchants*, p. 97; for the merchandise which was, for example, owned by Indian sailors on a ship heading to the Philippines—from which one can learn that an important part of the cargo was owned by the crew—see VOC/OB 1756, "A summary account of money handed to three Indian ships in Malacca."

45. For the manning and crew of Indian vessels see A.J. Quaisar, "Merchant Shipping in India During the Seventeenth Century," *Medieval India. A Miscellany*, ii, p. 196; and on Arab ships see R.B. Sergeant, "Maritime Customary Law off the South Arabian Coast," in M. Mollat (ed.), *Sociétés et compagnies de commerce en Orient et dans l'Océan Indien* (Beirut, Paris, 1970), p. 201.

46. VOC/HB 4457, 22 April 1682, fo. 621.

47. VOC/XVII 317, 12 April 1656, fo. 434 vo.

48. VOC/HB 4459, 7 July 1690; but see especially VOC/OB 1474, "Exhibits relative to the mutiny on board of *De Leck*," fo. 197–99.

49. See, for example, PRONI D 654/03/110, 24 May 1724, or VOC/OB 1388, 28 April 1685, fo. 52 vo., and comparable complaints about the Coromandel Coast in VOC/XVII 321, 8 October 1685, fo. 302 vo.

50. VOC/OB 1388, 31 March 1683, fo. 2028 vo.; VOC/OB 1379, 17 February 1682, fo. 2504–6 vo.

51. VOC/XVII 320, 31 August 1678.

52. *English Factories* 1634–1636, p. 107; Geleynssen 133, 11 January 1641; HAG, LM, 38, 2 December 1663, fo. 294.

53. W.H. Coates, *The Old "Country Trade" of the East Indies* (London, 1911).

54. See, for example, *English Factories* 1650–1654, p. 98; Geleynssen 283, 18 March 1645, fo. 96–97; VOC/OB 1224, 18 May 1658, fo. 819.

55. *Dagregister* 1663, pp. 143, 150; Bruce Watson, *Foundations*, p. 82; Bowrey, *An Account*, pp. 102–4.

56. G.W. Forrest, *Selections from the Records Preserved in the Bombay Secretariat, Home Series*, 2 vols. (Bombay, 1884, 1887), i, p. 225; *Gazetteer Bombay City*, ii, p. 188.

57. AHU, Índia, 27 bis, 33, 9 December 1669; AHU, Cód. 14, 18 September 1647, fo. 82; ANTT, DRI, 35, 15 March 1636, fo. 46; ANTT, DRI, 60, 13 December 1650, fo. 261–63.

58. VOC/XVII 318, 16 April 1658, fo. 25; VOC/XVII 317, 8 October 1654, fo. 350; VOC/OB 1215, "Account of the costs of the *Palicatta*," fo. 317 vo.; VOC/RXVII 221, 26 March 1692.

59. S. Das (ed.), *Selections from the Indian Journals*, 2 vols. (Calcutta, 1963), i, pp. 99–103; VOC/OB 1474, 13 January 1691, fo. 551; VOC/RXVII 323, 27 January 1692.

60. R.A. Wadia, *The Bombay Dockyard and the Wadia Masterbuilders* (Bombay, 1982), p. 121; Ajuda 51-VII-30, fo. 1 vo.; VOC/OB 1454, "Report on Surat shipbuilding," fo. 1363; the Bombay dockyard generally used wood from Karwar (*Gazetteer of Bombay*, ii, p. 188).

61. De Korte, *De jaarlijkse financiële verantwoording*, p. 38.

62. Quoted by C.H. Northcote Parkinson, *Trade in Eastern Seas 1793–1813* (Cambridge, 1937), p. 327.

63. Ibid., p. 245.

64. VOC/OB 1635, "Note on freight-rates," fo. 811–12; J.R. Wright, *Annesley of Surat and His Times: The True Story of the Mythical Wesley Fortune* (London, 1916), p. 164.

65. A. Das Gupta, *Indian Merchants*, p. 97.

66. Évora CXVII/2–14, 1703, fo. 12.

67. VOC/OB 1291, "Report of George Willemson," fo. 576; VOC/OB 1548, Surat diary, 27 February 1693, fo. 418 vo.; see P.J. Marshall, "Western Arms in Maritime Asia in the Early Phase of European Expansion," *MAS* 14 (1) (1980), p. 16; and G. Parker, *The Military Revolution: Military Innovation and the Rise of the West* (Cambridge, 1986), p. 220; however, at the end of the seventeenth century the gunnery of ships from Oman had much improved, due, to no small extent, to the assistance of English mercenaries (HAG, LM, 69, 19 January 1694, fo. 27).

68. VOC/OB 1559, 2 August 1693, fo. 711 vo.

69. ARA, Coll. van Hoorn van Riebeeck 12, "Description of Mocha"; Marshall, *East India Fortunes*, pp. 84, 88.

70. VOC/OB 1548, Surat diary, 17 March 1694, fo. 441; *English Factories* 1670–1677, i, p. 273; VOC/OB 1620, 15 June 1694, fo. 279; for the *dastaks*, in Bengal see Marshall, *East India Fortunes*, pp. 117–24.

71. D.K. Basset, "Early English Trade and Settlement in Asia," in J.S. Bromley and E. Kossman (eds.), *Britain and the Netherlands in Europe and Asia. Papers Delivered to the Third Anglo-Dutch Historical Conference* (London 1968), p. 108; see also Lequin, "Het personeel," i, p. 99.

72. Watson, *Foundations*, p. 124; C.S. Dalton, *Life of Thomas Pitt* (Cambridge, 1915); H. Bingham, *Elihu Yale: The American Nabob of Queen's Square* (New York, 1939; Hamden, 1968), pp. 65–75; VOC/OB 1638, "Note on ships arriving at Cochin," 23 December 1699; 10 September 1699; and 31 May 1700, fo. 154.

73. *Merchants, Companies and Commerce*, pp. 229–35.

74. *Court Minutes* 1677–1679, p. 302; Bruce Watson, *Foundations*, p. 239.

75. Khan, *East India Trade*, p. 199.

76. Winius, "The 'Shadow-Empire,' " p. 68; and, to be sure, an obvious Portuguese impact on the English in India was that the English habitually married Indo-Portuguese women: *Records of Fort St. George: Diary and Consultation Book* 1684–1692, p. 2.

77. D.K. Basset, "The British Country-Trader and Mariner in South-East Asia ca. 1660–1715," in *The British in South-East Asia During the Seventeenth and Eighteenth Century* (London, 1990); Furber, *John Company at Work*, p. 116; R.C. Wilson, *Early Annals of the English in Bengal, Being the Bengal Public Consultations for the First Half of the Eighteenth Century*, 3 vols. (Calcutta, 1895–1917), i, p. 54.

78. *Records of Ft. St. George: Diary and Consultation Book* 1687, p. 165.

79. Lubbock (ed.), *Barlow's Journal*, i, p. 194.

80. Watson, *Foundations*, p. 123; Lockyer, *An Account*, p. 16; H.H. Doddwel (ed.), *The Private Letter-books of Joseph Collett* (London, 1924), p. 142; and for the eighteenth century see P. Nightingale, *Trade and Empire in Western India 1784–1806* (Cambridge, 1970), pp. 45–47.

81. *Court Minutes* 1674–1676, p. 252; Forrest, *Selections*, p. 136; *English Factories* 1670–1677, ii, p. 202.

82. Bruce Watson, *Foundations*, pp. 130–34; Marshall, *East India Fortunes*, pp. 85–89.

83. VOC/UB, 21 August 1697, fo. 993; VOC/OB 1409, "Report on events at Mocha," fo. 1670; Love, *Vestiges*, i, p. 451.

84. *An Account*, p. 17.

85. Évora CV/1–17, "Sobre a conservação da Índia," fo. 14, 16, 19.

86. VOC/OB 1548, Surat resolution, 6 June 1693, fo. 244 vo.

87. Lockyer, *An Account*, p. 212.

88. Ibid. p. 212, see Yule, *Diary of W. Hedges*, ii, p. cclvii.

89. VOC/OB 1649, 10 September 1700, fo. 202 vo.; VOC/OB 1480, "Translation of a Gujarati contract signed by Jan Roelofsz. 'dated in the year of 1743, in the month of Cartek,' " fo. 219; and in same, "Extract from the diary of the commissioner," fo. 223; and in same, 12 May 1690, fo. 301 vo.

90. BNL, FG, Cód. 10836, 20 January 1677, fo. 93 vo.

91. *English Factories* 1664–1669, p. 254.

92. Forrest, *Selections*, i, p. 132; AHU, Índia 31, Cx. 49, "Copy of a petition of the principal Guzarate merchants."

93. HAG, LM, 42, 1679, fo. 128; the English Board thought, though (*English Factories*, 1670–1677, i, p. 183), that the new settlers in Bombay "are a miserable, poor sort of people and the very rabble of all sects who fly from the Moores and Portuguese persecution."

94. *Court Minutes* 1677–1679, p. 245; BNL, FG, Cód. 10703, "Discurso apologético."

95. M.D. David, *History of Bombay 1663–1713* (Bombay, 1974), pp. 125–40; *English Factories* 1670–1677, i, p. 183; *English Factories* 1677–1684, i, p. 284.

96. *English Factories* 1678–1684, ii, pp. 87–90; Burnell, *Bombay*, p. 61; *Gazetteer Bombay*, i, p. 80; HAG, LM, 51 bis, 24 March 1685; HAG, Livro da provincia do Norte, 1376, "Regiment for Antônio Teixeira," fo. 17 vo.

97. VOC/OB 1635, Diary H. Zwaardecroon, 23 November 1699, fo. 582; VOC/XVII 332, 30 September 1689, fo. 540 vo.; VOC/OB 1333, "Orders for chief-merchant Lefeber," 6 August 1678 fo. 473–74 vo.; *English Factories* 1678–1684, ii, pp. 8, 11; Forrest, *Selections*, i, p. 223; *Gazetteer Bombay*, i, p. 74.

98. VOC/OB 1582, 21 May 1696, fo. 137.

99. *English Factories* 1678–1684, pp. 151, 155, 161; Bruce, *Annals*, ii, p. 514.

100. W.S. Desai, *Bombay and the Marathas up to 1774* (New Delhi, 1982), p. 19; Forrest, *Selections*, i, p. 223; Campbell, *Gazetteer*, i, p. 74; *English Factories* 1670–1677, i, p. 70; BAC, A 497, 23 January 1671; VOC/OB 1313, "Report by A. Lefebvre," fo. 474 vo. 75; VOC/OB 1321, 29 April 1676, fo. 971 vo.

101. *English Factories*, 1678–1684, ii, pp. 8–11.

102. ARA, Coll. Hoppe, K.A. 8448, "Considerations" Schreuder paragraph 160.

103. Chaudhuri, *Trading World*, p. 49; Das Gupta, *Indian Merchants*, p. 8; Forrest, *Selections*, p. 114: "Here is nothing on ye island but coconuts and all things we want must come from abroad"; Bruce, *Annals*, ii, p. 423; *Gazetteer Bombay*, i, p. 479; Lockyer, *An Account*, p. 260; M. Kossambi, "Commerce, Conquest and the Colonial City," *Economic and Political Weekly,* 5 January 1985, p. 34; PRONI, D 654/61/1, 7 November 1729.

104. ARA, HRB 874, "Thorough description of Persia" paragraph 7.

105. VOC/OB 1295, 5 January 1673, fo. 479 vo.

106. R.W. Ferrier, "The Trade Between India and the Persian Gulf and the East India Company in the 17th Century," *Bengal Past and Present* 89 (1970), pp. 189–98; VOC/UB, 21 October 1682, fo. 1220; VOC/UB 919, 2 July 1692, fo. 501.

107. VOC/XVII 321, 24 June 1684, fo. 179 vo.; VOC/XVII 320, 4 November 1673, see Prakash, *Dutch East India Company*, pp. 177–82.

108. Lockyer, *An Account*, p. 225.

109. VOC/OB 1582, 15 March 1696, fo. 121.

110. Marshall, *East India Fortunes*, p. 80; VOC/OB 1652, "List of ships touching here," 21 July 1703; see too VOC/OB 1559, 30 October 1693, fo. 837 vo., and Yule, *Hedges*, ii, p. cccxvii.

111. Lockyer, *An Account*, p. 251.

112. HAG, Petições despachadas para o conselho da fazenda, 1129, 7 February 1687, fo. 39; HAG, LM, 56, 18 March 1676, fo. 136, and 18 January 1677, fo. 137; AHU, Índia, Cx. 28, 36, 1 March 1669; BAC, A 499, 25 December 1678.

113. See Bruce, *Annals*, ii, p. 291, and see for instance VOC/OB 1284, "Report by C. Coemans," fo. 2236.

114. Chaudhuri, *Trading World*, p. 371; *Court Minutes* 1677–1679, p. 237.

115. VOC/UB 922, fo. 432.

116. Holden Furber, *Bombay Presidency*, p. 25; and see the shipping lists in VOC 9116, Mocha diary, 1720; VOC 9117, Mocha diary, 1723; VOC 9118, Mocha diary, 1726.

117. PRONI D 654/81/13, 20 October 1723.

118. For the English trade to Surat see K.N. Chaudhuri, *The Trading World*, p. 229; Chaudhuri, *English East India Company*, p. 179; O.P. Sing, *Surat and Its Trade in the Second Half of the Seventeenth Century* (New Delhi, 1979), pp. 121–46.

119. Furber, *Rival Empires*, p. 74; see also ANTT, DRI, 45, 30 November 1638, fo. 273 vo.

120. AHU, Índia, Cx. 27, 87, 30 January 1667.

121. Marshall, *East India Fortunes*, p. 78; *English Factories* 1670–1677, i, p. 245; VOC/OB 9115, Journal of Kettelaar, 3 September; PRONI D 654/31/10, 6 September 1724; PRONI D 654/31/15, 8 November 1724; VOC/OB 1474, "Report van Raatsveld," 19 March 1689, fo. 338 vo.

122. VOC/OB 1474, 10 January 1690, fo. 11; BNL, FG, Cód. 8538, 24 January 1688.

123. Furber, *John Company*, p. 183; ARA, Coll. Hoppe K.A. 8448 "Considerations" Schreuder paragraph 172. According to Schreuder, in 1752 the total trade of the French was worth 70,000 to 80,000 rupees, that of the Portuguese 200,000 to 300,000; Dutch trade had declined from 1 million to 500,000, that of the EIC amounted to 800,000, imports of British private traders to 700,000, exports to 500,000, the excess being covered by bills on Bengal.

124. A. Martineau, *Dupleix et l'Inde français*, 4 vols. (Paris, 1932–34), i, p. 75 et seq.

125. N. Earl Pritchard, "Private Trade Between India and China During the Eighteenth Century," *JESHO* 1 (1956), pp. 109–37; *Gazetteer Bombay*, ii, p. 94; and H.B. Morse, *Chronicles of the East India Company Trading to China*, 4 vols. (Oxford, 1926–29), i, pp. 85–89.

126. VOC/OB 1548, Surat resolution, 23 April 1693, fo. 218.

127. VOC/OB 1569, 9 February 1695, fo. 24; VOC/OB 1611, Report Ketting, fo. 267–69.

128. *Court Minutes* 1652–1654, p. 116; VOC/HB 4458, 16 July 1687; VOC/HB 4455, 18 March 1658.

129. "Fortifications and the Idea of Force," p. 88.

130. A. Das Gupta, "The Merchants of Surat," p. 214.

10

# Private Deals

By 1700 a subtle web of global connections tied the two Indies together. Due to traditional academic divisions, these dependencies have all too often been ignored by the two separate strands of colonial historians: the Atlantic (Afro-) American specialists and those specializing in the greater Indian Ocean. The growth of the EIC's commerce was part of a rapid increase in English trade both in Europe and within England's Atlantic empire. The EIC was a component of this network of trade, which Westminster, through a host of laws and prohibitions, tried to develop into a neatly closed system excluding both foreign outsiders and outsiders who did not belong to the merchant elite of London. The English Navigation Acts indubitably constituted (after the Spanish *asiento*) the most complex system of mercantilist restrictions on trade and shipping. Not only were these strictures intended to prevent the Dutch from encroaching on English trade, they were focused on keeping the West Indian and the East Indian trades apart as well.[1]

Many other states used such divisions between west and east too, however, as we saw in the Portuguese case. The mercantilist system allowed the elites running the state to gather rent on products from the colonies for which a monopoly price was charged, but competitors had to be ousted and access to colonies restricted to achieve this. The English were much more successful in imposing such restrictions than the Portuguese were, for England was in the center instead of on the semi-periphery.

In contemporary tracts it was often asserted that—contrary to the trade with the colonies and Europe—Asian trade did not benefit the English commonwealth since the constant flow of bullion into Asian vaults tapped the very veins of the nation. Pamphlet writers, opposing this point of view—rightly, no doubt—adduced that the trade of the Atlantic was inseparably linked to that of Asia.[2] The trade with Guinea, for example, depended upon the regular supply of Guinea cloth from the Coromandel Coast. Again, for the trade on the Gold Coast one needed huge amounts of cowry shells from the Maldives, where they were the currency.[3]

Seen from the City of London, Asia was in theory, partly in practice, one angle of a quadrilateral: India—Africa—North America—England. The Indian angle was of importance since slaves, for example, could be more cheaply and conveniently clothed in Indian cotton than English wool. Again, in North America there was demand for Coromandel textiles for the trade between the North American and the Caribbean colonies (and for the illegal traffic with Spanish America too) as well as for sheets and handkerchiefs for the planters of Virginia or the merchants of Boston.

In principle, the City and Westminster tried to reserve this trade entirely for themselves through a system of monopoly companies. With good reason, it was argued in Westminster that since the colonies paid low taxes and Britain had to finance their defense it was but logical that the motherland be allotted the commercial gains to pay for it. But such neat political geometry existed on paper only. The rapid development of the British Atlantic economy made the navigation laws obsolete by 1690.[4]

**Smuggling Between the Circuits of the Arabian Seas and the Atlantic**

During the period of the Commonwealth momentous change was occurring in the economy of the Atlantic empire. On the one hand, the manufacture and trade of Barbados, the Leeward Islands, and, after 1690, Jamaica declined and those islands turned to plantation monocultures with a virtually all-black population ruled by a tiny oligarchy of white planters. Trade with the colonies in North America and England disappeared, though merchants in Barbados and Antigua still conducted some shipping and traded with the Spanish Main and the other islands. As the plantations exhausted the fertile soil along the coastline white settlers were forced into the mountainous interior of Jamaica as buccaneers: cattle drivers for the plantations. These needed vast herds of cattle for consumption, production of sugar, and transport. Partly, too, it forced the white settlers to seek their fortunes at sea.[5]

Massachusetts and, after 1686, New York and the Rhode Island chartered colony, on the other hand, developed from monocultures (trading in fur, fish, and wood) to differentiated economies trafficking in basic as much as in finished products. The tobacco colonies of the Carolinas and Delaware to an extent assumed an intermediate position in this spectrum. Thus, the trade of Boston and its satellites Salem and Gloucester, as well as that of Philadelphia, Newport, and Providence (Rhode Island), was booming after 1660 (this occurred later in New York). The colonial traders dealt in raw materials like furs, naval stores, and fish as well as in manufactured goods like rum and piece-cloth. The colonies were struggling with a constant deficit in trade with the motherland. This had to be replenished by trade in grain, fish, wood, and horses with the Caribbean and the Spanish Main; fish and wood with Portugal, Madeira, and the Azores;

and the smuggling of rum, steel, and weapons to West Africa, in exchange for African slaves.[6]

The concession for English trade to Africa, from the Cape of Good Hope westward, had been allotted in 1664 to a monopoly company—the Royal African Company. In view of the rampant costs of its African strongholds, the Company pleaded that ships sailing without a permit of the Company to Africa should be duly punished. The Royal African Company did possess a monopoly on the slave trade too. But all areas east of the Cape of Good Hope fell under the charter of the East India Company. From its very beginning the Royal African Company was faced with stubborn resistance in Parliament. The opposition considered the Royal African Company as a royal device to curb trade. Understandably, the EIC preferred not to singe its fingers in such conflicts and would not side with the Royal African Company. So the relation between the two Companies was tense. In spite of protests by the Royal African Company, the East India Company would not aid the former with its struggle against its interlopers—while the consuls of the Royal African Company were only too willing to sell provisions to interlopers on the EIC's monopoly.[7] So, though it was easy to bribe English consuls in Guinea or the Cape Verdes, English interlopers started to send ships for the slave trade to Madagascar, Mozambique; and the Mrima Coast.[8]

## *Harbors and Inlets in the Arabian Seas*

The Comoros and especially the port of Mutsamudu on Anjuan—or Joanna, as the captains of the East Indiamen called it—were one hub for such smuggling in the southwestern Arabian seas. The island—with its cheap and abundant supplies—was busily frequented by the Portuguese, French, and particularly the English, who had a warehouse and maybe an infirmary there.

*Johanna man, Englishman, one brother come*
*Englishman very good man, drinkee de punch*
*Fire de gun, beatee de French, very good fun.*

So went a rhyme in the Pidgin English used for commercial intercourse in the narrow seas of the Mozambique Channel in the seventeenth and eighteenth centuries. Anjuan developed to an entrepôt between country traders and ships from the Americas—no minor benefit for the sultan, who tried to control this trade by force. Flotillas from Anjuan, provided with arms by interlopers and joined by buccaneers and European adventurers, would fight the barges of Mayotte and Moheli. Each of these rival sultanates tried to control the waters of the Comoros and trade with the English, Madagascar, Mozambique, and the Swahili Coast. In 1704 Mayotte was said to be entirely controlled by pirates.[9]

But the focus for illegal trade in the southwestern Arabian seas was undoubtedly Madagascar. Madagascar was beyond the compass of either the VOC's or the Estado da Índia's control. Besides, interlopers and pirates were welcome as skilled auxiliaries in the continual wars tormenting the island of the moon and there was a tradition of *ghazi*s founding independent kingdoms. For there was but a thin line dividing armed horse or slave traders from *ghazi*s and *ghazi*s from thugs.[10]

It is difficult to say how substantial the trade to the island of the moon was, as much of it was smuggling and that, by nature, is hard to quantify. In Maselagache in the seventies, six or eight ships arrived from the Americas and Cape Town; in Augustin Bay in the eighties, six or seven arrived from the French Atlantic coast, as well as England and the Americas. Considering the evidence that has been uncovered so far, the trade can be guesstimated at 15 to 20 ships yearly at the end of the century.[11]

Both smugglers and their kindred, the pirates, sailed from and to Madagascar's bays to the Red Sea, Mozambique, and more remote destinations right up to Canton and the Pacific. Regarding China, three privateers from Ireland in 1694 cruised over Madagascar and Atjeh to Canton. And, as to the Pacific, since W. Sharpe in 1683 discovered Madagascar's potential as way station during his voyage round the world, ships that had preyed in the South Seas on Spanish settlements and colonists would often steer to Madagascar.[12]

The stronghold (or should we say the *vahema*?) of the buccaneers there, the island of St. Mary, in front of Antongil Bay, was described in 1699 by J. Caen, skipper of the yacht *De Tamboer*. He was searching for the missing *Ridderschap*. Nothing precise was known of its whereabouts on Madagascar. At Cape St. Mary people had seen drifting beams; in Maratoanga Bay fourteen wooden crosses had been erected—nobody knew by whom. The disappearance of the *Ridderschap* might well be blamed on heinous deeds of the buccaneers on St. Mary.

> The main rendezvous which the pirates here, in the Indies, are frequenting is on the isle Saint Mary in front of Antongil Bay at 17 degrees, southern latitude. They come wintering there, and conduct a large trade with ships, which come from New York (or else the New Netherlands), as well as from New England and Bermuda. On the interior side of the island is a good harbor which is a musket-shot wide and 5½ fathoms to 6 fathoms deep. . . . There is no fortress on the island, but roughly 45 to 50 pieces of cannon, mostly lying on the ground, some too mounted on the cliffs which are in front of this port.[13]

In the vicinity was Manawara Bay where logs were fetched on sloops to the pirates' ships, sheltering from the hurricanes in January or February. Nearby on the mainland, near present Tulear, could be found another robbers' den. Malagasy warriors with firearms, under the command of Martin Samuels, former mestizo shipmate of a buccaneer from Martinique and now king of Manawara Bay, fought the erstwhile ruler Tanoar Tamar, who had been overthrown by

Samuels and was hiding in the bush. Samuels had the auspicious marks on his face of a true king, and a soothsayer had divined that the kingdom had to be ruled by a black man coming from overseas; this had allowed him to gather a retinue. Samuels's suite entirely consisted of sea rovers and he was in close touch with them, briefing them when potential game entered Manawara Bay.[14]

It is uncertain when, why, and how the buccaneers established themselves on St. Mary Island. I venture a hypothesis, however. Not all Englishmen on Assade's island were killed, imprisoned, or ransomed. If they agreed not to erect another fortress, they might stay, King Assad promised them. By 1660 there were still a couple of Englishmen living at Nossi Bé. It is possible they traded in lumber at St. Mary, selling it to Fort Dauphiné and Mozambique. Buccaneers coming from Campeche in the middle of the eighties may have reinforced them.[15]

### *Harbors and Inlets in the Americas*

The slave ships to Madagascar were coming from all kinds of places, while constantly changing heading and banking on the pliability of rules and regulations or the venality of customs officials. And this was all too easy, for His Majesty's customs were sadly understaffed and underpaid. The situation only ameliorated somewhat with the installation of a central Board for Trade and Plantations in 1694.

There were many opportunities for interlopers and pirates to evade customs or the gallows. Many slave traders would sail to Bermuda, for instance. A tiny archipelago in the Atlantic, Bermuda was a good place to get certifications that slaves had been obtained at an allowed place, or obtain a letter of marque from the governor of Bermuda on behalf of the Admiralty. Such letters were quite popular among privateers active in the Bab al-Mandeb (the "Babs").[16] When the cultivation of tobacco languished—due to the financial troubles of the Summer Island Company and the subsequent mismanagement by the crown—the island turned into a haven of smugglers and pirates. Passes and letters of marque were freely available there and pirates could have prizes declared as being obtained in decent privateering. Or, again, one could procure a deed stating that one had sold one's human cargo at Barbados rather than at Martinique. By 1720 most of the archipelago, outside of the capital, was controlled by buccaneers. The former surgeon of a pirate's vessel was said to rule over the community.[17]

Even if the governors of Jamaica strove to combat piracy—and one could surely not expect this from a former comrade in arms like Governor Sir Henry "Harry" Morgan—one might presume them to be very forgiving. Finally, the incomes from privateering to the Main and the French possessions were a major source of income for Jamaica's thriving harbor of Port Royal—"the most wicked town in the Western Hemisphere"—on the island's south coast and for his majesty's customs officials there. However, should those customs officials not prove

**Map 8. The Caribbean and North American Colonies**

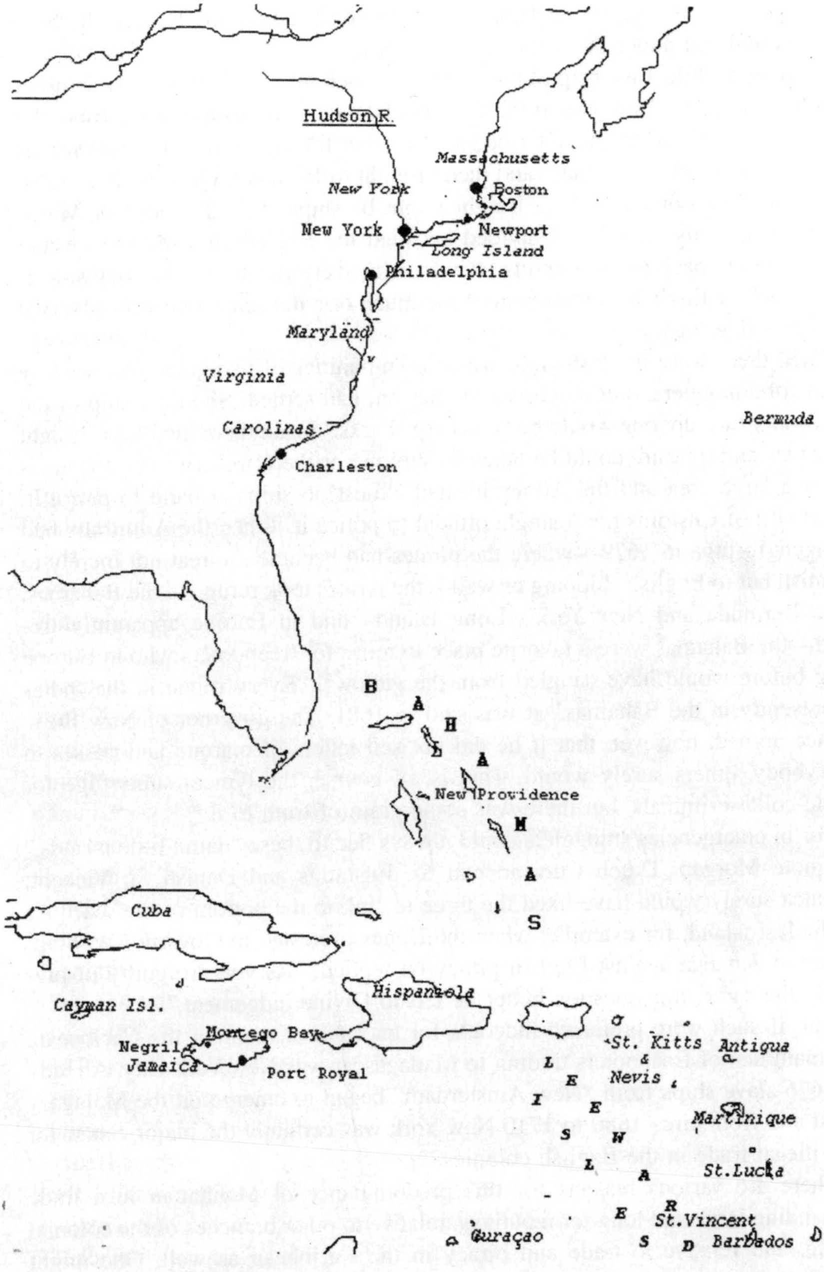

to be as accommodating as was normal, one could still bring booty ashore at Montego Bay and Negril on Jamaica's north coast, where the huts of the buccaneers huddled under the swaying palm trees.[18]

Once in a while a warship of the Admiralty anchored there. But treasure might still be fetched to Tortuga and the Cayman Islands. (The former until 1680, the latter afterward, were the intermediate stations for smuggling to Panama, as goods could be cleansed there and then brought to Jamaica). Or to St. Kitts (also called St. Christopher), where freight might be shipped to Barbados or Martinique. This puny island was divided between the English and the French and was a classic base for smuggling. It was effectively run by the bootleggers. If the French or English consuls proved too much of a nuisance, one simply raised the other flag.[19]

Then there were the Bahamas, where communities of fishermen followed by bands of smugglers, and much worse later on, had settled. Should a ship of the Admiralty turn up, one would be "catching sharks." From there the illegal freight of slaves and treasure could be taken to Virginia or the Carolinas. The Bahamas cover a large area and the Admiralty had almost no ships at hand to patrol it, the Board of Customs not a single official to police it. When the Admiralty had ravaged Tortuga in 1679—where the pirates had become a threat not merely to Spanish but to English shipping as well—the pirates took refuge in the Bahamas. Like Bermuda and New York's Long Island—and in Europe apparently Ireland—the Bahamas were a favorite place to retire for freebooters who in Europe long before would have dangled from the gallows. "Every rogue in the Indies is presently in the Bahamas," it was said in 1681. The governor of New Providence argued, however, that if he did not sell letters of marque and passes to everybody, others surely would. That is, of course, the typical subterfuge for white-collar criminals, but there was some grain of truth to it.[20]

For in emergencies smugglers could always flee to these "damn little islands," to quote Morgan: Dutch Curaçao and St. Eustatius and Danish St. Vincent; Jamaica surely would have liked the three to sink to the bottom of the sea.[21] As to the last island, for example: when the Danes protested to Governor W. Stapleton at Jamaica against English piracy he replied: "As you are guilty of precisely the same, this question better be left to Divine judgement."[22]

But, if such were preferred hideouts for buccaneers roaming the Caribbean, the main den of freebooters trading to Madagascar was New York City. Already in 1676 slave ships from "New Amsterdam" began to emerge on the Malagasy coast and from circa 1680 to 1710 New York was certainly the major center for this illegal trade in the English colonies.[23]

There are various reasons for this predominance of Manhattan in a trade demanding large and long-term outlays, relative to other branches of the colonial traffic, and relative to trade and piracy in the Caribbean as well. One might mention the strength of the municipality vis-à-vis the governor in New York, which inhibited strong measures against illegal trade. One might refer to the international character of the community, with its strong component of Dutch burghers, conducting illegal trade with the Republic and Curaçao; there was a large Scottish component too—another group not likely to heed prescriptions of the English crown. Finally, one might think about the manorial structure of landed property there. Manorial property was an ideal investment for—one might be tempted to say—"financial sharks," like Benjamin Harrison, one of the main organizers of privateering to the Babs and a landowner along the Hudson River.[24]

However, other ports in the colonies also dealt with Madagascar. Although Antigua and Bridgetown were mainly centers for trade within the Caribbean in the seventeenth century, unlike in the eighteenth, merchant houses there still engaged in slave trade themselves. And in the eighties two or three vessels were sent from Bridgetown and Antigua to Madagascar yearly.[25]

> The fame that this place hath borne in this western part of the world makes me somewhat digress about their church-integrity way of life. Which, in brief, is now almost wholly devoured with Christian policy of New England, with which means they have made their moderation their prime best commodity of merchandise and their zeal their best broker. And their occasion and affairs in the world shall require that these two shall pass as the greatest cheats in the world.

Thus commented Governor J. Holden when two ships from Madagascar had dropped anchor in Massachusetts Bay.[26]

Bostonian trade was, however, far more extensive and varied than that of New York and therefore far more dependent on official consent than the trade of Manhattan. The trade to Madagascar was also of less significance to the city on Massachusetts Bay than for that on the Hudson too. And, undoubtedly, Boston was not such a hub of unscrupulous speculators as New York. The vessels of New York's shipowners would generally first sail to Manhattan, whence the slaves were fetched to the Caribbean. Bostonian vessels would first set course to Jamaica or Bermuda. From there they would head to the Carolinas to vend the remaining slaves and would then, loaded with sugar and tobacco, sail to their port of origin.[27]

Yet the trade with Madagascar was more than merely a local affair of New York or Boston. The interlopers to Madagascar in the colonies were inextricably linked to the financiers and merchants of London—and beyond. Among the freighters of the New York bird of prey *Margaret*, only two, B. Harrison and J. Walton, lived in New York.[28] The major share in the voyage belonged to smugglers from the City of London. Various well-known interlopers from the city participated in outfitting two ships to Mozambique and Madagascar, the crew of which was imprisoned by the Portuguese and put on trial in Goa in 1687: S. Evans, R. Calvet, J. Blackman (whose manifold concerns, as Brenner has shown, touched on virtually every branch of illegal trade), and R. Allenby (of whom the same may be said). Blackman and Allenby were already involved in the Assade Company.[29] J. Davids, resident at Delfshaven (near Rotterdam) had his ship the *Providence* (100 tons, 6 guns) sail under English flag from the Meuse to Madagascar in order to procure slaves for Barbados there.[30]

Indeed, since the very governors of New York, Bellomonte and Fletcher, were involved in the voyages to the Bab, the tentacles of piracy would seem to have led into the very crofts of Parliament—a question that has long fascinated sleuths.[31]

### *Smuggling to Madagascar*

To form a clearer picture of smuggling operations, let us look at the orders from S. de Lancey, one of New York's major traders, a respected landowner and politician, to his agent at St. Mary, W. Shelley, a notorious pirate and smuggler who was supposed to have made several voyages to the Babs.[32] These orders were seized by the VOC at Cape Town in 1698 and are apparently one of the few samples of commercial orders that have survived—no doubt since smugglers are wont to destroy incriminating evidence.[33]

> I hope this will meet with you at Madagascar and that before the arrival of this vessel, you shall have bought what goods you can meet with, like the best sort of white and painted calicoes, large salempuris, skirting muslims and fine handkerchiefstuff (the fine calicoes in halff [sic] parts and the best). If you come next summer, the best will be at the place mentioned at the bottom of your orders. [These orders are not preserved but probably Gloucester, Mass., is meant.—Au.] I have the intent to write to the chiefest dealer of that part and send him a letter for you to give you an account of all transactions here, whereby you may be informed of what is to be done. It would not be inadvisable, if not too dangerous, to call at St. Helena, to get a clearance for the negroes. But if you hear that there is any man of war at that place and you have any quantity of goods on board, best will be to keep them from thence whatever you do. If you touch there do not come near any guns till you have sent your boat ashore, and heard how things stand effected. I am thinking to send a sloop to the place mentioned.

Let me make three observations in regard to this telling letter: First, as we see, smuggling is very much a part of European-Asian trade. It involved—except for the slaves—normal products involved in this trade.[34] Second, the commerce entailed merchant houses throughout the colonies. And, third, the commerce involved the personnel of the East India Company too. Provided the Admiralty would not demur, the Board of Directors permitted slave ships from Madagascar to anchor at St. Helena when paying dues of 20 shillings a ton. Albeit, the official permit of the Board of Directors does not mention the additional odd penny the director at St. Helena obtained by "handing clearances for the negroes."[35]

Given the VOC's complaints over the scant benefit of the Madagascar slave trade, it seemed to the high and mighty Company that the Americans were running the trade at much lower cost. In regard to this, van Rheede proposed one should allow the "New Netherlanders" a concession, whereby the VOC would pay them to deliver slaves to Cape Town.[36] The profits on the slave trade from Madagascar appear to have been minor in New York as well. But skippers could benefit from the sales of the piece-cloth and the boon of the occasional loot, which might amount to 200,000 pounds sterling. This looted treasure was badly needed, as New York was constantly suffering from a lack of means of exchange.[37] And, though many a small investor probably took a loss on this trade, F. Philipse, the main entrepreneur active in the trade from New York, certainly made no small profits on it.[38]

Governor J. Fletcher of New York, who was acting in collusion with pirates to an impermissible degree, adduced in defense that he could never have deterred such trafficking. If he had tried, this would have caused a constitutional conflict with a community in which everyone had some share in it. This is true enough, though he himself also had no objection to getting richer from it.[39]

These activities were important to the shipbuilding of New York. The vessels used in this traffic were of moderate size (on average 140 tons and often with only a few pieces of artillery) but for a small town like New York these were still sizeable keels. It seems that ships heading for the Babs were sometimes intentionally built to resemble dhows in order to hide their true colors. In the colonies there was usually a lack of capable sailors. The ships had to be manned as efficiently as possible: crews of 20 to 30 men. Both their small size and complement contributed to lowering the costs for the colonial traders. It is left to the reader to speculate on the life of the human cargo on such tiny vessels during a trip to New York, which took four to six months. Some ships—which were especially constructed for privateering—were larger, sometimes armed with as many as 22 guns and with a crew of up to 100 men.[40]

This smuggling provided an important stimulus to the trade within the colonies. The major products, which the colonial traders sold at Madagascar, were, in probable order of significance, weapons, spirits, iron, copper, and chains. Colonial America had an advantage in most of these products. The major article colonial traders had for sale in Africa was of course the legendary rum. The growth of the slave trade was related to an increase in its manufacture in New York. Most of this spirit was, however, brought by colonial traders from the Caribbean, although Boston and Providence also brewed this drink.[41]

But in Madagascar the sale of rum was less important than that of weapons and powder. Because of the wars with the French and the Indians, New York imported arms in bulk from England. Arms were produced in the colonies as well. The Americans were dominant in this trade since they sold arms more cheaply than the Dutch, the Breton, or the English vessels and furnished ammunition with them.[42]

New York developed into a slave entrepôt within the colonies. The city itself purchased only a few dozen slaves; most blacks were vended at Barbados and other Leeward Islands. After 1680 more slaves were sold to Jamaica, where the imports from Madagascar amounted to 30 to 40 slaves yearly, according to customs figures that may not tell the whole story. The "Madagascers" tended to form separate communities there, quite aloof from the West African slaves. They stuck to the Malagasy language and customs well into the eighteenth century. Even among the maroons the Malagasys—an exceptionally ferocious breed of blacks, the English thought—were detached from, and often fought, the other communities.[43]

What did a typical voyage from North America to Madagascar look like? Let us, to answer this question, consider the trip of Captain T. Edwards out of Boston.[44]

The *Royal James* departed from Boston on the 27th of August 1675. The voyage first led along a number of small ports, such as Salem and Gloucester, Massachusetts, where freight was embarked. Then the sails were hoisted and the ship cruised by way of the Cape Verdes, where salt was taken in as ballast, to the English stronghold Cape Coast Castle on the Guinea Coast. There, Edwards was faced with a nasty surprise. Former governors of the Royal African Company had cheerfully looked the other way when interlopers wanted to stock supplies there—if receiving a payoff. T. Mingay, the new resident, seized the ship, however. Only after twelve days' negotiating and offering a much higher bribe than he had intended did Edwards succeed in getting his ship off the chain, whereupon he hastened to the Cape of Good Hope.[45] He arrived there on the 8th of April, and, fortunately (for the VOC might also present a problem), the commander of Cape Town was willing to sell supplies to him.

On the 19th of May Madagascar was sighted, and on the 24th Edwards arrived at Augustin Bay. There were no slaves for sale there. Upon crossing to Mozambique, Edwards proceeded to the west coast of the island, where the mariners went ashore to try and catch a few prisoners. The Mahafaly fishermen were prepared, though, and fired poisoned arrows at the landing party while hidden in high trees, so it was necessary to beat a hasty retreat. Finally, Edwards arrived in Boina Bay on the 18th of July. The iron locks and bullion he had brought for Maselagache could not be bartered for slaves. Edwards decided to exchange them for Indian piece-cloth instead and sail with this back to Mozambique. Upon his return to Augustin Bay, a messenger was sent to King Marana Kaya, who requested that Edwards wait. After a long delay, Edwards was invited to the court, where the king and his concubines greeted him most enthusiastically, "all shouting and screaming, very delightful, in their fashion." Edwards bought 30 slaves in addition to the 80 slaves he had procured already from the kind Jesuits at Mozambique. Then the ships raised anchor and arrived at Cape Town in December, where a quarrel erupted with the VOC.

Trips to Madagascar were, as shown in this probably rather typical example, lengthy journeys sailing a seesaw course, dependent both on the venality of local officials and on supply. The Americans switched between looting, preying on Arab or French ships, and exchanging Indian textiles, ropes, sailcloth, arms, or munitions for coral, beads, or other products of use in other slave markets. For, besides going to Madagascar, the Americans traded at Mozambique, Dela Goa Bay, the Mrima Coast, and—if we are to believe Defoe—even at Mogadishu. The hold would contain, in addition to the inevitable arms and rum, a substantial array of other goods since it was unknown how much and where products had been traded by the French, Dutch, and metropolitan English competitors.[46]

To shorten such expensive wanderings it would be advantageous if a number of freebooters remained permanently at a strategic location in the Arabian seas. One could then fetch booty or smuggle on decent sails to the colonies. This was attained by the establishment of the entrepôt at St. Mary. By 1686 a division of labor was achieved. Pirates would carry out the dirty work: the slave trade, partly, and piracy. Merchants in the colonies would not have to risk dabbling in such risky bargains anymore. Instead, the loot was stocked at places like St. Mary, Anjuan, and, later on, the Seychelles and Mauritius. There, decent colonial vessels would exchange slaves, Asian goods, and bullion for naval stores like sailcloth, ropes, tar, weapons, munitions, and cloth.[47]

## From Smugglers to Pirates

The activities of illegal traders were very much mere robbery. Quite an acceptable matter—because piracy was still an everyday pursuit. It was, generally, in the seventeenth century not below the dignity of the average captain to supplement the treasure a bit by ransacking other vessels. To states, privateering was a way of privatizing warfare; it was a common institution in the seventeenth century, whether on land or at sea. One who had raised an army or warship at his own cost and risk should be permitted the spoils.[48]

But the buccaneers on Madagascar are no common privateers. They were far from merely "agents of empire," nor were they "corporate raiders"—agents of mercantile capitalism. They were perhaps rather "raiders incorporated," embodying the form of "European expansion" by fugitive outlaws that we already encountered on the Mozambique *prazos* and on the Swahili Coast, sometimes collaborating, sometimes at war, with the state, and always opposed to its elites.[49] Of course, the English sometimes provided buccaneers with letters of marque and so did the French. And the English state, if hesitantly, backed some of the buccaneers' enterprises, like Morgan's attack on Panama. However, both in the West and in the East Indies a letter of marque or a flag from French, English, Scottish, Swedish, Brandenburg, Danish, or Dutch representatives was largely a cover-up to carry on with robbery. The buccaneers obeyed their own interests, and those of states or local governors only if convenient—just as the *prazeiros* did.

The way of life and worldview of the buccaneers is probably related to that of European mariners and roving bands of mercenaries.[50] The historian also clearly meets with elements of the roaming gangs of beggars and bandits, wandering in the English and French countryside, in which members were adopted in early childhood and to which they were fettered for the remainder of a mostly brief and savage existence. The historian, too, finds elements of egalitarian ideas, akin to those of the levelers in the English civil war.[51] However, the image and most inside information on the buccaneers derives from Exquemelin and Captain Johnson—alias Daniel Defoe—and both are sources fraught with problems. The former in particular wanted to contrast these noble robbers with a corrupt society, whereas Defoe's is a mere compilation of amazing stories circulating in the inns of Bristol or London. It is thus hard to keep fancy and fact apart when dealing with this topic.[52]

Some buccaneers were true desperados, utterly foreign and hostile to the society ashore—those buccaneer ships were indeed "total institutions," as E. Gofman calls them, since there was nowhere to escape. But many better-known buccaneers were really privateers. For example, the buccaneers sailing the South Seas were mostly provided with a letter of marque, though from local authorities instead of from Westminster—or Paris.[53] Other buccaneers, roaming the Arabian seas, like Tew and Avery, were mainly smugglers who added to their contraband by preying on "Moorish" ships. They enjoyed the fullest right to do so, they believed: Islamic states were not included in the European system of international law—so their ships were a free prize.[54]

### *Buccaneers*

The background to the buccaneers' story is the reckless exhaustion of nature. Contract laborers who fled the miseries of life as indentured workers at Barbados told of the logging camps at Campeche and Tortuga, of the suffocating heat of the jungle on the Central American shores. Campeche was a merciless world of man against fellow man. It was a tale of succumbing to loneliness in the jungle or on god forsaken beaches. What other possibilities did the "white trash" of Barbados or those "baymen" of Campeche have but to fly to the sea? Yonder, over the briny deep, echoed a call of liberty—liberty from malaria, from the whip, from the scaffold.[55]

Over the burned forests, the fallow fields, the overgrown tillage of Hispaniola, Cuba, and Puerto Rico roamed wild cattle hunted by outlaws. Spanish patrols chased those bandits again. The cattle was vended to English, Dutch, and French smugglers or hawkers from Curaçao and Tortuga skimming the Caribbean shores. They sold the bulls to the tobacco colonies at Barbados and Martinique.[56]

The herds were hunted into extinction. There was no alternative but to flee to the sea. The existence of the "small privateers, or buccaneers as we call them," as Morgan described the outlaws at sea, is this lifestyle of migrant hunters and fishermen.[57]

From the logs of the South Sea buccaneers one gets an image of infinite wanderings, where the routes one sailed depended on the amount of game one might catch or shoot.[58] The quarry was meager for all the plenty of the Caribbean seas; the existence of buccaneers was haunted by a specter of hunger. On such errands the big catch was the exception; sometimes one might plunder a Spanish hamlet, capture a few slaves, or grapple a sloop with some food—but more often than not one ended up empty-handed.[59]

This was largely an underworld society. To some extent the mores on vessels of buccaneers were like "respectable society" ashore through the looking glass. Thus, sexually: against the straight heterosexual marriage propagated by the church, the buccaneers juxtaposed the marriage between males. In a kind of parody of heterosexual marriage, two men (for example, the ship boy and the boatswain) would give each other consent, and promise to share their property for good and bad times. However, if such practices existed; if, too, "buggering" was probably as common amongst buccaneers as it was in any navy; and if, finally, many persecuted homosexuals fled to the sea, this does not signify that most buccaneers were homosexuals, as B.R. Burg argues. There were more than sufficient women available to the buccaneers, though this surely was a man's world.[60]

As Burg reasons more convincingly, buccaneers often tended to identify with evil, and evil was often linked to "sodomy." Blackbeard used to throw his captives in the hold, where they might suffocate. "Life is hell, let's make hell of it," he explained. Many buccaneers were assumed to light candles for Satan and celebrate black masses.[61]

For satanic rituals were quite common among lowly sailors. If God guided the rich, Satan should shepherd the poorest of the poor. Sailor Johan Sigismundi from Stralsund, Germany, had in 1651, in a letter written in blood, sold his soul to Beelzebub. One surely believed in Evil in Batavia. (We are, of course, in the era of the witch craze.) Therefore, an extensive exorcism was staged whereupon Sigismundi was strangled, his body blown to pieces with powder, and his body parts fed to vultures.[62]

Sailors had their own views about creed or—as you like it—superstition. The piety of Catholic (French) pirates, who would solemnly celebrate mass before pillaging a town, contrasted to the religious indifference among Dutch or English pirates. Everywhere in the world deities are adored, the former lay preacher Carraciolo sermonized to the pirates—who may discern the true ones? Yet all favor the rich; this much is sure. On board the English buccaneer vessel that the pirates had baptized the *Good Fortune*, "it was an irregular, godforsaken life. One never prayed, and screamed 'let's have a feast!' *[val aan!]* if one began to eat without the slightest sign of religiosity."[63]

This was an underworld indeed. A privateer was a respected, even notable, figure. Thus Harry Morgan; thus too the former VOC servant Hubert Hugo, who after a colorful and distinguished carreer as privateer in the Babs for the Compagnies des Indes Orientales et Madagascar's service still ascended to the position of governor of Mauritius.[64] Pirates, on the other hand, were the lowest of miscreants. In Batavia they could be hanged without trial, and their bodies fed to birds of prey.[65] So pirates were at all-out war with society.

And yet, in spite of their often horrifying demise, such temptation for the poor sailors if mariners could be their own lord and smash the stifling bonds of the society of estates! An example: from the flute *De Hoogwagen* anchored in front of Purakkad in 1701 a sloop fled to the pirate ship of Captain Silvius, a Dutchman, yet manned with Englishmen, Frenchmen, Italians, Indians, and Malays. The VOC summoned Silvius to immediately return the sailors. "Sir," Silvius replied in the Dutch/English slang used on board:

> we knoweth of no man, but if they wereth 100 men or even a single one, they all would be wellekom, for our skip is a free skip, and were there be 1000 and our skip be kapable to fetch them all over the sea, they wouldeth be wellekom. As for you man, keep them on board, we shell not fetch them.[66]

One became a pirate by one's own choosing. When the *Good Fortune* grappled the *Westerwijck* at Madagascar the sailors could choose to be put ashore. They would then be picked up in due course by other vessels—no harm would be inflicted on them. Or they might join the buccaneers. And a number of them, indeed, "were embittered with us, because of bad pay and treatment. So they joined the pirates and they had to vow—like the English—that they would assail any nation they would meet with."[67]

As to the treatment of captives, there was a major difference between thugs like Blackbeard or the infamous Captain Blood—whose nickname suffices—and self-proclaimed "gentleman pirates" like Avery or W. Kidd (the best known of the Madagascar buccaneers since his grand public trial attracted a lot of publicity).[68] Among buccaneers in the Caribbean, "woolding" was normal: one would hang the victim, on a rope and kick his head till his eyes would goggle. Kidd did not butcher his "Moorish" victims, though, and "as to the Dutch or the Englishmen, they shell not be disadvantaged at all, be it skip, sloop or sail, whatever 't might be, and if it were a kanoe with one man, they would be wellekom, and not bee at any peril."[69]

Amid the buccaneers booty was divided among the crew. Kidd, however, locked looted treasure away in his cabin. The sailors could plunder the rest of the freight. Everybody had to support each other on buccaneer vessels. But if somebody infringed upon the discipline and thus imperiled the community, he might be tortured to death. The crew elected the captain; the others would obey him. But he had constantly to prove himself by fairly fighting anybody who might challenge him with the cutlass.[70]

The *pièce de résistance* of buccaneers' lore is the "communist republic" Libertalia, which Carraciolo is supposed to have established at Madagascar. There is no proof that Libertalia ever existed. It is possible that it is a compound of stories about St. Mary that went round the taverns of the seven seas. There is no evidence that communal property and communal living were practiced there, however. Libertalia was first dished up by Captain Johnson, an author best used with a great deal of caution.[71]

Libertalia seems to be a mixture of real elements of life at St. Mary with fancy; it is interesting lore, however. This is the idea of the Garden of Eden held by the poor wanderer over the oceans. To fish in abundant waters; to gather food without toil from a bountiful nature without money, lords, or greedy traders; to live in harmony and love with pretty native women—a community of races, creeds, and people with communal property (for Carraciolo was supposed to have freed the slaves brought to Libertalia).[72]

And, surely, what a gap between legend and life! The sea rovers' existence was one of want and thirst. On the *Good Fortune* one had to feed on sour flour, which the sailors baked into biscuit. The main problem was lack of water, however. Sails had been spread on the deck to catch rainwater. On the *Adventure Galley*, the rations were poor. "Their food, what little they have, is black rice, cooked once daily and nothing else but what they have taken from other sails—that is some beans, honey and biscuits which tasteth like leather [*die benne als leer*]." Apart from the empty stomach and thirst, life was dominated by two other concerns: the lack of munitions and the need of rope, wood, and tar—one had to obtain this from prizes.[73]

As pirate ships often were carrying a lot of crew and stowed munitions on the decks, grappling is rather fancy than fact. Buccaneer vessels were floating bombs: if pirates met with ships of the navy on the high seas, they would be defenseless against the grenades these would throw on the decks. Most ships taken by buccaneers were either anchored or taken by surprise. If Kidd, for example, assaulted a ship, he would use cunning rather than force. With some pretext one would first board a ship, then, "a barrel with powder was put on the poop-deck and the moors were threatened that if anybody would dare to go from board, they would blow-up the ship with everybody on it."[74]

Crews were recruited among sailors rambling around Massachusetts Bay or Manhattan. On the Hudson the naval press-gangs had great trouble recruiting mariners, since these would rather sail with the buccaneers. What a contrast between Philadelphia's Quakers and the pirates hanging around in the inns there! At Boston too there must have been quite a distinction between puritans and pirates. But on the lists of pirates captured by the VOC one finds men from throughout the colonies: not merely Massachusetts, Rhode Island, and New York are represented but Pennsylvania and Barbados too; the motherland—Bristol and

Plymouth; and buccaneers might come from still further away, like Genoa (Carraciolo), Amsterdam, Rotterdam, and, of course, Brittany.[75]

The color of the skin was of small concern to freebooters, so we should imagine buccaneer crews as many-colored palettes. Among the bandits who attacked the settlement at Mauritius in 1705 were 30 "Moorish *lascarins*," for example. Pirates active in the Gulf of Aden had "20 caffirs, as well as other kind of such people, to do the common ship's work" on board.[76]

In Asia the crews were also replenished with deserted servants of the Companies. "There are many deserters from the *Platluys*" on the *Adventure Galley*, for instance, "who say: 'we and the captain have always been waiting for such a wonderful guy.' "[77] Without such deserters the pirates could never have sailed the Arabian seas. As the "captive" Michael Dicker wrote from the *Adventure Galley* to his wife: "I, poor man, hav' to be their pilotte and helmsman, for they are all ignorante of the Indies." But the ranks of the pirates in Asia were mainly strengthened by the European freebooters, or rather plain bandits roaming the shores of the Arabian seas, rather than through desertion. Take the adventures of R. Simes, for example.[78]

Simes had sailed as boatswain on the pirate ship of R. Colton in the Bay of Bengal. Nigh St. Mary mutiny erupted. Colton was murdered; Simes was put overboard with ten fellows near the Malagasy Coast. With their sloop they succeeded reaching Augustin Bay. A schooner with smuggled goods from France was anchored there. They invited the crew ashore. At night our heroes grappled the vessel, and butchered the crew on deck. Then sail was hoisted and they set course for the Babs. To buy cattle they touched at Maratoanga Bay. The schooner was then in turn seized by 13 English and French freebooters staying ashore. Andramasira II, the Sakalava king, had nearly the entire gang of unfortunate freebooters shot—only Simes saved his skin by miraculously curing Andramasira of a tumor.

### Companies and Buccaneers

Pirates depended on the other Europeans in Asia not only by recruiting among them but also by selling to them, and they were, sometimes indeed supported by the companies. Various representatives of the English Company at Surat were buccaneers, the EIC adduced, and probably accurately. Anyway, merchants of the English Company would accept the goods of looted ships. Interlopers and country traders were involved in piracy too. On board the interloper ship *Benjamin* the booty taken from the *Ganj-i Sawai* was brought on shore at Surat, for instance. The notorious interloper Jerome Boucher, "a common robber" according to Annesley, sold part of the buccaneers' loot at Surat.[79]

To Viceroy Gonçalves de Câmera Coutinho, who was responsible for piracy was never in doubt:

> The sea is full of pirates, which will result in the ruin of commerce and—if robbery continues like this—its total destruction and it is rumored with good grounds that all pirates are Englishmen and that they go to Bombay to sell the treasures they have robbed. And if our frigates try to seize them they show us letter-patents of the East India Company, so that we cannot do them any harm.[80]

Assuredly, the buccaneers were especially collaborating with the Englishmen, yet dealing with buccaneers was far from merely a pursuit of the British. As the Dansk Ostindiske Kompagni did little business at Mocha, the Danish resident there in the mid-eighties worked part time as representative for the private trade of VOC personnel and interlopers. It seems, however, that some of his funds derived from the purses of pirates too. They needed an informer to brief them when prey sailed out of the Babs. English traders in Yemen also were suspected of mixing their activities as interlopers with that of informer—one such was E. Clive, captain of the interloper *Charles the Second*.[81]

Queried by the court of justice at Batavia, pirates declared that "they did conduct trade with the English, but not with the Dutch" on the Malabar Coast.[82] No, the Englishmen at Telicherry would have answered—in their view most treasures unloaded by bandits on the Malabar Coast roosted in the coffers of Cochin: "What inconvenience and injury must the master's subjects sustain under one who can truckle such treacherous and base means as corresponding and trading with pirates?"[83]

Whether or not the buccaneers were business partners of the personnel in Asia, there were—at least until 1697, when the Admiralty first sent warships rather than mere privateers like Kidd to Asia—no pressing reasons to deal with those smugglers and pirates on Madagascar harshly. Initially, buccaneers avoided ships of their own nationality. But everybody preyed on "heathens" and the ships from Surat with their huge treasures in particular. Therefore, the depredations of the sea rovers and the Danish corsairs initially mainly hit the shipping of Surat, especially that to Mocha.

This was apparently perceived by Aurengzeb as a Christian conspiracy to impede the hajj. And with good grounds: the damage to Indian shipping because of piracy must have amounted to millions of rupees. It measured more than 200,000 rupees with the plunder of the *Ganj-i Sawai* and the *Sulaimani* by Avery for Abdul Ghafur alone.[84] Apart from the treasure lost, there was the loss of the ships, the delays that sails incurred because of the danger of pirates, and the mounting costs for insurance and bottomry.

The loss of the *Ganj-i Sawai* sufficed for Aurengzeb. Though the ship did not fetch a beautiful Mughal princess who preferred "Long John" Avery's charms to those of her Indian solicitor, as Defoe fabled, it did carry alms to be distributed among the poor of Mecca on behalf of the emperor. [85] The English might well plea this was done by "rebels" but at court one did not bother to distinguish between the various "hat-wearers," let alone to discern whether they were rebels or not. If one European was misbehaving, the other members of his *natio* were accountable too.[86] They were all to be imprisoned and their property seized until they could repay the damages incurred by their pirates.

At Surat, where the governor wisely hushed up those harsh orders, they had meanwhile settled on a compromise: the VOC and EIC were to escort the ships to Mocha, for which they were to be paid. However, these payments were received late or not at all, which soon caused the VOC to demur. Ghafur, hesitantly supported by the government of Surat, protested that these costs should be entirely blamed on the Companies. The VOC had no cause to be discontented at that: were pirates not often former servants of the Company? Did all Companies not fence booty? The Dutch argued they should not be blamed for evils committed by English pirates, and were highly offended when Ghafur summarily dismissed their demands for higher convoy dues. This wrangle finally led to a war between the VOC and the Mughal empire in 1705.[87]

But likely Mughal reprisals at least prompted the EIC to insist on a much more active policy of the Admiralty toward pirates. The EIC even consulted the VOC on joint actions against the pirates, but they was unable to reach an agreement on how to deal with sea rovers in the East Indies. The VOC was disinclined to have an English squadron stationed at Cape Town, for example.[88]

## Conclusion

The web of regulations with which mercantilist states tried to hoodwink trade to serve their interest, broke both at the corners and in the center. It broke in the center as the merchant elites of Lisbon, London, Paris, or Amsterdam, closely associated with the state, were unable to curtail the activities of competing firms, both in the metropolis and in the Atlantic colonies.

To these elites the interlopers were free riders on the military, financial, and administrative infrastructure that had been built up by the Companies and the Estado in the Arabian seas, or by the WIC and the African Company in the Atlantic. They profited from it but did not want to contribute either men or finances, nor were they willing to shoulder any risks. Yet to the various interlopers and to the buccaneers the Estado and the Companies were little more than honorary pirates themselves, systematically advantaging a tiny ruling class: first and foremost the hated tax gatherers and financiers. Surely, the buccaneers claimed to themselves, we are like modern-day Robin Hoods![89]

However, the difference between commerce and smuggling, between Companies and interlopers, was by no means as clear as it might seem. With the sharp international competition in the West and East Indies, the welter of authorities in the metropolis and colonies with overlapping competencies, and the generally contradictory laws emanating from London, Lisbon, The Hague, or Paris, what was permitted and what was not was very fuzzy indeed.

And yet this very fuzziness was to a large extent precisely the strength of

Old Corruption—not merely in Britain but in Portugal's Atlantic colonies as well, as we observed already with the Brazil trade.[90] By the many institutionalized loopholes allowing one to avoid carrying out orders, Old Corruption gave authorities and communities in the American colonies considerable leeway to engage in trade, which did not benefit the metropolis and thus went against the gist of the mercantilist system. Winking at illegal trade allowed the inclusion of groups who were nominally to be excluded, while sticking to a fiction of bureaucratic control—in that respect Britain's Atlantic empire differed little from the VOC.

As in the case of the independent *fiscaals* of the VOC, occasional punishment of those who had transgressed limits to permissiveness—like the hanging of Kidd—served to set an example, to reaffirm royal control by means of the Navigation Laws, and therewith to prove that the king's writ ruled throughout the land.

The web broke on the edges too. In the southwestern Arabian seas neither the Companies nor the Portuguese disposed of means to implement their regulations. The population and the trade on this frontier were simply too small to support the kinds of elaborate bureaucracies with which the Dutch, British, and Portuguese tried to curtail colonial commerce.

In such a situation of effective lawlessness the private dealings of smugglers and ruffians prospered. Nuances of European law were also not very applicable to Madagascar. When was somebody a pirate, when a privateer? Such subtle distinctions were of little use in the Babs, especially when pirates took "Moorish" ships as prizes. Were Islamic states excluded from the European state system, in which case their ships were booty? Or were their ships protected by some European state if Europeans had extra-territorial settlements there? Could a privateer be summoned to a European court, then? Or should he be summoned to a Muslim court, but in that case would that not conflict with the extra-territorial status? Or, most importantly, if the Dutch at Cochin captured American sea rovers, where was the trial to be—Cochin, Bombay, Batavia, London, or Amsterdam? For the main problem inhibiting any effective action against buccaneers was that all Companies jealously guarded the area covered in their charter.

Nor were the profits of the Madagascar trade sufficient to allow for constructing factories there, as the Compagnie des Indes found out to its sorrow. The most efficient way of commerce was that of the interlopers since they were not burdened by the overhead costs of Companies. Piracy, moreover, was "no prey, no pay"—if there was no booty, the investor did not get his money back and all costs of the voyage were for the pirates. Overhead costs were shouldered by the outlaws, so this trade had a very advantageous cost structure, allowing buccaneers to deal with areas that were only marginally profitable for everybody else, such as the Madagascar slave trade.

Because of these competitive advantages, I doubt whether the war fleets, that the Board of Trade sent to Asia after 1705 were more successful in turning pirates into law-abiding citizens. Rather, by 1705 a *modus vivendi* was achieved between the Red Sea buccaneers and "Moorish" shipping. The former began to behave like normal interlopers, supplementing smuggled goods with occasional plunder. They would treat the crew of captured vessels well if these would immediately surrender. They would allow them to keep personal possessions and garb and not snatch their last piece of clothing, as Kidd still did.

And the buccaneers began to emulate the normal practices of pirates in the Arabian seas. *Nakhila, chulia*, Angria, or Sidhi corsairs were as a rule not provided with letters of marque, but there were certain customs of the sea. One could loot enemy keels, extort ransack from ports or ships, sometimes enslave crews, but not kill prisoners or unarmed persons. It seems the buccaneers at St. Mary in the eighteenth century merged with the trade network of the Swahili Coast. Former sea rovers, living in Madagascar with Malagasy girls, acted as intermediaries for the traders of Bourbon and Mauritius. There was in the Antongil area until very recently a separate clan refered to as the *zana malats* (the children of the mulattoes)—often with light eyes or red hair. The pirates also conducted the slave trade on American ships with the Comoros, Mozambique, and Madagascar on the French account. If demand from the Atlantic declined in the eighteenth century, with the growth of coffee plantations that from the Arabian seas—and from Bourbon and Mauritius in particular—increased.[91]

## Notes

1. I.A. Harper, *The English Navigation Acts: An Experiment in Social Engineering* (New York, 1939).

2. T. Munn, "English Treasure by Foreign Trade," in *East India Trade: Selected Tracts from the Seventeenth Century* (Cambridge, 1968); W.J. Barber, *British Economic Thought and India* (Oxford, 1975), p. 36; A.S. Khan, *The East India Trade*, pp. 207–40.

3. J. Hagendoorn and M. Johnson, *The Shell-Money of the Slave Trade* (Cambridge, 1986), pp. 91–97.

4. V.B. Platt, "The Trade in East India Commodities to the American Colonies 1690–1775" (Ph.D. diss., Iowa State University, 1940).

5. See R.S. Dunn, *Sugar and Slaves: The Rise of the Planter Class in the English West Indies 1624–1713* (Chapel Hill, 1972); R.J. Sheridan, *Sugar and Slaves: An Economic History of the British West Indies* (Baltimore, 1974).

6. R.J. Beer, *The Origins of the British Colonial System* (New York, 1922), pp. 145–80; H.L. Kammen, *Empire and Interest: The American Colonies and the Politics of English Mercantilism* (Philadelphia, 1978), pp. 48–54; C. Bailyn, *The New England Merchants in the Seventeenth Century* (New York, 1964/1972), p. 149.

7. K.G. Davis, *The Royal African Company* (London, 1957), p. 100; J.F. Platt, "The East India Company and the Madagascar Slave Trade," *William and Mary Quarterly*, 3rd series, 26 (1969), pp. 548–77.

8. C. Donnan (ed.), *Documents Illustrative to the History of the Slave Trade to America,* 3 vols. (Washington, D.C., 1935–37), i, pp. 93–95.

9. Martin, *Comores,* I, p. 37; on Moheli see R. Challe, *Journal d'un voyage fait aux Indes Orientales 1690–1691* (F. Deloffre and M. Menemencioglu, eds.) (Paris, 1979), pp. 236–52; and AHU, Moç. Cx. 3, 78, 23 December 1679; G. Shepperd, "The Comorians and the East African Slave Trade," in J.L. Watson (ed.), *African and Asian Systems of Slavery* (Oxford, 1980), p. 75; ANTT, DRI, 40, "Letter to the captain of Mombaçca," fo. 257 vo.; D. Defoe, *General History*, p. 407; B.D. Dubbins, "A Political History of the Comoro Islands" (Ph.D. dissertation, Boston University, 1972), pp. 45–63; R.J. Barendse, "Pirates of the West Coast: A Case Tried at the Court of Cochin in 1704," forthcoming in *Comptes rendus du colloque international sur l'esclavage à la côte ouest de Madagascar* (Tamatave).

10. See J. Gommans, *The Rise of Indo Afghan Empire c. 1710–1783* (Leiden, 1995).

11. J.T. Hardyman, "The Madagascar Slave Trade to the Americas," in M. Mollat (ed.), *Sociétés et compagnies de commerce en Orient et dans l'Océan Indien* (Beirut and Paris, 1971), pp. 501–26; P.D. Curtin, *The Atlantic Slave Trade: A Census* (Madison, 1975), p. 235; VOC/OB 4012, "Diary *Voorhouten,*" 10 August; and in same, "Brief relation," fo. 704; VOC/OB 4018, Diary Barry, fo. 200, 201, 202.

12. *COACM*, iii, p. 552–91; "Cowley's Journal," in W. Hacke (ed.), *A Collection of Original Voyages* (London, 1699), ch. iv; Furber, *Rival Empires*, p. 272; VOC/OB 1598, 30 March 1697, fo. 30; VOC/OB 1490, 12 January 1695, enclosure, "list of ships arriving here," 15 December 1695; HAG, LM, 71, 6 December 1698, fo. 4; VOC 1589, 8 May 1698, fo. 1678 vo.

13. VOC/OB 4043, "Report by Arnout Caen," fo. 822; there are two other translations of this report: one (probably based on the copy quoted here) in *COACM*, vi, p. 51, and another (based on the copy in the archives of Cape Town) in Liebrand, *Précis*, 2nd series, *In-letters*, p. 228, for English documents on St. Mary see *Cal. St. Pap. Col.* 1697–1698, p. 108.

14. Caen, "Report," fo. 823; R. Drury, *Madagascar, or Rubert Drury's Journal During Fifteen Years' Captivity on That Island* (P. Olivier, ed.) (London, 1890), pp. 100–6.

15. AHU, Índia, Cx. 35, 98, "Pareçer" Dom Francisco da Costa; AHU, Índia, Cx. 30, 104, March 1676; ANTT, DRI, 60, 15 December 1650, fo. 340.

16. For an example see VOC/OB 4031, fo. 410.

17. *Cal. St. Pap. Col.* 1677–1680, pp. 357–60; *Cal. St. Pap. Col.* 1677–1680, p. 392; H.C. Wilkinson, *Bermuda in the Old Empire* (Oxford, 1950); R.S. Dunn, "The Downfall of the Bermuda Company: A Restoration Farce," *William and Mary Quarterly*, 3rd series, 20 (1963), pp. 487–512; *Cal. St. Pap. Col.* 1714, p. 334; *Cal. St. Pap. Col.* 1716–1717, p. 155, 328; *Cal. St. Pap. Col.* 1719–1720, p. 286; *NYCD*, iv, p. 446.

18. M. Pawson and D. Buiseret, *Port Royal, Jamaica* (Oxford, 1975), pp. 32–41; D. Pope, *Harry Morgan's Way: The Biography of Sir Henry Morgan* (London, 1977). While the evidence for smuggling at Montego Bay is extensive—as, for example, in *Cal. St. Pap. Col.* 1677–1680, pp. 86, 93, 99, and *Cal. St. Pap. Col.* 1681–1685, pp. 6, 22, 145, 286—the traditional association in Jamaican lore of Negril with buccaneers and smugglers is not at all attested in the sources. But then, of course, neither is there evidence for the existence of Anne Boney (female buccaneer in man's clothing), who is traditionally also said to have been from Negril. At any rate *se non é vero é ben trovato . . .*

19. M.A. Peña Battle, *La isla de Tortuga. Plaza de armas, refugio y seminario de los enemigos de España en las Indias* (Madrid, 1951); Dunn, *Sugar and Slaves*, p. 32; *Cal. St. Pap. Col.* 1677–1680, pp. 99, 110, 223, 231, 242–49.

20. *Cal. St. Pap. Col.* 1681–1685, pp. 246, 287, 320; *Cal. St. Pap. Col.* 1697–1698, p. 313; *Cal. St. Pap. Col.* 1716–1717, p. 360; E.O. Callaghan (ed.), *A Documentary History of the State of New York*, 4 vols. (Albany, 1849–51), iii, p. 243.

21. C. Goslinga, *The Dutch on the Caribbean and the Wild Coast 1580–1680* (Assen, 1971), pp. 304–404; W. Klooster, *Illicit Riches Dutch Trade in the Carribean* (Leiden, 1998); A.P. Newton, *The European Nations in the West Indies 1493–1688* (London, 1933), p. 286; *Cal. St. Pap. Col.* 1661–1668, p. 281.

22. *Cal. St. Pap. Col.* 1681–1685, p. 235 "*quo semel est imbuta recens, servabit ordore testate Divina*."

23. J.G. Lydon, "New York and the Slave Trade," *William and Mary Quarterly*, 3rd series, 25 (1976), pp. 375–94.

24. R.C. Ritchie, *The Duke's Providence: A Study of Politics and Society in Colonial New York* (Chapel Hill, 1977), pp. 189–204; S.B. Kim, *Landlord and Tenant in Colonial New York: Manorial Society 1664–1775* (Chapel Hill, 1978); J. Bonomi, *A Factitious People: New York Society and Politics During the Colonial Period* (New York, 1974), pp. 54–102; Klooster, *Illicit Riches*, pp. 95–97.

25. VOC/OB 4018, Diary Cape Town, 7 March 1683; *NYCD*, iv, p. 303; *Cal. St. Pap. Col.* 1661–1668, pp. 253, 282.

26. *Cal. St. Pap. Col.* 1677–1680, p. 373.

27. Donnan, *Documents*, iii, p. 14; *Cal. St. Pap. Col.* 1697–1698, p. 480; VOC/OB 4019, Diary Cape Town, 29 January 1691; see J. Pope-Henessy, *Sins of the Fathers: A Study of the Atlantic Slave-Traders 1441–1807* (Guildford, 1967/1988), pp. 233–45; Baylin, *New England Merchants;* and W.B. Weeden, *Economic and Social History of New England*, 2 vols. (New York, 1890; Philadelphia, 1969), ii, pp. 420–25.

28. HAG, LM, 47, "Suit regarding the *Nossa Senhora da Ajuda*."

29. Brenner, *Merchants and Revolution*, pp. 146–47, 175.

30. VOC/OB 4022, Diary Cape Town, 24 March 1687.

31. J. Judd, "William Bellomonte and Captain Kidd," *New York Historical Society Quarterly* 49 (1965), pp. 69–74.

32. *NYCD*, iv, p. 721; Bonomi, *A Factitious People*, p. 63.

33. VOC/OB 4043, fo. 690–91; for another example of such correspondence see *COACM*, vi, 41.

34. Though it should be added that Portuguese Indiamen in the beginning of the seventeenth century brought hundreds of slaves to Portugal yearly. However, these were largely household slaves not imported for commercial purposes.

35. *Court Minutes* 1677–1678, p. 275; Bruce, *Annals*, ii, p. 47.

36. Van Dam, *Beschrijvinge*, I, ii, p. 658; VOC/OB 4029, 18 April 1687, fo. 35.

37. P.C. Nettels, *The Money-Supply to the American Colonies Prior to 1720* (Madison, 1934).

38. J.G. Lydon, *Pirates, Privateers and Profits: New York Privateering During the Colonial Period* (Upper Saddle River, NJ, 1970); J. Judd, "F. Philipse and the Madagascar Trade," *New York Historical Society Quarterly* 55 (1971), p. 361.

39. *NYCD*, iv, p. 327; J. Lemon, "Governor Fletcher's Recall," *William and Mary Quarterly*, 3rd series, 20 (1963), pp. 547–62.

40. *NYCD*, iv, pp. 323, 816; T.J. Archdeacon, *New York City 1664–1700: Conquest and Change* (Ithaca, 1976), pp. 65–8; *Cal. St. Pap. Col.* 1697–1698, p. 397; Callaghan, *A Documentary History*, iv, pp. 172–76; *Cal. St. Pap. Col.* 1697–1698, p. 397; *Cal. St. Pap. Col.* 1677–1680, p. 238; VOC/XVII 323, 10 December 1692; see too AHU, Moç.

Cx. 3, 99, 3 July 1682; VOC/OB 4015, Diary Cape Town, 15 December 1679; R.P. Goldenburg, *Ship-Building in Colonial America* (Charlottesville, 1976); C. Bailyn and L. Bailyn, *Massachussets Shipping 1679–1714: A Statistical Study* (Cambridge, MA, 1956), pp. 27–31.

41. Ritchie, *The Duke's Province*, p. 190; R.L. Pares, *Yankees and Creoles: A Study of Trade Between North America and the Caribbean Colonies Before the Revolution* (Cambridge, MA, 1968); J.J. McCusker and R.R. Menard, *The Economy of British America 1607–1789* (Chapel Hill, London, 1985), p. 290.

42. VOC/OB 4022, "Diary of *Jan en Marie*," fo. 859 vo; VOC 10812, "Diary of the *Ter Aa*," 28 July.

43. J.W. Gardner, *A History of Jamaica* (London, 1883/1973), p. 97; B. Kopytoff, "The Maroons of Jamaica: A Study of Incomplete Policies," (Ph.D. dissertation, University of Pennsylvania, 1973), pp. 16–23; O. Patterson, *The Sociology of Slavery. An Analysis of the Origins, Development and Structure of Negro Slave Society in Jamaica* (Cranburry, NJ, 1967), p. 135.

44. VOC/OB 4013, "Diary of Thomas Edwards."

45. This event is mentioned in Cape Coast Castle's diary, which, albeit, "accidentally" silences over the subsequent release of the ship. Donnan, *Documents*, i, p. 202.

46. See Theal, I, p. 417; VOC/OB 4018, "Diary Barry," fo. 195–202; VOC/OB 4187, Diary Cape Town, fo. 161 vo.; VOC/OB 4012, "Diary *Voorhouten*," fo. 680, 10 August.

47. *Cal. St. Pap. Col.* 1697–1698, pp. 287–89; H.L. Osgood, *The American Colonies in the Eighteenth Century*, 4 vols. (New York, 1932–34), i, p. 532–35; Furber, *Rival Empires*, p. 272.

48. See F. Redlich, *De Preada Militaris: Looting and Booty 1500–1815* (Wiesbaden, 1965).

49. A.P. Thornton, "Agents of Empire: The Buccaneers," in *For the File on Empire* (London, 1969), pp. 79–89; K. Pomeranz and S. Topik, *The World That Trade Created: Society, Culture and the World Economy 1400–the Present* (Armonk, NY, 1999).

50. F.C. Hill, "Radical Pirates?" in M. and J. Jacob (eds.), *The Origins of Anglo-American Radicalism* (London, 1984), pp. 17–32; M. Rediker, "Under the Banner of King Death: The Social World of the Anglo-American Pirate," *William and Mary Quarterly*, 3rd series, 29 (1983), pp. 203–28; J.S. Bromley, "Outlaws at Sea: Liberty, Equality and Fraternity Amongst Caribbean Freebooters," in *Corsairs and Navies 1660–1760* (London, 1987), pp. 1–21.

51. F.C. Hill, *The World Turned Upside Down: Radical Ideas in the English Revolution* (London, 1972); D. Underdown, *Revel, Riot and Rebellion: Popular Politics and Culture in England 1603–1660* (Oxford, 1985).

52. Captain Johnson was first identified as D. Defoe by J.R. Moore, *Defoe in the Pillory* (Bloomington, 1939), pp. 126–88; there are scores of books on Defoe but see for example W. Freeman, *The Incredible Defoe* (London, 1950). For a discussion of Oxmellin see C.S. Harring, *The Buccaneers in the West Indies in the Seventeenth Century* (London, 1910/Hamden, 1967), p. 16. Also see W.H. Bonner, *Pirate Laureate: The Life and Legend of Captain Kidd* (New Brunswick, 1947/1958), p. 125; and W.H. Bonner, *Captain William Dampier: Buccaneer-Author* (Stanford, 1934).

53. See *Cal. St. Pap. Col.* 1681–1685, pp. 203, 364.

54. There is a vast literature on piracy. However, much of it is unreliable; for instance, it normally dispenses with any scholarly apparatus, so that it is impossible to ascertain which assumptions are derived from where. Useful older studies would include G.F. Dow

and J. Edmonds, *The Pirates of the New England Coast 1630–1730* (Salem, MA, 1923); C. Grey, *Pirates of the Eastern Sea* (London, 1933); C. Mulligan, *Captain William Kidd: Gentleman or Buccaneer?* (Philadelphia, 1932); more recently see M. Mollat (ed.), *Course et piraterie. Études présentées à la commission internationale d'histoire maritime à l'occasion de son XVègeme colloque international pendant le XVe congrès des sciences historiques*, 2 vols. (Paris, 1975); and R.C. Ritchie, *Captain Kidd and the War Against Pirates* (Cambridge, MA, 1987). However, as will be apparent from the references, even Ritchie's painstaking research has not uncovered all sources on Kidd alone. Sources on piracy are literally spread throughout the world, and a massive amount of work has still to be done.

55. J. Juárez Moreno, *Corsarios y piratas en Veracruz y en Campeche* (Seville, 1971); C. Bridenbaugh and J. Bridenbaugh, *No Peace Beyond the Line: The English in the Caribbean* (New York, 1972).

56. J.P. du Têttre, *Histoire générale des Antilles*, 3 vols. (Paris, 1667–69; Fort de France, 1979), iii, p. 123; C.S. Harring, *The Buccaneers*, pp. 32–42; H. Friedländer, *Historia económica de Cuba*, 2 vols. (Havana, 1978), i, pp. 48–51.

57. *Cal. St. Pap. Col.* 1677–1680, p. 249.

58. W. Dampier, *A New Voyage Round the World*, 2 vols. (J. Masefield, ed.) (London, 1916); and W. Rogers, *A Cruising Voyage Around the World. First to the South Seas, then to the East Indies and Homeward by the Cape of Good Hope* (London, 1713), have to be used with some caution, since these are partly advertising texts for the South Seas Company; this is mainly based on G. Shelvocke, *A Voyage Round the World by the Way of the Great South Sea, Perform'd in the Years 1720–1722* (London, 1726), and on VOC/OB 1483, "A description of the voyage started by Captain Capistan 1702–1703," fo. 246–84.

59. There is a vast literature on the South Seas buccaneers, although the sources are far from exhausted; see O.K. Spate, *The Pacific Since Magellan: A History*, 2 vols. (Canberra, London, 1979/1983), ii, *Monopolists and Freebooters*, pp. 133–35; P.C. Kemp and C. Loyd, *The Brethren of the Coast: The British and French Buccaneers in the South Seas* (London, 1960); G. Wycherley, *Buccaneers of the Pacific* (Indianapolis, 1928).

60. B.R. Burg, *Sodomy and the Perception of Evil: English Sea Rovers in the Seventeenth-Century Caribbean* (New York, 1983), p. 133.

61. H. Deschamps, *Les pirates à Madagascar au XVII et XVIIIème siècle* (Paris, 1949/1958), p. 22; Defoe, *A General History*, pp. 351, 355.

62. VOC/RGGR 675, 15 March 1652.

63. VOC/OB 1418, "Extract from a letter regarding the capture of the Company's vessel *Westerwijck* at Madagascar," fo. 657 vo.; Defoe, *A General History*, p. 398; M. Rediker, *Between the Devil and the Deep Blue Sea: Merchants, Seamen and the Anglo-American Maritime World 1700–1750* (Cambridge, 1987), pp. 177–83.

64. F.W. Stapel, "Hubert Hugo. Een zeerover in dienst van de Verenigde Oost-Indische Compagnie," *BTLV* 89 (1932), pp. 615–35.

65. VOC/CR 9285, 8 July 1651.

66. VOC/OB 1655, 21 November 1701: "Sir, Wy wete van geen man, al voor 100 man, off eenige andere persoonel, hebbe welkomme, want ons schip is een vry schip en offer 1000 ware en ons schip was kapas om se over see te voere, souwe wellekom wese, als voor jou man, hou se aen boort, wy selle se niet kome haelen."

67. VOC/OB 1418, "Extract from a letter," fo. 676.

68. Avery pleaded that not he but his mutinous crew was guilty of outrages: Yule, *Diary of Hedges*, ii, p. cxxix.

69. *Cal. St. Pap. Col.* 1669–1675, p. 50; VOC/OB 1593, "Translation report by Charles Gibbons," fo. 558 vo.

70. See Rediker, *Between the Devil and the Deep Blue Sea*, p. 234; Bromley, "Outlaws," p. 14; VOC/OB 1684, "Written report by Mr. Herman de Wilde," fo. 2124.

71. Defoe, *General History*, pp. 152–66; and see for further material *COACM*, iii, pp. 480–542.

72. On the social content of the legend of Libertalia, see in particular Hill, "Radical Pirates," pp. 23–26. Deschamps, one of the foremost *malgachisants,* notes that the local details related by Defoe do tally with Malagasy uses. It is, thus, possible that "Libertalia" does contain at least a kernel of truth; and it is surely possible that St. Mary was known among sea rovers as Libertalia. However, in 1698 rumors went round in New York that the colony there had been evacuated because of attacks of "ferocious natives" (*NYCD*, iv, p. 413), so the chronologies of "Libertalia" and St. Mary are at variance.

73. VOC/OB 1593, "Relation," fo. 557; see R.C. Leslie, *Life Aboard a British Privateering Vessel* (London, 1899).

74. VOC/OB 1593, Cochin resolution, 16 December 1697; see for a description of a fight against buccaneer vessels VOC/OB 4023, "True and detailed account of the fight of the *Caesar*."

75. VOC/OB 1613, "Role of English pirates," fo. 492; VOC/OB 1699, "Account by Christoffer Wagenaer," fo. 2304; *NYCD*, iv, p. 460; C. Bridenbaugh, *Cities in the Wilderness: The First Century of Urban Life in Colonial America* (New York, 1938/1960), p. 222; A. Winslow, *No Purchase, No Pay: Sir Henry Morgan, Captain William Kidd and Captain Wooden Roogers in the Great Age of Privateers and Pirates* (London, 1967/ Boston, 1969), p. 89.

76. VOC/OB 1725, "Account of William Keystock," fo. 823; Defoe, *A General History*, p. 522.

77. VOC/OB 1539, Michiel Dekker to Maria Segers, fo. 334; on Dekker (mispronounced as Dicker in English) see Dalton, *Life of Pitt*, p. 289. However, our poor soul Dekker, whose married life was apparently far from ideal, had quite a nice time on board of the *Adventure Galley*. When Kidd took him ashore near Goa, he was so drunk that he pleaded he was unaware Kidd had put 40,000 guilders in his luggage to cashier there—which Zwaardecroon believed, given his clear state of inebriation. VOC/OB 1635, Diary of Zwaardecroon, 29 December 1699, fo. 588 vo.

78. VOC 10812, "Diary *Ter Aa*," 29 June 1705.

79. C.S. Hill, "Notes on Piracy in Eastern Waters," *The Indian Antiquary* 55 (1926), pp. 93–95; VOC/OB 1636, Diary Deodati, 26 January, fo. 141; Wright, *Annesley of Surat*, p. 180.

80. HAG, LM, 69, 2 January 1698; Iria, *Da navegação*, p. 230, omits this passage on the Company while giving the rest of the letter.

81. J. Macau, *L'Inde danoise: La première compagnie*, 2 vols. (Aix en Provence, 1969), ii, p. 117; Bruce, *Annals*, ii, p. 575; VOC/OB 1464, 11 October 1688, fo. 378 vo.

82. VOC/OB 1684, "Relation on the examination of five pirates," fo. 2133 vo.

83. Defoe, *A General History*, p. 127; for further evidence of the connivance of the VOC in piracy see Ritchie, *Kidd*, p. 266.

84. VOC/OB 1696, 27 September 1695, fo. 341.

85. *The King of Pirates, Being an Account of Famous Enterprises of Captain Avery* (London, 1724). This story has made it to most of the literature, and was inevitably even the topic of an Errol Flynn movie. One might, however, add that there were wives of Sanusi *sayyids* on board so that Defoe embellished things just a little.

86. BNL, Pombalina, Cód. 439, 3 June 1698, fo. 177; see also the documents on reprisals against the Danish, the Dutch, and the English in Y.S. Husain (ed.), *Selected Documents of Aurengzeb's Reign (1659–1706* A.D.*)* (Hyderabad, 1957), p. 5.

87. See for the above A. Das Gupta, *Indian Merchants*, p. 15; ARA, Coll. Van Hoorn Van Riebeeck 11, iii, "Copy of a Persian letter" 14 Muharam 1119/29 April 1706.

88. Welch, *Portuguese and Dutch*, pp. 320–40; I.K. Steele, *Politics of Colonial Policy. The Board of Trade in Colonial Administration* (Oxford, 1968), pp. 42–59; VC/XVII 322, 5 April 1692, fo. 677 vo.; VOC/RXVII 221, 31 March 1692.

89. F.J. Jameson (ed.), *Pirates and Piracy in the Colonial Period: Illustrative Documents* (New York, 1923), p. 304.

90. See on this E. Pijning, "Controlling Contraband: Mentality, Economy and Society in Eighteenth Century Rio de Janeiro" (Ph. D. dissertation, Johns Hopkins University, Baltimore, 1997), p. 368.

91. Brown, *History of Madagascar*, p. 78; Deschamps, *Les pirates*, p. 190; A. Lougnon, *L'île Bourbon pendant la regence. Desforges-Bouches les débuts du café* (Paris, 1956), p. 162; Defoe, *General History*, p. 61; *NYCD*, iv, p. 41; *Fort William–India House Correspondence*, iv, p. 11.

# 11

# Concluding Thoughts

At the end of our wanderings through the Arabian seas, let us consider two issues in closing: What was the significance of exchanges and markets in the Arabian seas, and what was the European impact on this region?

We saw the Arabian seas as an ancient network of commercial, social, and cultural relations linking India with the Middle East and East Africa. Though our main concern was with the sea lanes, maritime trade was closely linked with overland trade and the fortunes of many a port depended on this. While the city-states did have ancient institutions and might struggle through reversals of fortune, many ports were mere fairs: caravanserais with some surrounding dwellings. Such places might evaporate when their bonds with the interior were severed.

The relation between land and seaborne trade is a complex one: the choice between them partly depended upon the circuits covered, partly on protection rent. Trade along the caravan roads was not replaced by seaborne trade. In some cases seaborne trade might even stimulate caravan trade. In others, commerce partly shifted to the sea routes, particularly where overland trade became dangerous, as in India in the late seventeenth century.

Trade on the coast depended on that of the hinterland. Many fairs were mere satellites on the coast of metropolises in the interior: thus Barcelore of Vijayanagar, Dabhul of Bijapur, and—as its name indicates—Laribandar of Lahore. The centers of both manufacture and government were located in the hinterland, with the bulk of the agricultural production redistributed there. The rise of colonial enclaves rearranging production in the hinterland to their own benefit is an eighteenth-century development, however, rooted in the European city-states that developed on the Coromandel Coast in the seventeenth century.[1]

Though coast and interior were complementary, there were marked differences between society along the shores of the Arabian seas and in the hinterland. Certainly, as in the interior, the peasantry was far and away the most important occupational category on the coast, and likewise most trade conducted was commerce in bulk goods with the immediate surroundings. But long-distance trade was a magnet attracting capital and resources. The allocation of markets and the flow of trade on the coast cannot, therefore, be primarily explained through military and political factors; in the interior, on the other hand, it often squared with the might of empire or landholders.

The armed hold of the state on trade along the coast differed from the interior as well. Trade, fishing, or shipping are not stationary and are, therefore, hard to tax. Mostly revenues were gathered by local officials, very often tax farmers, who sent but part of the revenue to the center, so that coastal fiscal regimes were to some extent different from hinterland regimes. The coast eluded the central control and was hence in many ways an inner frontier of both the Mughal and the Safavid empires. And this is true not only in a fiscal sense but in a military sense as well, for the often indented and heavily forested terrain of the Indian west coast was typically badly fitted for the mainly cavalry forces of the hinterland states.[2]

But the central authorities were often not really that concerned with what was happening along the coast. And certainly Mughal or Safavid nobles felt uncomfortable with the sea, preferring the stirrup to the ship. They would have felt—had they ever chosen such company—uncomfortable with mariners and merchants as well. For both nobles and scholars tended to depreciate the mean pursuit of gain for its own sake. There was a cleavage between the world vision of the bureaucrats and warriors running the kingdoms and that of merchants along its seashore.

This was no unbridgeable gap, however. Quite a few nobles, often including the king, were involved in commerce. Separate institutional arrangements for ports did not necessarily proceed from a systematic neglect of trade by the ruler. Rather, it can be more conveniently taxed locally than centrally, and the king could not legally hamper commerce. Where the court was directly trading through a monopoly, like the Safavid empire with silk, this was seen as an adjunct to "foreign policy." It was perceived as an exchange of gifts; prices were based on prestige rather than demand. One might farm out revenues but not subject the inhabitants to taxes merely to obtain a marketable surplus, however.

We have seen that the Ja'ariba imamate and the Mughal, the Safavid, and the Maratha empires did have some economic interests. They sometimes intervened directly in shipping, reserved some goods as a monopoly, and in the Safavid empire we found something pretty much approaching "bullionism." Yet such was not an Eastern variation on the mercantilist theme: there is little proof that it was part of a systematic policy to further "the national interest" by stimulating "national prosperity." Such a doctrine would have been alien to Safavid or Mughal rulers alike: these were empires of conquest, not nation-states intent on managing the economy.

And in one crucial sphere—banking—Islamic states made little effort to create institutionalized safeguards for investments. Lending to the Mughal empire was a risky matter, dependent on one's ties with acquaintances at court and on the land revenue received—on war and the harvest essentially. As the Companies' fortunes were tied to the consolidated state debts of Europe, they benefited from a clear advantage over Islamic nobles and states. It seemed they could never go broke, whereas many an amir or even many a rajah did suffer bankruptcy.

Merchant communities were linked by the common tie of credit, encompassing cash lent on interest but contingent on patronage and bonds with networks of rule, legitimacy, and caste as well. Although the continuity of credit—the permanence of the firm—certainly depended on the profitability of the enterprise, it entailed factors more difficult to quantify, like upholding one's honor and status as well. However, the merchant's stress on continuity rather than gain was quite rational in an economy vexed by constant insecurity—ranging from highway robbery to famine.

Stark fluctuations of prices might occur in the bazaar, and peddlers certainly constituted the backbone of trade. But there were staples and portfolio merchants besides. The peddlers' markets described by Steensgaard and van Leur represent but one form of market. Peddlers' markets were found when supply or demand was unpredictable, information scarce, the state not involved in trade, and no rings of merchants functioned as a buffer. We do not find a single "Asian market," but instead an array of arrangements, ranging from cutthroat competition in Basra to the closely regulated bazaars of high Yemen to huge transactions and monopolistic deals in Surat.

Staple markets like Surat were thus found in Europe and elsewhere. But, like in Europe, the market was segmented, so that a monopolist staple market might exist next to the hog cycles of a peddlers' market.[3] Merchants could engage in monopolistic practices only with goods for which there was a predictable supply and demand. Furthermore, the ability to engage in such practices depended on the transaction costs and on that of information. Monopolist practices were in the Arabian seas, as in Europe, a way to reduce these or make them more predictable.

To some extent trade was arranged by a system of "central locus markets," the location of which essentially depended on the scale of transactions and on the transaction cost and availability of information. The paramount factor in the location of staple markets (such as Surat and earlier Laribandar) and thus of the rise or decline great ports was not the competitiveness of raw materials or of labor but rather that of transaction and (overland) transport costs. And there were some hierarchically arranged chains of production as well. It seems that trade and production were increasingly organized through such spatially diversified chains in the seventeenth century.

In view of the existence of such central markets and such regionally and functionally diversified chains of production, one might—and R. Palat and others have indeed done so—cherish the Arabian seas as a "world economy" in itself.[4] For the organization of commerce and production by an array of spatially arranged marketing and trade circuits showing some degree of hierarchical setup does not necessarily have to be confined to industrial societies. The term might certainly have some use to indicate a wider system of links between different modes of production.

The main factor involved in this arrangement was not the regional endowment of production factors (labor and raw materials); rather it was the transaction costs involved: information, services, "protection rent," and transport. This explained much of the location of manufacturing industry too—industry followed the merchant rather than the other way round. This allowed, for instance, Indian urban manufacturing to compete with rural manufacturing in spite of higher urban factor prices. As such a hierarchical structuring by transactions rather than factor costs does not tally with the unequal exchange implied in the original definition of a center-periphery structure, I doubt whether the term *world economy* has any added value over *network of trade* or some similar term.[5]

Rather than seeing the Arabian seas in the seventeenth century as a world economy apart, I would go one step further—following V. Magalhães Godinho long ago and more recently Perlin, Steensgaard, Bayly, Gumilev, and Gunder Frank—and argue instead that there was only one world economy rather than several, or for that matter an infinity.[6]

The Arabian seas were since antiquity part of the "ethnosphere," an ancient, large network of cultural and technological diffusions and commercial exchanges between China, Southeast Asia, India, Central Asia, the Middle East, and East Africa as well as West Africa and Europe, which has some conjunctural fluctuations in common. States tended also to respond to similar frictions in similar ways throughout these wide stretches of land: military changes, epidemics, nomadic incursions, shifts in world demand, and climatic changes.

Within the ethnosphere as Perlin, Bayly, and very eloquently K. Pomeranz and Gunder Frank have adduced, major changes were taking place in the seventeenth century: an increasing monetization of economic relations; a "rationalization" of exchange as it got more standardized and predictable; growing ties of local markets to international markets; an expanding role of bankers, traders, and manufacturers within the economy; and growing mass consumption. In view of such developments, Perlin has argued for the rise of a special kind of capitalism, which he calls "proto-capitalism," throughout Eurasia, the difference between "proto-" and "modern" capitalism being that the former focused essentially on trade rather than on production.

This, Perlin implies, is a necessary corrective to Wallerstein's emphasis on the European origins of the world-system, which grossly overrates the European impact. I sympathize with Perlin's case that there are many simarities between Europe and Asia, almost inevitably from the point of view of an historian of the Arabian seas, a region that has been in close touch with the Mediterranean since remote antiquity. After all, one cannot but be struck by the fact that ancient Dhilmun fulfilled many of the same functions as an offshore entrepôt for trade between Europe, the Middle East, and India as Hormuz, or by the fact that Dhilmun probably displayed many of the same characteristics as Hormuz did, and to an extent Dubai still does. But while agreeing with this case overall, I ought to make two cardinal reservations.

First, though one may well distinguish similar trends, there are still such major differences as to virtually deny any similarity between Europe and the Arabian seas. Technically Indian ships might well have sailed to Britain, but there were no Mughal fortifications in England.

Second and more important, is it true that the European role in such developments was insignificant? There is a tendency in recent studies to debunk "Eurocentric" colonial history—to the extent of exaggerating in the opposite direction. While colonial history often perceived the seventeenth century as the prelude to Europe's onward march to imperial glory, largely ignoring the environment, the present tendency is to ignore the European role altogether.

But the major product traded within Eurasia was American silver and African gold, mined and/or traded by Europeans, and connections between the various component parts of the global system (Europe, Africa, the Americas, and the greater Indian Ocean) were dominated—increasingly so—by European shipowners. The striking fact is that if Indian or Arab trade within Asia might have grown, European inter-Asian trade increased far more rapidly. Again, if the output of the manufacturing industry in the greater Indian Ocean did indeed increase, the European share in its export—however small—increased far more swiftly. In my view, the modern world-system emerging in the sixteenth and seventeenth centuries was based on Europe and European enterprises. Which is not to deny that Asian and African traders or empires played their own role, apart from the European impact. But while it is certainly not true that Europeans dominated the Arabian seas, it is equally untrue to say they were not significant; they were, and increasingly so.

When assessing this question of the European significance, we enter both a safer and a more intractable field. On the one hand, the development of trade and institutions of the Companies is quite easy to study. On the other hand, however, an external impact on any society can only be assessed through questionable "what if" and "why not" constructions. (The standard example being: Why didn't the Chinese "discover" Europe?)

Yet this is in many respects the critical issue. For, obviously, within a mere 60 years from the end of our period, those same small European factories and enclaves would develop to huge territorial empires with a huge impact on Asia as a whole as well. This seems to be the major flaw in the argumentation of the "California school" of Asian economic historians. In explaining the "rise of Europe" and the "fall of Asia" in the eighteenth century they tend to ignore or dismiss the impact of colonialism on Asia. Instead they focus on factors within Europe and Asia, and essentially on country-to-country comparisons—for example, on the "energy base" of England versus China, cultural advantages of

England versus China, and so on—rather than on the world-system in which both operated. And yet if it did not cause the rise of Europe, the fall of Asia was to a very large extent, perhaps mainly, caused by the rise of Europe in Asia. For the rise of British, French, Portuguese, and Dutch colonialism (or the integration of Asia in the modern world-system) slanted the terms of trade of the world-system to the advantage of Europe rather than of Asia for a long time.

One may of course plead that this "rise of Europe" in South and Southeast Asia was a freak coincidence: that "one morning the British rose up and found they had become a great empire" (in Asia), as J.R. Seeley is often (mis-) quoted as saying.[7] However, Steensgaard confesses he feels rather uncomfortable when explaining such historic milestones by flukes, and one can sympathize with this feeling.[8]

The obvious, simple, way to tackle this thorny issue of the European significance would be, as Om Prakash has tried, to make an analysis of how much employment and income the export of, say, textiles would have provided to the "relevant regional economy."[9] Now, in Om Prakash's case of Bengal (which, as mentioned, in the late seventeenth century accounted for 33 to 40 percent of the total exports of the Dutch and English East India Companies) European demand was a very major factor indeed. But for Persia and the West Coast the answer would be that the overall European share of the export trade was quite minor and was decreasing rather than increasing at the end of the seventeenth century. In the Dutch case so little was exported from Mocha (until 1700), Surat, Persia, and Vengurla that imports exceeded exports by far and the VOC exported bullion instead of local products from there. And in the case of the English country traders too, the trade with Persia and Surat was dominated by imports rather than exports.

However, though certainly not dominating the whole trade, this import trade was not insignificant either. In the case of Surat the aggregate total trade of the East India Companies constituted about 20 to 25 percent of the commerce of the *bandar-i mobarak*. In Persia L. Winninx estimated that the total revenue of the customs of Bandar Abbas in 1646—before the trade in the Gulf began to shift to Kung—amounted to 500,000 guilders, giving us an estimated value of the whole trade of 5 to 6 million. Since the VOC then imported goods to the value of about 700,000, the VOC accounted for about 10 to 15 percent of the total trade of Bandar Abbas.[10]

Finally, in the case of East Africa the trade in ivory and gold by the Portuguese from Mozambique certainly played a major role. But if East Africa was not very significant for the total volume of trade within the Arabian seas, that was also because commerce was not that important to East Africa. As we have seen, the demand there was quite small and the market was very easily glutted because Mozambique sought few products from outside, and the Mrima Coast even less. And even on the *feiras*—the major outlet for international trade of the Monomotappa confederation—most products traded were locally produced bulk goods. Nor—in spite of its rapid growth—was the slave trade sufficient to have a notable demographic effect on Mozambique or Madagascar.

But such numerical exercises are of limited use. When assessing the importance of the transactions of Companies to the relevant regional economy one needs to consider the profit on transactions and not only their size. One can argue that transactions with the Companies led to an accumulation of profits within a tiny circle of wealthy merchants while the proceeds on the caravan trade—and of dealings with Portuguese private traders—were much more equally divided. Prakash assumes too that the relevant products would not have been exported without the demand of the Companies and that their impact on employment and on output was altogether positive. This is debatable. One might think about the singular increase in the price of spices. No doubt, this must have induced some shift of capital resources from other sectors of investment to pay for this. It is apparent too that the Indian trade with the Indonesian Archipelago was severely damaged by the VOC's impact and that the market for Indian piece-cloth in Java was in decline.

Still, despite some negative effects, the trade with the Companies might have showed a positive balance to the economies concerned. At any rate, states were highly interested in attracting those settlements. In view of such mutually profitable relations Furber has styled the seventeenth century "an age of partnership"—an era of harmonious collaboration between Europeans and Asians motivated by mutual advantage.[11]

To some extent, the long debate over indigenous collaboration with European empire—as if "European," "Asian," and "African" were fixed groups or fixed identities—beg the real question. This in a way presumes the existence of a single source of sovereignty and allegiance—putting, say, the Mughal in the position of the premier of India, or the Monomotappa in that of the president of Zimbabwe. In the seventeenth century it was perfectly possible to have multiple sovereignties over the same area, and indeed to hold to multiple and shifting allegiances. Groups could also have several "assumed" identities as both European and African or Indian, depending on the context—as we have seen in treating the Portuguese *casados*. Rather than saying that Europeans and Asians were partners, one might rather say they were part of the same trade network.

For the Europeans were tied to, and part of, a set of informal pre-existing arrangements: a law of nations or, in the Sinologist's terms, an (informal rather than formal) "world order" relating to foreign traders.[12] They were tied reluctantly, as European communities were generally quite isolated from their surroundings, often as a matter of choice. There was a good deal of racial prejudice on the European side, and (at the very least) cultural prejudice on the Asian and—as we saw—African side. Not, of course, that Africans were wrong in fearing the white men wanted to enslave them!

Yet, under the cloak of cordial and equitable commercial relationships, the European presence was first and foremost built on a capacity to deploy armed force and on the contained use of force. One might collaborate with indigenous states and traders but if there was "no fear no friendship, if no naval force no trade," as C. Boone put it.[13] Typical of the European presence in the Arabian seas was not so much the peaceful conduct of trade but rather that the European merchant—unlike the Asian and the African—was legally endowed by European governments with the capacity to act like a sovereign state and to deploy military power. The use of violence is thus the critical issue when studying European trade in the Arabian seas.

Because of the monopoly of power one might see the Companies as states, even if they pretended to be mere peaceful merchants. We have discussed the differences between the Companies and the Estado at some length. The dissimilarity is quite simple and is obscured rather than clarified by the lengthy debate on whether the Estado was "modern" or "traditional." The Estado was part of the Portuguese state. Therefore its proceeds, and the trade carried out under royal control, could be sold or dealt with as fiefs. The Estado as part of the Portuguese state did not conduct trade within Asia. It merely taxed it. It used its navicerts, or customs, not to redirect trade, but rather to allow its beneficiaries to gather an income too.

The VOC, on the other hand, was a state for whom the conduct of trade was the main objective. To realize maximum profits, the VOC evinced an urge towards detailed planning and predictability. This would include what Steensgaard calls the "internalisation of protection-costs," but this was not the most important characteristic of the VOC; rather, it was its attempt to bureaucratically control trade. The VOC—ideally—only used force after having assessed the gains that could be attained by this. Among the Portuguese such was rarely the case; war was largely an affair of private entrepreneurs. To achieve predictability of supplies from producer to consumer and utilize its economy of scale, the VOC massively invested in naval and military force intended to restrain trade and shipping within Asia.

The VOC's effort to redirect and monopolize Asian trade was an important new development—as van Leur noted. And in some branches of trade—the trade with the Moluccas and, though for completely different reasons, with Japan too, the VOC was successful. However, van Leur later began to question his own thesis.[14] Although the presence of the Companies is conspicuous, one should not overlook the dynamics of Asian shipping and trade itself, van Leur reasoned, which cannot be explained by the European impact. Hence the Dutch impact was perhaps less dramatic than van Leur originally argued.

Above all, the impact of the Europeans was highly varied, which is why it is so difficult to make sweeping statements on their impact in Asia. In the Moluccas, Java, and in some respects Kerala and Ceylon, the Company developed to become the major military power with an enormous impact on the hinterland as, surely, was the case for the Portuguese in Mozambique. For although the Portuguese failed in controlling the gold trade—their ultimate objective—they were surely quite successful in firmly establishing agrarian "rooted property" on the Zambesi. And to obtain landed property was as important an objective for private Portuguese merchants as was gathering benefits from trade. Furthermore, if the specialized literature on Monomotappa tends to see the collapse of the kingdom as resulting from purely internal factors, the absorption of lands and offices by the *prazeiros* did hollow out the state from within. Thus the European impact on Mozambique was perhaps more important than is often admitted in the literature, as was likewise the case in Madagascar. On the other hand, the European impact on the Mrima Coast was of quite minor importance, and it was altogether nil on Ethiopia.[15]

But in Iran, Yemen, and the rest of India the sheer massiveness of those agrarian civilizations stymied any substantial European impact. A few cases of "limited and strategic use of force" excepted, both the Companies and the Estado largely fit into a pattern of Asian trade routes and communities.[16] The major impact of the VOC there was not the monopoly on the spice trade—if this undoubtedly made some Indian dishes less savory. Neither was it its hold on some sea routes. No, the main impact should be looked for in two other directions, shifts taking place within a much larger frame than merely the trade of the Companies.

One important influence was the centralized inter-Asian trade of the VOC, and the English country trade, on the pattern of routes and demand within Asia. Indirect connections were replaced by direct shipping links tying together a number of Asian markets and the demand for some products. The Dutch Company took the lead here by its centralized large-scale planning and the introduction of new products under its protective cover, as we saw in the case of Javanese sugar in Persia. One could say that, partly through the European impact, prices and supplies of Asian products began to show more intimately interlocked patterns, as did the supply of bulk products. The production was centralized in places where the costs of labor were lowest. This, not primarily low transport costs, explains the success of the VOC. But once the VOC had opened a market, it often offered ample leeway to its competitors.

Yet, as noted in the treatment of the trade in various commodities, activities of the Companies were but a part of a much larger development: the integration of the Arabian seas within the modern world-system. The trade flows in the Atlantic, and the sweat and tears of Indians and black slaves on which the commerce was erected, was the heartbeat of the conjuncture of the modern world, as P. Chaunu would put it.[17]

Cases in point are the activities of smugglers and buccaneers in the southwestern Arabian seas, the semi-illicit trade on the *carreira da Índia* with Brazil and Angola, and the increasing dominance of Brazilian products in Portuguese trade. This was linked to and financed by merchant houses in the Atlantic colonies. As those cases demonstrate, to confine the European impact to the Companies is too narrow an approach. The comparative cost advantages (e.g., the cheap tobacco, leather, and rum produced in the colonies) were pulling Asian and American markets together—regardless of mercantilist restrictions. Another case of this was the substitution for Indian, Arab, and Persian products like indigo, silk, sugar, pearls, cotton, and later on even coffee—the most profitable commodities traded in the Arabian seas in the late seventeenth century—by goods produced elsewhere, generally the American colonies, and on both European and somewhat later many Asian markets.

Due to this global process of product substitution, by 1680 the transit trade through the Levant of the Arabian seas with Europe had disappeared or was in decline. This was for a while cushioned by the rise of the coffee trade both with Europe and within the Arabian seas. But this decline contributed to a prolonged depression in the commerce between the Gulf, the Red Sea and the West Coast. Internal trade within the Arabian seas smoothed the decline of the transit trade too. However, the Middle East had to pay for its imports from India by selling bulk products in the Mediterranean, like grain or wool. This was a precarious balance, which spawned an inflationary pull, both on the Ottoman and the Safavid currency.

These separate filaments—the substitution of products in the Mediterranean, the rise of American involvement in the Arabian seas, and the ascent of European intra-Asian trade—were tied together in Europe's financial centers. European businessmen effected it, and the price of products traded depended upon those in London, Paris, or Amsterdam. Areas with high and low wage levels, with high and low reserves of capital and scarcity or abundance of land increasingly competed. The fixation of prices was increasingly done on the European markets. It seems reasonable to assume that the "seventeenth-century crisis" in the Arabian seas to a large extent originated in Europe.

To be sure, some elements contributing to this had their origin within the Arabian seas—or in heaven. The cycle of bad harvests in Gujarat, Mozambique, and the Konkan may have originated in climatic shifts; the epidemics there were not—or not primarily—due to human intervention. An important cause, the weight of taxation and war, which aggravated the decline of trade, was indigenous. The spread of firearms did contribute to this, however, as did the expansion of the use of money in the levy of the land revenues.

If that was so, why did states in the Arabian seas do so little to prevent such a disadvantageous trend? After all, Ethiopia was—voluntary or not—by and large isolated from the Europeans after 1634. In this respect one may refer to the theory of F. Moulder, who explains the separate roads of development of China and Japan through Japan's closure to the outside world.[18] Such would not have been a practical option for most states in the Arabian seas, however, for two reasons. First, contacts between Europe and the Arabian seas were far closer than between Europe and East Asia, Europe and Ethiopia. There were not only maritime links but caravan routes as well: Persia's supply of bullion depended upon its overland trade with Russia and the Ottoman empire, for example. And, though certainly far from critical to the imperial revenues, the royal trade in silk did nevertheless produce undeniable financial benefits. Even the powerful and prosperous Safavid empire seemed "like a body which, to survive, needs a lot from outside," as Gentlemen XVII put it in 1647.[19]

And, second, as has emerged from the treatment of the East African trade, while long-distance trade made up only a small portion of it and was not large enough to have any clear impact on production in the hinterland, it did yield both high and easily exploitable profits. To obtain these profits and constrict trade to members of the royal household on the African side and to officials on the Portuguese, both sides tried to restrict the size of trade as much as possible and to limit it to a quite narrow range of products. By trying to gather tribute through the exploitation of foreign trade, the Yao, Sakalava, and Monomotappa (and later the Rozvi) rulers were trying to exploit the Europeans as much as the other way around.[20]

And the exchange was of some benefit to Persia too, through earnings from re-exporting products. The balance of trade was highly favorable to the Zaidit imamate. And, although I have nuanced his view to some extent, K.N. Chaudhuri's judgment that the imports of bullion in India represented a payment for the exports of Indian products to Europe—so that the balance of trade was in India's favor and it was highly profitable for Indian states to attract European traders—is well justified.[21]

The advantage of trade with the Companies accrued to great Indian merchants—wealthy traders who could more conveniently be taxed than caravan traders—and to bankers, of whom some financed the Mughal empire. Consequently the trade yielded a double advantage to the Mughal, the Adilshahi, the Maratha rulers, and to those of Cochin: it generated and concentrated wealth, spatially in cities and market towns and socially among rich merchants and substantial farmers. For wealth did not accrue to "the Indian economy"[22] but to groups, classes, in India; there is no reason why commercial wealth should have trickled down to the poor. While certainly giving some short-run benefit to the rural producers, in the longer run it may have even exacerbated rural inequality. Peasants cultivating cash crops were far more dependent on rural credit and on links to the market than were mainly self-sufficient communities, strengthening the roles of rural moneylenders, merchants, landlords, and tax gatherers. Profits gathered in the pepper or indigo trade thus hardly made most poor *rayyat*s prosperous.

To those beneficiaries of trade the Companies and the Estado sold arms and protection—security from the perils of war and urban and rural insurgency, caused either by the corruption of the administration or by the increasing disparities of wealth and power occasioned by production for export.

Closely related to this marketing of protection was the fact that in the seventeenth century the Europeans began, with the threat of violence, to shift the boundary of jurisdiction in their favor. The European enclaves were surrounded by a frontier of low-key violence: the normal disorder during the levy of the land revenues. The European communities were bound to become entangled in conflicts in their surroundings, for they rarely had clear boundaries.

This was generally the kernel of conflict between companies and kings. The local conflicts between Goa, Bijapur, and the Marathas on the jurisdiction over areas adjacent to Daman and Goa are a case in point, and so are those between Cochin and Calicut.

Of course, such tussles were not always resolved to the favor of the Europeans—far from it. As we have seen, both the Dutch and the English attempts to force concessions on the Mughal empire by blockading Surat and the Hugly by and large failed. Likewise, the two attempts of the VOC to obtain favorable conditions of trade from the Safavid empire in 1645 and 1684 by bombarding Bandar Abbas and assaulting Khism were costly failures. Isfahan barely took note of the VOC's attempt to enhance its standing by the use of its "awesome weapons" in the Gulf. These weapons notwithstanding, the court continued to treat the Company's emissaries as mere humble supplicants at the "gate of bliss."

Yet from this ensued a broad and multifaceted degree of friction regarding the question of which law was applicable to whom, and when. In the seventeenth century a situation ensued, moreover, whereby indigenous traders became dependent (financially too) on the Estado and the Companies—or rather the Company states—and whereby the Companies claimed jurisdiction over them. And it was quite advantageous for indigenous bankers and nobles—enriched through transactions with the Companies—to seek their aid: the Companies were able to provide them with boundless credit. This had far-reaching consequences when a European credit circuit in Asia developed. Of course, the agency houses were not directly linked to the EIC, but since most of its servants had invested in them one could—during emergencies—fall back on the capital of the Company and recurrently its armed support as well. Indian merchants and rulers were seeking security by investments in several portfolios, both land revenues and commerce. Investments in Companies habitually did not yield high but did produce predictable profits. Therefore, many a merchant and noble would replenish loans from a *shroff* with loans from a Company. Those outlays served as backup for riskier ones, including political intrigues. If a quarrel arose during such deals, the Companies would claim they enjoyed preference above other suitors and that the persons involved resorted under their jurisdiction. Local officials, nobles, and finally and inevitably kings, were thus caught in a web of investments and loans, with territorial possession serving as collateral.

And while professing to be trade organizations, both the VOC and the EIC were states as well, and the interests of the trade organization became increasingly subordinated to those of the state. The urge was—as Van Hoorn put it—"to constantly fear decline; to shy away from any change which might be harmful; and to embrace, on the other hand, anything which may strengthen." And as J. Childe memorably said, the search was for "a sure and well grounded revenue for all times to come."

## Notes

1. R. Murphy, *The Outsiders: The Western Experience in India and China* (Ann Arbor, 1977).
2. J.C. Heesterman, "Warriors and Merchants," *Itinerário* 15 (1) (1991), p. 47.
3. See, for example, the criticism of P.W. Klein's views by J.W. Veluwenkamp, "Ondernemersgedrag op de Hollandse stapelmarkt in de tijd van de Republiek. De Amsterdamse handelsfirma Jan Isaac de Neufville & Comp. 1730–1764" (Academisch Proefschrift, University of Leiden, 1981), pp. 11–21.
4. R. Palat et al., "The Incorporation and Peripheralization of South Asia," *Review* 10, 1 (1986), pp. 173–76.
5. See the useful comments on Palat c.s. by S. Subrahmanyam, "World Economies and South Asia: A Sceptical Note," *Review* 12, 1 (1992), pp. 141–48.
6. V. Magalhães Godinho, "A viragem mundial de 1517–1524 e o imperio português," in *Ensaios*, ii, pp. 141–53; Perlin, "Proto-Industrialisation," p. 91; N. Steensgaard, "Asian Trade and World Market: Orders of Magnitude in the 'Long Sixteenth Century,' " in *L'histoire à Nice. Actes du Colloque international 1980* (Nice, 1981), iii, pp. 129–47; C.A. Bayly, *Imperial Meridian: The British Empire and the World 1780–1830* (London, 1988); pp. 18–34; A. Gunder Frank and B. Gillis, *The World System: 300 or 3000 Years?* (London, 1994).
7. Although—as normal with famous quotations—Seeley said nothing of the kind. What he tried to indicate in his *Expansion of England* was that the administration *in Westminster* only woke up late to the existence of the Asian empire and then accepted its existence only reluctantly.
8. N. Steensgaard, "Asian Trade and the World Economy from the 15th to the 18th Century," in de Souza (ed.), *Indo-Portuguese History*, p. 228.
9. Om Prakash, "The Dutch East India Archives as Source Material on Indian History," *Itinerário* 7 (2) (1983), p. 47.
10. Das Gupta, *Indian Merchants*, p. 136; VOC/OB, 1136, Diary of L. Winnincx, fo. 198 vo., 28 August 1646; VOC/OB 1144, 8 September 1646, fo. 562.
11. H. Furber, "Asia and the West as Partners Before Empire and After," *JAS* 28 (4) (1969), pp. 711–21.
12. L. Blussé, "Tussen geveinsde vrunden en verklaarde vijanden," inaugural lecture (Amsterdam/Leiden, 1999).
13. C. Boone quoted in K.N. Chaudhuri, *Trade and Civilisation*, p. 3.
14. "Over de mogelijkheid van de achttiende eeuw als een categorie in de Indische geschiedenis," originally published in *Tijdschrift voor Indische Taal-, Land- en Volkenkunde* 80 (1940); and in English in *Indonesian Trade and Society: Essays in Asian Social and Economic History* (The Hague, 1955), pp. 268–89.
15. Thus, I would not agree with Pearson's conclusion (*Port Cities and Intruders*, p. 154) that the Portuguese impact on the Swahili Coast was neglible, or that the Portuguese presence there was a failure. Nor, indeed—as we have seen in the case of northwestern Madagacar or in that of Khisn—would I argue that the Portuguese found "peaceful and free trade" there and that they (and only they) tried to monopolize it by force.
16. Van Santen, "Verenigde Oost-Indische Compagnie," p. 25.

17. P. Chaunu, *Sevilla y América*, p. 322; by implication I also support the famous thesis of E. Williams, *Capitalism and Slavery* (London, 1941), that slavery was paramount to the rise of capitalism, although of mercantile and perhaps not of industrial capitalism.

18. *Japan, China and the Modern World-Economy: Towards a Reinterpretation of East Asian Development ca. 1650 to ca. 1918* (Cambridge, 1977).

19. VOC/XVII 316, 16 August 1646, fo. 62 vo.

20. This refers to the "African mode of production" debate, to which I alluded in chapter 1. But though the African mode of production model might well be relevant to Monomotappa and Kiteve, it seems a questionable model for Madagascar. The cultivation of rice there did normally produce large surpluses, so that the Malagasy rural economy was less locked into a bolster of self-sufficient production than agriculture in southern Mozambique. In Madagascar states could rely less on incomes from trade, and the large-scale exploitation of agrarian resources by forced labor was much more important than on the East African mainland. See P. Boiteau, *Les Droits sur la terre dans la société malgache pré-coloniale. Contribution à l'étude du mode de production asiatique* (Cahiers d'étude et de recherches marxistes) (Paris, 1969).

21. And this is well attested in Mughal and Maratha sources besides. Thus it is in the *Ajñapatra*, where it is argued that, though the Europeans were potentially dangerous since they tended to mingle in politics and built fortifications, one had nevertheless to allow European settlements as their procurements of goods provided work for many poor people. See S.V. Punambekar, "The Ajñapatra or Royal Edict Relating to the Principles of Maratha State Policy," *Journal of Indian History* 8 (2, 3), pp. 81–105, 207–33.

22. I put "the Indian economy" in quotation marks as the formulation assumes that India was one (national) economy in the seventeenth century, a position I consider arguble.

# Appendix One: Currencies and Measures

## Currencies

### *Europe*

1 guilder = 20 stuivers
1 rixdollar (rijksdaalder)
= 48 stuivers
1 Mexican real = 2.5 guilders
1 pound sterling = 0.6 guilders
1 cruzado = 2 guilders
1 cruzado = 400 milreis

### *Netherlands Indies*

1 "light" guilder = 15 stuivers
1 rixdollar = 60 stuivers
1 Mexican real = 2.5 guilders
1 liondollar (leeuwendaalder)
= 48 stuivers

### *Portuguese Indies*

1 cruzado = 1.4 Spanish reales
1 xeraphin = 2.4 guilders
1 xeraphin = 5 tangas
1 tanga = 16 stuivers
1 xeraphin = 300 milreis
1 pardao = 1 milrei

### *Mozambique*

1 cruzado = 1.5 reales

### *Malabar*

1 ducaton = 2 reales
1 real = 5 fanam
1 fanam = 10 stuivers
1 pagoda = 10 fanams

### *Coromandel*

### *Pulicat*

1 pagoda = 24 fanams
1 pagoda = 84 stuivers

### *Masulipatam*

1 pagoda = 15 fanams
1 pagoda = 96 stuivers

### *Súrat*

1 real = 51 stuivers
1 rupee = 2.4 guilders
1 rupee = 2.5 mahmudis
1 rupee = 42 paisas

1 rupee = 16 annas
1 larin = 10 stuivers

***Persia***

1 toman = 40 guilders
1 toman = 10 oris
1 ori = 10 mahmudis
1 mahmudi = 10 annas
1 mahmudi = 1 quazbegi

***Vengurla and Canara***

1 larin = 20 stuivers
1 pagoda = 10 larins
1 larin = 1 fanams

***Yemen***

1 liondollar = 1.2–1.6 reales
1 real = 80 kabir

***Basra***

1 liondollar = 0.8 real

## Measures

***Europe***

1 Dutch pound = 494 grams
= 0.4 kilo
1 last = 3,000 pounds

***Netherlands Indies***

1 bahar = 3 picols
1 picol = 3.66 pounds

***Portuguese Indies***

1 quintal = 101 pounds
1 marques = 0.38 pound

***Mozambique***

1 bahar ivory = 540 pounds

***Persia***

1 bahar = 505 pounds
1 man-i shah = 10 pounds
1 man of Bandar Abbas
= 30 pounds

***Surat***

1 maund = 34 pounds
1 maund = 44 shirs
1 maund indigo in Agra
= 50 pounds
1 maund indigo in Ahmedabad
= 31 pounds
1 candil cotton = 610 pounds
1 candil spices = 690 pounds
1 carga textiles = 34 pieces

***Vengurla and Canara***

1 maund spices = 24 pounds
1 guni = 288 pounds
1 candil = 600 pounds

***Kerala***

1 candil = 500 pounds
1 candil cotton = 690 pounds
1 maund Kerala = 24.5 pounds
1 para = 40 pounds

# Appendix Two: Viceroys and Governors-General

### *1. Government of Portuguese India, 1629–1705*

| | |
|---|---|
| 1629–1635 | Viceroy Dom Miguel de Noronha (Count of Linhares) |
| 1635–1639 | Viceroy Dom Pedro da Silva |
| 1639 | Governor Antônio Telles de Menezes |
| 1640–1645 | Viceroy Dom João de Silva Telles de Menezes (Count of Aveiras) |
| 1645–1651 | Viceroy Dom Felipe Mascarenhas |
| 1651–1652 | Council Dom Frey Francisco de Martins, Antônio de Souza Coutinho, Francisco de Mello e Castro |
| 1652–1654 | Viceroy Dom Vasco de Mascarenhas (Count of Óbidos) |
| 1654 | Manuel Mascarenhas Homem (not recognized by crown) |
| 1655–1656 | Viceroy Dom Rodrigo Lobo de Silveira (Count of Sarzedas) |
| 1656–1661 | Council Manuel Mascarenhas Homem, Francisco de Mello e Castro, Antônio de Souza Coutinho |
| 1661–1662 | Council Luís de Mendonça Furtado, Dom Manuel Mascarenhas, Dom Pedro de Alencastre |
| 1662–1666 | Viceroy Antônio de Mello e Castro |
| 1666–1668 | Viceroy João Nunes de Costa |
| 1668–1671 | Council Antônio de Mello e Castro, Manuel de Corte Real, Antônio Vaz de Sampayo |
| 1671–1676 | Viceroy Luís de Mendonça Furtado (Count of São Vicente) |
| 1676–1678 | Viceroy Dom Pedro de Almeida (Count of Asumar) |
| 1678–1681 | Governors Antônio Pães de Sande, Frey Antônio Brandão |

| | |
|---|---|
| 1681–1686 | Viceroy Francisco de Távora (Count of Alvor) |
| 1686–1690 | Governor Dom Rodrigues da Costa |
| 1690–1691 | Governor Dom Miguel de Almeida |
| 1691–1692 | Council Frey Agostinho de Annunciação, Dom Fernando de Martim de Mascarenhas, Dom Pedro de Alencastre |
| 1693–1698 | Viceroy Dom Pedro Antônio de Noronha (Count of Villa Verde) |
| 1698–1701 | Viceroy Antônio Luís Gonçalves de Câmera Coutinho |
| 1701–1705 | Viceroy Antônio Caetano de Mello e Castro |

## 2. *Governor-General of Netherlands Indies*

| | |
|---|---|
| 1610–1614 | Pieter Both |
| 1614–1615 | Gerard Reynst |
| 1616–1619 | Laurens Reaal |
| 1619–1623 | Jan Pieterszoon Coen |
| 1623–1627 | Pieter de Carpentier |
| 1627–1629 | Jan Pieterszoon Coen |
| 1629–1632 | Jacques Speck |
| 1632–1636 | Hendrik Brouwer |
| 1636–1645 | Anthonie van Diemen |
| 1645–1650 | Cornelis van Lijn |
| 1653–1678 | Cornelis Maetsuycker |
| 1678–1681 | Rijkloff Volckertzoon van Goens |
| 1681–1684 | Cornelis Speelman |
| 1684–1691 | Johan Camphuys |
| 1691–1704 | Willem van Oudhoorn |
| 1704–1709 | Johan van Hoorn |

# Glossary

*Abunhado:* Serf tied to a village

*Akhbarat:* Provincial newsletter

*Aldeia:* Village, administrative district

*Alfândega:* Customs station

*Ali Kapu:* "Sublime gate," the Safavid court

*Ali Raja:* Hereditary ruler over the Muslim community in Cananore

*Alim*, pl. *ulama:* Islamic scholar

*Almazem:* Dockyard

*Almazem do reino:* Royal dockyards in Lisbon and Goa

*Almirante:* Commodore

*Amir:* Noble

*Analoatra:* Foreign (originally Muslim) settlers in Madagascar

*Bailardeira:* Indian nautch girl

*Bania:* Merchant caste, also Hindu merchant in general, especially from Gujarat

*Batta:* Premium

*Begam:* The king's mother or sister

*Beglarbeg:* Ottoman and Safavid provincial governor

*Bewindhebbers:* Members of the council of the supreme board of the Dutch East India Company, the Gentlemen XVII

*Bhora:* Follower of an Islamic Ismailite sect

*Bombara:* Dhow, especially with two or more sails

*Bottomry:* Form of maritime insurance whereby the sum lent is repaid upon the return of the keel with a percentage of interest

*Cabedal:* Investment

*Cabedal do reino:* Capital and merchandise sent by the Portuguese crown to invest in return goods

*Cafilla:* Caravan, or fleet of trading vessels with escort of warships

*Canarin:* Indian Catholic; in Mozambique, Hindu and Christian emigrants from Goa

*Capitão-mor:* Commodore

*Carreira da Índia:* Navigation between Portugal and Asia

*Cartaz:* Passport, navicert

*Casa da Índia:* "India office" responsible for conducting trade and navigation between Portugal, Asia, and Guinea

*Casa dos contos:* Council of the exchequer

*Casado:* Portuguese married man, dwelling in India

*Chaukidar:* Leaseholder of right to levy taxes on staple goods

*Chauth:* Percentage levy on the land revenue, generally amounting to about 15 percent

*Chettiar:* Merchant caste on the Coromandel Coast

*Chulia:* Collective term for Muslims dwelling along the South Indian coast

*Cola:* Monopoly of the captain of Bassein fortress on the trade with wood

*Colathiri:* Rajah of Cananore

*Collecta:* 1 percent levy on foodstuffs imported in Goa, levied by the senate of Goa, to finance a fleet to escort the rice trade from Canara.

*Commandement:* Presidency of the Dutch East India Company, comprising several main and out-factories

*Commenda:* Commercial arrangement whereby a couple of merchants pool their funds to pay an agent who is allowed a percentage profit on the transactions

*Concessionary voyage:* A monopoly to undertake a voyage along a stipulated route in return for a lump sum

*Conquista:* Conquest, conquests

*Conselho administrativo:* Plenipotentiary council

*Conselho da Fazenda:* Board of the exchequer

*Conselho do Estado:* Council of state

*Conselho Ultramarino:* Portuguese sovereign council for the overseas possessions

*Consulta:* Legal consultation

*Curva:* Impost on foreign traders in the Monomotappa kingdom

*Dastak:* Written free permit

*Dasturi:* Generally 1–2 percent share of the purchase price of a good, delivered by its buyer to the seller

*Desai:* Mostly hereditary proprietor of the right to collect landed revenues for one or several villages on behalf of the king

*Desembargador:* Justice of the peace, itinerant judge

*Desembargadores do paço:* Portuguese "privy council"

*Devassa:* Preliminary legal inquiry, instituted by any official with the power of judicial prosecution

*Divan:* Treasury

*Divan-i khassi:* Treasury of the royal domain

*Echelle:* Place where seaways are tied to routes to the interior

*Estanco:* Tax farm held in monopoly

*Estanco do Comércio:* Monopoly of a board on the conduct of trade; here especially used for the conduct of trade to Sofala

*Estanco do Tabaco:* Monopoly of the Portuguese crown to pound and sell tobacco

*Farman:* Royal charter

*Faujdar:* Regional governor (Bijapur)

*Feitor:* Merchant dealing on behalf of the Portuguese crown

*Feitoria:* Factory

*Fidalgo:* Knight

*Fiscaal:* Attorney

*Foro:* Usufruct of royal property for one generation; *foreiro:* proprietor of a *foro*

*Free burgher (vrjburger):* Dutch inhabitant of Asia not in the service of the VOC but within its jurisdiction

*Frotta do alto bordo:* High-seas fleet

*Frotta do estreito:* Fleets mustered by the Portuguese to the Red Sea and the Persian Gulf

*Frotta dos remos:* Escorted fleet of oared vessels, connecting Goa and Praças do Norte to Canara and Cambay

*Fumo:* Semi-independent confederate chief of the Monomotappa kingdom

*Gaokar:* Hereditary proprietor to the first use of land (Goa)

*Gentlemen XVII (Heren XVII):* Board of directors of the Dutch East India Company

*Ghaz:* Warrior of Islam

*Girasia:* General name for Rajput (warrior) junior subcastes in Gujarat

*Haagsch Besoigne:* Committee of correspondence of the VOC

*Hajjis:* Pilgrims to Mecca

*Hoge Regering:* Dutch governor-general and council of the Indies at Batavia

*Hoofdbouwer:* Large cultivator of indigo

*Inam* or *madad i-ma'ash:* Property or land exempt of taxation and mostly outside of jurisdiction, whereby the former is mostly endowed to an institution, the latter mostly to an individual

*Independent fiscaal:* Independent attorney named by and accountable to Gentlemen XVII

*Jilbas:* large flat-bottomed crafts tied together with ropes without use of nails, used within the Red Sea

*Junta do Coméralo:* Board running the new Portuguese East India Company

*Junta do Póvo:* Diet

*Junta do Tabaco:* Board conducting trade and sales of tobacco on behalf of the Portuguese crown

*Kaimal:* Feudatory of the king's family in Kerala

*Khatri:* Northwest Indian Brahmin caste

*Koli:* Native tribes of Gujarat and the Deccan

*Krankenbezoeker:* Dutch lay preacher

*Lançado:* Portuguese freebooter or outlaw living outside of Portuguese jurisdiction

*Lascarin:* Indian (especially Hindu) mercenary

*Maidan:* Large square

*Mansabdar:* Nobleman given land by the emperor for feeding horses

*Mappilas:* indigenous (*deshi*) Muslims of Kerala

*Misericórdia:* House of charity

*Muzungo:* Chiefs and merchants of the Kiteve kingdom around Sofala, allotted *praças da coroa* by the Portuguese

*Muzungulos:* The "twelve cities" of inhabitants immediately surrounding Mombasa

*Nakhuda:* Captain or supercargo of an Indian or Persian vessel

*Nayyar:* Warrior caste in Kerala

*Negus:* Emperor of Ethiopia

*Noorderkwartier:* Province of present-day Noord Holland from Amsterdam and Haarlem northward

*Ommelanden:* Surroundings of Batavia, conquered by Dutch East India Company

*Passos secos:* Passable fords between the islands of Goa, Bardes, and Salcete and the mainland

*Peshkash:* gifts or tribute

*Peta:* Small market town

*Praças do Norte:* Portuguese possessions along the littoral from Chaul to Daman

*Prazo da coroa:* Fief granted for one generation in return for a quit-rent after which the territory reverts to the control of the crown

*Prazeiros:* Persons being granted a *prazo da coroa*

*Qazi:* Religious judge

*Rahdari:* Road dues

*Rajadors:* Minister or lieutenant in Kerala

*Rayyat:* The Indian tiller of the soil

*Regenten:* Families with a predominant stake in communal councils in Holland

*Reinois:* Inhabitants of Portuguese Asia deriving from and intending to return to Portugal

*Relação:* Court of justice

*Renda do katvali:* Tax farm of fees on petty offenses

*Renúnçia:* Procedure whereby an official, upon the expiration of his term to office, is allowed to name three candidates for his succesion, and is mostly paid some cash in reward

*Saraswat:* Brahmin caste originally from the Konkan

*Senado da Câmera:* Municipal council

*Sepoy:* Indian mercenary

*Sertaneiros:* "Explorers of the bush"

*Shahbandar:* Master of the port

*Shamal:* Strong and unreliable wind in the Gulf from April to May

*Shastra:* Corpus of Hindu law

*Sheikh al-Islam:* Islamic supreme judge

*Shroff:* Local moneylender and moneychanger

*Sidhi:* Descendants of Ethiopian slaves

*Sipahsalar:* Generalissimo

*Subah:* Province of the Mughal empire

*Subehdar:* Governor of a province

*Tanahdar:* Governor of a district

*Tanaqin:* Flat-bottomed ship with one sail, used in shallow waters and on rivers in the Persian Gulf region

*Tombo:* Register of dues paid for fiefs

*Topaz:* Catholic Indian, especially of European descent

*Vahema:* Fortified compound, generally located on a hillock in Madagascar

*Vakil:* Agent, representative

*Vali:* Second in command, marshal

*Veador da fazenda:* Chancellor of the exchequer of Portuguese India

*Weeskamer:* Orphanage

*Werkbaas:* Foreman, jobber

*Westerkwartieren:* VOC factories in India and Persia

*Zambucca:* Dhow with two sails

*Zamindar:* Local landholder

*Zamorin:* Ruler of Calicut

# Bibliography

## Published Works


Aalbers, J. *Ryckloff Volckertsz. Van Goens. Commisaris en veldoverste van de Oost-Indische Compagnie en zijn arbeidsveld in Indië 1653/1654 en 1657/1658*. Groningen, 1916.

Abdulaev, M.G. *Politeceśkic, ekonomiceskic i socialnogo istorija Azerbaidjana v XVIII v. i vsaimotnošenije ego s Rossiejei*. Baku, 1967.

Abel, W. *Massenarmut und Hungerkrisen im vorindustriellen Europa*. Hamburg, 1974.

Abeyasinge, T. *Portuguese Rule in Ceylon*. Colombo, 1966.

Abir, M. "Southern Ethiopia." In R. Gray and D. Birmingham (eds.), *Pre-Colonial African Trade,* pp. 119–39.

———. *Ethiopia and the Red Sea: The Fall of the Solomonic Dynasty and European-Muslim Rivalry in the Region*. London, 1980.

Abramjan, R.A. *Armjanskie istocniki XVIII veka ob Indii*. Erevan, 1968.

Abu-Lughod, J. *Before European Dominion: The World System* A.D. *1250–1350*. New York, 1989.

Ahmad, A. *Indo-Portuguese Trade in Seventeenth Century*. New Delhi, 1991.

Aitchinson, A.H., ed. *A Collection of Treaties, Engagements and Sunnuds Relating to India and Neighbouring Countries*. 8 vols. Calcutta, 1862–67.

Akerlof, G. *An Economic Theorist's Book of Tales*. Cambridge, 1984.

Alam, M. *The Crisis of Empire in Mughal North India: Awadh and the Punjab 1707–1748*. Delhi, 1986.

Albuquerque, L. de, ed. "Diário da viagem de Dom Álvaro de Castro ao Hadramaute em 1548." *Revista da Universidade de Coimbra* 23 (1973), pp. 157–221.

Albuquerque, V. de. *O Senado da Goa. Memória histórica-archeológica*. Nova Goa, 1909.

Alexandrowicz, C.H. *An Introduction to the Law of Nations in the East Indies*. Oxford, 1976.

———. "A Persian-Dutch Treaty in the Seventeenth Century." *The International Handbook of International Affairs* (1958), pp. 201–6.

Alibert, G. *Mayotte. Plaque tournante et microcosme de l'Océan Indien*. Paris, 1984.

Allavi, R.A. "New Light on Mughal Cavalry." In *Medieval India: A Miscellany*, vol. 2, pp. 70–99. Bombay, 1973.

Allen, C.H. "The Indian Merchant Community of Muscat." *Bulletin of the School of Oriental and African Studies* 44 (1) (1981), pp. 39–54.

Allen, J. de V. *Swahili Origins*. London, 1993.

Allen, W.E.D. *A History of the Georgian People*. London, 1932.

Almeida Calado, A. de, ed. *Livro em que se tratta muito por extenso das cousas da Índia e do Japão*. Coimbra, 1957.

———. "Acclimatição de plantas do oriente no Brasil durante os séculos XVII e XVIII." *Revista Portuguêsa Da história* 15 (1976), pp. 339–81.

Alpers, E.A. "Towards a History of the Expansion of Islam in East Africa: The Matrilineal People of the Southern Interior." In T.O. Ranger and I.M. Kimambo (eds.), *The Historical Study of African Religion*, pp. 172–201. London, 1972.

———. *Ivory and Slaves in East Central Africa*. London, 1975.

———. "Gujarat and the Trade of East Africa." *IJAHS* 9 (1) (1976), pp. 368–90.

Amancio Gracias, J.R. de. *Floreal da nobreza da cidade de Goa*. Bastora, 1905.

———. "Bens pensionadas de Goa." *O Oriente Português*, Nova série, 4. Bastora, 1936, pp. 1–56.

Amaral Lapa, J.R. de. "O Brasil e a navegação para a Ásia." *Estudos históricos*. Marilla, 1968, pp. 110–73.

———. *O Brasil e as drogas do Oriente*. Amaril, 1973.

Ames, G.J. "The Estado da Índia 1662–1684: Strategies and Priorities in Europe and the East." *Studia* 48 (1989), pp. 214–42.

———. "The Carreira da Índia 1668–1682: Maritime Enterprise and the Quest for Stability in Portugal's Asian Empire." *Journal of European Economic History* 20 (1) (1991), pp. 7–27.

Andersen, J., and V. Iversen. *Orientalische Reisebeschreibung*. A. Olearius, ed. Deutsche Neudrucke Reihe Barock 27, Tübingen, 1980.

Andrade, A.A. de. *Relações de Moçambique settecentista*. Lisbon, 1956.

Andresyan, H.D. *Polonyali Simeon'un seyhatnâmesi*. Istanbul, 1964.

Antonova, A.A., ed. *Russko-Indiskie otnošenija v XVIII v*. Moscow, 1985.

Arasaratnam, S. *Dutch Power in Ceylon 1659–1676*. Amsterdam, 1958.

———. "Dutch Monopoly Policy in Ceylon and Its Effect on the Indo-Ceylon Trade." *IESHR* 4 (2) (1967), pp. 119–30.

———. "Monopoly and Free Trade in Dutch-Asian Commercial Policy." *Journal of Southeast Asian History* (1973), pp. 1–15.

———. "The Coromandel Southeast Asia Trade 1650–1740: Challenges and Adaptation of a Commercial System." *Journal of Asian History* 18 (1984), pp. 113–35.

———. *Merchants, Companies and Commerce on the Coromandel Coast 1650–1740*. New Delhi, 1986.

———. "India and the Indian Ocean in the Seventeenth Century." In A. Das Gupta and M. Pearson (eds.), *India and the Indian Ocean*.

Araujo, M.B. de. *O giro moçambiquano. Subsídio para a história de Moçambique*. Coimbra, 1992.

Archdeacon, T.J. *New York City 1664–1700: Conquest and Change*. Ithaca, 1976.

*Armas e inscrições do forte de Baçaim*. Lisbon, 1975.

Armstrong, G. "Madagascar and the Slave Trade in the Seventeenth Century." *Omaly sy Anio* 23/24 (1986), pp. 211–35.

Arregay, M.W. "A Reappraisal of the Impact of Firearms on the History of Ethiopia." *Journal of Ethiopian Studies* 13 (1) (1975), pp. 92–123.

Arunchalam, B. "The Heaven-Finding Art in Indian Navigational Tradition and Cartography." In S. Chandra (ed.), *The Indian Ocean*, pp. 191–221.

Ashton, T., ed. *Crisis in Europe 1550–1650*, London, 1964.

Ashtor, E. *The Levant Trade in the Late Middle Ages*. Princeton, 1985.

Athar Ali, M. *The Mughal Nobility Under Aurengzeb*. London, 1966.

———. "The Passing of Empire: The Mughal Case." *MAS* 9 (3) (1975), pp. 385–396.

*Atlas-i naghsheha-ye joqrafiya-'i va asnad baraye tarikhi dar Khalij-e Fars*. Teheran, 1971.

Attman, A. *Den Rysska marknaden i det 1500-talets Baltiska politik*. Lund, 1944.

———. *The Bullion Flow Between Europe and the East* (Acta Regiae Societatis Scientiarum et Litteraturum Gothenburgensis Humianora 20). Gotteborg, 1981.

Auber, A. *An Analysis of the Constitution of the East India Company*. London, 1826.

Aubin, J., ed. "Le Orçamento do Estado da Índia de Antônio de Abreu." *Studia* 4 (1959).

———, ed. *L'Ambassade de Gregório Pereira fidalgo à la cour du châh soltân Hosseyn*. Lisbon, 1971.

———. "Le royaume de Hormuz." *Mare Luso-Indicum* 2 (1972), pp. 120–231.

———. "Les persans au Siam dans le règne de Narain." *Mare Luso-Indicum* 4 (1980), pp. 95–126.

Austen, R. "The 19th Century Islamic Slave Trade from East Africa (Swahili and Red Sea Coast): A Tentative Census." In W.G. Clarence Smith (ed.), *The Economics of the Indian Ocean Slave Trade in the Nineteenth Century*. London, 1989.

Axelson, E. *Portuguese in Southeast Africa 1498–1699*. Cape Town, 1963.

Azevedo, L. de. *Épocas de Portugal económico*. Lisbon 1974/78.

Bacqué-Grammont, J.L. *Les Ottomans, les Safavides et leurs voisins: contribution à l'histoire des rélations internationales dans l'Orient islamique*. Leiden and Istanbul, 1987.

Baião, A., ed. *Itinerários da Índia athé o Portugal por terra*. Coimbra, 1923.

———. *A inquisição de Goa*. 2 vols. Lisbon, 1930/1945.

Bailyn, C. *The New England Merchants in the Seventeenth Century*. New York 1964/1972.

Bailyn, C., and L. Bailyn. *Massachussets Shipping 1679–1718. A Statistical Study*. Cambridge, MA, 1956.

Baladounian, V. "Armenian Trade with the English East India Company." *Journal of European Economic History* 15 (1) (1987), pp. 157–83.

Baldeus, F. *Nauwekeurige beschryvinge van Malabar en Coromandel, derzelver aangrensende rycken en van 't magtig eyland Ceylon*. Amsterdam, 1672.

Baldry, J. "The Early History of the Yemeni Port of al-Huddaydah." *Arabian Studies* 7 (1) (1985), pp. 37–53.

Barber, W.I. *British Economic Thought and India*. Oxford, 1975.

Barendse, R.J. "The Long Road to Livorno: The Overland Messenger Service of the Dutch East India Company in the Seventeenth Century." *Itinerário* 12 (1) (1988), pp. 25–45.

———. "Pirates of the West Coast: A Case Tried at the Court of Cochin in 1704." Forthcoming in *Comptes rendus du colloque international sur l'esclavage à la côte ouest de Madagascar*. Tamatave.

Barros, J. des and D. do Couto. *Da Ásia. Dos feitos que os portuguezes fizeram na conquista e descobrimento das terras e mares do oriente*. 25 vols. Lisbon, 1780; facsimile reprint, 1974.

Basset, D.K. "Early English Trade and Settlement in Asia." In J.S. Bromley and E. Kossman (eds.), *Britain and the Netherlands in Europe and Asia. Papers delivered to the Third Anglo-Dutch Historical Conference*. London, 1968.

———. "British 'Country Trade' and Local Trade Networks in the Thai and Malay States, 1680–1770." *MAS* 23 (4) (1989), pp. 625–45.

———. *The British in South-East Asia During the Seventeenth and Eighteenth Centuries*. London, 1990.

Bastani Parizi, M.A. *Siasat va eqtesad-i ʿasr-i Safavi*. Teheran, 1354.

Bastin, J. *The Changing Pattern of the Early South-East Asian Spice Trade*. Kuala Lumpur, 1956.

———. *The British in Western Sumatra*. London, 1965.

Bathurst, G. "Imamate and Maritime Trade: Two Principal Themes in the History of Oman." In D.K. Hopwood (ed.), *The Arab Peninsula: Society and Politics*, pp. 93–126. London, 1972.

Bayly, C.A. "Indian Merchants in a 'Traditional' Setting: Varaṇasi 1780–1830." In C.A. Dewey and A.G. Hopkins (eds.), *The Imperial Impact: Studies in the Economic History of India and Africa*. London, 1978.

———. *Rulers, Townsmen and Bazaars: North Indian Society in the Age of British Expansion*. Cambridge, 1983.

———. *Imperial Meridian: The British Empire and the World 1780–1830*. Oxford, 1988.

Bayly, S. "Hindu Kingship and the Origins of Community: Religion, State and Society in Kerala." *MAS* 18 (2) (1984), pp. 177–213

Beach, D. *The Shona and Their Neighbours*. Oxford, 1994.

Beachy, D.R. "The Arms Trade in East Africa in the Late Nineteenth Century." *JAH* 23 (4) (1982), pp. 451–67.

———. *A History of East Africa 1592–1902*. London, 1996.

Becker, H., V. Hohfeld, and H. Kopf. *Kaffee aus Arabien. Der Bedeutungswandel eines Weltwirtschaftgutes und seine siedlungsgeographische Konsequenz*. Wiesbaden, 1979.

Beer, R.J. *The Origins of the British Colonial System*. New York, 1922.

Bentley-Duncan, T. *Atlantic Islands: Madeira, the Azores and the Cape Verdes in Seventeenth-Century Commerce and Navigation*. Chicago, 1972.

———. "Niels Steensgaard and the Europe-Asia Trade of the Early Seventeenth Century." *Journal of Modern History* 47 (3) (1975), pp. 512–19.

Berg, C.R. "The Sacred Musket: Tactics, Technology, and Power in Eighteenth Century Madagascar." *Comparative Studies in Society and History* 27 (2) (1985), pp. 261–79.

Bhacker, M. Reda *Trade and Empire in Muscat and Zanzibar*. London, 1992.

Bidwel, S. *Swords for Hire: European Mercenaries in Eighteenth Century India*. London, 1974.

Biker, J.F., ed. *Collecção de trattados e concertos de paz que o* Estado da Índia *fêz com os reis e senhores delle*. 14 vols. Lisbon, 1883–87.

Bingham, H. *Elihu Yale: The American Nabob of Queen's Square*. New York, 1939; Hamden, 1968.

Birdwood, K.C. *Report on the Old Records Preserved in the Indian Office*. London, 1861.

Blake, S.P. "The Structure of Monetary Exchange in North India." In J.F. Richards (ed.), *The Imperial Monetary System of Mughal India*, pp. 100–137. New Delhi, 1987.

Bloch, H. "Mode of Production and Slavery in Madagascar: Two Case Studies." In J.L. Watson (ed.) *Asian and African Systems of Slavery*, pp. 100–134.

Blussé, L. *Strange Company: Chinese Settlers, Mestizo Women and the Dutch in VOC Batavia*. Dordrecht, 1986.

———, ed. "All of One Company: The Biographical Approach to VOC History." *Itinerário*, Special Issue 7, Leiden, 1986.

———. "The Run to the Coast: Comparative Notes on Early Dutch and English Expansion and State Formation in Asia." *Itinerário* 12 (1) (1988), pp. 195–215.

Blussé, L., and F.S. Gaastra, eds. *Companies and Trade: Essays on Overseas Trading Companies During the Ancien Régime*. Leiden, 1981.

Böeseken, A.J. *De Nederlandse commissarisen aan de Kaap 1657–1700*. The Hague, 1938.

Bog, I., ed. *Der Außenhandel Ost-Mitteleuropas*. Cologne and Vienna, 1971.

Boiteau, P. *Les Droits sur la terre dans la société malgache pré-coloniale. Contribution à l'étude du mode de production asiatique* (Cahiers d'étude et de recherches marxistes). Paris, 1969.

Boiteux, L.A. *Richelieu: Grand Maître de la navigation et du commerce de la France*. Paris, 1955.

Bolleo, A. "O 'Regimento novo para o comércio de Moçambique' de 1673." *Studia* 3 (1950), pp. 153–74.

Bonner, W.H. *Captain William Dampier: Buccaneer/Author*. Stanford, 1936.

———. *Pirate Laureate: The Life and Legend of Captain Kidd*. New Brunswick, 1947/1958.

Bonomi, J. *A Factitious People: New York Society and Politics During the Colonial Period*. New York, 1974.

Borges, J. *The Economics of the Goa Jesuits*. New Delhi, 1998.

Bouchon, G. "Les Musulmans du Kerala à l'époque de la découverte Portugaise." *Mare Luso-Indicum* 2 (1973), pp. 3–59.

———. *Mamale de Cananore. Un adversaire de l'Inde Portugais*. Paris, 1975.

———. "Sixteenth Century Malabar." In M.N. Pearson and A. Das Gupta (eds.), *India and the Indian Ocean*. New York, 1987.

Bowrey, T. *A Geographical Account of the Countries Around the Bay of Bengal*, R.C. Temple (ed.) London, 1911.

Boyajian, J.G. *Portuguese Trade in Asia Under the Habsburgs, 1580–1640*. Baltimore, 1993.

Boyer-Xambeu, M.T., G. Deleplace, and L. Gillard. *Private Money and Public Currencies: The 16th Century Challenge*. Armonk, 1994.

Boxer, C.R. "Anglo-Portuguese Rivalry in the Persian Gulf 1603–1635." In E. Prestage (ed.), *Chapters in Anglo-Portuguese Relations*, pp. 46–130. Watford, 1935.

———. "The General of the Galleons and the Anglo-Dutch Truce Celebrated at Goa in 1635." *Ethnos* 1 (1935), pp. 27–32.

———. "Fidalgos portuguêses e bailardeiras Indianas." *Revista da História* (São Paulo) 50 (1961), pp. 83–105.

———. *Race Relations in the Portuguese Empire*. Oxford, 1963.

———. *Portuguese Society in the Tropics: The Municipal Councils of Goa, Macao, Bahia and Luanda*. Madison, 1965.

———. *Francisco Veira de Figueiredo: A Portuguese Merchant Adventurer in Southeast Asia*. The Hague, 1967.

———. "On the Eighteenth Century as a Category in Indonesian History: A Reconsideration of J.C. van Leur." *Documentatieblad 18 e eeuw* 41/42 (1979), pp. 1–12.

———. *The Portuguese Seaborne Empire 1425–1825*. New York 1969/1989.

———. *Mary and Misogyny: Women in Iberian Expansion Overseas*. Duckworth, 1975.

———. "Some Possible Fields of Research in the History of Portuguese India." In J. Correia Alfonso (ed.), *Indo-Portuguese History*, pp. 172–190.

———. *A Índia portuguêsa em meados do século XVII*. Lisbon, 1981.

———. *From Lisbon to Goa. Studies in Portuguese Trade and Navigation*. Ashgate, 1984.

———. *The Dutch Seaborne Empire*. London, 1988.

Boxer, C.R., and L. de Azevedo. *Fort Jesus and the Portuguese in Mombasa*. Nairobi, 1962.

Boxhall, P.H., ed. "The Journal of a Mocha Coffee Merchant." *Journal of Arabian Studies* 1 (1974), pp. 113–38.

Bragança Pereira, A. de, ed. *Arquivo português oriental*. 11 vols. Bastora/Goa, 1932–36.

———. "Relações do Estado da Índia com os reis vizinhos." *O Oriente Português*, Velha Séria, 24 (1932), pp. 117–330.

———. *Notas para a história dos portugueses em Damão*. Bastora, 1936.

———. "Os portugueses em Bassein." *O Oriente Português*, Nova Séria, 1 (1936), pp. 1–185.

———. *Notas sobre as fortalezzas de Sofala, Moçambique, Mombaça, Mascate, Sohar e outras de Árabia e Diu*. Bastora, 1938.

Braudel, F. *The Mediterranean and the Mediterranean World in the Age of Philip II*. 2 vols. New York, 1972.

———. *Afterthoughts on Material Civilization and Capitalism*, Baltimore, 1977.

———. *Capitalism and Material Life, 15th–18th Century*. 3 vols. New York 1984–86.

Braun, H. "Ein iranischer Großwezir des 17 e Jahrhunderts: Muhammad Taqi." In W. Eiler (ed.), *Festgabe deutscher Iranisten für das 2500-Jahrfeier Irans*, pp. 1–7. Stuttgart, 1971.

Brenner, R. "On the Origins of Capitalist Development: A Critique of Neo-Smithian Marxism." *New Left Review* 104 (1977), pp. 25–92.

———. *Merchants and Revolution: Commercial Change, Political Conflict and London's Overseas Traders 1550–1653*. Cambridge, 1993.

Brenning, J. "Silver in Seventeenth Century Surat: Monetary Circulation and the Price Revolution in Mughal India." In J.F. Richards (ed.), *Precious Metals*.

———. "Joint Stock Companies of Coromandel." In B.B. Kling and M.N. Pearson (eds.), *The Age of Partnership*.

Bridenbaugh, C. *Cities in the Wilderness: The First Century of Urban Life in Colonial America*. New York, 1938/1960.

Bridenbaugh, C., and J. Bridenbaugh. *No Peace Beyond the Line: The English in the Caribbean*. New York, 1972.

Broeze, F., and K. MacPherson. *Brides of the Sea: Port Cities of Asia from the 16th to the 20th Centuries*. Honolulu, 1989.

Bromley, J.S. *Corsairs and Navies 1660–1760*. London, 1987.

Brouwer, C.G. "Die Madagascar Connection. Holländische Beiträge zur Erforschung der Yementische Sklavengeschichte." *Orientations: A Multidisciplinary Journal of the Dutch Association for Middle Eastern and Islamic Studies* (1992), pp. 56–86.

———. *Al Mukha: Profile of a Yemeni Seaport as Sketched by Servants of the Dutch East India Company*. Amsterdam, 1997.

Brown, B. "Muslim Influences on Trade and Politics in the Lake Tanganyika Region." *African Historical Studies* 4 (1971), pp. 617–29.

Brown, H. "Siyu: Town of the Craftsmen." *Azania* 23 (1988), pp. 101–33.

Brown, M. *A History of Madagascar*. London, 1995.

Bruce, J. *Annals of the Honourable East India Company 1600–1700*. 3 vols. London, 1810; Farnborough, 1970.

Brønstedt, J., ed. *Vore Gamle Tropenkolonier*. 2 vols. Copenhagen, 1967.

Buckridge, Nicolas, *The Journals of Nicolas Buckridge* (J.R. Jensen, ed.). Minneapolis, 1973.

Bulhão Patto, L. de, and A. da Silva Rego. *Documentos remettidos da Índia ou livros dos monções*. 7 vols. Lisbon, 1884–.

Burg, B.R. *Sodomy and the Perception of Evil: English Sea Rovers in the Seventeenth-Century Caribbean*. New York, 1983.

Burke, Edmund. *Works*. 8 vols. London, 1854–57.

Burnell, J. *Bombay in the Days of Queen Anne* (T. Sheppard, ed.). London, *WHS*, 1933.

Busev, V.V. *Istorija posolst'v i diplomaticeskich otnošenii Russkogo i Iranskogo gosudarei v 1586–1672 gc*. 2 vols. Moscow, 1976–1982.

Caetano, M. *O conselho ultramarino: Esboço da sua história*. Lisbon, 1967.

*Calendar of State Papers. Colonial Series. East Indies, Persia and Japan* (S. Sainsbury, ed.). 4 vols. London 1862–66.

Callaghan, E.B.O., ed. *A Documentary History of the State of New York*. 4 vols. Albany, 1849–51.

Callet, R., ed. *Histoire des rois. Tantaran' ny andriana*. 3 vols. Antananarivo, 1972–74.

Calmard, J. "Les marchands iraniens." In D. Lombard and J. Aubin (eds.), *Marchands et hommes d' affaire asiatique dans l'Océan Indien et la mer de Chine 13–20e siècle*, pp. 92–102. Paris, 1988.

*The Cambridge History of Africa*. Cambridge, 1975.

*The Cambridge History of Iran*. Cambridge, 1968–1989.

Campbell, G. "The Structure of Trade on Madagascar 1750–1823" *IJAHS* 26 (1) (1993), pp. 111–48.

———. "Madagascar and the Slave Trade 1810–1895" *Omaly sy anio* 23/24 (1986), pp. 279–311.

Campbell, G.N., et al. *Gazetteer of Town and Island of Bombay*. 3 vols. Bombay, 1893–94. Separate work considered as volumes 25–27 of *Gazetteer of Bombay Presidency*.

Campos, A. dos. *Os portugueses em Zanzibar e Pemba*. Bastora, 1936.

Canter Vischer, J.H. *Malabarse brieven*. Leeuwarden, 1743.

Capela, J., and E. Medeiros. *O tráfico de escravos de Moçambique para as Ilhas do Índico 1720–1920*. Maputo, 1987.

Carita, H. *Les palais de Goa. Modèles et typologies de l'architecture indo-portugais*. Paris, 1996.

Carlson S.H. *Trade and Dependency: Studies in the Expansion of Europe*. Uppsala, 1984.

Carruthers, D.S. *British Routes to India*. London, 1924.

———, ed. *The Desert Route to India*. London, *WHS*, 1929.

Celabi, E. *Seyhatnâmesi*. 6 vols. Istanbul, 1985.

Cerulli, E. *Somalia. Scritii varii e inediti*. 2 vols. Rome, 1957.

Cessi, R. "Mercanti veneziani nella 'India' nel secolo XVI." In *Studii in onore di Armando Sapori*, pp. 1098–1105. 2 vols. Milan, 1957,

Challe, R. *Journal d'un voyage fait aux Indes Orientales 1690–1691* (F. Deloffre Menemencioglu and M. Menemciogu, eds.). Paris, 1979.

Chandra, S. "Commercial Activities of the Mughal Emperors During the Seventeenth Century." *Bengal Past and Present* 78 (146) (1959), pp. 93–97.

———, ed. *The Indian Ocean: Explorations in History, Commerce and Politics*. London, 1987.

Chardin, J. *Voyages du chevalier Chardin en Perse et et autres lieux de l'Orient enrichis d'un grand nombre des figures* (L. Langlès, ed.). 11 vols. and atlas. Paris, 1811–14.

———. *La couronation de Suleiman. Roi présent de Perse.* Paris 1680; facs. reprint Teheran, 1984.

Charles-Roux, A. *Les échelles du Syrie et du Palestine au XVIIIe siècle,* Paris, 1928.

Chase-Dunn, C., and T.D. Hall. *Rise and Demise: Comparing World-Systems*. Boulder, 1997.

Chaudhuri, K.N. *The English East India Company: The Study of an Early Joint-Stock Company*. London, 1965.

———. *The Trading World of Asia and the English East India Company 1660–1760*. Cambridge, 1978.

———. *Trade and Civilisation in the Indian Ocean: An Economic History from the Rise of Islam to 1750*. Cambridge, 1986.

———. *Asia Before Europe: Economy and Civilisation of the Indian Ocean from the Rise of Islam to 1750*. Cambridge, 1990.

Chaudhuri, K.N., and J.I. Israel. "The East India Company and the Revolution of 1688–1689." In J.I. Israel (ed.), *The Anglo-Dutch Moment: Essays on the Glorious Revolution and its World Impact*, pp. 412–37. Cambridge, 1991.

Chaudhuri, S. *Trade and Commercial Organization in Bengal*. Calcutta, 1975.

Chaunu, P. *Les Philippines et le Pacifique des ibériques*. Paris, 1960.

———. *Sevilla y América siglos XVI y XVII*. Seville, 1983.

Chayanov, A.V. *On the Theory of Peasant Economies*. Delhi, 1981.

Chicerov, A.I. *India: Economic Development 16th to 18th Century: Outline History of Crafts and Industry*. Moscow, 1971.

Chick, V.B., ed. *A Chronicle of the Carmelites and of the Carmelite Mission in Persia in the Seventeenth Century*. 2 vols. London, 1936–38.

Choksey, R.D. *Economic Life in the Bombay Gujarat*. Bombay, 1968.

Cipolla, C.N. *Clocks and Culture*. London, 1965.

Coates, T.J. *Degredados e orfãs: colonização dirigida pela coroa no império português*. Lisbon, 1998.

Coetzee, J. de. *Die Kompagnie se besettinge van Dela Goa Baai*. Pretoria, 1947.

Cohn, B.S. *India: The Social Anthopology of a Civilization*. Englewood Cliffs, 1971.

Coleman, D.C., ed. *Revisions in Mercantilism*. London, 1969.

Collet, J. *The Private Letter-Book of Joseph Collet* (H.H. Doddwel, ed.). London, 1924.

Conlon, F.F. *A Caste in a Changing World: The Chitrapur Saraswat Brahmins*. New Delhi, 1977.

Coolhaas, W.P.H., ed. *Pieter van Den Broecke in Azië*. 2 vols. The Hague, *WLV*, 1963.

Cooper, F. *Plantation Slavery on the East Coast of Africa*. New Haven, 1977.

Coquery-Vidrovitch, C. "The Political Economy of the African Peasantry and Modes of Production." In P.C. Gutkind and I. Wallerstein (eds.), *The Political Economy of Contemporary Africa*, pp. 98–111. Beverly Hills, 1976.

Cordeiro, L., ed. *Batalhas da Índia: Como se perdeu Hormuz (Processo inédito do século XVII)*. Lisbon, 1896.

Correia Alfonso, J., ed. *Indo-Portuguese History: Sources and Problems*. Bombay, 1981.

Cortesão, A., and A.T. de Motta. *Portugaliae monumenta cartographica*. 6 vols. Lisbon, 1960–62.

Cortesão, A., and L. de Albuquerque, eds. *Obras de Dom João de Castro*. 2 vols. Coimbra, 1971.

Costa, J.F. da. "The Demolition of the Temples on the Island of Goa in 1540 and the Disposition of the Temple Lands." *Neues Zeitschrift für Missionswißenschaft* 18 (1962), pp. 161–71.

———. "Soccotra e o dominio português no oriente." *Annais. Academia Português da História*. Segunda séria, 24 (1) (1977), pp. 323–77.

[Costa, M. da?], *Arte de Furtar* (J. Ribeiro, ed.). 4 vols. in one. Rio de Janeiro, 1907.

Cousins, H.L. "The Antiquities of Sind with Historical Outline." *Archeological Survey of India,* XLVI Imperial Series. Varanasi, 1975.

Cultru, P. *Madagascar au XVIIIème siècle. Benyowski*. Paris, 1936.

Cummins, J.S., ed. and trans. *Travels and Controversies of Frey Domingo Navarette*. 2 vols. Cambridge *WHS*, 1962.

Cunha Rivara, H. da. "A Índia no governo do Vice-Rey Conde da Villa Verde 1693–1698." *O chronista do Tissuary* 18, 19 (1867–68).

Curtin, P.D. *The Atlantic Slave Trade: A Census*. Madison, 1975.

———. *Economic Change in Pre-Colonial Africa: Senegambia in the Age of the Slave Trade*. 2 vols. Madison, 1975.

———. *Cross-Cultural Trade in World History*. Cambridge, 1984.

Dale, S.B. *Islamic Society on the South Asian Frontier. The Mappillas of Malabar 1498–1922*. Oxford, 1980.

———. *Indian Merchants and Eurasian Trade 1600–1750*. Cambridge, 1994.

Dalton, C.S. *Life of Thomas Pitt*. Cambridge, 1915.

Dalton, R.C. "Karl Polanyi's Analysis of Long-Distance Trade and His Wider Paradigm." In C.C. Lamberg and K. Sabloff (eds.), *Ancient Civilisation and Trade*. Albuquerque, 1975.

Dampier, W. *A New Voyage Round the World* (J. Masefield, ed.). 2 vols. London, 1916.

Dan, M., and S. Goldberg. "Le commerce Balkano-Levantin de la Transylvanie au cours de la seconde moitié du XVI siècle et au début du XVIIe siècle." *Revue des études sud-est européenes* 5 (1967), pp. 97–106.

Dantwale, M.I. *The Marketing of Raw Cotton in India*. London, 1928.

Dapper, O. *Asia ofte nauwekeurige beschrijvinge van't rijk der grooten Mogol benevens een volkomene beschrijvinge van geheel Persiën*. 2 vols. in one. Amsterdam, 1672.

Darwish, M.A. *Saltanat 'Uman fi'l qarayn al-thamin 'ashar va al-tashi 'ashat*. Jedda, 1992.

Das, G. *The Norris Embassy to Aurengzeb*. Calcutta, 1947.

Das, S. *Selections from the Indian Journals*. 2 vols. Calcutta, 1963.

Das Gupta, A. *Malabar in Asian Trade*. Cambridge, 1967.

———. "De VOC en Suratte." In M.A.P. Meilink-Roelofs, *De V.O.C. in Azië*.

———. "The Merchants of Surat 1700–1750." In E. Leach and S.N. Mukherjee (eds.), *Elites in South Asia,* pp. 181–214. London, 1970.

———. "Gujarati Merchants and the Red Sea Trade." In B.B. Kling and M.N. Pearson (eds.), *The Age of Partnership*, pp. 123–58.

———. *Indian Merchants and the Decline of Surat*. Wiesbaden, 1976.

———. "Indian Merchants and the Western Indian Ocean: The Early Seventeenth Century." *MAS* 19 (3) (1985), pp. 481–95.

Das Gupta, A., and M.N. Pearson. *India and the Indian Ocean, 1500–1800*. New Delhi 1987.

Daskevic, J.C., ed. *Ukrainsko-Armjanskie sviazi v XVII veke. Sbornik, dokumentov*. Kiev, 1966.

Datoo, B.A. "Influence of the Monsoons on the Movement of Dhows Along the East African Coast." *East African Geographical Review* 12 (1974), pp. 23–33.

David, M.D. *History of Bombay 1663–1713*. Bombay, 1974.

Davis, K.G. *The Royal African Company*. London, 1957.

Davis, R. "English Imports from the Levant." In M.A. Coock (ed.), *Studies in the Economic History of the Middle East*, pp. 193–206. London, 1970.

De Souza, T.R. (ed.), *Indo-Portuguese History: Old Issues, New Questions*. New Delhi, 1985.

———. *Medieval Goa: A Socio-Economic History*. New Delhi, 1976.

———. "Glimpses of Hindu Dominance of Goan Economy in the Seventeenth Century." *Indica* 12 (1975), pp. 27–35.

Defoe, D. (alias Captain Johnson). *A General History of the Robberies and Murders of the Most Notorious Pirates of the English Nation* (M. Schlumhorn, ed.). Columbia, 1972.

———. *The King of Pirates; being an Account of Famous Enterprises of Captain Avery*. London, 1724.

Deloche, J. *La circulation en Inde avant la révolution des transports*. 2 vols. Paris, 1980.

———. *Recherches sur les routes de l'Inde au temps de Mogols (Étude critique des sources)*, Paris, 1968.

Dermigny, L. *L'Europe et la Chine. Le commerce à Canton au XVIIIème siècle*. 3 vols. and atlas. Paris, 1964.

———. "Les Européens aux 'Indes' du XVI au XVIIIème siècle." In Mehaud (ed.), *Mouvements des Populations*, pp. 209–16.

Desai, W.S. *Bombay and the Marathas up to 1774*. New Delhi, 1982.

Deschamps, H. *Les pirates à Madagascar au XVII et XVIIIème siècle*, Paris, 1949, 1959.

———. *Histoire de Madagascar*. Paris, 1959.

*Diário do terceiro conde de Linhares*. 2 vols. in one, Lisbon 1937/1943.

Dias Antunes, L.F. "The Trade Activities of the *Banyans* in Mozambique: Private Indian Dynamics in the Portuguese State Economy." In K.N. Mathews (ed.), *Mariners, Merchants and Oceans: Studies in Maritime History*, pp. 301–31. New Delhi, 1995.

Disney, A.R. *A decadência do império da pimenta* (Twilight of the pepper empire). Lisbon, 1981.

———. "The Portuguese Empire in India: Some Suggestions for a Less Seaborne and More Land-based Approach to its History." In J. Correia Alfonso, *Indo-Portuguese History*, pp. 148–62.

———. "Contrasting Models of Empire." In A.R. Duttra (ed.), *The Portuguese and the Pacific*, pp. 26–38. Santa Barbara, 1995.

Donnan, E. ed. *Documents Illustrative of the History of the Slave Trade to America*, 3 vols. Washington, D.C., 1935–37.

Dostal, W. "Der Markt von Sana." *Österreichische Akademie der Wissenschaften Sitzungsberichte* 354. Vienna, 1979.

Dow, F.G., and J. Edmonds. *The Pirates of the New England Coast 1638–1730*. Salem, MA, 1923.

Dowson, O., and C.H. Eliot, eds. *The History of India as Told by Its Own Historians: The Muhammadan Period*. 8 vols. London 1876–77; Calcutta 1954–60.

Dresch, P. *Tribes, Government and History in Yemen*. Oxford, 1989.

Drescher, S. *Econocide: British Slavery in the Age of Abolition*. Pittsburgh, 1977.

Drury, R. *Madagascar, or Robert Drury's Journal During Fifteen Years' Captivity on That Island* (P. Olivier, ed.). London, 1890.

Duffy, T.R. *Shipwreck and Empire: Portuguese Maritime Disasters in an Age of Decline*. Cambridge, MA, 1965.

Dunlop, H. *Bronnen tot de geschiedenis van de Oost-Indische Compagnie in Perzië 1611–1638*. The Hague, *RGP*, 1936.

Dunn, R.S. "The Downfall of the Bermuda Company: A Restoration Farce." *William and Mary Quarterly*, 3rd Series, 20 (1963), pp. 487–512.

———. *Sugar and Slaves: The Rise of the Planter Class in the English West Indies 1624–1713*. Chapel Hill, 1972.

Dzao, J.R. "Funerailles royales chez les sakalavas du nord de Madagascar." *Omaly sy anio* 25 (1987), pp. 9–19.

Eastman, C.M. "Service, Slavery and the Swahili Social Reality." *Afrikanistische Arbeitspapiere* 37 (1994), pp. 87–107.

Eaton, R.M. "Multiple Lenses: Differing Perspectives of Fifteenth Century Calicut." In L. Sears (ed.), *Autonomous Histories, Particular Truths*, pp. 71–86. Madison, 1983.

Ehrenberg, R. *Das Zeitalter der Fugger. Geldhandel und Creditverkehr im 16 Jahrhundert*. 2 vols. Frankfurt, 1896.

Ekelund, E.B., and R.D. Tolison. *Mercantilism as a Rent-Seeking Society*. College Station, 1981.

Ellert, H. *Rivers of Gold* (*Zambesiana* no. 21). Gweru, 1993.

Elphik, R. *Kraal and Castle: Khoikhoi and the Founding of White South Africa*. London, 1977.

Esparteiro, A.M. *Três séculos no mar. Ementa histórica das naos portuguêses*. 2 vols. Lisbon, 1974–75.

Falcon, J.F. *Mercantilismo e transição ao capitalismo*. São Paulo, 1981.

Falsafi, Nasrula. *Cand majala-i-tarikh va adabi*. Teheran, 1342.

Farinho de Carvalho, A. *Diogo do Couto. O soldado prático e a Índia*. Lisbon, 1979.

Farooqi, S. *Towns and Townsmen of Ottoman Anatolia: Trade, Crafts and Food Production in an Urban Setting 1520–1650*. Cambridge, 1983.

———. "Coffee and Spices: Official Ottoman Reactions to Egyptian Trade in the Late Sixteenth Century." In *Festschrift für Andreas Tietzke*. Sonderheft wiener Zeitschrift für die Kunde des Morgenlandes, vol. 76, pp. 87–96. Vienna, 1986.

Fawcett, C.H. *The First Century of British Justice in India*. Oxford, 1934; Aalen, 1979.

Fecner, M. *Torgovlija Russkogo gosudarst'va so stranami vostoka v XVI v*. Moscow, 1956.

Feiling, K.G. *British Foreign Policy 1660–1672*. London 1930/1968.

Feketé, L. *Einführung in die persische Paläographie*. Budapest, 1977.

Feldbœck, O. *Danmarks historien*. Vol. 6, *Kolonierne i Asien og Afrika*. Copenhagen, 1988.

Felipe Thomaz, L. "Les portugais dans les mers de l'Archipel au XVIe siècle." *Archipel* 18 (1979), pp. 105–25.

———. "Estrutura política e administrativa do Estado da Índia no século XVI." In A. Guerreiro and L. de Albuquerque, *IIo seminário*.

Feraud, D. *Du paludisme à Madagascar*. Montpelier, 1887.

Ferrand, G. *Les musulmans à Madagascar*. 3 vols. Paris, 1902.

Ferraz, M.L.E. dos Santos de Freitas. *Documentação histórica moçambicana*. Lisbon, 1973.

Ferreira, A. Rita, *Fixação portuguêsa e história pre-colonial de Moçambique*. Lisbon, 1986.

Ferreira Martins, J.L. *História da misericórdia de Goa*. 3 vols. Nova Goa, 1910–14.

Ferrier, R.W. "The Trade Between India and the Persian Gulf and the East India Company in the 17th Century." *Bengal Past and Present* 89 (1970), pp. 189–98.

———. "The Armenians and the English East India Company in Persia in the 17th and Early 18th Century." *EHR* 26 (1) (1973).

Filliot, J.M. *La traite des esclaves vers les Mascareignes au XVIIIème siècle*. Antananarivo, 1971.

Finlay, R. "The Pilgrim Art: The Culture of Porcelain in World History." *Journal of World History* 9 (1) (1998), pp. 141–87.

Fiorani Piacenti, A. *L'emporio ed'il regno di Hormuz (VII fino XV secolo di Christo): Vicende storiche, problemi ed aspetti di un civiltà costeira del Golfo Persico*. Milan, 1975.

Fisch, J. *Die europäische Expansion und das Völkerrecht*. Stuttgart, 1984.

Fishel, W. "Cochin in Jewish History." *Proceedings of the American Academy of Jewish Research* 30 (1962), pp. 37–59.

Fisher, A.G.B., and H.J. Fisher. *Slavery and Muslim Society in Africa*. New York, 1971.

Fitzler, M.A.H. "Die Handelsgesellschaft Felix von Oldenburgs. Ein Beitrag zur Geschichte des Deutschtums im Portugal zur Zeitalter des Absolutismus." *Beiheft VSWG* 23. Stuttgart, 1931.

Floor, W. "Pearl-Fishing in the Persian Gulf in 1757." *Persica* 10 (1982), pp. 215–19.

———. "Het Nederlands-Perzische conflict van 1645." *Stichting Cultuurgeschiedenis Nederlanders Overzee. Bijdragen en Mededelingen* (*Verslagen en Aanwinsten*) (1978/1979), pp. 1–8.

———. "Commercial Conflict Between Persia and the Netherlands." University of Durham Center for Islamic Studies Occasional Paper 37. Durham, 1988.

Flynn, D. *World Silver and Monetary History in the 16th and 17th Century*. Aldershot, 1996.

Fonseca, J.N. de. *An Historical and Archeological Sketch of the City of Goa*. Bombay, 1887.

Forán, J. "The Making of an External Area: Iran's Place in the World-System." *Review* 12 (1), (1989), pp. 79–119.

Forbes, A.W. "Southern Arabia and the Islamisation of the Central Indian Archipelago." *Archipel* 21 (4) (1981), pp. 55–91.

Ford, J. *The Role of Trypanosomiases in African History*. Oxford, 1971.

Forrest, G.W. *Selections from the Records Preserved in the Bombay Secretariat. Home Series*. 2 vols. Bombay, 1884, 1887.

———. *Fort William–India House Correspondence* (K.N. Datta et al., eds.). 23 vols. New Delhi 1949–.

Foster, W. "An English Settlement on Madagascar." *The English Historical Review* 27 (1927), pp. 29–50.

———, ed. *The Red Sea and Adjacant Countries at the Close of the Seventeenth Century*. London, *WHS,* 1947.

Fox, R.C. *King, Clan, Raja and Rule: State-Hinterland Relations in Pre-Colonial India*. Berkeley, 1973.

França, A. *Portugal na época da restoração*. São Paulo, 1951.

Freeman, W. *The Incredible Defoe*. London, 1950.

Freeman-Grenville, C.S.P., ed. and trans. *The East African Coast: Selected Documents from the First to the Early Nineteenth Century*. Oxford, 1966.

———. *The Mombasa Rising Against the Portuguese. 1634. From Sworn Evidence*. London, 1980.

Freitas, G. de. "A companhia geral de comércio do Brasil." *Revista da história*. São Paulo, 1950.

Freitas, S. de. *Do justo império asiático dos portugueses* (S. Leite, ed. and trans.). 2 vols. Lisbon, 1980.

Friedländer, H. *Historia económica de Cuba*. 2 vols. Havana, 1970.

Fryer, J. *A New Account of the East Indies and Persia, Being Nine Years' Travel 1672–1681* (W. Crooke, ed.). 3 vols. Cambridge *WHS*, 1909–15.

Frykenberg, R. "Company Sirkars in the Karnatak: The Inner Logic of Political Systems in India." In R. Fox (ed.), *Realm and Region in Traditional India*, pp. 117–64. Madison, 1968; New Delhi, 1979.

Fuentes, L.F. *El comercio español con América*. Seville, 1980.

Gaastra, F. "The Shifting Balance of Trade of the Dutch East India Company." In L. Blussé and F.S. Gaastra, *Companies and Trade*, pp. 47–69.

———. "De Verenigde Oost Indische Compagnie: de groei van een bedrijf. Geld tegen goederen. Een structurele verandering van het Nederlands-Aziatische handelsverkeer." *BMGN* 89 (1976), pp. 249–76.

———. "The Independent Fiscaals of the VOC." In L. Blussé (ed.), *All of One Company*, pp. 92–102.

———. *Bewind en beleid bij de VOC*. Zutphen, 1989.

Galetti, A. *The Dutch in Malabar. Selections from the Records of Madras Government. Dutch Records*. Madras, 1911.

Ganesh, R.B., and D.B. Parasnis. *Selections from the Satara Raja's and the Peishawa's Diaries. I Shahu Chatrapati*. 2 vols. Puna, 1432 v./1906.

Garçia Abranches, J. de. *Archivo da relação de Goa*. 2 vols. in one. Nova Goa, 1872/1874.

García-Baquero, G.A. de. *Andalucía y la carrera de Indias 1492–1824*. Seville, 1986.

Gardner, J.W. *A History of Jamaica*. London, 1883/1973.

Garlake, P. "The Value of Imported Ceramics in the Dating of the Rhodesian Iron Age." *JAH* 9 (1) (1968), pp. 21–31.

Gaube, H. "Ein Abschnitt der safavidische Bandar e-Abbas-Shiraz strasse: die Strecke von Seyyid Gemal al-Din nach Lar." *Iran* 17 (1979), pp. 39–47.

Genovese, F.D., and Hochberg H.G. *Geographic Perspectives in History*. London, 1989.

Gentil da Silva, J. *Alguns documentos para o comércio da Índia de Portugal existentes na Bibliotheca Nacional de Madrid*. Lisbon, 1951.

Germano da Silva Correia, A.G. *História da colonização portuguêsa na Índia*. 6 vols. Lisbon, 1948–58.

Gerson da Cunha, A. *Notes on the History and Antiquities of Chaul and Bassein*. Bombay, 1878.

Gilbin J. "Trypanosomiases Control in African History: An Evaded Issue." *JAH* 31 (1) (1990), pp. 59–80.

Glamann, K. *Dutch-Asiatic Trade 1620–1740*. The Hague 1956/1981.

Gode, A.K. "The History of Tobacco in India and Europe." In *Studies in Indian Cultural History*, pp. 429–39. Hosiapur, 1961.

Godefroît, S. "Reflexions sur la notion de royauté sacré à Madagascar. L'exemple du Sakalava de Menabe." *Studia Africana* 9 (1989), pp. 159–78.

Godelier, M.E. *Rationalité et irrationalité en économie*. 2 vols. Paris, 1969.
Godinho, M. *Itinerario que o fêz no anno de 1663 vindo da Índia para o Portugal por terra*. Lisbon, 1974.
Godinho, Vitorino Magalhães. *Ensaios*. 3 vols. Lisbon, 1969.
———. *Les finances de l'état portugais des Indes*. Paris, 1971.
———. *Os descobrimentos e a economia mundial*. 4 vols. Lisbon 1983–85.
Goffman, D. *Izmir and the Levantine World*. Seattle, 1990.
Gois, D. de. *Crónica do felicissimo Rey Dom Manuel*. 4 vols. Coimbra, 1949–53.
Goitein, S. "From Aden to India: Specimen of India Traders of the Twelfth Century." *JESHO* 22 (1) (1980), pp. 43–66.
Gokhale, B.G. *Surat in the Seventeenth Century: A Study in Urban History in Pre-Modern India*. London, 1979.
Goldenburg, R.P. *Ship-Building in Colonial America*. Charlottesville, 1976.
Goldstone, J.M. *Revolutions and Rebellions in the Early Modern World*. Berkeley, 1991.
Golikova, N.B. *Astrakhanskoe voštanije 1706 g*. Moscow, 1973.
Gommans, J. *The Rise of Indo-Afghan Empire c. 1710–1783*. Leiden, 1995.
Gonçalves Pereira, G.R. *História da administração da justícia no Estado da Índia*. 2 vols. Lisbon, 1964–65.
Gonçalves Salvador, J. *Os christãos novos e comércio no Atlântico meridional*. São Paulo, 1978.
Goody, J. *The East in the West*. Cambridge, 1996.
Goonewardene, K.W. *The Foundation of Dutch Power in Ceylon 1638–1658*. Amsterdam, 1958.
———. "A New Netherlands in Ceylon: Dutch Attempts to Found a Colony During Their First Quarter Century of Power in Ceylon." *Ceylon Journal of Historical and Social Studies* 2 (1959), pp. 203–44.
Gordon, S.N. "The Slow Conquest: Administrative Integration of Malwa into the Maratha Empire." *MAS* 11 (1) (1977), pp. 1–44.
Goslinga, C. *The Dutch on the Caribbean and the Wild Coast 1580–1680*. Assen, 1971.
Grandidier, A. *Histoire politique et colonial de Madagascar*. Vol. 3, *Histoire des peuples autre que les Merinas*. Paris, 1915.
Grant, C.P. *The Syrian Desert: Caravans, Travel and Exploration*. London, 1936.
Gray, J., and Birmingham D., eds. *Pre-Colonial African Trade: Essays on Trade in Central and Eastern Africa Before 1900*. London 1970.
Gray, R.W. "Portuguese Musketeers on the Zambezi." *JAH* 12 (4) (1972), pp. 531–34.
Gray, R.W., and S. Marks. "Southern Africa and Madagascar." In R. Gray (ed.), *Cambridge History of Africa*, vol. IV, Cambridge, 1975, pp. 384–468.
Gregson, R.E. "Trade and Politics in South-East Africa: The Moors, the Portuguese and the Kingdom of Mwene Mutapa." *African Social Research* 16 (1973), pp. 413–46.
Grey, C. *Pirates of the Eastern Seas*. London, 1933.
Groeneboer, K. *Weg naar het Westen. Het Nederlands voor Indië 1600–1950. Een taalpolitieke geschiedenis*. Leiden, 1993.
Groot, A.H. de. *The Ottoman Empire and the Dutch Republic. A Study of their Earliest Contacts*. Leiden and Istanbul, 1978.
———. "The Organization of Western European Trade in the Levant." In L. Blussé and F.S. Gaastra, *Companies and Trade*, pp. 231–41.
Grotius, H. *De iuri belli ac pacis libri tres*. Amsterdam, 1667.
Grove, R.N. *Green Imperialism: Colonial Expansion, Tropical Island Edens and the Origins of Environmentalism 1600–1860*. Cambridge, 1995.

Guerreiro, A., and L. de Albuquerque, eds. *IIo seminário internacional da história indo-portuguêsa (Actas)*. Lisbon, 1985.

Guinet, V. *La Turquie de l'Asie: Géographie administrative, statistique, descriptive et raisonnée de chaque province de l'Asie mineure*. 4 vols. Paris, 1892–96.

Gumilev, L.N. *Rhitm Evrazii*. Moscow, 1992.

———. *Etnosfera: Istorija lijudej i istorija prirody*. Moscow, 1993.

Gunder Frank, A. *Reorient: Global Economy in the Asian Age*. Berkeley, 1998.

Gunder Frank, A., and B. Gillis. *The World System: Five Hundred or Five Thousand Years?* London, 1994.

Haan, J.F. de. "De laatste der Mardijkers," *BTLV* 73 (1917), pp. 219–25.

———. *Oud Batavia*. 2 vols. Bandung, 1922/1935.

Habib, I. *The Agrarian System of Mughal India (1556–1707)*. London, 1963.

Habib, I., D. Kumar, and T. Raychaudhuri, eds. *The Cambridge Economic History of India*. 2 vols. Cambridge, 1983–85.

Hacke, W., ed. *A Collection of Original Voyages*. London, 1699.

Hagendoorn, J., and M. Johnson. *The Shell-Money of the Slave-Trade*. Cambridge, 1986.

Hall, G.S. *State and Statecraft in the Age of the Imperial Colas*. New Delhi, 1981.

———. "Price-Making and Market Hierarchies in Early Medieval South India." *IESHR* 14 (2) (1982), pp. 207–30.

Hall, R. *Empires of the Monsoon: A History of the Indian Ocean and Its Invaders*. London, 1996.

Halisey, R.G. *The Rajput Rebellion Against Aurengzeb: A Study of the Mughal Empire in Seventeenth Century India*. Columbia, 1977.

Hamilton, A. *A New Account of the East Indies* (W. Foster, ed.). 2 vols. London, 1930.

Haneda, M. *Le châh et les Qizilbâs. Le système militaire safavide*. Berlin, 1987.

Hanke, L. "The Portuguese in South America, with Special Reference to the Villa Imperial de Potosí." *Revista de história de América* 51 (1958), pp. 1–48.

Hanoteaux, G., and A. Martineau, eds. *Histoire de l'expansion française dans le monde*. 9 vols. Paris, 1903–12.

Hanson, C.A. *Economy and Society in Baroque Portugal*. London, 1981.

———. "The Luso-Brazilian 'Renovation' and the South-Atlantic Economy." *Review* 6 (4) (1983), pp. 475–521.

Haring, C.S. *The Buccaneers in the West Indies in the Seventeenth Century*. London, 1910; Hamden, 1967.

Harper, A.I. *The English Navigation Acts: An Experiment in Social Engineering*. New York, 1939.

Hasan, A. "The Silver Currency Output of the Mughal Empire and Prices in India during the 16th and 17th Century." *IESHR* 6 (1) (1969), pp. 85–116.

Hattocx, R.S. *Coffee and Coffeehouses: The Origins of a Social Beverage in the Middle East*. Seattle, 1985.

Haynes, S.D. "The Dynamics of Continuity in Indian Industry: *Jari* Manufacturing in Surat, 1900–1947." *IESHR* 23 (2) (1986), pp. 127–51.

———. "Merchant–State Relations in Surat." In S.D. Haynes and G. Prakash (eds.), *Contesting Power: Resistance and Everyday Social Relations in South Asia*. Delhi, 1991.

Hedges, W. *The Diary of William Hedges During His Agency in Bengal (1681–1687)* (H. Yule, ed.). 3 vols. London, *WHS*, 1887–9.

Heeres, J.E., ed. *Corpus diplomaticus Neerlando-Indicum*. 6 vols. The Hague, 1906–57.

Heeringa, J.K. et al., eds. *Bronnen tot de geschiedenis van den Levantschen handel.* 6 vols. The Hague, *RGP*, 1917–67.

Heesterman, J.C. "Warriors and Merchants." *Itinerário* 15 (1) (1991), p. 37–51.

Hekscher, E. *Der Merkantilismus.* 2 vols. Jena, 1932.

Hertzig, T.E. "The Iranian Raw Silk Trade and European Manufacture in the XVIIth and XVIIIth Century." *The Journal of European Economic History* 19 (1) (1990), pp. 73–91.

Hesse, E. *Goldbergwerke auf der Küste Sumatras* (S.C. Honoré Nabre, ed.). The Hague, 1931.

Hill, F.C. *The World Turned Upside Down: Radical Ideas in the English Revolution.* London, 1972.

———. "Radical Pirates?" In M. and J. Jacob (eds.), *The Origins of Anglo-American Radicalism.* London, 1984.

Hill, S.C. "Notes on Piracy in Eastern Waters." *The Indian Antiquary* 55 (1926), pp. 1–65.

Hinz, W. "Die spätmittelaltrichen Währungen im Bereich des persischen Golfes." In C.E. Bosworth (ed.), *Iran and Islam: In Memory of the Late Vladimir Minorsky,* pp. 303–14. Edinburgh, 1971.

Historical Manuscripts Commission, xiiith Report. *Manuscripts of J.B. Fortescue.* 6 vols. London, 1892–96.

Holden, Furber. *John Company at Work.* Cambridge, MA, 1948.

———. "The Overland Route to India in the Seventeenth and Eighteenth Century." *Journal of Indian History* 25 (1951), pp. 24–45.

———. *Bombay Presidency in the Mid-Eighteenth Century.* Bombay, 1967.

———. "Asia and the West as Partners Before Empire and After." *JAS* 28 (4) (1969), pp. 711–21.

———. *Rival Empires of Trade in the Orient.* Minneapolis, 1976.

Homsy, A. *Les Capitulations et la protection des chrétiens au proche Orient.* Harissa, 1956.

Hoppe, F. *Portugiesisch Ost-Afrika zur Zeit des Marques de Pombal.* Berlin, 1965.

Hornton M.C. "Asiatic Colonisation of the East African Coastline: The Mande Evidence." *Journal of the Royal Asiatic Society* (1986), pp. 1–21.

Horst, W.A. "De peperhandel van de Vereenigde Oost Indische Compagnie." *Bijdragen voor Vaderlandsche Geschiedenis en Oudheidkunde* 8 (3) (1941), pp. 95–122.

Hotz, A. ed. *Journaal der reis van den gezant der O.I. Compagnie Johan Cunaeus naar Perzië.* Amsterdam, 1908.

Hovy, L. *Ceylonees Plakaatboek: Plakkaten en andere wetten uitgevaardigd door het Nederlands bestuur op Ceylon 1638–1796.* 2 vols. Hilversum, 1991.

Hroch, Miroslav. "Die Rolle des zentraleuropäischen Handels im Ausgleich der Handelsbilanz zwischen Ost- und Westeuropa." In I. Bog (ed.), *Der Außenhandel,* pp. 1–47.

Hromnik, C.A. "Canarins in the Rios de Cuama." *Journal of African Studies* 6 (1) (1979), pp. 27–37.

———. *Indo-Africa: Towards a New Understanding of the History of Sub-Saharan Africa.* Cape Town, 1981.

Hullu, J. de. *Op de schepen der Oost-Indische Compagnie. Vijf artikelen van J. de Hullu* (J.R. Bruijn and J. Lucassen, eds.). Groningen, 1980.

Hunter, W.W. *History of British India.* 2 vols. London, 1899/1900.

Husain, Y. ed. *Selected Waqai of the Deccan (1660–1671).* Hyderabad, 1953.

Inalcik, H. "Osmanli pamuklu pazari. Hindistan ve Inglitere: Pasar rekabetinde emek maliyerin rolü." *ÖDTÜ gelisme dergisi* 2 (1979–80), pp. 1–65.

Innes, C.A. *Gazetteer of Malabar and Anjengo District*. 3 vols. Madras, 1908.

Ionissian, A. (ed.), *Armjano-Russkie otnosenija v pervoi tretii XVIII veka (Sbornik, dokumentov)*. 2 vols. Erevan, 1964.

Iria, A. *Da navegação portuguêsa no Índico no século XVII (Documentos do archivo histórico ultramarino)*. Lisbon, 1963.

Irvine, W. *The Army of the Indian Moghuls*. London, 1902.

Irwin, J., and K.B. Brett *Origins of Chintz*. London, 1970.

Isaacman, A.F. *Mozambique: The Africanization of a European Institution: The Zambezi Prazos, 1750–1902*. Madison, 1972.

Iuct, A.I. "Russko-vostočnaja torgovlija v XVII–XVIII v. i uctajnie v nei Indiskoi kupetsestva." *Istorija SSR* 6 (1978), pp. 40–61.

s' Jacob, H.K. *De Nederlanders in Kerala 1663–1701. De memories en instructiën betreffende het commandement Malabar van de Verenigde Oost-Indische Compagnie*. The Hague, *RGP*, 1976.

———. "Nana Parbhu. The Dutch and a Konkani Merchant." In L. Blussé (ed.), *All of One Company*, pp. 92–102.

———. *The Rajas of Cochin 1663–1726*. New Delhi, 1999.

Jameson, F.J., ed. *Pirates and Piracy in the Colonial Period: Illustrative Documents* (New York, 1923).

Janish, H.P. *Selections from St. Helena Records*. St. Helena, 1885.

Japikse, N. *De diplomatieke verwikkelingen tussen de Republiek en Engeland van 1660 tot 1665*. Leiden, 1900.

Jervis, T.B. *Geographical and Statistical Memoir of the Konkan*. Calcutta, 1840.

Jonge, J.K. de, ed. *De opkomst van het Nederlands gezag in Oost-Indië. Verzameling van onuitgegeven stukken uit het oud-koloniaal archief*. 11 vols. The Hague, 1862–83.

Joret, C. *Jean Baptiste Tavernier*. Paris, 1883.

Judd, J. "William Bellomonte and Captain Kidd." *New York Historical Society Quarterly*, 49 (1965), pp. 69–74.

———. "F. Philipse and the Madagascar Trade." *New York Historical Society Quarterly*, 55 (1971), pp. 359–72.

Kämpfer, E. Die Reisetagebücher Engelbert Kämpfers (*Wiesbadener Erdwiβenschaftliche Forschungen* II) (H. Maier-Lemgo, ed.). Wiesbaden, 1968.

Kaeppelin, F. *Les origines de l'Inde française. La Compagnie des Indes orientales et Françcois Martin*. Paris, 1908.

Kahan, A. *The Plow, the Hammer and the Knout: An Economic History of Eighteenth Century Russia*. Chicago, 1985.

Kamdar, K.H. "Virji Vora. The Profile of an Indian Businessman in the Seventeenth Century." *Journal of the Oriental Research Institute* 3 (4) (Baroda, 1979), pp. 96–107.

Kammen, H.L. *Empire and Interest: The American Colonies and the Politics of English Mercantilism*. Philadelphia, 1978.

Karim Rafiq, A. *The Ottoman Province of Damascus in the Eighteenth Century*. Beirut, 1966.

Kea, R. "Firearms and Warfare on the Slave and Gold Coast from the Sixteenth to the Nineteenth Century." *JAH* 12 (2) (1971), pp. 185–213.

Keay, F.A. *A History of the Syrian Church in India*. New Delhi, 1960.

Kellenbenz, H. "Les Frères Fugger et le marché international du poivre autour de 1600." *Annales ESC* 11 (1) (1956), pp. 1–28.

———. "Le front hispano-portugais contre l'Inde et le rôle d'un agence de renseignement au service des marchands allemands et flamands." *Océan Indien et Méditerranée*, Special issue of *Studia,* pp. 263–90. Lisbon, 1962.

Kelly, J.B. *Britain and the Persian Gulf 1795–1880*. Oxford, 1968.

Kemp, P.C., and O. Loyd. *The Brethren of the Coast: The British and French Buccaneers in the South Seas*. London, 1960.

Kent, R. *Early Kingdoms in Madagascar*. New York, 1970.

Kevounian, K. "Marchands arméniens au XVIIe siècle: à propos d'un livre arménien publié à Amsterdam en 1699." *Cahiers du monde russe et soviétique* 16 (1975), pp. 199–244.

Keyvani, A. *Artisans and Guild Life During the Late Safavid Period*. Berlin, 1982.

Khachikian, L. "Le Registre d'un négociant arménien en Perse, en Inde et au Tibet," *Annales ESC* 22 (1967), pp. 231–78.

Khan, A.S. *The East India Trade in the Seventeenth Century in Its Political and Economic Aspect*. Oxford, 1932; New Delhi, 1971.

Khan, Ali. Muhammad *Mirat i-Ahmedi: A Persian History of Gujarat*. 2 vols. (M.T. Lokhandwale, ed. and trans.). Baroda, 1965.

Khan, Y.H., ed. *Selected Documents of Aurengzeb's Reign (1659–1706 A.D.)*. Hyderabad, 1958.

Kim, S.B. *Landlord and Tenant in Colonial New York: Manorial Society 1664–1775*. Chapel Hill, 1970.

Kindleberger, C.A. *Spenders and Hoarders*. New York, 1992.

Kirkman, J. *Men and Monuments of the Swahili Coast*. London, 1964.

Klein, P.W. "Kapitaal en stagnatie gedurende het Hollandse vroegkapitalisme." In A.M. Geurts (ed.), *Economische ontwikkeling en sociale emancipatie*. The Hague, 1977.

———. "Japanse rendementen in de achttiende eeuw: Innovatie en inertie." *Economisch historische jaarboeken* 47 (1984), pp. 195–204.

———. "De wereldhandel in edele metalen 1500–1800: centraliteit of polycentrisme?" *Tijdschrift voor geschiedenis* 100 (2) (1987), pp. 184–97.

Kling, B.B., and M.N. Pearson, eds. *The Age of Partnership: Europeans in Asia Before Dominon*. Honolulu, 1979.

Klooster, W. *Illicit Riches: Dutch Trade in the Caribbean*. Leiden, 1998.

Knaap, G.J. *Kruidnagelen en christenen. De Verenigde Oost-Indische Compagnie en de bevolking van Ambon*. Dordrecht, 1987.

———. "Europeans, Mestizos and Slaves: The Population of Colombo at the End of the Seventeenth Century." *Itinerário* 5 (2) (1984), pp. 84–101.

Knippendorf, A. *Staatsverfaβung und Mächtepolitik. Zur Genese von Staatenkonflikten im Zeitalter des Absolutismus* (Berliner historische Forschungen). Berlin, 1975.

Koebner, R. "Despot and Despotism: Vicissitudes of a Political Term." *Journal of the Warburg and Courtauld Institute* 14 (6) (1961), pp. 275–305.

Kolff, D.H.A. "La nation chrétienne à Surat au début du XVIIe siècle." In R. Goutalier (ed.), *La femme dans les sociétés coloniaux,* pp. 7–16. Aix-en-Provence, 1984.

Koponen, J. *People and Production in Late Precolonial Tanzania: History and Structure*. Jyväskylä, 1988.

Korte, J. de. *De jaarlijkse financiële verantwoording in de Oost-Indische Compagnie*. Leiden, 1984.

Kossambi, M. "Commerce, Conquest and the Colonial City." *Economic and Political Weekly*, January 5 1985, pp. 32–35.

Kotsekaev, V.A. *Nogaisko-Russkie otnošenija v XV–XVIII vv.* Alma Ata, 1988.

Kriedte, P., H. Medick, and J. Schlumböhm. *Industrialisierung vor der Industrialisierung*. Göttingen, 1977.

Kumar, D. *Land and Caste in South India: Agricultural Labor in the Madras Presidency During the Nineteenth Century*. Cambridge, 1965.

Kurup, K.N.K. *The Aliraja of Cananore*. Trivandrum, 1972.

———. "Telicherry Factory: A Case Study in British Colonialism." In *Aspects of Kerala History and Culture*, pp. 50–60. Trivandurum, 1977.

Kuznetsovoi, N.A., ed. *Chodzdenie kuptsa Feodoša Kotova v Persiu*. Moscow, 1958.

La Roque, George. *Voyage dans l'Arabie heureuse*. Amsterdam, 1711.

Lach, D.H. *Asia in the Making of Europe*. 7 vols. so far. Chicago 1965–.

Lambart, D., ed. *Le "Spraak ende Woorde-boeck" de Frederick de Houtman. Première Méthode de Malais parlé (fin du XVI'e siècle)*. Paris, 1970.

Lane, F.C. *Venice: A Maritime Republic*. Baltimore, 1973.

———. *Profits from Power: Readings in Protection and Violence-Controlling Enterprises*. Albany, 1979.

Lannoy, M. de. *The Kulasekhara Perumals of Travancore: History and State Formation in Travancore from 1671 to 1758*. Leiden, 1997.

Larsen, Kay I. *De Dansk Ostindiske Kolonier Historie (Trankebar)*. Copenhagen, 1907.

Laspreyes, H. *Geschichte der volkswirtschaftliche Anschauungen der Niederländer und ihre Literatur zur Zeit der Republik*. Leipzig, 1863/Nieuwkoop, 1961.

Lattimore, O. *The Desert Road to Turkestan*. London, 1928.

———. *The Laws or Standing Orders of the East India Company*. London, 1621; Farnborough, 1968.

Le Guennec-Coppens, F. and P. Caplan, eds. *Les Swahili entre Afrique et Arabie*. Paris, 1991.

Le Roy Ladurie, E. *Histoire du climat depuis l'an mil*. 2 vols. Paris, 1972.

Leitão, H. *Os portugueses em Solor e Timor de 1512 a 1702*. Lisbon, 1948.

———, ed. *Os dois descobrimentos da ilha de São Lourenço mandado fazer pelo vice-rei D. Jerônimo de Azevedo*. Lisbon, 1970.

Lemon, J. "Governor Fletcher's Recall." *William and Mary Quarterly*, 3rd Series, 20 (1963), pp. 547–62.

Leonard, K.L. "The 'Great Firm' Theory of the Mughal Empire." *Comparative Studies in Society and History* 21 (2) (1979), pp. 151–61.

*Lettres édifiantes et très curieux des pères de la mission*. 12 vols. Paris, 1780–86.

Leupe, P.H. "Brievenvervoer over land naar Indië door de Verenigde Oost-Indische Compagnie in de zeventiende eeuw." *Bijdragen voor Vaderlandse Geschiedenis en Oudheidkunde* Nieuwe reeks 6 (1870), pp. 54–67.

———. "Nederlandse schilders in Perzië en Hindoestan in de eerste helft van de 17 e eeuw." *De Nederlandse Spectator* 1873, pp. 261–95.

Lewis, G. *The French Revolution: Rethinking the Debate*. London, 1993.

Lewis, W.A. "Economic Development with Unlimited Supply of Labor." In A.N. Agarawal and S.P. Singh (eds.), *The Economics of Underdevelopment: A Series of Articles and Papers*, pp. 400–449. London, 1958.

Liebrand, K.N., ed. *Précis of the Archives of the Cape of Good Hope*. 6 vols. Cape Town, 1896–1906.

Ligtenberg, G. *Willem Usselincx*. Utrecht, 1914.

Lima Cruz, M.A. "Exiles and Renegades in Early Sixteenth Century Portuguese Asia." *IESHR* 23 (3) (1986), pp. 249–62.

Lima Felner, J.R. de, ed. *Subsídios para a história da Índia portuguêsa*. Lisbon, 1868.

Lobato, A. *Estudos moçambiquanos. A expanção portuguêsa em Moçambique de 1498 a 1530.* 4 vols. Lisbon, 1959–63.

———. *Quatro estudios e um evocação para a história de Lourenço Marques.* Lisbon, 1961.

———. *Colonização senhoral no Zambesi e outros ensaios.* Lisbon, 1962

———. *Índia—relações luso-marathas.* Lisbon, 1967.

———. "Sobre os prazos da Índia." In A. Guerreiro and L. de Albuquerque, *IIo seminário*, pp. 459–75.

Lockart, L. *Famous Cities of Persia.* Middlesex, 1939.

Lockyer, J. *An Account of the Trade of India.* London, 1711.

Logan, W. *Malabar.* 3 vols. Madras, 1951.

Long, D.E. *The Persian Gulf: An Introduction.* Boulder, CO, 1977.

Longrigg, S. *Three Centuries of Modern Iraq.* London, 1956.

Lopes, D. *A expansão da lingua portuguêsa no Oriente durante os séculos XVI, XVII e XVIII.* Barcelos, 1936.

Lorrimer, L. *Persian Gulf Gazetteer.* 3 parts in 6 vols. Calcutta, 1903; reprinted London, 1969.

Lougnon, A. *L'île Bourbon pendant la Regence. Desforges-Boucher les débuts du café.* Paris, 1956.

Love, H.D. *Vestiges of Old Madras 1640–1800.* 3 vols. London 1913; New York, 1968.

Low, C.R. *History of the Indian Navy.* 2 vols. London, 1877.

Lubbock, E., ed. *Thomas Barlow's Journal of His Life at Sea.* 2 vols. London, 1954.

Lybyer, A.H. "The Ottoman Turks and the Routes of Oriental Trade." *English Historical Review* 30 (4) (1915).

Lydon, J.G. *Pirates, Privateers and Profits: New York Privateering During the Colonial Period.* Upper Saddle River, NJ, 1970.

———. "New York and the Slave Trade." *William and Mary Quarterly*, 3rd Series, 25 (1976), pp. 375–94.

Löfgren, Oscar, ed. *Arabische Texte zur Kenntnis der Stadt Aden im Mittelalter.* 2 vols. Uppsala, 1936/1950.

Macau, J. *L'Inde danoise. La première compagnie.* 2 vols. Aix-en-Provence, 1969.

Macaulay, T.B. *The History of England from the Accession of James II.* 4 vols. London, 1966.

MacCusker, J.J., and R.R. Menard. *The Economy of British America 1687–1789.* Chapel Hill, London, 1985.

MacGowan, B. *Economic Life in Ottoman Turkey.* Paris and Cambridge, 1985.

MacNiell, W.H. *De pest in de geschiedenis.* Amsterdam, 1974.

MacPherson, K. *The Indian Ocean: A History of the People and the Sea.* New Delhi, 1994.

Maçzak, A. "Der polnische Getreideexport und das Problem der Handelsbilanz." In I. Bog, *Der Außenhandel Ost-Mitteleuropas*, pp. 42–61.

Magalhães, J.R. "Uma estrutura do império português. O município." In *1o Ciclo das Conferências Portugal e o Oriente*, pp. 67–91. Lisbon, 1994.

Majid, Ibn Ahmad. *Três roteiros desconhecidos de Ahmad Ibn Majid, o piloto arabe de Vasco da Gama* (T.A. Chumkovsky, ed.). Lisbon, 1960.

Malabari, F.N. *Bombay in the Making.* London, 1910.

Malecki, I.M. "Die Wandlungen im krakauer und polnischen Handel zur Zeit der Türkenkriege des 16 und 17 Jahrhunderts." In O. Pickl (ed.), *Die wirtschaftliche Auswirkungen der Türkenkriege*, pp. 140–52. Graz, 1971.

Malotet, F. de. *Étienne de Flacourt ou les origines de la colonisation française à Madagascar*. Paris, 1858.
Mandeville, W.P.H. de. "The Ottoman Province of al-Hasha in the Sixteenth and Seventeenth Century." *Journal of the American Oriental Society* 90 (3) (1970), pp. 1179–91.
Mans, Raphael du. *Estat de la Perse en 1660* (C. Schefer, ed.). Paris, 1890.
Mansfeld, W.F. *Rechtsvorm en geldelijk beheer bij de Oost Indische Compagnie*. Amsterdam, 1922.
Mantran, R. *Istanbul dans le second moitié du XVIIe siècle*. Paris, 1962.
———. "Réglementations fiscaux ottomanes: le sanjaq de Bassorah." *JESHO* 10 (2) (1977), pp. 244–77.
Manucci, N. *Storia do Mogor or Mughal India* (W. Irvine, ed.). 4 vols. London, 1907–8.
Mar'ashi Safavi, Mirza Muhammad (A. Iqbal, ed.). *Majama al-tawarikh dar tarikh-i inqirad-i Safavija va vaqa-i ba'ad*. Teheran, 1328/1345.
Marcus, A. *The Middle East on the Eve of Modernity: Aleppo in the Eighteenth Century*. New York, 1989.
Marshall, P.J. "British Expansion in India in the Eighteenth Century: A Historical Revision." *History* 60 (1) (1975), pp. 28–43.
———. *East India Fortunes: The British in Bengal in the Eighteenth Century*. Oxford, 1976.
———. "Western Arms in Maritime Asia in the Early Phase of European Expansion." *MAS* 14 (1) (1980), pp. 13–28.
Martin, J. *Comores: quatre îles entre pirates et planteurs*. 2 vols. Paris, 1983.
Martin, E.B. *The History of Malindi*. Nairobi, 1973.
Martin, G.B. "Arab Migration to East Africa in Medieval Times." *IJAHS* 9 (1) (1978), pp. 368–90.
Martineau, A., ed. *Lettres et conventions des gouverneurs de Pondichéry*. Pondicherry, 1914.
———, ed. *Mémoires de François Martin*. 3 vols. Paris, 1931–34.
———. *Dupleix et l'Inde français*. 4 vols. Paris, 1932–34.
Martins, F. *Os vicereis da Índia*. Lisbon, 1935.
Masson, P. *Histoire du commerce de Marseille au XVIIe siècle*. Paris 1911; New York, 1967.
Masters, B.A. The *Origins of Western Economic Dominance in the Middle East: Mercantilism and the Islamic Economy in Aleppo*. New York, 1988.
Mathee, R. "Administrative Stability and Change in Late 17th Century Iran." *International Journal of Middle Eastern Studies* 26 (1) (1994), pp. 77–98.
———. "Coffee in Safavid Iran: Commerce and Consumption." *JESHO* 37 (1994), pp. 1–34.
Mathew, K.N. *Portuguese Trade with India in the Sixteenth Century*. New Delhi, 1975.
———. "Trade in the Indian Ocean and the Portuguese System of Cartazes." In M.D.D. Newitt (ed.), *The First Portuguese Empire*, pp. 63–84. Exeter, 1985.
Matos, A. Teodoro de. "The Financial Situation of the State of India in the Philipine Period." In T.R. de Souza (ed.), *Indo-Portuguese History*, pp. 90–101.
Mauro, F. *Le Portugal et l'Atlantique au XVIIe siècle*. Paris, 1960.
Mbwiliza, J.F. "The Hoe and the Stick: A Political Economy of the Heru Kingdom c. 1750–1900." In *La Civilisation ancienne des peuples des grand lacs: Colloque de Bujumbura*. pp. 95–112. Paris, 1981.

Mehaud, A., ed. *Mouvements des populations dans l'Océan Indien*. Paris, 1979.

Meillassoux, C. *Femmes, greniers et capitaux*. Paris, 1975.

———. *Terrains et théories*. Paris, 1977.

Meilink-Roelofs, M.A.P. *De vestiging der Nederlanders ter kuste Malabar*. The Hague, 1943.

———. *Asian Trade and European Influences in the Indonesian Archipelago Between 1500 and About 1630*. The Hague, 1962.

———, ed. *De V.O.C. in Azië*. Bussum, 1976.

———. "Een vergelijkend onderzoek naar de Nederlandse en Engelse koloniale instellingen." *BMGN* 91 (2) (1976), pp. 196–217.

———. "The Structure of Asian Trade: A Critical Appreciation of Steensgaard's *Asian Trade Revolution*." *Mare Luso-Indicum* 5 (1980), pp. 1–43.

Mendes da Luz F., ed. "Livro das cidades e fortalezas que a coroa de Portugal têm nas partes da Índia." *Studia* 5 (1960).

Mhamai, S.K. *The Sawants of Vadi and the Portuguese*. New Delhi, 1984.

Middleton, J. *The World of the Swahili: An African Mercantile Civilization*. New Haven, 1982.

Miles, S.B. *The Countries and Tribes of the Persian Gulf*. London, 1919/1969.

Miller, E.J. *Mappila Muslims of Kerala: A Study of Islamic Trends*. Bombay, 1976.

Minorsky, V.V., ed. and trans. *The tadhikarat al-muluk: A Manual of Safavid Administration*. London, 1943.

Misra, H.K. *Bureaucracy Under the Mughals*. New Delhi, 1989.

Mittelwalner, G. von. *Chaul. Eine unerforschte Stadt an der Westküste Indiens (Wehr-Sakral- und Profanarchitektur)*. Berlin, 1964.

Modi, J.J. *Asiatic Papers*. 4 vols. Bombay, 1927–29.

Mollat, M., ed. *Sociétés et compagnies de commerce en Orient et dans l'Océan Indien*. Beirut and Paris, 1971.

———. "Les Contacts historiques de l'Afrique et de Madagascar avec l'Asie du sud-est et le rôle de l'Océan Indien." *Archipel* 21 (1981), pp. 35–55.

———, ed. *Course et piraterie. Études présentées à la commision international d'histoire maritime à l'occasion de son Xème colloque international pendant le XVème congrès des sciences historiques*. 2 vols. Paris, 1975.

Mondain, G. *L'histoire de l'Imoro d'après un manuscrit arabo-malgache*. Paris and Algiers, 1910.

Moore, R.J. *Defoe in the Pillory*. Bloomington, 1939.

Moosvi, S. *The Economy of the Mughal Empire c. 1595: A Statistical Study*. New Delhi, 1987.

———. "The Silver Influx, Money Supply and Revenue Extraction in Mughal India." *JESHO* 30 (1987), pp. 47–98.

Mooy, J. *Geschiedenis van de Protestantse kerk in Nederlandsch-Indië 1 van de stichting der Oost-Indische Compagnie tot het optreden der Gouverneur-Generaal Antonio van Diemen*. Weltevreden, 1927.

Moreen, V.B. "The Status of Religious Minorities in Safavid Iran 1617–1661." *Journal of Near Eastern Studies* 40 (1981), pp. 128–33.

Moreland, W.H. *India at the Death of Akbar: An Economic Study*. London, 1902.

———. *From Akbar to Aurengzeb*. New York, 1975.

Moreno, H.B. *Os munícipios portuguêses nos séculos XIII a XVI*. Lisbon, 1986.

Moreno Juárez, J. *Corsarios y piratas en Veracruz y Campeche*. Seville, 1971.

Morineau, M. "Naissance d'une domination. Marchands européens et marchands du Levant au XVIII et XIXe siècle." *Cahiers de la Méditerranée* 1975, pp. 145–85.

———. *Incroyables gazettes et fabuleux métaux.* Paris and Cambridge, 1985.

Morree, P. *A Concise History of Dutch Mauritius: A Fruitful and Healthy Land.* London, 1998.

———. *"Met Vriend die God geleide": het Nederlands-Aziatische postvervoer ten tijde van de Verenigde Oost-Indische Compagnie.* Zutphen, 1998.

Morse, H.B. *Annals of the Honourable East India Company Trading to China.* 4 vols. Oxford, 1926–29.

Mosca, L. "La schavitù e la sua abolizione nel Madagascar." *Africa. Instituto Italiano per l'Africa e l'Oriente* 52 (4) (1997), pp. 497–535.

Moulder, F. *Japan, China and the Modern World-Economy: Towards a Reinterpretation of East Asian Development ca. 1650 to ca. 1918.* Cambridge, 1977.

Mudenge, S.I.G. "The Role of Foreign Trade in the Rozvi Empire: A Reappraisal." *JAH* 15 (3) (1974), pp. 379–92.

———. "Afro-Indian Relations Before 1900: A South-East African Perspective." In S. Ali and R.R. Ramachandi (eds.), *India and the Western Indian Ocean States*, pp. 223–35. New Delhi, 1981.

———. *A Political History of Munhumutapa c. 1400–1982.* Harare, 1988.

ibn Muhammad Ibrahim, Muhammad Rabi. *The Ship of Sulaiman* (J.D. Kane, ed. and trans.). London, 1972.

Mukhia, E. "Illegal Exactions from Peasants, Artisians and Menials in Eighteenth Century Rajasthan." *IESHR* 14 (2) (1977), pp. 231–41.

Mukherjee, C. *From Graven Images: Patterns of Modern Materialism.* New York, 1983.

Mulligan, C.C. *Captain William Kidd: Gentleman or Buccaneer?* Philadelphia, 1932.

Munn, Thomas. "English Treasure by Foreign Trade." In *East India Trade: Selected Tracts from the Seventeenth Century.* Cambridge, 1968.

Mijers, P., ed. *Verzameling van instructiën en reglementen voor de regering van Nederlandsch Indië.* Batavia, 1848.

Nachod, O. *Die Beziehungen der niederländischen ostindischen Kompagnie zur Japan im siebzehnte Jahrhundert.* Leipzig, 1897.

Nagashima, H. "Indigo Production and Circulation in North India During the 17th Century—A Study of the Bayana Tract." *The Shirin* 63, 4 (1980), pp. 527–60.

Nambiar, O. *The Kunjalis: Admirals of Calicut.* Bombay, 1963.

Naqvi, H.K. *Urbanisation and Urban Centers in Upper India 1556–1803.* Bombay, 1968.

———. *Population and Urban Centers Under the Great Mughals 1556–1706.* Simla, 1972.

Nayeem, S.B. *External Relations of the Bijapuri Kingdom.* Hyderabad, 1976.

Nettles, P.C. *The Money Supply to the American Colonies Prior to 1729.* Madison, 1934.

Newitt, M.D.D. *Portuguese Settlement on the Zambezi.* London, 1973.

———. "The Southern Swahili Coast in the First Century of Portuguese Expansion." *Azania* 13 (1978), pp. 111–26.

———. "Plunder and the Reward of Office in the Portuguese Empire." In M. Duffy (ed.), *The Military Revolution and the State 1500–1800*, pp. 10–25. Exeter, 1980.

———. "The Comoro Islands in Indian Ocean Trade Before the 19th Century." *Cahiers d' études africaines* 23 (1983), pp. 139–65.

———. "The East India Company in the Western Indian Ocean in the Early Seventeenth Century." *Journal of Imperial and Commonwealth History* 14 (1988), pp. 5–33.

———. *A History of Mozambique*, London, 1995.

Newton, A.P. *The European Nations in the West Indies 1493–1688*. London, 1933.

Niebuhr, C. *Reise nach Arabien*. Graz Reprint, 1969.

Nightingale, P. *Trade and Empire in Western India 1784–1806*. Cambridge, 1970.

Nogueira da Costa, A. de. *Penetração e impacto do capital mercantil português em Moçambique nos séculos XVI e XVII: o caso de Muenemutapa*. Maputo, 1982.

Novais, F. *Estrutura e dinâmica do sistema colonial*. Lisbon, n.d.

Ogot, A.C., ed. *Zamani*. Nairobi, 1975.

Ohlson, D. *The Ottoman Siege of Mosul and Ottoman-Persian Relationships*. Bloomington, 1974.

Oliveira, A. de. *Poder e oposição política em Portugal no período filipino*. Lisbon, 1990.

Oliveira Marques, F. de. *História militar e política dos portugueses em Moçambique*. 2 vols. Lisbon 1953/1956.

Orhonlu, Çangiz A. "XVI asrin ilk yarasinda Kizildenis sahilirinde Osmanlilar." *Türk Tarih dergisi* 12 (1962), pp. 1–34.

Osgood, H.L. *The American Colonies in the Eighteenth Century*. 4 vols. New York, 1932–34.

Ottino, P. "À propos de deux mythes malgaches du début du XVIIème siècle." *Taloha* 6 (1974), pp. 72–91.

Ottow, J. *Rijckloff Volckertsz. Van Goens. De carrière van een diplomaat*. Utrecht, 1955.

Ovington, J. *A Voyage to Surat in the Year 1689* (C.H. Rawlins, ed.). London, *WHS*, 1929.

Padmenabha Menon, K.P. *History of Kerala*. 3 vols. Ernakulam, 1924–37.

Paixão, A. *Monstruosidades do tempo e da fortuna* (D. Peres, ed.). 4 vols. in one. Porto, 1938.

Palat, R., and I. Wallerstein. "Of What World-System Was Pre-1500 'India' a Part?" In S. Chaudhuri and M. Morineau (eds.), *Merchants, Companies and Trade*. Paris and Brussels, 1996.

———. "The Incorporation and Peripheralization of South Asia." *Review* 10, 1 (1986), pp. 171–208.

Palombini, B. von. *Bündniswerben abendländischer Mächte um Persien 1453–1600*. Wiesbaden, 1968.

Pankhurst, R.R. *An Introduction to the Economic History of Ethiopia*. London, 1964.

———. "Some Notes on the Historical and Economic Geography of the Mesawa Area." *Journal of Ethiopian Studies* 13 (1) (1975), pp. 85–110.

———. "The Banya, or Indian, Presence at Massawa, the Dahlak Islands and the Horn of Africa." In A. Mehaud (ed.), *Mouvements des populations*, pp. 107–27.

Pannikar, K.N. *Malabar and the Dutch: Being the History of the Fall of Nayyar Power in Kerala*. Bombay, 1931.

Papazian, V.P.P. *Matendàrana parskeren vargenere (Persidski dokument Matendarana)*. 2 vols. Erevan, 1958/1956.

———. *Agrarnie otnošenije v vostocnoi Armenii XVI–XVII vc*. Erevan, 1972.

Parasnis, B.R., ed. and trans. *Shivaji Chatrapati*. Puna, 1932.

Pares, R.L. *Yankees and Creoles: A Study of Trade Between North America and the Carribean Colonies Before the Revolution*. Cambridge, MA, 1968.

Paris, R. *Histoire du commerce de Marseille de 1660 à 1789. Le Levant*. Paris, 1953.

Parker, G. *The Military Revolution: Military Innovation and the Rise of the West*. Cambridge, 1986.

Parker, G., and L. Smith, eds. *The General Crisis of the Seventeenth Century*. London, 1978.
Parkinson, C.H. Northcote. *Trade in Eastern Seas 1793–1813*. Cambridge, 1937.
Parry, M.L. *Climatic Change, Agriculture and Settlement*. Dawson, 1978.
Parthasarathi, P. "Rethinking Wages and Competiveness in the Eighteenth Century: Britain and South India." *Past and Present* 158 (1998), pp. 79–110.
Patterson, O. *The Sociology of Slavery: An Analysis of the Origins, Development and Structure of Negro Society in Jamaica*. Cranbury, NJ, 1967.
Pawar, A., ed. *Tarabai kalina kagadpatre*. 3 vols. Kolhapur, 1969–72.
Pawson, M., and D. Buiseret. *Port Royal, Jamaica*. Oxford, 1975.
Pearson, M.N., and A. Das Gupta. *India and the Indian Ocean*. Cambridge, 1981.
Pearson, M.N. *Merchants and Rulers in Gujarat: The Response to the Portuguese in the Sixteenth Century*. Berkeley, 1976.
———. "Shivaji and the Decline of the Mughal Empire." *JAS* 35, 2 (1976), pp. 221–35.
———. *Coastal Western India: Studies from the Portuguese Records*. New Delhi, 1981.
———. "Goa During the First Century of Portuguese Rule." *Itinerário* 8 (1) (1984).
———. "Littoral Society: The Case for the Coast." *The Great Circle* 9 (1987), pp. 1–12.
———. "Brokers in Western Indian Port Cities: Their Role in Servicing Western Merchants." *MAS* 22 (3) (1988), pp. 455–72.
———. *Pilgrimage to Mecca: The Indian Experience*. Princeton, 1996.
———. *Port Cities and Invaders: The Swahili Coast, India and Portugal in the Early Modern Age*. Baltimore and London, 1998.
Peers, D.M., ed. *Warfare and Empire*. Ashgate, 1997.
Pelsaert, Francisco, *De geschriften van F. Pelsaert over Mughal India. Kroniek en remonstrantie* (D.H.A. Kolff and H.W. van Santen, eds.). The Hague, *WLV*, 1979.
Penrose, A. *Goa Rainha do Oriente/Goa Queen of the Orient*. Lisbon, 1960.
Peña Batlle, M.A. *La Isla de Tortuga. Plaza de armas, refugio y seminario de los enemigos de España en las Indias*. Madrid, 1957.
Perlin, F. "Of 'White Wale' and Countrymen in the Eighteenth Century Maratha Deccan: Extended Class Relations, Rights and the Problem of Rural Autonomy Under the Ancien Régime." *Journal of Peasant Studies* 5 (2) (1978).
———. "South Asia and Western Penetration from the Sixteenth to the Nineteenth Century: A Problem of Epistemological Status." *Review* 6 (2) (1980), pp. 267–306.
———. "The Pre-colonial Indian State in History and Epistemology: A Reconstruction of Societal Formations in the Western Deccan from the Fifteenth to the Early Nineteenth Century." In M. Claessen and P. Skalnik (eds.), *The Study of the State*, pp. 275–303. The Hague, 1981.
———. "Proto-Industrialisation and Pre-Colonial South Asia." *Past and Present* 98 (1983), pp. 30–95.
———. "Money use in Late Pre-colonial India." In *Studies in Late Pre-colonial Indian Society and Economy*. Academisch Proefschrift: Leiden, 1984, iv, p. 210.
Pereira, J. *Baroque Goa: The Architecture of Portuguese India*. New Delhi, 1995.
Peres, D., ed. *Monstruosidades do tempo e da fortuna*, 4 vols. Porto, 1938, attributed to A. Paixão.
Pescatello, A.M. "The African Presence in Portuguese India." In P. Manning (ed.), *Slave Trades 1500–1800: Globalisation of Forced Labor*. pp. 279–91. Aldershot, 1996.
Petruševski, I. *Ocerki po istorii feodalnie otnošenije v Azerbaidjane i Armenii v XVI–nacale XIX vc*. Leningrad, 1949.

Phillips, W. *Oman: A History*. Beirut, 1971.

Pigulewskaja, N. *Byzanz auf der Wege nach Indien. Aus der Geschichte des byzantinischen Handels mit dem Orient im 4 bis 6 Jahrhundert.* Berlin, 1969.

Pillai, K.N. *Studies in Kerala History.* Trivandrum, 1978.

Pinto, J. *Slavery in Portuguese India.* Bombay, 1992.

Pissurlencar, P.P.S. *Portuguese Documents on Rustamji*. Bastora, 1936.

———, ed. *Regimentos das fortalezas da Índia*, Bastora, 1951.

———. *Agentes da diplomacia portuguêsa na Índia (Hindus, Muslims e Parçias)*. Bastora, 1964.

———. *The Portuguese and the Marathas.* Puna, 1974.

Pissurlencar, P.P.S., and U.M. Guha (eds.), *Assentos do conselho do estado da Índia*, 6 vols. Bastora and Goa, 1953–74.

Pitot, A. *T'eylandt Mauritius. Esquisses historiques*. Port-Louis, 1905.

Platt, J.F. "The East India Company and the Madagascar Slave Trade." *William and Mary Quarterly* 3rd Series, 26 (1969), pp. 540–77.

Polanyi, K. *The Great Transformation*. New York, 1944.

———. "Ports of Trade in Early Civilisation." *Journal of Economic History* 23 (1) (1963), pp. 30–45.

Pomeranz, K. *The Great Divergence: Europe, China and the Making of the Modern World.* Princeton, 2000.

Pomeranz, K., and S. Topik. *The World That Trade Created: Society, Culture and the World Economy 1400–the Present*. Armonk, NY, 1999.

Pope, D. *Harry Morgan's Way: The Biography of Sir Henry Morgan*. London, 1977.

Pope-Hennessy, J.L. *Sins of the Fathers: A Study of the Atlantic Slave Traders 1441–1807*. Guildford, 1967/1988.

Posnadski, M. "Connections Between the Lagustine People and the Coast." In N.H. Chittick and R.I. Rotbert (eds.), *East Africa and the Orient*, pp. 212–23. New York, 1975.

Postma, J. *The Dutch Participation in the Slave Trade: Slaving on the Guinea Coast.* Cambridge, 1981.

Poujade, J. *La Route des Indes et ses navires.* Paris, 1947.

Prakash, Om. "The Dutch East India Company in Bengal: Trade Privileges and Problems." *IESHR* 9 (3) (1974), pp. 258–87.

———. "European Trade and South Asian Economies: Some Regional Contrasts." In L. Blussé and F.S. Gaastra (eds.), *Companies and Trade,* pp. 189–205.

———. "The Dutch East India Company Documents as Source Material on Indian History." *Itinerário* 7 (2) (1983), pp. 38–50.

———. *The Dutch East India Company and the Economy of Bengal*. Princeton, 1986.

———. "Restrictive Trade Regimes: VOC and the Asian Spice Trade in the Seventeenth Century." In R. Ptak and D. Rothermund (eds.), *Emporia, Commodities and Entrepreneurs in Asian Maritime Trade ca. 1400–1750*, pp. 113–32. Stuttgart, 1981.

———. "Precious Metal Flows, Coinage and Prices in India in the 17th and Early 18th Centuries." In E.H.G. van Cauwenberge (ed.), *Money, Coins and Commerce: Essays in Monetary History of Asia and Europe*. pp. 55–74. Louvain, 1991.

Prakash, Om, and J. Krishnamurty. "Mughal Silver Currency—a Critique." *IESHR* 7 (1) (1970), pp. 139–50.

Pritchard, N.E. "Private Trade Between India and China During the Eighteenth Century." *JESHO* 1 (1957), pp. 109–37, 2 (1958), pp. 221–56.

Priolkar, A.K. *The Goa Inquisition.* Bombay, 1961.

Punambekar, S.V. "The Ajnapatra or Royal Edict Relating to the Principles of Maratha State Policy." *Journal of Indian History* 8 (2, 3), pp. 81–105, 207–33.

Purosthama, M.N. "Saraswats in History with Special Reference to Kerala." *Journal of Kerala Studies* 4 (1) (1977), pp. 75–83.

Puturidze, V.S. *Sparsuli Kartli cenobis Pars lehist (Persidskii dokument v knichgranil'itsa Gruznii)*. Tibilisi, 1961.

Pyrard de Laval, F. *The Voyages of François Pyrard of Laval to the East Indies, the Moluccas and Brazil (1611)*. 3 vols. London, *WHS*, 1887–1900.

Quadros, J.R. *Diu. Appontamentos para sua história e chorographia*. Nova Goa, 1899.

Quaisar, A.J. "Merchant Shipping in India During the Seventeenth Century." In *Medieval India. A Miscellany*, ii (1972), pp. 195–220.

Quaison, S.D. *English "Country-Trade" with the Philippines 1644–1765*. Quezon City, 1966.

Queiroz, F. de. *Vida do veneravel irmão Basto*. Lisbon, 1687.

Rabb, T.K. *Investment in Empire: Merchant and Gentry Investment in the Expansion of England*. Cambridge, MA, 1967.

Rabino di Borgomale, H.L. *The Coins and Seals of the Shahs of Iran, 1500–1941*. Hertford, 1945.

Rachmani, A. *Azerbaidjan v konce XVI i XVII v*. Baku, 1974.

Radzbali, A.M. "O mednom zekanie v Sefevidskom gosudarst've (XVI- nacale XVII v.)." In *Azerbaidjane tarikhine dair materiallar* 6 (Baku, 1963), pp. 47–72.

Rana, R.P. "Agrarian Revolts in Northern India During the Late 17th and Early 18th Century." *IESHR* 18 (3) (1981), pp. 287–326.

Randles, W.G. *L'empire du Monomotappa du XV au XIX siècle*. The Hague, 1975.

Rau, V. "Nobrezza portuguêsa e fortunas ultramarinas no século XVII." *Revista Portuguêsa da História* 8 (1961), pp. 1–55.

Rau, V. and G. Gomes. *Os manuscritos do arquivo da casa de Cadaval respeitante ao Brasil*. 2 vols. Coimbra, 1953/1956.

Rawlinson, C.H. *English Beginnings in Western India 1600–1650*. London, 1926.

Ray, I., ed. "Of Trade and Traders in Seventeenth Century India. An Unpublished Memorandum by G. Roque." *The Indian Historical Review* 9 (1982), pp. 125–57.

Raymond, A. *Marchands et commerçants du Caire au XVIIIe siècle*. 2 vols. Damascus, 1973.

Razi, Sheikh Muhammad Ibn. *The Ship of the Sulaiman* (J.D. Kane, ed. and trans.). London, 1972.

Rea, W.G. *The Economics of the Zambesi Mission 1580–1795*. Rome, 1976.

*Records of Fort Saint George*. 125 vols. Madras, 1910–50. Including *Despatches to England*, Madras, 1919–. *Diary and Consultation Books*, Madras, 1910–. *Letters to Ft. St. George*, Madras, 1916–.

Rediker, M. "Under the Banner of King Death: The Social World of the Anglo-American Pirate." *William and Mary Quarterly* 3rd Series 29 (1983), pp. 203–28.

———. *Between the Devil and the Deep Blue Sea: Merchants, Seamen and the Anglo-American Maritime World 1700–1750*. Cambridge, 1987.

Redlich, F. *De Praeda Militaris: Looting and Booty 1500–1815*. Wiesbaden, 1965.

Reid, A. *Southeast Asia in the Age of Commerce*. Vol. 2, *Expansion and Crisis*. New Haven, 1993.

Reinhold, J. *Polen/Litauen auf den leipziger Messen des 18 e Jahrhunderts*. Weimar, 1971.

Rennefort, Guy de. *Rélation du premier voyage de la Compagnie des Indes Orientales en l'île de Madagascar*. Paris, 1668; Ann Arbor, 1987.
Ribeiro, J., ed. *Arte de Futar*, 4 vols. Rio de Janeiro, 1907, attributed to M. da Costa.
Richards, J.F. *Mughal Administration in Golconda 1687–1724*. Oxford, 1975.
———. "Mughal State Finances and the Premodern World Economy." *Comparative Studies in Society and History* 21 (2) (1979), pp. 285–308.
———, ed. *Precious Metals in the Late Medieval and Early Modern Period*. Durham, NC, 1983.
———. "The Seventeenth Century Crisis in South Asia." *MAS* 24 (4) (1990) pp. 625–38.
Riedlmaier, A. "Ottoman-Safavid Relations and the Anatolian Trade Routes, 1603–1618." *Turkish Studies Association Bulletin* 5 (1981), pp. 7–10.
Risso, P. *Oman and Muscat: An Early Modern History*. London, 1986.
———. *Merchants and Faith: Muslim Commerce and Culture in the Indian Ocean*. Boulder, CO, 1995.
Ritchie, R.C. *The Duke's Province: A Study of Politics and Society in Colonial New York*. Chapel Hill, 1977.
———. *Captain Kidd and the War Against Pirates*. Cambridge, MA, 1987.
Robinson, J. *The Economics of Imperfect Competition*. London, 1956.
Rogers, W. *A Cruising Voyage Round the World. First to the South Seas, then to the East Indies and Homeward by the Cape of Good Hope*. London, 1713.
Röhrborn, K. "Die safavidische Zentralverwaltung." *Handbuch der Orientalistik*. II Regierung und Verwaltung des vorderen Orient in islamischer Zeit. Leiden, 1979.
———. *Provinze und Zentralgewalt Persiens im XVI und XVII Jahrhundert* (*Der Islam Beiheft*). Berlin, 1972.
Rosabi, M. "The 'Decline' of the Central Asian Caravan-Trade." In J.D. Tracy (ed.), *The Rise of Merchant Empire*. 2 vols. Cambridge, MA, 1990.
Ross, D.H. "Annals of Oman from Earliest Times to the Year 1728 A.D." *Journal of the Asiatic Society of Bengal* 43 (1) (1874).
Ross, R. *Cape of Torments: Slavery and Resistance in South Africa*. London, 1983.
Rueb, P. "Un mine d'or à Sumatra. Technologie saxon et méthodes indigènes au XVIIe siècle." *Archipel* 41 (1991), pp. 13–32.
Russel-Wood, A.J. *Fidalgos and Philanthropists: The Santa Casa da Misericórdia of Bahia*. Berkeley and London, 1968.
Sadid al-Saltanah, M.A. *Bandar Abbas va Khalij-i Fars* (A. Iqtidari, ed.) Teheran, 1342/1354.
Sahilioglu, H. "The Role of International Monetary and Metal Movements in Ottoman Monetary History." In J.F. Richards (ed.), *Precious Metals*.
Salgado, G. (ed.) *Fiscais e meirinhos. A administração no Brasil colonial*. Rio de Janeiro, 1985.
Salil ibn Razik. *History of the Imams and Seyyids of Oman* (G.P. Badger, ed. and trans.). London, 1871.
Salim, A., ed. *State Formation in Eastern Africa*. Nairobi, 1984.
Salim, M. *Al muʿarrikhun al Yamanijun fi 'l ahd al-ʿUthmani al awwal*. Cairo, 1971.
San Bernardino, Frey Gaspar de. *Itinerário da Índia athé a ilha de Chypre por terra* (A. Reis Machado, ed.). Lisbon, 1953.
Sanceau, E., ed. *Cartas de Dom João de Castro*. Lisbon, 1954.
———. *Mulheres portuguesas no ultramar*. Porto, 1979.

Saraiva, A., et al., eds. *História de Portugal*, 9 vols. Lisbon, 1979–82.
Sardesai, E.S. *A New History of the Marathas*. 3 vols. Bombay, 1963–65.
Sarkar, Jadunath. *A Short History of Aurengzeb*. Hyderabad, 1979.
———. *The House of Shivaji*, Hyderabad, 1987.
Sarkar, Jagadish, N. *Studies in Economic Life in Mughal India*. Delhi, 1975.
Sassoon, G. *Chinese Porcelains in Fort Jesus*. Mombasa, 1975.
Scammel, G.V. *The World Encompassed: The First European Maritime Empires ca. 800–1650*. London, 1985.
———. "European Exiles, Renegades and Outlaws and the Maritime Economy of Asia c. 1500–1750." *MAS* 26 (4) (1982), pp. 642–63.
———. "The Pillars of Empire: Indigenous Assistence and the Survival of the Estado da Índia." *MAS* 22 (2) (1988), pp. 473–89.
Schimkoreit, R. *Regesten publizierter safawidischer Herscherurkunden*. Berlin, 1982.
Schofeld, J.F. "The Ancient Workings of South East Africa." *Native Affairs Department Quarterly* (Bulawayo) (1971), pp. 1–32.
Schouten, J. *Oost Indische Voyagie*. Amsterdam, 1676.
Schubert, E. *Einführung in die Grundprobleme der deutschen Geschichte im Spätmittelalter*. Darmstadt, 1992.
Schulte, A. *Geschichte der großen ravensbürgischen Handelsgesellschaft*. 3 vols. Stuttgart, Berlin, 1931.
Schurhammer, G. *Franz Xavier. Sein Leben und seine Zeit*. 4 vols. in two parts. Freiburg, 1952–62.
———. *Die zeitgenößische Quellen zur Geschichte portugiesisch Asien und seine Nachbahrstaaten zur Zeit des heiligen Franz Xaviers*. Freiburg, 1956.
Schuster-Walser, S. *Das safavidische Persien im Spiegel europäischer Reiseberichten (1502–1722)*. Baden-Baden, 1970.
Schutte, G.J. *De Nederlandse patriotten en de koloniën: een onderzoek naar hun denkbeelden en optreden*. Groningen, 1974.
Schwartz, S.B. *Sovereignity and Society in Colonial Brazil: The High Court of Bahia and Its Judges*. Berkeley, 1973.
Schwarz, R.P. *Printing on Cotton at Ahmadabad, India, in 1678*. Ahmedabad, 1969.
Scott, G.W. *Constitution and Finance of English, Scottish and Irish Joint-Stock Companies*. 3 vols. London, 1903–7.
Seddon, D., ed. *Relations of Production: Marxist Approaches to Social Anthropology*. London, 1978.
*Selections from Papers from the Records of the Government of India*. 4 vols. London 1820–6.
Sen, S.N. *Shiv Chatrapati: Being a Translation of Sabhasad with Extracts from Chitnis and Shivadigvija*. Calcutta, 1920.
———. *Foreign Accounts of Shivaji*. Calcutta, 1927.
———. *The Administrative System of the Marathas*. Calcutta, 1976.
Sergeant, R.B. "Maritime Customary Law off the South Arabian Coast." In M. Mollat (ed.), *Sociétés et compagnies de commerce*.
———. "The Ports of Aden and Shihr." In *Les grandes escales dans le monde (Recueils de la société Jean Bodin)*, pp. 207–44. Brussels, 1974.
Sérgio, A. *Breve interpretação da história de Portugal*. Lisbon, 1975.
Serra, G. *Subsídios para a história da arte militar moçambicana*. Maputo, 1983.
Serrão, J.V. *História de Portugal*. 9 vols. Lisbon, 1972–87.

Sharma, G.D., ed. *Vakil Reports Maharajganj*. New Delhi, 1986.

Shastri, B.G. *Studies in Indo-Portuguese History.* Bangalore, 1981.

Shaw, S.J. *The Financial and Administrative Organization of Ottoman Egypt.* Princeton, 1962.

———, ed. and trans. *Ottoman Egypt in the Eighteenth Century. The Nizâmnâme-i-Misr of Cezzâr Ahmad Pasha.* Cambridge, MA, 1962.

Shelvocke, G. *A Voyage Round the World by the Way of the Great South Seas p'rformed in the Years 1720–1722*. London, 1726.

Shepperd, G. "The Comorians and East African Slave Trade." In J.L. Watson (ed.), *Asian and African Systems of Slavery*, pp. 73–89.

Sheridan, W.J. *Sugar and Slaves: An Economic History of the British West Indies*. Baltimore, 1974.

Sheriff, A.M. "Trade and Underdevelopment: Economic History of the East African Coast from the 9th to the 15th Century." *Hadith* 5 (1975), pp. 1–23.

Sicard, H. von. "Reiche und Köningstume der Rozwi vom Ende des 17 bis zum Anfang des 19 e Jahrhunderts." In *Festschrift für A.E. Jensen,* ii, pp. 641–62. 2 vols. Munich, 1964.

Sideri, S. *Profit and Power: Informal Colonialism in Anglo-Portuguese Relations.* Rotterdam, 1970.

Silva y Figueiroa, Don Garçia de. *Commentarios de Don Garçia de Silva y Figueiroa de la embajada que de parte del rey de España Don Felipe III hizo al Rey Xa Abbas de Persia.* 2 vols. Madrid, 1905.

Silva Gracias, F. da. *Health and Hygiene in Colonial Goa*. New Delhi, 1994.

Silva Rego, A. de *Portuguese Colonisation in the Sixteenth Century: A Study of Royal Ordinances*. Johannesburg, 1957.

———, et al., eds. *Documentação ultramarina portuguêsa.* 4 vols. Lisbon, 1960–.

Silveira, F.R. *Reformação da milícia e governo da Índia oriental* (B.N. Teensma, ed.). Lisbon, 1996.

Simonsen, R. *Historia econômica do Brasil*. São Paulo, 1957.

Sing, O.P. *Surat and Its Trade in the Second Half of the Seventeenth Century*. New Delhi, 1979.

Sinha, K.N. *The Economic History of Bengal from Plassey to the Permanent Settlement.* 2 vols. Calcutta, 1956/1962.

Skinner, G.W. "Marketing and Rural Structure in Rural China." *JAS* 24 (1964), pp. 195–229.

Smirnov, N.A. *Politika Rosii na Kavkaze XVI–XIX vekac.* Moscow, 1950.

Smith, A. "Dela Goa Bay and the Trade of Southeast Africa." In J. Gray and D. Birmingham (eds.), *Pre-Colonial African Trade*, pp. 265–91.

Souza, G.B. *A sobrevivência do império. Os portugueses na China (1630–1745)*. Lisbon 1991.

Spate, O.K. *The Pacific Since Magellaen. A History*. 3 vols. Canberra, London, 1972–86.

Spear, P. *The Nabobs: A Study of the Social Life of the English in Eighteenth Century India*. London, 1963.

Spears, T. *The Kaya Complex: A Study of the Mijikenda People of the Kenya Coast to 1900*. Nairobi, 1978.

Spears, T., and D. Nurse. *The Swahili: Reconstructing the History and Language of an African Society*. Philadelphia, 1984.

Spooner, F. *The International Monetary Economy and Monetary Movements in France*. Cambridge, MA, 1982.

Stanfield, J.R. *The Economic Thought of Karl Polanyi*. London, 1986.

Stapel, F.W. "Johannes Hudde over de balansen van de Verenigde Oost-Indische Compagnie." *Economisch-historische jaarboek* 13 (1927).

———. "Hubert Hugo. Een zeerover in dienst van de Verenigde Oost-Indische Compagnie." *BTLV* 89 (1932), pp. 615–35.

———. "Cornelis Janszoon Speelman." *BTLV*, 94 (1936), pp. 1–122.

Steele, I.K. *Politics of Colonial Policy: The Board of Trade in Colonial Administration*. Oxford, 1968.

Steensgaard, N. "Consuls and Nations in the Levant." *Scandinavian Economic History Review* 14 (1) (1967), pp. 1–23.

———. "European Shipping to Asia 1497–1700." *Scandinavian Economic History Review* 18 (1) (1970), pp. 1–25.

———. *Carracks, Caravans and Companies: The Structural Crisis in European-Asian Trade in the Early Seventeenth Century*. Copenhagen, 1973.

———. "Violence and the Rise of Capitalism: F.C. Lane's Theory of Protection." *Review* 5 (2) (1981), pp. 247–73.

———. "The Indian Ocean Network and the Emerging World Economy ca. 1500–1700." In S. Chandra (ed.), *The Indian Ocean*, pp. 223–35.

———. "Asian Trade and World Market: Orders of Magnitude in the 'Long Sixteenth Century.' " In *L'histoire à Nice. Actes du colloque international 1980*, vol. 3., pp. 129–47. 3 vols. Nice, 1981.

———. "Commodities, Bullion and Services in Inter-continental Transactions Before 1790." In H. Pohl (ed.), *The European Discovery of the World and Its Economic Effects on Pre-industrial Society*. Stuttgart, 1990.

Stein, B. "Does Culture Make Practice Perfect?" In *All the King's Mana: Papers on Medieval South Indian History*, pp. 90–117. Madras, 1984.

Stein, R.L. *The French Slave Trade in the Eighteenth Century: An Old Régime Business*. Madison, 1979.

Steur, J. *Herstel of ondergang. De voorstellen tot redres van de VOC*. Utrecht, 1984.

Stols, E., and G. Verberkmoere. *Aziatische omzwervingen. Het levensverhaal van Jacob de Coutre. Een Brugse diamanthandelaar 1591–1627*. Berchem, 1988.

Strandes, J. *Die Portugiesenzeit deutsch und englisch Ostafrikas*. Berlin, 1899.

Streusand, D.E. *The Formation of the Mughal Empire*. New Delhi, 1989.

Struijs, Johan. *Drie aanmerkelijke en seer rampspoedige reysen door Italiën, Griekenland, Lijfland, Moskoviën, Tartarije, Persiën, Oost Indiën en verscheydene andere Gewesten*. Amsterdam, 1676.

Subrahmanyam, S. "Staying On: The Portuguese on the Coromandel Coast in the Late Seventeenth Century." *IESHR* 22 (4) (1985), pp. 445–63.

———. "Cochin in Decline: Myth and Manipulation in the Estado da Índia." In R. Ptak (ed.), *Portuguese Asia: Aspects in History and Economics*. Stuttgart, 1987.

———. "The *Kagemusa* Effect: The Portuguese, Firearms and the State in Early Modern South India." *Moyen Orient et Océan Indien* 4 (1987), pp. 249–62.

———. "Persians, Pilgrims and Portuguese: The Travails of Masulipatam Shipping in the Western Indian Ocean 1590–1685." *MAS* 22 (3) (1988), pp. 503–30.

———. *Improvising Empire: Portuguese Trade and Settlement on the Bay of Bengal 1500–1700*. Delhi, 1990.

———. *The Political Economy of Commerce: Southern India 1500–1650*. Cambridge, 1990.

———. "The Portuguese, the Post of Basrur, and the Rice Trade, 1600–50." *IESHR* 21 (2) (1989), pp. 433–62.

———. "The Portuguese, Thatta and the External Trade of Sind 1515–1635." *Revista da Cultura* 13/14 (1991), pp. 48–58.

———. "World Economies and South Asia: A Skeptical Note." *Review* 12 (1) (1992), pp. 141–48.

———. *Portuguese Asia 1498–1700: A Political and Economic History*. London, 1993.

———. "Precious Metal Flows and Prices in Western and South-Asia: Some Comparative and Conjunctural Aspects." In S. Subrahmanyam (ed.), *Money and the Market in India 1100–1700*. New Delhi, 1995.

Subramanian, L. "Banias and British: The Role of Indigenous Credit in the Process of Imperial Expansion in Western India in the Second Half of the Eighteenth Century." *MAS* 21 (3) (1987), 487–510.

Sutherland, L. *A London Merchant 1695–1774*. Oxford, 1933.

Swaminathan, K.D. *The Nayyakas of Ikkeri*. Madras, 1957.

Tabatai, Said Ali Husain. *Burhan i-ma'athir*. Hyderabad, 1300/1936.

Talett, J. *War and Society in Early Modern Europe 1495–1715*. London, 1992.

Tavernier, J.B. *Travels in India* (V. Ball, ed.). 2 vols. London, 1887.

Taylor, J. *Smeltkroes Batavia. Europeanen en Euraziaten in de Europese vestigingen in Azië*. Groningen, 1988.

Teixeira, P. *The Journey of Pedro Teixeira from India to Italy by Land, with his Chronicles of the Kings of Hormuz* (W.F. Sinclair, ed.). London, *WHS*, 1901.

Teixeira de Aragão, A.C. *Descrição geral e histórica das moedas cunhadas em nome dos reis, regentes e governadores de Portugal*. 3 vols. Lisbon, 1874–83.

Terpstra, H.A. *De Nederlanders in Voor-Indië*. Amsterdam, 1947.

Têttre, J.P. du. *Histoire générale des Antilles*. 2 vols. Paris, 1667, 1669; Fort-de-France, 1979.

Thekkedath, A. *History of Christianity in India*. Vol. 5, *From the Middle of the Sixteenth to the Seventeenth Century*. Bangalore, 1982.

Thomas, P.J. *Mercantilism and the East India Trade*. London, 1926.

Thompson, E.P. *The Poverty of Theory and Other Essays*. London, 1978.

Thompson, I.I.A. *War and Society in Habsburg Spain 1580–1640*. London, 1986.

Thornton, A.P.*For the File on Empire*. London, 1969.

Thurston, A.N. *The Castes and Tribes of the Madras Presidency*. 7 vols. Madras, 1909–13.

Tiele, P.A. *Bouwstoffen voor de geschiedenis van de Nederlanders in den Maleischen Archipel*. 3 vols. The Hague, 1866–95.

Tindall, A. *City of Gold. The Story of Bombay*. London, 1982.

Torri, Mugliemo. "Trapped Inside the Colonial Order: The Hindu Bankers of Surat and Their Business World During the Second Half of the Eighteenth Century." In G. Borsa (ed.), *Trade and Politics in the Indian Ocean: Historic and Contemporary Perspectives*, pp. 47–81. New Delhi, 1990.

———. "In the Deep Blue Sea: Surat and Its Merchant Class During the Diarchic Era." *IESHR* 19 (3) (1982), 267–99.

Toussaint, A. *History of the Indian Ocean*. London, 1966.

———. *Histoire de l'Île Maurice*. Paris, 1973.

———. *L'Océan Indien au XVIIIème siècle.* Paris, 1974.
*Travancore Archeological Series.* 8 vols. Trivandrum, 1908–15.
Trinidade, Frey Gaspar de. *Conquista espiritual do Oriente* (F. Lopes, ed.). 3 vols. Lisbon, 1967–69.
Tucci, U. *Mercanti, navi e monete nel cinquecento veneziano.* Bologna, 1981.
Tuck, R. *Natural Right Theories: Their Origin and Development.* Cambridge, 1979.
Tuson, P., ed. "Lieutenant Wyburd's Journal of an Excursion into Arabia." *Arabian Studies* 5, Cambridge, 1979.
Udalova, G.M. *Yemen v period pervogo Osmanskogo zavoevanija.* Moscow, 1988.
Udovitch, A. *Partnership and Profit in Medieval Islam.* Princeton, 1970.
Underdown, R. *Revel, Riot and Rebellion: Popular Politics and Culture in England 1603–1660.* Oxford, 1985.
Utterstrom, G. "Climatic Fluctuations and Population Problems in Early Modern History." *Scandinavian Economic History Review* 3 (1955), pp. 3–47.
Üzünçarsili, H. *Mekke i-müherimijie emirleri.* Ankara, 1970.
Valentijn, F. *Oud en nieuw Oost-Indië.* 6 vols. Dordrecht, 1724–26.
van Dam, Pieter. *Beschrijvinge van de Oost-Indische Compagnie* (F.W. Stapel and C.W.T. van Boetzelaar, eds.) 7 vols. The Hague, *RGP*, 1927–63.
van der Kan, L. *Uit de rechtsgeschiedenis der Oost-Indische Compagnie.* 2 vols. Batavia, 1930/1935.
———. "De rechtstitels van de Vereenigde Oost-Indische Compagnie." *Medelingen van de Koninklijke Akademie van wetenschappen.* Nieuwe Reeks. Afdeling Letterkunde 5/8, Amsterdam, 1942.
van der Kooy, T.P. *Hollands stapelmarkt en haar verval.* Amsterdam, 1931.
van der Sleen, W. *A Handbook on Beads.* Liege, 1967.
van der Veen, K. *Huwelijk en hiërarchie bij de Ananvil Brahmanen van zuidelijk Gujarat. AZOA*-publikaties 12. Amsterdam, 1969.
van Donzel, E. *Foreign Relations of Ethiopia 1642–1700. Documents Relative to the Journeys of Khodja Murat.* Istanbul, 1979.
———, ed. and trans. *A Yemenite Embassy to Ethiopia 1647–1649: Al Haymi's Sirat al-Habasha.* Stuttgart, 1986.
van Gelder, R. *Het Oost-Indisch avontuur. Duitsers in dienst van de VOC.* Ninwegen, 1997.
van Goens, Rijkloff, Volkertszoon. *Memoir of Ryckloff van Goens.* (J. Reimers, ed.). Colombo, 1932.
van Goor, J. *Kooplieden, predikanten en bestuurders overzee. Beeldvorming en plaatsbepaling in een vreemde wereld.* Utrecht, 1982.
van Klaveren, J. "Die historische Erscheinung der Korruption in ihrer Zusammenhang mit der Staats- und Gesellschaftsstruktur betrachtet." *VSWG* 54 (1957), pp. 289–324.
———. "Fiskalismus, Merkantilismus und Korruption. Drie Aspekte der Sozial- und Wirtschaftspolitik des Ancien régime." *VSWG* 55 (1958), pp. 443–504.
van Leur, J.C. *Eenige beschouwingen omtrent den ouden Aziatischen handel.* Middelburg, 1976.
van Linschoten, J.H. *Itinerario ofte schipvaart* (J. Kenn and H. Terpstra, eds.). 2 vols. The Hague, *WLV*, 1903.
van Rees, O. *Geschiedenis der staatshuishoudkunde in Nederland tot het einde der achttiende eeuw.* 2 vols. Utrecht, 1856/1868.
van Twist, J. *Generale Beschrijvinge van Indië.* Amsterdam, 1648.

Varadarajan, L. "The Brothers Bora and Virji Vora." *JESHO* 17 (1967).

———. "Traditions of Indigenous Navigation in Gujarat." *South Asia,* New Series, 3 (1) (1982), pp. 28–35.

Varady, R. "North Indian Banjaras: Their Evolution as Transporters." *South Asia,* New Series, 1 (1) (1980), pp. 1–19.

Veth, P.H.J. "H.A. van Rheede tot Drakensteyn." *De Gids* (3) (1887), pp. 423–75; (4), pp. 113–61.

Verger, P.*Flux et réflux de la traite des nègres entre le Golfe de Bénin et Bahia de Todos os Santos du 17 au 19e siècle*. Paris, 1968.

Verin, P. *The History of Civilisation in Northern Madagascar*. Rotterdam, 1986.

Viceconde de Goa. *Grandes e humildes na epopeia portuguêsa no Oriente*. 2 vols. Lisbon, 1942/1943.

Vink, M.P.M. "Passes and Protection Rights: The Dutch East India Company as a Redistributive Enterprise in Malacca, 1641–1662." *Moyen Orient et Océan Indien* 7 (1990), pp. 73–101.

Vogel, J. *De opkomst van het Indocentrische geschiedsbeeld. Leven en werken van B.J.O. Schrieke and J.C. van Leur*. Hilversum, 1992.

———. "J.C. van Leur 1908–1942: A Short Life in History." In F. Gaastra and L. Blussé (eds.), *On the Eighteenth Century as a Category in Asian History: A Retrospect*. Aldershot, 1998

Volker, T. *Porcelain and the Dutch East India Company*. Leiden, 1954.

Voll, J.O. "Islam as a Special World System." *Journal of World History* 5 (1) (1994), pp. 213–27.

Vrijmans, J.C. *Slavenhalers en slavenhandel*. Kampen, 1937.

Wadia, R.A. *The Bombay Dockyard and the Wadia Masterbuilders*. Bombay, 1982.

Wagle, N. "The History and Social Organization of the Gauda Saraswat Brahmins of the West Coast of India." *Journal of Indian History* 47 (1970), pp. 498–508.

Wake, C.H. "The Changing Pattern of Europe's Pepper and Spice Imports." *Journal of European Economic History* 47 (3) (1975), pp. 361–405.

Wallerstein, I. *The Modern World System*. 3 vols. so far. New York, 1974–.

Walz, T. "Gold and Silver Exchanges Between Egypt and Sudan 16th–18th Century." In J.F. Richards (ed.), *Precious Metals*. pp. 305–29.

Warren, J. *The Sulu Zone, 1768–1898: The Dynamics of External Trade, Slavery and Ethnicity in the Transformation of a Southeast Asian Maritime State*. Singapore, 1981.

Wätjen, H. *Die Niederländer im Mittelmeergebiet zur Zeit ihrer höchste Machtsstellung*. Berlin, 1909.

Watson, I.B. "Fortifications and the Idea of 'Force' in Early English East India Company Relations with India." *Past and Present* 88 (1976), pp. 70–87.

———. *Foundations for Empire: British Private Trade in India 1659–1760*. New Delhi, 1984.

Watson, J.L., ed. *Asian and African Systems of Slavery*. Oxford, 1980.

Webb, S.G. *The Governors-General: The English Army and the Definition of Empire*. Chapel Hill, 1979.

Weber, M. *Wirtschaft und gesellschaft. Grundriß der verstehende Soziologie*. 2 vols. Cologne and Bonn, 1964.

Weeden, B.W. *Economic and Social History of New England*. 2 vols. New York, 1890; Philadelphia, 1960.

Welch, S. *Portuguese and Dutch in Southern Africa*. Cape Town and Johannesburg, 1951.

Westera, L.D. "Boekhouding en management bij de Verenigde Oostindische Compagnie." *Economisch-historische jaarboek* 55 (1992), pp. 75–105.

White, D.I. "Parsis in the Commercial World of Western India." *IESHR* 24 (2) (1987), pp. 183–202.

White, G. "The Impact of Firearms on Africa: An Introduction." *JAH* 18 (2) (1977), pp. 173–84.

Wilding R. *The Shorefolk: Aspects of the Early Development of Swahili Culture*. Mombasa, 1987.

———. *Swahili Bibliography of the East African Coast*. Nairobi, 1990.

Wilkes, J.R. *Historical Sketches of the South of India*. 2 vols. Mysore, 1932.

Wilkinson, H.C. *Bermuda in the Old Empire*. London, 1950.

Wilkinson, J.C. *The Imamate Tradition of Oman*. Cambridge, 1987.

Williams, E. *Capitalism and Slavery*. London, 1941.

Wilson, C.H. *Profit and Power: A Study of England and the Dutch Wars*. London, 1957.

Wilson, R.C. *Early Annals of the English in Bengal, Being the Bengal Consultations for the First Half of the Eighteenth Century*. 3 vols. Calcutta, 1885–1917.

Winius, G.D. *The Fatal History of Portuguese Ceylon: Transition to Dutch Rule*. Gainesville, 1977.

———. "Two Lusitanian Variations on a Dutch Theme: Portuguese Companies in Times of Crisis." In L. Blussé and F.S. Gaastra (eds.), *Companies and Trade*, pp. 119–35.

———. "The "Shadow-Empire" of Goa in the Bay of Bengal" *Itinerário* 7 (2) (1983), pp. 83–101.

———. *The Black Legend of Portuguese India: Diogo do Couto, His Contemporaries and the "Soldado Prático."* New Delhi, 1985.

Winius, G.D., and M.P.M. Vink. *The Merchant-Warrior Pacified: The VOC (the Dutch East India Company) and Its Changing Political Economy in India*. New Delhi, 1991.

Wink, A. "*Al-Hind:* India and Indonesia in the Islamic World-Economy." *Itinerário* 12 (1) (1988), pp. 33–70.

———. *Land and Sovereignity Under the Eighteenth Century Maratha Svaraj*. Cambridge, 1989.

———. *Al Hind: The Making of the Indo-Islamic World*. 3 vols. so far. Leiden, 1991–.

Winstow, A. *No Purchase No Pay: Sir Henry Morgan, Captain William Kidd and Captain Woodes Rogers in the Great Age of Privateering and Pirates*. London, 1967; Boston, 1989.

Witsen, N. *Noord en Oost Tartarye. Behelsende eene beschryvinge van verscheydene gewesten in de noorder en oostelycke delen van Asiën en Europa*. 2 vols. Amsterdam, 1672/1776.

Wong, R.B. *China Transformed: Historical Changes and the Limits of the European Experience*. Ithaca, 1997.

Wood, A.G. *A History of the Levant Company*. Oxford, 1935.

Worden, N. *Slavery in Dutch South Africa*. Cambridge, 1985.

Wright, H.T., et al. "The Evolution of Settlement Systems in the Bay of Boeny." *Azania* 31 (1996), pp. 35–75.

Wright, J.R. *Annesley of Surat and His Times: The True Story of the Mythical Wesley Fortune*. London, 1916.

Wycherley, G. *Buccaneers of the Pacific*. Indianapolis, 1928.

Wycki, J. "Die Laienbruderschaft der Misericórdia in portugiesisch Asien." In *Das Laienapostolat in den Missiones. Festschrift für Dr. J. Bechman*, pp. 79–97. Schöneck, 1961.

———, ed. "Duas relações sobre a situação da Índia portuguêsa nos annos 1568 e 1569." *Studia* 8 (1961), pp. 123–221.

———, ed. *O livro do pai dos christãos*. Lisbon, 1969.

———. "Unbewältigte Problemen in Indien, Ceylon und Burma." In *Sacra Congregatione de Propaganda Fide: Memoria Rerum*, ii, pp. 547–72. 2 vols. Rome, Freiburg, 1972.

Wycki, J., et al., eds. *Documenta Indica Societate Iesu*. 26 vols. so far. Rome, 1956–.

Xavier, F.N. *Bosquejo histórico das communidades das ilhas de Goa, de Bardes e de Salcete*. 2 vols. in one. Nova Goa, 1853; Bastora, 1905.

———. *Defesa dos direitos das Gão-carias, Gão-cares e de seus privilégios*. Nova Goa, 1858.

Yajima, H. "Some Problems on the Formation of the Swahili World and the Indian Ocean Maritime World." *Senri Ethnological Studies* 43 (1996), pp. 319–55.

Ylvisaker, M. "Ivory Trade in the Lamu Area." *Paideuma* 28 (1982), pp. 221–31.

Yogev, G. *Diamonds and Coral: Anglo-Dutch Jews and Eighteenth Century Trade*. Leicester and New York, 1978.

Zahir ud Din Babur. *Babur Nama [Memoirs of Babur]* (A.S. Beveridge, ed. and trans.). London, 1922; Delhi, 1979.

Zwaardecroon, C. *Memoir of Zwaardecroon* (S. Pieters, ed.). Colombo, 1911.

## Unpublished Theses and Papers

Bardwell, R. "The Governors of Portugal's South Atlantic Empire in the Seventeenth Century: Social Background, Qualifications and Rewards." Ph.D. diss., University of California at St. Barbara, 1974.

Barendse, R.J. "Zijde, zamboeks en zilver: de Verenigde Oost-Indische Compagnie in Iran." Doctoraalscriptie, Leiden, 1984.

———. "The Ottoman Empire and the Mediterrenean." Paper presented to the VIth Conference of the World History Association. Pamplona, 1996.

Berg, F.J. "Mombasa Under the Busaidi Sultanate: The City and Its Hinterland in the Nineteenth Century." Ph.D. diss., University of Wisconsin, 1971.

Blussé, L. "Tussen geveinsde vrunden en verklaarde vijanden." Inaugural lecture, Amsterdam/Leiden, 1999.

Disney, A.R. "The Estado da Índia and the Caravan Trade." Paper presented to the International Conference of Human Sciences in Asia and Africa, Tokyo, 1983.

Dubbins, B.R. "A Political History of the Comoro Islands." Ph.D. diss., University of Boston, 1972.

Eastman, C.M. "Winawaka, Watumwa na Wageni: African Cultural Influences in the Formation of the Northern Swahili." Paper presented to the 29th Annual Meeting of the African Studies Association, Madison, 30 October–2 November 1986.

Emerson, G. "Ex Occidente Lux: Some European Sources on the Economic and Social Structure of Safavid Persia." Ph.D. diss., University of Cambridge, 1968.

Gupta, V.B. "The Dutch East India Company in Gujarat Trade: A Study of Selected Aspects." Ph.D. diss., Delhi School of Economics, 1991.

Hafkin, D. "Politics and Trade in Northern Mozambique in the Late qEighteenth and Early Nineteenth Century." Ph.D. diss., Indiana University, 1974.

Hamid Hiyed, A.A. "Relations Between the Yemen and South Arabia During the Zeyd Imamate of Abd al-Qasim." Ph.D. diss., University of Edinburgh, 1973.

Kolff, D.H.A. "An Armed Peasantry and Its Allies: Rajput Tradition and State Formation in Hindustan 1450–1850." Academisch Proefschrift, Leiden, 1983.

Kopytoff, B. "The Maroons of Jamaica: A Study of Incomplete Policies." Ph.D. diss., University of Pennsylvania, 1973.

Lequin, F. "Het personeel van de Verenigde Oost-Indische Compagnie in de achttiende eeuw, méér in het bijzonder in de vestiging Bengalen." 2 vols. Academisch Proefschrift, Leiden, 1982.

Lewis, D. "The Dutch East India Company and the Straits of Malacca." Ph.D. diss., Australian National University, Canberra, 1970.

Meilink-Roelofs, M.A.P. "Van geheim tot openbaar." Inaugural lecture, Leiden, 1970.

Nagazumi, Y. "From Company to Individual Company Servants. Dutch Trade to Japan in the Eighteenth Century." Paper presented to Workshop on Asia in the Eighteenth Century, Leiden, 1993.

Nagtegaal, L. "Rijden op een Hollandse Tijger. De Noordkust van Java en de VOC." *Academisch proefschrift,* Utrecht, 1988.

Niemeijer, H. *Calvinisme en Koloniale Stadscultuur. Batavia, 1619–1725.* Academisch Proefschrift, Leiden, 1996.

Perlin, F. "Studies in Late Pre-Colonial Indian Society and Economy." Academisch Proefschrift, Leiden, 1984.

Pijning, E. "Controlling Contraband: Mentality, Economy and Society in Eighteenth Century Rio de Janeiro." Ph.D. diss., Johns Hopkins University, 1997.

Platt, V.B. "The Trade in East India Commodities to the American Colonies 1690–1775." Ph.D. diss., University of Iowa, 1940.

Saxe, E.L. "Fortune Tangled Web: Trading Networks of English Merchants in Eastern India." Ph.D. diss., Yale University, 1979.

Sherman, A.A. "Commerce, Colonies and Competition: Special Interest Groups and English Commercial and Colonial Policy 1660–1673." Ph.D. diss., Yale University, 1973.

Smith, D.G. "The Mercantile Class of Portugal and Brazil in the Seventeenth Century: A Socio-Economic Survey of the Merchants of Lisbon and Bahia." Ph.D. diss., University of Texas at Austin, 1975.

Takeshi, Ito. "The World of Adat Aceh: A Historical Study of the Sultanate of Aceh." Ph.D. diss., Australian National University, Canberra, 1984.

Thorbahn, E.A. "The Precolonial Ivory Trade of East Africa: Reconstruction of a Human-Elephant Ecosystem." Ph.D. diss., University of London, 1970.

van der Werff, P. "Frontier Poverty: Labour Household Strategies and Limited Economic Circulation in the Foothills of Kerala, India." Academisch Proefschrift, Gemeenteuniversiteit, Amsterdam, 1987.

van Santen, H.W. "De Verenigde Oost-Indische Compagnie in Gujarat en Hindustan." Academisch Proefschrift, Leiden, 1982.

van Spengen, H.W. "Tibetan Borderlands: A Geo-Historical Analysis of Trade and Traders." Academisch Proefschrift, Vrije Universiteit Amsterdam, 1992.

van Wee, A. "Aziatische Produktiewijze en Mughal India." Academisch Proefschrift, Nijmegen, 1985.

Veluwenkamp, J. "Ondernemersgedrag op de Hollandse stapelmarkt in de tijd van de Republiek. De Amsterdamse handelsfirma Jan Isaac de Neufville & Comp. 1730–1764." Academisch Proefschrift, Leiden, 1981.

Vos, R. "Koopman en koning. De VOC en de Maleise tinhandel." Academisch Proefschrift, Utrecht, 1990.

# Index